A Custom Edi

THINK Critically

Taken from:

THINK Critically, Second Edition
by Peter Facione and Carol Ann Gittens

PEARSON

Cover Art: *Wheel Head*, by Christian Stolte.

Taken from:

THINK Critically, Second Edition
by Peter Facione and Carol Ann Gittens

Upper Saddle River, New Jersey 07458

This special edition published in cooperation with Pearson Learning Solutions.

Pearson Learning Solutions, 501 Boylston Street, Suite 900, Boston, MA 02116
A Pearson Education Company
www.pearsoned.com

Printed in the United States of America

25

000200010271677714

RH

ISBN 10: 1-256-78202-5
ISBN 13: 978-1-256-78202-5

To students and teachers everywhere,
may developing critical thinking help you stay
forever young.

BRIEF CONTENTS

CONTENTS

ANALYZE ARGUMENTS AND DIAGRAM DECISIONS 86

EVALUATE THE CREDIBILITY OF CLAIMS AND SOURCES 108

EVALUATE ARGUMENTS: THE FOUR BASIC TESTS 130

EVALUATE DEDUCTIVE REASONING AND SPOT DEDUCTIVE FALLACIES 150

EVALUATE INDUCTIVE REASONING AND SPOT INDUCTIVE FALLACIES 164

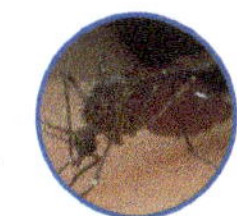

15 

SPECIAL FEATURES AND EXERCISES

01 THE POWER OF CRITICAL THINKING

02 SKILLED AND EAGER TO THINK

03 SOLVE PROBLEMS AND SUCCEED IN COLLEGE

04 CLARIFY IDEAS AND CONCEPTS

05 ANALYZE ARGUMENTS AND DIAGRAM DECISIONS

06

EVALUATE THE CREDIBILITY OF CLAIMS AND SOURCES

07

EVALUATE ARGUMENTS: THE FOUR BASIC TESTS

EVALUATE DEDUCTIVE REASONING AND SPOT DEDUCTIVE FALLACIES

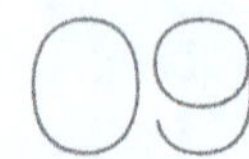

EVALUATE INDUCTIVE REASONING AND SPOT INDUCTIVE FALLACIES

10

THINK HEURISTICALLY: RISKS AND BENEFITS OF SNAP JUDGMENTS

ACKNOWLEDGMENTS

Just as teaching and learning critical thinking is a collaboration, so is putting together all the words, images, exercises, video clips, page layouts, and Web site materials for *THINK Critically*. This project could not have happened were it not for the wonderful participation, support, and guidance of a great many people.

The biggest thank you of all goes to my coauthor, Carol Gittens. She is a faculty member of Santa Clara University, where she will soon begin serving as Associate Dean of the College of Arts and Sciences. Every chapter of the second edition benefits from her hard work, her humane sensitivity, her insights, and her attention to the finer points of authoring for learning. Dr. Gittens authored the Instructor's Manual for the first and the second editions of *THINK Critically*. A wonderful resource, her Instructor's Manual offers strategies on teaching *for* thinking.

The second edition benefited from the helpful comments and suggestions provided by many reviewers. New chapters and familiar chapters all were improved by their recommendations. We thank, again, the great support we received from exercise contributors, PowerPoint builders, and test-bank authors. It was again a pleasure be working with the professionals at Pearson Education. Carol and I are grateful to each and every person there, including the publisher, the marketing director, the editor, the permissions and images people, the MyThinkingLab content input person, the designers, the copyeditors, and many more. Melissa Sacco, Carly Czech, and Elsa van Bergen deserve special acknowledgement because of how well the three of them guided the second edition from an author's hopeful ideas to the completed book and package of support materials.

For me, good ideas come from thinking and discussing things with other people. Great ideas come when that other person happens to be brilliant and wise. The ideas in this book come from a lifetime of those kinds of experiences, but mostly from talking and thinking with the one brilliant and amazing person who has shared that lifetime with me. Through her words and ideas, she contributed inestimably to this book, to other books, to a myriad of projects both professional and domestic, and to every other part of my life. No "thank you" can do justice to all that I owe to her. But let me say it anyway. Thank you, Noreen.

Co-author, Carol Gittens adds, "When Pete asked me to join him as a main author, I jumped at the opportunity to add my voice to a text that is designed to nurture students' critical thinking skills and habits of minds, not only to promote success in the academic arena, but to promote success in life. I would like to express my gratitude to my long-time research colleague and professional mentor Peter Facione and by extension his wife and fellow colleague, Noreen, for extending our scholarly partnership to include this project. Even more importantly, I want to acknowledge and thank my wonderful husband William who supported me unconditionally even when my efforts on this book required more of my attention than he or our children would have wished to share."

PREFACE

In "Forever Young" the songwriter Bob Dylan expressed my hopes for all who learn from and teach from *THINK Critically.* What more could one person wish for another than that he or she should always seek to know the truth, walk in the light of well-trained reason, be courageous, and have the intellectual integrity to stand strong, and that, no matter what the chronological age, that he or she should stay forever young?

This book aims to strengthen critical thinking skills and nurture the courageous desire to seek truth by following reasons and evidence wherever they lead. We all may have different beliefs, values, perspectives, and experiences influencing our problem solving and decision making. But we share the human capacity to be reflective, analytical, open-minded, and systematic about thinking through our problems and choices, so that we can make the best judgments possible about what to believe or what to do. That process of well-reasoned, reflective judgment is critical thinking. Exercising our critical thinking helps our minds become stronger, healthier, and more youthful.

Our approach is simple, practical, and focused. To strengthen critical thinking skills, we have to use them. To build positive critical thinking habits of mind, we have to engage our beliefs, intentions, and values around the importance of thinking critically as the optimal means of solving problems and making decisions, particularly in contexts of risk and uncertainty. Every chapter of this book builds critical thinking skills and engages critical thinking habits of mind in every way possible. Questions, exercises, video clips, controversial examples, contemporary issues, practical life problems, classic questions, science, technology, religion, politics—all of these, and more, are represented.

Why? Because my co-author and I believe with every fiber of our beings that critical thinking is all about real life, and so the only way to build up one's skills and desire to engage practical problems and important decisions is to use material from real-life situations in teaching and learning critical thinking.

It is more important, in my judgment, that a person use all of his or her strength as a critical thinker to try to make the best judgments possible than that the person memorize a lot of vocabulary or theory about critical thinking. Learning about critical thinking certainly helps one become a better critical thinker. But knowing music isn't playing music. Knowing the rules of a game well is not the same as playing the game well. Knowing military strategy is not the same as making strategic decisions. A person must pick up the instrument and practice, or play the game, or engage the conflict. The same goes for critical thinking. We learn it by doing it, not just reading about it or watching someone else do it.

That is why there are hundreds of exercises woven into the text itself, and still more at **www.mythinkinglab.com**. Some are group exercises and some are individual exercises, because critical thinking is something we do occasionally individually and at other times with friends, family, or co-workers. The exercises in the textbook and the supplementary exercises, which faculty colleagues from around the nation contributed, are crafted to be engaging, fascinating, entertaining, and provocative as well as instructional. The book references more than 75 video clips, news stories, and Internet URLs. Text is not enough by itself; critical thinking in real life calls for analyzing and interpreting images, body language, gestures, contexts, and much more. The video clips and other links build upon the words in print to give you a more well-rounded body of examples and exercises from which to learn. One suggestion: Don't just read the book, *do* the book.

We think developing your own critical thinking is absolutely the most valuable and beneficial thing you can do for yourself. But, to let you know what we hope for you, and to help you understand why we wrote a book on critical thinking as our gift to you, we offer this Dylanesque blessing: That you should have a strong foundation, even in the shifting winds of change, that joy should fill your heart and learning guide your life, and, of course, that by using your mind to reflect on what to believe and what to do, that you should stay forever young.

HOW THE BOOK IS ORGANIZED

Chapters 1 and 2 explain what critical thinking is and why it is so vitally important to all of us individually and collectively. These chapters show how critical thinking connects to our academic studies and to our personal, professional, and civic lives. Chapter 3 builds immediately on the theme of the practical value of critical thinking by describing the IDEAS approach to problem solving and then applying that approach to the kinds of problems typically encountered by college students of all ages. Chapter 3 is an important new element in the second edition. It connects critical thinking with something we all must do everyday throughout our lives: solve problems. The examples in the chapter are about college life, but the skills apply throughout all dimensions of our lives.

Chapters 4 and 5 focus on the skills of interpretation and analysis; when we can understand what people are saying, we can articulate the reasons being advanced on behalf of a particular claim or choice. Without these vital critical thinking skills we wander in a cloud of confusion, not really knowing what things might mean or why people, including ourselves, think what they think.

Chapters 6, 7, 8, and 9 are essential building block chapters. In these, we focus on the skill of evaluation as applied to the truthfulness of claims, the trustworthiness of so-called experts, and the quality of arguments. These chapters focus on reasoning patterns that are logical and strong, and contrast those with reasoning patterns that are misleading and fallacious.

Chapters 10 and 11 are on decision making. Chapter 10 focuses on importance of snap judgments and the grip of our previous decisions have on how we live and act as we go through our day. These two chapters emphasize the essential critical thinking skills of self-monitoring and self-correction, along with the habits of truth seeking and open-mindedness, as the best defense against mistaken snap judgments and unreflective decision making.

The three most important chapters of this book are Chapters 12, 13, and 14. Why? Because comparative reasoning, ideological reasoning, and empirical reasoning are the three most fundamental and most widely used methods human beings have for supplying reasons on behalf of their beliefs and ideas. These three chapters focus on the core critical thinking skills of inference and explanation, because drawing conclusions and explaining one's reasons in real life are the products of comparative, ideological, and empirical reasoning. The other chapters enable you to get the most out of these three chapters.

Chapter 15 provides strategies for writing sound and effective arguments. Effective writing, a skill that turns out to have huge practical value, becomes much easier when a person learns how to "think like a writer" instead of thinking like a student doing a writing assignment. Chapter 15 addresses that goal. This new chapter gives the second edition of the book a whole new dimension because it connects critical thinking with sound and effective writing.

Thinking like professionals, instead of simply studying about them or reading what they have said, is way more fun and more effective for learning. Some versions of this book include one or more of the four supplementary chapters designed expressly for the purpose of helping you think like a social scientist, or a natural scientist, or an ethical decision maker, or a logician. We hope that you have the chance to work through one or more of these four supplementary chapters either with the aid of your instructor or on your own. Each one connects critical thinking with the subjects you are learning in college and with the many professional fields that depend on those disciplines.

PETER FACIONE, PhD, has dedicated himself to helping people build their critical thinking to become better problem solvers and decisions makers. He does this work not only to help individuals and groups achieve their own goals, but also for the sake of our freedom and democracy. Facione draws on experience as a teacher, consultant, business entrepreneur, university dean, grandfather, husband, and avid "old school" pickup basketball player. Now he is taking his message about the importance of critical thinking directly to students. For improving reasoning skills for use in one's personal, professional, and civic life, there may never before have been a more practical, enjoyable, important, comprehensive, and engaging text than this.

"I've paid very close attention to the way people make decisions since I was 13 years old," says Facione. "Some people were good at solving problems and making decisions; others were not. I have always felt driven to figure out how to tell which were which." He says that this led him as an undergraduate and later as a professor to study psychology, philosophy, logic, statistics, and information systems as he searched for how our beliefs, values, thinking skills, and habits of mind connect with the decisions we make, particularly in contexts of risk and uncertainty.

"I seem always to be focused on problem-solving and decision-making strategies. Whether as a teacher, consultant, or manager, I find it is always valuable, when working with groups or individuals, to be mindful of how they applied their cognitive skills and habits of mind to solve a problem, make a decision, or troubleshoot a situation. When I am working with a client or a student, this helps me be of more value to them. By knowing how they think, I am able to help them improve their thinking and make better decisions. As a competitor on the basketball court or in business dealings, I find that I am better able to outmaneuver the opposition if I know what and how they are thinking. As a scholar and scientist, and as a citizen in our complex, pluralistic democracy, I am absolutely convinced that careful analysis and open-minded truth-seeking always work better than any other way of learning the truth and solving our problems."

A native Midwesterner, Facione earned his PhD in Philosophy from Michigan State University and his BA in Philosophy from Sacred Heart College in Detroit. He says, "Critical thinking has helped me be a better parent, citizen, manager, teacher, writer, and friend. It even helps a little when playing point guard!"

In academia, Facione served as provost of Loyola University–Chicago, dean of the College of Arts and Sciences at Santa Clara University, and dean of the School of Human Development and Community Service at California State University–Fullerton. "As a dean and provost, I could easily see that critical thinking was alive and well in every professional field and academic discipline."

"I've focused my research on the teaching and measurement of critical thinking since my earliest years as a faculty member in the 1960s and 1970s. But before you can measure something that crosses into every aspect of life, you have to be sure that you understand what it is. So, in the 1980s, I first had to see whether there was a consensus among experts about the term *critical thinking*. After two years of research, a solid consensus emerged. That plus all the stats and behavioral science research I had studied and taught for years enabled me and my research team, during the 1990s, to design and validate tools to assess critical thinking skills and habits of mind. In the first decade of this century, our team has explored the connections between critical thinking and human decision making in its broadest sense."

In fact, Facione spearheaded the international study to define critical thinking, sponsored by the American Philosophical Association. His research formed the basis for numerous government policy studies about critical thinking in the workplace, including research sponsored by the U.S. Department of Education. Today, his tools for assessing reasoning are used around the world in educational, business, legal, military, and health sciences.

Today, Peter operates his own business, *Measured Reasons*. He is a speaker, writer, workshop presenter, and consultant for organizations large and small. His work focuses on strategic planning and leadership decision making, in addition to teaching and assessing critical thinking. With his wife, who is also his closest research colleague and co-author of many books and assessment tools, he now lives in sunny Los Angeles, which he says, "suits [him] just fine." He welcomes questions from students and instructors—you can reach him at pfacione@measuredreasons.com.

CAROL ANN GITTENS, PhD, is deeply committed to support the development of critical thinking in learners of all ages. With a doctorate in Psychology and faculty experience in programs focused on teacher development, she has gained a national reputation for her excellent work in the measurement of critical thinking in K-12 learners. "For children, success in school," says Gittens, "comes down to building critical thinking skills and positive habits of mind. With strong critical thinking, there is no school subject that a child cannot master. Deep learning comes about when a child understands the *why* and the *how*—the explanations and the thinking processes—of the subject. Rote memorization—as useful as that may be when children are learning the *what*, the distilled content knowledge of a subject—is never sufficient in the long term." She worries that too many elementary school and high school students learn too late that memorization by itself is not going to make them successful in college or in their work and family life outside of school. In those arenas problem-solving and decision-making skills are essential, and these vital processes are built upon critical thinking. So passionate is Gittens about the importance of the development of critical thinking in K-12 educational programs that she would love to see inscribed on the wall of every classroom the motto "Think to Learn and Learn to Think."

Dr. Gittens is on faculty of Santa Clara University, where she holds a tenured joint appointment in the Education Department and the Liberal Studies Program. Gittens received her PhD in Psychology from the University of California–Riverside and her BA in Psychology and Women's Studies from the University of California–Davis. At Santa Clara she teaches undergraduate and graduate courses in educational assessment, research methods, instructional technology and curriculum innovation, critical thinking pedagogy, psychological foundations of education, developmental psychology, and community health education. She describes her philosophy of teaching this way: "I have applied my background in psychology to my career in teacher education. In my courses I emphasize the centrality of both critical thinking skills and dispositional habits of mind. By creating a rich critical thinking environment in my courses and modeling critical thinking teaching techniques, I help my students develop their skills of teaching for critical thinking that they will carry into their careers as educators." It is this focus on the practical applications of critical thinking that she brings to her co-authorship of *THINK Critically*.

The central focus of Gittens's research supports and grows out of her philosophy of teaching. She publishes on the interface of critical thinking, motivation, mathematical reasoning, and academic achievement of adolescents and young adults from diverse cultural and ethnic backgrounds. Dr. Gittens is an author or co-author of numerous articles on critical thinking skills and dispositions. Her essay in *Critical Thinking Education and Assessment* (Althouse Press, 2009) argues for the necessity for assessing critical thinking dispositions in an era of K-12 high-stakes standardized testing.

She not only urges that more scholarly attention be focused on *meaningful* educational testing, she engages in that research herself. Deeply concerned about the accurate and meaningful measurement of critical thinking in children and adolescents, Gittens has developed tools to assess their critical thinking habits of mind and their critical thinking skills. She is first-author of the *California Measure of Mental Motivation* (CM3), a critical thinking disposition assessment instrument for children, adolescents and adults, and the *California Critical Thinking Skills Test-M20*, a critical thinking skills test for children in grades 3 through 8.

Dr. Gittens has served as department chair, associate dean, and most recently as Director of Santa Clara University's Office of Assessment. After devoting her 2011–2012 sabbatical to research, she takes up duties as an Associate Dean in the College of Arts and Sciences at the start of the 2012–2013 academic year. As Assessment Director, she chaired the University Assessment Committee, performed key activities related to institutional re-accreditation, was a consultant to academic and co-curricular programs on the assessment of student learning, and designed and oversaw the campus's innovative multi-year, rubric-based assessment plan for the Core Curriculum. Gittens is a recognized leader in the assessment of student learning and educational effectiveness. Gittens's consulting activities include working with college administrators, faculty and staff, K-12 educators, as well as business executives, managers, and employees. Gittens's areas of expertise include assessment of student learning outcomes, critical thinking pedagogy and assessment, integrating critical thinking across the curriculum, critical thinking and co-curricular programs, as well as statistics and assessment design for individuals and institutions.

Gittens and her husband live in California's Silicon Valley with their teen-aged daughter and son and their 1-year-old daughter. Gittens volunteers her time with the local chapter of National Junior Basketball, where she has been a youth coach and board member for the past six years. She is an active parent volunteer in her older children's school, and is involved with K-12 schools in the local community, offering teacher training workshops on nurturing and assessing students' critical thinking.

THINK
CRITICALLY

STATION
2
STATION
2

Read the Chapter on mythinkinglab.com

Listen to the Chapter Audio on mythinkinglab.com

CHAPTER 01

The Power of Critical Thinking

WHAT does "critical thinking" mean?

WHY is critical thinking important?

HOW can we evaluate our critical thinking?

Walking down 10th

Street in Hermosa Beach the other day, I saw a helmetless young man skillfully slalom his skateboard downhill toward the beach. Ignoring the stop sign at Hermosa Boulevard, he flashed across all four lanes of traffic and coasted on down the hill. My immediate reaction was "Whew! Lucky that dude wasn't killed!" because I had often seen cars on Hermosa roll through that particular stop sign. Whatever was occupying his attention, the skateboarder did not appear to have self-preservation on his mind that day!

Whether he reflected on it or not, the skater *decided* to run the stop sign. Similarly, we all make decisions all the time, with some of our choices made more thoughtfully than others. We've all underestimated obstacles, overlooked reasonable options, and failed to anticipate likely consequences. Life will continue to present us with our full share of problems, and when we err, we often think about the better decisions we could have made if we'd given it a little more thought.

Critical thinking is the process of reasoned judgment. That is, judgment which is both purposeful and reflective. Because this book is about that process, it is about *how to go about deciding* what to believe or what to do. This is not a book about what we should believe or do. The purpose of the book is to assist you in strengthening your critical thinking skills and habits of mind. Why should you strengthen these skills and habits? To solve problems and make decisions more thoughtfully.

<<< Michelle Obama visits an elementary school to promote nutritious lunches and physical activity in schools as part of the "Let's Move!" Campaign. What decision-making factors contribute to our own choices to exercise regularly and eat healthily?

Risk and Uncertainty Abound

We might not skateboard through an intersection, but none of us can escape life's risks and uncertainties. Uncertainties apply to potentially good things, too. For example, people might be uncertain when choosing a major, taking a part-time job, making a new friend, or responding to a disaster stricken nation's call for volunteers. You never know what new friendships you will make, what new skills you will acquire, what new opportunities might emerge for you, how your efforts will benefit other people, or how much satisfaction you may feel. Whenever a choice is being contemplated, to maximize our chances for welcome outcomes and to minimize our chances for undesirable outcomes, we need to employ purposeful, reflective judgment. Sure, winning is great, but it's just not a good idea to play poker unless we can afford to lose. We need to think ahead, to plan, and to problem solve. This means we need **critical thinking**.

All of us encounter opportunities in our daily lives to engage problems and decisions using strong critical thinking. In a nation that values self-reliance and initiative, the stronger our critical thinking skills and habits of mind, the greater our prospects for success. Imagine a population that made thoughtful and informed judgments about the policy issues and social questions of its day. It is unlikely that such a citizenry would blindly accept whatever the authorities said was true or unquestioningly comply with whatever those leaders commanded. Some have argued that corporations that hope to succeed in a global high-tech world will have to cultivate exactly the kind of internal culture that fosters strong critical thinking.[ii] Fortunately, a great many leaders in government, business, education, military, and religious organizations truly value critical thinking.

"You will recall how you were inspired to THINK CRITICALLY and to question without fear, to seek out radically different solutions and to voice them without reprisal, to read widely and deeply, and to examine without end and grow intellectually. . . . What I ask is this: pass it on."

Navy Adm. Mike Mullen Ret., June 11, 2009[i]

The late comedian, George Carlin, offers his comical take on education and critical thinking. Using satire, irony, and his characteristically vulgar language, Carlin warns us not to swallow the mental junk food being served up by those whose only purpose is to maintain their own personal and corporate power and control.

Positive Examples of Critical Thinking

- A person trying to interpret an angry friend's needs, expressed through a rush of emotion and snide comments, to give that friend some help and support
- A manager trying to be as objective as possible when settling a dispute by summarizing the alternatives, with fairness to all sides to a disagreement
- A team of scientists working with great precision through a complex experiment in an effort to gather and analyze data
- A creative writer organizing ideas for the plot of a story and attending to the complex motivations and personalities of the fictional characters
- A person running a small business trying to anticipate the possible economic and human consequences of various ways to increase sales or reduce costs
- A master sergeant and a captain working out the tactical plans for a dangerous military mission.
- A soccer coach working during halftime on new tactics for attacking the weaknesses of the other team when the match resumes
- A student confidently and correctly explaining exactly to his or her peers the methodology used to reach a particular conclusion, or why and how a certain methodology or standard of proof was applied
- An educator using clever questioning to guide a student to new insights
- Police detectives, crime scene analysts, lawyers, judges, and juries systematically investigating, interrogating, examining, and evaluating the evidence as they seek justice
- A policy analyst reviewing alternative drafts of product safety legislation while determining how to frame the law to benefit the most people at the least cost
- An applicant preparing for a job interview thinking about how to explain his or her particular skills and experiences in a way that will be relevant and of value to the prospective employer
- Parents anticipating the costs of sending their young child to college, analyzing the family's projected income, and budgeting projected household expenses in an effort to put aside some money for that child's future education

The quote from Retired Admiral Michael Mullen, formerly the Chairman of the Joint Chiefs of Staff, is only one example.[iii]

Obviously, a society of knowledgeable people determined to apply strong critical thinking skills to evaluate the policy decisions of their leaders might pose major difficulties for those in power. Not everyone in a leadership position has the confidence and the wisdom to want to cultivate critical thinking. A master of irony, the late comedian George Carlin says it could be "Dangerous!" Go to **www.mythinkinglab.com** to access a video clip of Carlin on critical thinking. Some are so worried about the risks to their own power and position that they do not see the benefits to their organization's core purposes if its people are strong critical thinkers. Unscrupulous Machiavellian leaders might well ponder the question of how to distract, divert, or derail other people's critical thinking so that they can maintain their own power and control. After viewing the George Carlin clip we can almost hear the answer he might have imagined: Force-feed the population mental junk food by filling the popular media with celebrity inanities, sports trivia, exaggerated reports of imminent catastrophes, and outrageous opinions pumped out by extremist talk-show hosts like methane over a Coalinga cattle yard. Carlin uses a lot of vulgarity and potentially offensive language in this clip, which is unfortunate. The question for critical thinkers is: Can we identify the good ideas and claims a person may be making in spite of the person's off-putting way of expressing himself?

Watch the **Video** on **mythinkinglab.com**

To get a sense of perception management in action, rent the movies, *Wag the Dog* starring Robert De Niro and Dustin Hoffman, or *Syriana* with George Clooney. The novel, *The Whole Truth*, by the *NY Times* best-selling author, David Baldacci, does a superb job of showing the extent to which some could take perception management to achieve their self-interested purposes.

CRITICAL THINKING AND A FREE SOCIETY

If information is power, then controlling the flow of information is wielding power. As we saw with the Iranian elections in 2009, an organization that can withhold information or distort it to fit official orthodoxy is in a much better position to suppress dissenters and maintain its position of control. The Iranian government curtailed Internet access, blamed the United States and Great Britain for fomenting opposition, and used the coercive power of the police and the social status of the ruling clergy to maintain its control. Thus, the desire to know who truly won the election, voiced by the hundreds of thousands who at first protested in the streets of Tehran, soon dissipated. Even those with strong critical thinking skills could not get the information needed to make a correct application of those skills. It was hard to know what to think. And the fear of imprisonment and retaliation put a major damper on efforts to find out.

More recent history offers similar examples. Governments in Syria, Egypt, Yemen, Libya, China, and elsewhere have cut off social media, expelled foreign journalists, put out inaccurate press releases, and tried in many other ways to curtail the free flow of accurate information. Yes, we must not forget that assuring public safety and maintaining law and order are important goals. And living in a harmonious and peaceful society is highly desirable. That said, the bottom line is that it is difficult to foster the free and open questioning and the fair-minded search for the truth that is characteristic of strong critical thinking when education is reduced to uniformity of belief, when asking challenging questions leads to punishment, and when those in authority are determined to withhold information and distort the truth.[iv]

Education in a free society is about learning to think, the powers of the state are used to protect the right to free and open inquiry, people have the courage and the brains to ask hard questions, and there is unfettered access to accurate information. In a free society "perception management" is far more difficult. *Perception management* is the carefully choreographed manipulation of the beliefs and feelings of large numbers of people. Going beyond marketing and spin, perception management uses fear, anger, distortion, disinformation, and deceit—whatever it takes, including creating martyrs for the cause, faking enemy threats, lying to the media, destroying documents, etc.,—to achieve its goals. Those goals are always to influence people's beliefs and behavior, typically toward one outcome rather than another. The important thing is that

"Our whole constitutional heritage rebels at the thought of giving government the power to control men's minds."

Thurgood Marshall, Former U.S. Supreme Court Justice[v]

the people would probably not accept those beliefs or make those decisions if they had access to all of the relevant information. We will see an example of intentional dishonesty in Chapter 2 with a transcript of an interview with Victor Crawford, a man who spent his career doing perception management on behalf of the tobacco industry.

One reason higher education in America is internationally admired and yet feared is that it has the potential to teach critical thinking. The upside is great progress in learning and culture, and hence huge benefits for society. Problem solvers using critical thinking have achieved massive breakthroughs in science, technology, commerce, and the arts, such as cell phone technology, cancer treatments individualized to a person's unique DNA, global e-business, and new forms of music and architecture. But, at the same time, all that critical thinking can make interactions awkward at times. When people begin thinking for themselves, not only does that make things harder for would-be tyrants but people are apt to disagree, policy issues become more complicated to resolve, public discourse is more confusing, and decision making takes more time.

History shows what happens when people are not vigilant defenders of open, objective, and independent inquiry. We saw the results to a greater or lesser extent in Hitler's Germany, in Stalin's Russia, Mao Tse Tung's China, and, sadly, even in the twenty-first century. Too often governments aggrandize their own power by fear-mongering and projecting doomsday scenarios. Some governments stifle free and open inquiry not just by temporarily shutting down the Internet, but by outlawing potentially life-saving science (e.g., medical research involving human organ cloning). Some governments intimidate and imprison dissenters who object to their policies or who challenge their authority. (See, for example, the book *And Then They Came for Me*, by Maziar Bahari, 2011, and then Google the phrase "and then they came for me" for several examples of similar incidents around the world.) And some governments brand critics and whistle-blowers as traitors (e.g., the U.S. Justice Department's accusations against NSA employee Thomas Drake—accusations which were withdrawn after its legal case collapsed). In the name of security some governments—especially in Europe and North America—encroach on personal privacy with surveillance cameras, facial recognition software, computerized cell-phone and e-mail conversation monitors. Even if we assume the best of intentions, the maximum attention to avoiding mistakes, and the complete assurance that none of the information will be misused for personal political or economic gains, we should not be lulled into complacency.

Strong critical thinking demands a healthy skepticism where government power is concerned. None of us want to wake up one fine day groggy and hungover from overindulging in Fantasy Football, 3D action movies, fast foods, Hollywood gossip, shopping sprees, video games, margaritas, and chips and salsa, only to discover that while we were otherwise occupied our rights and freedoms were quietly, yet systematically, stripped away. We believe that one way to protect our cherished and hard-won freedoms is by using our critical thinking to assure open scientific inquiry, access to complete and accurate information, and the right to ask challenging questions and follow the reasons and the evidence wherever they may lead.

THE ONE AND THE MANY

Individual decisions can seem isolated and yet when they accumulate, they can have a far-reaching impact. For instance, in China the one-child policy has been in force for about 30 years. Culturally, there has always been a strong preference for male children; and if families could only have one child, most wanted a boy. In household after household, family after family made the choice to do whatever seemed necessary, including infanticide, to ensure a male heir. The collective impact of those millions of individual decisions now burdens that nation. In some villages, the ratio of unmarried men to unmarried women is 20 to 1. Today brides fetch payments as high as five

"Very few really seek knowledge in this world. Mortal or immortal, few really ask. On the contrary, they try to wring from the unknown the answers they have already shaped in their own minds—justification, explanations, forms of consolation without which they can't go on. To really ask is to open the door to the whirlwind. The answer may annihilate the question and the questioner."

Spoken by the *vampire* Marius in *The Vampire Lestat*[vi]

years of family income. Those parents who decided to raise their first-born daughters sure look smart now.

Around seven billion members of our species, give or take, share a planet in which economic, cultural, political, and environmental forces are so interconnected that the decisions of a few can impact the lives of many. Short-sighted and self-interested decisions made by corporate executives, bankers, stock traders, borrowers, and government regulatory agencies plunged the world into a global economic depression, which has cost trillions of dollars, devastated honest and well-run companies, bankrupted pension plans, destroyed families, and put tens of millions of people out of work. What were the decision makers thinking? What blinded all of us to the foreseeable consequences of our choices? Did we think that there wouldn't be adverse consequences if we all ran our credit card and mortgage debts to levels that were beyond our capacity to repay those debts? For some insights into the poor critical thinking that contributed to this global economic problem visit www.mythinkinglab.com for links to the HBO film *Too Big To Fail.*

Watch the **Video** on **mythinkinglab.com**

Another reason why we need to think critically: Acting on beliefs accepted without reflection and decisions made impulsively can be devastating to us and to our families, friends, co-workers, society, environment, and planet. We might believe that, in the great sweep of history, we generally are making progress toward the good. Karl Popper, a leading political theorist of the twentieth century, argued that this notion can be comforting particularly to authoritarian and totalitarian organizations.[vii] But the evidence suggests that civilizations rise and fall, that economies flourish and flounder, that the arts are encouraged and suppressed, that advances in learning are made and then forgotten. As a species we have very few advantages, other than our oversized brain and the critical thinking it can generate. We would be unwise not to use what little we have.

What Do We Mean By "Critical Thinking?"

At this point you might be asking yourself, "OK, I get it. Critical thinking is important. But what *is* critical thinking, exactly"? To answer that question precisely, an international group of 46 recognized experts in critical thinking research collaborated. The men and women in this group were drawn from many different academic disciplines, including philosophy, psychology, economics, computer science, education, physics, and zoology.

EXPERT CONSENSUS CONCEPTUALIZATION

For more than a year and a half, from February 1988 through September 1989, the group engaged in a consensus-oriented research process developed by the Rand Corporation and known as the "Delphi" method.[viii] The challenge put to the experts was to come up with a working consensus about the meaning of "critical thinking," which could serve instructional and assessment purposes from K-12 through graduate school and across the full range of academic disciplines and professional fields. They also asked themselves questions that relate to Chapter 2, namely: "What are the core critical thinking skills and subskills? How can we strengthen those skills in students? Who are the best critical thinkers we know, and what habits of mind do they have that lead us to consider them the best?"

Long story short, the expert consensus defined *"critical thinking"* as *"the process of purposeful, self-regulatory judgment."*[ix] The purpose is straightforward: to form a well-reasoned and fair-minded judgment regarding what to believe or what to do. The "self-regulatory" part refers to our capacity to monitor our own thinking process and to correct any mistakes we might detect.[x]

Strong critical thinking—making well-reasoned judgments about what to believe and what to do—is essential to consistently successful decision making. For many years we authors have consulted with various branches of the U.S. military, including Special Ops, with senior business executives and mid-level managers, and with educators, policy makers, health care professionals, scientists, jurists, and engineers. Time and again we learn that strong critical thinking can contribute to achieving goals and that poor critical thinking contributes to mission failure. Strong critical thinking is essential wherever the quality of one's decisions and the accuracy of one's beliefs make a difference.

Critical thinking is not the *only* vital element, don't get us wrong. Knowledge, dedication, training, and ethical courage also factor into the formula for success. We often learn more from our failures than from our successes; when we examine unsuccessful operations we often find that individuals or groups have failed, someplace along the line, to make well-reasoned judgments. Failures of critical thinking can result in some truly unfortunate outcomes, as the examples in the figure indicate. Can you think of any such instances in your own experience?

Failures of critical thinking contribute to...

patient deaths / lost revenue / ineffective law enforcement / job loss / gullible voters / garbled communications / imprisonment /combat casualties / upside down mortgages / vehicular homicide / bad decisions / unplanned pregnancies / financial mismanagement / heart disease / family violence / repeated suicide attempts / divorce / drug addiction / academic failure / ... / ... /

Failure of critical thinking often contributes to some of the saddest and most unfortunate accidents. In 2009, for example, 288 people died in the crash of an Air France jet liner. Investigators who examined the crash and its causes indicated that the pilots might have had enough time to prevent the disaster had they realized that the plane was stalling, instead of climbing to a safe altitude. But they appear to have misinterpreted the warning signals and wrongly analyzed their problem, which led them to make the wrong inferences about what they should do.[xi]

Occasionally we see in the news that some poor individual has had a tragic lapse in good judgment. Like the three young people who stepped passed the guard rails to take pictures at Yosemite Park's Vernal Falls. Other park visitors called to them, urging them to get back to safety, but they did not. Then suddenly one fell, the other two tried to help, and all three were swept over the falls to their deaths.[xii] Sad as it was, we have to ask ourselves, what were they thinking? If they had thoughtfully considered the risks and benefits, we doubt that they would have made the tragic decision to ignore the posted warnings.

Realizing that strong critical thinking often results in positive outcomes, but failures of critical thinking could lead to major problems, the experts who were asked to define critical thinking determined that it was best to focus on the *process of judgment.* What they wanted to capture was that strong critical thinking was reflective, well-reasoned, and focused on a specific purpose, such as what to do or what to believe. "Should we ignore the posted warnings?" "Is the aircraft gaining altitude or have we caused it to stall?"

Given the expert consensus definition of critical thinking as purposeful reflective judgment, one of the first things the experts realized was that critical thinking was a "pervasive human phenomenon." Critical thinking is occurring whenever an individual or a group of people makes a reasoned and reflective judgment about what to believe or what to do. They also realized that strong critical thinking was thoughtful and informed, not impulsive nor knee-jerk reactive.

How important did the experts think critical thinking was? They put their answer to that question this way: "Critical thinking is essential as a tool of inquiry. As such, critical thinking is a liberating force in education and a powerful resource in one's personal and civic life. While not synonymous with good thinking, critical thinking is a pervasive and self-rectifying human phenomenon."

So long as people have problems to solve and decisions to make, so long as they have things to learn and issues to resolve, there will be ample opportunities to use our critical thinking skills and habits of mind.

"CRITICAL THINKING" DOES NOT MEAN "NEGATIVE THINKING"

Critical thinking is not about bashing what people believe just to show how clever we are. Nor is critical thinking about using our skills to defend beliefs that we know are untrue or decisions we know are poor. Critical thinking is intended to be used to seek truth (small "t") with intellectual energy and with integrity. Thus, critical thinking is skeptical without being cynical. It is open-minded without being wishy-washy. It is analytical without being nitpicky. Critical thinking can be decisive without being stubborn, evaluative without being judgmental, and forceful without being opinionated.

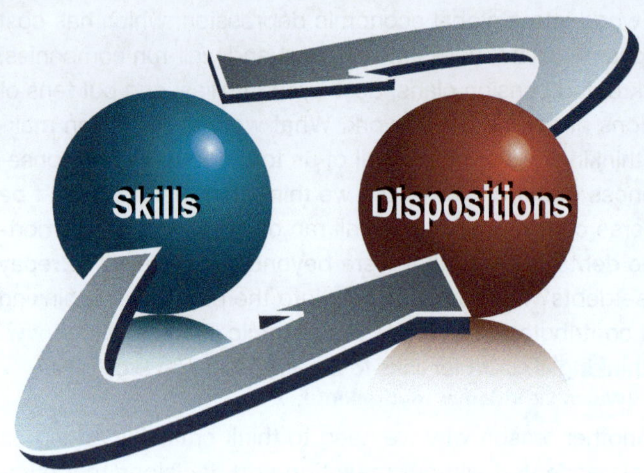

Critical Thinking Willing and Able

HOW TO GET THE MOST OUT OF THIS BOOK

Growth in critical thinking is about becoming more skillful and mentally disciplined. To maximize your growth, this book offers a variety of exercises, examples, and topics to think about. Some of these are intentionally jarring. Those among us who find it frightening to follow reason and evidence wherever they may lead, even if they go against cherished beliefs, will find it difficult to make progress in critical thinking. The same is true for those of us who try to avoid making decisions that involve uncertainty or risk or who try to live without ever questioning our own assumptions.

Think for a moment about learning to play a musical instrument or learning to play a sport. In both, improvement comes from practicing the requisite skills and strengthening our resolve to keep at it until we begin to see improvements. As we experience success at the skills part, enjoyment increases, and our disposition to keep applying ourselves grows. And, having an ever more positive attitude about striving to improve, we tend to enjoy more success as we seek to refine our skills. Each aspect feeds the other. To be a success the player must become not only able but willing, not just skillful but disposed to use those skills.

We learn to play a musical instrument so we can enjoy making music. We learn a sport to enjoy playing the game. We work on our skills and mental dispositions not for their own sake, but for the sake of making music or playing the game.

Thinking Critically Group Discussion: Critical Thinking and Risk Taking

Why do so many vacationers and sightseers foolishly risk their lives each year that our government must post warnings against even the most obvious dangers?

1 According to the National Park Service, over 250 people need to be rescued each year after they have tried to hike down into the Grand Canyon to reach the Colorado River and back up to the rim all in one day. More interestingly, these people tend to be young, healthy males. Why might this be? Is there something about the decision making of young healthy males that leads them, more than any other demographic, to take the kinds of risks that result in their needing to be rescued?

2 Not all risks are unreasonable. Parents worry all of the time about keeping their children safe, but what is the role of risk taking in childhood and adolescence? Visit www.mythinkinglab.com to read and listen to the National Public Radio discussion of "Teaching Kids to Take Healthy Risks" **http://www.npr.org/templates/story/story.php?storyId=126608357** and then read "Helicopter parents, who are they really protecting?"at www.mythinkinglab.com. Discuss the question: Should children be encouraged to climb trees? Rather than taking one side or the other, as in a debate, try instead to identify and elaborate on the best reasons for both sides of that question.

Listen to the **Podcast** on **mythinkinglab.com**

This is true with critical thinking, too. The defining purpose of critical thinking is to make reflective judgments about what to believe or what to do. We will work on both the skill part and the dispositional part as we move through this book. But we want to keep in mind that our purpose is to use them as tools to come to good judgments about what to do or what to believe.

Evaluating Critical Thinking

Even when we are first learning a musical instrument or a sport, we can tell that some of our peers are better at the instrument or the sport than others. We all make progress, and soon we are all doing much better than when we first started. We do not have to be experts to begin to see qualitative differences and to make reasonable evaluations. This, too, is true of critical thinking. There are some readily available ways to begin to make reasonable judgments concerning stronger or weaker uses of critical thinking. The following example illustrates some of these methods.

The Students' Assignment—Kennedy Act

Imagine a professor has assigned a group of four students to comment on the Edward M. Kennedy Serve America Act. Among other things, this bill, signed into law on April 21, 2009, designates September 11th as a National Day of Service and Remembrance. The group has access to the information about the bill reproduced here and on the Internet.

- "The bill encourages voluntary service. The legislation provides for gradually increasing the size of the Clinton-era AmeriCorps to 250,000 enrollees from its current 75,000. It outlines five broad categories where people can direct their service: helping the poor, improving education, encouraging energy efficiency, strengthening access to health care, and assisting veterans."
- "AmeriCorps offers a range of volunteer opportunities including housing construction, youth outreach, disaster response, and caring for the elderly. Most receive an annual stipend of slightly less than $12,000 for working 10 months to a year."
- "The bill also ties volunteer work to money for college. People 55 and older could earn $1,000 or more in education awards by getting involved in public service. Those education awards can be transferred to a child, grandchild, or even someone they mentored."
- "Students from sixth grade through senior year of high school could earn a $500 education award for helping in their neighborhoods during a new summer program."[xiii]
- "The new grant competitions carried out under the Serve America Act have generated a high volume of applications across all programs, reflecting growing recognition that national service is a valuable way to build capacity and

Corporation for National & Community Service

America's Promise Alliance

Peace Corps

Teach For America

Martin Luther King Jr. Day of Service

Learn and Serve

United Way

Habitat for Humanity

Americorps

Idealist

Senior Corps

Citizen Corps

Network for Good

Volunteer March Where Volunteering Begins

City Year

YSA Youth Service America

Selected National Service Organizations. Find out more at http://www.serve.gov/

address community challenges." For example, "The Social Innovation Fund ($50 million) will help effective nonprofits replicate their services in low-income communities."[xiv]

More information is available at **http://www.americorps.gov/**, and a summary of the legislation can be downloaded from **http://www.nationalservice.gov/about/serveamerica/index.asp**. The site **http://www.serve.gov/** is a clearinghouse of volunteer opportunities. Visit **www.mythinkinglab.com** for these links. **Read** the **Document** on **mythinkinglab.com**

The Students' Statements—Kennedy Act

Student #1: "My take on it is that this bill requires national service. It's like, . . . a churchy-service-sorta-thing. But, you know, like run by the government and all. We all have to sign up and do our bit before we can go to college. That's a great idea. Think about it, how could anyone be against this legislation? I mean, unless they are either lazy or selfish. What excuse could a person possibly have not to serve our country? The president is right, we need to bring back the draft so that our Army has enough soldiers, and we need to fix Wall Street and Social Security. I don't want to pay into a system all my working life only to find out that there's no money left when it's my time to retire."

Student #2: "Well I think this bill is a stupid idea. Who's going to agree to work for a lousy $12,000 a year? That's nuts. I can earn more working at Target or by enlisting in the Navy. This legislation is just more foolish liberal nonsense that takes our nation one step closer to socialism. Socialism is when the government tries to control too many things. And now the president is trying to control volunteer service. Maybe you want to build houses for poor people or clean up after hurricanes, but I don't see how any of that is going to help me pass physics or get me a better job after college."

Student #3: "I think there are problems with the legislation, too. But you're wrong about people not wanting to volunteer. The number of hits on the AmeriCorps Web site keeps going up and up each month. Retired people, students, and people who just want to make a difference go there and to Serve.gov to see what opportunities might exist near where they live. On the other hand, I do have issues with the government being the organizing force in this. Volunteerism was alive and well in America before Big Brother got involved. I don't see why we need to spend billions of dollars getting people to do what they were already going to do anyway. We shouldn't pay people to be volunteers."

Student #4: "That's the point, some of them wanted to do volunteer service but they need a small incentive. Nobody is going to get rich on the stipends the government is offering. But the new grant competitions for nonprofits, schools, and universities to create programs for at-risk youth in low-income communities and academic and service program for all young people is a way of directing government funds toward proven effective organizations that need money to keep doing good things for kids, teens, and families especially in these tough economic times. I think that people who want to keep government at arm's length are going to have problems with this bill. They are right that it is another way that government is worming itself into every facet of our lives. But a lot of people feel that way about religion, too; that's why they do not want to volunteer in programs sponsored by religious groups, because they don't want to be seen as agreeing with all the beliefs of that group. The real question for me is the effect that this legislation might have on the future politics of our nation. All these volunteers could become, in effect, people the administration can call on in the next election. Organizing tens of thousands Americans who basically agree with the idea of public service at public expense is like lining up the Democratic voters who will want to be sure these policies are not reversed by the Republicans. I'm not talking about a vague idea like "socialism," I'm talking about clever politics, positioning the Democratic Party for success in 2012. I'm not sure what I think about that yet. But we need to understand that this legislation will result in more than just a lot of wonderful work by a large number of generous Americans who are willing to give of their time to help others."

Having reviewed the information about this legislation and read the statements by each of the four students, how would you evaluate those statements in terms of the critical thinking each displays? Remember, base your evaluation on what the statements reveal about the quality of the reasoning, not on whether you agree or disagree with their conclusion. We'll offer our evaluative comments on these four statements in the paragraphs below. But before you read on, first make a preliminary assessment. Which of the four student statements would you rate right now as showing strong critical thinking and which do you regard at this point as showing the weak critical thinking?

> **"We need your service, right now, at this moment in history. I'm not going to tell you what your role should be; that's for you to discover. But I am asking you to stand up and play your part. I am asking you to help change history's course."**
>
> **President Barack Obama, April 21, 2009**[xv]

THE HOLISTIC CRITICAL THINKING SCORING RUBRIC

Every day we all make decisions about what to believe or what to do. When we are being reflective and fair-minded about doing so, we are using our critical thinking skills. The idea behind a critical thinking course is to help us strengthen these skills and fortify our intentions to use them when the occasion arises.

If that is true, then there probably is room for improvement—just as with other things we do that we may not have formally studied. But we are not starting from zero. We have critical thinking skills, even if we have not yet refined them to their maximum potential. We know what it means to be open-minded and to take a systematic and objective look at an issue. We are familiar with the ordinary English meanings of common words for talking about thinking such as *interpret, analyze*, *infer*, *explain*, *reason*, *conclusion*, *fallacy*, and *argument*. And, in a broad sense, a lot of the time we can tell the difference between strong reasoning and weak reasoning, even if we do not yet know all the details or terminology.

So, given that none of us are novices at critical thinking, we should be able to make a reasonable first stab at an evaluation of the thinking portrayed by the four students in the example on pages 10–11. Just using our experience and common sense we can agree that #4 and #3 are stronger than #2 and #1.

A tool designed to help us with this process of evaluation relies on the ordinary meanings of common terms used to talk about thinking. Called "The Holistic Critical Thinking Scoring

The Holistic Critical Thinking Scoring Rubric[xvi]

A Tool for Developing and Evaluating Critical Thinking

Peter A. Facione, Ph.D., and Noreen C. Facione, Ph.D.

Strong 4. Consistently does all or almost all of the following:

- Accurately interprets evidence, statements, graphics, questions, etc.
- Identifies the salient arguments (reasons and claims) pro and con.
- Thoughtfully analyzes and evaluates major alternative points of view.
- Draws warranted, judicious, non-fallacious conclusions.
- Justifies key results and procedures, explains assumptions and reasons.
- Fair-mindedly follows where evidence and reasons lead.

Acceptable 3. Does most or many of the following:

- Accurately interprets evidence, statements, graphics, questions, etc.
- Identifies relevant arguments (reasons and claims) pro and con.
- Offers analyses and evaluations of obvious alternative points of view.
- Draws warranted, non-fallacious conclusions.
- Justifies some results or procedures, explains reasons.
- Fair-mindedly follows where evidence and reasons lead.

Unacceptable 2. Does most or many of the following:

- Misinterprets evidence, statements, graphics, questions, etc.
- Fails to identify strong, relevant counterarguments.
- Ignores or superficially evaluates obvious alternative points of view.
- Draws unwarranted or fallacious conclusions.
- Justifies few results or procedures, seldom explains reasons.
- Regardless of the evidence or reasons, maintains or defends views based on self-interest or preconceptions.

Weak 1. Consistently does all or almost all of the following:

- Offers biased interpretations of evidence, statements, graphics, questions, information, or the points of view of others.
- Fails to identify or hastily dismisses strong, relevant counter-arguments.
- Ignores or superficially evaluates obvious alternative points of view.
- Argues using fallacious or irrelevant reasons and unwarranted claims.
- Does not justify results or procedures, nor explain reasons.
- Regardless of the evidence or reasons, maintains or defends views based on self-interest or preconceptions.
- Exhibits close-mindedness or hostility to reason.

Rubric" (HCTSR), this tool can aid us in evaluating real-life examples of critical thinking because it requires us only to consider the four evaluative descriptions: "strong," "acceptable," "unacceptable," and "weak" and see which of the four fits best. At this point, before we have worked through any of the other chapters of the book, this simple tool/approach is sufficient to get us started evaluating critical thinking. Naturally, as we learn more about critical thinking, we will become better at applying the rubric and more facile at using the terminology it contains. Our evaluative judgments will improve, and our ability to explain our judgments will improve as well. In this way, the rubric actually helps us to improve our critical thinking. Where we may disagree with one another at first about the evaluative levels that best fit, in time as we work with the rubric and with others on applying it, we will begin to form clearer ideas of the differences not only between the extreme examples, but between examples that fall between the extremes.

To apply the HCTSR, take each student's statement and see *which level of the Rubric offers the best description of the reasoning evident in that statement*. You will see that they line up rather well with the four levels of the HCTSR. Statement #4 is a good example of the top level, "strong"; student statement #3 is "acceptable"; student statement #2 is "unacceptable" because it displays the problems listed in the HCTSR in category 2; and statement #1 is so far off base that it qualifies as "weak."

Now that you have the HCTSR available to evaluate examples of real-life critical thinking, let's try it again with another set of four essays. As you read each essay response, compare what you are reading to the language on the HCTSR to determine which of the four descriptions, "strong," "acceptable," "unacceptable" and "weak" fits the best.

The Students' Assignment—Haiti

This time imagine a professor has asked her students to respond to the following essay question "Did the international community abandon Haiti or not? – give reasons and evidence to support your claim." The group has access to the information about the earthquake in Haiti reproduced here and on the Internet.

- On January 10, 2010, Haiti experienced its most deadly earthquake in the country's history. The quake left the capital city of Port-au-Prince flattened and the country devastated.
- The death toll is estimated to be upwards of 250,000 individuals, with 300,000 others being injured.
- The estimated cost of damage due to the earthquake is between 8 and 14 billion dollars.
- The international humanitarian effort has resulted in billions of dollars pledged and the creation of an Interim Haiti Recovery Commission being co-chaired by former U.S. President Bill Clinton.
- Over a year later, an estimated 375,000 people remain displaced with nearly 66,000 living in camps, and a newly elected president is facing a cholera epidemic in addition to recovery and reconstruction efforts.[xvii]

The Students' Statements—Haiti

Student #1: "I wouldn't say that the international community has abandoned Haiti as much as I would say that the international community has done nothing but make matters worse! That impoverished county had an earthquake that killed nearly 250,000 people and injured 300,000 more. I saw on Facebook that the cholera epidemic was caused by a Red Cross volunteer. That means that someone from the outside world caused a deadly disease to run rampant through the country. Everyone knows that developed countries only help out when there is something in it for them—like oil or bananas. Why else would the relief effort be run by a former U.S. president? What's his political motivation? One could say that the Haitian government or lack thereof is the main reason why Bill Clinton's commission has to run the recovery efforts and coordinate the funds for reconstruction, but I heard somewhere that Clinton's commission collected a ton of money for Haiti relief but hasn't spent even half of it yet. I don't get why not. You can be sure, however, that when the commission does spend the money it will only harm the Haitian economy. Clinton will probably give it all away like some kind of welfare program. The international community should abandon efforts so that no further harm is done."

Student #2: "I don't think the international community abandoned Haiti after the devastating earthquake. Even a year later you could still find news coverage of Haiti pretty much every day on the Internet. That means that Haiti has not been forgotten. Though the number of people who are still homeless is high, there are organizations over there that are rebuilding camps and schools. *60 Minutes* even showed a story about a guy who was

Thinking Critically — Who's Supposed to Help?

If you lost your home in a natural disaster, how many months and years would you and your family be willing to live in a temporary tent city? What if your government was unwilling or unable to provide more suitable housing, food, water, and loans to rebuild your home and business? Perhaps it is not the government's responsibility to offer those kinds of assistance. If not, is it any organization's responsibility? Perhaps a church, a university, or a charity? Or should the hurt and homeless after a natural disaster simply be left to fend for themselves? Whatever your view, articulate your reasons and then evaluate your reasoning using the HCTSR.

Semi-permanent post-earthquake tent city outside Port-au-Prince Haiti.

rebuilding a soccer field. They say that thousands of people have been able to go home and kids are able to attend the schools that have been reopened. I know the United States is not the only country that is helping in Haiti because the United Nations has sent money and workers—this means it is an international effort. Given that Haiti is not the only country needing our help, like Japan who had the tsunami, not to mention the hurricanes and tornados right here in America, the fact is that everyone is doing all that they can to help Haiti. What more can we possibly expect? I mean, we all have our problems. The biggest challenge is the cholera epidemic which is slowing down efforts to rebuild the country. Nobody knew what to do about that. But now that the president has been elected it should be possible to move forward with getting medicines to that country."

Student #3: "Haiti was abandoned by the international community. How else might we explain why numerous countries all over the world would have promised billions of dollars but then reneged on payment? Yes, lots of money and hundreds of emergency aid workers have been sent to that impoverished country, along with food, medicine, water, temporary shelters, and heavy machinery to clear the collapsed buildings that once were homes, schools, and businesses. But at the end of the day (or year in this case!) there is still so much left to be done. Several thousands of people are still living in camps, and those who are able to go home are afraid to live inside because they don't trust that their houses won't still collapse. At first there were no major issues related to diseases that typically follow a major natural disaster, and this was touted as a successful part of the relief effort, but now we see the country stricken with a cholera epidemic. The international community has made big promises to the people of Haiti but those promises have not yet been fulfilled. I support the people who are asking for an explanation of what is being done with the money that has been collected from the international community. If there is a reason to hold back on distributing the funds then that should be stated so that everyone knows the short- and long-term plan to achieve recovery and so that the people of Haiti know that the world still cares about them. And if we find no good reasons for holding back the money, then we should be told why it was not used sooner."

Student #4: "This is a really difficult question, but I'd have to say that the international community has not abandoned Haiti. This is not to say that the relief effort has been smooth, or that the country has been totally rebuilt in the 18 months since the deadly earthquake leveled Port-au-Prince. Nevertheless, an important distinction needs to be made between relief and recovery. Immediately following the earthquake monies and aid workers including doctors were rushed to Haiti. These monies and humanitarian aid were contributed by almost 40 different countries around the world, and involved organizations such as the United Nations, American Red Cross, and NGOs that are still hard at work in Haiti. These funds and workers were able to provide food, shelter, water and medicine to the survivors who were left homeless. Yes, many countries have pledge billions to help Haiti, and not all of the money has been spent. This has angered some—particularly the Haitian people and individuals directly involved in the organizations who are on the ground in Haiti trying to make the recovery effort move more quickly. It has got to be frustrating to know that monies have been pledged or collected but remain unspent, but the turmoil over the contested Presidential elections has to be considered—an unstable government is a liability when it comes to a wise and efficient use of public funds, even in the best of times. Finally, though it was once thought that the prevention of looting and disease in the immediate aftermath of the quake was evidence of the relief effort working, we should consider the cholera epidemic as evidence that the international community has forsaken Haiti. The cholera was entirely predictable when thousands are living in unsanitary camps. On the other hand, some international humanitarian organizations have stepped up their efforts to curtail the spread of cholera by provided medicine, sanitation, and fresh water which has effectively lessened the number of people who are dying from the outbreak. For these reasons I feel that the world has not given up on helping Haiti."

Like we did with the first set of student essays, we can apply the HCTSR to determine which level of the Rubric offers the best description of the reasoning evident in that statement. When reading these four student essays on Haiti in order we find that each displays stronger critical thinking than the one before. Statement #4 is a good example of the top level, "strong"; student statement #3 is "acceptable"; student statement #2 is "unacceptable" because it displays the problems listed in category 2 on the HCTSR; and statement #1 has many errors in thinking thereby qualifying it as "weak."

At this early stage in our discussion of critical thinking you only need to begin to differentiate among the four essays in

"Critical thinking is skeptical without being cynical. It is open-minded without being wishy-washy. It is analytical without being nitpicky. Critical thinking can be decisive without being stubborn, evaluative without being judgmental, and forceful without being opinionated."

Thinking Critically — Apply the Holistic Critical Thinking Scoring Rubric

1 Do restrictions on teacher-student interactions on social networking sites go too far? The *Kansas City Star* thinks so. And its editorial of June 14, 2011, explains why. Access the editorial at www.mythinkinglab.com (**http://www.kansascity.com/2011/06/14/2950695/the-stars-editorial-missouri-restrictions.html**). Read the editorial carefully and consider the quality of reasons presented, and then evaluate the editorial using the HCTSR.

2 In May of 2011 the U. S. Supreme Court ordered that California should reduce by 40,000 the number of prisoners in its jails if it could not properly incarcerate these inmates. An editorial appearing in stltoday.com warns that Missouri and Illinois should learn from California's errors. Read the editorial at www.mythinkinglab.com, (**http://www.stltoday.com/news/opinion/columns/the-platform/article_72f191c4-23e1-509a-862d-d71d53c18a22.html**) and consider the reasons presented. Visit credible national news Web sites and review summaries of that Supreme Court ruling so that you can confirm independently whether the editorial gets the relevant facts right. Then evaluate the reasoning presented in the editorial using the HCTSR.

3 When people first begin using a rubric like the HCTSR, it is important they calibrate their scoring with one another. Some individuals might initially rate something higher and others rate it lower. However, through mutual discussion, it is possible to help one another come to a reasonable consensus on a score. Identify two editorials and two letters to the editor that appear in your campus newspaper. Working with four classmates, individually rate those four things with the HCTSR. Then compare the scores that each of you initially assigned. Where the scores differ, discuss the critical thinking evident in the editorials or letters, and come to consensus on a score.

Read the Document on mythinkinglab.com

terms of the quality of the critical thinking they displayed. As we go though the chapters in this book the more technical explanations for their relative strengths and weaknesses will become much clearer. In the meantime, what is important is that you are able to recognize that the critical thinking generally improves as you go from the initial essay in the series on through to the fourth essay. As in real life, none of these four is absolutely dreadful and none is superbly stellar. But they do differ in the quality of the critical thinking displayed. Their differences will come into better focus as you get deeper into this book and progress in developing your own critical thinking.

The HCTSR is a great tool to use to evaluate the quality of the critical thinking evident in lots of different situations: classroom discussions, papers, essays, panel presentations, commercials, editorials, letters to the editor, news conferences, infomercials, commentator's remarks, speeches, jury deliberations, planning sessions, meetings, debates, or your own private thoughts. Keep the focus on the reasoning, and do not let the fact that you may agree or disagree with the particular conclusions being advocated sway you. Do not worry if you feel unsure of yourself, having used the HCTSR only a couple of times so far. There will be plenty of additional opportunities for you to practice with it in the exercises in this chapter and in future chapters. Like a new pair of shoes, the use of the tool will feel more comfortable with time. Think of it this way: The more you use the HCTSR, and the more adept you become at sorting out why something represents stronger or weaker critical thinking, the more you will improve your own critical thinking.

CHAPTER 01 REVIEW

Study and Review on mythinkinglab.com

CRITICAL THINKING is purposeful, reflective judgment that is focused on deciding what to believe or what to do. Critical thinking is a pervasive human phenomenon. We all have some level of skill in critical thinking and we have the capacity to improve those skills. Critical thinking skills are used to engage purposeful and reflective judgment. Critical thinking habits of mind motivate us to use those skills and incline us toward adopting critical thinking, rather than using some other approach, when we must make important decisions about what to believe or what to do. In the next chapter we will examine more deeply the specific skills and habits of mind that are central to critical thinking. These, then, are the skills and habits of mind we will be developing in focused ways as we work though this book. By building these skills and cultivating these habits of mind we become ever more willing and able to engage problems and make decisions using reflective judgment. That is, we become stronger critical thinkers.

Why critical thinking? Neither negative nor cynical, but thoughtful and fair-minded, critical thinking is essential for inquiry and learning. Neither reactive, nor impulsive, critical thinking is a liberating force in education and a precondition for a free and democratic society. Strong critical thinking is a powerful resource and tremendous asset in one's personal, professional, and civic life.

KEY TERM

Critical thinking is purposeful, reflective judgment that manifests itself in giving reasoned and fair-minded consideration to evidence, conceptualizations, methods, contexts, and standards in order to decide what to believe or what to do. (p. 4)

FIND IT ON MYTHINKINGLAB.COM

Explore the Concept on mythinkinglab.com This chapter features the ironic and at times caustic observations of the late George Carlin, comedian and social critic. I invite you to view video clips for this chapter and the dozens of other video clips cited throughout this book by going to www.mythinkinglab.com. Be advised, however, that Carlin is known not only for his humor and insight, but also for his vigorous use of profanity.

Why are we inviting you to mythinkinglab.com? You have the right to ask that, given that this is a book about giving reasons and making strong arguments. Strengthening our critical thinking for use in real-life contexts requires that we practice with realistic examples. As valuable as text-based examples will be for us in this book, we must also use examples that are visual, auditory, and culturally complex. The best examples require us to analyze and interpret body language, gestures, and unspoken but implicit assumptions. Video clips, particularly if we watch them carefully and analyze them in detail, are powerful devices for engaging our critical thinking.

In this chapter we put George Carlin's liberal views side by side with Admiral Mullen, whom we can consider a strong and articulate representative of a more conservative perspective. This juxtaposition is intentional. There are strong critical thinkers on all sides of the political spectrum. We would be mistaken to categorize people who agree with us as strong critical thinkers and those who disagree as weak critical thinkers. Please be careful about this as you work through the exercises in this chapter and throughout the book. In this book, as in real life, we often encounter vivid images, topics, issues, people, and events that trigger immediate positive or negative reactions. Critical thinking in real life must find its way through our initial reactions and locate that place in our minds where reflective thinking, a full and accurate understanding of the relevant facts, and wise judgments guide what we believe and what we do. This takes practice.

We invited you to visit www.mythinkinglab.com several times in this chapter.

- To hear what George Carlin has to say about critical thinking. (p. 5)
- To get materials relevant to exercise questions, e.g., on risk taking in childhood. (p. 9)
- To links to more articles on the 2010 Haiti's recovery from the earthquake, as well as articles discussing the recovery efforts in Japan after the 2011 Tsunami and New Orleans after Hurricane Katrina in 2005.
- To locate videos—e.g., the HBO Film *Too Big To Fail*. (p. 7)
- To do the background reading for the HCTSR exercises. (p. 15).
- And when you go there, you will also find additional HCTSR exercises and more learning aids for this chapter.

Exercises

REFLECTIVE LOG

Think back over today and yesterday. Describe a problem you faced or a decision which you considered. Who was involved, and what was the issue? Describe how you thought about that problem or decision—not so much what you decided or what solution you picked, but the process you used. Were you open-minded about various options, systematic in your approach, courageous enough to ask yourself tough questions, bold enough to follow the reasons and evidence wherever they led, inquisitive and eager to learn more before making a judgment, nuanced enough to see shades of gray rather than only stark black and white? Did you check your interpretations and analyses? Did you draw your inferences carefully? Were you as objective and fair-minded as you might have been? Explain your decision in your log with enough detail that would permit you to go back a week or two from now and evaluate your decision for the quality of the critical thinking it demonstrates.

EACH OF THESE CLAIMS IS MISTAKEN IN SOME WAY. EXPLAIN WHAT IS WRONG IN EACH CASE

1. Critical thinking has no application in day-to-day life.
2. "Critical thinking" means criticizing other people's thinking.
3. Democracies get along just fine even if people do not think for themselves.
4. Decisions about how I want to live my life do not affect other people.
5. Reflective decision making requires little or no effort.
6. Deciding what to believe or what to do is not possible without critical thinking.
7. If we disagree on something, then one of us is not using critical thinking.
8. Every time I make a judgment I am engaged in critical thinking.
9. It will only undermine authority, if we teach young people to think critically.
10. Reasons are irrelevant; having the right opinion is the only thing that matters.
11. Some people achieve popularity, wealth, and power without appearing to be strong critical thinkers, but you're saying that this can't happen to me.
12. I'm already very confident in my critical thinking ability, so there is no reason for me to go any further in this book.
13. If critical thinking is a mental process, then it will not help me learn the informational content of my other college courses.
14. You only are going to make trouble for yourself by rocking the boat with challenging questions and demands for reasons and evidence. Hey, you got to go along to get along.
15. I'm always disagreeing with authority figures, so I must be a great critical thinker.
16. I like many of the things that my city, county, state and national government does, so I must be a weak critical thinker.
17. It is fine to apply critical thinking in education, business, science, law enforcement, and international problems, but there is no place for critical thinking in religious matters.
18. Looking at the HCTSR, I find that my family and friends do not seem to be very good critical thinkers, so I don't have much of a chance to become one either.
19. If you are a strong critical thinker you will automatically be an ethical person.
20. Once you become adept at engaging problems and decisions using strong critical thinking, it is easy to quit.

GROUP DISCUSSION #1: THINK NOT!

Critical thinking takes effort! Why work so hard? Imagine what it would be like to live in a community where critical thinking was illegal. What might the risks and benefits of such a life be? How would the people living in that community redress grievances, solve problems, plan for the future, evaluate options, and pursue their individual and joint purposes? Now imagine what it would be like to live in a community where critical thinking was unnecessary. Can there be such a place, except perhaps as human specimens in some other species' zoo?

GROUP DISCUSSION #2: WHAT WERE WE THINKING?

If we learn best from our mistakes, then what can the international community learn about how best to assist a nation in recovering from catastrophic events given the experiences like Hurricane Katrina in 2005, the 2010 earthquake in Haiti, and the 2011 tsunami that hit Japan? Provide reasons and evidence in support of your response to the question.

Read the Chapter on mythinkinglab.com

Listen to the Chapter Audio on mythinkinglab.com

After training

for every conceivable contingency, the unexpected happened. Initially, the challenge was simply to figure out what the problem was. If it could be correctly identified, then there might be some slim chance of survival. If not, the outcome could be tragic.

Watch the Video on mythinkinglab.com As you watch the video clip at www.mythinkinglab.com, keep in mind that you are seeing a dramatic reenactment. The actors, music, camera angles, staging, props, and lighting all contribute to our overall experience. That said, this portrayal of individual and group problem solving is highly consistent with the research on human cognition and decision making.[i] The clip dramatizes a group of people engaged in thinking critically together about one thing: *What could the problem be?* Their approach is to apply their reasoning skills to the best of their ability. But, more than only their thinking skills, their mental habits of being analytical, focused, and systematic enabled them to apply those skills well during the moment of crisis. We suggest that you watch the brief video prior to reading the summary analysis of *Apollo 13*.

<<< In *Apollo 13* Tom Hanks and Kevin Bacon portray astronauts working together using critical thinking to identify the exact problem threatening their mission and their lives.

CHAPTER 02

Skilled and Eager to Think

HOW can I cultivate positive critical thinking habits of mind?

WHAT questions can I ask to engage my critical thinking skills?

WHAT are induction and deduction, and how do they differ?

HOW can I best use this book to develop my critical thinking skills?

Positive Critical Thinking Habits of Mind

The *Apollo 13* sequence opens with the staff at Mission Control in Houston and the three-person crew of *Apollo 13* well into the boredom of routine housekeeping. Suddenly, the crew of *Apollo 13* hears a loud banging noise and their small, fragile craft starts gyrating wildly. The startled look on Tom Hanks's face in the video reenactment is priceless. A full fifteen seconds elapses before he speaks. During that time his critical thinking is in overdrive. He is trying to interpret what has just happened. His mind has to make sense of the entirely unexpected and unfamiliar experience. He neither dismisses nor ignores the new information that presents itself. His attention moves between checking the craft's instrument panel and attending to the sounds and motions of the spacecraft itself. He focuses his mind, forms a cautious but accurate interpretation, and with the disciplined self-control we expect of a well-trained professional, he informs Mission Control in Houston, Texas that they most definitely have a problem![ii]

At first, the astronauts in the spacecraft and the technicians at Mission Control call out information from their desk monitors and the spacecraft's instrument displays. They crave information from all sources. They know they must share what they are learning with each other as quickly as they can in the hope that someone will be able to make sense out of things. They do not yet know which piece of information may be the clue to their life-or-death problem, but they have the discipline of mind to want to know everything that might be relevant. And they have the confidence in their collective critical thinking skills to believe that this approach offers their best hope to identify the true problem.

One member of the ground crew calls out, that O_2 Tank Two is not showing any readings. That vital bit of information swooshes by almost unnoticed in the torrents of data. Soon a number of people begin proposing explanations: Perhaps the spacecraft had been struck by a meteor. Perhaps its radio antenna is broken. Perhaps the issue is instrumentation, rather than something more serious, like a loss of power.

The vital critical thinking skill of Self-Regulation is personified in the movie by the character played by Ed Harris. His job is to monitor everything that is going on and to correct the process if he judges that it is getting off track. Harris's character makes the claim that the problem cannot simply be instrumentation. The reason for that claim is clear and reasonable. The astronauts are reporting hearing loud bangs and feeling their spacecraft jolt and shimmy. The unspoken assumption, one every pilot and technician understands in this context is that these physical manifestations—the noises and the shaking—would not be occurring if the problem were instrumentation. The conclusion Harris's character expressed has the effect of directing everyone's energy and attention toward one set of possibilities, those that would be considered real problems rather than toward the other set of possibilities. Had he categorized the problem as instrumentation, then everyone's efforts would have been directed toward checking and verifying that the gauges and computers were functioning properly.

There is a very important lesson for good critical thinking in what we see Ed Harris doing. Judging correctly what kind of problem we are facing is essential. If we are mistaken about what the problem is, we are likely to consume time, energy, and resources exploring the wrong kinds of solutions. By the time we figure out that we took the wrong road, the situation could have become much worse than when we started. The *Apollo 13* situation is a perfect example. In real life, had the people at Mission Control in Houston classified the problem as instrumentation, they would have used up what little oxygen there was left aboard the spacecraft while the ground crew spent time validating their instrument readouts.

Back on the spacecraft, Tom Hanks, who personifies the critical thinking skills of interpretation and inference, is struggling to regain navigational control. He articulates the inference by saying that had they been hit by a meteor, they would all be dead already. A few moments later he glances out the spacecraft's side window. Something in the rearview mirror catches his attention. Again, his inquisitive mind will not ignore what he's seeing. A few seconds pass as he tries to interpret what it might be. He offers his first observation that the craft is venting something into space. The mental focus and stress of the entire Houston ground crew are etched on their faces. Their expressions reveal the question in their minds: What could he possibly be seeing? Seconds pass with agonizing slowness. Using his interpretive skills, Tom Hanks categorizes with caution and then, adding greater precision, he infers that the venting must be some kind of a gas. He pauses to try to figure out what the gas might be and realizes that it must surely be the oxygen. Kevin Bacon looks immediately to the oxygen tank gauge on the instrument panel for information that might confirm or disconfirm whether it really is the oxygen. It is.

"If we were compelled to make a choice between these personal attributes [of a thoughtful reasoner] and knowledge about the principles of logical reasoning together with some degree of technical skill in manipulating special logical processes, we should decide for the former."

John Dewey, *How We Think*[iii]

Critical Thinking Disposition Self-Rating Form

Answer yes or no to each. Can I ***name any specific instances over the past two days*** when I:

1 ____ was courageous enough to ask tough questions about some of my longest held and most cherished beliefs?

2 ____ backed away from questions that might undercut some of my longest held and most cherished beliefs?

3 ____ showed tolerance toward the beliefs, ideas, or opinions of someone with whom I disagreed?

4 ____ tried to find information to build up my side of an argument but not the other side?

5 ____ tried to think ahead and anticipate the consequences of various options?

6 ____ laughed at what other people said and made fun of their beliefs, values, opinion, or points of views?

7 ____ made a serious effort to be analytical about the foreseeable outcomes of my decisions?

8 ____ manipulated information to suit my own purposes?

9 ____ encouraged peers not to dismiss out of hand the opinions and ideas other people offered?

10 ____ acted with disregard for the possible averse consequences of my choices?

11 ____ organized for myself a thoughtfully systematic approach to a question or issue?

12 ____ jumped in and tried to solve a problem without first thinking about how to approach it?

13 ____ approached a challenging problem with confidence that I could think it through?

14 ____ instead of working through a question for myself, took the easy way out and asked someone else for the answer?

15 ____ read a report, newspaper, or book chapter or watched the world news or a documentary just to learn something new?

16 ____ put zero effort into learning something new until I saw the immediate utility in doing so?

17 ____ showed how strong I was by being willing to honestly reconsider a decision?

18 ____ showed how strong I was by refusing to change my mind?

19 ____ attended to variations in circumstances, contexts, and situations in coming to a decision?

20 ____ refused to reconsider my position on an issue in light of differences in context, situations, or circumstances?

If you have described yourself honestly, this self-rating form can offer a rough estimate of what you think your overall disposition toward critical thinking has been in the past two days.

Give yourself 5 points for every "Yes" on odd numbered items and for every "No" on even numbered items. If your total is 70 or above, you are rating your disposition toward critical thinking over the past two days as generally positive. Scores of 50 or lower indicate a self-rating that is averse or hostile toward critical thinking over the past two days. Scores between 50 and 70 show that you would rate yourself as displaying an ambivalent or mixed overall disposition toward critical thinking over the past two days.

Interpret results on this tool cautiously. At best this tool offers only a rough approximation with regard to a brief moment in time. Other tools are more refined, such as the *California Critical Thinking Disposition Inventory*, which gives results for each of the seven critical thinking habits of mind.

Being by habit inclined to anticipate consequences, everyone silently contemplates the potential tragedy implied by the loss of oxygen. As truth-seekers, they must accept the finding. They cannot fathom denying it or hiding from it. Their somber response comes in the form of Mission Control's grim but objective acknowledgment that the spacecraft is venting.

OK, now we have the truth. What are we going to do about it? The characters depicted in this movie are driven by a powerful orientation toward using critical thinking to resolve whatever problems they encounter. The room erupts with noise as each person refocuses on their little piece of the problem. People are moving quickly, talking fast, pulling headset wires out of sockets in their haste. The chaos and cacophony in the room reveal that the group is not yet taking a systematic, organized approach. Monitoring this, Ed Harris's character interjects another self-correction into the group's critical thinking. He may not yet know how this problem of the oxygen supply is going to be solved or even whether this problem can be solved, but he is going to be sure that the ground crew addresses it with all the skill and all the mental power it can muster. He directs everyone to locate whomever they may need to assist them in their work and to focus themselves and those others immediately on working the problem.

As depicted in this excerpt, the combined ground crew and spacecraft crew, as a group, would earn a top score on "Holistic Critical Thinking Scoring Rubric." The emotions and stresses of the situation are unmistakable. The group's powerfully strong critical thinking habits of mind enable the group to use that energy productively. It gives urgency to the efforts. Thus, the message about our thinking processes that emerges is that emotion need not be the antithesis to reason; emotion can be the impetus to reason.

THE SPIRIT OF A STRONG CRITICAL THINKER

The scene shown in the video clip was well staged. Skillful actors displayed the behaviors and responses of strong critical thinkers engaged in problem solving at a moment of crisis. Authors of screenplays and novels often endow their protagonists with strongly positive critical thinking skills and dispositions. The brilliantly insightful Sherlock Holmes, played in films by Robert Downey Jr., the analytical and streetwise NYPD Detective Jane Timoney from the NBC series *Prime Suspect*, played by Maria Bello, or the clever and quick witted Patrick Jane in the CBS series *The Mentalist*, played by Simon Baker, come to mind as examples. A key difference, however, is that fictional detectives always solve the mystery, while, as we all know, in the real world there is no guarantee. Critical thinking is about *how* we approach problems, decisions, questions, and issues even if ultimate success eludes us. Being disposed to engage our skills as best we can is the "eager" part of "skilled and eager" to think. First we will examine the "eager" part, beginning with taking a closer look at the overall disposition toward critical thinking. Later in this chapter we will examine the "skilled" part, the core critical thinking skills.

POSITIVE AND NEGATIVE HABITS OF MIND

A person with a strong *disposition* toward critical thinking has the *consistent internal motivation* to engage problems and make decisions by using critical thinking.[iv] Operationally this means three things: The person consistently *values* critical thinking, *believes* that using critical thinking skills offers the greatest promise for reaching good judgments, and *intends* to approach problems and decisions by applying critical thinking skills as best as he or she can. This combination of values, beliefs, and intentions forms the habits of mind that dispose the person toward critical thinking.[v]

Someone strongly disposed toward critical thinking would probably agree with the following statements:

- "I hate talk shows where people shout their opinions but never give any reasons at all."
- "Figuring out what people really mean by what they say is important to me."
- "I always do better in jobs where I'm expected to think things out for myself."
- "I hold off making decisions until I have thought through my options."
- "Rather than relying on someone else's notes, I prefer to read the material myself."
- "I try to see the merit in another's opinion, even if I reject it later."
- "Even if a problem is tougher than I expected, I will keep working on it."
- "Making intelligent decisions is more important than winning arguments."

Persons who display a strong positive disposition toward critical thinking are described in the literature as "having a critical spirit," or as people who are "mindful," "reflective," and "meta-cognitive." These expressions give a person credit for consistently applying their critical thinking skills to whatever problem, question, or issue is at hand. People with a critical spirit tend to ask good questions, probe deeply for the truth, inquire fully into matters, and strive to anticipate the consequences of various options. In real life our skills may or may not be strong enough, our knowledge may or may not be adequate to the task at hand. The problem may or may not be too difficult for us. Forces beyond our control might or might not determine the actual outcome. None of that cancels out the positive critical thinking habits of mind with which strong critical thinkers strive to approach the problems life sends their way.

A person with weak critical thinking dispositions might disagree with the previous statements and be more likely to agree with these:

- "I prefer jobs where the supervisor says exactly what to do and exactly how to do it."
- "No matter how complex the problem, you can bet there will be a simple solution."
- "I don't waste time looking things up."
- "I hate when teachers discuss problems instead of just giving the answers."
- "If my belief is truly sincere, evidence to the contrary is irrelevant."
- "Selling an idea is like selling cars; you say whatever works."
- "Why go to the library when you can use made-up quotes and phony references?"
- "I take a lot on faith because questioning the fundamentals frightens me."
- "There is no point in trying to understand what terrorists are thinking."

When it comes to approaching specific questions, issues, decisions or problems, people with a weak or negative critical thinking disposition are apt to be impulsive, reactive, muddle-headed, disorganized, overly simplistic, spotty about getting relevant information, likely to apply unreasonable criteria, easily distracted, ready to give up at the least hint of difficulty, intent on a solution that is more detailed than is possible, or too readily satisfied with some uselessly vague response.

PRELIMINARY SELF-ASSESSMENT

It is only natural to wonder about our own disposition. The "Critical Thinking Disposition Self-Rating Form," found on page 21, offers us a way of reflecting on our own values, beliefs, and intentions about the use of critical thinking. As noted on the form itself, "This tool offers only a rough approximation with regard to a brief moment in time." We invite you to take a moment and complete the self-assessment. Keep in mind as you interpret the results that this measure does not assess critical thinking skills. Rather, this tool permits one to reflect on whether, over the past two days, the disposition manifested in behavior was positive, ambivalent, or averse toward engaging in thoughtful, reflective, and fair-minded judgments about what to believe or what to do.

RESEARCH ON CRITICAL THINKING HABITS OF MIND

The broad understanding of being disposed toward using critical thinking, or disposed away from using critical thinking, has been the object of empirical research in the cognitive sciences since the early 1990s. The purpose of this research has been to give greater precision to the analysis and measurement of the dispositional dimension of critical thinking.

Seven Positive Critical Thinking Habits of Mind

One research approach involved asking thousands of people to indicate the extent to which they agreed or disagreed with a long list of statements not unlike those in the two short lists presented above. Using statistical analysis, these researchers identified seven measurable aspects within the overall disposition toward critical thinking. We can think of these as the seven positive critical thinking habits of mind.[vi] Based on this research, we can describe someone who has all seven positive critical thinking habits of mind as a person who is:

- **Truth-seeking** – meaning that the person has intellectual integrity and a courageous desire to actively strive for the best possible knowledge in any given situation. A truth-seeker asks probing questions and follows reasons and evidence wherever they lead, even if the results go against his or her cherished beliefs.
- **Open-minded** – meaning that the person is tolerant of divergent views and sensitive to the possibility of his or her own possible biases. An open-minded person respects the right of others to have different opinions.
- **Analytical** – meaning that the person is habitually alert to potential problems and vigilant in anticipating consequences and trying to foresee short-term and long-term outcomes of events, decisions, and actions. Another word to describe this habit of mind might be "Foresightful."
- **Systematic** – meaning that the person consistently endeavors to take an organized and thorough approach to identifying and resolving problems. The systematic person is orderly, focused, persistent, and diligent in his or her approach to problem solving, learning, and inquiry.
- **Confident in reasoning** – meaning that the person is trustful of his or her own reasoning skills to yield good judgments. A person's or a group's confidence in their own critical thinking may or may not be warranted, which is another matter.
- **Inquisitive** – meaning that the person habitually strives to be well-informed, wants to know how things work, and seeks to learn new things about a wide range of topics, even if the immediate utility of knowing those things is not directly evident. The inquisitive person has a strong sense of intellectual curiosity.
- **Judicious** – meaning that the person approaches problems with a sense that some are ill-structured and some can have more than one plausible solution. The judicious person has the cognitive maturity to realize that many questions and issues are not black and white and that, at times, judgments must be made in contexts of uncertainty.

Negative Habits of Mind

After the measurement tools were refined and validated for use in data gathering, the results of repeated samplings showed that some people are strongly positive on one or more of the seven positive dispositional aspects. Some people are ambivalent or negatively disposed on one or more of the seven.

There is a name associated with the negative end of the scale for each of the seven attributes, just as there is a name associated with the positive end of the scale. The "Critical Thinking Habits of Mind" chart on page 26 lists the names, for both positive and negative attributes. A person's individual dispositional portrait emerges from the seven, for a person may be positive, ambivalent, or negative on each.

In the film *Philadelphia*, Denzel Washington plays a personal liability litigator who is not above increasing the amount a client seeks for "pain and suffering" by hinting to the client that he may have more medical problems than the client had at first noticed. Watch the scene where a new potential client, played by Tom Hanks, visits Washington's office seeking representation. Access this clip at www.mythinkinglab.com. **Watch** the **Video** on **mythinkinglab.com**

The clip from *Philadelphia* starts out with Denzel Washington talking to a client who wants to sue the city over a foolish accident that the man brought upon himself. The scene establishes that Washington is a hungry lawyer who will take almost any case. Tom Hanks comes into the office and says that he wants to sue his former employer, believing that he was wrongly fired from his job because he has AIDS. You would think that Washington would jump at this opportunity. There is a lot of money to be made if he can win the case. Truth-seeking demands that the real reason for the firing be brought to light. But at this point in the story, Washington declines to take the case.

Notice what the filmmakers do with the camera angles to show what Washington is thinking as he considers what to do. His eyes focus on the picture of his wife and child, on the skin lesion on Hanks's head, and on the cigars and other things Hanks touches. The story takes place during the early years when the general public did not understand AIDS well at all. It was a time when prejudices, homophobia, and misinformation

The Disposition toward Critical Thinking

nonverbal thinking cues are so well done by the filmmakers that we are not surprised when Washington, having thought things through, refuses to take the case.

There is no question that critical thinking is wonderfully powerful. Yet, by itself it is incomplete. We need knowledge, values, and sensitivities to guide our thinking. Washington's character is sensitive to what he thinks are the dangers of the disease and what he believes (wrongly) about the ways it might be transmitted. His character uses his critical thinking skills, which turn out to be quite formidable as the film progresses. But his beliefs about AIDS are simply wrong. He makes a judgment at the time not to represent Hanks's character. It is not the same judgment he will make later in the film, after he becomes better informed. Fortunately, he has the open-mindedness to entertain the possibility of representing Hanks's character, that perhaps Hanks's character does have a winnable case, and that perhaps the risks associated with AIDS are not as great as he had at first imagined. He has the inquisitiveness and the truth-seeking skills to gather more accurate information. And he has the judiciousness to reconsider and to change his mind.

surrounded the disease. Washington's character portrays the uncertainty and misplaced fears of the U.S. public at that time. Not understanding AIDS or being misinformed, Washington's character is frightened for himself and for his family. Notice how he stands in the very far corner of his office, as physically far away from Hanks's character as possible. He wipes his hand against his trousers after shaking hands. The

Thinking Critically — How Does TV Portray Critical Thinking?

1 **You can do this exercise by yourself or with a classmate.** This exercise requires watching TV for two hours. Begin with a clean piece of paper and draw a line down the page. Mark one side + and the other –. With pencil and paper in hand, watch CBS, NBC, or ABC or a cable network that shows commercials along with its regular programming. Pay close attention to the commercials, not the regular programming. Note each of the people who appear on screen. If you judge that a person is portrayed as a strong critical thinker, note it (e.g., Woman in car commercial +). If you think a person is portrayed as a weak critical thinker, note that (e.g., Three guys in beer commercial – – –). If you cannot tell (e.g., in the car commercial there were two kids riding in the back seat but they were not doing or saying anything), do not make any notation. After watching only the commercials during one hour of programming, total up the plusses and the minuses. Now do the same thing for another hour, but this time pay attention only to the regular programming, not the commercials. Again note every character who appears and indicate on the paper if the person is portrayed as a strong critical thinker (e.g., evil bad guy +, clever detective +) or a weak critical thinker (e.g., victim who foolishly walked into the dark alley alone –). Tally up the plusses and minuses. Based on your observations, is there a tendency or pattern that might be evident regarding the critical thinking strengths or weaknesses of children, adolescents, young adults, middle-aged people, and senior citizens?

2 **Group Project – 4-page mini-paper:** Attitudes, while not immutable, are shaped and formed as we mature. To the extent that the disposition toward critical thinking is attitudinal, it can be affected by our experiences growing up. Begin by locating research reports (not just opinion pieces) in which credible experts report findings based on solid data about the impact of the images of ourselves we see on television and whether those images influence how we behave. Research on the power of TV stereotypes, for example, can be a good place to start. Consider what you learn through your review of the materials you found, and drawing too on your own life experience, formulate your response to this question: What is the potential impact that the characters portrayed on TV have on the disposition toward critical thinking, which is developing in adolescents? Explain your opinion on this by providing reasons, examples, and citations. In the last part of your short paper, respond to this question: What kind of evidence would lead you to revise or reverse the opinion you have been presenting and explaining?

In *Philadelphia*, the plaintiff, played by Tom Hanks, and his lawyer, played by Denzel Washington, wade through a crowd of reporters. How does Denzel Washington's character use critical thinking throughout the course of the film?

"The expressions *mental disciplines* and *mental virtues* can be used to refer to *habits of mind* as well. The word *disciplines* in a military context and the word *virtues* in an ethical context both suggest something positive. We will use *habits of mind* because the word *habit* is neutral. Some habits are good, others bad. As will become evident, the same can be said with regard to critical thinking habits of mind. Some, like truth-seeking, are positive. Others, like indifference or intellectual dishonesty, are negative."

IS A GOOD CRITICAL THINKER AUTOMATICALLY A GOOD PERSON?

Thinking about Denzel Washington's character in *Philadelphia* raises the natural question about how critical thinking might or might not be connected with being an ethical person. We have been using the expression "strong critical thinker" instead of "good critical thinker" because of the ambiguity of the word *good*. We want to praise the person as a critical thinker without necessarily making a judgment about the person's ethics. For example, a person can be adept at developing cogent arguments and very adroit at finding the flaws in other people's reasoning, but that same person can use these skills unethically to mislead and exploit a gullible person, perpetrate a fraud, or deliberately confuse, confound, and frustrate a project.

A person can be *strong* at critical thinking, meaning that the person can have the appropriate dispositions, and be adept using his or her critical thinking skill, but still not be an ethical critical thinker. There have been people with superior thinking skills and strong habits of mind who, unfortunately, have used their talents for ruthless, horrific, and immoral purposes.

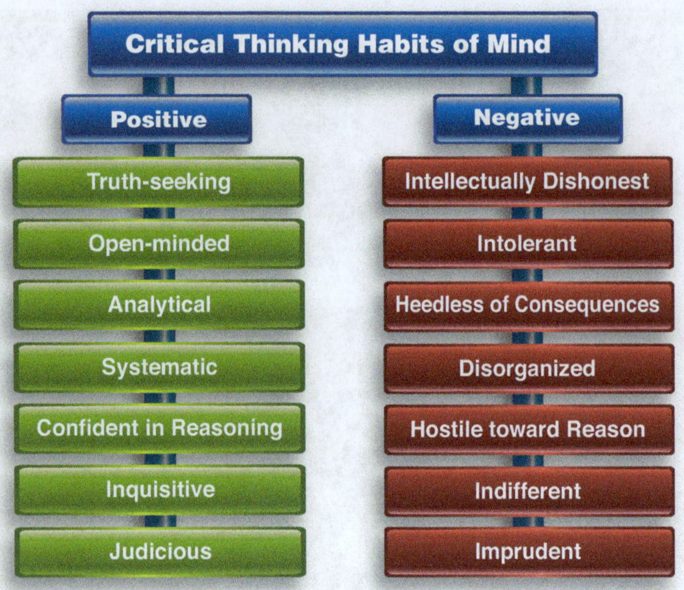

To get some sense of the colossal problems that result from our collective failures to anticipate consequences, watch the documentary film *The Unforeseen* (2007, directed by Laura Dunn). It is the remarkable story of the loss of quality of life and environmental degradation associated with real estate development in Austin, Texas, over the past 50 years.

It would be great if experience, knowledge, mental horsepower, and ethical virtue were all one and the same. But they are not.

Consider, for example, the revelations that Victor Crawford, a tobacco lobbyist, makes in the clip from his *60 Minutes* interview with Leslie Stahl. You can access a transcript of the interview at www.mythinkinglab.com. He admits that he lied, falsified information, and manipulated people in order to advance the interests of the tobacco indu stry. Ms. Stahl calls him out, saying that he was unethical and despicable to act that way. Crawford admits as much. He used his critical thinking skills to help sell people a product that, if used as intended by its manufacturer, was apt to cause them grave harm. Now, all these years later, he regrets having done that. The interview is part of his effort to make amends for his lies and the harm they may have caused to others. www.mythinkinglab.com and some printed versions of this book include a chapter exploring the relationship between critical thinking and ethical decision making more deeply.

Read the **Document** on **mythinkinglab.com**

BUILDING POSITIVE HABITS OF MIND

Critical thinking skills can be strengthened by exercising them, which is what the examples and the exercises in this book are intended to help you do. Critical thinking habits of mind can be nurtured by internalizing the values that they embody and by reaffirming the intention each day to live by those values.[vii] Here are four specific suggestions about how to go about this.

1. **Value Critical Thinking.** If we value critical thinking, we desire to be ever more truth-seeking, open-minded, mindful of consequences, systematic, inquisitive, confident in our critical thinking, and mature in our judgment. We will expect to manifest that desire in what we do and in what we say. We will seek to improve our critical thinking skills.
2. **Take Stock.** It is always good to know where we are in our journey. The "Critical Thinking Disposition Self-Rating Form," presented earlier in this chapter (page 21), will give us a rough idea. If we have general positive critical thinking habits of mind, that should show up in the score we give ourselves using this self-rating form.
3. **Be Alert for Opportunities.** Each day be alert for opportunities to act on the desire by translating it into words and actions. Make a conscious effort each day to be as reflective and thoughtful as possible in addressing at least one of the many problems or decisions of the day.
4. **Forgive and Persist.** Forgive yourself if you happen to backslide. Pick yourself up and get right back on the path. These are *ideals* we are striving to achieve. We each need discipline, determination, and persistence. There will be missteps along the way, but do not let them deter you. Working with a friend, mentor, or role model might make it easier to be successful, but it is really about what you want for your own thinking process.

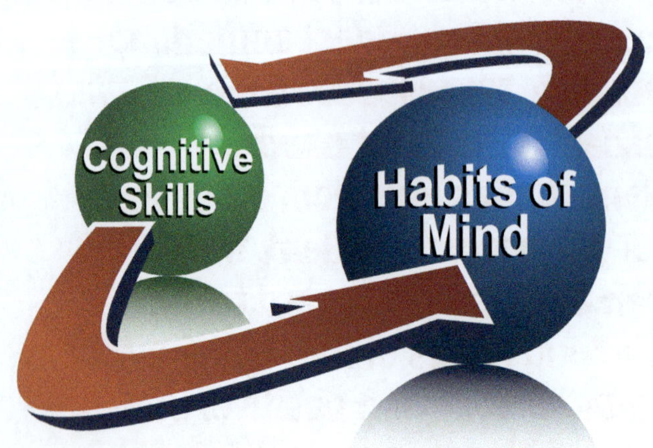

The Experts Worried That Schooling Might Be Harmful!

The critical thinking expert panel we talked about in Chapter 1 was absolutely convinced that critical thinking is a pervasive and purposeful human phenomenon. They insisted that strong critical thinkers should be characterized not merely by the cognitive skills they may have, but also by how they approach life and living in general.

This was a bold claim. At that time schooling in most of the world was characterized by the memorization of received truths. In the USA, the "back to basics" mantra echoed the pre-1960s Eisenhower era, when so much of schooling was focused on producing "interchangeable human parts" for an industrial manufacturing economy. Critical thinking that frees the mind to ask any question and evaluate any assumption naturally goes far beyond what the typical classroom was delivering. In fact, many of the experts feared that some of the things people experience in our schools could actually be harmful to the development and cultivation of strong critical thinking.

Critical thinking came before formal schooling was invented. It lies at the very roots of civilization. The experts saw critical thinking as a driving force in the human journey from ignorance, superstition, and savagery toward global understanding. Consider what life would be like without the things on this list, and you will appreciate why they had such confidence in strong critical thinking. The approaches to life and living which the experts said characterized the strong critical thinker included:

- inquisitiveness and a desire to remain well-informed with regard to a wide range of topics,
- trust in the processes of reasoned inquiry,
- self-confidence in one's own abilities to reason,
- open-mindedness regarding divergent world views,
- flexibility in considering alternatives and opinions,
- understanding of the opinions of other people,
- fair-mindedness in appraising reasoning,
- honesty in facing one's own biases, prejudices, stereotypes, or egocentric tendencies,
- prudence in suspending, making, or altering judgments,
- willingness to reconsider and revise views where honest reflection suggests that change is warranted,
- alertness to opportunities to use critical thinking.

The experts went beyond approaches to life and living in general to emphasize how strong critical thinkers approach specific issues, questions, or problems. The experts said we would find strong critical thinkers striving for:

- clarity in stating the question or concern,
- orderliness in working with complexity,
- diligence in seeking relevant information,
- reasonableness in selecting and applying criteria,
- care in focusing attention on the concern at hand,
- persistence though difficulties are encountered,
- precision to the degree permitted by the subject and the circumstances.

Table 5, page 25. American Philosophical Association. 1990, Critical Thinking: An Expert Consensus Statement for Purposes of Educational Assessment and Instruction. ERIC Doc. ED 315 423.

Putting the Positive Critical Thinking Habits of Mind into Practice

Here are a few suggestions about ways to translate each of the seven positive aspects of the disposition toward critical thinking into action.

Truth-seeking – Ask courageous and probing questions. Think deeply about the reasons and evidence for and against a given decision you must make. Pick one or two of your own most cherished beliefs and ask yourself what reasons and what evidence there are for those beliefs.

Open-mindedness – Listen patiently to someone who is offering opinions with which you do not agree. As you listen, show respect and tolerance toward the person offering the ideas. Show that you understand (not the same as "agree with") the opinions being presented.

Analyticity – Identify an opportunity to consciously pause to ask yourself about all the foreseeable and likely consequences of a decision you are making. Ask yourself what that choice, whether it be large or small, will mean for your future life and behavior.

Systematicity – Focus on getting more organized. Make lists of your most urgent work, family and educational responsibilities, and your assignments. Make lists of the most important priorities and obligations as well. Compare the urgent with the important. Budget time to take a systematic and methodical approach to fulfilling obligations.

Critical Thinking Confidence – Commit to resolve a challenging problem by reasoning it through. Embrace a question, problem, or issue that calls for a reasoned decision and begin working on it yourself or in collaboration with others.

Inquisitiveness – Learn something new. Go out and seek information about any topic of interest, but not one that you must learn about for work, and let the world surprise you with its variety and complexity.

Judiciousness – Revisit a decision you made recently and consider whether it is still the right decision. See if any relevant new information has come to light. Ask if the results that had been anticipated are being realized. If warranted, revise the decision to better suit your new understanding of the state of affairs.

Thinking Critically — What Is Wrong with These Statements?

Each of the following statements contains a mistake. Identify the mistake and edit the statement so that it is more accurate.

1 Having a "critical spirit" means one is a cynic.

2 Critical thinking habits of mind are always positive.

3 If you are open-minded, you must be a truth-seeker. Hint: open-mindedness is passive.

4 Calling on people to be systematic means that everyone must think the same way.

5 If a person is confident in his or her critical thinking, then he or she must have strong critical thinking skills.

6 If a person has strong critical thinking skills, then he or she must be confident in his or her critical thinking.

7 Truth-seeking is fine up to a point, but we have to draw the line. Some questions are too dangerous to be asked.

8 People with strong desire to be analytical have the skill to foresee the consequences of options and events.

9 If a person can see the value of critical thinking, then the person is disposed toward critical thinking. That's all it takes.

10 People who have not taken a course in critical thinking cannot have strong critical thinking skills.

If you feel comfortable with the idea, you may want to ask a close friend or two to rate you using the "Critical Thinking Disposition Self-Rating Form." To do this your friend would replace the words *I* or *my* with references to *you*. This assessment could provide valuable information about how your critical thinking disposition manifests itself to others.

Core Critical Thinking Skills

We have talked about the "eager" in the phrase "skilled and eager" to think critically. Now let's explore the "skilled" part by examining those mental skills which are at the core of purposeful reflective judgment.

INTERPRETING AND ANALYZING THE CONSENSUS STATEMENT

When thinking about the meaning and importance of the term "critical thinking" in Chapter 1, we referred to an expert consensus. That consensus identified certain cognitive skills as being central to critical thinking. Their research findings are shown below.[viii]

Let's unpack their quote. The experts identify six skills:

- Interpretation
- Analysis
- Inference
- Evaluation
- Explanation
- Self-Regulation

When thinking critically, we apply these six skills to:

- Evidence (facts, experiences, statements)
- Conceptualizations (ideas, theories, ways of seeing the world)
- Methods (strategies, techniques, approaches)
- Criteria (standards, benchmarks, expectations)
- Context (situations, conditions, circumstances)

We are expected to ask a lot of tough questions about all five areas. For example, How good is the evidence? Do these concepts apply? Were the methods appropriate? Are there better methods for investigating this question? What standard of proof should we be using? How rigorous should we be? What circumstantial factors might lead us to revise our opinions? Good critical thinkers are ever-vigilant, monitoring and correcting their own thinking.

THE JURY IS DELIBERATING

In *12 Angry Men* by Reginal Rose a jury deliberates the guilt or innocence of a young man accused of murder.[ix] The jury room is hot, the hour is late, and tempers are short. Ten of the twelve jurors have voted to convict when we join the story. In the classic American film version of Rose's play, one of the two jurors who are still uncertain is Henry Fonda's character.[x] That character first *analyzes* the testimony of a pair of witnesses, putting what each said side by side. Using all his critical thinking skills, he tries to reconcile their conflicting testimony. He asks how the old man could possibly have heard the accused man threaten the victim with the El Train roaring by the open window. From the facts of the situation Fonda's character has inferred that the old man could not have been telling the truth. Fonda then *explains* that inference to the other jurors with a flawless argument. But the other jurors still want to know why an old man with apparently nothing to gain would not tell the truth. One of the other jurors, an old man himself, *interprets* that witness's behavior for his colleagues. The conversation then turns to the

question of how to *interpret* the expression "I'm going kill you!" that the accused is alleged to have shouted. One juror wants to take it literally as a statement of intent. Another argues that context matters, that words and phrases cannot always be taken literally. Someone asks why the defense attorney did not bring up these same arguments during his cross examination of the witness. In their *evaluation*, the jury does seem to agree on the quality of the defense—namely, that it was poor. One juror draws the conclusion that this means the lawyer thought his own client was guilty. But is that so? Could there be some other explanation or interpretation for the half-hearted defense?

"We understand critical thinking to be purposeful, self-regulatory judgment which results in interpretation, analysis, evaluation, and inference, as well as explanation of the evidential, conceptual, methodological, criteriological, or contextual considerations upon which that judgment is based."

— *The Delphi Report*, American Philosophical Association [xi]

The jury has the authority to question the quality of the *evidence*, to dispute the competing *theories* of the case that are presented by the prosecution and the defense, to find fault with the investigatory *methods* of the police, to dispute whether the doubts some members may have meet the *criterion* of "reasonable doubt" or not, and to take into consideration all the *contextual* and *circumstantial* elements that may be relevant. In other words, a good jury is the embodiment of good critical thinking that a group of people practice. The stronger their collective skills, the greater the justice that will be done. Access the El Train video clip from *12 Angry Men* at www.mythinkinglab.com. **Watch** the **Video** on **mythinkinglab.com**

CRITICAL THINKING SKILLS FIRE IN MANY COMBINATIONS

One way to present critical thinking skills is in the form of a list. But lists typically suggest that we move from one item to another in a predetermined step-by-step progression, similar to pilots methodically working down the mandatory list of preflight safety checks. Critical thinking is not rote or scripted in the way that a list of skills might suggest.

Critical thinking is a form of judgment—namely reflective, purposeful judgment. The skills are what we use to make that judgment. Imagine for a moment what it is like looking for an address while driving on a busy and unfamiliar street. To do this, we must simultaneously be coordinating the use of many skills, but fundamentally our focus is on the driving and not on the individual skills. We are concentrating on street signs and address numbers while also interpreting traffic signals such as stoplights, and controlling the car's speed, direction, and location relative to other vehicles. Driving requires coordinating physical skills such as how hard to press the gas or tap the brakes and mental skills such as analyzing the movement of our vehicle relative to those around ours to avoid accidents. In the end, however, we say that we drove the car to the destination. We do not list all the skills, and we certainly do not practice them one by one in a serial order. Rather, we use them all in concert. Critical thinking has certain important features in common with looking for an address while driving on a busy and unfamiliar street. The key similarity to notice here is that critical thinking requires using all the skills in concert, not one at a time sequentially.

The intricate interaction of critical thinking skills in real-life problem solving and decision making may begin with an analysis, an interpretation, an inference, or an evaluation. Then, using self-regulation, we may go back and check ourselves for accuracy. On other occasions, we may first draw an inference on the basis of an interpretation and then evaluate our own inference. We may be explaining our reasoning to someone and realize, because we are monitoring our own thinking, that our reasoning is not adequate. And this may lead us to recheck our analyses or our inferences to see where we may need to refine our thinking.

That was what the jury, considered as a whole, was doing in *12 Angry Men*—going back and forth among interpretation, analysis, inference, and evaluation, with Henry Fonda's character as the person who called for more careful self-monitoring and self-correction. The jury's deliberation demanded reflection and an orderly analysis and evaluation of the facts, but deliberation is not constrained by adherence to a predetermined list or sequencing of mental events. Nor is critical thinking.

No, it would be an unfortunate and misleading oversimplification to reduce critical thinking to a list of skills, such as the recipe on the lid of dehydrated soup: first analyze, then infer, then explain, then close the lid and wait five minutes. To avoid the misimpressions that a list might engender, we need some other way of displaying the names of the skills.

We[xii] have always found it helpful when talking with college students and faculty around the world about critical thinking skills to use the metaphor of a sphere with the names of the skills displayed randomly over its surface.[xiii] Why a sphere? Three reasons.

- First, organizing the names of the skills on a sphere is truer to our lived experience of engaging in reflective judgment, as indicated above. We have all experienced those moments when, in the mental space of a few seconds, our minds fly from interpretation to analysis to inference and evaluation as we try to sort out our thoughts before we commit ourselves to a particular decision. We may go back and forth interpreting what we are seeing, analyzing ideas and drawing tentative inferences, trying to be sure that we have things right before we make a judgment.
- Second, a sphere does not presume any given order of events, which, for the present, is truer to the current state of the science.
- Third, a sphere reminds us about another important characteristic of critical thinking skills, namely that each can be applied to the other and to themselves.[xiv] We can analyze our inferences. We can analyze our analyses. We can explain our interpretations. We can evaluate our explanations. We can monitor those processes and correct any mistakes we might see ourselves making. In this way, *the core critical thinking skills can be said to interact*.

Core Critical Thinking Skills Interact

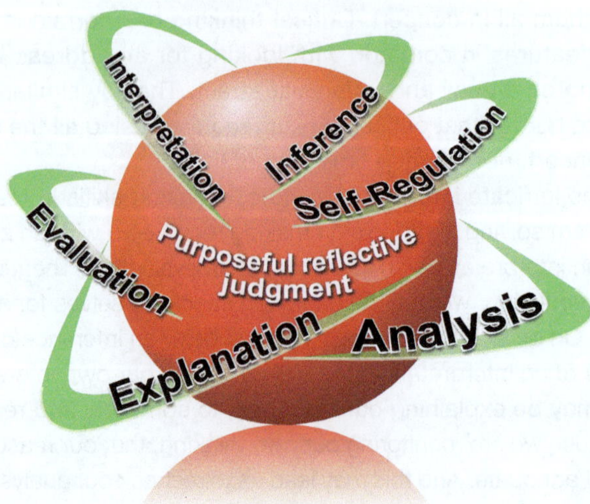

Professionals Measure Outcomes

STRENGTHENING OUR CORE CRITICAL THINKING SKILLS

Musicians, salespeople, athletes, nurses, teachers, and soldiers strive to improve their likelihood of success by strengthening the skills needed in their respective professions. Even as they train in one skill or another, working people must not lose sight of how those skills come together in their professional work. The quality of the concert, the number of sales made, the games won, the health care outcomes achieved, the learning accomplished, and the success of the mission—these are the outcomes that count. The same holds for critical thinkers. Success consists of making well-reasoned, reflective judgments to solve problems effectively and to make good decisions. Critical thinking skills are the tools we use to accomplish those purposes. In the driving example, our attention was on the challenges associated with reaching the intended street address. In real-world critical thinking, our attention will be on the challenges associated with solving the problem or making the decision at hand.

THE ART OF THE GOOD QUESTION

There are many familiar questions that invite people to use their critical thinking skills. We can associate certain questions with certain skills. The table below gives some examples.[xv] Often, our best critical thinking comes when we ask the right questions.[xvi]

Asking good questions, ones that promote critical thinking, is a highly effective way to gather important information about a topic, to probe unspoken assumptions, to clarify issues and to explore options. Asking good questions promotes strong problem solving and decision making, particularly when we encounter unfamiliar issues or significant problems.

Questions to Fire Up Our Critical Thinking Skills	
Interpretation	• What does this mean? • What's happening? • How should we understand that (e.g., what he or she just said)? • What is the best way to characterize/categorize/classify this? • In this context, what was intended by saying/doing that? • How can we make sense out of this (experience, feeling, statement)?
Analysis	• Please tell us again your reasons for making that claim. • What is your conclusion/What is it that you are claiming? • Why do you think that? • What are the arguments pro and con? • What assumptions must we make to accept that conclusion? • What is your basis for saying that?
Inference	• Given what we know so far, what conclusions can we draw? • Given what we know so far, what can we rule out? • What does this evidence imply? • If we abandoned/accepted that assumption, how would things change? • What additional information do we need to resolve this question? • If we believed these things, what would they imply for us going forward? • What are the consequences of doing things that way? • What are some alternatives we haven't yet explored? • Let's consider each option and see where it takes us. • Are there any undesirable consequences that we can and should foresee?
Evaluation	• How credible is that claim? • Why do we think we can trust what this person claims? • How strong are those arguments? • Do we have our facts right? • How confident can we be in our conclusion, given what we now know?
Explanation	• What were the specific findings/results of the investigation? • Please tell us how you conducted that analysis. • How did you come to that interpretation? • Please take us through your reasoning one more time. • Why do you think that (was the right answer/was the solution)? • How would you explain why this particular decision was made?
Self-Regulation	• Our position on this issue is still too vague; can we be more precise? • How good was our methodology, and how well did we follow it? • Is there a way we can reconcile these two apparently conflicting conclusions? • How good is our evidence? • OK, before we commit, what are we missing? • I'm finding some of our definitions a little confusing; can we revisit what we mean by certain things before making any final decisions?

Source: © 2009. Test Manual for the California Critical Thinking Skills Test, published by Insight Assessment. Used with permission.

Thinking Critically — Ask Good Critical Thinking Questions

Using the discussion about shale gas drilling as an example, practice formulating good critical thinking questions about the topics listed below. Look too at the table entitled "Questions to Fire Up Our Critical Thinking Skills" on page 31 to get ideas about how to target specific critical thinking skills with your questions. Write at least four good critical thinking questions about each of the topics below. The materials supporting this exerice are available at www.mythinkinglab.com.

1 Perhaps with more foresight strong critical thinkers might have anticipated this problem. But when the one-child policy was put in place, China was also beginning to experience a phenomenon that has continued for many decades, namely the migration of young people into urban areas in search of better jobs and a lifestyle different from what is available "back on the farm." Recently China was considering a regulation requiring children to visit their elderly parents who lived in the countryside. Review the story at www.mythinkinglab.com and then formulate good critical thinking questions about this policy and its the potential benefits and difficulties.

2 *USA Today* reported that 40 percent of all pregnancies across the United States were "unwanted or mistimed." The report was based on a study of 86,000 women who gave birth and 9,000 women who had abortions. The study itself appeared online in the journal *Perspectives on Sexual and Reproductive Health*. Review the study itself and the newspaper story at www.mythinkinglab.com and then formulate good critical thinking questions about this phenomenon.

3 The plant called quinoa offers "an exceptional balance of amino acids; quinoa, they declared, is virtually unrivaled in the plant or animal kingdom for its life-sustaining nutrients," according to a *New York Times* story about the problems of too much success. As global demand skyrockets, quinoa producers and other Bolivians may not be receiving either the nutritional or the economic benefits of this crop. Learn more about quinoa and the problems of its success by reading the news story at www.mythinkinglab.com. Then formulate four good critical thinking questions about this issue. Let one of the questions be about the importance of foresightfulness.

4 The Buddhist nation of Bhutan has a Commission for Gross National Happiness, and the head of that commission has a problem: Domestic violence appears to be rampant among a population whose religion abhors any kind of violence. Review the news story at www.mythinkinglab.com and then formulate good critical thinking questions from the perspective of the head of the Commission for Gross National Happiness.

5 How could a voluntary parent participation program that resulted in increased test scores go so wrong? That's what parents and school administrators are asking themselves in San Jose, California. Read the story by Sharon Noguchi, which appeared in the June 16, 2011 *San Jose Mercury News* at www.mythinkinglab.com, and then formulate good critical thinking questions to further analyze what happened and to guide in the formulation of possible next steps to resolve the situation.

Read the Document on mythinkinglab.com

Consider for a moment the topic of drilling to extract natural gas from shale. Natural gas as an alternative fuel source has not enjoyed the attention of the American population like solar energy or wind energy, mostly because it has been thought to be in short supply—until recently, that is. It turns out that natural gas can be harvested from shale rock formations two miles beneath the Earth's surface. The technology behind shale gas drilling involves sideways drilling and a process called "fracking." Over 30 states in the U.S. have underground shale beds and drilling in those regions has made some homeowners into overnight millionaires. The drilling has given a boost to the local economies in terms of jobs and retail sales. But, as reported by Lesley Stahl on *60 Minutes*, accidents and other safety concerns that have people who live in drilling communities concerned. Those living near shale gas drill sites are questioning the contamination of the drinking water by the chemicals involved in the fracking process. Go to www.mythinkinglab.com to listen to Lesley Stahl's full report.

Watch the Video on mythinkinglab.com

Thinking Critically — Holistic Critical Thinking Scoring Rubric

1 Look at the descriptions of each of the four levels of the "Holistic Critical Thinking Scoring Rubric" on page 12. In each, underline the elements that call out positive or negative critical thinking habits of mind.

2 Go online and locate two editorials from this week's *New York Times* or *Washington Post*. Select any issue or topic you wish. But find something that is controversial enough that the paper published at least one pro and one con editorial. Approach the two editorials with an open mind. Resist forming a judgment about the issue at least until you have read and considered both carefully. Evaluate both using the "Holistic Critical Thinking Scoring Rubric." Explain in detail the reasons for the score you assigned.

Before forming an opinion for or against fracking under residential real estate in your community, as a strong critical thinker you first would want to know more about this natural gas extraction method. Let's try to think of good critical thinking questions to ask. You might ask "What is known about the environmental risks of the chemicals involved in the fracking processes?" or "What exactly is involved in establishing a new drill site in my community?" to promote **interpretation**. You could also ask "What are the statistics on the frequency and severity of the accidents and safety violations associated with shale gas drilling?" to promote **inference**. Perhaps we would ask "If our community were to permit fracking, what would be the economic impact of that decision, and for whom, and how long would we have to wait before seeing those benefits?" to promote **evaluation.** Or you could ask "Do my past statements in support of alternative energy policies, or my financial interests in residential real estate, or my fears for the health and safety of myself and my family bias my review of the information about shale gas drilling?" to exercise our judiciousness habit of mind and our **self-regulation** skills.

SKILLS AND SUBSKILLS DEFINED

The six core critical thinking skills each has related subskills, as shown in the table below. The descriptions in the table of each core skill come from the expert consensus research discussed earlier.[xvii] The experts provided this more refined level of

Core Critical Thinking Skills

SKILL	Experts' Consensus Description	Subskill
Interpretation	"To comprehend and express the meaning or significance of a wide variety of experiences, situations, data, events, judgments, conventions, beliefs, rules, procedures, or criteria"	Categorize Decode significance Clarify meaning
Analysis	"To identify the intended and actual inferential relationships among statements, questions, concepts, descriptions, or other forms of representation intended to express belief, judgment, experiences, reasons, information, or opinions"	Examine ideas Identify arguments Identify reasons and claims
Inference	"To identify and secure elements needed to draw reasonable conclusions; to form conjectures and hypotheses; to consider relevant information and to educe the consequences flowing from data, statements, principles, evidence, judgments, beliefs, opinions, concepts, descriptions, questions, or other forms of representation"	Query evidence Conjecture alternatives Draw conclusions using inductive or deductive reasoning
Evaluation	"To assess the credibility of statements or other representations that are accounts or descriptions of a person's perception, experience, situation, judgment, belief, or opinion; and to assess the logical strength of the actual or intended inferential relationships among statements, descriptions, questions, or other forms of representation"	Assess credibility of claims Assess quality of arguments that were made using inductive or deductive reasoning
Explanation	"To state and to justify that reasoning in terms of the evidential, conceptual, methodological, criteriological, and contextual considerations upon which one's results were based; and to present one's reasoning in the form of cogent arguments"	State results Justify procedures Present arguments
Self-Regulation	"Self-consciously to monitor one's cognitive activities, the elements used in those activities, and the results educed, particularly by applying skills in analysis, and evaluation to one's own inferential judgments with a view toward questioning, confirming, validating, or correcting either one's reasoning or one's results"	Self-monitor Self-correct

Source: Critical thinking skill definitions cited are from APA Report: Expert Consensus Statement on Critical Thinking. (ERIC ED 315 423)

analysis of the concept of "critical thinking skills" to assist students and teachers in finding examples and exercises that could help strengthen these skills. But, remember that "critical thinking" does not refer to a package of skills. Rather, critical thinking is what we do *with* the skills—which is making purposeful reflective judgments about what to believe or what to do. So, make sure to use this table as an awareness tool, not a map.

A First Look at Inductive and Deductive Reasoning

The table describing the core critical thinking skills (see page 33) mentions "inductive or deductive reasoning" in the subskill column of the "inference" row and on the "evaluation" row. Conceiving of inferential reasoning as being either induction or deduction has a long and rich history going back to Aristotle (384–322 BCE).[xviii] Over the centuries, logicians studying deductive reasoning developed deductive logic systems that are useful in fields like mathematics and computer science.[xix] Statisticians have developed advanced techniques of statistical analysis that are useful for the kinds of probabilistic inductive inferences characteristic of scientific research and economics.[xx] But, as you will see from the examples in this section and later in the book, we all use inductive and deductive reasoning in making everyday inferences about what to believe or what to do. Let's take a quick preliminary look first at inductive reasoning and then at deductive reasoning. In later chapters we will return again and again to explore how critical thinking skills relate to induction and deduction.

NURSES' HEALTH STUDY—DECADES OF DATA

One powerful example of research that uses inductive reasoning is the Nurses' Health Study. This project is perhaps the most comprehensive descriptive investigation of health-related behavior ever conducted. Since its inception in 1976, over 238,000 nurses have provided information.[xxi] The details in the box entitled "Early Life Factors and Risk of Breast Cancer," report findings based on statistical analyses of millions of data points. As you can see, some remarkable, unexpected, and important correlations were discovered.[xxii] Measured expressions like "investigations . . . suggested . . .", ". . . is associated with reduced risk . . .", and "strong correlations . . . support . . ." characterize the report. The scientists who conducted this research are presenting *probabilistic conclusions*. Their conclusions are warranted because the statistical analyses provide sufficient confidence to assert that the relationships on which they report are highly unlikely to have occurred by random chance.

INDUCTIVE REASONING

Drawing probabilistic inferences regarding what is most likely to be true or most likely not true, given certain information, is known as **inductive reasoning**. Here are some examples.

- When I stop at a traffic light, I hear this funny, rattling sound coming from under my car. It is sort of in the middle or maybe toward the back, but definitely not toward the front. I only hear it when the car is idling, not when I'm driving along at a reasonable speed. My Dad said once that the metal baffles inside a muffler can loosen up if the muffler is old and rusty. He said that a loose baffle makes a rattling sound when it vibrates, like when the engine is idling or when the tires are out of alignment. My muffler is at least nine years old. So, I'm thinking that probably the rattling sound is coming from the muffler.
- We interviewed three people, and each one was very personable. I think that the first person had the strongest resume. But the second person seemed a lot smarter. I liked the enthusiasm and energy that the third person had, but

Early Life Factors and Risk of Breast Cancer

"Epidemiologic investigations conducted by our group and others have suggested that during childhood and early adult life breast tissue is particularly sensitive to factors that influence the likelihood of developing cancer many years later. For example, if the breast is exposed to multiple x-rays or other types of radiation during this early period, the risk of breast cancer rises steadily with higher doses, but after age 40 radiation has little effect. Also, we have seen that being overweight before age 20 is paradoxically associated with a reduced risk of breast cancer for the rest of a woman's life, although subsequent weight gain and becoming overweight after menopause increases risk of breast cancer in these later years. These findings led us to develop sets of questions focusing on diet and physical activity during the high school years. . . . In addition, to assess the validity of the recalled dietary data, we invited a sample of mothers of NHS II participants to also complete a questionnaire about the high school diets of their NHS II daughters; strong correlation between the mother–daughter reports supported the validity of our dietary data. We have now begun to examine the relation of high school diet and activity patterns to subsequent risk of breast cancer. We have seen that higher intake of red meat during high school years is related to a greater risk of premenopausal breast cancer. Also, higher levels of physical activity during high school were associated with lower risk of breast cancer before menopause. This is particularly important, as many schools do not include regular physical activity in the curriculum, and many girls are now quite inactive during these years."

that person never worked for an organization like ours before. It's a tough choice. But I'm thinking that probably the second person would be the best of the three for us to hire since innovative ideas are more important to us than experience or enthusiasm.

- In the past whenever the TV news programs in Chicago ran headline stories featuring a sketch artist's drawing of a fugitive, the Chicago Police Department (CPD) hotline received over 200 phone calls from people all over the city who said that they spotted the person. Tonight the Chicago TV news programs are going to feature a sketch artist's drawing of a fugitive whom the police are trying to locate. This will probably yield hundreds of calls to the CPD hotline.
- Suppose we imagine electricity flowing through wires in the way that water flows through pipes. With this analogy in mind, it would be reasonable to infer that wires that are larger in circumference should be capable of carrying greater electrical loads.

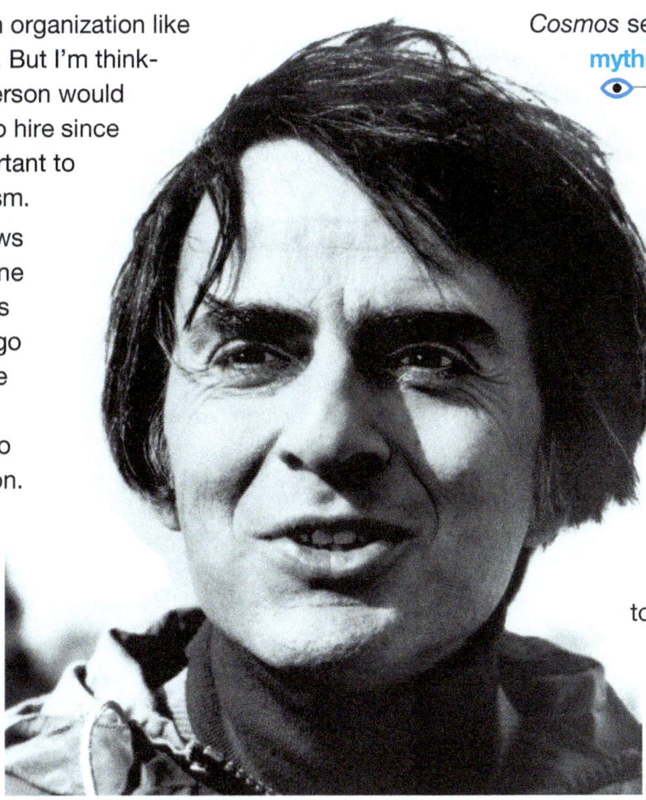

Inductive reasoning is used when we are trying to diagnose what the problem might be or deciding which of several promising options would be the most reasonable to select. Scientists use inductive methods, such as experimentation, and inductive tools, such as statistics. The Nurses' Health Study report was an example of scientific findings derived inductively. When we base our predictions on our past experiences about how things will happen in the future, we are using inductive reasoning. Reasoning by analogy, exemplified in the example about electricity being like water, is inductive. In strong, inductive reasoning, the evidence at hand gives us a reasonable assurance that the conclusion we are drawing is probably true. *As long as there is the possibility that all the reasons for a claim could be true and yet the claim itself could turn out to be false, we are in the realm of inductive reasoning.*

COSMOS VS. CHAOS

The idea that the earth is a planet revolving around the sun is often attributed to the fifteenth-century Polish astronomer-priest named Copernicus. But, in fact, the first scientist known to have reasoned to that view of the solar system was the Greek astronomer mathematician Aristarchus, who lived more than two millennia earlier. Centuries before telescopes were invented, Aristarchus had only his eyes and, of course, his mind. Carl Sagan describes the reasoning Aristarchus used in a clip from the *Cosmos* series, which you can access at **www.mythinkinglab.com**.

Watch the **Video** on **mythinkinglab.com**

Sagan tells us that Aristarchus "deduced that the Sun had to be much larger" from "the size of the Earth's shadow on the Moon during a lunar eclipse." Aristarchus used deduction to infer that the Sun was much larger than the Earth because there was no other possible explanation for the size of the shadow of the Earth on the Moon during a lunar eclipse than that the shadow is being made by a hugely larger source of light shining toward the Earth and the Moon from a very great distance away.

DEDUCTIVE REASONING

Drawing inferences in which it appears that the conclusion cannot possibly be false if all of the premises are true is called **deductive reasoning**.

Here are some examples:

- San Francisco is west of Denver. Denver is west of Detroit and Newark. Therefore, we can infer with deductive certitude that San Francisco is west of Newark.
- Every successful president of the United States was both diplomatic and decisive. General Dwight D. Eisenhower served in WWII as the Commander of the Allied Armies in Europe and then went on to become a successful U.S. president. Therefore, President Eisenhower was decisive and diplomatic.
- Either we attended the campus Halloween party last year or we were in Texas visiting your folks that day. We did not go to Texas at all last year. So, we must have attended the campus Halloween party last year.
- Assume that 'a,' 'b,' and 'c' are any three numbers. Where 'w' and 'y' are numbers, assume that '*f*' is a mathematical function such that '*f*wy' yields 'z' where 'z' is the number that is the product of 'w' multiplied by 'y.' It follows deductively then that '(*f*a(*f*bc))' yields to the product of 'a' multiplied by the product of 'b' multiplied by 'c.'
- If God intended marriage for the sole purpose of human reproduction, and if same-sex couples are entirely incapable of human reproduction, then it follows that God did not intend marriage for same-sex couples.
- Not every argument is of equal quality. Therefore, at least one argument is better than at least one other argument.

Thinking Critically

What Are Your Professors and Textbooks Asking of You?

1 A good education includes learning content knowledge and learning skills. Because there is so much to learn, it is understandable that many instructors focus a lot of attention on helping students get the content knowledge right. These profs often call on students in class to answer questions that show that they know the meanings of technical terms or have learned the material from a previous lesson. Sprinkled in among those questions from time to time are critical thinking skills questions like those given in the table on page 31. Here is your challenge: In each of your classes over the next two class days, keep a list of the questions that the instructors ask students. Then, take the complete list and evaluate each question to see which were intended to evoke the use of critical thinking skills. Which skills were most often evoked?

2 Some textbooks include exercises at the end of each chapter or unit. Those exercises can address content knowledge to be sure it is well understood. They can also invite students to apply their critical thinking skills to that knowledge—for example to interpret some data, to analyze arguments, to draw out the consequences of certain principles or facts, or to explain the right methods to apply. Take the textbooks for your other subjects and review the exercises at the end of the unit or chapter you are on. Identify those questions, if any, that are intended to evoke critical thinking skills. In the case of each textbook, write five additional "exercise questions" that evoke critical thinking about the content of the chapter.

Mathematics, algebra, geometry, and computer programming rely heavily on deductive reasoning. Activities that require us to apply strict protocols, rules, or regulations that leave no room for independent judgment call on our deductive reasoning skills. People often enjoy games and puzzles that test their deductive reasoning skills, such as Sudoku. When we seek to resolve questions and doubts by appeal to first principles, commandments, or beliefs that are assumed to be absolute certitudes, we are often using our deductive powers.

Deductive reasoning is a very important form of inference, as is inductive reasoning. We require both forms of inference to be successful in critical thinking. There is a lot more to learn about inductive and deductive reasoning. We will explore the uses and evaluation of both kinds of reasoning in more detail later. Chapter 8 is on deduction and Chapter 9 is on induction. As a matter of fact, this is a good place to talk about how this book is organized and how you can use this book to plan your learning to strengthen your critical thinking skills and habits of mind.

How to Get the Most Out of this Book

Our plan from here forward is to use each chapter to emphasize different critical thinking skills, always remembering to apply those skills with strong positive critical thinking habits of mind. To strengthen our critical thinking skills, we will emphasize first one skill and then another.

But first things first! Chapter 3, on problem solving, applies critical thinking to something we all care about, namely your being successful academically. From there we focus on strengthening specific skills.

We begin with interpretation and **analysis** in Chapters 4 and 5 when we examine how to clarify the meanings of individual claims and how to visually display the reasoning we use to support our claims and conclusions. In Chapters 6 through 9 we will work on evaluation, looking first at how to assess the credibility of individual claims and then at how to evaluate the quality of arguments. Strengthening our self-regulation skill will be our emphasis in Chapters 10 and 11 as we take a closer look at how to strengthen our real-life decision making. Snap judgments and reflective decisions are the topics for those two chapters.

We draw everything we've learned about critical thinking back together in Chapters 12, 13, and 14. In this set of chapters, which emphasize inference and **explanation,** as we focus on how human beings use their powers of reasoning to acquire new knowledge by means of analogies, inferences drawn from core ideological beliefs, and inferences drawn through methodical scientific investigative inquiry. These chapters explore the benefits, uses, strengths, and weaknesses of the three most powerful forms of argument making: comparative ("this is like that") reasoning, ideological ("top down") reasoning, and empirical ("bottom up") reasoning.

We complete the core set of fifteen chapters with one that addresses the vital skill of communicating in writing the critical thinking you have invested in a given question, issue, decision, or point of view. Effective writing and critical thinking just might be the two most important things to learn—period. The two are connected not only in the world of education but in every professional field and all throughout life.

If your instructor has elected to supplement the basics we present in these fifteen chapters, she or he may have added one or more of the four additional optional chapters to your version of this book. One of those supplemental chapters is on how social scientists think, one on how natural scientists think, one on ethical decision making, and one is on the logic of declarative statements. Building the connections between critical thinking and each of those different domains was both enjoyable and interesting for us, as authors. We sincerely hope that you have the opportunity to enjoy and learn from one or more of those chapters too. We think each of them, like the 15 we proudly included in the basic version of THINK Critically, will further strengthen your critical thinking skills and habits of mind. And that, after all, is our the whole point. It's about you, building up your critical thinking skills and habits of mind, and you capitalizing on your critical thinking to achieve success in college and throughout your whole life.

The key to getting the most out of this book is to practice your critical thinking skills as often as possible. There are literally hundreds of exercises in this text. Look for them not only at the ends chapters but in the "Thinking Critically" boxes within each chapter. There are more exercises for you at www.mythinkinglab.com. You'll find that some of these exercises ask you to think to yourself while others ask you to think in groups. This mirrors real life in that critical thinking is both an individual process on some occasions and a group problem-solving and a group decision-making process on other occasions. The point of including all of these exercises is that it is not enough to simply read about critical thinking as a topic, or passively view others thinking critically. We humans learn by doing. Building expertise at reflective judgment—that is, at critical thinking—takes practice, and lots of it! **Explore** the **Concept** on **mythinkinglab.com**

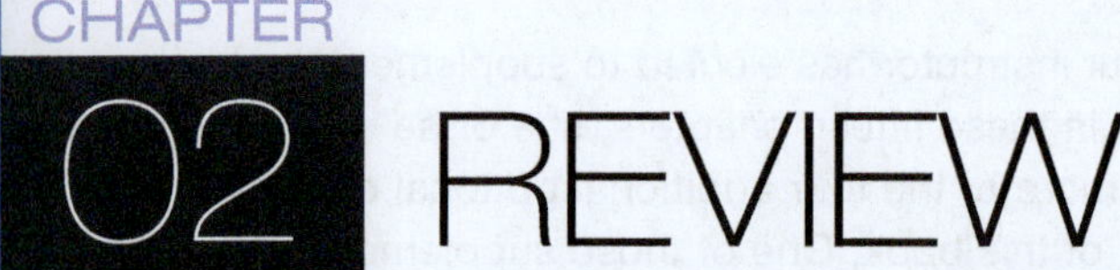

CHAPTER 02 REVIEW

Study and Review on mythinkinglab.com

We defined *critical thinking* and inquired into its value for ourselves individually and for society in Chapter 1. In this chapter we analyzed first the "eager" and then the "skilled" parts of the phrase, "skilled and eager to think critically." The willingness comes in the form of the seven positive habits of mind that dispose us toward engaging problems and making decisions using our critical thinking. For each of these seven habits, there is an opposite habit of mind that disposes us to be averse or hostile toward using critical thinking as our way of problem solving and decision making. We can fortify our critical thinking habits of mind by valuing critical thinking, taking stock of our current disposition toward critical thinking, looking for opportunities to translate the habits into practice, and being persistent in our efforts to engage problems using our critical thinking skills.

Being skilled at thinking is only part of the story. We examined the six core critical thinking skills: interpretation, analysis, inference, evaluation, explanation, and self-regulation. By asking good questions, we fire up those skills and their subskills. The skill of inference included both of the domains that are traditionally known as "inductive reasoning" and "deductive reasoning." To clarify the difference between induction and deduction we pointed to examples and presented definitions. But because this was only our first look at induction and deduction, we did not go as deeply into these topics here as we will in later chapters.

Knowing the plan for one's learning provides benchmarks for progress and helps a person to clarify his or her expectations. If the goal of this book is to assist you in building up your critical thinking skills and habits of mind, then there had better be a plan for achieving that goal. There *is* a plan, and we wanted to share it with you early in the book. We will first look at problem solving, then delve deeper into the different critical thinking skills, with the reminder to always apply those skills with strong positive critical thinking habits of mind.

KEY TERMS

truth-seeking means that a person has intellectual integrity and a courageous desire to actively strive for the best possible knowledge in any given situation. A truth-seeker asks probing questions and follows reasons and evidence wherever they lead, even if the results go against his or her cherished beliefs. (p. 23)

open-minded means that a person is tolerant of divergent views and sensitive to the possibility of his or her own possible biases. An open-minded person respects the right of others to have different opinions. (p. 23)

analytical means that a person is habitually alert to potential problems and vigilant in anticipating consequences and trying to foresee short-term and long-term outcomes of events, decisions, and actions. "Foresightful" is another word for what "analytical" means here. (p. 23)

systematic means that a person consistently endeavors to take an organized and thorough approach to identifying and resolving problems. A systematic person is orderly, focused, persistent, and diligent in his or her approach to problem solving, learning, and inquiry. (p. 23)

confident in reasoning means that a person is trustful of his or her own reasoning skills to yield good judgments. A person's or a group's confidence in their own critical thinking may or may not be warranted, which is another matter. (p. 23)

inquisitive means that a person habitually strives to be well-informed, wants to know how things work, and seeks to learn new things about a wide range of topics, even if the immediate utility of knowing those things is not directly evident. An inquisitive person has a strong sense of intellectual curiosity. (p. 23)

judicious means that a person approaches problems with a sense that some are ill-structured and some can have more than one plausible solution. A judicious person has the cognitive maturity to realize that many questions and issues are not black and white and that, at times, judgments must be made in contexts of uncertainty. (p. 23)

interpretation is an expression of the meaning or significance of a wide variety of experiences, situations, data, events, judgments, conventions, beliefs, rules, procedures, or criteria. (p. 33)

inference identifies and secures elements needed to draw reasonable conclusions; it forms conjectures and hypotheses, it considers relevant information, and it educes or draws out the consequences flowing from data, statements, principles, evidence, judgments, beliefs, opinions, concepts, descriptions, questions, or other forms of representation. (p. 33)

evaluation assesses the credibility of statements or other representations that are accounts or descriptions of a person's perception, experience, situation, judgment, belief, or opinion; also assesses the logical strength of the actual or intended inferential relationships among statements, descriptions, questions, or other forms of representation. (p. 33)

self-regulation is a process in which one monitors one's cognitive activities, the elements used in those activities, and the results educed, particularly by applying skills in analysis, and evaluation to one's own inferential judgments with a view toward questioning, confirming, validating, or correcting either one's reasoning or one's results. (p. 33)

inductive reasoning is drawing probabilistic inferences regarding what is most likely to be true or most likely not true, given certain information. (p. 34)

deductive reasoning is drawing inferences in which it appears that the conclusion cannot possibly be false if all of the premises are true. (p. 35)

analysis identifies the intended and actual inferential relationships among statements, questions, concepts, descriptions, or other forms of representation intended to express belief, judgment, experiences, reasons, information, or opinions. (p. 37)

explanation states and justifies reasoning in terms of the evidential, conceptual, methodological, criteriological, and contextual considerations upon which one's results were based; also presents one's reasoning in the form of cogent arguments. (p. 37)

FIND IT ON MYTHINKINGLAB.COM

Watch the **Video** on **mythinkinglab.com**

- Dramatic reenactment is not real life, but then neither are so-called "reality" shows. However, dramatic reenactments can be very valuable because they often highlight ideas and decision making in tense situations where uncertainties and risks abound. The clips from *Apollo 13* and *Philadelphia* certainly do that. The transcript of Leslie Stahl's interview with Victor Crawford is dramatic for what it reveals. Access all three of these clips at www.mythinkinglab.com.

- When we reference a video clip in the exercises, as with the "truthiness" clip from Comedy Central's *The Colbert Report*, you can also find it at www.mythinkinglab.com.
- The video clip of the El Train scene from *12 Angry Men* is a classic. Please view that scene and analyze it carefully, noticing how the argument unfolds and how the "train of reasoning" is often interrupted yet always stays on track. The movie itself is terrific, and we urge you to watch it all the way through. Do you think we've made much progress on the issue of racial profiling in the past 50 years? How about on a citizen's duty to render service as a thoughtful and diligent juror? (p. 29)

Exercises

SMALL GROUP DISCUSSIONS

1. Consider this claim: *"If textbooks used more critical thinking exercises, students would learn the material better."* What are the best arguments for and against that claim? Do not take a position on this. Rather, work to develop the strongest arguments possible for both sides. What additional information would you need to investigate, in order to ground each side's arguments in solid facts? What assumptions about learning and schooling are required to make each side's arguments as strong as possible? Again, do not evaluate (yet).
2. Consider this claim: *"Professors should ask content questions, not critical thinking questions. It's the responsibility of the professor to lay out the content, but it's the job of the student to think critically about the subject matter."* What are the best arguments for and against that claim? As with the question above, do not take a position on this. Rather, work to develop the strongest arguments possible for both sides. What additional information would you need to investigate, in order to ground each side's arguments in solid facts? What assumptions about learning and schooling are required to make each side's arguments as strong as possible? Again, do not evaluate (yet).

REFLECTIVE LOG

1. Mark Twain is reported to have said, "I have never let my schooling interfere with my education."[xxiii] Connect that sentiment with the information on page 27 in the box, "The Experts Worried That School Might Be Harmful!". What is your reasoned opinion on the matter? If you were critical of schooling, what would you recommend be done to improve it? What evidence do you have that your suggestions would actually work in the real world? Now ask someone who is 10 years younger than you what Mark Twain meant. Note the response in your log. Then ask someone who is at least 20 years older than you what Twain's saying might mean. Log the response. Compare the three opinions: yours, the younger person's, and the older person's. End this notation in your log by reflecting on these final questions: Should K-12 schooling be designed to prevent students from learning to think critically for themselves? Why or why not?
2. You were specifically asked not to "defend," "evaluate," or to "argue for" one side or the other in the previous two exercise items. Here's your new challenge: Keeping an open mind and maybe stirring up a bit of courage, too, interview two professors and two students *not* in your critical thinking class. Present them with the same two claims, but invite them to agree or disagree with each one and to give their reasons. Note their reasons respectfully, and ask follow-up questions aimed at evoking more critical thinking. You should be able to base your follow-up questions on the group work you did earlier when you developed the best arguments for and against each claim. Then, in your reflective log, record the conversations and highlight some of the places where the people you interviewed did, in fact, engage in some deeper critical thinking about the topic.
3. Using the "Holistic Critical Thinking Scoring Rubric" from Chapter 1, how would you evaluate the critical thinking displayed by each of the four people you interviewed? Quote some of the things each side said that led you to evaluate them in the way that you did. [We know you caught it, but just in case you didn't, that was another critical thinking skills question. This one asked you to *explain* the evidence you used for your *evaluation.*]

GROUP EXERCISE: WHAT WOULD IT BE LIKE?

Our habitual attitudes affect our behavior and the way that we interact with one another. People who are habitually intellectually dishonest, intolerant, or indifferent act differently in household and workplace settings than those who have opposite, positive habits. This exercise invites you to draw on your experience to describe what it would be like to interact regularly with a person with negative critical thinking habits of mind.

Scenario #1. You have a brother, close to your age, who is habitually intellectually dishonest, intolerant, and imprudent in making decisions. He has been like this since junior high school, and he recently enrolled at your college. Now he wants to share your apartment, borrow your car, and get you to help him with his academic assignments. What is it like to have this person as your family member? Given that you have the power to say "no" to his requests, what are your plans with regard to his requests?

Scenario #2. You have a part-time job in a department store as a clerk. Your old manager used to let your group solve a lot of the store's own problems, like who is going to cover a shift if someone can't work on a given day. But now you have a new manager. This person makes scheduling decisions arbitrarily, and is disorganized, and this means that your group always seems to be rushing to meet deadlines. She also habitually does not think about the consequences of her actions. What is it like to work for this supervisor? Given that you have the right to complain to management about your new supervisor, is that an option you will pursue? What other plans might you make to help you cope with the approach taken by this new supervisor?

THE COLBERT REPORT

Watch the **Video** on **mythinkinglab.com** Stephen Colbert, a master of humor and irony, offers "truthiness" as his word of the day. How does "truthiness," as Mr. Colbert defines it, relate to "truth-seeking"? Go to www.mythinkinglab.com to view the clip.

APOLLO 13 QUESTION

Group or Individual Exercise: The scene in *Apollo 13* when the engineers are put in a room and given a task is a memorable dramatization of a critical thinking challenge. Their task is to engineer something that will reduce the toxicity of the air in the spacecraft (a) as quickly as possible because time is running out, (b) using only the things the astronauts have at their disposal, and (c) using methods that the astronauts can repeat so that they can build the device themselves. Go to www.mythinkinglab.com, and watch the scene two or three times. The second or third time through, focus on trying to identify evidence of the critical thinking skills and habits of mind. Listen to what the characters say and watch their body language. Discuss the scene in detail, and then prepare a brief description of the scene, like the description that begins this chapter. Your description should highlight those critical thinking skills and habits of mind you noticed the characters displaying either individually or as a group.

Watch the **Video** on **mythinkinglab.com**

WEB VIDEO PROJECT

Consider this claim: *"Effective writing and critical thinking are the two most important things to learn in college."* Do not take a position on that claim; instead present the strongest possible arguments pro and con. One way to gather information about this is to ask other people their views and the reasons they have for those views. Ask at least three teachers or professors, ask three successful people in business and three in other professions, and ask three people who graduated at least 20 years ago what they think. Get their reasons, not just their opinions. Then formulate the arguments pro and con. Make and post a Web video that shows both sides.

Read the Chapter on mythinkinglab.com

Listen to the Chapter Audio on mythinkinglab.com

Solve Problems and Succeed in College

WHAT are the five steps of the "IDEAS" critical thinking process for problem solving and decision making?

HOW can we use the IDEAS critical thinking process to navigate the day-to-day challenges of being a college student?

A door down the hall slammed and John's eyes popped open. Immediately he blinked them shut. What time is it? He opened one eye to peer at the huge yellow-faced clock his roommate, Trent, had put on the wall. Almost noon!

John sat up in bed and groaned as he realized he was still wearing his jeans and jacket from yesterday, and even his shoes. He wondered how he had made it back to the dorm. But somehow he had. I need a shower, bad, he thought. He struggled to his feet and looked for some clean clothes. Nothing. Maybe he could borrow a shirt from Trent? He pulled open the drawer where Trent kept his T-shirts and socks and saw a piece of paper with his name on it.

"John, No. Don't touch my things. Get a new roommate. Get some help. Stay away from my things. Trent." John pulled open a couple of other drawers and saw copies of the same message.

John's phone was dead, so he plugged it into the charger. He booted his laptop to check his e-mail. There were four new messages. He opened the oldest one. John recognized that it was from his Math 101 Prof who used Blackboard to message the whole class with a one-liner. "Midterm exam is Thursday." Aw, no.

The next one was from Dad. "Hi, John. It's official, your mother and I are getting divorced. I'm moving to Dallas. After I get settled maybe you could visit. Keep in touch. Oh, and let me know if you want me to call the Business School Dean about getting you into the Finance program. Dad."

Aw, man. Dad's back on that B-School thing. I told him that I wanted to be a cop. If I had gone to Oakland Community College maybe I'd be in the law enforcement program right now. But noooo. He and mom insisted I go to a four-year school. Finance?! What, and end up like dad—an overweight, stressed-out banker? What's the rush? There're no jobs anyway. Undeclared is fine.

The third e-mail was from Rodney, a guy in his Intro Sociology course. "John, what are you doing? We need your section for the group paper. We're meeting tonight at Samira's apartment. She's going to cut and paste all our pieces together and make sure the paper reads okay. Tomorrow we proof it. It's due Friday. We need your section now!"

OK, so today the group's proofreading. Maybe not too late to get a couple of pages together. No sense trying to study for the math test anyway. Hadn't been to that boring class in three weeks. Should probably drop it. Wonder if it's too late? But the Sociology paper. There must be something in Google about, what was the goofy topic anyway, ah . . . , something about retired Baby Boomers taking part-time jobs. . . . Who picked that topic anyway? Ugh.

Three text messages chimed into John's phone. He was about to open the first one when he noticed the date on the phone's display. There was something wrong. It wasn't Thursday at all. It was Friday. Ah, no.

The Soc class met at 10:00 AM. It was almost noon!

He saw a text from Rodney. "Handed in group paper. Your name left off. See e-mail."

John looked back at his e-mail. There was another, more recent message from Rodney. "We talked with the Prof about you. She said we should turn in the paper without including your name. She said it would be academic dishonesty to put you as an author. You're busted, man."

Noon, Friday! He had just enough time to get to his 12:30 Philosophy course. John wondered how he'd ended up in a senior honors seminar on nineteenth-century European ideologists anyway. He hefted the 2-inch-thick book of readings off the shelf to put it into his backpack. John hated the philosophy readings. Did these guys get paid by the word or what? But the Prof was funny, the class discussions were lively, and, although they were seniors and never talked to him, the girls looked good.

His phone rang. John let it go to voice. A moment later the message came and John listened to it.

"Hey, dude! How you doing, man? You were really messed up the other night. Thought you were going to puke in the stairwell or something, man. Zach and I literally poured you into bed. It was like three in the morning and your roommate was pissed that we woke him up. Hey, like I need the thirty dollars you owe me from earlier this week, man. OK. So, text me or something when you get this. It's Friday, man. Weekend! Dude. Parrrrrtaaaayyy."

John groaned. He looked out the window at the October gray Michigan sky. His head throbbed. This was not how college was supposed to be! I'm screwed. Maybe his roommate was right, he thought. "Get some help." But, how? Who?

Obviously, John's life is in disarray. He is beset with problems of many kinds: social, vocational, academic, physical, emotional, and spiritual. And John appears not to know how to begin sorting out his problems and resolving them. John's situation may be familiar to you. You may have had this experience yourself or you may have seen it happening around you. John's story illustrates the downside of not having the critical thinking skills and the positive critical thinking habits of mind associated with successful problem solving. In this chapter we'll develop a process of problem solving that relies on those core critical thinking skills and habits of mind, and we'll apply that process to the kinds of problems college students can encounter.

There is no one stereotypic kind of college student. Some college students are younger people, recently graduated from high school, who are attending full-time and living on campus. Others are working adults with family responsibilities who enroll in only one or two courses at a time. Some college students attend nationally known research universities, some attend regional colleges and universities, some attend community colleges or liberal arts colleges. Some have disabilities, some are military veterans, some are going back to college after years of raising families. Some college students are deeply religious, some are politically active, some enjoy music more than sports, some have plenty of money, some are scraping it together with loans and part-time jobs. Some live at home with parents and siblings, some live alone, some live in apartments with friends, some on military bases around the world. Some take classes online, some face-to-face in classrooms. Some are enthusiastic about their chosen major, and some are totally undecided about a major. About the only thing we can say about "all college students" is that from time to time they all have problems that are social, academic, physical, emotional, vocational, or spiritual. Not in all those domains all the time, and certainly not all the same problems. Oh, and one other thing, those college students who have an effective process of problem solving stand a greater chance of successfully earning a degree and achieving their other goals.

"If you don't know where you are going, you will wind up somewhere else."

Yogi Berra

No guarantees, mind you. This is the real world. External factors beyond our control, like accidents, illness, natural disasters, social upheavals, economic downturns, etc. can delay our progress toward our goals and, occasionally, lead us to change our minds about those goals entirely. I'm reminded of a college student I knew, a real one—not a fictional one like the John in the opening story—who enrolled as a full-time student, living on campus, and majoring in English Literature. She soon met someone, fell in love, married, and had a child. So the student dropped out of college and, together with her husband, began raising their family. A few years later, with three small children, she decided that she wanted to return to get her degree. Instead of going back as an English Lit major she chose health sciences, because it seemed more practical to her as a young mother. She went to school part-time for many years and sure enough, 11 years after first enrolling, she graduated with her baccalaureate degree. She often used the critical thinking problem-solving process developed in this chapter to work though the many expected and unexpected problems and obstacles that came along during those years.

I know another young man, again a true story, whose college experience started out very similarly, good high school education, full-time resident student, attending a solid university. But he was not able to manage the burden of his new-found freedoms. He let his courses get away from him, found it very difficult to balance the distractions of his social life and the demands of school, and, being hundreds of miles from home, never let his friends or family back home know about how badly things were going. He ended up making such a mess of his first year at college that he withdrew. Three years passed before he decided to give it another try, this time at a local community college. He was determined to complete his studies while working a full-time job, living on his own and attending AA meetings. And today he's doing much better, but he regrets what he calls his "lost opportunities."

And, of course, I know another college student who came to college, her mind firmly set on becoming a high school science

Thinking Critically — Institutional Programs and Measures of Students' Success

Each individual student has a concept of what it means for him or her to be successful in college. And the colleges have an idea as well of how they seek to define and to measure student success. Colleges, accreditation agencies, and the media often think of student success in terms of graduation. At the undergraduate level the metric most often used is the "6-year graduation rate," which refers to the percentage of entering freshmen who complete a baccalaureate degree within six academic years. That metric, however, often fails to capture the successes of some students. Specifically that metric often misses successful degree-completing students who may have transferred from one institution to another, or who may have taken more than six years because they could not attend full-time or to attend continuously due to family, job, health, military service, or financial reasons. Each year *U.S. News & World Report* puts out its *Best Colleges* edition. In 2011 the editors refined this particular metric by calculating a comparison between an institution's actual graduation rate and the rate that it might be predicted to have based on its financial resources and on its students' entry test scores. The aim was to reward institutions that succeed in graduating at-risk students.

Another metric used by *U.S. News & World Report* and by many higher education leaders and researchers to gauge the quality of an institution is the percentage of last year's full-time freshmen that the institution is able to retain into their sophomore year. Unfortunately some institutions are revolving doors, taking in large freshmen classes only to fail to retain them as sophomores. But institutions committed to the academic success of their students work hard to assist them make a successful transition to college life. Learning communities, first-year experience courses, internships, study abroad programs, undergraduate research opportunities, creative and collaborative projects, writing in the disciplines, service learning programs, strong academic advising services and student success service centers, faculty committed to the enterprise of teaching, welcoming and helpful staff, good physical facilities, a campus culture of learning, institutional pride, and a positive school spirit are all elements that contribute to higher student retention rates.

Woody Allen said, "Eighty percent of life is just showing up." And while that hardly tells the whole story, there is a kernel of wisdom there. If you are a freshman, showing up as a sophomore next year is a very important part of graduating some time, if not on time.

Visit www.mythinkinglab.com to link to the *U.S. News & World Report* Web site, or get a copy of its latest issue of *Best Colleges*, and look up your institution. Then look up 10 or a dozen institutions like yours. Compare their stats on freshmen retention and graduation rates. What programs does your institution offer that are specifically designed to help ensure undergraduate student success? Are you participating in one or more of those programs?

Read the Document on mythinkinglab.com

teacher. She dedicated herself to her studies, majored in Biology and in Secondary Education, and graduated in four years.

Your situation may be like these folks or it may be different. Your success in college depends, for the most part, on you. Other people's stories about their college days are *their* stories. How those stories turned out does not determine how your story will turn out.

In addition to the abstract goal of describing a critical thinking process of problem solving which can be very widely applied, this chapter has a very practical goal. Namely assisting you to be successful as a college student. That starts with a basic question: What does being successful as a college student mean *to you*?

IDEAS: A 5-Step Critical Thinking Problem-Solving Process

Each of us must learn how to solve our own problems—in other words, to take responsibility for our own lives. In my own life I found that there was quite a difference between saying that I was ready to take full responsibility for myself and actually being ready. I had to learn a lot about myself, my friendships, and, most importantly, about how to think through the difficulties and challenges in my life. What really turned out to help me was a critical thinking process I could rely upon whenever a major problem arose. Calling my parents all the time made me feel more dependent than independent, and I knew what advice they were going to give anyway.

And that's the heart of this chapter. There's no way this chapter can cover every possible problem or fit exactly every person's individual unique situation. That is why the critical thinking problem-solving process is so valuable. The process can be applied no matter what kind of problem is at hand—social, vocational, academic, physical, emotional, or spiritual. So even if the specific examples in this chapter don't exactly fit your particular situation, there's plenty in each section that a good critical thinker will easily be able to adapt. One other note: Resolving a problem does not mean that it will never come back. Often the resolutions to our difficulties are sufficient only for a time, or only if conditions do not change.

For the sake of clarity, we define **problem solving** as moving from the point at which we initially realize that we have a difficulty that requires our attention to that point where we regard the difficulty as being sufficiently resolved for the current time and circumstances. There are five steps to reflective, well-reasoned problem solving about what to believe or what to do—that is, to engage in good critical thinking as we work through the problems and challenges in our lives. The process is universally applicable, but in this chapter the examples are the kinds of concerns that are more likely to occur

IDEAS

A 5-Step Critical Thinking Problem Solving Process

- **I** = IDENTIFY the Problem and Set Priorities (Step 1)
- **D** = DEEPEN Understanding and Gather Relevant Information (Step 2)
- **E** = ENUMERATE Options and Anticipate Consequences (Step 3)
- **A** = ASSESS the Situation and Make a Preliminary Decision (Step 4)
- **S** = SCRUTINIZE the Process and Self-Correct as Needed (Step 5)

in the lives of college students. We have named the process *IDEAS*. IDEAS is a 5-step critical thinking problem-solving process that is comparable to the critical thinking used in many professional settings including health care, legal analysis, arbitration and negotiation, scientific research, engineering and architectural design, financial planning, marketing and advertising, agricultural advancement, criminological investigations, etc. It is highly valuable in real-life situations such as buying a car, dealing with a difficult boss or co-worker, making a career change, ending a bad relationship, investing, starting or operating a small business, or selecting a candidate in the upcoming election.

With our research team we have studied problem solving in business, education, health sciences, the military, law, and a number of other fields and in all of these domains critical thinking and problem solving comes down to the same five things. The 5-step IDEAS critical thinking process is simple to understand and to apply and yet powerful enough to work with problems of significant complexity. The steps are straightforward. And yet, in response to the demands of the problem at hand, each step in the process can involve substantial analysis, inference, and evaluation. The IDEAS process calls for good critical thinkers to take the time to make well-reasoned, reflective and yet timely decisions about how to resolve their problems. We need to be patient enough to apply the process well, and yet savvy enough to avoid "paralysis by analysis" because in fact a judgment must at some point be made. The name of the process, IDEAS, is a mnemonic, which simply means that it is a device to help us to remember more easily these five steps:

- Step 1, represented by the "I" is **Identify Problems and Set Priorities**. The first step in problem solving is to realize that we have a difficulty that needs our attention. Knowing our priorities helps us identify situations which are or could become problems for us. In turn, examining the characteristics of the problem helps us clarify our priorities.
- Step 2, represented by the "D" is **Deepen Understanding and Gather Relevant Information**. Gathering relevant information helps us deepen our understanding of the problem. In turn, deepening our understanding of the problem helps us see what information might be relevant.
- Step 3, represented by the "E" is **Enumerate Options and Anticipate Consequences**. Enumerating genuine options helps us focus on those consequences that have a greater likelihood of occurring, rather than fantasizing about extreme and remote possibilities. In turn, anticipating consequences helps us discard the infeasible options quickly, thus saving energy and time so we can address the more realistic and practical options.
- Step 4, represented by the "A" is **Assess the Situation and Make a Preliminary Decision**. Assessing our situation thoughtfully helps us make an initial tentative decision about what steps we are going to take to resolve the problem. In turn, making a preliminary decision helps us clarify our expectations so we can better assess what level of resolution will be good enough, given the current circumstances, for us to consider the problem to be resolved at least for the present.
- Step 5, represented by the "S" is **Scrutinize the Process and Self-Correct as Needed**. Scrutinizing the whole process enables us to see possible flaws and gaps in our thinking so that we can correct ourselves before we make a mistake. In turn, self-correcting can lead us to necessary reconsiderations of any aspect of our problem-solving process: We may realize that we should reassess the nature of the problem, rework our priorities, gather more information, identify a new option, more carefully anticipate likely consequences, reassess our situation, reevaluate our expectations, and, in the end, make a better decision. This final step is our assurance that the problem has been resolved sufficiently for the current time and circumstances.

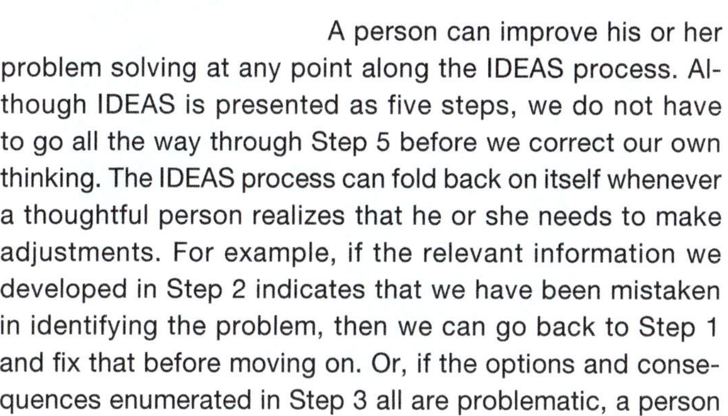

A person can improve his or her problem solving at any point along the IDEAS process. Although IDEAS is presented as five steps, we do not have to go all the way through Step 5 before we correct our own thinking. The IDEAS process can fold back on itself whenever a thoughtful person realizes that he or she needs to make adjustments. For example, if the relevant information we developed in Step 2 indicates that we have been mistaken in identifying the problem, then we can go back to Step 1 and fix that before moving on. Or, if the options and consequences enumerated in Step 3 all are problematic, a person can go back and reconsider his or her priorities from Step 1 or revisit Step 2 to determine whether additional information might be available to assist in expanding the options. IDEAS is a thoughtful and reflective process, not rigidly linear. We never have to wait for Step 5 to correct mistakes or make improvements on the work of earlier steps.

Using the IDEAS process well takes practice and that is what we are going to do in this chapter.[i] So here's our plan: To develop an understanding of this process and how to apply it to real problems in our lives we will explore each of the five steps, emphasizing how the step applies to actual problems faced by a wide range of college students. In the second part of this chapter we present six mini case study scenarios. The mini cases illustrate problems that typify the kinds of issues that arise in six different domains of college life: social, vocational, academic, physical, emotional, and spiritual. We will use the first five scenarios to explore each of the five IDEAS steps individually, emphasizing a different step with each scenario. Then in the final section of the chapter we'll put the five IDEAS steps back together. Every problem worth solving requires that we apply all five steps of the IDEAS process.

Educating the Whole Person

Armed with IDEAS, let's attack a few problems. In this section of the chapter we will explore the kinds of problems that college students often face. With each scenario we will take another step into the IDEAS process to illustrate how to apply strong critical thinking skills and positive critical thinking habits of mind to the problem or issue at hand. There are individual and group exercises suggested along the way because the best way to strengthen critical thinking is to engage those skills and habits of mind to solve problems.

"Education delivers a variety of benefits. Higher educational attainment is associated with better labor market outcomes including higher earnings, lower poverty, and lower unemployment. In addition, education is linked to various other benefits including higher job satisfaction, better fringe benefits, and better health."

Women in America: Indicators of Social and Economic Well-being (White House, March 2011); http://www.whitehouse.gov/sites/default/files/rss_viewer/Women_in_America.pdf. Link to this report at www.mythinkinglab.com

Research about college students of all different ages and backgrounds often focuses on how the experience of attending college impacts and shapes their lives. Our development as human beings continues throughout our lives. But the decade or so from late adolescence through young adulthood is particularly important because during these years we are

- developing the competencies we will need to make a living in a complex society,
- learning to manage our emotions,
- moving through autonomy toward interdependence,
- developing mature interpersonal relationships,
- establishing our personal identity,
- developing and refining our sense of purpose,
- developing a greater integration of who we are with what we say and do in all circumstances.[ii]

Although the domains into which problems might fall remain pretty much constant throughout the arc of our lives as human beings, the particular issues and concerns college students experience are not the same as those expressed by children or as those expressed later in midlife. Our success in college, as in life, depends on our ability to address these concerns and issues, as these are manifested in the problems of our day-to-day lives.

The table on the next page illustrates some of the issues and concerns typically experienced and expressed by college students. Again, we are all different. You may not have personally wrestled with each of these issues or concerns. Don't worry if the problems which hound your life in these different domains

Domain	Example Issues and Concerns of College Students
Social	How do I build lasting friendships and relate in a positive way to other people? What responsibilities do I have as a member of a community? What can I expect of others, what contributions do they have the right to expect of me?
Vocational	What major or career field shall I choose? What knowledge, skills, and experiences do I need to be successful in that career? How do I get started in that field?
Academic	How do I study, when and where? How do I prepare for tests? How can I improve my writing skills? How can I connect what I'm learning in one course with what I'm learning in another?
Physical	What should I eat or not eat? How can I stay fit? I know I'm free to do anything I want, but what kinds of risks with my health and safety are just too stupid to take?
Emotional	How do I cope with the stress and pressure of grades and the expectations that parents and others put on me? How do I cope with being alone, away from my family and the friends I grew up with? How do I get out of bed in the morning when I feel so depressed?
Spiritual	What are my true values? What do I really care about? What do I hope to achieve in my life? What about God, religion, patriotism, democracy, and all those things I used to believe without question?

do not happen to be listed here. The important thing is to realize that we all experience problems and challenges, and that there is a sensible process for working through them. So, let's begin.

SOCIAL RELATIONSHIPS

Social relationships are complex. The meanings that we attach to what others say or do can differ vastly. What one person might see as an apology, another might interpret as sarcasm. What one person thinks of as a harmless prank, another might experience as a deeply hurtful personal assault. What one person intends as respectful silence, another sees as unwitting acquiescence or as cold indifference. Seeing ourselves as others see us is not an easy thing. But throughout our lives those rare moments when we are able to see ourselves as others see us often yield valuable insights for personal reflection and growth.

Consider Jill's situation in this story: There was a huge party at a nearby night club last Saturday night after the football team's victory. Jill and her roommate went to the party, and Jill drank a few too many. A cute guy from her Communication class was there and he was buying Jill and her roommate a new drink every time they finished their old ones. The next day Jill learned from her roommate that something made Jill get into a shouting match with another female partygoer. In a fit of anger Jill screamed, cursed, and called the other girl several nasty and unflattering names. Ultimately, Jill was subdued and escorted out of the club by the bouncer. This verbal display was in front of a big crowd at the party. Or at least Jill thought it was only the partygoers. She quickly learned that someone at the party had posted pictures of her performance on Facebook and posted the video on YouTube. Jill's younger sister, a high school senior, had already left a voice mail because she was Jill's friend on Facebook and she had seen the video. Jill wondered who posted the video to the Web, who else had seen her act this way, and what was going to happen to her as a result. This was bad, really bad, Jill thought.

How would Jill's roommate interpret what happened? Did Jill lose respect in her eyes? How about in the eyes of the young man, whom she'll be seeing in her Comm class? And what about Jill's sister, the high school senior? What might she be thinking about her older sister and about college life in general when she sees the YouTube video? What if Jill's mother is one of her Facebook friends?

STEP 1: IDENTIFY the Problem and Set Priorities

Jill regards what happened as "bad, really bad." But there are no do-overs.

If Jill really wants to repair some of the damage, she's first going to have to identify the problem as accurately as she can, or in this case, problems that she's created for herself by her drunken indiscretion.

In some cases, the problem will be relatively straightforward, meaning that you can state your problem directly and simply. This doesn't mean that your problem is simple! It means, however, that you have clarity on what exactly the problem is that you need to thinking critically about. For example, "I'm going to see that guy in class and I have to think about what I'm going to say."

Other times your problem may be part of a constellation of related problems and your task in this first step is to clarify and prioritize the problems at hand so that you can systematically address the main or most pressing problem. For example, "I know that my sister and probably Mom, too, will have seen the YouTube posting. I'm going to want to apologize and make it clear to them all that nothing like that is going to happen ever again. But should I talk to my sister and my Mom together, or separately? And if separately, which one first?"

You may have experienced a situation where you spent a great deal of time thinking about a problem and coming up with a solution only to find out later that the thing that you *thought* was the problem turned out to be not really what you needed to work on. You were solving the wrong problem!

Thinking Critically Malicious Intent or a Prank Gone Horribly Wrong?

It was not supposed to end with his suicide! In September 2010 Rutgers University freshman, Tyler Clementi, 18, jumped off the George Washington Bridge to his death. Dharun Ravi, 18, and Molly Wei, also 18 at the time, are alleged to have streamed video of Tyler engaged sexually with another man. The authorities initially charged both Ravi and Wei with the crime of invasion of privacy. Clementi's family was devastated, and the University community was shocked by the tragedy. In the months that followed, Ravi received additional indictments for tampering with evidence, witness tampering, and for a hate crime with anti-gay motive. In order to avoid conviction, Wei has entered into a plea bargain that involves three years of community service, testifying at any proceedings, counseling for cyberbullying, and cooperation with authorities in this ongoing case. Both Ravi and Wei made bail, but dropped out of Rutgers. Facing deportation or trial, Ravi's lawyer said his client was innocent.

We do not want to second guess what happened that sad September, but these vivid events do raise the question of what must Tyler have been thinking after learning about the video. How could the young man have conceived of *the problem* such that his recourse was suicide? Was his fear that, having been outted for his homosexuality, his family and friends would forever reject him? We will never know. But what we do know is that to this young man the monumental character of his problem, whatever it was, must have seemed absolutely insurmountable.

And, in the aftermath, what now are the problems for Ravi, Wei, the Clementi family, and for the Rutgers university community?

Visit www.mythinkinglab.com for news stories and more about these tragic events.

Read the **Document** on **mythinkinglab.com**

What questions might we ask ourselves in order to be sure we have accurately identified the problem? For example, what might Jill ask herself to help her clarify the *main problem(s)* in this situation and to establish her priorities going forward?

- What aspects of last Saturday cause me the most concern or embarrassment?
- Should I be concerned about my drinking?
- Should I make it a priority to address the drinking issue?
- Has a verbal rage like this happened before and is it a pattern?
- Am I excessively vulnerable to peer pressure?
- Are my friends worthy of my trust?
- How badly have I hurt my relationship with my sister and my family?
- Have I jeopardized my enrollment at this university?
- What should I do first to repair my relationships with others?

Let's assume that Jill prioritizes mending her relationships with others. There are four more steps to the IDEAS process before Jill will have made a fully reflective and thoughtful decision about what to do to repair her damaged relationships. Before going on in this chapter, as an exercise, work though those four steps as if you were Jill and your first priority was to repair your relationship with your sister. You can do this exercise yourself as a personal reflection, or as a group discussion.

VOCATION

The word *vocation* means "calling," and it is associated with the kind of work for which one is most suited or "called to do." One's vocation is intimately associated with one's identity. People often describe themselves in terms of the professions they have pursued or the work they have done throughout their careers. "I'm an apprentice carpenter." "I'm a physical therapist at the Med Center." "I'm a teller at BofA." "I'm in marketing." Etc. A combination of temperament, knowledge, skill, and desire goes into forging one's sense of what one "ought to become"—that is, the career one ought to pursue. But the reality for college students often is that the jobs they happen to have during college do not represent the careers to which they aspire nor the majors they are pursuing. Rather, the forging of one's future identity as a contributing member of society through the vocation one will pursue is, for college students, focused in the selection of one's major. Many factors go into the selection of a major, and one's sense of one's potential career or vocation is certainly one of the central factors in that mix. But it is not the only factor. And whenever many different forces are at play, some can converge to make a decision easier, but others can diverge or even conflict, making the choice more difficult. We have all felt these pushes and pulls.

Consider this scenario: Deshan was sitting in the college library pouring over the university catalog and clicking through the campus Web site. Staring at the multitude of departmental Web pages, each featuring pictures of smiling, successful students, had made Deshan frustrated that he didn't have a major yet. Even though he had just started college, he felt pressure from his family to have his career plans all laid out. His parents had made it very clear that college was expensive. Unless he picked a major he felt like he was wasting time and money. He agonized over which major would be the best. Which would fit his interests and talents? Which would be the most enjoyable? Which might lead to the most exciting and lucrative career? And which would honor his parents' sense of worthy respectability and also their wishes that he get through college and out into the work world as quickly as possible? There were so

many possibilities! Deshan wanted to yell out loud with frustration. He did not know where to begin!

Your first reaction to Deshan's situation may be this, "Since when did having a lot of good choices become a problem?" Think back to a situation when you felt overwhelmed by your choices. The 5-step IDEAS problem-solving process can help counter the feelings of being overwhelmed by a challenging decision, like this one, which appears to have such momentous consequences. For Deshan, the first step would be to analyze the situation in order to identify the main problem and set his priorities. From there he could focus on deepening his understanding, not of every option, but rather of those options that were most relevant to his priorities.

"I don't know the key to success, but the key to failure is trying to please everybody."

Bill Cosby

STEP 1: IDENTIFY the Problem and Set Priorities

Deshan is in the library gathering information about all the academic majors his college offers. But his efforts are less than effective because, not yet having clearly established his priorities, he does not know what information is the most relevant to his particular situation. What is Deshan's problem, really? Is it that he must choose a major? No, that's a solution to some other problem. Clearly Deshan has a substantial wish list: He believes that he must declare a major in order to be happy like the students on the campus Web site. He wants to make his parents happy. He wants to graduate on time. He wants to have a good job when he is out of school. He wants a major that fits his interests and skills, to be enjoyable, and to fit his parents' sense of what is worthy and respectable.

Part of Deshan's problem is that he is trying to satisfy too many demands at once. Treating each demand as equal only pulls him apart. First he needs to figure out if selecting a major is vital at this very moment in his college career. It might be, if he is interested in a major that requires a large number of units. But it might not be if he is enrolled in courses that will count toward his graduation requirements no matter which of several majors he might select. He needs more information about this because it can be a mistake to make a decision that does not yet have to be made.

Deshan also needs to set some priorities. For example, is fulfilling his parents' expectations the top priority or not? Is it more important to select a major one's parents find worthy or one that fits your interests and talents? In the chapter on the positive critical thinking habits of mind, we identified courageous truth-seeking which plays an important role in clarifying priorities. In this case Deshan will need to muster the courage to ask himself some tough questions, like whether or not he wants to spend his college years preparing for a career that does not interest him. His parents may want him to become a lawyer, scientist, business executive, or physician. But Deshan may have other interests.

"Success is not the key to happiness. Happiness is the key to success. If you love what you are doing, you will be successful."

Albert Schweitzer

After reflecting on what is most important to him, let's assume that Deshan has determined that his primary problem is how to identify a major that will motivate him the most because it fits with his skills and interests. The more passion and motivation he has for the major, the more likely he is to enjoy his studies and do well. Even with his priorities in mind, Deshan might imagine that this major or that major is going to be the right one for him, but to continue to make progress on solving his problem he now needs to gather more information.

STEP 2: DEEPEN Understanding and Gather Relevant Information

After the main problem has been identified, Deshan would be ready to systematically gather the relevant information needed to inform his choice(s) of major. Other positive critical thinking habits of mind discussed in Chapter 2 alongside of truth-seeking include systematic inquiry and inquisitiveness. These are valuable habits during information gathering. Deshan would be wise to organize his inquiry the same way he would if this were an important academic assignment. He might begin by listing several questions related to the problem at hand so that he could understand the problem better and so that he could focus his information-gathering efforts. Here are a few examples:

- What do I know about myself in terms of my knowledge, skills, and values?
    - What topics do I find most interesting?
    - In which academic subjects do I excel?

Thinking Critically The "Gap Year"—Advantage or Liability?

The idea of a full-time student taking a year to do something other than study or start a career appears to be gaining some traction. Sometimes referred to by the media as "Gap Year" or the "Gap Year Advantage," the idea is that a person may gain valuable life experience doing volunteer service or working for a year by taking "a year off" before, during, or after college. To learn more about this concept visit www.mythinkinglab.com for a link to the article "The Lure of the Gap Year" in *U.S. News & World Report's Best Colleges, 2011 edition*. Evaluate pros and cons of a gap year at each of the three possible junctures (before, during or after college). If this concept is appealing, what policies and expectations would need to change in order to facilitate a "Gap Year Program"?

Read the Document on mythinkinglab.com

- What careers am I most interested in pursuing?
- What kinds of problems do I find most compelling?
- What can I learn from talking to other people?
  - What might my academic advisor be able to do to help me?
  - What could my professors this term do to help me?
  - What might my friends who are juniors and seniors be able to tell me about picking a major?
  - What could I learn from talking to people who work in careers that I think are interesting?
- What can I learn by consulting other available resources?
  - What resources exist on campus to help students pick a major or pick a career?
  - What could I look for on the Internet to learn more about career options?
  - Where do I look to find out what careers are possible with what majors?
- If I can narrow it down to two or three best options, are there any experiences, maybe internships or site visits, that might help me learn more?
- Does it really matter what major I choose, or could I get into the career field I want with any of several different majors?

Part of deepening our understanding of a problem is gathering information that is *relevant*. Determining what information is relevant involves the critical thinking skills of *interpretation and analysis* which are discussed in Chapters 4 and 6, on clarifying ideas and evaluating the credibility of sources of information. This is a two-way process. As we gather more information we deepen our understanding of the problem. Developing our understanding helps us see what additional relevant information might still be needed.

Deshan's decision will not be well made until he finishes the three remaining steps in the IDEAS process. But let's assume that he has narrowed his choices to these three possible majors: Criminal Justice (to become a Police Officer), Forensic Chemistry (to become a Criminologist or Crime Scene Investigator), and Psychology (with a view toward attending Law School in order to become a Criminal Defense Attorney.) As an individual exercise or as a group project, find out what programs your institution offers that most closely fit with these vocational choices. Investigate the next steps, beyond graduation from your institution with an Associate of Arts Degree or a Baccalaureate Degree, that a person would have to pursue to actually prepare for one or more of those careers. And then play out the conversation between Deshan and his parents, assuming they had been hoping he would become a physician or an engineer, as he explains to them that he has decided to dedicate his efforts during college to preparing for one of these three professional careers instead. Having worked your way through these steps in detail, what are the lessons that you might now bring to your own efforts to solidify your long-term career and vocational decisions?

ACADEMICS

Effective preparation for exams and assignments in college is not the brute memorization that many find works well enough in high school. College assignments and exams often require the application of critical thinking skills, like analysis, explanation, evaluation, interpretation, and inference. For years we have given "open book and neighbor" tests, allowing students to collaborate with one another and to look things up online or in their textbooks. But success on exams like that is never only about getting the informational content correct. They always demand a deeper understanding borne of reflective analysis, thoughtful interpretation, warranted inferences, and clear explanation based on reasons and evidence. And good exams often require, in addition to knowledge, thoughtful application, and informed analysis, a measure of skill at effective writing. What's the point of a college course otherwise? Today,

Thinking Critically How Can We Use Our Study Time Most Effectively?

Given how busy college students are these days, it is important to get everything possible out of every minute we can devote to studying and preparing for exams. It is better to study with highly focused intensity for 30 solid minutes, and then to take a mental break, than it is to waste an hour or two on a distracted, disengaged, disjointed, and half-hearted effort. Successful studying at the college level means becoming intimately, actively, and at times even passionately engaged with the material. Some students find it useful to make outlines of chapters, to write sample test questions, to make lists or tables or charts, or to create line drawings and diagrams showing interrelationships and linkages. A casual read is not enough—it might be a mile-wide overview but it will end up being only inch-deep understanding. On the other hand, if you can simulate teaching each section and each paragraph to yourself—or better, actually teach the material to someone else—you will have significantly magnified your comprehension and your chances of earning high marks on tests. Memorizing definitions, facts, and theories is not enough. Beyond just being able to find or to recite the facts a successful student is able to interpret them in a sensible and meaningful way and to apply them correctly when drawing inferences and giving explanations. Simply being able to identify names, events, objects, and dates is not the same as being able to analyze those objects and to explain the key relationships among those objects. Reading through a set of exercises does not pay half the dividends that actually working the exercises provides. And, figuring out exactly why a mistaken answer is an error can be more valuable for deeper learning than happening to get the answer right but not being sure why.

information—some of it reliable and some not—is as abundant as sand on an LA beach. If a college education were no more than a game of *Jeopardy*, then everyone with a smart phone would have a doctorate.

Consider Maria's situation. In high school, where memorization was the main cognitive skill needed, Maria had always considered herself a good student. Maria earned excellent grades in high school and was in the Advanced Placement or Honors classes in most subjects. So, when Maria got her first test back in college—it was in an Introduction to Cultural Anthropology course—she was shocked to see the big, red "F" at the top of her exam. What the heck happened? She thought she knew the material! She had memorized the terminology and read the chapters, highlighting almost every sentence it seemed. She was definitely confused because she had come to college thinking she was pretty smart. Maria was right about that, too; she was a very smart woman. But the demands of college work clearly were not going to be the same as high school. Maria knew she had to do something different if she was going to pass this class.

What should someone in Maria's shoes ask themselves? Following the 5-step IDEAS process in this situation, the first two steps would be to analyze the situation in order to identify the problem and set priorities and then systematically gather the relevant information needed to deepen understanding of the problem and change future behavior.

The First Two IDEAS Steps in Maria's Case

STEP 1: What is Maria's problem and what is her priority? The "F" grade is not the problem. It is the result. The problem, in retrospect, became very clear to Maria: She quickly realized that she was not sufficiently prepared to take the kind of exam that the college professor gave. Her priority

"The definition of success: fall down seven times, stand up eight times."

Japanese Proverb

is to reverse that situation. Like going into an important game without appreciating how much it would take to be successful, she had no idea how much critical thinking, as compared with information recall, the professor expected. And now she intends never to put herself in that disadvantageous situation again. Okay, but how? That brings us to the second step.

STEP 2: How can Maria deepen her understanding and gather relevant information? What questions could a student ask in order to learn what the professor expects? The question, "Is this going to be on the exam," is not one of them. In college everything and anything might turn out to be on the exam. A more helpful question might be "Can you give us an example or two of the kinds of questions we might expect on the exam?" The purpose of that question is not to find out if the questions are essay, short answer, or multiple choice, but to find out, no matter what the format, whether the questions demand interpretation, analysis, inference, evaluation, or explanation. What other questions would you ask? How about, "Can you share with us some examples of really strong papers or exams from the last time you taught this course?" If yes, then the professor is providing you with benchmarks and paradigms of the kinds of performances on assignments and tests that this professor hopes to see.

STEP 3: ENUMERATE Options and Anticipate Consequences

The twin goals of this third step in the 5-step IDEAS process are to generate potential choices and to reflect on their ramifications. One way to think about this is to visualize yourself standing in the center of an intersection, with paths heading in multiple directions around you. The first thing to do is to imagine as many options, or potential paths, as you can. This sounds easy, but it can be difficult to see all the options because of our natural human tendency to lock into a one possible solution or option prematurely, without giving due consider to the other options. Chapter 11, Think Reflectively: Strategies for Decision Making, offers a great many suggestions on how to avoid the common mistake of locking into an inferior option before having seriously considered some better possibilities.

Suppose you were worried or disappointed, or downright embarrassed, about your poor academic performance. Each of these questions could generate options for future behavior.

- Are my study habits effective, and if not, how can I change them?
- What could I ask my professor that would improve my performance in each class?
- How might I engage with my classmates to help us all do better on the next test or assignment?
- How could I utilize the textbook or class sessions to help my learning? The section about introductory college courses and language communities in Chapter 4 on clarifying ideas can be helpful. The same for the three important chapters (12–14) on ideological, comparative, and empirical reasoning, because those chapters explain the kinds of thinking which characterize knowledge acquisition in different academic domains of inquiry.
- What distracts me or takes me away from my studies? Can I eliminate, contain, or control these factors?
- How might my family or friends help me improve as a student?
- What campus resources are available to students who are trying to bring up their grades? Most student success centers at colleges these days are intended to help average students become good students and to help good students become superior students.

> **"Always bear in mind that your own resolution to succeed is more important than any other one thing."**
>
> **Abraham Lincoln**

The second part of this step is to consider what is likely to happen if you choose a particular option and, obviously, to be able to explain to yourself why that is the likely outcome. The positive critical thinking habit of mind of striving to anticipate consequences as objectively as possible is particularly valuable to cultivate. There are some helpful tips on how to do this in Chapter 2's section on critical thinking habits of mind. Some of us overestimate our capacity to control events, and others of us underestimate our potential. But the wise person is one who thinks ahead when considering choices, and tries to figure out what is likely to happen or not happen if a given choice is made. The more we can understand ourselves and the reasons we make certain choices, the more likely we are able to capitalize on opportunities and avoid negative or disappointing results. As explained in Chapter 10 on heuristic thinking and snap judgments, pausing to consider first the potential consequences of our decisions will make us help us become wiser, more reflective decision makers. It certainly helps us eliminate the kinds of impulsive, reactive, shoot-from-the-hip choices that so often lead to unexpected problems.

> **For every one of us that succeeds, it's because there's somebody there to show you the way out. The light doesn't always necessarily have to be in your family; for me it was teachers and school.**
>
> **Oprah Winfrey**

Let's practice anticipating the consequences of some potential actions in response to getting a less than fully satisfying grade on an academic assignment or test. Considering your own personal situation, how would you fill in the blanks?

- If I spend twice as much *time* studying as compared to last time, it is likely that ______________ because ______________ .

- If I spend the same amount of time, but studied more intensely and more frequently than last time it is likely that ______________ because ______________ .
- If my attendance in class stays the same that will likely ______________ because ______________ .
- If I participated more in class discussion this will likely ______________ because ______________ .
- If I go to my professor's office hours, or send an e-mail asking for some help with a particularly confusing or difficult concept, he or she will likely tell me that ______________ because ______________ .
- If I study with one of my classmates we will likely ______________ because ______________ .
- If I looked for a campus office that is designed to assist students I will likely find ______________ because ______________ .
- If I increased the amount of sleep I get at night that would likely result in ______________ because ______________ .
- If I continue to eat the way I have been eating, this will likely ______________ because ______________ .

One more hypothetical for you to consider: Suppose that Maria, who likes to e-mail and text her mother every day, told her mother about the failing grade on that Cultural Anthropology exam. And suppose that, without informing Maria of her intentions, Maria's mother decided to phone the academic dean or the Anthropology Department chairperson to complain about the professor's "impossibly unfair tests" and to ask the dean to void that exam score or transfer Maria to a section of the course taught by some other professor. What do you think will happen in such a case? Apart from guessing or speculating about what the dean or the department chairperson might do, how can you find out for sure what is likely to happen at your institution if this kind of a situation should arise? Once you know what is likely to happen, would you want your partner, parent, or best friend making such a call on your behalf unbeknownst to you? Explain why or why not?

HEALTH AND PHYSICAL WELL-BEING

Attributed to the Roman poet Juvenal, the popular saying, *"Mens sana in corpore sano"* ("A sound mind in a sound body") suggests that human happiness is intimately connected with one's emotional and physical well-being. That Latin phrase, which has become the motto of many educational institutions,

Thinking Critically — What Is the Relationship between Education and Income?

Anticipating consequences, like the other steps in the 5-step IDEAS critical thinking problem-solving process, applies to big decisions as well as small ones. Consider the big decision of whether or not to go to college and graduate. One of the consequences of various options has to do with the financial impact of those options on a person's future earnings potential. Sure, there are always stories about someone who made it big financially but never went to college. Just like there are stories about people who smoked for decades but never contracted heart disease, lung cancer, or emphysema. But, statistically speaking, those celebrated examples are the rare exceptions. Like winning a fortune in a casino, it can happen; but the smart money says don't bet your life on it.

In its May 8, 2010 issue, when the public mood was growing severely impatient with the continuing U.S. economic problems, *The Economist* published a graphic "Richer by degrees" (page 33) based on data from the Brookings Institution. The graphic describes the relationship between academic attainment, gender, and income. As a critical thinking exercise, how would you interpret what this graphic is telling us about the changes in real hourly earnings by sex and educational attainment? What do you suppose explains the generally better numbers for women at every educational level? Do you believe that the next 30 years will be different than the previous 30 with regard to earnings by educational level? What are the reasons and the evidence for your view?

Visit **www.mythinkinglab.com** to link to this story in *The Economist* and these data from the Brookings Institution.

Read the **Document** on **mythinkinglab.com**

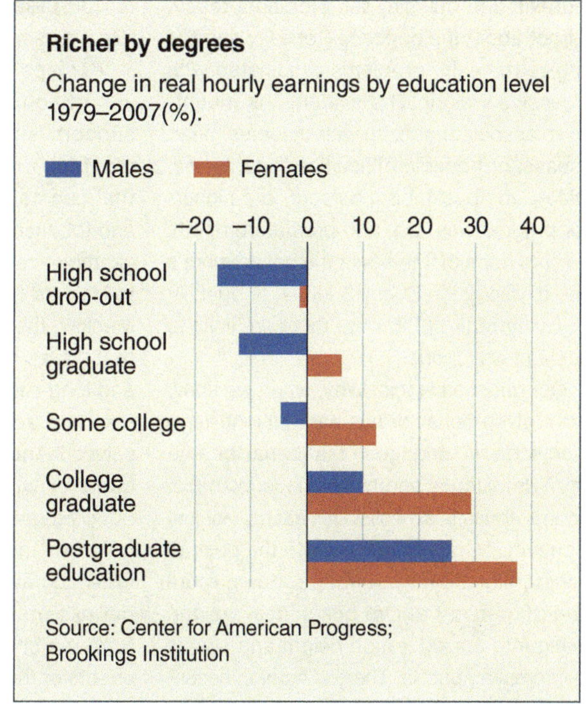

Mens sana in corpore sano

sports clubs and products, and military organizations, has echoed through the centuries in the writings of poets, presidents, and educational philosophers. Today, attending to physical health and well-being covers a lot of territory: diet and dietary supplements, fatty fast foods, fitness products, exercise regimens, drugs and alcohol usage, safe and risky sexual activity, etc. And, when we care about others, we often find ourselves worried about their physical well-being, not just our own.

Consider this scenario: Leah could not believe how much she was agonizing over whether or not to say something to her roommate Stephanie. It was the beginning of the semester, and she had been with Stephanie in the cafeteria talking with two other girlfriends about their summer breaks. Stephanie had clearly surprised her friends when she told them how she was still seeing Brett and that they spend most every night together these days. One friend at the table blurted out "I hope he at least uses a condom!" and Stephanie replied 'Nah, he got so mad when I asked him to wear one . . . he says he HATES those things. Anyway, I am on the pill and I know he is a good guy so we're good." Leah had been stunned by Stephanie's reply, but her friends seemed not to be. Without missing a beat their conversation immediately moved to a discussion of the lunch entrées they were eating. Three days later Leah was still trying to decide if she should talk to Stephanie about her relationship with Brett. Brett was pressuring Stephanie to gamble with her health and Stephanie was dismissing it. This concerned Leah greatly. She cared about Stephanie a lot and wanted to see their friendship grow. But Leah was still getting to know her roommate, and she was not sure how Stephanie would react if she seemed to be criticizing Stephanie's love life.

Thinking Critically

How Can We Protect Ourselves from Ourselves?

Scientifically we know a lot about the relationships between dietary habits and health. A generation ago colleges worried about anorexia and bulimia, still problems today, but not about the opposite—obesity and the long-term health problems associated with excessive weight. The evidence is mounting to associate obesity with diabetes, heart disease, orthopedic difficulties (hips, knees, ankles, and back), birth defects, and higher-risk pregnancies. Oh, and premature death. We sure hope that this isn't the government's plan for fixing the Social Security budget! At www.mythinkinglab.com there are links to recent news reports.

Our question is this: Why, when we know that a given behavior has harmful long-term effects, do we engage in that behavior anyway? Smoking is another obvious example. Alcohol abuse is as well. Over-eating, not just occasionally, but consistently to the point of gaining significant poundage, going more than 20 percent above one's ideal weight, taking into consideration height and sex, is an interesting puzzle. There is nothing necessarily wrong with eating. Food, unlike cigarette smoking, does not necessarily introduce anything harmful into a person's body. And, unlike alcohol, eating a lot all at once does not cause intoxication. But consistently eating too much does ruin a person in the long run. Just like consistently eating too little can ruin a person.

Perhaps the answer to this dilemma can in part be found in the arguments used to support "sin" taxes. A sin tax is a government tax on various products or activities that can cause us harm. Taxes on alcohol and tobacco products, and on gambling, for example, can be called sin taxes. According to Harvard Economics Professor N. Gregory Mankiw, the best argument for "sin" taxes is that "taxes on items with short-run benefits and long-run costs tell our current selves to take into account the welfare of our future selves." Another good argument is that the costs of which the professor speaks are not paid only by the sinner. Often there are costs to the rest of the society—namely other taxpayers—too, for example for medical expenses to treat people who suffer from the chronic diseases and debilitating effects of their own unwise behavior.

Professor Mankiw's remarks were published in an opinion piece he wrote on the topic of taxing soda. His question is "Is a soda tax a good idea?" You can access his essay at www.mythinkinglab.com. Consider his perspective, consider the various options and their consequences, and then formulate one of your own and explain your point of view using good reasons and solid evidence.

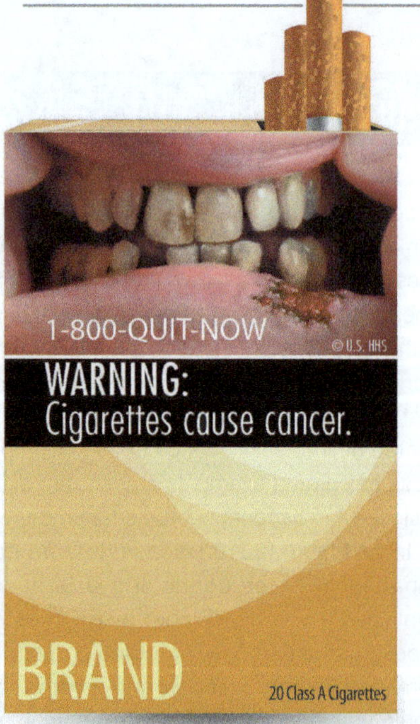

Read the Document on mythinkinglab.com

The First Three Steps in Leah's Case

Suppose Leah had been introduced to the 5-step IDEAS process. What might her thinking have been as she worked through the first three steps in the process? Here's one possibility.

STEP 1: Identify the problem and set priorities. Leah would first analyze the situation in order to clarify her priorities and determine the main problem. Clearly one of her objectives is to develop her friendship with Stephanie. That Stephanie has unprotected sex seems unnecessarily risky to Leah, and Leah is concerned that perhaps Stephanie perceives herself to be invulnerable for one reason or another. Getting to be a better friend to Stephanie becomes Leah's paramount objective. But being a person's friend means acting in their best interests. So Leah's problem is to find a way to be honest with Stephanie about her concerns, even if acting in such an honest way puts their relationship at risk. For if the relationship is to blossom into a lasting friendship, then that level of honesty is mandatory. Friends do not lie to each other or withhold their concerns.

STEP 2: Deepen understanding and gather relevant information. The goal of Step 2 is to clarify the parameters of the situation, illuminate the relevant perspectives, and bring whatever needs to be known to the table. In this situation, Leah thought about how she didn't know Stephanie well enough to simply begin a conversation by telling her that she was foolish for taking such risks. Leah decided to ask the other two women who were at the table that day what they thought she should do. Their responses were mixed; one said Leah should definitely talk to Stephanie because that would show her that someone cared (even if Leah was a relative stranger). The other told Leah that Stephanie seemed like a smart person and that Leah shouldn't feel like she had to say anything. In fact, maybe, she said, what Stephanie did was none of Leah's business. It looked like the outcome of this step in the IDEAS process for Leah was going to be ambiguous. And then Leah asked herself how the idea of having unprotected sex based on a guy's opposition to wearing a condom fit with her own sense of being a smart person. To Leah those two ideas didn't go together in her mind at all.

STEP 3: Identifying Options and Anticipating Consequences. When Leah imagined bringing the subject up with Stephanie she could see her reacting in many different ways—appreciation, anger, embarrassment, defensiveness, helplessness, happiness, etc. Leah realized she didn't know Stephanie well enough to predict which of these would actually happen. But when she imagined her other option, not approaching Stephanie, Leah envisioned a variety of futures. Stephanie might continue to take risks with her sexual health, or she might insist on using a condom from here on out. She might be told one day by a doctor that she has contracted a sexually transmitted disease. Or she might realize that she had been lucky in her relationship with Brett, even though no one said anything to her. But to Leah, the risks for Stephanie were rather large, and the benefits of not bringing up the issue were almost zero, particularly since Leah wanted to cultivate a deeper friendship with Stephanie. On the other hand, there were risks associated with bringing up the topic. If Stephanie reacted with anger or hostility, that could prevent the friendship from ever happening. As with many difficult problems, it was not easy for Leah to infer what would be the better option. She knows that she needs to think carefully about these options and that she needs to make a choice.

Leah realized that procrastinating or failing to make any decision in a case like this is the same for all practical purposes as explicitly deciding to do nothing. Ignoring the problem is not the same as resolving it. Leah realized that a timely decision was essential. And so she moved on to Step 4.

STEP 4: ASSESS the Situation and Make a Preliminary Decision

The goal of Step 4 is to evaluate the relevant information, use it to inform your understanding of the problem at hand, and to come to a tentative initial decision about what to believe or what to do. Even in contexts of uncertainty and risk it is often necessary to find the courage to make a decision and stick with it. Chapters 10 and 11 on human decision making focus on the differences between reactive and reflective decisions, warn us about typical human decision-making errors, and provide helpful guidance on how to make timely and well-reasoned decisions without being locked prematurely into a less than optimal choice. The box on page 58 "Critical Thinking Problem-Solving and Decision Making Strategies" includes many of those recommendations. Each of these derives not only from research about how humans can make better decisions, but from the practical school of hard knocks. Some of the best decision makers are people and organizations that debrief their past decisions looking for why they may have been wise or unwise. From as impartial an analysis as possible, they derive for themselves some "lessons learned" to help with future decision making.

What questions could Leah ask herself in this specific situation to reflect on her options and come to a decision of what to do about her concern for Stephanie? Here are three. Can you think of others she might ask?

- Will I be able to live with myself if I don't approach Stephanie with my concerns for her health and well-being?
- Am I confident that approaching Stephanie and risking a negative response on her part is worth it, because showing my concern is the right thing to do?

Critical Thinking Problem-Solving and Decision Making Strategies
First of all, be sure you have correctly identified "the problem."
Specify which factors and priorities are most critical.
Gather relevant information from multiple reliable sources.
Identify and clearly differentiate viable options.
Be clear about why each option is in or out.
Evaluate viable options with disciplined impartiality.
Listen to both sides first—hear the pros and cons before evaluating them.
If new critical factors or priorities emerge use those as well.
Evaluate options in terms of all the critical factors and priorities, not just a sub-set.
Treat all the viable options equally—don't focus only on the advantages of the one you like and the flaws of the ones you don't like.
Have the courage to follow the reasons and evidence wherever they lead and to ask all the hard questions before making a final decision.
Seek advice from independent, informed, and unbiased sources
Decide when it is time to decide, and then make the decision in a timely way.
Check to see that the process you used has been reflective, complete, and fair-minded.
Check to see that the outcomes anticipated are the outcomes being attained. If not, make mid-course corrections to get back on track.
Have the maturity of judgment to stick with a decision if it is well made, but to change direction if there is good reason to reconsider and revise the decision.

- Will I be able to handle the rejection if she doesn't want to talk to me about something so intimate?

In the end one question Leah asked herself seemed to make all the difference. She asked herself this: "If Stephanie and I were real friends and the situation were reversed, what would I want or expect Stephanie to do to help me?" And her answer then became clear to her: "I would want her to tell me about her concerns, even if she thought that it would be difficult to raise the issue with me." And so Leah's tentative decision was to find an appropriate opportunity in the very near future to have a friend-to-friend conversation with Stephanie about how much it worried her that Stephanie took the risk of having unprotected sex with Brett and how troubling it was that he seemed to reject the idea of doing everything possible to keep them both healthy

There is one more step to the IDEAS process, and we will focus on it with the next scenario. But first, this question for you: "When you last had a conversation with a good friend about a health risk behavior—such as abusing alcohol or drugs, or overeating or not exercising, or not sleeping enough, or bulimia, or whatever worried you—how did that conversation go? Specifically, did having that conversation hurt your friendship, help it, or not affect it at all? How do you know?"

EMOTIONAL WELL-BEING

The decision we reach in Step 4 is called "preliminary" or "tentative" because it is not the end of the problem-solving process. Yes, that preliminary decision is our best candidate for what often becomes our final decision. But before we embrace it and consider our problem to have been resolved, we must first double-check how we got where we are. Step 5 challenges us to scrutinize our own decision-making process with as much rigor and objectivity as we can muster, and then to correct any lapses or errors we might find. As psychologically challenging as being our own tough critic might be, this step is vital, if we hope to be consistently successful at problem solving and decision making.

Consider, for example, Angelica's situation: Angelica walked into the student lounge and flopped down on the couch across from her classmates Shawna and Bree. The three of them had a formidable group project deadline looming. There was a lot of work to do before the end of the week. But, before they could start talking about their group project tears started to well up in Angelica's eyes. Her grades were slipping, and today that was weighing heavy on her mind. Nevertheless, what Angelica didn't anticipate was getting emotional in front of her classmates. She hated the weakness she felt in herself and she did not want to be telling her classmates about all of the things that were stressing her out. But it just all started pouring out. She had so many responsibilities; in addition to carrying a full load of units this term Angelica was working nights and weekends waiting tables. And since her parents both had multiple jobs, she was expected to be at home with her little brothers and sisters when she wasn't in class or working. She was also expected to contribute some of her tip money each week to cover the family's expenses. Angelica didn't resent the responsibility because she loved her family, but she was in college now and she wondered how she was going to get it all done without failing out of school. By the time she was done talking she was obviously distraught.

In this scenario we have three participants, Angelica, Shawna, and Bree, and they all could apply our 5-step IDEAS process. But would they all focus on the same problem (Step 1)? Maybe not. Bree may determine that the main problem they are facing right now is how to successfully finish the group project. Shawna may determine that the main problem is to help her classmate with her troubles. Meanwhile Angela can't focus on the group project because she is distraught about keeping her grades up.

Let's take Bree's version of the problem at hand. As Bree navigates the remaining steps in the process, she will seek to clarify the situation, analyze the available options, evaluate the likelihood of success from choosing a particular option, and then after reflection, choose a course of action. To accomplish this, Bree may want to review the assignment with her two classmates, and go over what they had decided to do separately and together over the next day or two before the due date. She may ask the group to think about whether the plan is still realistic. Specifically she may ask Angelica whether she will have the time to complete her part of the project. She may also ask Shawna whether she can take on some additional work to assist Angelica. Bree would reflect on her own ability to assist Angelica.

Only gods and fools never reconsider!

Anonymous

STEP 5: SCRUTINIZE Processes and Self-Correct as Needed

Let's assume that Angelica regained her composure and promised Shawna and Bree that she will get her parts of the project done on time. In light of this new information, Bree would need to consider the ramifications of trusting Angelica (Step 4). Bree would also want to ask questions that would help her anticipate the consequences of accepting Angelica's promise (Step 3). Ultimately, Bree accepts Angelica's promise and is confident about this decision. Does this mean that Bree's critical thinking about this situation is done? Actually no. The final step in the 5-step IDEAS process includes ongoing monitoring, analyzing, and evaluating the consequences of our chosen actions or beliefs. Mid-course corrections may always be necessary, no matter what the decision.

Step 5 directs us to be deliberately mindful of our decisions and whether or not they are leading to our desired outcomes. Sometimes when we move forward with a decision we are rewarded with things going as we had envisioned them. But as often as not, our planning is imperfect or the unexpected happens. Or, if there are competitors in the mix, they respond to our moves by making tactical adjustments that counteract or nullify our own efforts. The situation changes, people do not fulfill their responsibilities, or events beyond anyone's control intervene. Things go awry. Bad stuff happens!

Monitoring progress toward important goals and successfully achieving intermediary benchmarks and objectives are very much a part of thoughtful and effective problem solving. And, when we see things beginning to slip, revising our assumptions, reviewing our options, investigating why, and self-correcting are essential. This applies as much to beliefs—as the Chapters 12, 13, and 14 on comparative, ideological, and empirical reasoning explain—as it does to actions.

Here are some questions to help when reviewing and revising a decision:

- What is actually happening as a result of my decision, and is it what I thought would happen?
- If my decision was related to a short-term goal, was the goal achieved? Why or why not?
- If my decision was related to a mid-range or long-term goal, what evidence can I collect to gauge whether I am still on the path to achieve my goal?
- Whom might I consult in order to get feedback on my decision and the ramifications of my chosen action (or belief)?
- If my decision impacts the actions of another person, what can I do to support this relationship?
- If I need to make a self-correction, where should I start? Do I have the problem and the priorities right? Is there new information to consider? Are some options looking better now than before? Was I mistaken about the consequences? Did I act prematurely or delay too long on some aspect of this?
- If the situation did not turn out as I had anticipated, how might I rethink this problem, minimize the damage my error may have caused, and make the best out of the position I now find myself in?
- Are there some questions that I should have asked, some techniques or methods for information gathering I should have used, some assumptions or expectations that I made which were unfounded, some standards of performance or quality that I failed to apply, and some contextual factors which I failed to take into consideration?

SPIRITUAL DEVELOPMENT

In the previous sections we emphasized first one then another step in the IDEAS process. Along the way we have seen examples of problems in five of the six domains listed in the section on educating the whole person: social, vocational, academic, physical health, and emotional well-being. The one remaining domain is called the "spiritual" domain. *Spiritual* can be a troubling word for some of us; so if it helps to think of this domain as the province of one's core values, ethical principles, and deep commitments, that is fine as well.

Here's the situation: Max had been feeling ambivalent about the community service project he got sucked into over spring break. A group from his residence hall had signed up to spend the week building houses with Habitat for Humanity. His friends had coaxed him to join in by pointing out that Max's father was in construction so Max would be a natural asset. Max knew that his friends were mostly joking about his being "an asset" and that they just wanted more hands working on the project so they would finish faster. What they didn't know is that Max's father was constantly telling Max that a college education would be his "ticket out of Pop's blue collar life, and don't look back." Max always found that statement puzzling, but he knew that Pop was thrilled when Max announced that he was majoring in Engineering Management. Max never saw the curveball coming, but his life was irrevocably changed by his experience during spring break. Max had never witnessed poverty like that before, nor the tearful gratitude from the families who were receiving the new houses. Ever since, Max can't stop thinking about how his own family actually has it pretty good. Max finds himself asking hard questions about privilege, social justice, and what is fair in the world. He's not only wondering what happened, he's wondering now about the advice his Pop gave and about a lot of societal and political values and beliefs that he had never before questioned.

During one's college experience the central themes linked with the category we are calling "Spiritual Development" pertain to nurturing a positive and enthusiastic outlook on life and the future, setting goals for oneself, and achieving those aspirations—by cultivating open-mindedness, forming a personal value system and appreciating others' value systems, establishing a sense of ethics and ethical behavior, and engaging existential questions about life and the world around us. If your instructor assigned a version of this book that includes the supplementary chapter on ethical decision making, you will find that chapter useful in this regard.

Throughout this chapter we have highlighted the important factors that shape our college experience: social relationships, vocational direction, academics, physical health, and emotional well-being. These are not discrete domains; the life decisions we make during college inevitably touch on and are influenced by many of these factors in complex ways. The 5-Step IDEAS Critical Thinking Problem-Solving Process works well for the practical, day-to-day problems that vex and at times torment us. Now, we end this chapter by acknowledging and celebrating the "big questions" that are likely to be raised by the experiences you'll have while in college. In fact, the big questions are likely to be ones that we come back to more than once throughout our lifetime. It seems that every stage of life holds its share of experiences that can cause a person or a community to revisit core values, principles, and commitments. Let's take a brief look at how the five IDEAS steps might apply.

Max is grappling with the big question of "Who am I in this world?" Reflecting thoughtfully about one's identity is a hallmark of the college experience. Erik Erikson and other developmental psychologists remind us that many of the elements of the college environment—academic, co-curricular, administrative and community-based—facilitate college students' identity formation and social development.[iii] The table "Levels of Thinking and Knowing" in Chapter 6 on page 111 describes a progression from the naïvely trusting ways children deal with ideas all the way to the subtle and complex ways that "truth-seekers" and "sages" think. Critical thinking, and the cultivation of a healthy skepticism, can aid our cognitive development and help us not to be trapped in any one stage along the way. Max finds that he can no longer accept his father's views about society and about work without questioning. Max's experiences during the service learning project reveal a troubling disconnect between what he had believed before and what he has learned since about relative wealth and poverty, and the conditions under which people live. Max is not so naïve as to think that he can go out and "save the world." But neither is he so insensitive as to think that "none of this is about me."

Applying the 5-step IDEAS process can help counteract the feeling of being overwhelmed by the magnitude of big questions, such as those with which Max is wrestling. Forming a clear, solid, and durable sense of self takes time. Max is not going to have this all figured out in a day or two. But he does have the courage to face his question. He wants to know who the man is that he is going to become. And he knows that choices along the way are going to affect how he reacts each morning when he looks at the face of the man in the mirror. Rather than doing anything drastic that might impact his future options, Max is not going to drop out of college to take up missionary work in the inner city. Although that is one option that some might pursue. Nor is Max going to turn his back on his Habitat for Humanity experiences, trying to pretend that they never happened. Again, that is an option some others might pursue. Max is probably going to end up agreeing with his father that a college degree is essential, but that will be an inference Max draws for his own reasons, and not simply because his father may or may not have said so. Max will see the value of a college degree for the work he wants to do in life. Max may or may not decide to stick with his Engineering Management major. Either way, again, this decision will be for his own reasons, and whether it pleases or displeases his father will be of secondary consideration. Probably Max will gather data information about Engineering Management careers that have the potential to combine employment and service to the greater good. It is highly unlikely that Max would take a job that fulfilled only one of those two compatible objectives. Max may then decide to seek summer internships with firms that appear to offer those kinds of job opportunities after graduation. Not only would taking those kinds of internships help Max review and validate or amend his thinking about the man he will become, but internships can position him to be a stronger job candidate in those firms, if it turns out that the experiences affirm the direction he thinks he wants to take in his life.

Max's case reminds us that the 5-step IDEAS process can work over an extended period of time when applied to larger problems and dynamic circumstances, just as it can work with smaller, more well-defined problems. The key thing is that good problem solving and decision making during our college experience, and for all the rest of one's life, demands purposeful reflective judgment—that is, critical thinking.

Thinking Critically

Religious Practices and Beliefs—What *Do* We Know?

Whether it is through a religious tradition or a personally defined spiritualism, faith in a higher power, for many students, is a recognizable expression of their value system. How important is religion in your life—very important, somewhat important, not too important, or not at all important?

And how important is religion to the other students in your classes? Do you practice your religion at least once a week? Do other students practice theirs? Given the diversity of religious views, practices, and traditions among college students, perhaps a more fundamental question is how much do we really know about the practices and beliefs of those other religions . . . or even of our own?

According to a recent Religious Knowledge Survey conducted by the Pew Research Center nearly 60 percent of U.S. adults said religion is "very important" to them. And 40 percent of adults said they regularly (at least once a week) attend religious services. Nevertheless, a large numbers of Americans could not correctly identify the tenets, practices, history, and leading figures of *their own faith tradition,* let alone those of other major world religions.

The strongest predictor of religious knowledge wasn't having a religious upbringing, but it was a *person's years of schooling*. Other important factors included a person's religious affiliation, overall levels of religious commitment and frequency of reading religious materials, their gender and ethnicity, and where in the country a person resides.

Review the survey findings at Report of survey results: **http://pewforum.org/Other-Beliefs-and-Practices/U-S-Religious-Knowledge-Survey.aspx**. How can we explain the relationship between education and religious knowledge?

How well do you know the Bible and Christianity, world religions, or the constitutional restrictions on religion in the public schools? Take the Pew Research Center's Religious Knowledge Quiz for yourself: **http://features.pewforum.org/quiz/us-religious-knowledge/**

What do expert theologians think of the Pew Religious Knowledge Survey results? Check out this blog **http://blogs.ssrc.org/tif/2010/10/05/religious-knowledge/**

Read the **Document** on **mythinkinglab.com**

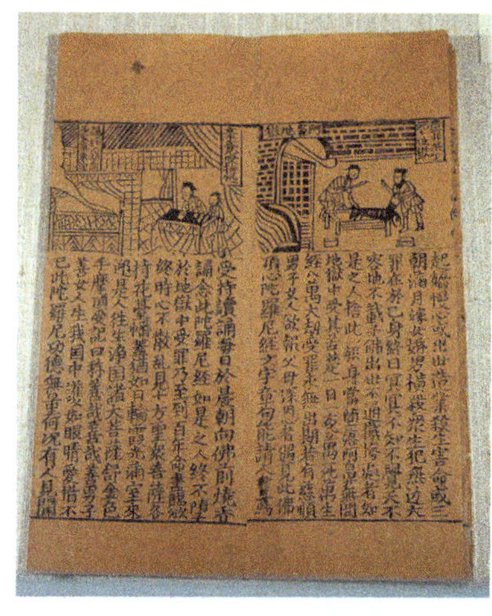

CHAPTER 03 REVIEW

Study and Review on mythinkinglab.com

Your success in college, as in many other endeavors, depends on how well you are able to solve problems. Critical thinking—that is reasoned and reflective judgment aimed at deciding what to do or what to believe—can be your key to successful problem solving. This chapter presents a 5-step critical thinking process that we can apply to the many different kinds of day-to-day challenges and difficulties college students encounter. Those problems might have to do with social relationships, vocational choices, academic challenges, physical health, emotional well-being, or spiritual concerns. Whatever they may be in any of our cases, this 5-step IDEAS critical thinking problem-solving process can assist us in getting a grip on those problems and making some progress in resolving them. The steps are straightforward; they call on us to apply our critical thinking skills and positive critical thinking habits of mind thoughtfully. The 5-step critical thinking process, IDEAS, can be applied to a very wide range of problems throughout our lives. Applying IDEAS helps us move from realizing that we have a challenge or difficulty that needs our attention to that point where we can reasonably regard that problem as having been resolved, at least for the current time and circumstances.

IDEAS

A 5-Step Critical Thinking Problem Solving Process

I = IDENTIFY the Problem and Set Priorities (Step 1)

D = DEEPEN Understanding and Gather Relevant Information (Step 2)

E = ENUMERATE Options and Anticipate Consequences (Step 3)

A = ASSESS the Situation and Make a Preliminary Decision (Step 4)

S = SCRUTINIZE the Process and Self-Correct as Needed (Step 5)

KEY TERM

problem solving is moving from the point at which we initially realize that we have a difficulty which requires our attention to that point where we regard the difficulty as being sufficiently resolved for the current time and circumstances. (p. 46)

FIND IT ON MYTHINKINGLAB.COM

Read the Document on mythinkinglab.com There are so many differences between college students that success for each individual can take on very different meanings. By contrast, at the institutional level success often comes down to graduation rates and retention rates. And at the national level, higher-education success or failure can mean the difference between scientific and technological progress or economic difficulties. Visit www.mythinkinglab.com to link to the news stories about the tragic case at Rutgers, the stats on your institution's retention and graduation rates, the Brookings Institution's data on the relationship between educational success and hourly earnings, and articles relating obesity to problem pregnancies, Professor Mankiw's opinion piece on the question of taxing soda, and the 2011 White House report, *Women in America: Indicators of Social and Economic Well-being* and the PEW survey on religious knowledge.

Exercises

REFLECTIVE LOG: WHAT'S ON MY LIST?

No doubt every one of us has small problems, if not big problems, that can aptly be classified as social, vocational, academic, physical, emotional, or spiritual concerns. Take a moment to jot down some of your issues, questions, and problems in each of these areas. When you have done that, reflect for a moment on which of the ones you've listed appears to you to be the most challenging. Having done that, now ask yourself what constructive steps are you taking to address that/those issues, questions, and concerns? How are those approaches working out for you? If not as well as you had hoped or expected, what might you do differently? Remember what Albert Einstein said, "Insanity is doing the same thing over and over again and expecting a different result."

BELIEVING OUR OWN PRESS RELEASES

Films like *The Social Network* and *Catfish* dramatize the complexity of online relationships. They bring home the need to evaluate how trustworthy the information might be that someone posts about themselves. Hundreds of millions of us have Facebook pages and hundreds of thousands more of us have Internet home pages and listings on matchmaking social networks. While we may be cautious about believing how honest others are being when they talk about themselves, have we applied a comparable degree of healthy skepticism to what we say about ourselves? Or, do we fall prey to the problem of believing our own press releases? Do a picture-by-picture and line-by-line analysis of your own postings about yourself. Are there some exaggerations, omissions, or misleading descriptions there? Is the impression we are trying to give people about ourselves an honest one? Not that we should post all of our flaws and fears for the whole world to see, but we might ask: To what extent might some degree of depth, substance, and sincerity actually present a truer picture? And if we know we are not being fully honest ourselves, then how can we trust what others are saying about themselves?

APPLY THE PROCESS

In the section on emotional well-being, Angelica, Shawna, and Bree each had a different sense of the key problem that required attention. Shawna may determine that the main problem is to help Angelica with all the emotional stress she was feeling. Angelica seemed to have focused only the immediate issue of keeping her grades up, given her many other responsibilities. And Bree was worried most about the looming group project deadline. Take up "the problem" first as seen by Shawna and then as seen by Angelica. Apply the 5-step IDEAS Critical Thinking Problem-Solving Process and identify the most promising options in each case. Do any options or combination of options appear to adequately address the problem in both of the ways it is being conceived? What signs would we look for to tell us that we are on the right track in the approaches we've taken to solving the problem as Shawna sees it and as Angelica sees it?

GROUP EXERCISE: #1–WHO ARE "TODAY'S COLLEGE STUDENTS"?

The concept "today's college student" refers to a very large and diverse set of people. What characteristics make college students different from one another and where can we look to see our similarities? How do these differences and similarities promote or hinder our likelihood of success in college? Apart from arming ourselves with a process we can use to address our many and varied day-to-day problems, what else might we do to help assure that we achieve academic success?

GROUP EXERCISE: #2–INVESTIGATE, CLASSIFY, AND RANK ORDER THE PURPOSES OF COLLEGE

Students have their reasons for attending college, parents and family members have their hopes and expectations, governments and foundations have their reasons for funding colleges, religious communities have purposes in mind for starting and sustaining colleges, and the colleges themselves have mission statements and Web sites proclaiming all the worthy things they expect all their graduates to have learned. Compare those lists. What are the commonalities of purpose, if any? Which are the most worthy and reasonable, even if they are not the most common? Which do the faculty, staff, alumni, and financial supporters of your college most value and spend the most effort to achieve? Which do you prize most and focus your greatest efforts on achieving? Which define the college and you as a success?

COMPLIMENTS
MASON'S

Read the Chapter on mythinkinglab.com

Listen to the Chapter Audio on mythinkinglab.com

You interpret!

The verbal gauntlet is hurled at the over-confident prosecution witness, Harrison Brady, by defense attorney Harry Drummond in *Inherit the Wind.*[i] Drummond is defending a school teacher fired for teaching evolution, something which Brady maintains is demonstrably false, given the creation story presented in *Genesis,* the opening book of the Bible. The Harrison Brady character is a staunch advocate of reading every word and verse in the Bible as the exact historically truth in all respects. But, thinks Drummond, if Brady is offering an interpretation, then Brady has strayed from his strictly literal reading of the sacred text. An interpretive analysis would be a crack in Brady's mental armor, a weakness that Drummond, like any good attorney, vigorously exploits. Drummond challenges Brady's thinking with questions about how to make sense of the word *day* as that word is used in Genesis. How long is a day to the eternal Creator, particularly if the Sun had not yet been created? There would be no way to measure a day, there would be no sundown to sundown, for example. So, is a "day" necessarily a 24-hour day; or might a day have been longer (or shorter) than 24 hours? Might it have perhaps been a year, hundreds of years, thousands of years, or, who knows, maybe millions of years?

<<< In one of the most dramatic moments of the the academy award winning film version of *Inherit the Wind* two of the great actors of the previous century confront one another. Spencer Tracy, playing Harry Drummond, cross-examines Fredric March, playing Harrison Brady, on this point: How shall we interpret the Biblical meaning of *day*? Rent this wonderful film, the scene is near the end. It is such a famous scene that you may be able to locate it on YouTube.com.

CHAPTER 04

Clarify Ideas and Concepts

HOW do context and purpose affect the quality of an interpretation?

HOW much precision does a good interpretation require?

HOW can I resolve problematic vagueness and ambiguity?

WHAT are language communities, and am I a member of any?

Scientific advances over recent centuries have reshaped our understanding of ourselves, our world, our solar system, and our universe. Without diminishing the value of the biblical book of Genesis for other purposes, to offer the book as a historical record of actual events occurring within the specific time frames stated there is to invite precisely the kind of exposure that *Inherit the Wind* delivers. On a literal level, Genesis's obvious contradictions (e.g., daylight on earth being created before the Sun) and vast inconsistencies between that text and all that we have learned scientifically pose too great an intellectual obstacle for reason to vault. But, what if the authors and editors of Genesis had other purposes in mind as they told their marvelous and meaningful stories around the campfires of their nomadic kinsmen?

This chapter is about interpreting the meanings of ideas as they are conveyed in language. Our goal, in the exercise of our critical thinking skill of interpretation, is to achieve as much accuracy and precision as may be required for the purposes and the context at hand.

Interpretation, Context, and Purpose

The authors and editors of Genesis meant to communicate their faith perspective. By telling of the powerful and awe-inspiring Yahweh, the authors of Genesis wanted to reassure the Israelites that Yahweh was far superior to the pagan gods. The tales of fearsome divine reprisals for straying from the teachings of Yahweh (e.g., death for those who went with the Moabite women to ceremonies honoring the god Baal) were meant to reinforce compliance. Genesis is meant to bind the Israelites as a group by giving them a common religious heritage and identity. To do this, the authors and editors of Genesis used some of the most memorable stories known to man.[ii]

We do not expect a scientific publication to be a musical score. And we do not defend it or criticize it using the standards that are meant to be applied to music. The purposes and context of the material determines how it should be interpreted and used. Take the book of Genesis, for example—to interpret it as a scientific work would be a mistake. First, as indicated earlier, it is very probably not an accurate understanding of the purposes of the authors. Second, the historical, social, and cultural context within which the work was produced was prescientific. The investigatory methodology we know as science was foreign to the authors and the audience of Genesis. Thus, it would be equally wrongheaded either to criticize or to defend that collection of religious stories as if it were astronomical, biological, or geophysical science. In fact, the whole question of the Bible's historical context and purpose is fascinating. And given the political, moral, religious, and social significance of the Bible in today's world, it is a question well worth examining carefully.[iii] As we shall see throughout this chapter, a grasp of context and purpose forms the starting point for interpretation.

HOW PRECISE IS PRECISE ENOUGH?

We apply our core critical thinking skill of interpretation and our habit of judiciousness when endeavoring to determine the meaning and significance of what is being communicated. *The first rule of fair-minded interpretation is to be sensitive to context and purpose.*

From: Mom and Pop
To: Susan, Bill, and Karl

Dear Susan, Bill, and Karl,

You probably never thought you'd see our last will and testament sent by e-mail, but here it is. We know that you are all over 40, but Pop and I still think of you as our kids. We're getting old and we've been thinking a lot lately about passing our belongings on to the three of you. We have no plans to do this in the near or foreseeable future. But, you never know. We have our aches and pains, and we are getting to that point when it is important to be sure that our ideas are known before it gets to be too late.

So, here's what we want. We want all our money to go to each of you equally. Bill, we want you to have our business, which is no prize because it takes a lot of work. But we love it, and it has been good to Pop and me over all these years. Each year it provides us with a little profit, so we can't complain. And you are the only one who ever really took an interest in it. Susan, we want you to have our house in Milwaukee. We had some fun times there when you kids were growing up. Maybe you can sell it if the economy improves. Karl, we want you to have the house here in Lakeland we're living in now. The real estate market is the pits right now. And the house needs a new roof and the plumbing is a mess. But you know all that because you're living here now. So, Karl, it's yours.

Divide up our furniture, pictures, books, and personal things, and give everything you don't want to Goodwill.

The main thing is for you three to divide everything equally. Including whatever might be left in our 401K. Please respect our wishes about not squabbling over what little there will be in our estate.

We love you.

Oh, and Karl, you get our dog, Lobo Loco. Lucky you.

To uncover context and purpose, we can use a few basic questions. For example, assume that someone texts this message: "Torch in boot." At first this message appears nonsensical. Here is some context: The message was sent in response to a question, "Do we have a torch?" A Liverpool teenage driver sent this message at night to her dad. The dad's purpose in sending "Torch in boot" was to respond to his daughter's question. OK, now we can make a reasonably accurate interpretation of the message. It means, "Yes, we do have a torch (flashlight). You'll find it in the boot (trunk) of the car you are driving."

Use these questions to initiate the interpretation of written material:

- In what social–cultural–historical context was this written?
- What was the author's purpose in writing it?
- Who was the author's intended audience?
- What does the author believe that the audience already knows?

LANGUAGE AND THOUGHT

Our use of language and our thinking are so closely connected that most of us think in our native language. As children, years before formal schooling, we begin to learn how to express our ideas in words and sentences. As we grow and learn more, our vocabulary expands, as does our ability to express ourselves with greater precision. If we try to learn a new language as an adult, we often find ourselves translating from the new language into English (if English is our native language) and then back into the target language.

Some anthropologists maintain that the capacity to use language gave the young species *Homo sapiens* great advantages over the other hominids, such as Neanderthals, who had greater numbers and greater physical strength.[iv] Using language, early human beings were able to coordinate efforts in combat and refine strategies for acquiring the resources our species needed to survive. Early human language may have included, along with words and pictographs, sounds like clicks and whistles, which we do not use in English. Because communication was almost always face-to-face in the centuries before writing, gestures and movements were also used to facilitate communication. Taken in its broadest sense, language in the earliest millennia of our species was a rich and varied system of gesticulations, sounds, pictures, and symbols.

As human society became more complex and agreements and ideas became so important that they had to be passed down to future generations, written language evolved to capture those ideas and agreements. Whether it was the location of the family plot of land in a river delta that flooded each spring, or the dictates of the monarch, some things needed to be remembered. Written language became our means of commemorating important things like these. Yet words on a page are poor messengers compared to a face-to-face conversation, in which facial expressions, gestures, and body language add so much. When immediate face-to-face communication is reduced to words on a page, we run the risk that vagueness or ambiguity can make accurate interpretation more difficult. We risk stripping vital cues to purpose and context out of our messages when we text and tweet. But, we gain a huge benefit: speed. Most often we interpret texts and tweets correctly when we know the person with whom we are communicating. If we know that person, then we often are able to infer his or her purpose and the context of their communication correctly. If we do not know the person who is sending the text or the tweet (or e-mail, or Web post, or letter), we are at risk of misunderstanding, or worse, of being duped or conned. A strong critical thinker will always ask "Who sent me this, and why?"

Occasionally even longer and more carefully prepared messages can be difficult to interpret. Consider the example of the e-mail letter (page 66) written by an older couple to their adult children. Suppose several years later, the day has come when the three adult children pull out their parents' letter and try to figure out how to honor what it tells them. Imagine the three of them, Susan, Bill, and Karl, discussing their parents' letter:

- **Susan:** "Our parents said that their whole idea was to divide everything equally. But the house in Milwaukee is worth only 70 percent of what the house in Lakeland, Florida, is worth. So, how is that equal?"
- **Bill:** "The business was making money back in the day when Mom and Pop were more active, but the last few years it has been a struggle to break even. These days, it is nothing but headaches. Even if I sold the business I would have almost nothing left after I paid off the loans they needed just to keep operating these past couple of years. How is that equal to a house in Milwaukee or a house in Lakeland?"
- **Karl:** "Look, they didn't want us to fight over things like this. So, why don't we put a value on each house and on the business, then sell everything, and divide the proceeds equally?"

- **Susan:** "Well, that makes financial sense. But would it really be what they wanted? After all, they were very specific about which one of us would receive each of the houses and the business."

As we review the parents' letter, we can see the problems that the three siblings are having. The parents thought that their instructions were clear and precise. But, as it turned out, they were wrong. The instruction to "divide everything equally," is problematic in two ways. First the word *everything* is vague. Did the parents intend that "everything" should include the two houses and the business, or does it apply to all their money and possessions other than the real estate and the business? The siblings need to clarify what's in and what's out so that they can fulfill their parents' intent and divide "everything" equally. The letter is vague. Arguments could be made for both interpretations.

The second problem has to do with the word *equally*. Should the siblings interpret that word to mean "financially exactly the same dollar value," or should they interpret "equally" to mean each gets one major asset, each gets one third of the books, furniture, and personal possessions, and each gets one third of the dollar value remaining in the parents' 401K? In this second sense of "equally," the result may not be that each person would receive the exact same total dollar value, but each would have been given an equal share of each category of objects in the parents' estate. The letter is ambiguous. Arguments could be made for both interpretations.

In the sections that follow we will first talk about the problem of vagueness and then the problem of ambiguity. The good news is that both kinds of problems can be reasonably resolved through the wise application of our critical thinking skills and habits of mind.

VAGUENESS: "WHERE ARE THE BOUNDARIES, DOES THE TERM INCLUDE THIS CASE OR NOT?"

Common sense tells us that we should not bring animals to the airport. Cows, chickens, cats, goldfish, snakes, and monkeys are not welcome there. Although we all can agree with the general principle, it would still be reasonable to ask, "What about companion animals and assistance animals?" And as soon as the question is asked, we realize that our common sense understanding, while generally correct, is not precise enough for practical purposes.

A guide dog is an assistance animal, which we would not *intend* to prohibit from the airport. We can address the uncertainty about whether the term "animal" *in this context* is meant to refer to guide dogs or not by adding a qualification or exception to our initial statement. We could say, as they do in Tampa, "No animals are allowed in the airport terminal except assistance animals."

OK, but now what about "companion animals"? For example, for reasons of psychological health, in some states elderly people and others are permitted to legally register certain animals as "companion animals." Often this registration permits the owner of the companion animal to be granted exceptions to restrictions that generally apply to pets. So, we might want to make a further amendment to our dictate about no animals at airports to permit another exception. In this case, for "registered companion animals." Again, the uncertainty about whether the word *animals* applies *in this context* to companion animals needs to be resolved. Our intent is to permit them to be brought to the airport. So, for our current purposes, a dog that is either an assistance animal or a companion animal is permitted. In real-life situations, we think about our purposes and about the context to decide how to resolve uncertainties just like these.

Notice that we did not ask whether human beings were excluded from airports on the grounds that human beings were animals. In terms of the purpose and context, it simply was not a reasonable question. But in other contexts or for other purposes, it could be, as for example in the question of whether or not a viral strain, say avian flu, can jump animal species. In that situation, human beings are animals, rather than plants.

Consider this question: Given the purposes for not permitting animals at airports, how would you resolve the vagueness in the word *airport* if a child were to ask, "Is it OK if we bring our pet dog with us in the car when we take Grandma to the airport? Please, we are only going to drop Grandma off." Does "airport" in this context and for these purposes include or not include the interior of vehicles that use the departure street outside the terminal building?

Problematic vagueness is the characteristic of a word or expression having an imprecise meaning or unclear boundaries in a given context or for a given purpose. However, as the "animal" and "airport" examples illustrate, vagueness is best considered *not as an absolute feature, but as being relative to the context within which and purposes for which the term is being used*.

PROBLEMATIC VAGUENESS

Imagine you work in the marketing department at H&M, and you receive the following memo from corporate for the next campaign: "We want to go after a young adult demographic." Does that mean married yuppies in their mid-20s or urban hipsters? In the sentence "We have to find those who were responsible for causing this terrible car accident," does the expression "those who were responsible" include only the drivers who were involved, or does it also include any or all of these other persons: the manufacturers of the vehicles involved in the accident, the engineers who designed the street, the city officials who refused to install a stoplight, the people living along the street who never trimmed or pruned their shrubs and

Thinking Critically Interpreting "Dependent"

The term *dependent* in the sentence, "Are you dependent on your parents?" can be interpreted to mean "needy" or "reliant" as contrasted with "independent." But for purposes of filing federal income tax, the term "dependent" has a far more precise meaning that is stipulated in the tax code. For individuals, IRS Publication 17, which is available free from the **www.irs.gov** Web site, is the basic source of information on how to interpret "dependent" in the context of our tax rules and for the purpose of correctly filing a federal tax return. The table below is from page 28 of Publication 17. By interpreting the table, answer each of the following questions and write out the explanation for why you believe your answer is correct.

1. Can you claim your child as your dependent if you are claimed as a dependent on your parent's or parents' tax return? __________ Explanation:
2. Is it possible for you to claim a person as a dependent if that person is a resident of another country? __________ Explanation:
3. If you adopt a child and the adoption is finalized by the court on December 10, can you claim that child as your dependent for that year? __________ Explanation:
4. Say you are 22 years old, a full-time student, and you live at home. You pay fair-market rent and provide for more than half of your own support (food, clothing, travel expenses, tuition, books, cell phone, etc.). Can your parents claim you as a dependent on their tax return? __________ Explanation:
5. Say you are divorced and have a multiple-support agreement that awards your ex the right to claim your child as a dependent on his/her tax return, but you actually provide more than half of the child's support. Can you claim the child as your dependent on your tax return, too? __________ Explanation:
6. Can you claim the child of your stepbrother as your dependent? __________ Explanation:
7. Can you claim your grandmother as your dependent if she lives in your home all year, earns less than $7,500, and you provide more than half of her support? __________ Explanation:
8. Can you claim your 10-year-old child as your dependent if your child lives with you all year, receives $50,000 in movie royalties each year that are deposited into a trust fund that cannot be touched until the child is 25 years old, and you provide more than half of the child's support? __________ Explanation:

Table 4-1. Overview of the Rules for Claiming an Exemption for a Dependent

Caution. This table is only an overview of the rules. For details, see the rest of this chapter.

- You cannot claim any dependents if you, or your spouse if filing jointly, could be claimed as a dependent by another taxpayer.
- You cannot claim a married person who files a joint return as a dependent unless that joint return is only a claim for refund and there would be no tax liability for either spouse on separate returns.
- You cannot claim a person as a dependent unless that person is a U.S. citizen, U.S. resident alien, U.S. national, or a resident of Canada or Mexico, for some part of the year.[1]
- You cannot claim a person as a dependent unless that person is your qualifying child or qualifying relative.

Tests To Be a Qualifying Child	Tests To Be a Qualifying Relative
1 The child must be your son, daughter, stepchild, foster child, brother, sister, half brother, half sister, stepbrother, stepsister, or a descendant of any of them.	1 The person cannot be your qualifying child or the qualifying child of any other taxpayer.
2 The child must be (a) under age 19 at the end of the year, (b) under age 24 at the end of the year and a full-time student, or (c) any age if permanently and totally disabled.	2 The person either (a) must be related to you in one of the ways listed under *Relatives who do not have to live with you*, or (b) must live with you all year as a member of your household[2] (and your relationship must not violate local law).
3 The child must have lived with you for more than half of the year.[2]	3 The person's gross income for the year must be less than $3,500.[3]
4 The child must not have provided more than half of his or her own support for the year.	4 You must provide more than half of the person's total support for the year.[4]
5 If the child meets the rules to be a qualifying child of more than one person, you must be the person entitled to claim the child as a qualifying child.	

[1]There is an exception for certain adopted children.

[2]There are exceptions for temporary absences, children who were born or died during the year, children of divorced or separated parents, and kidnapped children.

[3]There is an exception if the person is disabled and has income from a sheltered workshop.

[4]There are exceptions for multiple support agreements, children of divorced or separated parents, and kidnapped children.

Do you think this ad hits the "young adult" market? Will this ad appeal to any other markets as well?

trees (which grow so thick that the vision of the drivers was limited), or the business owner who put up the huge, distracting billboard?

The H&M example does not pose major problems. If married yuppies decide to buy H&M clothing, the corporation will sell them the clothes and take the profit even if the marketing campaign had no particular effect on the yuppies' decision. However, the corporation does care whether the campaign is reaching those who are clearly members of the target audience. Marketing campaigns are expensive. But they're also like shotgun blasts. As long as the campaign hits its main target, it is not a problem if some of the pellets spray raggedly around the edges. Yuppies are probably someplace along the borderline of the marketing campaign's target audience. So, for the purposes of the campaign and in the context of selling clothes, resolving the question of whether "young adults" does or does not refer to yuppies is not going to be a problem that the corporation will worry about.

The car accident example is different. There the vagueness of the expression "those who were responsible" could become the object of highly contentious legal battles. If it is proven that vehicle manufacturers knew of some defect in the braking system of one of the cars but did not recall the vehicle for repairs, then a jury may decide to hold the manufacturer partially responsible for the accident. Similarly, it might be argued that the others listed each knew something, did something, or failed to do something that contributed to the accident. The vagueness of the term *responsible* as it applies to the car accident needs to be resolved for the purposes of determining criminal and financial responsibility. This matter is so problematic and yet so important that our society has instituted a specific methodology for resolving the applicability of the term "responsible" in situations like this. That method almost always involves negotiation between lawyers representing interested parties, and, in the most extreme situations, litigation.

When the use of a term results in imprecision sufficient to cause problems for the interpretation of that term in a given context and for a given purpose, we call that *problematic vagueness.*

AMBIGUITY: "WHICH SENSE OF THE TERM ARE WE USING, DOES IT MEAN THIS, OR DOES IT MEAN THAT?"

In the hilarious comedy *My Cousin Vinny,*[v] Ralph Macchio's, character has been brought in by an Alabama sheriff for questioning about a crime. Did he do it, or not? Listen carefully to the exact words Macchio uses when he confesses to the sheriff. Macchio's character is referring to his having walked out of a convenience store with a can of tuna fish in his jacket pocket. He forgot it was there and so left without paying for it. He is trying to confess to inadvertent shoplifting. The sheriff, on the other hand, is investigating the killing of the cashier at that same convenience store. The sheriff interprets Macchio as having said, "I killed the cashier" when Macchio apologizes for having left the store stupidly forgetting to pay for the can of tuna. The ambiguity triggers a chain of events that includes Macchio and his traveling companion, played by Mitchell Whitfield, being charged with murder.

Watch the **Video** on **mythinkinglab.com**

When a word, expression, or statement has more than one meaning, we call it ambiguous. A quick look at the dictionary shows that a great many words have more than one meaning. Why, then, are we not confused on an almost constant basis? Because, again, knowing the context of the conversation and the purpose of the speaker, we can readily pick out the speaker's intended meaning. "Heads up!" shouted at the people sitting behind first base at a baseball game is not a command to look toward the sky; it is a warning to duck because the batter has just fouled off a pitch. "It's 30–love," at a tennis match is intended to reveal the score, not someone's amorous relationships. "That's sick!" is slang in some high schools for "That's terrific." And, "Baby, you're the greatest!" is Hollywood hyperbole for "You're no better than average."

PROBLEMATIC AMBIGUITY

Macchio's ambiguous confession is problematic because the misunderstanding results in his arrest. Were it not for the stunning defense put on by Joe Pesci, Macchio's character could easily have been convicted of murder and sentenced to the electric chair. The ambiguity of *equal* in the parents' letter about dividing up their estate was problematic because it left the three siblings uncertain how to fulfill their parents' wishes. When ambiguity leads to troublesome misunderstanding or uncertainty about how to proceed, it is **problematic ambiguity**, which is the characteristic of a word or expression having more than one meaning in a given context or for a given purpose.

Resolving Problematic Vagueness and Ambiguity

Resolving problematic vagueness and problematic ambiguity requires us to apply our critical thinking skills and habits of mind. In the case of problematic vagueness, we must make a judgment about where the borderlines of the term are to be located. In the case of problematic ambiguity we must decide which of the possible meanings of the term is the one the author intended. In other words, using thoughtful, reasoned judgment, we must solve the practical problem of what a term or expression means in a given context and for a given purpose.

There are at least five ways to address problematic vagueness or problematic ambiguity:

- Contextualizing
- Clarifying intent
- Negotiating
- Qualifying
- Stipulating

CONTEXTUALIZING

AAA can refer to the American Automobile Association, the American Anthropological Association, the American Accounting Association, the American Academy of Audiology, the Amateur Astronomers Association, the American Association of Anatomists, the American Ambulance Association, the Aikido Association of America, and the Arkansas Activities Association, just to name a few. So, if a person were to say, "I'm joining the AAA," we might find the ambiguity in that statement to be problematic.

Contextualizing resolves problematic ambiguity by reminding us of the topic being discussed or the circumstances within which a statement was made. In the "I'm joining the AAA" example, simply noting that the person was an undergraduate physics major talking about her interest in astronomy would clarify which AAA she meant.

Consider another example. "We need to find some more offensive people," can mean one thing in the context of sports and quite another thing spoken as irony after someone has made a particularly rude remark during a meeting. In the first context, the discussion is about building up the team's capacity to score more points by improving its offense. In the second context, the speaker probably intends to express a negative opinion about the behavior of one of the other people at the meeting.

To establish context we ask questions like these:

- Who said it to whom?
- When and where was it said?

These are just two meanings of the word offensive. Can you think of any other meanings?

- What was the topic of the conversation?
- Was the comment meant to be ironic, hyperbolic, misleading, or deceptive?
- Were technical terms, abbreviations, symbols, slang, code words, double entendre, euphemisms, or acronyms used?

That final question is important because often knowing that the conversation took place among members of a particular interest group or professional group helps us immediately recognize that a given word or expression is used with the special meaning that the given group attaches to that expression. We will talk more about this in the section on language communities later in the chapter.

Words taken out of context can be misleading. Consider, for example, "I smoked 50 years . . . today I can run a marathon." We might interpret this to be a reasonably unambiguous statement suggesting that smoking is not always physically detrimental. The only clue that there may be more to the story is the three-dot ellipsis. What were the words that the author omitted? The misleading quotation was pulled from the text in the box to the right. Seeing the author's words in context, our interpretation becomes the opposite of what it was. Now we know that the author is advising people not to smoke, instead of saying that it might not be a problem.

Putting an author's words in context not only permits us to make an accurate interpretation, it helps us not be misled by unscrupulous individuals. Intellectual integrity and a strong habit of truth-seeking are needed when we synopsize and de-contextualize the words and ideas of others. Accuracy is important, but so is a truthful preservation of the author's original intent. Deceitful politicians like to quote their opponent's words out of context; accurate, yes, but intentionally untruthful.

"I smoked 50 years ago, when I was in high school. But only a few cigarettes just to see what it was like. It was cross-country season, and my coach told me that I was one of the best in the state. He said that if I started smoking, I could kiss the state championship good-bye. So, I quit smoking before I ever really got started and stayed away from cancer sticks ever since. Because I quit smoking and because I've worked out several days a week all of my life, today I can run a marathon."

CLARIFYING ORIGINAL INTENT

Because problematic vagueness and ambiguity emerge when we are trying to interpret what someone means, one reasonable way to resolve the vagueness is simply to ask for clarification. Let's go back to the marketing department at H&M. One of the first things we will want to do is clarify the target audience that the executives have in mind for the campaign.

We would not want to put all our effort into designing the marketing approach until we were clear whom corporate H&M wants to reach. And our best method for doing this would be to ask the executives, "Can you clarify for us exactly which demographic you have in mind when you say 'young adults'?" We might hear back that we should target single men and women between the ages of 22 and 29 who are college graduates and employed at jobs that pay $35,000 to $60,000 per year. If so, that would add a lot of useful clarification, and we might be able to apply our critical thinking to the question of how best to reach that market segment.

On the other hand, we might hear back from our client that "young adults" is as clear as the client can be at this time about the target audience. In this case, we would probably try to help clarify that problematic vagueness. Given our experience and expertise in producing marketing campaigns, we might explain that the approach we would take to reach a single person who is a college graduate and has a good job is not the same as the approach we would use to market a product to someone who is the same age but married with children, or the same age but not a college graduate, or the same age but not currently employed.

Clarifying the speaker's intent becomes more challenging when multiple alternative wordings are possible and it is not possible to ask the author for clarification. For example, suppose our job was to resolve problematic phrases such as "unreasonable search and seizure," "the right to bear arms," or "freedom of assembly." The framers of the U.S. Constitution and the Bill of Rights are not available, and times and conditions have changed over the centuries. Although not the only way to interpret the U.S. Constitution, endeavoring to discern the framers' intent is one recognized approach.[vi] And, although we do not have benefit of access to the original authors, we do have a large number of previous rulings that established important precedents. In fact, endeavoring to discern intent is part of the process of interpreting the law in general. It is essential to our criminal justice system.[vii]

Fine, but what if the problematic vagueness was intentional? The framers of the U.S. Constitution and the Bill of Rights were wise enough to realize that times and conditions would change and that therefore it would be prudent to write in ways that left room for future generations of Americans to interpret these fundamental documents to fit their times and circumstances. Wise judgment is a very good thing. We want to cultivate that in ourselves and leave room for it to be exercised by others, too, because it is absolutely impossible for any individual or any group to anticipate every kind of problem and every set of circumstances. The habit of judiciousness, which we talked about in Chapter 2, inclines us toward wisdom and prudence in making judgments. It is precisely this virtue that the framers of the Constitution trusted that future generations of Americans would need and would have if the young Republic were going to survive and flourish.

On the other hand, at times intentional vagueness can be frustrating when precise, practical answers are what people desire. Imagine the blustery Senatorial candidate who pounds the electorate with bromides like these: "I will bring transparency and fiscal accountability to Congress!" "Our educational system is such a mess that we need a war on ignorance." "When I'm in office, our nation will never again negotiate from weakness." "Too many hard-working Americans are fed up with Washington politicians who take a business-as-usual approach." As voters, we might do well to demand greater clarity and operational precision, rather than accepting platitudes like those.

NEGOTIATING THE MEANING

Suppose you decide to hire me and we come to a handshake agreement that you will pay me a fair wage. As it turns out, we then discover that it is your position that "fair wage" has an upper limit of $25 per hour and it is my position that "fair wage" means $30 per hour. Because we both want the working relationship to start out being friendly, we decide to try to negotiate away the problematic vagueness by trying to reach a compromise between our two divergent positions. So, for our purposes in this context we can negotiate the mutual agreement that "fair wage" means $27.50 per hour.

Successful negotiation in complex real-world contexts involves much more than the simple compromise this example indicates.[viii] The box "Thinking Critically about Successful Negotiation" describes a process for negotiating that is far more satisfying. Strong critical thinking skills are valuable assets in reaching mutually acceptable agreements.

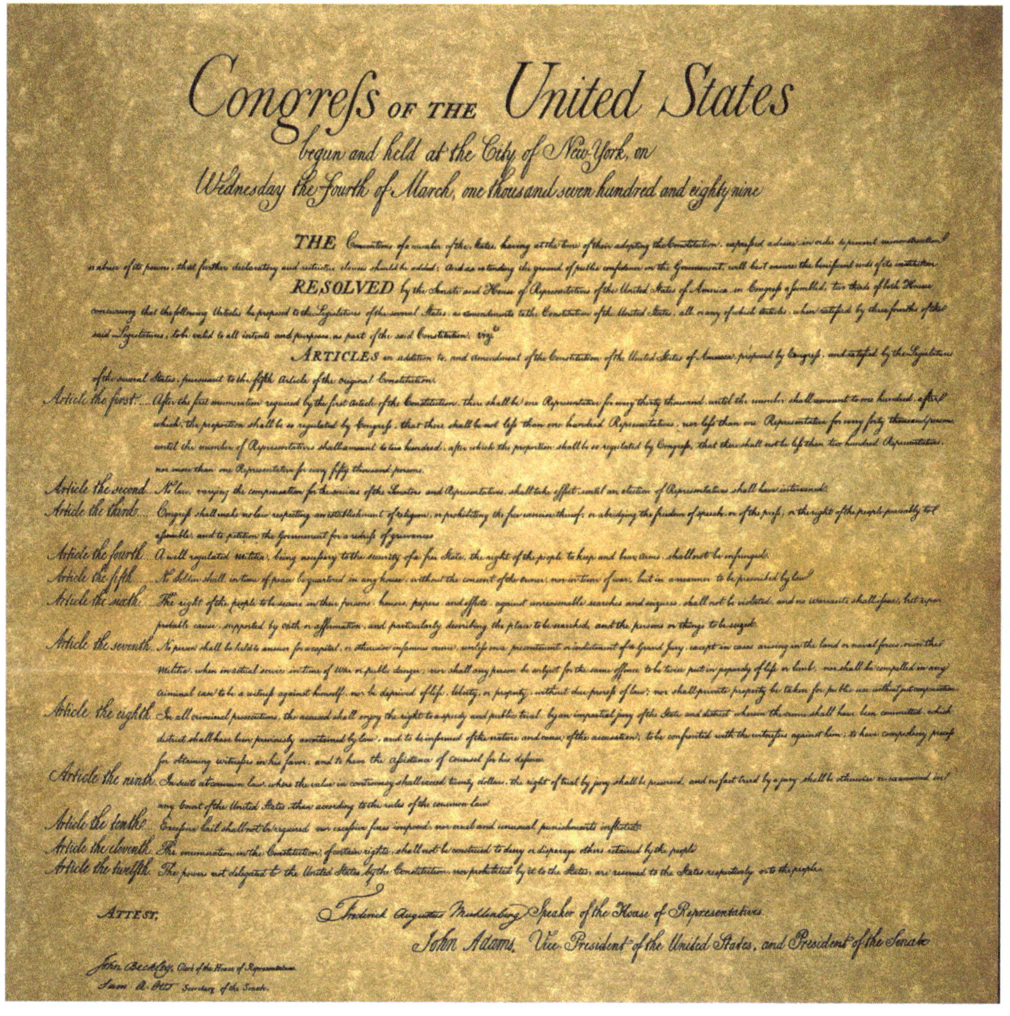
Congreſs of the United States
begun and held at the City of New-York, on
Wednesday the fourth of March, one thousand seven hundred and eighty nine

ATTEST,

Frederick Augustus Muhlenberg Speaker of the House of Representatives.

John Adams, Vice-President of the United States, and President of the Senate

John Beckley, Clerk of the House of Representatives.

Sam. A. Otis Secretary of the Senate.

Framers of the U.S. Constitution and the Bill of Rights were intentionally vague so future generations could interpret these documents to fit changing times and national circumstances which the framers themselves wisely knew they could not anticipate.

In this example, we have negotiated the meaning of "fair wage" to fit our purposes in the context of a hiring agreement. Must we resolve the meaning of "fair wage" for all the other workers and all the other jobs that there are? No. That would not only be impractical and unlikely to succeed—it may not even be desirable. *There is nothing inherently wrong with vagueness or ambiguity unless it introduces problems in a given real-life context.*

Now that we have agreed that I will work for you, I ask you if there is a dress code of some kind that I should know about. You say, "Why, yes. Glad you asked. We expect everyone who works in our office to wear a shirt with a collar. No T-shirts, tank tops, or V-necks."

I think, "What if we don't mean the same thing by 'shirt with a collar'?" I imagine a golf shirt with a soft collar, a loud Hawaiian shirt with a big collar, and a conservative dress shirt with a button-down collar. The expression "shirt with a collar" is causing problematic ambiguity. So, I ask you to be more specific and you say, "Oh, I meant a dress shirt. You don't have to wear a tie, but we expect everyone to wear a dress shirt to work."

Still some vagueness, I'm thinking. What about colors? Or will only white shirts count as what you mean by "dress shirt"? But I decide not to ask about that because I can just keep my eyes open the first couple of days on the job to see if anyone wears a dress shirt that isn't pure white. I do want to ask one more question—kind of a mini-negotiation. "What about Fridays? Do you have casual Fridays?" And happily you respond, "Of course, we do. You'll see a lot of golf shirts on Fridays at our office."

"Shirt with a collar" as a problematic ambiguity—gone!—for our purposes in this context.

The phrase "shirt with a collar" is problematically vague without context or clarification. How many different types of shirts with collars can you think of?

USING QUALIFICATIONS, EXCEPTIONS, OR EXCLUSIONS

One of the most practical ways of resolving problematic vagueness and ambiguity is to introduce qualifications that clarify which cases are included or excluded. Here are some examples of using qualifying expressions to introduce a measure of clarity.

veteran	→	person with prior experience, as contrasted with beginner
veteran athlete	→	player who was with the team last season, as contrasted with rookie
military veteran	→	soldier who has been honorably discharged from service
military veteran	→	soldier who served in combat
cold weather	→	chilly enough to need a jacket
cold weather	→	outdoor air temperatures lower than 45 degrees Fahrenheit
cold weather	→	chill factor the equivalent of 32 degrees Fahrenheit or lower
expensive car	→	more than I want to pay for that car
expensive car	→	more costly than other similar cars
expensive car	→	car that costs more than $100,000
expensive car	→	a new Bentley, Lamborghini, or Bugatti
bad language	→	curse, a solemn invocation of misfortune to be visited upon some person, group or object
bad language	→	blasphemy, an expression that is contemptuous of a religiously significant person, object, custom, or belief
bad language	→	vulgarity, an expression that is crude, unseemly, not in good taste
bad language	→	obscenity, an expression that is lewd, licentious, or indecent

bad language	→	indecent expression, one that is improper with respect to prevailing social standards especially in sexual matters
bad language	→	profanity, an expression that is irreverent or contemptuous of what is considered sacred
bad language	→	offensive expression, one that inflicts or is intended to inflict emotional pain such as ridicule, abuse, mockery, or hate speech
bad language	→	expletive or swear word, a grammatical term classified as profane, indecent, vulgar, or obscene by a given language community

Visit www.mythinkinglab.com to see a clip of comedian and social commentator Lewis Black discussing "bad language." **http://www.youtube.com/watch?v=uFr6P2BtE3k** Why are some terms regarded as "swear words" or "expletives" by some groups, but not by others? Can the same sound be a forbidden expletive in one language and a perfectly acceptable word in another? Should "clean language" directed at someone in anger be regarded as more or less offensive than "dirty words" used for the sake of humor? Give reasons and examples to support your opinion.

Watch the **Video** on **mythinkinglab.com**

As the examples above suggest, we can clarify expressions a lot or a little, depending on our purposes, by using descriptive phrases, contrasts, technical terminology, and thorough examples.

In the "animals at the airport" example, we clarified the problematic vagueness by making exceptions for two kinds of animals. Our exception allowed us to make a statement that actually appears self-contradictory. "Companion animals are not animals as far as airport policy is concerned." But, in fact, the statement makes good sense given the purpose and context.

If you are getting the sense that critical thinking in real-life contexts requires refining our skill at making good judgments relative to the circumstances and situations at hand, you are correct. The judicious habit of mind impels us to strive to make judgments about what to believe or what to do that are as precise as the subject matter, context, and purposes permit. But no more precise than that. In fact, it would be unwise to strive to be more precise than that. Real-life judgments are often made in contexts in which absolute certitude is not attainable.

STIPULATING THE MEANING

When the determination of the exact meaning of a term has major consequences for one or more of the parties involved, then adding qualifications or noting exceptions and exclusions may not be sufficient. This often happens in financial and legal matters, when a word's meaning must be circumscribed as precisely and completely as possible.

We would not want the legal definition of "driving under the influence" to be left to each individual police officer, judge, or prosecuting attorney to define in any way he or she might wish. There would be too much variability in practice. One person might show favoritism to locals, but eagerly arrest folks from out of town. Another person might rely on a person's answer to the question "How many drinks have you had?" Still another might believe that being drunk meant that the driver slurred his words or could not walk a straight line.

It is in the interest of justice and public safety to use a uniform definition of the term "driving under the influence." Ideally, the definition would provide for some objective way of

One way to define "expensive car" is to show what the words refer to—in this case a Bugatti, a Lamborghini, and a Bentley. The base price of a 2009 Bugatti Veyron 16.4 Grand Sport is €1.4 Million, that's about $2,000,000.

Tips on the Strategy of Interest-Based Negotiation

Many people see negotiation as the process of trying to find a compromise between conflicting positions. They think of stories about bitter contract negotiations between management and a labor union. Or they remember buying their first condo and finding it stressful because they felt at a disadvantage when bargaining for a good price against the more experienced seller. Negotiating with an insurance company over settlements or negotiating with an ex over child support and visitation rights are more examples of things people would rather avoid. The problem is that when people try to find a compromise between two positions, each party thinks that it is going to be forced to "give up something."

Traditionally, negotiating has been thought of as trying to reach a compromise between two initial positions on the issue. This kind of negotiation, called *positional negotiation*, is often adversarial. The process tends to end up with both sides being dissatisfied with the final outcomes because the process makes them feel forced into making concessions.

Good critical thinkers realize that the methods used to achieve a result and the criteria used to evaluate the result are, themselves, open to review and reconsideration. What if there were a better way to negotiate around problematic vagueness and simply a better method for negotiation, period? What if we evaluated the outcome of the process of negotiation as good only if both sides were satisfied, rather than if both sides were dissatisfied? These questions led to the development of an alternative method of negotiation called *interest-based negotiation.*

Instead of competing in an effort not to give up more than the other guy, interest-based negotiation begins with trying to figure out what each party's interests are and then it works to find a way to achieve the interests of both parties. Interest-based negotiation calls for collaboration and creativity. Both parties strive to find a way for their own interest and the interests of the other party to be achieved. Neither party is expected to give up its interest.

Let's revisit the hiring example. Using positional-negotiating, we agreed on $27.50 per hour for 40 hours of work, five days a week. You may have felt that you were paying me too much, and I may have felt that my work was undervalued. There is a reasonable chance that the job will not start on the friendly basis we had hoped.

Using interest-based negotiation, we might have reached a different and far more amiable result. Suppose that we explore why you want to set the limit of "fair wage" at $25 and why I want it to be $30. Your interest is to preserve the pay structure you have for all the workers who are doing the same job as I would be doing. You cannot hire me for more than $25 per hour without creating an unaffordable precedent, from your perspective. You explain that you have done an industry study and the average hourly wage for the kind of work I will be doing for you is actually $23.65. But you pay $25.00 per hour.

For my part, it is not the dollars per hour that concerns me. Rather, my interest is in the total number of dollars I will make in a week and the number of hours I have to be away from my mother because I am her primary caregiver. I explain that I need to make $1,200 per week because I am expecting to pay $250 per week ($50 per day) for her dependent care expenses if I must commute to work five days a week. And I am not happy about the long commute, almost 90 minutes each way. With the commute time added in, I was expecting that my workdays would require me to be away from home for 11 hours each day of the workweek. And I was worried about what that would mean in terms of my mother's care.

Knowing each other's interests permits us to explore more creative resolutions. We might discover, for example, that I would accept $1,100 per week if you would permit me to telecommute from home two days a week. Working at home those two days saves me six hours of commuting time per week and $100 of dependent care expenses per week. In return, I guarantee you that I will give you 44 hours of work each week. This agreement permits you to preserve your $25-per-hour pay policy, which is fine with me. Notice too that we have now expanded the meaning of "fair wage" beyond simply dollars per hour. Now it can include telecommuting and a variable number of work hours per week. Our negotiation resolved our problem without promoting greater conflict. In fact, neither of us feels dismayed, disrespected, or dissatisfied with the process or the result.

A tip on negotiating for a job on campus: Most colleges hire large numbers of students part-time. They work as assistants in academic and non-academic departmental offices all over campus, or they work in the library, food services, recreation, and residence life. Colleges often have rigid pay structures that do not permit room for negotiating the hourly wage. It is in the student's interest simply to secure a job, given that pay often cannot be a negotiating point. But the person doing the hiring has other interests: They want to hire students who are flexible about how many hours of work they will do per week and flexible about which hours and which days they will work. (They also want students who are friendly, professional, quick to learn, and show initiative.) So, if it is in your interest to get a job that you might be able to count on for some part-time income not only this year but in future years, and if it is in your interest that the job be close to where you live and go to class (e.g., on campus), then you would want to show that you are willing to be flexible about your work schedule. When you interview you might say that you know how important it is that the supervisor should be able to find students who are flexible about scheduling. Showing you understand the other person's interests is as pleasant for the person who is hiring you as it is for you when that person shows that he or she understands your interests.

telling which drivers it applied to and which it did not. Knowing exactly how many drinks a person had, for example, will not work. Some drinks have a higher alcohol content than others, some people weigh more than others, and some metabolize alcohol at different rates than others.

As in other states, California lawmakers stipulated the meaning of the expression "driving under the influence." Stipulating meaning is intended to remove problematic vagueness and problematic ambiguity by establishing what a term shall mean for a specific set of purposes. In this case, for legal purposes within the state of California the term "driving under the influence" means exactly what Section 23152 of the state's motor vehicle code says it means. No more. No less.

Your Language Communities

In this chapter, we have stressed that knowing the context and purpose of a communication provides a vital basis for making an accurate interpretation. As item #18 in the "Resolving Vagueness and Ambiguity" exercise on this page suggests, if we know we are talking about psychology then "defensive" means one thing. And if we are talking about sports, "defensive" has

Driving Under Influence of Alcohol or Drugs

California Vehicle Code 23152 states:

(a) It is unlawful for any person who is under the influence of any alcoholic beverage or drug, or under the combined influence of any alcoholic beverage and drug, to drive a vehicle.

(b) It is unlawful for any person who has 0.08 percent or more, by weight, of alcohol in his or her blood to drive a vehicle.

For purposes of this article and Section 34501.16, percent, by weight, of alcohol in a person's blood is based upon grams of alcohol per 100 milliliters of blood or grams of alcohol per 210 liters of breath.

In any prosecution under this subdivision, it is a rebuttable presumption that the person had 0.08 percent or more, by weight, of alcohol in his or her blood at the time of driving the vehicle if the person had 0.08 percent or more, by weight, of alcohol in his or her blood at the time of the performance of a chemical test within three hours after the driving.[ix]

Thinking Critically — Resolving Vagueness and Ambiguity

EXERCISE Each of the *italicized terms in the statements below introduce a degree of vagueness.* The underlined terms are ambiguous. Use qualifications, exceptions, exclusions, or stipulations to rewrite each statement with sufficient precision to resolve the problematic vagueness or ambiguity.

1 America is *overeating.*

2 *Successful people* should *give back.*

3 In *an emergency*, please *proceed* to the nearest exit.

4 She had the *good judgment* to dump the *creep*.

5 The *tennis star* had to forfeit the match due to *unsportsmanlike conduct*.

6 Kate Winslet was riveting in her portrayal of a *desperate* housewife in "Revolutionary Road."

7 The high schools in our state are a *mess*.

8 We do not negotiate with *terrorists*.

9 The measure of our *greatness* is our ability to *change*.

10 I want to live a meaningful life.

11 Every living breathing *person* has rights.

12 We need to talk *tomorrow*?

13 We never had sex.

14 I was shocked when *she left*.

15 *Usher's lyrics* move me.

16 Direct *inquires* to the front desk.

17 Kathleen Madigan is hysterical.

18 It's defensive. [Hint: Soccer vs. Military vs. Psychology]

19 *The crowd* carried signs that said "*Free* Republic"

20 Workers carried signs *downtown* that read "Free *Health Care*."

21 In a nonviolent protest, five hundred off-duty firefighters carried signs outside the mayor's office that read "Free Education for *Low-Income* Families."

22 *Everything and everyone* has a cause. [Hint: Physics vs. Philanthropy]

23 *Nobody* under 6 is permitted in the ER or the ICU. [Hint: Hospitals]

24

1	2	1
2	3	0

[Hint: Hockey vs. Baseball]

25 *For you,* connection *with all who came before cannot be helped.* [Hint: Horoscope]

Watch Out for Donkey Cart Words

"Donkey cart words" change the meaning of an otherwise perfectly good word. And, at the same time, the use of donkey cart words is designed to make anyone who tries to use that word in the correct way feel a bit humiliated for not knowing the word's "true meaning." The use of donkey cart words is not a sign of wisdom, rather it is a signal that someone is being a bit of a pompous jackass.

Authority figures often use donkey cart words to impose on their gullible disciples a way of talking that then becomes immunized against normal criticisms. By talking a special way, they are able to say things that may sound normal to non-initiates, but that have coded meanings for themselves and their followers, thus forming an inner circle of people who know what was meant, while those outside the group only *think* that they know what was meant. The six most common donkey cart words are:

"True ________," "Real ________,"
"Genuine _______," "Authentic _______"
"Natural _______", and "Pure ________"

"*True freedom* means not choosing to do what you know you cannot do."

"*Real love* requires emptying your identity as a gift for the other."

"*Genuine power* rests only with those who rule by unchallenged will."

"*Authentic human beings* ride their emotions without question."

"*Natural water* is better for you than water out of a tap.

"*Pure* courage ignores all risk to self."

Although each of these seems like a pearl of wisdom, they are in fact donkey dung. They are nothing more than thinly disguised stipulations, offered without backing of any kind. They are intended to change the meaning of the word that rides in the donkey cart—that is, the word that follows behind *true*, *real*, *genuine*, *authentic*, *natural*, or *pure*. The *NBC Nightly News with Brian Williams* carried a story on September 20, 2011 nicely illustrating how food manufacturers and retail food stores manipulate naïve consumers with "natural." [x]

The only useful thing about the donkey cart word is the clanging bell that we should hear warning us every time one of these words comes along. We should take note because the speaker is inviting us to depart from the community of those who use these words as they are defined in the dictionary. Instead we are being told that we must venture forth, like the video gamers, into a fictional world where words do not mean what they should mean. The person who drives the donkey cart is the person who controls that fictional world and those of us who would follow that cart.

By learning the "truths" proposed by the donkey cart driver, we are not necessarily gaining new knowledge about the universe or anything else. We are only learning the special vocabulary that the donkey cart driver wants us to use. It is a stinky and manipulative game played with language.

a different meaning. In the case of military weapons systems it means something else again. It is helpful to think of the people who use terms the way psychologists do to be members of a community; we might call it the "Psychology Language Community." And, at the same time, those who use terms the way players, coaches, and sportswriters do might be referred to as the "Sports Language Community." And those who use "defensive" in the context of weaponry and military strategy and tactics might be conceived of as the "Military Language Community." It is precisely because we might be members of, or familiar with, all three language communities that we are able to appreciate the ambiguity of item #18.

NATIONAL AND GLOBAL LANGUAGE COMMUNITIES

Over the millennia our species developed many languages in order to facilitate effective communication between people living in various regions of the world. Sounds became words and took on different meanings within the communities. To preserve ideas, various systems of writing were invented that used symbols, words, and icons that meant specific things to the people of a given tribe, region, or nation. People who shared an understanding of the meanings of the words and icons can be thought of as a community defined in part by its shared language, or a **language community**.

The meanings of the words that form a given language are conventional. The words mean what they mean in a given language by virtue of the tacit mutual agreement of the people who speak that language. Those tens of millions of us who speak English never voted what each English word should mean. We learned our shared language by learning the conventions for how words are used by the English-speaking language community. Dictionaries were invented to record a language community's conventions for what its words shall mean. But, as Mark Twain Prize winner George Carlin illustrates in his bit "I'm a Modern Man," English is a very dynamic language. New words are invented, and old words take on new meanings.

Listen to the **Podcast** on **mythinkinglab.com**

Dictionaries need updates. Access this clip at **www.mythinkinglab.com**.

Language Communities Around the World	
English	Love of learning is the first step toward wisdom.
Arabic	حب التعلم هو الخطوة الأولى نحو الحكمة
Chinese (Mandarin)	愛學習的第一步智慧
Greek	Η αγάπη της μάθησης είναι το πρώτο βήμα προς την σοφία.
Italian	Amore di apprendimento è il primo passo verso la saggezza.
Polish	Mi łość nauki jest pierwszym krokiem na drodze do mądrości.
Spanish	Amor por el aprendizaje es el primer paso hacia la sabiduría.
Thai	รักของการเรียนรู้ที่เป็นขั้นตอนแรกที่ไปภูมิปัญญา
Vietnamese	Tình yêu và học tập là bước đầu tiên hướng về trí tuệ.

At the national and global levels the expression *language community* refers to the community of people who can communicate in a given language (e.g., Thai-speaking people, Polish-speaking people and English-speaking people form three language communities). A given person may be a member of one or more of these communities, or none of them, being instead a member of some other language community, such as those who speak Italian, or those who speak Arabic, Bahasa, Dutch, Farsi, Tagalog, Turkish, or Yoruban.

LANGUAGE COMMUNITIES FORMED OF PEOPLE WITH LIKE INTERESTS

Today the idea of a language community has taken on even richer meaning. Those who understand and use the technical vocabulary of a more specialized field of human endeavor can also be called a "language community." For example, there are language communities of musicians, mathematicians, electrical engineers, military officers, bankers, biochemists, health professionals, and model train hobbyists. The words and symbols used within these communities have conventional meanings that are known and used by the members of the community. Look at the "Do You Know Members of Any of These Language Communities?" chart to see examples of sets of symbols that are well known to those who are members of specific language communities, but not well known to other people.

A speaker seeking to communicate with a listener whom he or she knows to be a member of the same language community will use the special language and symbols of that community. For example, a hobo wanting to warn other hobos to beware of the local authorities will use a particular symbol that to the members of the hobo language community has that particular conventional meaning. *To make a correct interpretation, we need to know how words and symbols are used by the members of the language community.*

ACADEMIC DISCIPLINES AS LANGUAGE COMMUNITIES

When we are novices relative to a given area of human endeavor—for example, the subject fields represented by the academic departments of a college or university—we may feel somewhat intimidated by those language communities. We know those who have already been initiated into that community—for example the faculty, graduate students, and undergraduate majors—know vocabulary we do not know. They are able to speak with one another about that subject field in ways that we cannot yet comprehend.

As newcomers to those language communities, we may not fully understand the textbooks or lectures senior members of that community have prepared for us. One reason is that the terminology differs from one discipline to another. *Freedom*, for example, has different meanings depending on whether the discipline is political science, mathematics, economics, philosophy, statistics, or chemistry.

Another reason understanding what is being said can be difficult for novices is because there are different conventions within the different disciplines for how one conducts inquiry and communicates findings. As we shall see in Chapter 14 on empirical reasoning, science proceeds by seeking evidence to confirm or disconfirm hypotheses. In science the professional papers that present research findings follow a specific outline in which methods, findings, and results are described separately; data are displayed in charts and graphs; and often statistical analyses are used to establish that the data are not simply the result of random chance.

In contrast, in the humanities, scholars work to refine the meanings of terms and provide textual analyses based on the author's intentions, cultural context, word choice, and historical time and place. We illustrated this briefly at the beginning of this chapter in the Genesis example. Charts and graphs displaying experimental data are almost never found in the humanities, although its scholars take due note of evidence, such as historical and cultural facts. Their work is presented in papers that often begin by stating a problem and then proceed by introducing important distinctions and parsing out alternative meanings.

Historians, musicians, accountants, political scientists, poets, nurses, civil engineers, journalists, physicists, social workers, lawyers, and all the other academic language communities at a university each follow the standards of their professional or academic field for how to conduct inquiry and communicate findings.

CRITICAL THINKING AND COLLEGE INTRODUCTORY COURSES

There is a strong connection between critical thinking in general and critical thinking in specific fields of study. Often college freshmen and sophomore general studies requirements are intended to introduce students to the array of different academic language communities. To help us understand how a given academic discipline functions, the typical introductory course is designed to explain

- The kinds of questions that the discipline seeks to address
- The evidence the discipline understands to be relevant to resolving its questions
- The concepts, terminology, and basic theories of the discipline
- The methods and techniques of inquiry used in the discipline
- The criteria the discipline applies when evaluating the quality of work produced
- The contexts within which the discipline conducts its work

Notice how well this list matches the list presented by the expert consensus researchers as they described critical thinking, cited in the opening chapters of this book [xi]: "We understand critical thinking to be purposeful, self-regulatory judgment that results in interpretation, analysis, evaluation, and inference, as well as explanation of the *evidential, conceptual, methodological, criteriological,* or *contextual* considerations upon which that judgment is based."

Critical thinking within a disciplinary language community is like critical thinking within any language community. Different language communities, and in particular different academic disciplines, focus on the specific evidence, concepts, methods, criteria, and context. But the critical thinking skills and habits of mind apply across all language communities. As a result, strengthening our critical thinking skills and habits of mind helps us when we venture into different academic language communities.

Through steady effort, practice, and attention to the language conventions of the different communities, we gain warranted confidence in our own ability to speak effectively and interpret accurately. In our introductory college courses, our challenge is to learn the terminology and the way that the discipline conducts its work—its questions, evidence, concepts, methods, criteria, and context of inquiry. By applying our critical thinking skills, and in particular the skill of interpretation, we can begin to take a few successful steps along the path toward fuller membership in these different academic language communities.

Supplementary chapters to *THINK Critically* assist in bridging to specific introductory college courses. There are chapters available from the publisher, Pearson Education, on Social Science, Natural Science, Ethics, and Logic. Like Chapter 14, on making written arguments, these special chapters connect the ideas presented here about critical thinking with the ways in which those ideas are expressed and used in the different academic language communities college students encounter.

The term *gadget* may mean one thing to you but something completely different to a member of the military.

Do You Know Members of Any of These Language Communities?	
Examples of Special Terms & Symbols	Language Community
LOL, ROFL, TMI, BFF, BFN, RTFM, BIOYE, SNAG	Cell phone texters
Pt, Au, Hg, H_2O, CO_2	Chemists
Stet, ^, :/, tr, ?/	Copy editors
SATCOM, SEABEE, UNSC, SOP	Department of Defense employees and contractors
	Electrical engineers
	Hobos
	iPhone owners
3 4 0 = +	Mathematicians
	Military field commanders
	Musicians
	Racist prison gangs

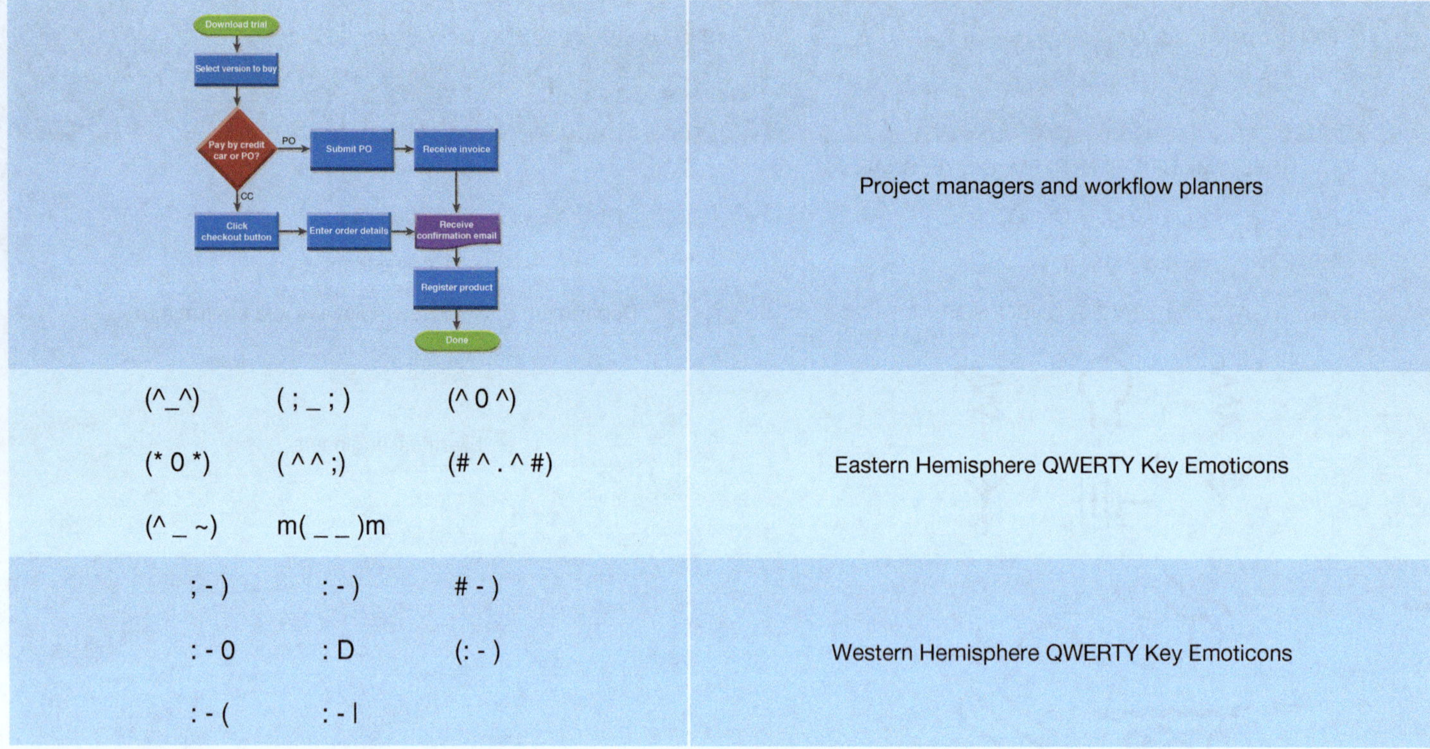

[flowchart]	Project managers and workflow planners
(^_^) (; _ ;) (^ 0 ^) (* 0 *) (^ ^ ;) (# ^ . ^ #) (^ _ ~) m(_ _)m	Eastern Hemisphere QWERTY Key Emoticons
; -) : -) # -) : - 0 : D (: -) : - (: - I	Western Hemisphere QWERTY Key Emoticons

Learn more about these organizations at **www.mythinkinglab.com**.

"How Are We As We Are?"

Different academic fields and disciplines interpret the question "How are we as we are?" in different ways or from different perspectives. To some extent noting how scholars and practitioners from different areas respond to this question helps us understand how the various academic language communities differ from one another. It gives us an insight into what each regards as "important" and "interesting." From the practical perspective, knowing this helps a person do better in his or her courses and it invites adventurous minds to explore the wonderful and varied landscape of human learning.

For example, biologists and physical scientists see this as a question about how our species and our world evolved, how all the parts interact at every physical level from the galactic to the subatomic, and in particular how human beings function as complex organisms with biological, chemical, and physical characteristics. Psychologists and behavioral scientists interpret this as a question about our human-to-human interactions, how we think about ourselves and how we relate to others in socially complex and culturally distinct communities.

Humanities and arts disciplines seek ways of expressing answers to "How are we as we are?" using creative and narrative means, such as poems, novels, dances, drawings, sculptures, songs, and plays. History responds by recounting the complex and often unpredictable or unexpected sequence of events that brought us individually and as different communities to this juncture in the human story.

The health professions respond by diagnosis of how we are as we are, if we are not as we might hope to be physically or mentally. These disciplines go on to proposing treatments that might be useful in moving us to our own levels of optimal health and functioning. Educators do the same with regard to the skills, knowledge, attitudes, and values that may be seen as needed or underdeveloped. Business-oriented fields see this question in terms of our economic interactions and our needs for organization, leadership, and teamwork. Engineers see the question as a call for equipment, infrastructure, tools, and devices that would enable us to do what we otherwise could not do, since we are as we are.

Philosophers respond to "How are we as we are?" by trying to fathom and to articulate the fundamental characteristics of the human condition, and they occasionally ask how we ought to behave if we were to desire to be at our best. And theologians explore the question of how we are as we are by considering the extent to which forces revealed only through the mysteries of a faith perspective offer possible glimpses into the supernatural forces which may shape human destiny in general and personal lives in particular.

One way to think about your own academic major, or about choosing a major, is to ask yourself which way of understanding or interpreting this question resonates most with you.

REVIEW

In this chapter we applied our critical thinking to the problem of interpreting ideas expressed in language. Knowing the context within which a word or expression is used and the intent of the speaker in using that word or expression is essential to making an accurate interpretation. Vagueness and ambiguity are unproblematic if the context and purpose make the speaker's meaning clear to the listener. But vagueness and ambiguity can be problematic in those contexts in which multiple plausible interpretations are possible. We may not be sure exactly what cases a problematically vague term is intended to include or exclude. We may not be sure which meaning of a problematically ambiguous term the speaker intends.

There are strategies we can use to resolve problematic vagueness and ambiguity. Using our critical thinking skills, we can ask probing questions to contextualize, to clarify intent, to negotiate the meaning, to establish exclusions and exceptions, or to stipulate the meaning for a given purpose.

People with a shared understanding of the meanings of words and icons can be thought of as a language community. Academic language communities, also known as professional fields or academic disciplines, are defined not only by their terminology, but by the sets of questions, kinds of evidence, conceptualizations, methods, and standards of proof that they accept. Critical thinking calls for us to give reasoned consideration to precisely this same list of things when we are making a reflective judgment about what to believe or what to do. The core critical thinking skill of interpretation is vital for this, because using it well enables us to understand what words and symbols mean in a given context and, therefore, what the members of these different language communities are saying.

KEY TERMS

problematic vagueness is the characteristic of a word or expression having an imprecise meaning or unclear boundaries in a given context or for a given purpose. (p. 68)

problematic ambiguity is the characteristic of a word or expression referring to more than one object or as having more than one meaning in a given context or for a given purpose. (p. 71)

language community is a community in which people share an understanding of the meanings of words and icons. Dictionaries were invented to record a language community's conventions for what its words *shall* mean. (p. 78)

FIND IT ON MYTHINKINGLAB.COM

- Both *Inherit the Wind* (p. 65) and *My Cousin Vinny* (p. 70) send us to www.mythinkinglab.com. There are so many great scenes in these two wonderful films that it's difficult to know which to offer as examples of strong or weak critical thinking. Both films are courtroom dramas set in Southern states, and both bring to mind the importance of precise language and rigorous thinking.

Watch the Video on mythinkinglab.com

- George Carlin's bit "I'm a Modern Man" (p. 78), found at www.mythinkinglab.com, is not only fun but is also a masterful display of linguistic dexterity. The precision with which Carlin uses language is matched by the troubling sloppiness with which some toss around the word *science*. That's why the Small Group Exercise invites you to visit the National Science Foundation link at www.mythinkinglab.com.

Exercises

ANALYZE AND INTERPRET

Reword each of the following to expose the problematic ambiguity or vagueness, if any, that each statement contains. Add context as needed. Remember that a given statement might be both ambiguous in some respects and vague in other respects. Mark as "OK AS IS" any that are crystal clear and entirely unproblematic no matter what the context or purpose.

1. America is the land of opportunity.
2. If you can't afford food, then you're not free.
3. I love my brother and my wife, but not in the same way.
4. God is love.
5. When in doubt, whistle.
6. Organic foods are healthier.
7. Clean coal is a green business!
8. *Hamlet* contains timeless truths.
9. Music soothes the savage beast in all of us.
10. Ignoring lazy thinking is like snoozing on a railroad crossing—not a problem until it's too late.

SMALL GROUP EXERCISE: INTERPRETING "SCIENCE" AND "PSEUDOSCIENCE"

For many years the National Science Foundation (NSF) has conducted surveys of the public attitudes and understanding about science and scientific knowledge. The results inform policy development, legislation, and funding for scientific research and science education in the nation. NSF reports: "In 2002 the survey showed that belief in pseudoscience was relatively widespread. . . . For example 25% of the public believed in astrology . . . , at least half the people believe in the existence of extrasensory perception, . . . 30% believe that some of the UFOs are really space vehicles from other civilizations, . . . half believe in haunted houses and ghosts, faith healing, communication with the dead, and lucky numbers." Form a small working group with one or two others in your class. Do steps 1, 2, and 5 as a group. Divide the work among yourselves for steps 3 and 4.

1. Review the public information on the NSF Web site, particularly the report "Science and Engineering Indicators–2002." Access the NSF report at **www.mythinkinglab.com**.
   Read the **Document** on **mythinkinglab.com**
2. Define the words *pseudoscience* and *science* in a fair-minded and reasoned way.
3. Survey 10 of your friends and family members about their views on astrology, extrasensory perception, and ghosts. In each case invite them to use their critical thinking skills and explain why they believe what they believe.
4. Objectively summarize the reasons pro and con for each of the three topics.
5. Using the Holistic Critical Thinking Scoring Rubric in Chapter 1, evaluate the quality of the thinking pros and cons for each of the three topics. Explain your evaluation.

MEANING MATTERS

A great many public policy issues turn on our understanding of words that evoke strong emotional responses, either positive or negative. But before taking a stand for or against something, strong critical thinkers will step back to be sure that they really understand what is being said. This exercise challenges you to use contextualization, clarification of intent, negotiation, qualification, or stipulation to clarify the underlined term(s) in each passage. This is not an exercise aimed at evaluating the claims being made in these passages. Rather the goal of the exercise is to achieve as clear an understanding of the key term(s) as possible. Correct analysis and interpretation comes before thoughtful evaluation. Otherwise, like a slimy eel, poorly defined terms make it difficult to get a grip on exactly what is being argued.

1. "In today's world truthfulness is at risk. To quote what Dr. House is often heard saying on the TV drama *House MD*, House says, 'People lie'." [Hint, lying includes more than trying to mislead a person by telling them something the speaker believes to be be untrue.]
2. "Misrepresentation by deceptive naming has become an art form. Today pollsters, political pundits, and populist politicians attach misleading names to ballot propositions, Web sites, and campaign contribution mailers. Often the public is not deceived. But occasionally a name creeps into common usage. Take for example "Clean Energy." What exactly is that?" [Suggestion: Begin with the interview with Noble Award–winning physicist, Steven Chu, and watch "Power Surge" and other recent shows available for free Web viewing from NOVA. **http://www.pbs.org/wgbh/nova/** Access the NOVA Web site through **www.mythinkinglab.com**
3. "When you tell me that I should buy your telephone because it has high-speed Internet, I just have to laugh. What's so great about 4G? Consumers in South Korea already have 5G! And

cellular communications technology does not always use the Internet anyway!"

4. "Former Senator, and one-time presidential hopeful, John Edwards, was indicted by the U.S. Justice Department for the misuse of campaign funds. He responded by saying that he had done something immoral that was not illegal. By contrast, advocates of civil disobedience, like Gandhi and King, say that at times breaking the law, which is obviously an illegal act, can be moral. I don't understand. What's the difference between illegal and immoral?", [Suggestion: The Harvard vs. Wiley College debate in the 2007 film *The Great Debaters*, starring Denzel Washington, illustrates the important distinction between morality and legality. Likewise the 1983 Best Picture Academy Award-winning film *Gandhi*, starring Ben Kingsley.
5. "I worry about the pornographic, vulgar, and lewd commercials and television shows that pour forth from the cable and satellite TV vendors today. Even the big networks are producing programming that would have been considered indecent only a generation ago. Yes, I realize that in July of 2010 the U.S. Court of Appeals dealt a serious blow to the American Family when it struck down the TV indecency rules that the FCC and the Congress had put in place. Which is partly why I'm so upset—we have to do something to protect the children.
6. "My grandfather said that he did not want the doctors to use extraordinary measures to prolong his life. I never expected to have his medical power-of-attorney. But that's how things in our family have worked out. So, now that I find myself legally responsible for his medical decision making, I'm really wondering what he meant."

VIDEO EXERCISE: SIGNS OF THE TIMES

For years Jay Leno has featured "Headlines" on his NBC *Tonight Show*. Create and post your own video clip of ambiguous signs, headlines, want ads, or slogans. One of our favorite is the highway sign that reads, "Slow Chidren Play Here." Is it advising drivers to reduce their speed, or lamenting the weak academic performance of the children in the neighborhood?

REFLECTIVE LOG

Song lyrics and poetry often contain references to emotions, ideas, issues, persons, or events well known to the members of the language community for whom the song was written. Select a song you particularly enjoy. Write out the lyrics. Research the song and the composer or author in order to learn what you can about the purpose and context of that work. Restate what is being said to explain what the composer or poet is trying to communicate with each verse.

Locate and listen to Bob Dylan's original version of "Forever Young," then listen to Rod Stewart's 1988 version. Compare those interpretations to each other and to Will.i.am's rap rendition, which was used in the 2009 Pepsi Super Bowl commercial. Use your critical thinking skills to explain how each artist's interpretation slightly modifies what the song is intended to mean.

Read the Chapter on mythinkinglab.com

Listen to the Chapter Audio on mythinkinglab.com

CHAPTER 05

Analyze Arguments and Diagram Decisions

Making arguments and giving reasons to explain the basis for our beliefs and decisions are universal in our species. There is a way to ask "Why?" in every language. For example, were we to ask Karen why she believes pot should be legalized, Karen might say, "Because then the state could get sales tax when people buy pot, just like with alcohol." To the question "Why did you order a moratorium on Illinois death penalty executions in January 2000?" former Illinois Governor George Ryan might have responded, "Because our state's criminal justice system has made mistakes, and innocent people have been wrongly executed. There is no way to undo that kind of a mistake."

Our goal in this chapter is to analyze exactly what people's claims are and the reasons they use to back up those claims. We will use a technique called *mapping* to help clarify how a person's reasoning flows from initial statements taken as true to the conclusion the person regards as being supported by those statements. Like a Google map showing how to get from point A to point B, the maps we will draw show how people reason from their beliefs and assumptions to reach a particular belief or decision.

<<< Preschoolers learn to ask why-questions early and often. Adults reinforce this behavior by responding with explanations and reasons. For a three year old, asking why may only be a way to get attention. But by the time children start school they have come to expect that there are reasons and explanations for events, decisions, and beliefs. There are reasons why the Santa Claus story can't be true. And yet we still want to pretend it is. Why? Because little brother or sister still believes in Santa.

HOW are reasons, conclusions, and arguments related?

HOW can we analyze and map these basic relationships?

HOW do context, personal experience, and unspoken assumptions affect the way we express reasons and conclusions?

WHERE do wit, irony, sarcasm, and humor come in?

HOW can we map the reasoning in decisions made by a group of people?

Analyzing and Mapping Arguments

In the *Law & Order: Special Victims Unit* clip that accompanies this chapter, a mother explains why she decided not to vaccinate her son against measles. Access the clip at www.mythinkinglab.com. Her reason was her worry about the possible risks to her son associated with being vaccinated. She says many other things as well. For example, that as a parent, it's her right to make this decision. She asserts that she is not accountable for the consequences of her decision. And she says that for her child the outcome was exactly as she had hoped. Without incurring the risk she associated with a vaccination, her son got sick with measles and then recovered. In the final analysis, her reason is this: "Measles vaccinations have dangerous side effects. Those risks worry me a lot." In view of this, her decision was not to have her son vaccinated. Independently we know that those risks are exceedingly rare and that the disease itself is a far greater risk to her child and to other children.[i] And so, we may want to evaluate her decision negatively. **Watch** the **Video** on **mythinkinglab.com**

But our task in this chapter is not to evaluate. For now, our job is to analyze the person's judgment about what to believe or what to do based on the reasons the person gives in support of those judgments. Analysis calls for us to be as accurate and objective as possible, even if we totally disagree with that judgment or personally would have used other reasons—in fact, especially if we disagree. When the time comes for evaluation, we will want to be sure that we are being true to the speaker's position with no alteration or revisions from other sources, including from ourselves. Evaluating an argument requires first having made a thoughtful and insightful analysis. We will work on the critical thinking skill of argument evaluation in chapters that come later in the book. Our focus for now is on the critical thinking skill of analysis.

"ARGUMENT = (REASON + CLAIM)"

Consistent with common usage, we will use the expression **make an argument** to refer to the process of giving a reason in support of a claim.[ii] Here are some examples of arguments:

1 [Reason] Student journalists should have the same rights as professional journalists. [Claim it is intended to support] So, laws that shield professional journalists from imprisonment should apply to student journalists, too.

2 [Reasons] A journalist's confidential sources of information would be in danger if they were publically identified. To legally require journalists to tell the names of their confidential sources to the police will have the effect of publically identifying those confidential sources. It is never a good thing to put people in danger unnecessarily. [Claim] Therefore, no, the law should not require journalists to reveal their confidential sources.

3 [Claim] Encephalitis (swelling of the brain) cannot be said to be a side effect of measles vaccination. [Reason] Here's why: "This happens so rarely—less than once in a million shots—that experts can't be sure whether the vaccine is the cause or not."[iii]

4 [Claim] I need to get a better job! [Reason] My boss is a total moron.

4′ [Reason] I work for a total moron. [Claim] Man, do I need to get a better job or what?

The term **claim** refers to the statement that the maker of the argument is seeking to show to be true or probably true. We will often refer to an argument's claim as the argument's **conclusion**. The other sentences in the argument, namely those that are used to show that the claim is true or that it is probably true, constitute the **reason**. We can use the term **argument** to refer to the combination of a person's claim and the reason a person presents in support of that claim.

Two Reasons, Two Arguments

It is common in natural conversation to give more than one reason in support of a claim. We will treat each separate combination of reason-plus-claim as a separate argument. To help see why, consider this: "I should buy the thin crust pizza because it costs less and it tastes better." It is reasonable to analyze that sentence as expressing two arguments:

5 [Reason] Thin crust pizza costs less.
[Claim/Conclusion] I should buy thin crust.

6 [Reason] Thin crust pizza tastes better.
[Claim/Conclusion] I should buy thin crust.

Now suppose someone tried to argue against that claim that I should buy thin crust this way: "What? You're wrong about the 'tastes better' part. The last time we had thin crust, you said it tasted like cardboard." Let us concede that the person's memory is accurate, and I remember. "Oh, yeah, the last thin crust I had tasted like pavement-baked Wyoming roadkill." And so we all agree that the argument is defeated. Even so, the claim that I should buy thin crust still is being supported by the reason that it costs less.

Two Confusions to Avoid

There are a couple of confusions to avoid. First, by using the word *argument*, we do not mean "quarrel" or "disagreement." The discussions that result when making arguments and giving reasons can be civil, constructive, respectful, and collaborative. Second, when using the word *conclusion*, we do not mean to suggest that the person's conclusion must come at the end. Examples #3 and #4 above demonstrate that the conclusion—that is, the claim that the speaker intends to support—can be the first statement in the speaker's argument. In natural discourse, it often is.

"Reason" and "Premise"

In example arguments #1, #4, #5, and #6 above, the reason is expressed in a single statement. In #2 three statements are

Words That Signal Conclusions	Words That Signal Reasons
So . . .	Since . . .
Thus . . .	Given that . . .
Therefore . . .	Whereas . . .
Hence . . .	Because . . .
We can now infer . . .	For the reason that . . .
It follows that . . .	Suppose . . .
This means that . . .	Assume . . .
This implies . . .	Let us take it that . . .
These facts indicate . . .	Let us begin agreeing that . . .
The evidence shows . . .	The evidence is as follows . . .
Let us infer that . . .	We all know that . . .
So it would seem that . . .	In the first place . . .
And so probably . . .	Is supported by . . .
We can deduce . . .	Is implied by . . .
This supports the view that . . .	Is derived from the fact that . . .
You see, therefore, that . . .	For the reason that . . .

used together to express the reason. In #3, grammatically only one sentence is used. But when we analyze what that sentence tells us, we see that it expresses two statements[iv]:

- For every 1 million measles vaccinations administered, 1 case of encephalitis occurs.
- The rate of 1 in 1 million is so rare that experts cannot be sure if the vaccine was the cause or not.

The statement or statements that comprise a reason are commonly referred to as the **premises** of the argument. Often in natural conversation we do not find it necessary to articulate each and every premise in a given reason. The context and our shared understanding of the topic we are discussing permit us to put into words only as much as we believe to be sufficient to communicate our thinking. Here are two examples. In their proper contexts, the makers of these arguments correctly believe that they can afford to leave a premise unexpressed.

7 Optimus Prime and Bumblebee are Transformers. So, obviously they are made of metal.

8 Salerno is south of Napoli. So, it is south of Roma.

The premise missing from #7 is "All Transformers are metal," which is a true statement within the fictional universe of the many Transformers action adventure movies. If you know that fictional universe, then it is unnecessary, redundant, and even a little insulting to remind you of such an obvious fact. But if you do not know that fictional universe, argument #7 may not even make sense. Too much information is missing. The implicit premise of #8 is about the relative location of two cities in Italy. Specifically, "Napoli (Naples) is south of Roma (Rome)." It is unnecessary to remind anyone who knows Italy about the location of Naples. But, if the speaker thought that he or she was making argument #8 to someone who did not know the locations of major cities in Italy, then the speakers would be wise to voice the unspoken premise about Naples being south of Rome.[v]

Distinguishing Reasons from Conclusion

Our language is rich with words we can use to communicate our intentions when it comes to expressing arguments. Some words signal our conclusion, and others signal our reason. The table lists some of the most common words and phrases used when we want to be sure people know we are making an argument. Naturally, it would be an error to think that we always are so clear and obvious about our argument making. Context is everything. Miscommunication happens.

MAPPING CLAIMS AND REASONS

When we are trying to be precise in our analysis of an argument, especially a complex argument or a conversation in which several arguments are made, many of us find it useful to display the reasoning visually. In effect, we try to map the arguments. Using familiar shapes and connecting lines, we express how we understand the ideas to be related. As analysts, our main responsibility is to develop as accurate an understanding as possible of what the person expressing the argument had in mind. Like the TV show *CSI*, we analyze the evidence and map out our findings. Our aim is to show how that person intended to support the claims being made by the reasons that were used.

Let's map a few simple examples to get started. We will use a ***rectangle*** to represent the argument's conclusion. Let's use an ***oval*** to represent the reason. And we will simply draw an ***arrow*** from the reason to the conclusion to show that the person who made the argument intends to support that claim with that reason. Remember, just because the speaker intends that a given reason should support a given claim, it does not follow that the reason actually does support that claim. Some reasons fail. But, determining whether or not an argument fails is evaluation, and we are only analyzing arguments in this chapter. Now, think back to Karen's argument in the introduction to this chapter. Map 1 shows that

MAP > it > OUT 1

The state can get sales tax when people buy pot, just like with alcohol. → Pot should be legalized.

argument using our simple oval-arrow-rectangle mapping conventions.

Suppose Karen was to have said, "I think pot should be legalized because, just like alcohol, the state could get sales tax revenues and because people over 21 could buy pot legally. Oh, and another thing, then we could regulate it to ensure the pot-buying public gets consistent quality, man." The argument Map 2 shows that Karen offers three separate reasons for believing that pot should be legalized.

MAP > it > OUT 2

When the topic of an argument is important to us we may become tempted to want to "repair," "reword," or "supplement" what the person said. For example, we might want to build an argument concerning legalizing pot by using public opinion polls or the outcomes of recent ballot initiatives.[vi] Or we may want to editorialize about the economic impact of farming the cash crop, cannabis.[vii] Be that as it may, at the point when we are analyzing arguments, we must resist the temptation to improve, to diminish, or to editorialize. As analysts our responsibility is to unearth and to describe the speaker's arguments, not to bolster nor to undercut them. We must be as intellectually honest and as rigorously objective as possible as we point out the claims, reasons, and unspoken assumptions. Our aim here is to display with accuracy *the arguments as the speaker made them*.

Mapping a Line of Reasoning

There are times when a claim becomes a reason for another claim, thus forming a *chain of reasoning*. For example, say a person named Sara were to share her reasoning for having rented an apartment on State Street this way: "I wanted a place near the library because I love to study there. It was the closest rental available." Were we to ask Sara why she loves to study in the library, she might give as her reason, "Because it's quiet there." And if we push her to say why quiet is important to her, especially in a world where background music seems to assault us all the time, she might say, "I like music, but I need quiet when I study. Music, or anything that disturbs the quiet, distracts me from my work." The analysis of Sara's reasoning would map out this way:

Sara's line of reasoning begins with a fundamental thing she knows about herself ("anything that disturbs the quiet causes me to be distracted") and concludes with the idea that she should rent an apartment on State Street. If she learns that any of the links along that chain of reasoning is not well connected, then she may well decide to reconsider and rent someplace else.

A diagram like Map 3, which shows a chain of reasoning, suggests that we might want to reserve the word *conclusion* for that claim that the speaker is ultimately trying to establish. The other claims along the way are intermediate relative to the conclusion. OK, we could do that. But, on the other hand, every additional tweak or restriction on how we will use any given word raises the question Why? Can't we make ourselves understood to more people without that rule?

MAP > it > OUT 3

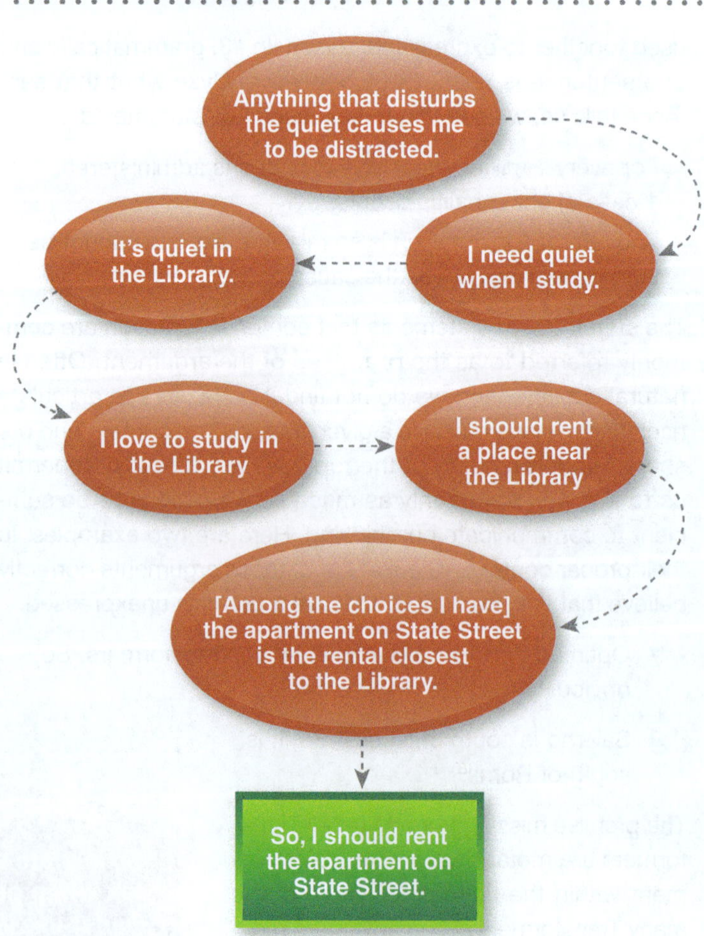

Mapping Implicit Ideas

In natural conversational contexts when people give their reasons for a claim, they typically offer a specific fact, opinion, observation, or belief. "Thin crust pizza costs less." "It's quiet in the library." "The state can get sales tax." "Optimus Prime and Bumblebee are Transformers." The speaker typically believes that he or she has said enough, given the context, his or her purpose in communicating, and the understandings to be shared with the others in the conversation. That is, unless someone asks for a clarification. In the case of argument #7 about the Transformers, if we did not know the movie reference, we might well ask how the person jumped all the way to "So, Optimus Prime and Bumblebee are made of metal." The response would be to articulate the implicit but unspoken premise, "All transformers are made of metal." But for the most part, most days, in most contexts, we get it. Argument making and reason giving are highly efficient processes.

So, cutting to the chase, how should we map argument #7 if we want to show both the expressed premise and the implied premise? We can simply put both statements in the oval. To note that the speaker implicitly relied on an idea, but did not actually express that thought, we can use a ***cloud shape***, like in a comic strip. The cloud shape is one of the devices we can use to keep track of things we have added to the analysis beyond what the speaker actually said. Looking at the cloud shapes, we will know exactly which ideas we have attributed to the speaker, and we can double-check to see whether our interpretations are reasonable or need to be refined. Map 4 describes argument #7 about the two Transformers characters.

"Students trying to understand an academic discipline that is new to them need to learn the specialized language of the discipline to be successful."

About Technical Vocabulary

Specialized terminology is valuable because it improves communication among the members of a specific language community. Professional fields, businesses, government agencies, religions, social organizations, clubs, and societies of all kinds inevitably generate specialized vocabulary—words that have special definitions for the members of that language community, definitions that differ from what those words might mean when used by the rest of the people who are not members of that language community. There are many important reasons to generate specialized terminology; often the reasons relate to the activities the language community is engaged in together and the nuanced understandings those activities require. Think of medical or legal terminology as examples.

To become a participating member of that language community, we must learn to use words that have specialized meanings for that community in the same ways that others in the community use those words. We need to internalize the special meanings the group attaches to certain words. But along with the benefit of clarifying the precise meanings of key terms for the members of the language community comes the risk that the members of the community will find it more difficult to communicate effectively with people who are not privy to the specialized meanings they attach to those words. The more a language community generates specialized terminology, the less people who are not members of that language community can understand what is being said, even if the words being used are familiar words that have been around for centuries.

In the previous chapter, on clarifying ideas, we suggested that to make progress in an academic discipline that is new to you, it is vital to discover how to communicate using the specialized language of that discipline. Learning technical terminology means acquiring the facility to use words that have specialized meanings the same way that the other members of the disciplinary language community use those words when conversing with one another.

That said, specialized vocabulary poses major problems for talking with people about their critical thinking. Critical thinking is a pervasive human phenomenon. It is evident everywhere, in all academic disciplines, in every professional field, in all language communities. So, the more we want to talk with people about how to analyze, evaluate, or explain reasoned judgments about what to believe or what to do, the more important it is for us *not* to create a specialized vocabulary. Instead, to be able to talk to everyone about critical thinking we need to use the vocabulary of human thinking in ways that are consistent with the ordinary, everyday meanings of words. We need to be able to talk about these things with people no matter what discipline, profession, political party, religion, business, club, or other language community they may be a member of. If we attach special meanings to common words like *reason*, *claim*, *analysis*, *open-mindedness*, etc., we only limit the utility of those words to communicate across the greatest possible span of people, topics, and real-life situations. The language community for critical thinking includes everybody. So, the words have to be used in ways that can be understood by everyone . . . even if they were not fortunate enough to have attended college or to have read this or any other book about critical thinking.

MAP > it > OUT 4

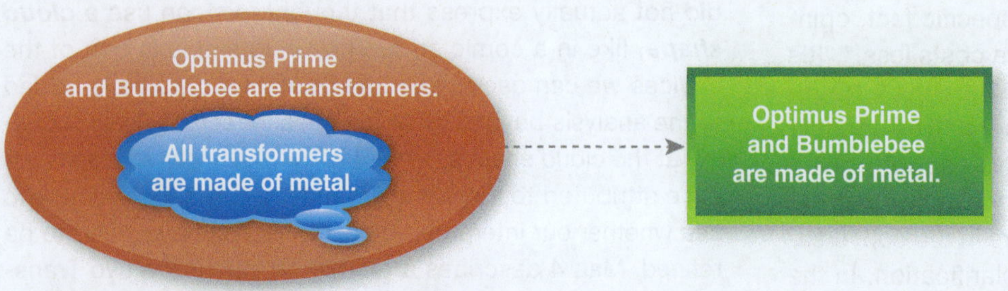

shared experiences, common knowledge, and similarities of cultural backgrounds. But, obviously, what we leave unspoken can cause problems. From time to time, we all have experienced such a situation. Either we get someone else's unspoken assumptions wrong, or they are mistaken about our unspoken assumptions. Fortunately, these problems are easy to spot and easy to fix. Going back to the pot example, clarification could go like this: "Karen, are you saying that the state should raise the sales tax?" "No, I'm saying that an entirely new source of revenue, namely a tax on the sale of pot, will be beneficial to the state budget."

INTERPRETING UNSPOKEN REASONS AND CLAIMS IN CONTEXT

Teammates are talking about next Saturday's softball game. One says, "Look, we shut out State last week, and the week before that State buried Western. So, Saturday should be easy." Before we can map this argument, we need to interpret it so that the reasoning is more fully expressed, and we may have to restate it for the sake of clarity.

- Our team defeated State's team last week.
- State's team defeated Western's team the week before that.
- [Our team is scheduled to play Western's team on Saturday.]
- [So, our team will probably defeat Western's team on Saturday.]

How many reasons does the speaker use to support the claim? Only one. The context permitted the speaker to communicate successfully by offering only two facts. Our interpretation of what she said revealed that the team's shared knowledge of their game schedule enabled the speaker to omit the third fact. Map 5 shows that this argument includes both of the elements not spoken in the original: a premise and the conclusion itself.

When we give reasons, we naturally assume that the others in our conversation understand us. Much is left unsaid because it very often does not need to be said, given factors like context,

MAP > it > OUT 5

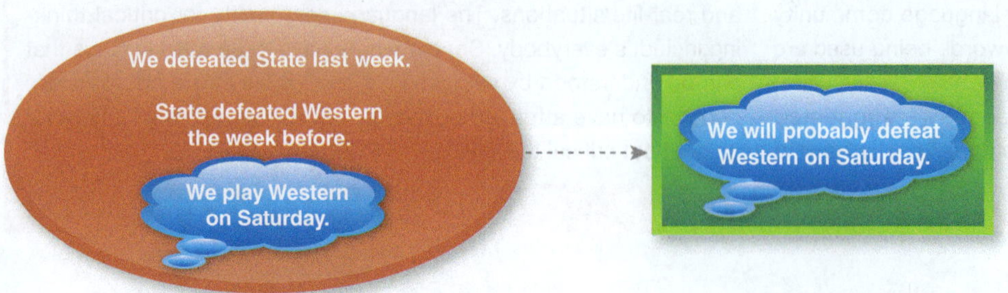

INTERPRETING THE USE OF IRONY, HUMOR, SARCASM, AND MORE

As we saw in Chapter 4 on clarifying ideas, interpretation is an essential critical thinking skill—one we need to refine. To understand what people really mean, we cannot always take their words at face value. We spice up our conversations with wit, humor, irony, sarcasm, smack talk, innuendo, double entendre, exaggerations, understatement, slang, imagery, emotion, provocation, and much more. These language tools can give a single word a variety of meanings. For example, the words "Nice tat!" can mean that a person thinks your tattoo is awesome, thinks your tattoo is silly, thinks your tattoo should not be showing, thinks your tattoo makes a poignant statement, etc. As we did with the softball team example above, interpretation and restatement are vital preliminary activities to analysis and mapping.

Before mapping an ironic or sarcastic comment, switch the statement from the positive that was spoken to the negative that was intended (or from the negative spoken to the positive that was intended). For example, in one context "He was wonderfully diplomatic" can be meant as sincere praise. In this context it supports the claim "Let him represent us." But in another context it can be intended sarcastically. There the speaker would be using it to support the opposite claim: "Don't let him represent us." In the latter case, since the correct analysis must reflect the speaker's intent, and since we know the speaker was making a negative comment, we would restate the reason as, "He was [not at all] wonderfully diplomatic."

As we have already done a couple of times above, we can use words in ***[brackets]*** to clarify a statement so that it can be read in the argument map the way the speaker intended it to be understood. We can also use bracketed text to describe the impact on the reasoning process of nonverbal cues.

For example, people frown, scoff, cross their arms, or roll their eyes to show that they disagree. Such nonverbal cues can be represented in an argument map in this way: "[Arms are crossed and he's shaking his head—John strongly disagrees with Karen about legalizing pot.]"

Giving Reasons and Making Arguments in Real Life

Asking someone about their reasons and having them share their thinking honestly and fully are complex human social interactions. The context, a gesture, a look, a facial expression, the past history between people, unspoken assumptions, and all kinds of other things can enter into how we interpret what people really mean. As we mature, we gain the skills, knowledge, and experience to understand others and to express ourselves better. As our skills advance, we can handle more challenging arguments, such as the ones in this next section.

THE EL TRAIN ARGUMENT

The famous El Train scene from *12 Angry Men* offers examples of sarcasm, irony, expressive body language, and raw emotion, all of which may or may not be influencing the thinking of the various members of the jury as they deliberate.[viii] Let's apply our argument-mapping techniques to the argument offered in support of the claim that the old man was lying when he testified that he actually heard the defendant threaten to kill the victim. In the classic 1957 film version, the scene runs from 39:30 [minute:second] to 43:00.

One of the responsibilities of any jury is to determine the facts of a case. Using testimony and their good judgment, the jurors must decide whom to believe. In the El Train scene the jury is trying to determine whether to believe the testimony of an older gentleman who lives in the apartment building where the murder had taken place. The old man testified under oath that he heard the accused shout that he was going to kill the victim just one second before he heard the victim's body hit the floor. The jury wonders whether the old man could have heard the accused make such a threat. Is it possible for a person in one apartment to hear what someone in another apartment is shouting? Well, yes, under ordinary circumstances it might be possible, the jury reasons, particularly if the apartment windows are open. And they were open, according to the witnesses. So perhaps the old man heard the threat through his open window. The jury has vital information about the moments during which the threat was supposed to have been heard. Another witness has testified that the murder occurred just as a noisy elevated train went shrieking past the window of the apartment where the victim was killed. Several members of the jury comment about how incredibly noisy an elevated train can be, and this train passed so close to the side of the apartment building that the clatter of its passing might have been unbearably loud. So the question becomes: Could the old man have heard the killer shout a threat over the racket made by the passing train? The jury determines that it took the train roughly ten seconds to pass the apartment window. According to the testimony of the other witness the killing happened just as the last part of the train passed by the window. Putting the testimony of the old man together with what the other witness said implies that the threat was shouted while the train was roaring past the window. Not possible, reasons the jury. We have a major conflict in the testimony of these two witnesses. Either we believe the eyewitness who said that the murder occurred just as the train went past the window, or we believe that the old man could hear the threat being shouted over the roar of a passing train. No, the jury decides, the old man's testimony is not credible. Because of the noise of the train the old man could not possibly have heard anything people in another apartment were saying, even if they were shouting threats.

The summary of the scene we have provided here leaves out things that the playwright has the characters doing while the argument was unfolding. For example, two of them start playing tic-tac-toe instead of paying attention. The summary also omits the snide comments and exasperation some of the jurors express, which also interrupts the flow of the reasoning. But even with these distractions not present in our summary, many of us would still have a difficult time following the twists and turns of a complicated argument like this one when all we have is a long paragraph of text. We need some way to organize the ideas, to diagram the flow of the reasoning, to clarify and to display for ourselves and others our analyses of relationships between reasons and claims. Argument maps provide the solution. And, because the reasoning is presented using simple shapes and arrows, the flow of the thinking quickly becomes apparent. It is easier to collaborate on the analysis of complicated arguments using visuals, which can spread across a page in all directions, versus a text-based approach, which can only move from left to right and from top to bottom line by line.

Of course, to appreciate the advantages of visual mapping when analyzing more complicated passages, one must understand the mapping process. Practice. That's the ticket. So, how about we try to map an argument for not believing the testimony of the old man from our summary of the El Train scene?

Here are a few tips. It often works best to begin an argument map by identifying the speaker's final conclusion. In this case, it is easy because the whole scene builds up to the claim the old man did not hear the accused make the threatening statement. Let's put that down first, and then, working backward from that conclusion, let's add the two strands of reasoning, which collide at the point where the old man's testimony about what he says he heard conflicts with the fact of how noisy it is when an El Train roars by. The dilemma for the jury is that they either have to reject the facts about noisy

MAP > it > OUT 6

The train was roaring by the open window of the old man's apartment for nearly 10 seconds before the body of the victim hit the floor.

When an elevated train roars by an open window the noise is almost unbearable.

This means that the old man would have had to have heard the boy make his threat over the noise of the train roaring past his open window.

The noise from the train passing his open apartment window would have prevented the old man from hearing the accused man's voice through the open window.

Either the other witness who said the murder took place as the train passed the window was mistaken, or the old man who said he heard the threat being shouted a second before the body hit the floor was mistaken.

The old man did not tell the truth when he said he heard the accused threaten the victim.

trains or reject the old man's testimony. Map 6 shows that dilemma too.

The map above is not complete. The scene includes arguments that lead to the two ovals with "The train was roaring by . . ." and "When an elevated train . . ." Try for yourself to map each of those lines of reasoning back to their respective starting points. Expect to do more than one or two drafts before you are satisfied with your analysis. Mapping is like writing. The key to quality comes from drafting and redrafting.

HUCKABEE AND STEWART DISCUSS "THE PRO-LIFE ISSUE—ABORTION"

Let's try another moderately difficult example: On June 18, 2009, the former governor of Arkansas, Mike Huckabee, visited with Jon Stewart on *The Daily Show* specifically to discuss the controversial topic of pro-life/abortion. Access this clip at **www.mythinkinglab.com**.

Watch the **Video** on **mythinkinglab.com**

The conversation's first 90 seconds is taken up with humor and comments acknowledging that two middle-aged men may have no business addressing this topic. The next 60 seconds is on point. Governor Huckabee presents the standard pro-life argument. Like many others, he interprets the question as being about whether every human life has intrinsic worth and value. Of course the obvious issue then becomes the point at which we are dealing with a human life that is as deserving of all the protections accorded to people like you and like me. It would be unfair in the extreme to characterize everyone who defends the right of a woman to choose to have an abortion as savagely indifferent to human life. In fact, the history of the past decades' long debate on this controversial issues

MAP > it > OUT 7

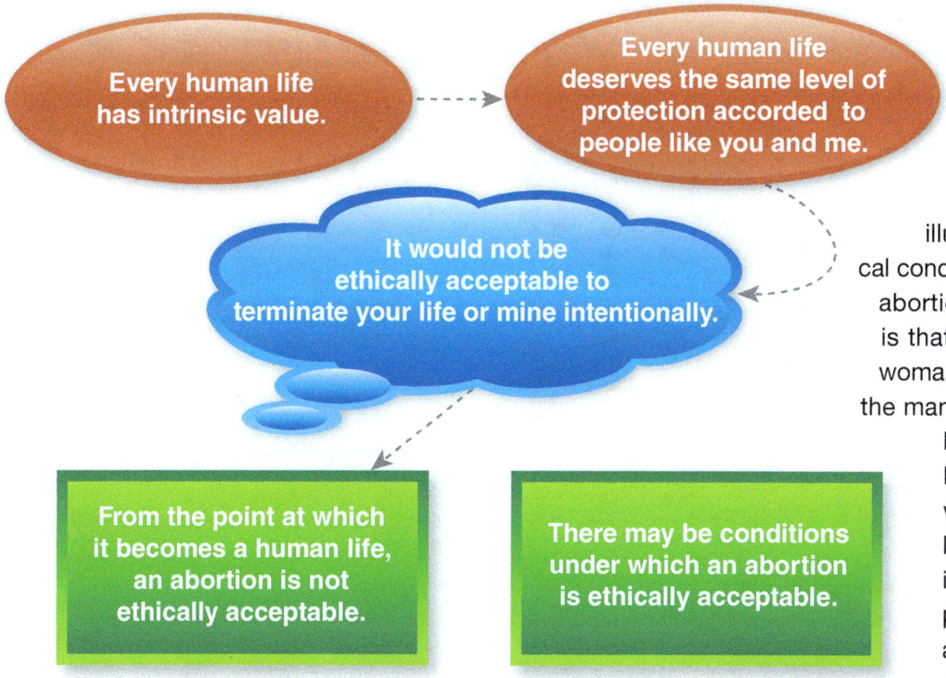

Every human life has intrinsic value.

Every human life deserves the same level of protection accorded to people like you and me.

It would not be ethically acceptable to terminate your life or mine intentionally.

From the point at which it becomes a human life, an abortion is not ethically acceptable.

There may be conditions under which an abortion is ethically acceptable.

has shown that people on both sides can agree that every human life has value. Map 7 displays the familiar anti-abortion position, but that map does not display the pro-choice reasoning which would flow toward the alternative "there may be conditions under which an abortion is ethically acceptable."

Many who want to make abortion illegal take the view that human life begins with conception because biologically the living embryo is human. For many who advocate the pro-life side of this debate, nothing further need be said. But, as often happens in these kinds of discussions, the defender of one side takes a moment to anticipate possible objections people on the other side might make. The defender presents counterarguments to those potential objections, even before the other side advances those objections. To put forth counterarguments, experienced debaters like to point out undesirable consequences of their opponent's position. Huckabee employs this debate strategy in his interview with Jon Stewart. We can paraphrase Huckabee's counterargument this way. Suppose we raise our sons and daughters to believe they may take a human life whenever that life represents an interference to their lives. What will happen when we are old and infirm? Would we really want to give our sons and daughters the opportunity to terminate our lives simply because putting us in a nursing home was inconvenient or too expensive for them? A person who would make this counterargument assumes that people representing the other side of the debate would say, "Certainly we would not!"

Stewart challenges the analogy Huckabee had offered, which compared one's elder parent and an unborn embryo. Is the inconvenience of the situation sufficiently comparable? Jon Stewart observes that one important difference is that the elderly parent is not living inside of their son or daughter.

The pro-choice side of the debate can also employ the strategy of showing that the other side's position results in unwanted consequences. Jon Stewart illustrates this when he objects that the logical conclusion we should draw, given the claim that abortion is the unethical taking of a human life, is that abortion is murder. It follows then that a woman who has an abortion should be jailed and the man by whom she became pregnant ought to be considered an accessory to murder. From the perspective of the defender of a woman's right to choose, these are ridiculous ideas that illustrate that the other side is mistaken. But what if the people on the pro-life side of the argument do not find it absurd at all to put a woman in jail for murder if she has an abortion?

We acknowledge that this is a disturbing debate. People on both sides value human life and human freedom. These important values collide in this situation. You may be wondering why we elected to use such a highly charged issue in a chapter that about argument mapping, when we could have picked examples that did not evoke such strong responses from people on both sides. We decided to use the abortion issue precisely because it is so familiar and so divisive. The key to good argument mapping is to focus on achieving an objective analysis of the pros and cons, regardless of one's own point of view. Evaluation is for later. It is difficult for people who have strong opinions on a given issue to acknowledge that the other side has anything going for it at all. But strong critical thinkers realize that it is essential to give both sides a fair and objective hearing before rendering an evaluative judgment on the merits of either side. So we picked this issue because we wanted to challenge you to remain as objective as possible during the analytical phase. In this phase our purpose is to render a map that displays an objective account of the case each side makes, regardless of which side we support.

Getting back to the mapping, although we could use ovals to represent objections and counterarguments, that shape undersells the intended logical force of these elements. Objections and counterarguments are intended to show that some position the speaker does not agree with is seriously flawed. Objections and counterarguments are used to reverse the flow of the reasoning away from the conclusion being rejected and back toward the speaker's position on the issue. They are examples of the use of reasons to disprove, refute, invalidate, or show that a given claim is not true. Let's

MAP > it > OUT 8

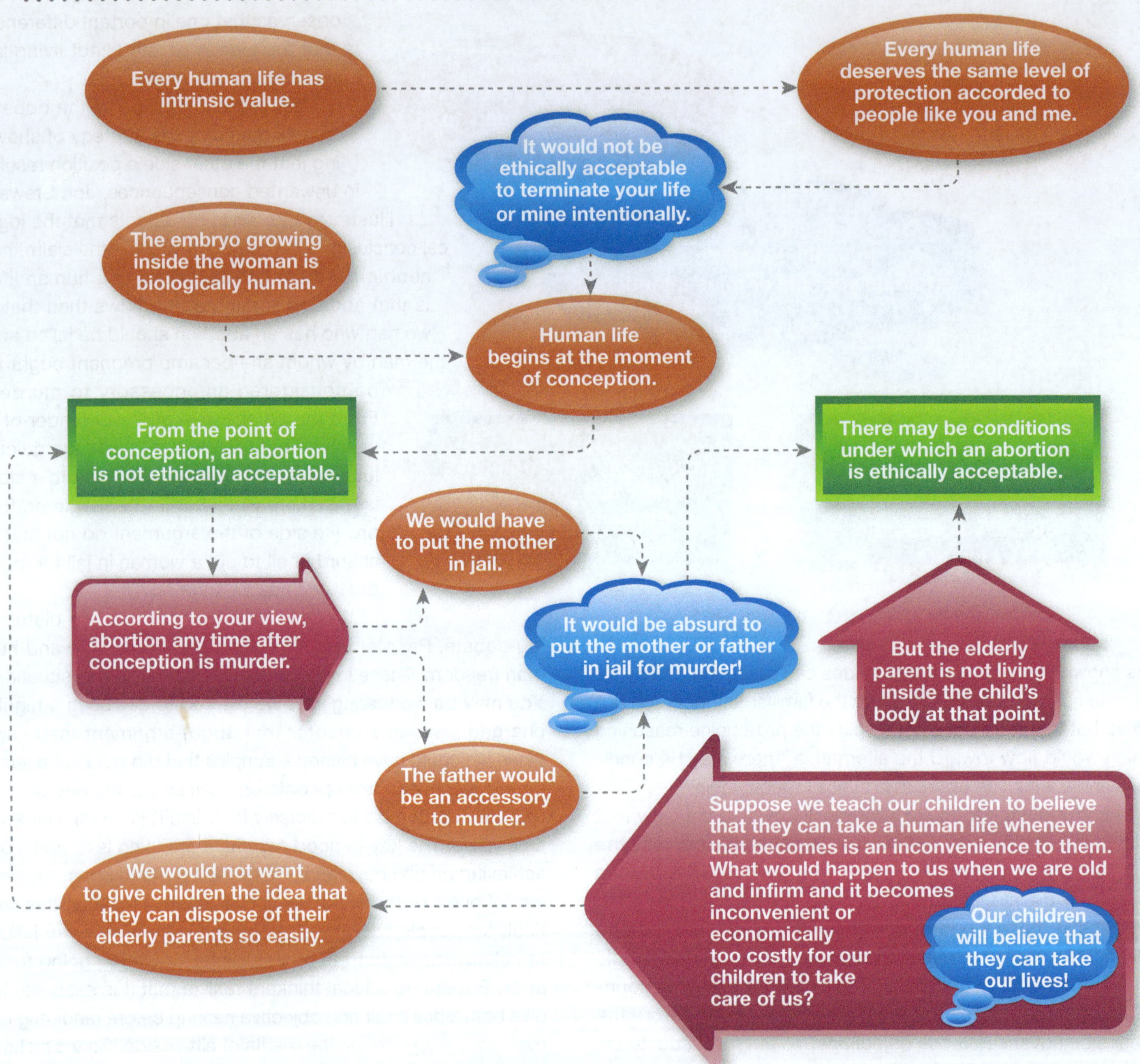

use a ***wide arrow*** with words inside to depict objections and counterarguments. Map 8 incorporates the arrow device in its analysis. The map includes the elements shown in Map 7 and adds the Huckabee and the Stewart counterarguments that we paraphrased afterward.

Before moving on, we do want to acknowledge that it was tough for us, and probably for you too, to go through the Huckabee interview and to revisit the abortion question in such detail without evaluating the case each side was making. So many ideas cried out for clarification, so many distinctions should have been made, so many more considerations should have been brought forward. One lesson, reinforced again and again over the years, is that those with whom we disagree are almost never as evil or as stupid as we imagine. Good critical thinkers know that it is wise not to demonize, underestimate, or disrespect those arguing for a different conclusion.

Analyzing and Mapping Decisions

Argument maps are intended to depict in a helpful way the analysis of the reasons presented in support of a given conclusion. And if our purpose in learning critical thinking was only to

Expressions that Often Signal Objections or Counterarguments	Examples
But	As in Map 8, "... But the elderly parent is not living inside the child's body at that point."
However	You say you heard the body hit the floor, however the El Train was roaring by your open apartment window at precisely that moment.
Yet	The body hit the floor just as the El Train was roaring by the open window. All that noise and yet the old man heard the body hit the floor? No, I don't think so.
On the other hand	Public polls do support legalizing medical marijuana. On the other hand the majority of people in our state do not support total legalization of all uses of pot.
Nevertheless	Public polls support legalizing medical marijuana. Nevertheless it remains a dangerous drug.
Notwithstanding	"Notwithstanding the importance of respect for free choice, the life of the fetus is the central consideration."
Regardless of	"Regardless of the risks to other children, I have to put the safety of my children first."
Still	As in Map 11, "No he doesn't. We still have the problem about ... "
Despite	"Despite what the esteemed ambassador is saying, according to reports from independent journalists the facts on the ground are quite different."
If we were to accept the view that ..., then ...	If we accept the view that an embryo has all the rights of a fully developed human person, then abortion at any time during a pregnancy is unethical.
..., all the same ...	A option may be unethical, all the same it can still be legal.
Be that as it may ...	The Fukushima Daiichi nuclear power plant passed all inspections. Be that as it may, the plant was not prepared for the 2011 tsunami.
That being said, ...	The international community generously responded with millions of dollars in relief after the Haiti hurricane disaster. That being said, the international response to the Haitian cholera epidemic that followed was far from impressive.

be able to present, analyze, and evaluate arguments, then we might be able to end the chapter here and go directly to the exercises. However, as we said in the beginning of the book, critical thinking is extremely practical because it is about judging, in a reasoned and reflective way, what we should actually believe and what we should actually do in real-life situations.

If the abortion issue were not presented as an abstract debate between two middle-aged men, but rather as the private and highly personal question a woman was trying to think her way through, we would know that she might be wrestling with a myriad of thoughts, feelings, worries, and questions. In her mind she may be able to see several reasons why she should and why she should not have an abortion. In a situation like this, a decision at some point one way or the other is inevitable, for even the decision to delay deciding becomes a decision with very real consequences.

When people are interviewed about difficult decisions they have made, they often talk about how they considered various options and, for various reasons, came to select one rather than any of the others.[ix] In effect, they are describing a series of arguments. *A decision map depicts all the arguments, pro or con, which are used in the decision-making process during the consideration of various options and the selection of the final choice.* Decision maps can be thought of as argument maps used to analyze and depict the deliberations involved in individual or group decision making. To show how to build decision maps, and for more practice mapping critical thinking, consider the following extended example about a spring trip.

"WE SHOULD CANCEL THE SPRING TRIP" #1

The planning committee of a student club called the High Sierra Hikers is talking about a camping trip the club hopes to take during spring break. Eve is the chairperson of the group, Melissa is the treasurer, and James and Felix are the trip coordinators.

Meeting Transcript:

Eve: How are the plans coming for the spring camping trip?

Felix: Bad news. The room rates at the Base Camp Lodge have doubled since last year.

Melissa: Yes, and the money we've set aside for the trip won't cover the difference. Our budget is already a problem because of the all other events we have planned.

Felix: Even if we could get the money, the Lodge has no available rooms during spring break. The only available rooms are during finals week.

MAP > it > OUT 9

James: But wait. We've been planning this trip for almost a year. People are all excited about going. It's going to be a lot of fun.

Eve: So, Felix, you're saying we have to cancel the trip. What about other places we can stay?

Felix: Yes, I am. There aren't enough rooms in any one other place. We'd have to split up our group.

Melissa: It would be a hassle to organize transportation from different sites. And we could use the money for the other events this year.

Eve: OK, we'll cancel. I agree with Melissa, let's use the money we would've spent on the camping trip some other way.

An analysis of this transcript reveals that the planning committee is making a decision between cancelling and not cancelling the trip that the club had planned for spring break. They are alerted to the need to make a decision when Felix responds with, "Bad news" to Eve's question. We can interpret the expression "Bad news" in this context to mean, "There's a problem about our spring trip." At this early point in the conversation, though, we would not know what that problem might be. We could use an oval to represent that idea. But, as before, an oval does not seem to suggest enough about the impact of this realization on the reasoning process. Recall the line from *Apollo 13* when the pilot calls down to Mission Control in Houston to say there is a problem. The rather commonplace assertion that there was a problem was actually a stunning realization. That declaration alerted everyone that they needed to be thinking about what could possibly be happening.

To capture the sense that some assertions put us on notice that we have to start thinking—although we may not yet know which direction our thinking will go, or what the nature of the problem really is—we can opt for a more dramatic shape than the humble oval. As illustrated in Map 9, we can use a ***diamond*** to represent the realization that a decision needs to be made or the realization that deliberation is needed. The content is typically a statement that is *neutral relative to the various options* and draws attention to the opportunity, need, or appropriateness of engaging in decision making with regard to the issue at hand.

In the final map of a decision there will be lines of reasoning flowing toward each of the options considered. One of them will end up being the choice that is made, and the others will be options not selected. We already have the rectangle shape for the final conclusion of an argument map, so let's continue to use that shape for each of the options. This gives us the fundamental structure of the decision at hand. Since we know that the group decided to cancel the trip, we can represent the rejected option by a ***shaded rectangle***. If the group had considered a couple of other options, we would have put them in as rectangles. The only one we would not have shaded would be the option that the group actually chose.

After we have this, we can add the argument for and against the options. When the reasoning to be mapped is more complex, as it is here, it takes a couple of drafts to design an effective decision map. Redrafting helps refine the analysis and clarify exactly what is being said. Redrafting also lets you move the shapes around on the page so that the flow of the reasoning, as you have analyzed it, can be seen moro readily.

Decision Map 10 emerged after producing two or three earlier versions. Same for the El Train scene map and the maps of the abortion issue; in each case there were two or three preliminary drafts.

"WE SHOULD CANCEL THE SPRING TRIP" #2

Surely, we could make a plausible case not to cancel the trip. Maybe the logistical problems could be overcome, and it might not be so bad if the whole group wasn't able to be in the same hotel. Perhaps some money could be shifted from those other events toward this spring trip. But, as decision analysts, it's not our job to solve the problems, but rather to uncover the reasoning process behind them.

Suppose that James, still wanting to go, pushes the group to reconsider.

MAP > it > OUT 10

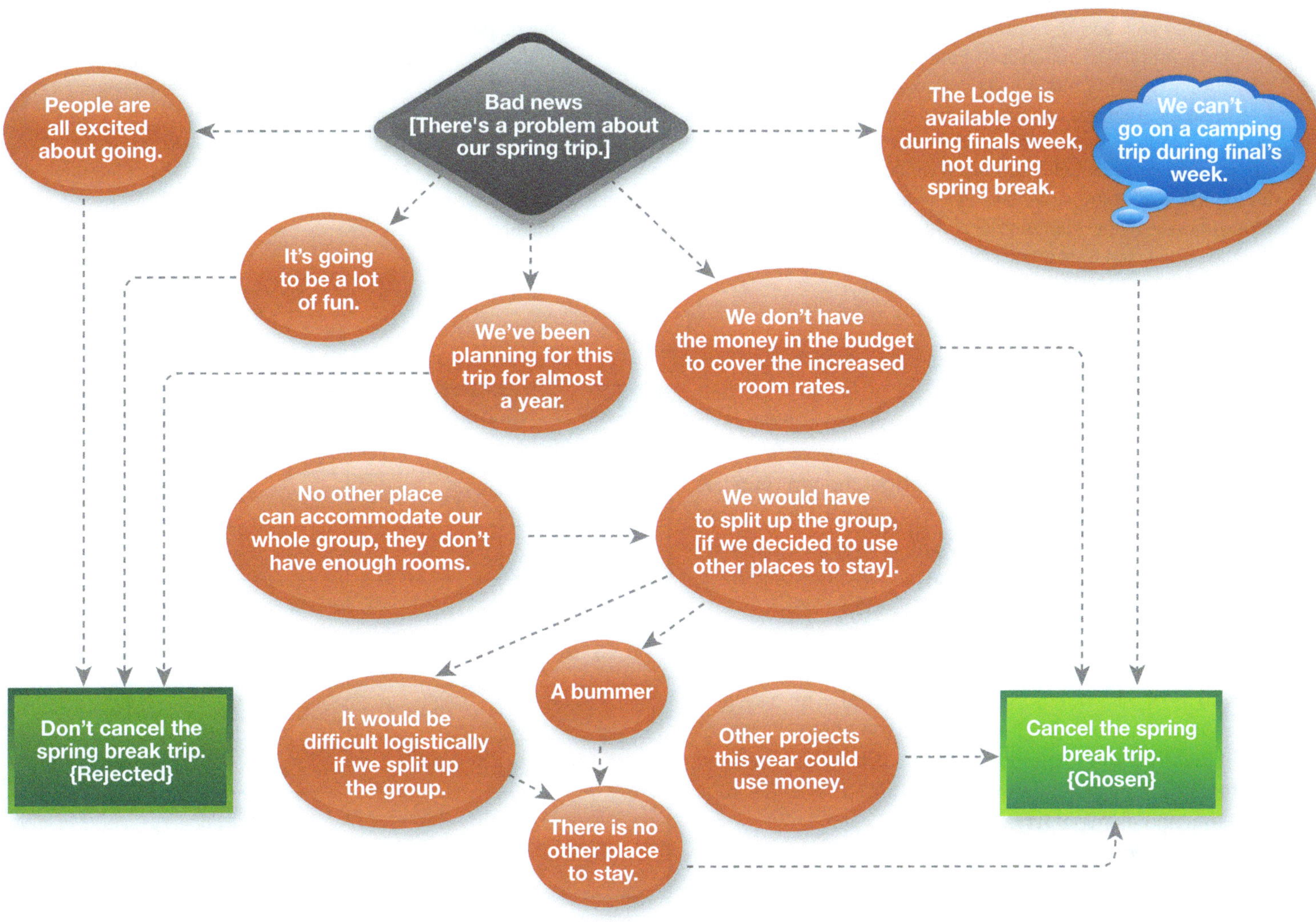

Meeting Transcript Continued:

James: I know we have to think about the budget. But we could pay for this year's trip using next year's funds.

Melissa: That would be great. Let's just raid the coffers for next year.

Felix: Spoken like a true graduating senior, James!

Eve: Calm down, you guys. Maybe James has a point.

Felix: No, Eve, he doesn't. We can't take the trip during finals week. And we still have problems with where to stay if we go during spring break. It just doesn't make sense.

James: Forget it.

James begins by acknowledging there's a budget problem. From this point of consensus, arguments could flow in either direction, so we can treat it as another invitation to the group to engage in deliberation. We will use the diamond shape for this when we map the group's decision-making process. It opens up the possibility that a new decision can be made. But James's invitation to reconsider is immediately met with a flurry of objections and counterarguments. From the context we can interpret Melissa's "That would be great" as something not meant to be taken literally. Using irony and the slanted and emotionally charged word *raid*, she rejects James' proposal. Felix joins in with his contemptuous "graduating senior" remark. Felix is implying that James doesn't care about what future problems he might be making for the club because he will have graduated and left. Eve tries to keep things civil and to reopen the deliberation with a respectfully neutral observation, "Maybe James has a point." But Felix counters by reminding everyone about the issues James's proposal simply ignored. In the end James abandons the effort to salvage the trip. He's so frustrated he says, "Forget it."

How should we map that remark? "Forget it" is a powerful signal that James is abandoning the effort to salvage the

Thinking Critically — Interpret with Care and Precision

The first 90 seconds of the Huckabee interview contains so much interpersonal respect and warmth that it invites its own interpretation. Perhaps Jon Stewart and his guest were trying to demonstrate that people who disagree can still treat each other as friends. Knowing the sensitivities of his studio and viewing audience around the abortion issue, Jon Stewart makes it a point to acknowledge that both he and his guest are white men.

Claims like the following can often be heard in a discussion about abortion. With as much truth seeking and open-mindedness as you can muster, do some research first and then develop the strongest reasons for each of the claims. Write out and map the arguments in support of each.

(A) A living human embryo is a living human being.

(A′) A living human embryo is not a person.

(B) It is never ethically justifiable to take another person's life intentionally.

(B′) At times the intentional killing of another person is ethically justifiable.

trip. Discontinuing a line of reasoning can be a very important turning point in the decision-making process. We could map it with an oval, but that would not fully convey the force of this element in the group's critical thinking about the trip. Another shape would be better. We will use a ***hexagon*** to convey that a line of reasoning has been abandoned. A hexagon marks an ending point of a line of reasoning that otherwise would have eventually connected to a conclusion. See Map 11.[x]

To separate any notes or interpretive comments added by the analyst from what the speakers themselves said, simply put the analyst's notations inside ***{braces}***. The hexagon with the word *silence* inside the braces is the analyst's way of showing that the group abandoned the possibility of moving in that direction, toward not cancelling the trip, after Eve's suggestion that James might have a point.

Looking for more example maps? There are several in the Appendix that display real decisions people have made about important personal and public issues. This Appendix also illustrates some creative ways to use and to extend the basic argument and decision-making system presented in this chapter.

Mapping Conventions[vii]

(green rectangle)	Rectangle	Conclusion or Decision
(shaded rectangle)	Shaded Rectangle	Choice not Selected
(oval)	Oval	Reason Supporting a Claim
- - - - - - ->	Connecting Lines with Arrowheads	Intended Flow of Reasoning from Reason to Claim
[....]	Brackets	Clarification of Speaker's Intended Meaning
(cloud)	Cloud	Implicit but Unspoken Element
(wide arrow)	Wide Arrow	Objection or Counterargument
(diamond)	Diamond	Recognition of the Need to Decide Invitation to Deliberate
(hexagon)	Hexagon	Abandonment of a Line of Reasoning
{....}	Braces	Analyst's Note or Interpretive Comment

Thinking Critically — Analyze and Map the Arguments or Decisions in These Quotes

1. "Swimming is a great workout. When you swim you use all your muscles."
2. "It's no use texting her. She lost her phone yesterday."
3. "If it weren't for how much it costs and how big it is, I'd buy that TV for our bedroom."
4. Why did *Billboard* stop listing older albums on its "Billboard 200" web page? Simple—it's about money. The recording companies make money selling the most popular new albums. There is no money for them in the old releases people can download from iTunes.
5. "Michael Jackson was truly the 'king of pop.' Just look at all that he achieved. He was a pop sensation by the time that he was 11 years old. His album, *Thriller*, was the best-selling album of all time. He started out in show business when he was only 5, and he performed for more than 40 years. And he had millions of fans all over the world."
6. "People believe that small class sizes are essential for better learning. I'm not convinced. I say that a good teacher with a large group can be just as effective as a lousy teacher with a small group."
7. "A study in the San Mateo County schools of second grade students' reading and math skills shows that students from classes averaging 15 to 20 students scored significantly higher than students from classes averaging 25 to 35 students.

A second study looking at the same test scores for fourth and fifth grade students in the Fresno County schools showed the same results. Kids from the schools with average class sizes around 30 had significantly lower scores, on average, than did kids coming from schools with class sizes around 17. Three other studies, all of them conducted several years ago in Los Angeles, San Diego, and Anaheim, reported similar findings. So, it is reasonable to conclude that average class size makes a difference when it comes to elementary school students' test score results in math and reading."

8 "Whoever loves winter loves cold, snow, and warm sweaters. Uncle Bill loves those things. I guess it's fair to say that he loves winter."

9 "Everyone believes that change is possible. So, change is definitely possible!"

10 "Nobody really believes in climate change. You can tell that by how people act. Political leaders don't pass the legislation needed to change our nation's dependence on coal and oil. Consumers don't install solar heating, and they don't buy electric cars. We keep building hotels and condos along the ocean in places that will flood as the sea levels rise. We pave over our farms to build suburbs. Instead of wearing a sweater, we keep the thermostat too high in the winter. Instead of taking off our suit jackets, we keep our office buildings too cold in the summer."

11 "Many families who have pet dogs also have children. Julio and Teresa have a cute pet dog named Bowser. I know because Teresa was talking about Bowser and how he loves to put his paws on the windowsill and bark at the passing cars. I overheard her telling Arnold about Bowser and the cars last week. So, long story short, Julio and Teresa probably have a couple of kids, too."

12 "I need a break! It's been nothing but nonstop work since last Thursday. I didn't even get a weekend. My parents visited unexpectedly, and that was majorly stressful."

13 "So, let me get this right. You're Harvey's sister's husband. And you're saying that Harvey is actually my uncle. So, this makes his sister my aunt. And, I guess that makes you my uncle, too. Wow."

14 "I think we should have a law to limit salaries for fat-cat CEOs if their companies are receiving government bailout money. That money comes from our taxes. I don't want it going to those same CEOs who screwed up in the first place. Why should we reward them for failing?"

15 The new store manager called the staff together and said, "Looking at our marketing, I think we need to make some changes. First, the display in the store window looks like something out of the 1980s. It's dated and shabby looking. Second, our in-store signage isn't colorful. There are no pictures of happy people. The signs are so small they are hard to read. And they are positioned in places that make them unnecessarily hard for our customers to find. Third, we have to do something about our Web site. When was the last time it was updated—2001? It is clunky, confusing, wordy, and has lots of out-of-date information. Our phone number on the Web site is wrong, for heaven's sake! Finally, our newspaper ads are a total waste of money. Why are we paying graphic designers and printers to produce things nobody pays any attention to? We keep printing 10 percent coupons in those newspaper ads but we have not had any customers bring in a coupon from one of those ads in over three months."

16 "Everyone has two biological parents. Each of them in turn had two biological parents. So, it must be true that in our grandparents' day there were four times as many people as there are today!"

17 "I was about to register online for music updates, but decided not to. The thing was that if you registered they gave you an e-mail account. You couldn't use any of your existing e-mail accounts. And the last thing I wanted was one more e-mail account. It takes too much of my day to check the three I already have."

18 Analyze and map the argument "sovereignty" which Jon Stewart makes in the extended Huckabee interview: Access the interview at **www.mythinkinglab.com**.

Watch the **Video** on **mythinkinglab.com**

19 *Frontline*, the PBS documentary series, describes how for-profit colleges are changing how Americans think about higher education. The PBS Web site highlights the May 4, 2010 *Frontline* broadcast, "College Inc." with "The business of higher education is booming. It's a $400 billion industry fueled by taxpayer money." Analyze and map the arguments and counterarguments as presented in that PBS documentary for the claim that the business is booming and that its boom is being fueled by taxpayer money. Connect to it at **www.mythinkinglab.com** or on the Web at **http://video.pbs.org/video/1485280975**

Watch the **Video** on **mythinkinglab.com**

20 The long-running Showtime series *Penn & Teller: Bullshit!* examines the arguments for some of the most cherished urban myths, popular misconceptions, and "Internet Truisms" in our culture. The show is definitely not PG. There is always a dollop of vulgarity and sexual explicitness to these broadcasts. But each show does make an argument, not necessarily a strong argument, but an argument nevertheless. In the case of show 10 of season 8, "Vaccinations" (August 28, 2010), Penn and Teller argue that the anti-vaccination movement is, well, not to put too fine a point on it, thoroughly mistaken. Analyze and map their arguments as objectively as possible. You can access this show and many episodes directly from the Showtime Web site or visit **www.mythinkinglab.com** for the link.

Watch the **Video** on **mythinkinglab.com**

MAP > it > OUT 11

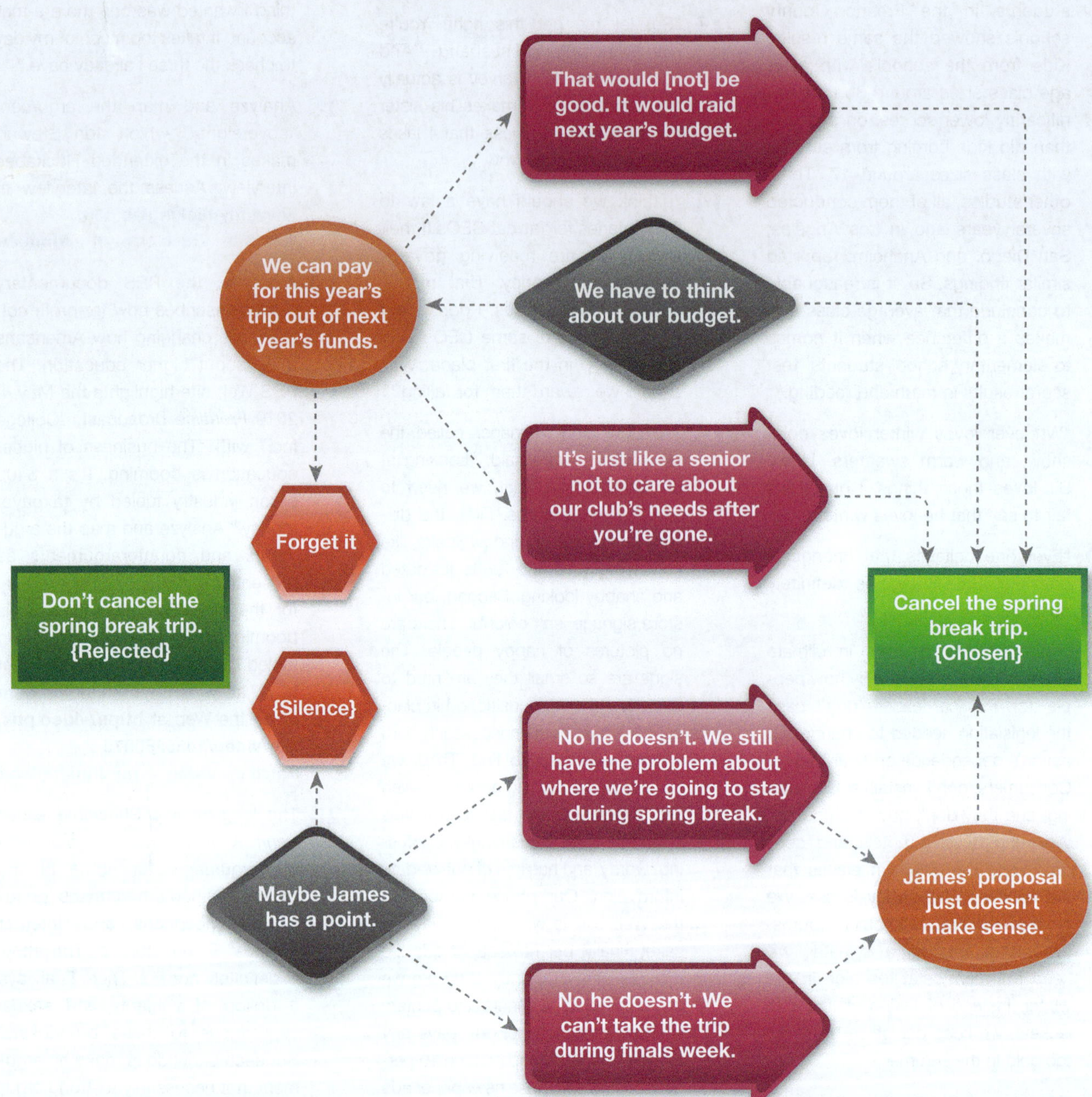
That would [not] be good. It would raid next year's budget.
We can pay for this year's trip out of next year's funds.
We have to think about our budget.
It's just like a senior not to care about our club's needs after you're gone.
Forget it
Don't cancel the spring break trip. {Rejected}
Cancel the spring break trip. {Chosen}
{Silence}
No he doesn't. We still have the problem about where we're going to stay during spring break.
James' proposal just doesn't make sense.
Maybe James has a point.
No he doesn't. We can't take the trip during finals week.

CHAPTER REVIEW 05

An argument is a claim plus the reason offered in support of the truth of that claim. We make arguments and offer reasons to explain our decisions and to reason through our problems. Often, we make multiple arguments, pro and con, when we are deliberating. In real life, human communication is highly expeditious. Verbal and nonverbal elements comprise human communication. It is also layered with humor, irony, sarcasm, and, quite often, complex and potentially divergent purposes. In a given context, people often express aloud some, but not all, of the elements of their arguments because so much is implicit and understood by the people with whom we are conversing. But to properly interpret what people mean and to analyze their arguments in an objective and fair-minded way, we must make explicit all the premises contained in a person's reason and all the unspoken assumptions that the person relies upon to support his or her claim.

Mapping is a technique for analyzing arguments and decisions. In mapping a person's reasons and claims, we make explicit and accessible the ideas that the person has advanced for the conclusion he or she has reached or the decision made. The map displays the flow of the person's reasoning from reasons through intermediate claims to the final conclusion. The map of a human decision can display the realization that a decision or deliberation is needed, lines of reasoning pursued, implicit but unspoken ideas relied upon, choices not selected, objections or counterarguments advanced, and lines of reasoning that may have been abandoned. Maps not only aid us in our interpretation and analysis of a person's thinking or a group's thinking, but they permit other people to collaborate with us in making and improving the interpretation and analysis. The goals of this chapter are (1) to strengthen our skills in analyzing people's claims and their reasons accurately and with precision, and (2) to provide a product of our analyses that others can improve and critique. Argument and decision mapping achieve both goals. Applying this technique strengthens our analytical and interpretive skills. And the product of our analyses, namely the argument and decision maps, are open to others to review, evaluate, and assist us to refine.

KEY TERMS

make an argument is the process of giving a reason in support of a claim. (p. 88)

claim refers to the statement that the maker of the argument is seeking to show to be true or probably true. (p. 88)

conclusion is another way of referring to an argument's claim. (p. 88)

reason is the basis provided by the argument maker to show that the claim is true or probably true. (p. 88)

argument refers to the combination of a person's claim and the reason a person presents in support of that claim. (p. 88)

premises are the statements, explicitly asserted or contextually assumed and implicit, that comprise an argument's reason. Each reason is a separate set of premises. (p. 89)

FIND IT ON MYTHINKINGLAB.COM

- The *Law & Order: Special Victims Unit* clip that opens this chapter follows a mother's decision not to vaccinate her child against measles. The argument is similar to some heard as parents weighed the risks of H1N1 vaccination against the risks of the disease itself. Visit www.mythinkinglab.com to view the clip. Visit **http://www.cdc.gov/measles/** to learn more about this disease, the most recent statistics on its prevalence, and recommendations of precautions for unimmunized international travelers and parents to consider. Watch the Video on mythinkinglab.com
- Jon Stewart's interview with Mike Huckabee has been viewed more than 100,000 times online. You can access it directly from the hotlink at www.mythinkinglab.com. View the entire interview; it's remarkable. And look at the comments too. It was fascinating to see the critical thinking, or lack thereof, displayed on occasion in some of the comments. Watch the Video on mythinkinglab.com
- The final two Bonus Exercises are challenging. Both rely on material you can access at www.mythinkinglab.com. One uses a clip from *The Daily Show* and the other uses an interview with Dennis Miller. They make us wonder about the relationship between critical thinking and the kinds of skills required to be a successful comedian-commentator. Watch the Video on mythinkinglab.com

Exercises

REFLECTIVE LOG

In regard to a choice a friend has made, ask, "Why do you decide to do that?" After the friend gives his or her initial response, ask that she or he elaborate so that you can understand his or her thinking. In your log, explain why you decided to ask that friend about that particular decision, describe the context within which your conversation occurred, and write down the questions you used to get a full and accurate understanding of your friend's reasoning. Then write your friend's response as fully as possible. Capture not only the option chosen, but the other options considered and the reasons leading to rejecting those options and selecting the option chosen. Carefully analyze what your friend said, but do not evaluate. In your log, map the decision your friend made, showing the reasoning process as objectively and fair-mindedly as possible, whether you agree or disagree with it. In fact, go out of your way *not* to reveal your evaluation of your friend's decision—be as analytical as possible without being evaluative. Share a draft of the map with your friend and explain to your friend how to interpret it. Listen to your friend's comments about the accuracy of your analysis as it is revealed in the draft decision map you made. Note in your log all the amendments or revisions your friend wants to offer. Make another draft of the decision map in your log and compare the two side by side. Reflect on what you learned by allowing your friend to view and comment on your analysis. Did your friend change his or her story, add more reasons in favor of the selected choice, add more reasons opposed to rejected choices, ask you to remove argument strands that looked like weak reasons, or ask you to bolster argument strands that looked flimsy?

Using the Holistic Critical Thinking Scoring Rubric from Chapter 1, add a final part to this section of your reflective log in which you permit yourself a few evaluative comments on your friend's decision making.

THREE-PERSON GROUP

Working in a team with two other students, identify an issue in this week's campus newspaper. Then, go to the office of the faculty members or administrators involved and respectfully ask for 15 or 20 minutes to talk about the issue. Bring a tape recorder and ask permission to tape the person's comments. Be open about this; never secretly tape conversations. Explain that the purpose is so that you can be accurate in your portrayal of the person's point of view. Then interview the person with particular emphasis on questions such as:

- Why did you think that?
- Why did you do that?
- Why is that a problem?
- Why is that a good way to resolve the issue?

After the interview, transcribe the things the person said and number each sentence or statement made so you can refer to that statement more easily in your analysis. Then make a map of the person's reasoning. If the interview transcript is too long, focus instead on shorter segments.

EXPLAIN WHAT IS WRONG

1. A good analyst will fix the obvious mistakes in a person's argument.
2. Every line of reasoning in a map eventually connects to a conclusion.
3. Unless people actually say what's on their minds, we can't tell what they are thinking.
4. Every sentence in an argument gets represented by an oval.
5. Argument maps differ from decision maps because argument maps are used when an individual's reasoning is being displayed, but decision maps are used when a group's reasoning is being displayed.

ANALYZE AND MAP THE FRIENDS' DECISION MAKING

1. Decision to join ROTC

Ana: Hey, girl! Guess what? I just came from the recruitment office. I think I should join ROTC. I have always been interested in the Army.

Caroline: It's just . . .

Ana: What?

Caroline: I don't know. There is a war going on. You could be sent. Isn't that, like, dangerous?

Ana: This is the best time to join—when I can make a difference.

Caroline: I could so totally see you in fatigues, looking cute.

Ana: Be serious.

Caroline: I am being serious, at least about the danger part. I'd be afraid.

Ana: ROTC is a way to pay for my education. By the time I graduate, the war will be over anyway.

Caroline: Whatever. It's not for me. But you'd be great, Lieutenant!

2. Decision to buy a gun

A young woman who lives alone hears that a neighbor's apartment was broken into. She knows that neighbor. The woman is just like her—single, full-time job, pet cat, part-time student. Not one of those old-white-guy-NRA-gun-nuts by any means. It's terrifying to think that somebody is breaking into apartments in the neighborhood. What does the person want, money? What if it's a rapist? So, the young woman decides to purchase a gun and keep it, loaded, in the top drawer of her nightstand. She thought about moving, but that would have cost her a lot of money, and it would have been really disruptive and time consuming. She thought about getting a watch dog, but then she would have all the responsibilities that go along with having another pet. Dogs are more trouble than cats by a lot. She thought about trying to find a roommate, but she wasn't sure she could find anyone whom she really would want to share her apartment with. And finding someone would take a lot of time and effort, too. Forget that, the burglar-rapist-whatever-jerk is in the neighborhood right now. And she thought about just doing nothing; after all she has a deadbolt on the door and she's on the third floor so sleeping with a window open isn't that much of a risk.

3. Decision not to have heart valve surgery
An elderly widower sits alone in his silent house. He is short of breath, and sleeping is difficult because aortic heart valve stenosis has caused fluid to accumulate in his chest. The cardiologist he saw earlier in the week recommended surgery. Yes, he knows he must decide whether to have the operation before it is too late. The doctor said in a year or so without an operation his heart will fail completely, and he will die. His children, now all middle-aged and living far away, have phoned to urge him to have the surgery. He knows they are worried about him and that they are trying to talk some sense into him. Ah, but they are young. Is it really worth all the pain and bother of heart surgery just so that afterward he can return to his current life? He'll still be alone most days. He'll still be struggling with the problems of old age. He might not survive the surgery. He thinks not.

4. Decisions to donate a live kidney to a friend.
"Ah, well, I found that, um, I saw a very dear friend of mine in trouble and, ah . . . I didn't like the uh, the uh, prospects for him if he didn't get a live donor. I didn't like the idea of him being on dialysis or waiting for a kidney for several years. And I love him and I love his wife and his baby daughter. And I felt that I've got two kidneys, I don't need both and it was, it was a decision that I made in about 60 seconds or so. Yeah. . . . So, as soon as I found out from him, . . . He said, "And it looks like I'm going to need a transplant," I thought about it for maybe 60 seconds and said, "Well, count me in as a possible donor if you want to have a test done on me."[xi]

5. Decision to buy the '10 model instead of the 2013
"You see, I need a car to get to work and school. And I plan to keep it a long time; I'll probably drive it till the wheels come off or I get to 250,000 miles. Beside durability, I'm big on safety. So I visited **www.SaferCar.gov** to see which models had 5-star ratings, and a Honda Civic seemed the best way to go. It was affordable—which is big—and reliable; and it had good safety ratings too. Then I went to **www.Cars.com**, **www.Edmunds.com**, and **www.AutoTrader.com** to find out more about the Civic and a few other makes and models, just to compare prices. I even went to the home pages of Honda, Acura, Nissan, Mazda, Subaru, Ford, Hyundai, Chevrolet, Dodge, and Chrysler. That took a lot of time! I used the "build your own" feature, which they all have, to see what it would cost to get exactly what I was looking for. Long story short, it turns out I'm back looking at Civics. The other makes and models each had some good features, but none that I could find were able to combine price, reliability, trade-in value, safety, size, style, and fuel efficiency the way the Civic did. So I settled on looking at Civics. I liked the Si Coupe, which is very sporty. I found I could get a 2013 for about $28,500, including leather seats and 6-speed manual transmission. That is very fun to drive! There were some new 2012 models available, but the prices were only 1K lower. Then I found this great-looking racing-blue 2010 Civic Si. It's a four door, but that's not a problem. The dealer had used it as a demo model and it was fully loaded with all the accessories. The car had only 100 miles on it, too, which is as good as new as far as mileage goes. The price was $25,500 out the door, and that includes taxes, fees, and destination charges. I figured I could save $3,000 and get a machine that was in every way identical to the 2013. And in a color I like a lot better! So that's how I decided to buy the 2010 for $25,500."
[Hint: This passage includes a description of a process of fact finding and a series of arguments whereby the speaker narrows the choices until eventually deciding on one in particular. Your challenge is to sort through the passage and find the reasons, the intermediary claims, and the connecting points that show why the one option was selected and all others rejected. This is a challenging passage and your map will probably go through three or four revisions. Although not an easy decision to map, it is authentic. It comes from an interview with a person who spent several days learning the facts and reflecting on options. To that person it was effort well spent because of how much money the car would cost and because of how long the person expected to have the car.]

BUT WHAT DOES FOX AND MSNBC SAY?

Every election year offers strong critical thinkers plenty of delicious arguments. They are made by proponents and opponents of both sides of every ballot initiative and the supporters and detractors of every major candidate. Radio and television entertainers/commentators on Comedy Central, FOX, HBO, MSNBC, and CNN comment extravagantly, provocatively, and convincingly (to some). Pick an issue or a candidate. Locate an editorial/discussion/debate as presented on one or more of the networks listed, and map the arguments presented. This exercise may challenge not only your analytical skills but also your ability to remain objective and "above the fray" as you dig out the reasons, counterarguments, intermediary claims, and, most importantly, the unspoken assumptions.

VIDEO AND ANALYZE

We all know people with whom we disagree. For this exercise identify one such person in your life. Perhaps it's a friend, classmate, sibling, whomever. The two conditions are that the person has to be articulate enough to make arguments that you do not accept and that the person has to agree to help you with this exercise. With the peron's knowledge, permission, and consent, videotape the person and yourself discussing a topic about which you disagree. Your job in the videotape is to interview the person. Explain to the person that you you will be asking the person to give reasons for their point of view on the topic. But you will not be debating the person. Instead you will be asking questions aimed at eliciting the person's assumptions and premises and the person's counterarguments to the most obvious objections. But, again, remind the person that you are not bringing up the objections in order to make the opposite argument. Only to make explicit the fullness of the person's own position. Then, after the video session, and after the person agrees that indeed it does capture his or her thinking, map out the person's arguments for his or her claim. Save the videotape because you may well want to review the tape in order to practice your argument evaluation skills when we get to the chapters on evaluating arguments.

BONUS EXERCISE: #1 THE CRAMER SMACKDOWN

The generally affable host of *The Daily Show*, Jon Stewart, lashes out at his guest, Jim Cramer, calling him a snake oil salesman and accusing him of contributing to the devastation of the financial security of millions of Americans. In the third part of his interview with Jim Cramer, Jon Stewart claims that the financial news industry has certain ethical responsibilities to the viewing public. Here's your challenge: Map Stewart's arguments indicating which elements were actually spoken in the interview and which are unspoken but still functionally part of his thinking as Stewart makes his case. Locate the interview at www.mythinkinglab.com.

Watch the Video on mythinkinglab.com

By the time Cramer appeared on *The Daily Show*, he and Stewart had already gone back and forth about this. Stewart's stinging criticisms had been leveled against Cramer, and Cramer had responded on his own CNBC show.

To analyze Stewart's arguments, we have to step past his strident angry tone, his puns, his humor, and his sarcasm. We have to dig out his claims and reasons. Stewart's main claim is that Cramer is ethically culpable for having caused great harm. Stewart's argument goes like this: On CNBC, a financial news network, Jim Cramer presents himself as a financial expert and gives his viewers financial advice. Stewart reasons that: If you have a show on a network that portrays itself as providing financial news, and if your job there is to give financial advice, then you have the ethical duty to be honest with your audience. Within this statement is the implication that you have the ethical duty to provide advice in the financial interest *of your audience*.

(Not just to get higher Nielsen ratings and to make more money for CNBC.) But, the fact is, John Stewart says, Mr. Cramer, you were not honest. Instead, you knowingly gave misleading information, and you did this consistently over a long period of time. Your viewers trusted you, and you conned them. You should be ashamed of yourself; you are ethically culpable.

Stewart's argument depends heavily on the key assertion that Cramer knowingly gave misleading information. If this step in the argument strand is mistaken, then Stewart's case against Cramer disintegrates. So, Stewart bolsters that intermediary claim with evidence in the form of video clips. These become the reasons Stewart uses to demonstrate that Cramer knew better, but kept on giving bad advice.

BONUS EXERCISE: #2 THE DENNIS MILLER CHALLENGE

Known for his caustic wit, expansive vocabulary, and conservative politics, Dennis Miller often entertains on FOX. Access his October 21, 2009 interview with Bill O'Reilly at www.mythinkinglab.com. Listen to Miller's arguments for his claim that Sarah Palin is not going rogue in spite of the title of her recent book. And listen, too, for Miller's arguments accusing Balloon Boy's father of being a horrible parent. Map Miller's arguments, as given in that interview, for those two claims.

Watch the Video on mythinkinglab.com

Read the Chapter on mythinkinglab.com
Listen to the Chapter Audio on mythinkinglab.com

Evaluate the Credibility of Claims and Sources

WHICH sources should I trust?
WHICH claims should I believe?
HOW can I evaluate a claim's truth or falsity for myself?

RIP Selma Goncalves,

born April 30, 1988, on Cape Verde, an island off the west coast of Africa. Shot to death January 21, 2009, in Brockton, MA, USA, a victim of hate in America.

On January 21, 2009, Selma Goncalves, age 20, was shot to death as she fled her apartment in Brockton, Massachusetts. Inside that apartment her sister lay critically wounded after being raped and shot. The hate-filled killer had driven off in his van in search of other non-whites and had shortly thereafter shot to death a 72-year-old West African man who happened to be out walking. When arrested, the shooter, Keith Luke, age 22, told police that he had gone to the women's apartment intent on murder and rape. He said that he planned later that night "to go to a local synagogue and open fire on bingo players." Having purchased his weapon and ammunition six months earlier, he told authorities that his plan was to "kill as many nonwhites and Jews as possible."[i] Prior to his trial, Luke's defense attorney claimed that Luke, who had a history of mental illness, came to believe that he should kill to "defend the white race." He had apparently developed some of his ideas by repeatedly visiting Web sites that glorified racially motivated murder and lone-wolf domestic terrorism. These white supremacist hate-based Web sites display skinheads beating and killing nonwhite people and immigrants.[ii] Watch the emotionally moving video clip from Selma's funeral.

Watch the Video on mythinkinglab.com

Tragic events like these are all too frequent. Inevitably, the aftermath produces an outpouring of

<<< Morris Dees of the Southern Poverty Law Center has dedicated his life to critical thinking in the real world by working on behalf of social justice.

grief and sympathy as well as soul-searching questions: Are there constitutional ways to prevent people like this killer from acquiring guns and ammunition? How can we protect ourselves from violence and hate crimes committed by our fellow citizens without violating their rights? As repugnant as they may be to most of us, can visiting hate-mongering Web sites cause a person to go on a killing rampage? Some people will claim yes, and others no, in response to difficult yet important questions like these. Some people may give reasons, and some may simply assert their opinions with great conviction.

As critical thinkers, how can we evaluate claims like these, particularly when reasons are not given? Answering this question is the focus of this chapter.

Assessing the Source—Whom Should I Trust?

As critical thinkers, we are inquisitive truth-seekers with a healthy sense of skepticism. Positive critical thinking habits of mind incline us not to accept naively every claim someone may happen to make. Like a store clerk examining a twenty dollar bill to be sure it is not counterfeit, strong critical thinkers use their knowledge and skills to assess the *credibility of the source* and the *plausibility of the claim* itself.

CLAIMS WITHOUT REASONS

In the previous chapter on analyzing arguments, we defined the term *argument* as the combination of a claim plus the reason given to support that claim. But what if the speaker simply makes the claim and does not give any reasons? A tweet, a sound bite, a headline, a poster, a passing comment, a billboard, a rumor—there are so many situations in real life in which people make claims without giving their reasons. Here are some examples:

1. Salesclerk to customer trying on a sports jacket: "That looks great on you."
2. Political commentator speaking about a member of the opposition party: "So-and-so's proposal will cripple the economy."
3. Person under arrest to police investigator after hearing that if he implicates others he will receive a lighter sentence: "Well, now that I think of it. There was this guy. He calls himself "B-Lucky." The whole thing was his idea in the first place."
4. U.S. top military commander: "It will take another 40,000 troops."
5. Candidate interviewing for a job: "I have a college degree and three years of experience."
6. Best friend: "You really need to do something about how much you drink at parties."
7. Parent to daughter in the eighth grade: "No, it is not a good idea to go out with a high school junior."
8. Co-worker to new employee: "Everybody here plays fantasy football using their office computer."
9. Roommate: "The apartment manager was looking for you this morning."
10. Doctor to patient: "The lab test came back positive."

The question that comes to mind for critical thinkers when they hear a claim made but no reason given is, "Can I trust this person to be telling me the truth or even to know the truth?" Looking back over those ten examples, we can think of reasons why we probably can or probably cannot trust the speaker in each case. For example, in #1 maybe the salesclerk's compliment is nothing more than an insincere sales tactic used to get the customer to buy the jacket. Maybe the salesclerk would have said the same thing if the jacket looked dreadful. In #2, unfortunate as it may be, the criticism that a political commentator representing one party hurls at a member of the other party is occasionally exaggerated, inaccurate, and alarmist. In #3, the person who was arrested might say anything

that the police would find credible in order to reduce his sentence. So, in the first three examples we would be inclined to discount the claims because each of the speakers has an ulterior motive: to make a sale, to prevent you from voting for or supporting the other party, to receive a lesser punishment.

On the other hand, in #7 why shouldn't the daughter trust her parent's judgment in that case? She may not like the advice at all. And she may ignore it. But there is no obvious reason in normal circumstances to think that the parent has some ulterior motive that makes the parent untrustworthy. In fact, the opposite. Typically a parent has the child's best interests at heart, even if the child does not like the guidance the parent is offering and even if the parent can anticipate an unpleasant confrontation will ensue. In #10, the doctor example, we would also expect that the doctor has no ulterior motive. In normal circumstances, why would the patient not trust the doctor about the lab results? Yes, we can imagine a scenario or two in which a child should not trust her parent and a patient should not trust the doctor. But more likely than not, such scenarios would be implausible—interesting as movie scripts, but not likely to happen to most people in real life. When we do not know if a claim is true or false, and if we cannot independently evaluate it, then the question becomes one of trust. We ask ourselves *how can we use our critical thinking skills to evaluate the credibility of the source of the claim. Whom should we trust? Whom should we not trust?*

COGNITIVE DEVELOPMENT AND HEALTHY SKEPTICISM

The issue of trust—in particular, trust of authorities—is connected to our maturation. The below table "Levels of Thinking and Knowing" describes seven stages of maturation.[iii] For children in those early stages, trust in authority figures—primarily

Levels of Thinking and Knowing
(7) **"Sages"** – We can seek and discover many truths and we can address ill-structured problems with greater or lesser levels of success. But even what we call "knowledge" inevitably contains elements of uncertainty, for as we build from the known toward the unknown, new ways of organizing knowledge often yield unforeseen conceptual revolutions. Even well-informed opinion is subject to interpretation and reasoned revision. Yet, justifiable claims about the relative merits of alternative arguments can be made. We can assert with justifiable confidence that some judgments are rightly to be regarded as more reasonable, more warranted, more justifiable, more sensible, or wiser than others. We solve problems the way a truth-seeker does, but we realize that judgments must often be made in contexts of risk and uncertainty, that some issues admit greater precision than others, that at times we must reconsider our judgments and revise them, and that at other times we must hold firm in our judgments. Wisdom comes as we learn which are which.
(6) **"Truth-Seekers"** – Some claims are true and some are not; some evaluations or approaches are not as good as others. Some reasons, perspectives, and theories are actually superior to others. Information is essential, uncertainty is real, and context is important. But not everything is context bound. We can reasonably and rationally compare evidence, opinions, theories, and arguments across contexts. We solve problems by following the reasons and the evidence with courage wherever they lead, by asking the tough questions, by being inquisitive, by being open-minded and tolerant about a wide range of ideas and possible explanations, by being persistent and systematic in our inquiry, and by not fearing what this process will turn up as possible answers.
(5) **"Relativists"** – Facts exist, but always and only in context. Everything is relative. There are no absolutes. Ill-structured problems abound. Every theory and every perspective is as good as every other theory or perspective. Proof and evidence are entirely context dependent. Disagreements about basic theories and fundamental principles cannot be resolved by any rational means because the criteria themselves are perpetually contested.
(4) **"Collectors"** – All knowledge is idiosyncratic—a collection of isolated facts to be memorized for later retrieval if needed. There are many separate databases—for example, scientific, business, political, and religious. They are not combinable. Information in one of them may or may not be consistent with information in another one of them. Uncertainty is real; external validation is impossible. So-called authorities and experts are just as limited as everyone else. To solve any problem, look for all the information you can find about that topic.
(3) **"Feelers"** – Authorities know everything that can be known now, but the evidence is incomplete, even to the authorities. Some things may never be known because of the limitations of the human mind. Uncertainty is real, so we need to be cautious or we are apt to stray and make mistakes. The best policy is to stick with beliefs that feel right to us because they are familiar, comfortable, and conform to what everyone else in our peer group thinks.
(2) **"Trusters"** – Truth is knowable. We have absolute confidence in the authorities who share the truth with us. All problems have solutions, and all questions have answers. What we do not know today will someday be known by somebody. Anyone who disagrees with the truth as presented by our authorities must be wrong. To question any element of the truth is to abandon all of it. We must learn to defend ourselves from any person or idea that threatens the truth.
(1) **"Touchers"** – To touch is to know. Knowledge is nothing but direct personal experience. Facts are absolute, concrete, and readily available. There are no lenses on experience; things are exactly as they appear to be.

their parents and teachers—is a major factor in shaping what young minds believe. Karen Kitchener and Patricia King, on whose work the "Levels of Thinking and Knowing" table is primarily based, report that most students entering college are stage 3 or stage 4, what we are calling "Feelers" and "Collectors." Many college students become "Relativists" as their studies progress. And there is still room for growth. Even the "Truth-Seeker" stage, which critical thinkers greatly value, is not the highest we can achieve.

Strong critical thinkers cultivate a healthy sense of skepticism. They do not trust the word of authority figures in the same uncritical way that those in the early stages of their cognitive development might. Nor are strong critical thinkers satisfied merely to collect information, even though it is important to be well informed. While valuing context and perspective, strong critical thinkers understand that some reasons, perspectives, and theories are actually superior to others. Strong critical thinking habits of mind—such as truth seeking, inquisitiveness, and judiciousness—impel us to try to apply our critical thinking skills to the question of trustworthiness. We know that there are many reasons why we should not always trust everything that anyone might tell us. Some people lie, some speak of things about which they have no expertise, some say things under duress that are not true, and some may have been deceived themselves and pass on misinformation unwittingly. We can be skeptical without being cynical. And certainly one good time to keep this in mind is when it comes to evaluating the credibility of sources.

AUTHORITY AND EXPERTISE

We have been using the word *authority* to refer to a person who is potentially a trustworthy source of information and good advice. In the context of cognitive development, the typical examples of authorities for children would be parents, grandparents, teachers, ministers, and police officers. But that is where "authority," as we have been using it, begins to reveal its problematic ambiguity and problematic vagueness.

"Authority" can also mean "a person with the rightful power to control the behavior of another." Parents and teachers have authority, in that sense of the word, over children. But as we mature, we realize that a police officer, our boss at work, our landlord, or even a teacher or parent may have the rightful power to control our behavior, but that does not necessarily make the person more knowledgeable than we are on a given topic.

The sense of the word *authority* we are looking for is "person with expertise." To a child, parents, ministers, teachers, and police officers are authorities in both senses of the term; children perceive them to be experts with the power to control behavior. Okay. But we are not children anymore. The authorities we may wish to trust are those with *expertise*.

Wikipedia offers a useful starting point for a discussion of expertise, including this characterization:

> An expert is a person with extensive knowledge or ability in a particular area of study. Experts are called in for advice on their respective subject, but they do not always agree on the particulars of a field of study. An expert can be, by virtue of training, education, profession, publication or experience, believed to have special knowledge of a subject beyond that of the average person, sufficient that others may officially (and legally) rely upon the individual's opinion. Historically, an expert was referred to as a sage. The individual was usually a profound thinker distinguished for wisdom and sound judgment. . . . An expert is someone widely recognized as a reliable source of technique or skill whose faculty for judging or deciding rightly, justly, or wisely is accorded authority and status by professional peers or the public in a specific well distinguished domain. . . . Experts have a prolonged or intense experience through practice and education in a particular field.[iv]

Thinking Critically — *Wikipedia!* OMG!

The bitter irony of citing *Wikipedia* in a discussion about the trustworthiness of sources screams out. Why should we trust *Wikipedia*, you may well wonder. *Wikipedia* is not a source; it's a vehicle. Anyone can edit a *Wikipedia* entry. How can we know if what it says is actually true? It might be plagiarized, it might be wrong in some important but subtle ways. Hey, it might be outright fiction! In fact, that's the same problem we have for everything we see on the Internet or in print: Who wrote that, and can we trust that person (or that government agency, corporation, or organization)? These days there is so much untruth, disinformation, misdirection, propaganda, and outright deceit on the Internet that we dare not believe it simply because we see it in Wikipedia or anywhere else on the Internet or in a tweet, text message, or TV infomercial.

Your challenge in this exercise is to fact-check the *Wikipedia* entry for "expertise" for its accuracy. We suggest you use three different ways to do this: (1) Go to the entry itself and see if you can tell who wrote it and what references it uses. Fact-check those references and Google the authors using *Google Scholar* to see if they are credible authorities on the topic of expertise. (2) Seek independent confirmation by looking up "expertise" in other, more trusted sources, including dictionaries, encyclopedias, and books on expertise. (3) Show the *Wikipedia* characterization of "expertise" to people who have expertise in their various fields, like your professors, and ask them if they would agree with the *Wikipedia* interpretation. If all three ways point to the accuracy of the entry, then good, we'll go with it. If the three ways diverge or contradict each other, we have problems. Use your analytical and interpretive skills to articulate an accurate understanding of "expertise" if the one in *Wikipedia* is defective.

Learned and Experienced

Two things a person must establish in order to be recognized as an expert on a given topic are that he or she is learned with regard to that topic and that he or she has significant relevant experience. The first condition, being learned, can be accomplished through formal education or through training under the guidance of good mentors and coaches. The second condition, having relevant experience, means that the person is not a novice or a beginner when it comes to the activities and practices associated with that topic.

We will use the word **expert** to refer to someone who is both experienced and learned in a given subject matter area or professional practice area. Establishing that a person is both learned and experienced is important in the legal context, because that person's expert testimony on matters within the domain of his or her expertise can be relied upon by juries when they deliberate the guilt or innocence of a person accused of a crime. We all have seen courtroom dramas where a pathologist, a fingerprint expert, or a psychiatrist is put on the witness stand to provide expert opinion with regard to the cause of death, the match of the fingerprints found at the scene of the crime and the fingerprints of the accused, or the mental state of the accused at the time of the crime. In standard examples, the people that the defense or the prosecution introduce as expert witnesses are considered to be qualified due to their many years of professional experience, formal education, and relevant state licenses.

As the movie *My Cousin Vinny* so aptly illustrates, on-the-job training and many years of practical experience can qualify a person as an expert in certain domains. Marisa Tomei, who plays a hairdresser and the fiancée of the defense attorney, played by Joe Pesci, is put on the witness stand as an expert in automobiles. The prosecuting attorney tries to discredit her as an expert, but fails. The judge accepts her as an expert on automobiles. We're told that this clip might be on YouTube.com or Hulu.com, but you can access it through Netflix or at www.mythinkinglab.com. Watch the Video on mythinkinglab.com

Determining that a person qualifies as an expert witness is a matter of serious concern for strong critical thinkers because the person's expertise, if established, gives us a good reason to consider putting our trust in what the person has to say regarding the area of his or her expertise.

Assuming that a person qualifies as an expert on X by virtue of prolonged, relevant experience, training, or education, what else could go wrong that would lead us not to find the person credible? Lots of things!

- The expert on X may be speaking about some other topic.
- The expert, having qualified long ago, may have failed to stay current on X.
- The expert on X may not be able to articulate exactly how X is done.
- The expert may be biased.
- The expert may lie or mislead.

- The expert may have a conflict of interest.
- The expert may give advice that is not in the interest of his or her client.
- The expert may be under duress, threatened, or constrained in some way.
- The expert may be uniformed or misinformed about the facts of the specific situation.
- The expert may have become mentally unstable.

On-Topic, Up-to-Date, and Capable of Explaining

Expertise with regard to a topic, X, implies that the expert is knowledgeable about X. But suppose that someone—say, an accomplished musical virtuoso—makes the claim, "The best way to eliminate pesky aphids from a rose garden is by spraying on a mix of water, mineral oil, and Murphy's soap." That concoction might work. But wait—gardening is not the virtuoso's area of expertise. Whatever measure of trust we would reasonably extend to the expert, were she or he speaking about music, does not carry over to claims the expert may make that are off-topic. Regarding gardening, the musical virtuoso is no more nor less of an expert than any other person. To be credible, the expert must be speaking on-topic.

A good friend of ours was an accomplished physician. She retired about 15 years ago and moved to Sarasota to enjoy her retirement playing golf and bridge. One of her friends asked her the other day about a cancer treatment that another physician had recommended. Unlike traditional chemotherapy, the treatment was one of the newer pharmacological approaches that targets the protein receptors on the cancer cells. Our friend rightly declined to offer an expert opinion about the new treatment method. Why? Because she knew that she had not kept up-to-date about advances in cancer treatment since her retirement. Although as a doctor she had the credentials to

An Expert on Hate in America?

Who keeps track of the haters? The shocking news stories about how some who hate express themselves through criminal violence always alarm and disappoint. Our hearts go out to the victims of hate attacks, like the awful events in Norway where a hate-filled extremist killed workers and injured passersby when he bombed the government building in Oslo and then, on the island, massacred so many innocent children at the youth camp.

There may be no one organization monitoring every hate group in the world, but at least one is trying to identify hate groups in America. The Southern Poverty Law Center is "a nonprofit civil rights organization dedicated to fighting hatred and bigotry, and to seeking justice for the most vulnerable members of society. Founded by civil rights lawyers Morris Dees [pictured at the beginning of this chapter] and Joseph Levin, Jr. in 1971, the SPLC is internationally known for tracking and exposing the activities of hate groups." To promote tolerance and respect in our nation's schools, "the Center produces and distributes documentary films, books, lesson plans and other materials free of charge." The disturbing but engaging 2011 documentary film, *Erasing Hate*, "chronicles the redemptive story of a violent, racist skinhead" who risks his life to renounce the white power movement. Over a period of almost two years "he undergoes an excruciating series of laser treatments to remove the racist tattoos that covered his face and hands."

In 2010 the SPLC identified 1,002 active hate groups in the United States. The SPLC defines a hate group as an organization that has "beliefs or practices that attack or malign an entire class of people, typically for their immutable characteristics." The Center compiled its 2010 list "using hate group publications and Web sites, citizen and law enforcement reports, field sources and news reports."

According to the SPLC, "hate group activities can include criminal acts, marches, rallies, speeches, meetings, leafleting or publishing." Appearing on the SPLC list "does not imply a group advocates or engages in violence or other criminal activity." While over one thousand hate groups were identified, the list does not attempt to represent everyone engaged in spewing hateful messages. The SPLC notes "Web sites appearing to be merely the work of a single individual, rather than the publication of a group, are not included in this list."

Citations are from the Southern Poverty Law Center Web site: **http://www.splcenter.org.** Dr. Facione, the lead author of *Think Critically*, has been a financial supporter of the SPLC for decades and has arranged for the Center's founder, Morris Dees, to speak on college campuses and to national organizations of academic leaders. Knowing where you can learn more about the SPLC for yourself, and knowing about Dr. Facione's endorsement and support of the Center's work, evaluate this claim made by Dr. Facione: "The SPLC is an expert on hate in America." www.mythinkinglab.com.

Norway children massacre story: **www.bbc.co.uk/news/world-europe-14265094**

See also, "The Invisible Hate Crime: How to combat hate crimes against people with disabilities," Jack Levin, *Miller-McCune,* March-April 2011, page 50.

Read the **Document** on **mythinkinglab.com**

provide an expert opinion about cancer treatment in general, as a responsible expert she knew that it would be wrong for her friend to rely on her expertise in this case.

We trust experts when they speak within their areas of expertise in part because we assume that, were they challenged, they could explain exactly why their claim is true or their advice

Does earning an advanced degree, a professional license, or a certification of advanced training mean that one is an expert?

is good. The capacity to explain why is a critical component of expertise. The second half of the *My Cousin Vinny* video clip illustrates this. Marisa Tomei offers the expert opinion that the defense's theory of the crime does not hold water. So the defense attorney, Joe Pesci, who had called her as a defense witness, demands that she explain exactly why she thinks that. She draws upon her extensive knowledge and experience as an expert to provide a factual, precise, and cogent explanation. And, in the process, the explanation she offers exonerates the defendants as well.

What if the expert cannot articulate the explanation? For example, a superstar athlete fails as a head coach and we learn afterward that the star was not able to teach others all that he or she knew about the game. The successful head coach turns out, instead, to be a former athlete who was good but not great. Unlike the person blessed with extraordinary natural ability, this person had to think constantly as a player about how to maximize his or her own talents to compete effectively against other, more skilled players. And those years of reflective practice translate later into the ability to teach and coach others.

There are many reasons why experts may fail to provide adequate explanations.

- Some may never have developed the practice of reflecting on their experiences to explain to themselves why events occurred as they did.
- Lacking the critical thinking habit of being foresightful, they may have failed to anticipate the likely effects of decisions and actions.
- Lacking the critical thinking habit of inquisitiveness, they may have failed to examine the implications of new information for their field of expertise.
- Experts who have weak skills in self-monitoring and self-correcting may not take the time to be sure that they can explain their current beliefs to themselves.
- Being unreflective, they may describe their own thinking using expressions like "I go with my gut" or "I just instinctively knew what I had to do." Unfortunately, statements like those explain nothing and teach nothing.[v]

It is difficult to place trust in experts when they cannot explain why they believe what they believe or why they do what they do. For the same reason, it is challenging to learn from these experts. Although we may be able to copy what they are doing, and it may even work, what we most need for learning is to know *why* it works. And these experts have a difficult time communicating that.

Consider this example: Suppose it is the first day of class and your Biology professor says, "This course will require more time than most other courses. So if you haven't got a job, don't bother getting one. If you thought you could work and study Biology in my class, think again." Suppose that someone asks the professor to explain the basis for that advice. Here are two possible responses:

Professor #1:
"Why did I say that? Because I say it to every class to warn them. I give out F's to people who can't perform in my class.

Professor #2:
"Working puts great demands on your time. In this course, you have three lecture hours each week plus a required lab each week. I demand experiments in each lab, and the reports from these experiments must be submitted in written form each week. If you do not pass in-class pop quizzes, I require you to attend review sessions. Our goal together is for you to learn biology, and I provide you with every opportunity to be successful. But I will not lower my standards, nor will I accept any excuses about your being too busy with other obligations. I grade on a curve and this course attracts the most serious and academically competitive students in biology. You will have to put a lot of time into this course just to get a passing grade. So I recommend that you not take on other responsibilities, like a job, that will pull you away from your studies."

Professor #1 offered nothing more than a statement of his or her own past practice and a veiled threat. Professor #2 explained why the course would demand a lot of time and why taking on outside responsibilities could become a problem for a student enrolled in this course.

We now have five conditions we can check when we are deciding whether or not a source is credible when that source makes a claim about topic X: Is the source experienced, learned, on-topic, up-to-date, and capable of explaining why his or her opinion on the matter is right?

Unbiased and Truthful

Experts are human beings and, like the rest of us, they may have biases. Olympic gymnastics and figure skating judges, every one an expert in his or her sport, are often accused of being biased in favor of athletes from some countries or against athletes from other countries. Or they are accused of showing favoritism toward more experienced athletes and being tougher when evaluating the performances of athletes who may be newer to that high level of competition. Ask anyone who has tried to umpire a baseball game or referee a high school basketball game, and they will tell you that accusations of bias are a regular feature of officiating.

If an expert is called as a witness in a trial and that expert happens to be biased in favor of or against defendants of a certain race or age or socioeconomic status, that fact alone should be enough to cause the jury not to trust that expert's testimony. Expert claims are supposed to be grounded in learning and experience, not in prejudices, biases, or favoritism of any kind.

But even unbiased experts may elect not to speak the truth. Recall that great scene in the 1992 film *A Few Good Men* where Jack Nicholson tells Tom Cruise that he couldn't handle the truth. Nicholson's character, a senior military officer and clearly an expert by training and experience, loses his temper. In his outburst, he explains why Tom Cruise, like so many of his

complacent countrymen, does not want to know the truth about what, in Nicholson's opinion, the military must do to keep this nation safe and free. In other words, Nicholson's character is condoning our nation's defense experts' practice of misdirecting and lying to the American people. Access this clip at **www.mythinkinglab.com**. **Watch** the **Video** on **mythinkinglab.com**

We can interpret Nicholson's character as practicing the "Noble Lie," as proposed by Plato in *The Republic*.[vi] In Plato's opinion, most people do not recognize their own best interests, nor can they fully comprehend what is in society's best interests. Plato's recommendation was that well-informed leaders who know the whole truth should guide the rest of us by using, when necessary, the "Noble Lie." That is, Plato proposes that the leaders should flat out lie to the people, if they are impelled by the most beneficent and purest of motives. In other words, the Noble Lie is a lie our leaders tell us because the lie is in our best interests. Not knowing the truth, we would be passive, content, and compliant. Social harmony would be preserved, unrest and discontent prevented. Of course, when the lie is discovered, the people may

Thinking Critically: Who Checks What the Experts Claim?

We tend to think of our elected leaders and those who comment regularly on Washington issues as people with expertise and experience. But because of conflicts of interest, we have reason to be skeptical. After all, aren't the first three rules of politics "Get Elected, Get Re-elected, and Get Re-Re-elected"? And aren't the first three values in broadcasting "Ratings, Ratings, and Ratings"? So when we hear claims like these, what can we do to check the facts?

> "In the first year of the Obama administration, more jobs were created in the private sector than in the eight years of the Bush administration."—Rep. Nancy Pelosi, Speaker of the House, 2007–2011.
>
> The Bush tax cuts "created about 8 million jobs over the first 10 years that they were in existence. We've lost about 5 million of those jobs during this recession."—Rep. John Boehner, Speaker of the House, 2011–
>
> "The clear majority of Republican voters think that any deficit reduction package should have a balanced approach and should include some revenues."—President Barack Obama
>
> Nevada will be "energy independent within the immediate future."—Senator Harry Reed, Majority Leader of the U.S. Senate.
>
> "A clause hidden in the Obamacare bill, which is now law, gives Obama the right to form a private army."—Victoria Johnson, columnist for the WorldNetDaily (and former SNL cast member).
>
> "The only growth sector that we've had in the last two years in America is government growth."—Senator Kay Bailey Hutchinson, Texas

To see which of the above statements were "Barely True" and which were "Pants on Fire False," visit the Web site of the 2009 Pulitzer Prize–winning *St. Petersburg Times*, **www.Politifact.com**. When you are there, look at the evidence that is presented in order to back up the evaluation. That Web site pulls together documentation and statistical evidence to support its assessment about the truth or falsity of the claims being made—far more work than any of us individually could undertake on our own, but necessary to the democracy so we voters can make informed decisions.

We were talking with a political observer the other day who cynically suggested that one or both of the major political parties might intentionally dissuade young people and independents from voting. Here is what that person said:

> By repeatedly making outlandish claims, one of the parties, or maybe both, is trying to turn off independents and young voters. That party wants these two groups to become so cynical about Washington politics that they decide not to support any candidate. Because this party (or these parties) believes that young voters and independents will not support their party's slate, they just want those voters out of the mix entirely. "If they will not vote for us, let's be sure that they don't vote for the other guys either" seems to be the strategy. "So let's turn them off and tune them out." The tactic is to make Washington politics so scummy and fraudulent that young people and independents will not want to be contaminated by the rot and the stench. "It's not important that what we say is true, it's only important that we get media attention, excite our base to go out and vote for us, and to repel independent thinkers and young people from voting at all."

What do you think? Are the two major U.S. political parties (the Democratic Party and the Republican Party, including the Tea Party) trying to drive young people and independents away from the national political process? Or, the opposite? Is one or both trying to appeal to those groups? Since opinions without reasons are thin soup at best, how might you investigate this question and get some hard evidence upon which to base an informed opinion? **www.mythinkinglab.com**.

Explore the **Concept** on **mythinkinglab.com**

become more than a little disenchanted with their "benevolent" leaders. The leaders would surely lose all credibility. We should not trust an expert source who believes that lying and misdirecting are acceptable when making expert claims and offering expert opinions.

WikiLeaks notwithstanding, there are a great many things that corporations, governments, and individual people have good reason not to make public—for example, the plans for developing and marketing new products, military battle strategies and contingency plans, the vulnerabilities of public buildings, the answers to the final exam, personal medical information, bank account PIN numbers. But hold on for a moment! The Noble Lie! My, how convenient for totalitarian leaders intent above all on maintaining power for themselves. Surely they would be able to rationalize just about any propaganda they wished to put out as being "in the best interests of the people." A little healthy skepticism would be very useful about here!

Free of Conflicts of Interest, and Acting in the Client's Interest

If an expert's personal interests diverge from the interests of the person he or she is advising, then there is good reason not to trust what that expert may have to say. Suppose you go to a mortgage broker seeking guidance about how to finance a condo you want to buy. The broker offers you three options with three different banks: A, B, and C. The broker strongly recommends bank B, saying that in his expert judgment bank B best meets your needs. At this point you may be inclined to accept the broker's expert opinion because mortgages are complicated and difficult for many of us to understand.

What if, unbeknownst to you, bank B has agreed to pay your broker a large fee for bringing his mortgage clients to that bank? And suppose that neither bank A nor bank C will pay the broker nearly as much. This puts the broker in a conflict-of-interest situation. It is in the broker's interest for you to go with bank B because he will get a larger fee. But would the broker have been so enthusiastic about bank B if bank B paid the same fee that banks A and C pay? If the answer is "no," then this broker's conflict of interest has made him an untrustworthy source of advice. Many professionals take it upon themselves, or are required by law, to disclose conflicts of interest to their clients. That way, the client can take that into consideration when evaluating the trustworthiness of the professional whose advice is being sought.

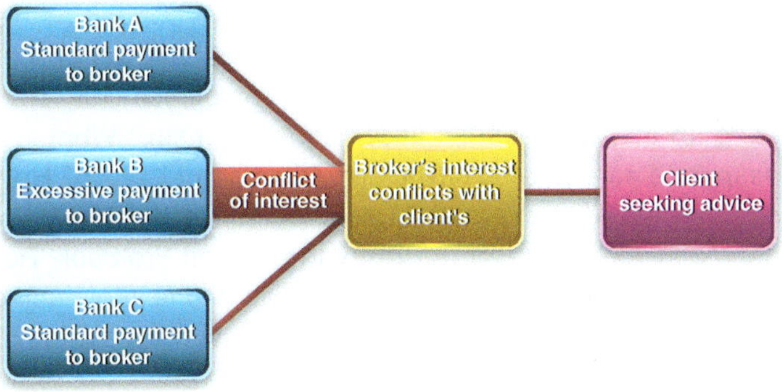

In an effort to protect us from unscrupulous experts who might give us bad advice, there are laws that require that health care professionals, real estate professionals, bankers, lawyers, high-level executives, and members of governing boards act in the interests of their clients or in the interests of their organizations. Under the law, this obligation is called their fiduciary responsibility. The president of the university has a fiduciary responsibility as the institution's chief executive officer to make decisions that are in the best interests of the university. A doctor has a fiduciary responsibility to make medical decisions and offer medical advice that is in the best interests of the patient.

If the university president makes decisions that are not in the university's best interests, but rather are in the best interest of some other organization (e.g., the city, the employees of the institution, the department of athletics, or to some other organization to showcase his own reputation) to the detriment of the university as a whole, then the president has failed to fulfill his or her legal obligations. Having broken trust with the institution by that decision, the president might be fired. If a doctor gives medical advice that is in the best interest of a scientific experiment but not in the best interest of the patient, then the doctor has broken trust. In cases where the expert makes claims or offers opinions that are not in the best interest of the person or organization to which the expert owes a fiduciary responsibility, the expert cannot be trusted as a reliable source of truthful information or sound advice.

Unconstrained, Informed about the Case at Hand, and Mentally Stable

Constrained: When being tortured, people are apt to say anything to stop the pain. Intelligence services, knowing this, have devised other tactics to extract accurate and useful information. Torture is one form of constraint that can cause an expert to make claims that are not reliable. Also, an expert may be legally constrained from offering advice or information on a given topic. For example, the expert may have signed an agreement with a former employer that prohibits the expert from revealing proprietary business secrets that are the property of the former employer for a certain period of time, typically a year or two. In this case, even if the expert goes to work for a new employer, the expert cannot legally violate the agreement with the previous employer. Under this constraint, the expert's claims will not rely on the expert's full range of knowledge. This is a reason not to fully trust what the expert has to say.

Informed about the Case at Hand: A friend of ours is a personal trainer with great expertise. People he happens to meet often ask him casually for advice. They want to know which exercises to do in order to gain greater strength, speed, or endurance. He could give them broad general answers, but he declines. Why? Because in these causal encounters, he does not have the opportunity to fully evaluate the person's physical status, so he worries that any advice he may offer or any claims he may make might be wrong for this particular person. As an expert, he realizes that knowing a lot about exercise in general is not always enough to give this particular person the right advice. The expert must also become informed about this particular person's individual circumstances and condition. To use another example, general advice about how to prepare for a job interview may or may not be the right advice to give one particular person who is preparing for one specific interview for one specific job. An expert's claims and advice gain credibility if the expert has taken the time to inform himself or herself about the specific case at hand.

Mentally Stable: We have come quite a long way in developing our list of things to think about when evaluating the credibility of a source. And there is only one more issue to add, and that is that the expert is mentally competent, unimpaired, and, to use a layman's term, "stable." Drugs and alcohol can impair judgment, including expert judgment. Psychosis, severe clinical depression, and recent traumatic experiences can cause people who may ordinarily have good judgment to make mistakes. And, as research with health care providers and pilots shows, long hours in stressful situations and sleep deprivation are associated with increased risk of errors. An expert who is not mentally stable cannot be trusted to provide reliable information or advice.

Twelve Characteristics of a Trustworthy Source

In summary, when evaluating a **trusted source** on topic X, it would be reasonable for us to trust a person (or the words of a person) who fulfills all twelve of the criteria below.

1. Learned in topic X
2. Experienced in topic X
3. Speaking about X
4. Up-to-date about X
5. Capable of explaining the basis for their claim or their advice about X
6. Unbiased
7. Truthful
8. Free of conflicts of interest
9. Acting in accord with our interests
10. Unconstrained
11. Informed about the specifics of the case at hand
12. Mentally stable

This may seem like a formidable list, but asking people who have a healthy skepticism to take one's claims and advice on faith is a sizable request. So it is reasonable that we should have high standards when it comes to establishing and maintaining trust. You may already have noted many of these positive characteristics in people whose advice you trust.

Autism is a heartbreaking diagnosis and a growing medical problem. How do the 12 characteristics of a trustworthy source factor into a parent's decision about seeking care for an autistic child? In its January 14–21, 2011 issue, the *San Francisco Business Times* ran a story, "In Autism's Storm," about a wealthy CEO and philanthropist, Zach Nelson, and his wife, who are advocates for families with autistic children. The Nelsons support the work of British physician, Andrew Wakefield, who claims, contrary to what many physicians and medical researchers believe, that autism originates from digestive problems and can be cured. Dr. Wakefield has written a book, *Callous Disregard: Autism and Vaccines—The Truth Behind the Tragedy*, and the Nelsons, along with filmmaker Elizabeth Horn, have produced a film, setup a Web site, and raised money in support of his work. Meanwhile, the *British Medical Journal* published an editorial denouncing Wakefield, and Wakefield has been stripped of his license to practice medicine by the British medical authorities. Read the article and apply the 12 characteristics to evaluate the trustworthiness of claims made by the Nelsons, Ms. Horn, and Dr. Wakefield. **http://www.bizjournals.com/sanfrancisco/print-edition/2011/01/14/in-autisms-storm.html** **Read** the **Document** on **mythinkinglab.com**

Dr. Mark Geier of Maryland developed a drug called Lupron for the treatment of autism and he is marketing the "Lupron Protocol" across the country by opening clinics in several states. Dr. Geier's theory is that autism is caused by a harmful link between testosterone and mercury, according to a story that appeared in the *Los Angeles Times* on May 24, 2009. Leading pediatric endocrinologists say that the Lupron Protocol is baseless. Experts warn that the protocol can have harmful effects on young children, "disrupt normal development, interfering with natural puberty and potentially putting children's hearts and bones at risk." But the protocol is FDA approved, albeit for the treatment of an extremely rare condition that has little if anything to do with autism. Like Dr. Wakefield, defenders of Dr. Geier claim that mainstream medicine condemns his work because he has been vocal about his criticism of "pediatricians, health officials, and drug companies" for "covering up the link between vaccines and autism." What is a desperate parent to do? Who should a parent believe? How can parents who love their autistic child and want only the best, decide whether or not to try the Lupron Protocol? Research the Lupron Protocol and Dr. Geier on the Intenet, and then apply the 12 characteristics of a trustworthy source to Dr. Geier's claims.

Assessing the Substance—What Should I Believe?

In the previous section, we focused on assessing the credibility of a person who makes an assertion without supplying reasons. Often, the claim stands alone, its source is unknown, and no reasons in support of it are supplied. Here are a few examples:

1 "Rumor has it that the dean is going to resign."

2 "I heard that she was so angry with her boyfriend that she keyed his new car."

3 "An unnamed source close to the police investigation told us that murder indictments were going to be handed down soon for as many as 35 gang members."

4 "According to a high-ranking administration official, the President is not happy with the leadership of his own party."

5 "Wind power generation of electricity will cost so much to implement that reliance on coal is financially a better option."

6 "Wind power has to be in the mix of alternative renewable sources of energy."

7 "The nursing staff knows that what happened today in room 314 was assisted suicide."

8 "The patient in 314 was dying of cancer and had less than a week to live."

9 "Doctors recommend getting your annual flu shot early this year."

10 "A huge killer anaconda lives in the utility tunnels under the main campus quad."

In this section, we will look at ways of evaluating the truth or falsity of assertions in the absence of supporting reasons and in the absence of identifiable sources.

DONKEY DUNG DETECTOR

Except for two rare situations that we will take up a bit later in this section, there is no reliable way of telling that a claim, standing alone, is true or false. We may have some initial impressions or some common-sense notions—for example, that a claim like #10, about a killer anaconda, is highly unlikely and that a claim like #9, about getting a flu shot early, seems plausible. But initial impressions are not proof, and so-called

Thinking Critically — Whom Do *You* Trust?

When you think about it, you have known a great many people now and throughout the years, such as family, friends, teachers, coworkers, and classmates. Identify two people you trust. Then review the list of 12 criteria and see how many of them are fulfilled by each of the people on your list. Did either of those people do things or say things that lead you to evaluate them highly on one or more of the 12 criteria? Did either ever do anything that would disqualify them from being trusted by you because they missed on one or another of the 12 items? Next, think of two people you do not trust. Has either done something or said something relating to one or more of the 12 critiera that leads you to regard him or her as untrustworthy? What did he or she do and how did you connect that to being untrustworthy? Do you notice that it takes much effort to build trust and little effort to lose it?

Thinking Critically Blogs and Web Pages

Web pages and blogs can be posted by reliable and informed experts and by unscrupulous people bent on fraud, hate, or mischief. Truths and falsehoods spread as people cite other Web pages as their sources, as they e-mail URLs to friends, and as they blog, tweet, and comment about things they have seen on the Web. Blogs and Web sites can provide pros and cons for almost any idea. Question: In addition to healthy skepticism, what are the most reasonable, most reliable, and smartest strategies to determine what on the Web can and cannot be trusted?

common sense is not something that a person with a healthy sense of skepticism is going to rely upon. In fact, a healthy sense of skepticism (which is the alternative name for our personal "Donkey Dung Detector") turns out to be our best defense against being deceived by false claims.

A strong critical thinker with a healthy sense of skepticism would probably respond to the 10 numbered claims in this section by asking a number of probing questions. Here are some examples. Note that some questions focus on trying to identify the source of the claim and that others focus on the plausibility of the claim itself.

1 Who said that about the dean and how would that person know?

2 Who told you that? Did the person actually see her key the car? Are we sure that the car was keyed? If so, might it not have been someone else who vandalized his car?

3 Why would the police leak information like that to anyone? Revealing their plans for a major bust would only cause the suspects to flee, if they knew that they were going to be arrested.

4 Did anyone else in the President's administration confirm that rumor? Isn't the President the leader of his political party, so you're saying he's unhappy with himself?

5 Can you show me the financial projections that support this?

6 Why? What if wind power turns out to be inefficient and not cost-effective? Let's not just go along with something because nobody seems to be questioning the party line on this.

7 Oh, and how do you know that?

8 Did someone on the hospital staff share information about that patient's diagnosis with you?

9 Which doctors, the ones working for the pharmaceutical company, doctors with independent practices, who? Why do they recommend getting a flu shot? And who should get flu shots? Everyone? What does "early" mean? September? December?

10 Right. And it eats what? Freshmen who happen to go exploring in those tunnels?

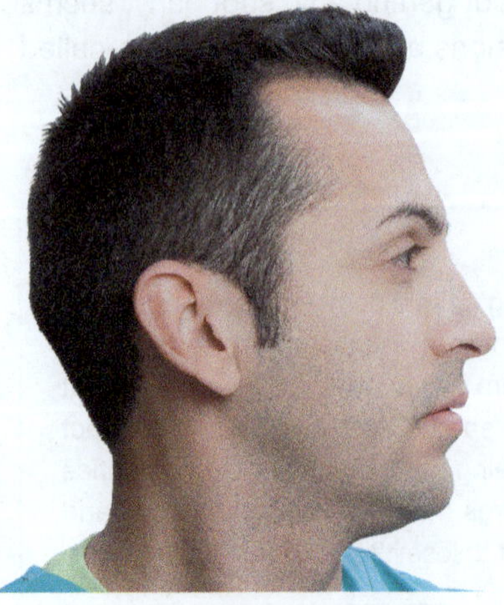

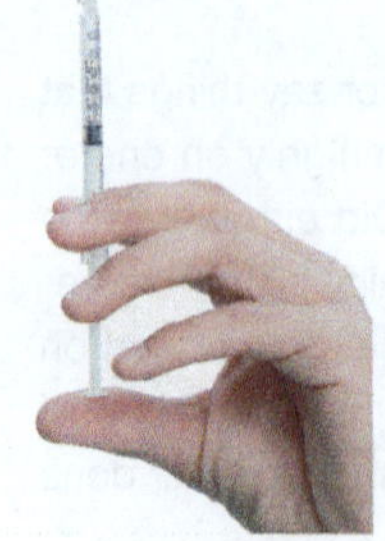

SELF-CONTRADICTIONS AND TAUTOLOGIES

We said that there were two rare situations where we actually could know that a given claim was false or was true just by what it says. The first situation is when the claim is self-contradictory, as in these examples:

- No point on the circumference of a circle is the same distance from the center of the circle as any other point on the circumference of the circle.
- The moon orbits the earth and does not orbit the earth.
- Everyone in our club despises our club president, and there are only one or two people who still admire her.

A **self-contradictory statement** cannot be true. The self-contradiction comes about because of the meanings of the words used to form the claim. For example, the definition of the word *circle* is not consistent with the notion that the circumference is variable distances from the center. Conveniently, self-contradictions, when you stop and think carefully about them, do not make sense. As they stand, they are un-interpretable. In real life, if someone happens to make a self-contradictory claim, strong critical thinkers use their question-asking skills to seek clarification from the speaker.

- If you are talking about a circle, then by definition every point on the circumference is the same distance from the center. Or else you are not talking about a circle. Which is it?
- Which is it, does the moon orbit the earth or not? Pick one. Both can't be true.

- That does not make any sense. You can't say that everyone despises the president but some do not. Can you clarify what you mean?

Some may worry that they will not always be able to identify self-contradictions in real life. But as a practical matter, what is important is that we recognize that a person's claim is not making sense to us for whatever reason. As we saw in Chapter 4 on clarifying and interpreting ideas, whenever we are trying to interpret a claim correctly, we should be prepared to ask the author respectful but challenging questions about what the author intends to communicate, by making the claim that we find to be confusing or self-contradictory.

Just as some claims cannot be true by virtue of what their words mean, other claims cannot be false by virtue of what their words mean. Here are examples:

- Every student enrolled in this university is a student enrolled in this university.
- Two straight lines on a plane that are not parallel to each other intersect at one and only one point.

- If God is all-powerful, then there is nothing that God cannot do.

The first example almost sounds as redundant as "if a student is enrolled, then a student is enrolled." The second is a truth of plane geometry. The third is equivalent to saying, "If God is all-powerful, then God is all-powerful" except that a definition for "all-powerful" is used in the predicate. In each of these cases, the statements must be true based simply on what the words mean. A statement that is true entirely because of the meanings of the words it contains is called a **tautology**. Here's one more example:

- You gotta do what you gotta do.

Imagine James Gandolfini playing the character Tony Soprano saying something like this to one of his Mafia lieutenants. Yes, technically he is speaking a tautology. But we might ask ourselves, "Why?" In context, people use statements like these for purposes other than to communicate informational content. Here, the Mafia don may be giving a murderous assignment to that underling, saying, in effect, "This decision to act is absolutely necessary." From the point of view of critical thinking and in order to make a full and accurate interpretation, we still must look to context and purpose, as was emphasized in Chapter 4, rather than only the literal meaning of a claim.

A more serious threat to good judgment is generated by speakers whose claims appear to be information culled from careful observation, but in reality turn out instead to be empty tautologies. I listened to a professional motivational speaker recently during a conference for upward-climbing corporate junior managers. They were looking for ideas about how to get ahead in their careers. The speaker had made a name for himself advising business audiences just like this one. As the next speaker on the program, I had the opportunity to listen to what he was telling our audience and to watch their reactions. I wrote down some of the claims he made. Here are three: "Every job pays exactly what it is worth in terms of its contribution to society." "There is no skill you cannot learn." "We all start off equal in life."

Whoa, I thought. Those claims are not true. A teacher is worth far more to society than what he or she is paid, and, arguably, a Wall Street financier who trades in junk bonds and mortgage derivatives is worth far less to society that the salary and bonus she or he takes home. Given that the context is not just fumbling through a skill like a beginner, but becoming professionally competent at the skill, then his claim is false. No, not everyone can play basketball at the level of a college or professional athlete, not everyone can write a best seller novel, not everyone can perform a concert-quality violin sonata. And a child born in a peaceful and prosperous community with loving parents and to a household that enjoys a modest but adequate income starts off life in a far more optimal position than a child born in a war-ravaged land, orphaned at birth, and struggling each day to scrounge for food while at the same time trying not to be killed or raped.

The speaker, it seemed to me, was either an idiot or a charlatan. He was no idiot. And yet the more than 300 people in the audience seemed to be eating up every word he said. Why? I wondered. Why do they not see that either his claims are objectively false, or if true, they are true by definition, nothing more than empty tautologies? If he meant to say that a teacher is worth no more nor less than she is paid when we factor her value into the mathematical formula for calculating the gross national product, then okay, I can understand that. But it is a disservice to underpaid teachers and to overpaid corporate executives to lead people to think that they can measure their social worth by the size of their salaries. And that is what he appeared to want the audience to believe. And if he meant to say that something is not a skill unless it can be learned, then thanks again, but that's not helpful. Because if he is telling the audience that they can learn to be more effective negotiators, that is one thing. But what he appeared to want them to believe was that each and every one of them had an equal chance to become the corporate CEO, if they only worked hard and learned the skills. A great message from the point of view of senior management, because it leads those on the lower rungs of the ladder to keep trying hard at their jobs, but a little unrealistic just on the sheer numbers, because for

Thinking Critically Cultivate a Healthy Sense of Skepticism

Each of the following claims may be true. But as they stand, cut off from their authors and without reasons being supplied, it is difficult to know whether they are true or false. For each claim, write four questions that, if answered, are likely to yield information that would help evaluate the claim's plausibility or implausibility.

1 The composer Richard Wagner (b. 1813) was a racist and anti-Semite whose music Hitler enjoyed and employed to further his Nazi political agenda.

2 Within five weeks after his death, over 10 million recordings and MP3 downloads of Michael Jackson's music were sold worldwide.

3 Your presence will be powerfully felt by your acquaintances and loved ones if you eliminate what does not add value to your life.

4 You can get cash for your old and unwanted gold jewelry from our friendly, professional staff of experienced appraiser-buyers.

5 If you exhume my father's grave and move his casket to another location, he will never rest in peace again.

6 Subscriptions to online pornography Internet sites are more prevalent in states "where surveys indicate conservative positions on religion, gender roles, and sexuality."[vii]

7 "Forgiveness liberates the soul. It removes fear. That is why it is such a powerful weapon."—Spoken by Morgan Freeman playing Nelson Mandela in the 2010 film about South Africa, *Invictus*.

8 The vulnerable workers in Zimbabwe's diamond fields are protected from external violence and lawlessness by the presence of Zimbabwe's military, which has restored order in the Marange district.

9 Steve Carell has signed an agreement for cameo appearances in a total of four episodes of *The Office* over each of the next two seasons.

10 Shiny striped gym bags and long-sleeve micro-mesh miniskirts are the newest fashions sweeping the nation.

11 More children between the ages of 13 and 17 have been killed playing football in the past 60 years than have been killed by other children with firearms.

12 Teen virginity pledges are effective in reducing the percentage of teens who have sex and in reducing the number of unwanted pregnancies among teenagers.

13 Unaware of how long they have to live and not knowing how chemotherapy will affect their lives, more than 20 percent of Medicare patients who have advanced cancer start a new chemotherapy regimen two weeks before they die.

14 Seamus Hogan of Rathkeale, County Limerick, Ireland claims that the tree stump with the image of the Blessed Virgin Mary brings people of all ages, races, and religions together in prayer. Seamus adds that as far as he can tell it is doing no harm.[viii]

15 When choosing colors for your favorite room, remember that "the antidote to fog is color. . . . A warmer color temperature in a room is a really good approach, so you don't feel like you're living on a glacier."[ix]

every 300 junior executives only one becomes a senior vice president. And that is not because none of the other 299 worked hard. And if he meant to say that each individual's economic contributions at birth is equal, that is zero, then, as the dolphins said in the *Restaurant at the End of the Universe*, "Good bye and thanks for all the fish." The speaker did motivate me to do something, however. And that was to include this warning in *Think Critically*: Be vigilant! Do not let yourself be misled by empty tautologies masquerading as informative facts. A strong critical thinker will be skeptical and ask, "What exactly do you mean when you say . . . ?" If you have ever found yourself arguing with someone only to discover that what she or he is saying is, in that person's view, true by definition, then you understand the problem.

MARKETING, SPIN, DISINFORMATION, AND PROPAGANDA

Claims without supporting reasons are the stock and trade of people who have ulterior motives. A marketer, wanting us to purchase something, makes claims about the virtues of the product. Extremist organizations eager to discredit someone make claims about the opponent's position on controversial issues. Sports promoters trying to generate press coverage and audience interest for a forthcoming game exaggerate the rivalry between the competing teams and over-interpret the significance of the game. Typical examples:

- Over 75 percent of the cars we make are still on the road.
- Supreme Court Justice Sonia Sotomayor supports Puerto Rican terrorists.
- This week's grudge match between the Bears and the Lions could determine which team will make it to the Super Bowl.

Those with a healthy sense of skepticism are ever on the alert for the donkey dung being distributed by people with ulterior motives. Whether they wrap it in humor, sincerity, or vitriolic rhetoric, it comes to the same thing: They are unsubstantiated claims made specifically for the purpose of getting us to do something that we otherwise would not do—such as to buy something we do not really need, to vote for something we don't believe in, or to support a cause we might not otherwise support. Or perhaps it is simply a way of responding to the desire some have to be the center of everyone's attention.

Skepticism is not cynicism. We need to remember that open-mindedness is a positive critical thinking habit of mind. So, when we evaluate the plausibility or implausibility of claims, we must discipline ourselves to be open-minded. Fortum, a Scandinavian energy company, won a Clio Award for its ad that features that claim that Fortum

- fills its brand with positive energy by activating its customers rather than only sending them bills.

Is this only a clever marketing gimmick, or might there be something more to the idea? Before you propose an evaluation, you will need to understand how to interpret Fortum's curious claim. Begin by watching the video that won the Clio Award. Access the video at **www.mythinkinglab.com**. **Watch** the **Video** on **mythinkinglab.com**

Given that consumers can become jaded and skeptical, marketers often try to separate us from our money using humor and entertainment, rather than with extravagant claims. This is particularly true if the product being marketed is something familiar, rather than a new program as in the Fortum example. Many Clio Award–quality commercials employ entertainment value and humor. We easily found many great examples by visiting YouTube and searching "Clio Award Commercials." The Guinness "tipping point" ad, Dr. Pepper's take-off on the "Hunchback of Notre Dame," and the Skittles "touch" commercial were some of our favorites. Does it make sense that we should be more inclined to purchase a product after seeing a funny and entertaining ad? And if so, why? It often takes imagination, good critical thinking, a team of professionals, and millions of dollars to produce commercials of this quality. What does it take not to be drawn in by them?

SLANTED LANGUAGE AND LOADED EXPRESSIONS

Often, it is difficult to evaluate claims that use language that carries a positive or negative emotional charge. Some expressions are so loaded down with social and cultural baggage that the very use of them excites strong positive or negative reactions. Here are sets of three statements each. The first in each set is intended to elicit a generally positive response to the topic, the second is neutrally factual, and the third is slanted negatively.

- John is a true American hero.
- John is a New York City firefighter.
- John is just another overpaid municipal employee working in public safety.

- Basketball combines finesse, grace, power, and skill.
- Basketball combines passing, dribbling, shooting, and defense.
- Basketball combines sweat, aggression, cunning, and brute force.

- Love is you and me together happily forever in each other's arms.
- Love is a strong emotional attachment to another.
- Love is that stupefying feeling you had before you really knew the bastard.

Slanted language and loaded expressions are not always easy to recognize. Certainly if we disagree with a claim we can often pick out the slanted language and loaded expressions. A good percentage of Keith Olbermann's show *Countdown* on the Current TV network is devoted each night to pointing out the slanted language, half-truths, exaggerations, and loaded expressions used by those on the extreme right of the American political spectrum. Many would say that Mr. Olbermann and others who share his far left wing political views also use some of the very same tactics.

The problem for all of us is that if we happen to agree with what is being said, we have great difficulties seeing anything particularly unfair, loaded, or egregious with the claims being made. Everyone likes to think of himself or herself as objective and able to see all sides of an issue. But the psychological fact is that most of us have a very difficult time putting ourselves in the minds of people with whom we disagree. Rather, we tend to prefer to make an idiot out of our opposition in our own minds, underestimating the merits of what the person may be saying and overestimating the clarity and strength of our own views. We saw this with the choice vs. life debate in Chapter 5 and we will learn more about the psychology behind this common human propensity in Chapter 11. That said, evaluating claims that tug at our emotions, either positively or negatively, by virtue of the language those claims employ must be done with care. A strong truth-seeking habit of mind can dispose us to approach this evaluation more objectively.

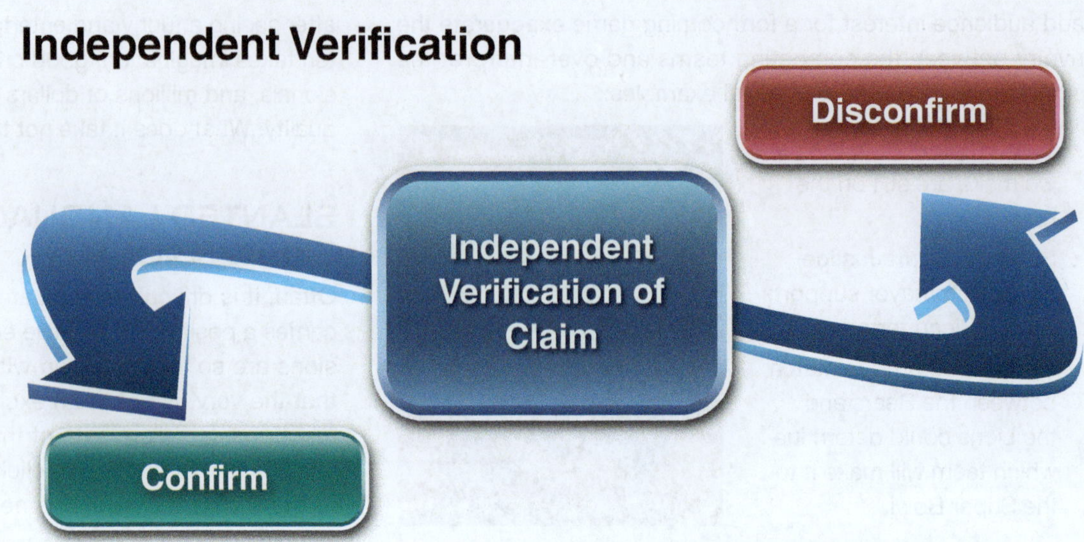

To sum up this section, we need a healthy skepticism when trying to evaluate claims that stand alone, without their authors and without reasons. Except for self-contradictions and tautologies, it is almost impossible to evaluate the claims by themselves as either true or false. Through tough questioning, we may find some claims more plausible and others less plausible. But even then, other factors, including the ulterior motives of the people who are making the claims and the emotion-laden language that is often used, make it difficult, if not impossible, to evaluate a claim standing alone. Almost, but not entirely impossible. There is another strategy, and that is to take upon ourselves to investigate the claim independently.

Independent Verification

Suppose we encounter a claim on the Internet and we hear it being repeated by friends and talked about in the media. Assume that on its face the claim appears plausible, yet we are skeptical. We know no claim is true simply because it is widely believed and frequently repeated. What can we do if we need to make a decision and this particular claim, if true, would lead us to make one decision, but, if false, would lead us to make a different decision? Is there any other way to figure out if we should believe the claim or not? Yes. One way to do this is to ask if the claim can be confirmed. The other is to ask if it can be disconfirmed. Let's look briefly at both.

CAN THE CLAIM BE CONFIRMED?

A claim becomes more plausible if we can find confirmatory information or information that is consistent with the claim. For example, suppose someone claims:

- Mother's Day is the most popular holiday celebrated in the United States.

How might we go about finding confirmation for this? First, we would need a measure of "popularity" as applied to holidays. For example, we could use the number of greeting cards sold per holiday, the money spent sending flowers per holiday, restaurant revenues per holiday, telephone calls made per holiday, or an opinion survey with an appropriately structured sample.

Another approach when attempting to confirm a claim is to ask ourselves if the claim in question is consistent with other things we may know. If it is, then the claim takes on more plausibility in our minds. Consider this claim:

- Samuel was the last person to leave this morning, and he forgot to lock the apartment door.

To confirm this claim, we might begin by asking how many people live in Samuel's apartment, and then we might ask each of those people what time he or she left the apartment this morning and whether he or she noticed who was still there when he or she left. But suppose that this line of questioning results in uncertainty because people can't recall the exact

Thinking Critically Your Best and Worst Commercials

We see or hear dozens of ads and commercials each day on TV, on the radio, on Web pages, in the newspaper, on T-shirts, on billboards, etc. (Have you ever asked yourself why we pay for clothing that sports a logo or promotes a brand name, instead of demanding that the corporation pay us to wear that clothing?) Mark the time. For the next 24 hours, keep track of the ads and commercials you see or hear. Focus on the ones you think are the very best and the ones that are the very worst. Keep two lists and refine the lists by crossing off and adding candidates as you hear or see another that is better or worse. After 24 hours, analyze your top three and your bottom three. What makes them the "best" and the "worst" in your mind? Were they funny, informative, creative, and effective in influencing you to want the product they were promoting? Or were they boring, stupid, confusing, and ineffective?

time they left or because they are not sure if others may or may not have been in the apartment when they left. Then we would go to things we know about Samuel, looking for something that may be consistent with the claim being evaluated. For example, we may learn that Samuel is often the last one to leave in the morning because he does not have any early classes. We may learn that in the recent past Samuel admitted to having forgotten to lock the apartment door when he left. And we may learn that Samuel is a generally irresponsible and unreliable person, often neglecting his responsibilities and not keeping his promises. If things should turn out this way upon investigation, then we would have reason to evaluate the claim as highly plausible.

CAN THE CLAIM BE DISCONFIRMED?

An alternative to trying to confirm that the claim is true is setting about trying to establish that it is false. Consider the claim. While the burden of proof would ordinarily be on those seeking to confirm a claim, at times it becomes desirable to try to disconfirm a claim. Consider these two claims:

- You are the person who murdered Mrs. X on Sunday at noon in her home in Boston.
- President Obama does not have a valid U.S. birth certificate.

In the first case, to disconfirm the accusation, the accused would have to establish a solid alibi. For example, "No, sir, I did not kill Mrs. X. I was onstage in Orlando, making a speech to 2,000 people exactly on the date and time that the murder occurred in Boston. My proof is the videotape of the speech, which is date-stamped, and the testimony of the audience members and technical support staff who were present at the time."

Some claims, like the second example about the President's birth certificate, are more challenging to disconfirm for reasons that go beyond the substance of the claim itself. All that would appear to be required to disconfirm that claim would be presenting the President's birth certificate for public inspection. Although we may not personally be able to access the president's birth records, presumably the President or his attorney can. "Public inspection" in a case like this would then be the responsibility of the news media.

Prior to the general election in November 2008, the *Chicago Tribune*'s Washington Bureau did post a story confirming that both presidential candidates were natural-born U.S. citizens, Obama having been born in the state of Hawaii and McCain at a naval hospital in the then U.S.-controlled Panama Canal Zone.[x] But then in the summer of 2009 a U.S. Army reserve soldier named Stefan Cook, a "Birther," refused to be deployed to Afghanistan on the grounds that he was being sent by a commander-in-chief who was not eligible to be president because he was not a native-born U.S. citizen. It turned out that Mr. Cook was misleading the public, for he had in fact volunteered for the military assignment in Afghanistan. And when he changed his mind about volunteering for military service in that country, his orders to deploy to Afghanistan were revoked, which is standard policy in the case of volunteers. But with the media attention to the initial story, these subsequent facts went relatively unnoticed and the rumors about Obama's birth certificate lived on. Ever the celebrity publicity seeker, Donald Trump jumped on the Birthers bandwagon early in 2011. But when the President again released his birth certificate, the teapot tempest settled down again, of course with Mr. Trump vigorously patting back himself on the back in self-congratulations for having sorted all of that out on behalf of the rest of the nation. If someone were to claim that the Trump-Birther episode helped the Republican Party, they might be surprised to discover that some Republican Senators and Governors disagree. For the counterargument visit **http://articles.latimes.com/2011/may/02/nation/la-na-gop-birthers-trump-20110502.** **Read** the **Document** on **mythinkinglab.com**

The durability of claims like the one about Obama and his birth certificate is fascinating in its own right. Some claims—call them "urban legends"—seem to endure no matter what investigative findings reveal. Even when the claim has been plausibly refuted, there are those who will not accept the evidence. Alex Koppelman offers an interesting analysis of why "conspiracy theorists" will never be satisfied about the validity of the birth certificate or the eligibility of Obama to be president.[xi]

But with due respect to the conspiracy theorists of every stripe, there is a difference between healthy skepticism and stubborn refusal to abandon a discredited position. In fact, the difference is rather profound. The skeptic is asserting that he or she is uncertain what the truth of the matter is. The conspiracy theorist is making a claim, often one that can be neither confirmed nor disconfirmed, that a certain version of events is the truth and that all other versions are false. This puts an enormous burden of proof on the conspiracy theorist, not the skeptic. The conspiracy theorist must do much more than discredit all other known versions of

Thinking Critically — The Endangered Pacific Northwest Tree Octopus

"The Pacific Northwest tree octopus (*Octopus paxarbolis*) can be found in the temperate rainforests of the Olympic Peninsula on the west coast of North America. Their habitat lies on the Eastern side of the Olympic mountain range, adjacent to Hood Canal. These solitary cephalopods reach an average size (measured from arm-tip to mantle-tip,) of 12–13 in. (30–33 cm). Unlike most other cephalopods, tree octopuses are amphibious, spending only their early life and the period of their mating season in their ancestral aquatic environment. Because of the moistness of the rainforests and specialized skin adaptations, they are able to keep from becoming desiccated for prolonged periods of time, but given the chance they would prefer resting in pooled water." For pictures and more background on this problem visit **http://zapatopi.net/treeoctopus/**

Question: Why did the tree octopus problem cause such a stir among teachers?

events. The conspiracy theorist must confirm his or her version of events. That is the step that most often is not rigorously fulfilled.

INDEPENDENT INVESTIGATION AND THE Q-RAY BRACELET CASE

The case of the Q-Ray bracelet offers us an excellent example of the value of independent investigation into the veracity of the claims people make to promote products and reap profits at the expense of gullible consumers. Perhaps you have seen the ads for the Q-Ray bracelet. Millions of Q-Ray bracelets have been marketed and sold, at prices ranging from $50.00 to $250.00, to people seeking relief from chronic pain caused by a variety of illnesses and medical conditions, including pain from chemotherapy. Its inventor, an infomercial entrepreneur, formed a company, QT Inc., to manufacture and sell the Q-Ray bracelets. Initially, the bracelets had been described as having been made from special metals that offer natural and effective pain relief. The fundamental claim made in the promotional infomercials and on the Q-Ray Web site between the years 2000 and 2003 was that an "activated" Q-Ray bracelet relieves pain. Whether or not the Q-Ray works or not turned out to be a multimillion-dollar question because of lawsuits charging that the product was ineffective. In 2002, the Mayo Clinic conducted an independent investigation into the effectiveness of the "ionized" Q-Ray bracelet as to whether it did or did not relieve pain.[xii]

The independent Mayo Clinic researchers set up a clinical trial like the ones used to test the effectiveness of pharmaceuticals and medical devices. Subjects (people with chronic pain) were randomly assigned to two different groups. The first group of subjects was given authentic activated Q-Ray bracelets to wear. The other group was given non-active replicas of Q-Ray bracelets to wear. At the end of the trial, 75 percent of the people in the first group reported experiencing pain relief. None of the subjects knew whether he or she had an "activated" or "non-active" bracelet.

What do you suppose was the percentage of people in the second group, those with the non-active replicas, that reported experiencing pain relief? It turned out to be the same percentage: 75 percent! This investigation established that the Q-Ray bracelet has a placebo effect only. It is the equivalent of taking a sugar pill instead of taking medication that has been demonstrated to be effective. Based on the research at the Mayo Clinic, the judge dealing with the lawsuits ruled that the Q-Ray promoters were guilty of false advertising.[xiii]

Did this put an end to the sale of Q-Ray bracelets? Hardly. To see for yourself what new claims are being made, visit **www.qray.com**.

On November 21, 2011 the company that produced power bracelets filed for bankruptcy. The founders admitted that claims that the rubber wristbands improved flexibility, balance, and strength were unsubstantiated. Celebrities, like Koby Bryant who had $ 400,000 endorsement deal, would not get paid their fees. Customers could apply for refunds. Our question is not "What went wrong?" but instead, "How could we be so gullible?" Really, a rubber band on the wrist is the secret to athletic success! What about human decision making enables such obvious nonsense to separate people from their hard earned money so easily?[xiv]

Read more about the rise and fall of the power bracelet at **www.mythinkinglab.com**.

Read the Document on mythinkinglab.com

SUSPENDING JUDGMENT

Judgments in contexts of uncertainty are unavoidable, given the human condition. The critical thinking habit of judiciousness disposes us toward prudence and caution when deciding what to believe or what to do. Our healthy sense of skepticism tells us that if we can neither confirm nor disconfirm a claim through independent investigation, then the wisest course would be to suspend judgment with regard to that claim. The best judgment about the plausibility or implausibility of some claims may be to make no judgment at all.

REVIEW

Study and Review on **mythinkinglab.com**

In this chapter, we approached the evaluation of claims in three ways. First, we established twelve criteria we could use to evaluate the credibility of the source of the claim. Second, we explored interrogating the plausibility of the claim itself and inquiring into the context within which the claim is positioned and the possible ulterior motives behind the use of the claim. And third, we envisioned conducting an independent investigation seeking either to confirm or to disconfirm the claim. In the next chapter, we reunite claims and the reasons their authors give in support of those claims so that we can explore the application of the critical thinking skill of evaluation to arguments.

KEY TERMS

expert refers to someone who is both experienced and learned in a given subject matter or professional practice area. (p. 113)

trusted source on topic X is a person (or the words of a person) who is learned in X, experienced in X, speaking about X, up-to-date about X, capable of explaining the basis for their claim or their advice about X, unbiased, truthful, free of conflicts of interest, acting in accord with our interests, unconstrained, informed about the specifics of the case at hand, and mentally stable. (p. 118)

self-contradictory statement is a sentence that is false entirely because of the grammatical construction and the meanings of the words used to form the sentence. (p. 120)

tautology is a statement that is necessarily true because of the meanings of the words. (p. 121)

FIND IT ON MYTHINKINGLAB.COM

- The moving story of Selma Goncalves opens this chapter. Visit **www.mythinkinglab.com** and view the clip there to make this tragedy more real and personal.
  Watch the Video on **mythinkinglab.com**
- In contrast to the sadness of that video we have the delightfully funny "Expert Witness" scene from *My Cousin Vinny* (p. 113). For that clip, and for the memorable "You Can't Handle the Truth" speech by Jack Nicholson in *A Few Good Men* (p. 116), visit **www.mythinkinglab.com**. Watch the Video on **mythinkinglab.com**
- TV commercials provide a rich source of material to analyze. Begin your analysis by asking, "What reasons, if any, am I being given to lead me to want to buy this product?" Often, commercials do not overtly state the reasons; instead, they use music, staging, gestures, and visual cues to subtly suggest the ideas they want us to have. We probably will not find a commercial that comes right out and says that buying someone a bottle of perfume or piece of jewelry will lead to a fulfilling love life, but several holiday commercials certainly intimate as much.

It takes skill, imagination, and a lot of excellent problem solving to produce award-winning commercials. On page 123, I invite you to link through **www.mythinkinglab.com** to the Fortum commercial and to look for a few other Clio Award winners while you are at it. Can you pick out the implicit and unspoken assumptions that the commercial maker wants you to accept so that you will buy the company's product? Or, if the commercial is not encouraging you to buy a product, then you are being asked to trust a company, appreciate a company's work, contribute to a worthy cause, or join an organization.

Once you start applying your critical thinking skills to TV commercials, you will never passively watch them again. Analyzing them is more fun. This is tough on the advertisers because they want our minds to be on cruise control when we're watching. Commercials are designed so that their messages sneak into our minds under the radar. A lot of commercials do not work at all if the viewing audience actually thinks about what it is seeing!

Exercises

WHAT IS WRONG WITH THESE INACCURATE STATEMENTS?

For each of the following, explain the mistake that makes it untrue.

1. A statement is a tautology if it is true.
2. A statement that is self-contradictory is seldom true.
3. We can tell if a claim is true or false by looking at what it means.
4. If a claim cannot be confirmed by an independent investigation, then it must be false.
5. If an independent investigation produces evidence that is consistent with a given claim, then the claim must be true.
6. Experts have the rightful authority to impose their beliefs on other people.
7. Relativism is the highest stage of cognitive development college students can achieve.
8. To doubt the truthfulness of a rightful authority means that a person is being disrespectful.
9. If a celebrity endorses a product, you can be sure that the product is of high quality.
10. If we do not believe that a claim is true, then we must believe that the claim is false.
11. No one can evaluate emotionally charged claims.
12. Critical thinking forces people to be cynical.

REFLECTIVE LOG: YOUR FAVORITE NUTRITIONAL SUPPLEMENT[XV]

The ads and testimonials for nutritional supplements are among the most effective marketing tools ever, as is supported by the unprecedented growth in the sales of energy drinks, dietary supplements, vitamin beverages, and stimulants. Select for this exercise one of these products you are already purchasing for your own use or any product of this kind that interests you. Use information provided on the product label and from the product's Web site as needed to respond to these questions in your log:

1. What claims are made about the benefits of the product?
2. What research is cited or what evidence is supplied to support the truth of these claims?
3. Who are the people who have provided testimonials in support of the product?
4. What level of expertise do these individuals have with regard to human nutrition?
5. Were any of these individuals paid to provide their endorsement?
6. What warnings, risks, or potentially harmful side effects are presented?
7. What ingredients does the supplement contain?
8. Biologically and nutritionally, what does each ingredient do? In other words, what is its function?
9. Is the supplement "specially formulated" in any way that is purported to enhance its efficacy?
10. Who are the target consumers of the supplement? Who should use it?
11. What have you been told about the supplement by friends, coaches, and salespeople?
12. Who produces/manufactures the supplement? What is that producer's reputation?
13. Is the supplement approved as "safe and effective" by the federal Food and Drug Administration?
14. In terms of the nutritional benefits and risks, how does the supplement compare to the items on this list: orange juice, milk, coffee, standard multivitamin tablets, carrots, apples, broccoli, ordinary yogurt, cottage cheese, peanut butter, tuna fish, baked turkey breast, and wheat bread?
15. Reflect on your answers to questions #2–14 and then evaluate the claims you wrote down in #1. Are they true, plausible, implausible, or untrue, or should you suspend judgment about those claims?

SELLING RISK

Watch the national news on CBS, NBC, or ABC. Focus on the commercials and make a list of each one and what it is advertising. In each case, the product can benefit people, and yet each comes with a measure of risk. The job of the commercial is to lead us to desire the product in spite of its inherent risks. When a commercial for a drug or medical device comes on, listen very carefully to the list of side effects and cautions. Write down as many as you can for each drug or medical device that is advertised. When a car commercial comes on, note what the manufacturer is using to sell the car (e.g., sex, power, prestige, popularity, comfort, fuel economy, safety, or resale value). When a banking or investment commercial comes on, record the disclaimers, cautions, and exceptions, like "not a guarantee," "read the prospectus carefully before investing," and "rates and conditions subject to change without notice." After the news broadcast is over, review your lists. Which of the commercials, in your judgment, was the most misleading with regard to the risks associated with the product? Why? Which company provided the least substantive guarantees with regards to the product's expected benefits in its commercial? Explain your choices.

GROUP EXERCISE: THE MOST POPULAR HOLIDAY ON CAMPUS

Suppose you see a claim in the campus paper, published on February 10, that says, "Valentine's Day is the most popular holiday on this campus." Develop a strategy by which you can determine which holiday is the most popular among the students enrolled in your university or college. Write up your recommended procedure in draft form. Work with up to two other students to combine the best ideas from your approach and their approaches. Then, develop a final recommendation for how to conduct the investigation.

The critical thinking involved in this strategy includes the question, "What sorts of evidence should we be able to find if we assume that the claim is true?" And our answer to that question in the Mother's Day example was evidence about cards, flowers, phone calls, etc., which would reflect that if people valued this holiday, they would show that in their behavior. The strategy is a good one if cards, flowers, phone calls, etc., are part of other holidays too. As you discovered in doing the exercise, another aspect of attempting to confirm or disconfirm a claim is to be sure exactly what the claim means. Interpreting the expression "most popular" required finding a way to measure popularity. Interpreting "holiday on this campus" required coming up with a list of holidays, some of which might have been unique to your specific campus (e.g., a "Founders Day" holiday or a religious holiday not celebrated at other colleges or universities).

GROUP EXERCISE: CLAIMS THAT COST MONEY AND CAUSE PAIN

1. Occasionally reputable sources present apparently divergent claims. But strong critical thinkers can still sort through the divergent claims and assess them by looking for the reasons and evidence upon which they are based. Many reputable investigators have looked into the health claims for the dietary supplement ginkgo biloba. It is said to improve cognitive functioning, assist memory, and help focus attention. Google "Ginkgo biloba health study" and review the research published in respected sources over the past four years. Focus on Web sites that provide information to the educated public, but which are not simply promoting particular products or medical services. You will find some serious research studies, some excellent summaries of multiple studies, and some detailed criticisms about the methods or the analyses of other studies. As strong critical thinkers, work through those reports and make a well-reasoned and thoughtful evaluation of the claim, "Ginkgo biloba supplements are beneficial for human cognitive functioning."
2. The U.S. Supreme Court ruled on a case brought by the father of a young serviceman killed in combat. The father sought to prohibit protests at military funerals. The group that had disrupted his son's funeral was from the Westboro Baptist Church. The protestors waved signs and shouted things like, "America is Doomed," and "Thank God for Dead Soldiers." They wore T-shirts that said "GodHatesFags.com" Their claim is that God is punishing America because it supports homosexuality and abortion. Lower courts held that the protestors were offensive and caused needless pain to grieving family members. The protestors claim that their right to demonstrate at military funerals is protected by the First Amendment of the U.S. Constitution. Evaluate that claim. To assist you in learning more about this before you render an opinion, use these text and video resources:

   Profile on Pastor Phelps and Westboro Baptist Church:
   http://www.youtube.com/watch?v=6PcU_iSXdw4

   ABC News Summary and Report of Court Ruling:
   http://abcnews.go.com/Politics/Supreme_Court/supreme-court-westboro-protests-military-funerals/story?id=13037219

   NY Times report on Issue and Court Ruling:
   http://www.nytimes.com/2011/03/03/us/03scotus.html?pagewanted=all

   Summary of U.S. Supreme Court ruling:
   http://www.youtube.com/watch?v=gYsVdIRURZc

   Christian Veterans Protect Families at Military Funerals:
   http://www.godvine.com/Christian-Veterans-Protect-the-Funeral-of-a-Fallen-Soldier-278.html>>

   Read the **Document** on **mythinkinglab.com**

   Watch the **Video** on **mythinkinglab.com**

MUSTANGS

Read the Chapter on mythinkinglab.com

Listen to the Chapter Audio on mythinkinglab.com

CHAPTER 07

Evaluate Arguments: The Four Basic Tests

WHAT presumptions do we make when we offer arguments to support our claims?

WHAT four tests must an argument pass to be worthy of acceptance?

HOW do we apply the four tests when evaluating arguments?

HOW can we recognize common reasoning mistakes more readily?

"I don't get why you want to quit," said Malcolm. "You came here to play volleyball. Volleyball is all you ever want to talk about! Now suddenly you want to quit?"

Caitlin looked at Malcolm. He couldn't possibly be this dense. "Look, I explained it all to you already."

"You said that you didn't like Coach Williams. So what? She's your head coach. Nobody likes a head coach. I don't like the marching band director, but you don't see me quitting the band," said Malcolm.

"Coach was screaming at everyone again. She's so negative, always screaming at the players, and that doesn't motivate me to try harder. I just hate all her yelling! Anyway, it's the setter, Jenny; she kept putting the ball too far from the net. It messed up everybody. But coach kept yelling at the rest of us, when it was all Jenny's fault."

"So," said Malcolm, "you're quitting because the coach yells at you? Williams has been a screamer since she took over as head coach two seasons ago. Her yelling never bothered you before. Or is it something else?"

"Yes! No. I don't know," replied Caitlin in exasperation. "Who cares? It's not like I have a future in volleyball after college."

"What does that have to do with anything? You knew a spot on the Olympic team or the AVP beach volleyball pro tour was like a near-impossible long shot before you came here. And another thing: Don't tell me you don't get motivated when the coach is fired up. I've seen you in games. You're angry because you know you can play Jenny's position better than she can. But the coach doesn't let you. So, you're pissed at the coach. It's not about the yelling."

"You're right. Jenny's terrible. I don't understand how she ever made the team."

"But, Caitlin, nobody can spike and defend at the net like you. Coach knows that, and so does everyone else on the team. So, you're going to play the front line. Which is great. I'll bet that Jenny wishes she could play where you play."

"Well, I don't care about any of that anymore. I'm quitting and therefore I'm quitting. End of story. Let's talk about something else. . . . Tell me how your marching band practice was today."

"Fine, I hear you. You're going to quit. And, yes, we can change the subject. But let me just say for the record that I still don't think you're really being honest about why you're leaving the team and the sport you love. And just saying over and over again that you plan to quit does not explain why you plan to quit."

In the scene that just played out, Caitlin explains her decision to quit the college volleyball team. Her stated reason is that she is not motivated to play harder by the coach's constant criticism. Ergo, she's going to quit the team. That may be a reasonably logical argument, if we also assume that Caitlin is the kind of athlete who does not respond well to that coaching style. But her friend Malcolm knows better. He does not accept her argument because he has seen her respond positively to the coach's style in game situations. The truth is that Caitlin does get motivated to play harder when the coach is fired up. Although Malcolm does not make the point, we might observe that the word *yelling* is negatively slanted. It fits Caitlin's current negative attitude toward the coach. But "yelling" is probably not the best word to use when talking about those times when the coach is successful in motivating Caitlin.

Caitlin offers another argument, saying that she has no future in volleyball. Malcolm points out the irrelevance of that consideration, and then he suggests that her real reason for being upset with her coach has to do with which position she wants to play. Caitlin ends the conversation about volleyball with a definitive and somewhat defensive, "I'm quitting and so I'm quitting." Malcolm makes it clear that her final statement forcefully affirms her intention, but it is not an acceptable answer to the question "Why?"

Throughout their conversation Malcolm has been evaluating his friend Caitlin's arguments. This chapter focuses on building argument evaluation skills. It presents a comprehensive and straightforward evaluative process that we can apply in everyday situations, much in the way that Malcolm did in the opening conversation with Caitlin. The process includes four specific tests. An argument must pass all four tests to be considered worthy of acceptance as proof that its conclusion is true or very probably true. Each of these four criteria is rooted in the natural and universal human practice of making arguments and giving reasons. Because critical thinking requires skill at evaluating arguments in real-life contexts, we begin with the expectations and responsibilities associated with giving reasons and making arguments.

Giving Reasons and Making Arguments

The practice of giving reasons for our claims—that is of making arguments—is part of every human civilization and culture. Every natural human language includes terminology and social conventions for making arguments as well as for evaluating them. But argument making is sensible only because of a set of presumptions we all implicitly rely upon to engage in this practice successfully. These presumptions are operative wherever and whenever people engage in a sincere effort to make arguments to one another regarding a decision about something of serious mutual concern. These presumptions form the basis for the expectations the listener has—and the responsibilities the argument maker has—when offering reasons to explain that the argument's claim is worthy of acceptance as true or very probably true.

TRUTHFULNESS

The practice of argument making rests in part on the presumption upon which so much of human discourse depends, namely that the speaker is telling the truth. In other words, when making arguments we expect that *the statements offered as premises are, in fact, true.*[i] As a rule, people collaborating with one another to think something through do not intentionally use erroneous information or lie to one another. If a disagreement about the truth of any premise arises, then the people involved have two options. They can make a reasonable effort to review the evidence for that premise, or they can qualify the force with which they assert and maintain any claims in the line of reasoning that relies on that premise. Of course, people do lie on occasion. And so this presumption often goes unfulfilled.

The assumption that premises are true provides a reasonable basis for moving to consider whether those premises imply that the conclusion is true or very probably true. But without first really considering the truthfulness of the premises, it becomes

Thinking Critically It's All Thanks to the Ionians!

Where did our persistent practice of trying to resolve problems by making arguments and giving reasons originate? Today the practical "pro-and-con" approach is applied to problems of every kind by people throughout the globe. There are other ways that human beings used in the long history of civilization, like accepting as true whatever the king, high priest, or soothsayer declared. Today in many places around the world people are less inclined to accept an authority figure's declarations on blind faith. The give-and-take of public argument making and reason giving aimed at solving practical problems, while not unknown in more ancient times, is a three-thousand-year-old cultural legacy of the Ionians. Watch the fascinating account of the rise and the impact of this approach to resolving practical problems offered by Burke in the video "The Way We Are," episode 1 of his captivating series, *The Day the Universe Changed.* Question: How would we decide, individually or as a community, what to believe or what to do if we did not have the practice of reason giving and argument making? Would we go back to trusting authority figures? Or would we perhaps try to apply a method that was developed in more recent centuries—empirical investigation? **www.mythinkinglab.com**

Watch the **Video** on **mythinkinglab.com**

only an exercise, rather than a matter of practical significance, to consider the argument's logical strength. Here are two arguments with true premises.

- Chicago is north of St. Louis. St. Louis is north of New Orleans. Therefore, Chicago is north of New Orleans.
- There are 325 children registered in grades 1 through 6 at the Carver Elementary School. We have tested 40 percent of these children for reading skills. We also have taken a number of physiological measurements of each of those same children. Our data show that there is a strong positive statistical correlation between the size of a child's feet and the child's reading skill level.

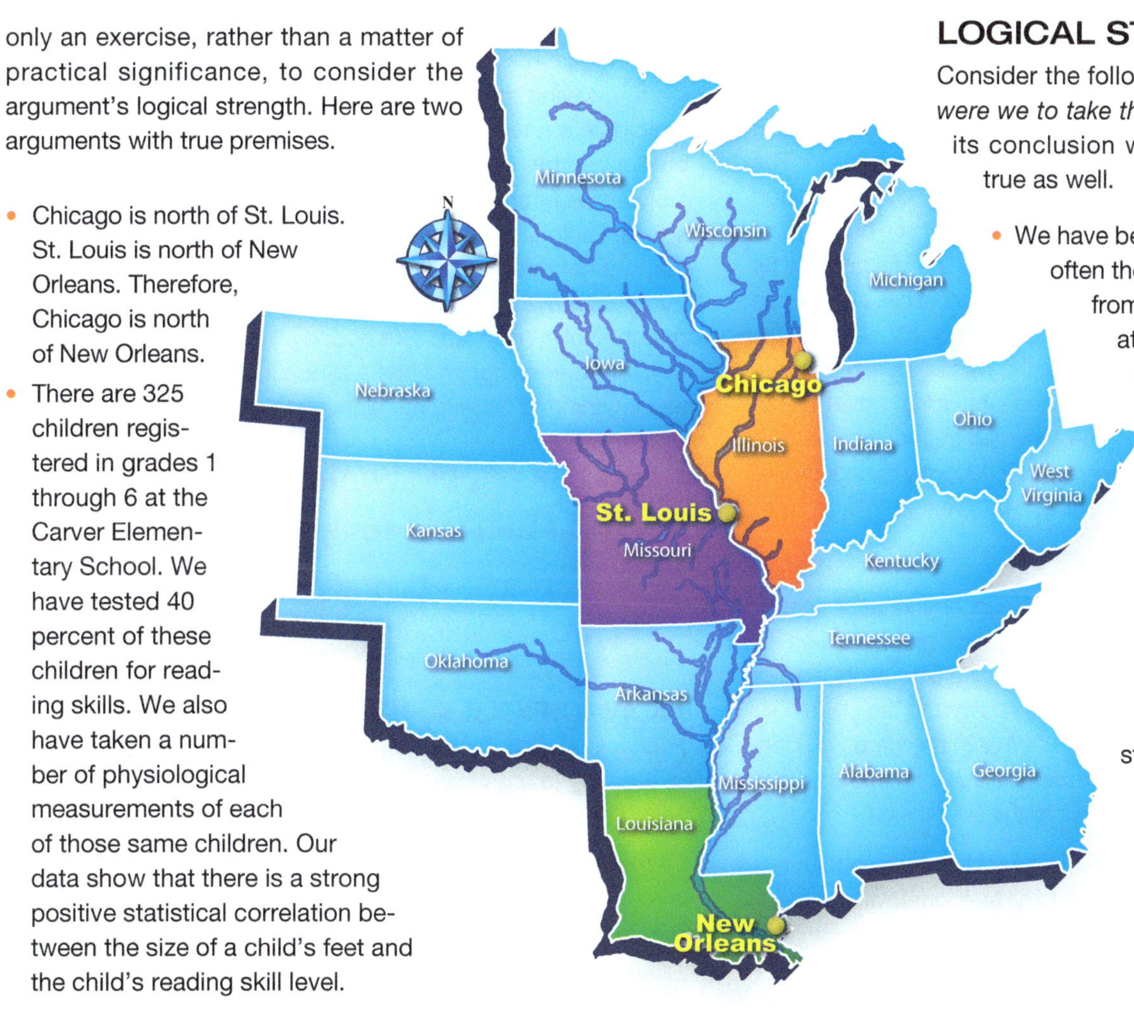

Mississippi River Basin

The map verifies that the cities are positioned the way the first example's premises indicate. Regarding the second example, one obvious question is whether the measurements mentioned in the third sentence included foot size. If not, we may want to call into question the truthfulness of what the speaker is saying. If the speaker does not have any information about the children's foot sizes, then the speaker's argument falls apart.

LOGICAL STRENGTH

Consider the following example. In this case, *were we to take the premises to be true*, then its conclusion would have to be taken as true as well.

- We have been keeping track of how often the weekday 6:56 am Caltrain from San Francisco arrives late at the Millbrae station. We conducted three 6-week surveys over the past 12 months. In each survey the weekday train arrived at the Millbrae station late 24 out of 30 times. Therefore, there is an 80 percent probability that the weekday 6:56 am Caltrain will arrive late at the Millbrae station.

Next we have an example in which all the premises are true as well, but the reasoning is an unacceptable leap from a simple association to an assertion of a causal relationship. The premises of this argument, although in fact true, do not logically justify accepting the truth of the conclusion.

- All throughout Europe data collected on children between the ages of 5 and 12 show a strong positive correlation between height and reading skill level. Therefore, learning to read makes European children grow.

To repeat what others have said, requires education; to challenge it, requires brains.

—Mary Pettibone Poole, *A Glass Eye at a Keyhole*, 1938[ii]

Physical development and reading level! How are they related?

When someone offers an argument, the speaker's reason is supposed to be the logical basis for the speaker's claim. The point of giving reasons for our claims is that the reasons support the claims. The second presupposition of the practice of argument making is that the speaker's reason, if true, is the logical basis for the speaker's claim. Notice that this is a hypothetical. *Were we to assume that the reason a person gives for his or her claim is true,* that assumption would then imply that the person's claim is probably or necessarily true as well. In the language of logic, this presupposition is expressed this way: The assumed truth of the premises of an argument justifies or implies, either inductively or deductively, that the conclusion of the argument also be taken as true.

RELEVANCE

It happens that a conclusion might be true *independent of* whether the premises are true or whether the premises logically support the conclusion; because this is so, when we make arguments we also presume that the truth of the reason is *relevant* to the claim. This presumption might be called the "So What?" presumption. Consider this example, where the premises are true and the conclusion is true, but the reason is not relevant to the claim.

- To many around the world, the Statue of Liberty symbolizes the welcome our nation extends to all freedom-loving people. So, as the great Yogi Berra says, "You can observe a lot just by watching."

This argument is so odd that it would get a squawk out of the Aflac duck. The reason given has no relevance to the truth of the claim. Their only connection is that Yogi Berra happened to have been a player for the New York Yankees, and the Statue of Liberty happens to be in New York. For us that is not sufficient to say that the one is relevant to the other. If anyone were to seriously present this reason as the basis for the truth of the conclusion we would say, "So What? That's not relevant!" And this reveals our third presupposition: *the listener takes the reason given by the speaker to be relevant in believing the speaker's claim.*

There is no point to giving reasons if the listener is not going to rely on those reasons in deciding what to believe with regard to the claim. Recall that in our opening example, Caitlin changed her story about why she wanted to quit the volleyball team. At first she talked about how the coach's yelling and berating players was her issue. But then she gave a different reason, saying that she was going to quit because she did not anticipate a future as a professional volleyball player. Malcolm challenged her on that, noting that it was not even relevant, in his view. A future in professional volleyball was never her reason for joining the college team, and the absence of that opportunity is not relevant to why Caitlin now wants to quit the team. Everyone, including Caitlin, may believe that Caitlin wants to quit the volleyball team. But nobody, not even Caitlin, believes that whether or not she has a future in professional volleyball has anything to do with her wanting to quit at this point in time.

Many people would sooner die than think; in fact, they do so.

—Bertrand Russell British author, mathematician, & philosopher (1872–1970)

NON-CIRCULARITY

Our fourth precondition when we give reasons for our claims is that *the claim must not be part of the basis for believing in the truth of the reason.* Argument making in real life is essentially a one-way street: The reasons are used to establish

Scott Adams, Inc, United Media/United Feature Syndicate, Inc.

Anyone ever say something circular like this to you at school, home, or work?

Four Tests of an Argument's Worthiness		
Test Name	**Order of Application**	**Test Condition**
Test of Truthfulness of the Premises	First	The reason is true in each of its premises, explicit and implicit.
Test of Logical Strength	Second	If the reason were true, then the conclusion (claim) would be true or very probably true.
Test of Relevance	Third	The truth of the claim depends on the truth of the reason.
Test of Non-Circularity	Fourth	The truth of the reason does not depend on the truth of the claim.

the acceptability of the claim. But we do not use the claim to explain the reason. We use the premises of the argument to support the conclusion, not the conclusion to support the premises. In other words, there is directionality to argument making. The flow of reasoning is from reason toward claim, not the other way around. All the examples of mapped arguments in Chapter 5 show this, because in mapping arguments we used the arrow convention to display the intended directionality of the argument maker's reasoning.

In the Dilbert's cartoon strip the boss criticizes Dilbert's presentation for being full of technical words and way too long. We naturally think that the boss came to those conclusions about the presentation by having seen it and evaluated it. But no. The boss then turns around and uses those same two claims as his reasons for not seeing or evaluating the presentation. It makes no sense to give a reason as the basis for one's claim and then to use that claim as the basis for one's reason. In a comic strip, circular reasoning is funny, and in real life it can be infuriating.

The Four Tests for Evaluating Arguments

The four presumptions about argument making as an interpersonal human activity form the bases for the four evaluative criteria applicable to all arguments. In other words, it would be reasonable to accept a person's argument if it met all four of the conditions implied by those presumptions. These are the four conditions:

1 To the best of our knowledge and understanding, the reason is true.

2 The logical relationship between the reason and the claim is such that the claim must be true or very probably true if the reason is taken to be true.

Thinking Critically *The Name of the Rose*

Consider an example from the film adaptation of *The Name of the Rose.* Early in the story the abbot in charge of a fourteenth-century monastery comes to a visiting Franciscan scholar-detective, played by Sean Connery, to explain why he believes that a recent death there was caused by the devil. This attribution of the cause of death to a supernatural intervention occurs about 9 minutes and 15 seconds into the film.

Access the scene at **www.mythinkinglab.com**. Listen carefully to the abbot as he makes his argument. It begins with the abbot saying that the monks had found a body after a hailstorm. The abbot's argument is only a few lines. Transcribe it so that you can have the language in front of you. Evaluate it for logical strength. Can you think of how the monk might have died other than at the hand of the devil, given the information you have at that point in the story? Is there a set of circumstances so that all the premises of the abbot's argument could remain true but the claim still be false? How plausible or implausible are those circumstances? For example, if someone were to answer, "Yes, an alien from another galaxy could have transported into the closed room and killed the monk," we probably would regard that as highly implausible.

As you watch the film, new information is presented visually. The director gives us a shot looking up a steep ravine at the abbey, which wraps around the crest of the hills above the ravine. There appear to be two towers. Sean Connery's character and the viewer can use that information to show the logical flaw in the abbot's argument about the death being caused by the devil. Connery as he completes his alternative explanation to his young apprentice, played by Christian Slater by saying that there's no need of the devil to explain this death. The death was natural. Go 6 minutes and 29 seconds further into the movie and view this short scene. Transcribe Connery's alternative explanation. Map it, and after reading this chapter, evaluate it for logical strength.

Watch the **Video** on **mythinkinglab.com**

What is Connery's argument for the claim that there is no need for the devil?

3. The relevance of the reason to the claim is such that the truth of the claim actually depends on the truth of the reason.
4. The truth of the claim must not be used to support the truth of the reason.

An argument that satisfies all four conditions is worthy of our acceptance as a proof that its claim is true or very probably true. We will apply the adjectives *good* and *worthy* to those arguments. A **good argument** or a **worthy argument** is an argument that merits being accepted as a proof that its conclusion is true or very probably true. The four conditions listed to define four tests to apply when evaluating arguments are to be applied in the order given. As soon as an argument fails to meet one of the four, it is no longer eligible to be considered a good or worthy argument. Let's see how to apply each of these four to determine whether or not an argument is worthy of acceptance.

TEST #1: TRUTHFULNESS OF THE PREMISES

In everyday situations and in critical thinking, the truth or falsity of premises is our first concern. If one or more of the premises of an argument is not true, then, for practical purposes, there is little point in moving forward to evaluate other aspects of the argument. If we do not have the best information (actually we have some false information built into our reasoning), our first job is to get our information straight. The critical thinking habit of truth-seeking demands that we courageously endeavor to learn what we can before moving forward with claims and arguments based on incomplete knowledge.

The Test of the Truthfulness of the Premises is a favorite in police dramas. We have all seen the scene in which detectives interrogate someone who gives a lame alibi like this one: "My friends and I were at a movie the night the crime took place." The detectives check the story and discover it is a lie. Having exposed his lack of truthfulness, the detectives no longer accept the person's alibi and may even make the liar their prime suspect.

TEST #2: LOGICAL STRENGTH

One way to apply the Test for Logical Strength is to challenge yourself to imagine a situation, if possible, in which all the premises of an argument are true, but the conclusion is false. If there is no possible scenario in which all the premises of an argument can be true while at the same time its conclusion is false, or if such a scenario is extremely improbable, then the argument passes the Test of Logical Strength. However, to the extent that such a scenario is possible, plausible, likely, or actually true, the argument fails this test.[iii] If an argument is deductively valid, then there is no conceivable counterexample to disprove that argument.[iv] If there is a possible scenario, but it is remote and implausible, perhaps as unlikely as 1 chance in 20 or 1 chance in a 1,000, then we can maintain a comparable degree of confidence in the argument's logical strength. Logicians call an argument with true premises that has also passed the Test of Logical Strength a **sound argument.**[v] *Sound* is used here in the sense of "healthy," meaning that such an argument ordinarily is rather robust and deserves our attention as we deliberate what to do or what to believe.

What if there is more than one reason given to support a claim? Does discovering that one reason has a false premise make the claim unacceptable? Consider this example; here a claim is supported by two reasons.

- "I'm not an alcoholic. Look, I only drink beer. And, in fact, I've never been drunk in my life."

Review Map #1 below to see how we would map these arguments.

Suppose we discover that the speaker is telling the truth when he says that he only drinks beer. However, the implicit but unspoken premise ("Someone who only drinks beer cannot be an alcoholic") is false. So, the first argument fails the Test of the Truthfulness of the Premises. Suppose we then discover that the speaker is also being truthful when he says that he has never been drunk in his life. This, along with the generally accepted truth of the implicit, but unspoken, premise "A person who has never been drunk cannot be an alcoholic," indicates that his second argument passes the Test of Truthfulness of the Premises.

That second argument also passes the Test of Logical Strength. It is difficult to imagine a case where a person who has never been drunk is an alcoholic, although it is not impossible to imagine such a case. So, it would seem reasonable to accept that our speaker is not an alcoholic, even though one of his reasons (that he only drinks beer) was poor. His second argument, based on the other reason (he has never been drunk in his life), which is independent of the first, was sound.

MAP > it > OUT 1

People often provide multiple reasons for a given claim and some of those reasons may turn out to be false. One may be inclined to dismiss the claim itself, having heard the speaker present one unsound argument. Dismissing an otherwise-worthy claim simply because one or more of the arguments made on its behalf contains false reasons is one of the most common human reasoning errors. Each reason-claim combination is a separate argument. Thus, before determining that a claim should be rejected, a strong critical thinker would first need to find problems with the soundness of *all* the arguments being advanced.

Because there are so many important varieties of deductive and inductive arguments, which require special attention when testing for logical strength, we will cut this discussion short at this point. We will devote the next two chapters to issues of logical strength as they are manifested in deductive reasoning and in inductive reasoning. For the moment, let's complete our review of the four tests of an argument's worthiness to be accepted.

TEST #3: RELEVANCE

The Test of Relevance requires making a reasoned judgment that the truth of the conclusion *depends upon* the truth of the reason given. If an argument passes the first two tests, then The Test of Relevance is the next one to apply. Recall that the presumption we are seeking to fulfill is that the author's reason is, in fact, the basis for believing the claim. And the listener must judge if accepting the claim as true depends on support derived from that reason. For example, the following example passes the Test of Relevance.

- A study from the Harvard Center of Risk Analysis estimates that cell phone use while driving contributes to 6 percent of crashes, which equates to 636,000 crashes, 330,000 injuries, 12,000 serious injuries and 2,600 deaths each year. The study also put the annual financial toll of cell phone–related crashes at $43 billion. The research investigated whether or not a hands-free device was less dangerous. The statistical evidence suggests not. It appears from the data that the fact that the driver was distracted by the conversation was a greater factor than was the type of cell phone technology, hands-free or not, that was being used. The researchers concluded that using cell phone technology of any kind while driving was associated with a greater risk of automobile accidents.[vi]

Is the fact that you like Golden Gate Park relevant to wanting to travel to Europe?

Is it fair for another driver to expose you to greater risk just so he or she can text a friend?

By contrast, the next argument fails the Test of Relevance.

- Yeah, like I'm really wanting to visit Italy, you know, Old Europe, man. Why is too obvious. See, I've been working part-time at the Golden Gate Park in San Francisco. It's incredible there. Beautiful, open, free. There's this one garden there that kind of reminds me of pictures I've seen of Italy. I love being outside in the spring, the flowers and the fresh air, the smell of fresh-cut grass. And all that makes me think how great it would be to just live slow and relaxed, like they do in Europe, taking life as it comes. You know what I mean?

That the research on car accidents and cell phone usage is relevant to the conclusion in the first example is obvious in the first example. The connection between visiting Italy and working part-time in Golden Gate Park in the second example

Thinking Critically Pythagoras and the Shape of Immortal Perfection

Pythagoras, the controversial Greek metaphysician (570 to ca. 490 BCE) and his followers, the Pythagoreans, have had a significant influence on Western thinking. They were among the first to suggest that human beings possessed immortal souls, that the heavens moved with harmonious mathematical precision, and that unchanging stability was a characteristic of divine perfection. The Pythagoreans took a special interest in mathematical relationships (e.g., the Pythagorean Theorem) and often attributed moral characteristics to them. Note, for example, that certain two-dimensional shapes can be made into three-dimensional solids with the same number of sides: a circle into a sphere, a triangle with three equal sides into a three-sided pyramid, a square into a box. Noting these relationships, the Pythagoreans regarded the circle, triangle, and square to be "Perfect" shapes. And, because perfection was evident in the universe, it made sense to them to infer that the source of that perfection was divine. Hence what Carl Sagan called the "God-Hypothesis" in the first episode of the *Cosmos* series. Today we might take issue with a leap from geometric observations to theology. We would question the relevance of the one to the other. Likewise, we might question the leap from "unchanging" to "incorruptible" to "immortal" and on to "perfect." We would perhaps challenge an unspoken assumption by asking, "Why would the attribute of being unchanging be considered relevant to the concept of perfection?" What do you think? **www.mythinkinglab.com**

For more on this extremely influential and fascinating progression of ideas from geometric shapes to perfection to the divine, revisit the first episode of *Cosmos* where Sagan is talking about the influence of the ancient Greek philosophers on modern thinking. Located around the same place in the episode where he tells the story of Aristarchus, which we mentioned in Chapter 2.[vii]

Watch the **Video** on **mythinkinglab.com**

seems to be tenuous at best, more based on the person's free association of ideas than on any actual evidence. Even if the speaker imagines a connection, the listener can judge that the reason given, even if true, is not a basis for believing that the speaker wants to visit Italy. In fact, if the speaker had simply said, "I want to visit Italy," that might have been more credible than his having come up with the far-fetched and irrelevant dissertation about the glories of a part-time job in a city park—even if it is one of the greatest public parks in this nation.

Applying the Test of Relevance is substantially easier for people with knowledge and experience appropriate to the context and issues under discussion. For example, U.S. laws prohibiting using gender as the basis for workplace promotions express American society's judgment that a person's gender is not a relevant consideration when deciding whether the person merits a promotion. In another country with a different set of cultural mores, gender-based promotion decisions might be considered both legal and reasonable. The Test of Relevance is important because people often make the argument that they should be excused from responsibility for certain actions. However, as a people, having heard these arguments before, we have come to the judgment that certain reasons are not going to be accepted as relevant. For example:

- Claiming that one was following the direct orders of one's superior is not a relevant defense against charges of war crimes.
- Claiming that one's judgment was impaired by drugs or alcohol is not a relevant defense against charges of vehicular manslaughter resulting from driving while under the influence.
- Claiming that one must protect his or her GPA because one plans to become a doctor is not a relevant defense against charges of academic dishonesty in any course, including general education elective courses.

TEST #4: NON-CIRCULARITY

The fourth and final test of logical acceptability is the Test of Non-Circularity. This test requires that a claim is not being relied upon either implicitly or explicitly as part of a chain of reasoning used to support its own reason. If such a chain looping back on itself is found, then the argument maker is reasoning in a circle. An argument is like a river that flows in one direction, from reasons and evidence toward the conclusion. A river cannot feed itself and still be described as a river; rather, it becomes a stagnant moat. So it is with good arguments: Claims cannot be the bases for their own reasons. If they were, then the reasoning would simply be stagnant and self-justifying in the most unflattering sense.

The final argument Caitlin made about quitting the volleyball team was "I'm quitting and therefore I'm quitting." Here the circle is so tight that the reason and the claim are identical. If we were to map it, it would look something like Map 2 above.

Circular reasoning, like a moat around a castle, is stagnant thinking.

We can interpret this way of speaking as a way of emphasizing one's claim, but not as a way of proving one's claim. It is like saying "I'm quitting" real loud. But volume is not proof.

Reasoning in a circle results most frequently from the use of multiple arguments in combination with each other. At times people lose track of the reasons for their beliefs, forgetting, for example, that their basis for believing one idea, *X*, was because they accepted another idea, *Y*, and that their reason for accepting *Y* had been their belief in *X*. The result is that the person has high confidence, although misplaced, in both ideas. However, because their support for *X* is *Y* and their support for *Y* is *X*, the reasonable thing would be to have no confidence in either. For example, consider the pair of arguments in this passage:

- I'm sure we can make this marriage work. That's why we're talking through our problems, which shows that we still care for each other. And that's why I'm sure we can make this marriage work.

MAP > it > OUT 3

We can make this marriage work.

We still care for each other.

We're talking through our problems.

The speaker's reason for the claim that the marriage is salvageable is the belief that both parties still care for each other. And the basis for believing that goes back to the idea that the marriage can be saved. If we were to map these arguments, it would look like Map #3 below. This reasoning is as fragile as a house of cards; touch it in the least with an analytical finger and it collapses upon itself.

CONTEXTS FOR ARGUMENT MAKING AND EVALUATIVE TERMS

There is nothing about argument making for purposes of coming to a decision that requires the format to be a debate or in any way an adversarial confrontation. In fact, it does a great disservice to decision making to imagine the process as a confrontation of opponents pro and con. In such an adversarial frame, it is too easy to forgo truth-seeking in the false belief that argument making is simply the search for facts that support one's preconceptions. Too often, the courageous desire for best knowledge is trumped by the competitive need to vanquish the opposition. In that case, the honest pursuit of reasons and evidence, wherever they may lead, even if the reasons and evidence go against one's preconceptions or interests, is abandoned because intellectual honesty and integrity are not always suitable virtues for warriors who must bring home the victory for their side.

Good arguments—subtle and yet effective as solid proofs that their claims are worthy of being accepted as true—occur within a variety of linguistic behaviors and activities. In natural language contexts, argument making takes many forms. It can be a personable and friendly conversation exploring options and considering ideas. It can also be embedded in warnings, recommendations, preambles to policy statements, public addresses, conversations, group meetings, negotiations, monologues, reflections, and even the lyrics of songs.[viii]

The vocabulary we use to evaluate arguments must be as flexible as our understanding of the contexts of argument making. A conversation with a colleague about an impending decision can be helpful, even if we would not think about calling it *valid*, or *persuasive*. Natural language offers such richness in its evaluative repertoire that it seems wise, at least at this early point, not to close our options by prematurely stipulating a set of evaluative categories. Thus, with the understanding that the terms listed in the table "Evaluative Adjectives for Arguments and Their Elements" are not meant to be interpreted rigidly or in some special technical way, let us simply go forward with our evaluation of arguments using common language.

Thinking Critically Evaluate Argument Worthiness and Explain

Assume that all the premises that are asserted are true. Apply the remaining three tests to evaluate each argument to see if it is worthy of acceptance. Remember, if the argument fails a test, you do not have to apply any further tests because at that point the argument is not worthy to be accepted. In each case, give a detailed explanation to support your evaluation. State in your own words why the argument is worthy of acceptance, or why it is not a good argument.[ix]

1 When I stop at a traffic light, I hear this funny rattling sound coming from under my car. It is sort of in the middle or maybe toward the back, but definitely not toward the front. I only hear it when the car is idling, not when I'm driving along at a reasonable speed. My dad said once that the metal baffles inside a muffler can loosen up if the muffler is old and rusty. He said that a loose baffle makes a rattling sound when it vibrates, like when the engine is idling or when the tires are out of alignment. My muffler is at least nine years old. So, I'm thinking that probably the rattling sound is coming from the muffler.

2 Every successful president of the United States was both diplomatic and decisive. General Dwight D. Eisenhower served in WWII as the Commander of the Allied Armies in Europe and then went on to become a successful U.S. president. Therefore, President Eisenhower was decisive and diplomatic.

3 In a perfect world, the government should investigate whether any laws were broken relating to the treatment of wartime detainees. But this is not a perfect world. So, it would be a mistake for the government to engage in such an investigation.

4 Vancouver is east of Toronto. Toronto is east of Montreal. So Vancouver is east of Montreal.

5 Having turned up some new information, a cold case homicide detective interviewed the victim's husband some years after his wife's death. The distraught husband said, "I have been praying all these years, asking God to send us something. My wife's murder could not have been simply a random accident. God would not permit that."[x]

6 Generally, forest fires at this time of the year are caused by careless campers. From where I'm standing I see a column of dark smoke rising out of the forest across the valley. So, some camper must have caused a forest fire.

7 In hot dry regions of the country, new fires can be caused by lightning, arson, or sparks from other nearby fires. Therefore, in the summertime all the fires in states like California, Arizona, and Nevada must be caused by mentally deranged individuals or lightning strikes.

8 If a little child is happy then the child will jump around. Little Marcus is jumping around. So, he must be a happy child.

9 If God intended marriage for the sole purpose of human reproduction, and if same-sex couples are entirely incapable of human reproduction, then it follows that God did not intend marriage for same-sex couples.

10 We interviewed three people and each one was very personable. I think that the first person had the strongest resume. But the second person seemed a lot smarter. I liked the enthusiasm and energy that the third person had, but that person never worked for an organization like ours before. It's a tough choice. But I'm thinking that probably the second person would be the best of the three for us to hire since innovative ideas are more important to us than experience or enthusiasm.

11 Torturing prisoners of war often results in poor-quality intelligence. Experience has shown that people in pain will say anything to get the pain to stop. The pain can be either physical or psychological—it does not matter. People crack under the pressure of an experienced interrogator using torture methods. So, we cannot trust the information that comes from that source.

The table on page 141 offers suggestions regarding the range of evaluative adjectives that might reasonably be applied when evaluating the different elements of major concern, data, warrants, claims, and arguments.

Common Reasoning Errors

Humans learn from their mistakes. We can capitalize on that truism to strengthen our skill in evaluating arguments by studying those errors of reasoning that have over the centuries earned themselves a reputation as alluringly deceptive and misleading. As a group they are called "fallacies." **Fallacies** are deceptive arguments that appear logical and seem at times to be persuasive, but, upon closer analysis, fail to demonstrate their conclusions. Many types of fallacies have their own name, as we shall see.

Learning to recognize common fallacies and learning how to explain in ordinary, non-technical terms the mistaken reasoning they contain is a great aid to evaluating arguments. The seven fallacies of relevance described in this chapter are types of arguments that will fail the Test of Relevance. In Chapters 8 and 9, to help with the application of the Test of Logical Strength, we will expand the list of fallacies to include several that masquerade as logically strong deductive or inductive arguments.[xii] Skill in recognizing when someone is making a fallacious argument is a strong defense against being mislead about what to believe or what to do.

FALLACIES OF RELEVANCE

For centuries logicians have supplied lists of the kinds of deceptive arguments that people have tended to find persuasive.[xiii] When it comes to being deceived by the rhetoric of gifted speakers, eloquent writers, or clever advertisements, many of us are no wiser or more sophisticated than people were in Aristotle's time. Yet in our effort to make an honest argument to another person about what to believe or what to do, we are asking that person to accept the truth of the claim

12 Torturing prisoners may be against the Geneva Conventions, but it is a legitimate means of gathering potentially valuable intelligence. There have been cases where the information given to us by prisoners who have been repeatedly waterboarded, for example, has turned out to be correct. Therefore, we are justified in using torture on prisoners even if our laws explicitly prohibit such methods.

13 Assume that *a*, *b*, and *c* are any three numbers. Where *w* and *y* are numbers, assume that *f*-is a mathematical function such that *fwy* yields *z* where *z* is the number that is the product of *w* multiplied by *y*. It follows deductively then that (*fa*(*f*bc)) yields to the product of *a* multiplied by the product of *b* multiplied by *c*.

14 In the past whenever the TV news programs in Chicago ran headline stories featuring a sketch artist's drawing of a fugitive, the Chicago Police Department hotline received over 200 phone calls from people all over the city who said that they spotted the person. Tonight the Chicago TV news programs are going to feature a sketch artist's drawing of a fugitive whom the police are trying to locate. This will probably yield hundreds of calls on the CPD hotline.

15 Suppose we imagine electricity flowing through wires in the way that water flows through pipes. With this analogy in mind, it would be reasonable to infer that wires that are larger in circumference should be capable of carrying greater electrical loads.

16 James Harris: "I made a commitment, threw balls 'til my arm got sore. They always talked about the down-and-out in the NFL, so I went to the park—nobody there but me—to test myself. I was going to throw at this tree blindfolded. I figured if I hit the tree, I'm ready. If I miss the tree, I've got to walk and get the ball. The first time I tried, I missed. The ball was way downfield. I debated about trying it again. I dropped back and threw, heard the ball hit, and something went through me—gave me all the confidence in the world."[xi]

17 The novice pointed eagerly in the direction of the pier and said, "There, do you see them? What fine specimens of brown pelicans." His instructor asked, "Why do you think that they are brown pelicans." "Because," answered the novice, "they look just like the brown pelicans in this picture that I just took of them with my phone. It's really a great shot. Come and see."

18 As you all know, there has been a successful Chinese experiment that used a single cell from a laboratory rat to generate a living chimera of that rat. In the chimera, which lived to adulthood, 95 percent of its genetic material was identical to the donor rat. Noted cell biologist Dr. Kastenzakis believes tinkering with nature is just what scientists do. Therefore the Chinese experiment raises no ethical questions and poses no ethical risks.

19 My client did not intend to use the weapon, and so he is not guilty of armed robbery. Yes, we agree with the prosecution that he committed the robbery. And, yes, we agree that he was carrying a weapon and that he brandished the weapon to intimidate the store clerk and the customers. We agree that the law reads, "Anyone who carries a weapon in the commission of a robbery shall be guilty of armed robbery." And, yes we admit that he shouted, "Everyone down on the floor or I'll shoot." But, and here is the key fact, the weapon was not loaded. He did not have ammunition anyplace on his person or in his possessions. He never intended to use that weapon. And, therefore, the crime that he is guilty of is robbery, but not armed robbery.

20 Not every argument is of equal quality. Therefore, at least one argument is better than at least one other argument.

because of the reason given. This expectation of relevance at times goes unfilled. Instead we provide a reason that is not relevant. Creative questioning is a powerful tool for uncovering the false assumptions that lie at the core of fallacies of relevance. Whatever the specific application of the question, the fundamental issue is "What does the reason actually have to do with the claim?" From this fundamental concern we can derive a number of specific queries.

Evaluative Adjectives for Arguments and Their Elements		
PREMISES	POSITIVE NEGATIVE	True, Possible, Probable, Verifiable, Believable, Precise, Clear, Accurate, Factual, etc. False, Improbable, Self-Contradictory, Fanciful, Fabricated, Vague, Ambiguous, Unknowable, etc.
REASONS	POSITIVE NEGATIVE	Certain, True, Probable, Verifiable, Relevant, Wise, Sensible, Well-Applied, Plausible, Believable, etc. False, Improbable, Self-Contradictory, Poorly Applied, Irrelevant, Foolish, Irrational, Fanciful, Unknowable, Vague, Equivocal, Ill-Conceived, Circular, etc.
CLAIMS / CONCLUSIONS	POSITIVE NEGATIVE	Well-Documented, Strongly Supported, Well-Argued, Certain, True, Reasonable, Plausible, Probable, etc. Improbable, Poorly Supported, Unfounded, Self-Contradictory, Uncertain, False, Biased, Preposterous, Implausible, etc.
ARGUMENTS	POSITIVE NEGATIVE	Worthy, Good, Acceptable, Sound, Valid, Logical, Strong, Persuasive, Reasonable, etc. Unworthy, Poor, Unacceptable, Unsound, Fallacious, Illogical, Incomplete, Unreasonable, Bad, Trivial, etc.

Thinking Critically Worthy of Acceptance?

Evaluate the following arguments using all four tests, applied in their proper sequence.

1 Being a sports writer offers challenges that writing standard news stories do not. Here's why. Unlike with standard news stories where the writer is telling the reader something that the reader does not yet know, most of the time the reader knows who won the game before reading your article. Readers probably watched the game on TV. This means a sports writer has to find some angle or some clever and captivating way of telling the story.

2 The *Seattle Post-Intelligencer* and *Denver Rocky Mountain News* are going to close unless they find a buyer. Same for the *San Francisco Chronicle* and the *Miami Herald*. The *Minneapolis Star-Tribune* may file for bankruptcy. The *Los Angeles Times* Sunday edition has shrunk to half its former size. And the list of newspapers in financial trouble goes on and on. I think it is safe to say that the newspaper business may be dying.

3 [In this case assume the premises are true.] Look, officer, you can't arrest me on felony rape charges just because she's 17 and I'm 21. Yes we had sex. But it was consensual. And anyway, in two weeks she's going to be 18, and we plan to get married.

4 [Again, assume the premises are true.] I like the President's approach to trade with China, and I haven't heard anyone give any evidence that his approach is not going to be effective. So, it must be the right thing for our country to do at this time.

5 Our male enhancement pills are so effective, that we'll give you your first bottle of pills for free. How could we afford to do that if everything we say about them wasn't true?

There are so many ways that a reason might be irrelevant to the claim being made that it is impossible to list them all. Some arguments appeal to tradition, others, particularly in marketing, try to sell us something simply because it is new. Some use emotions such as fear to move us to accept the claim being made. Others try flattery, praise, trust, or affection to move us to accept a claim that we otherwise would not believe.

- We've always done it this way. I don't want to change our policy.
- Try Sudsy Detergent in your dishwasher. It's new!
- It would be a grave mistake to think that there is no Hell. In fact, an eternal error.
- Hey, trust me. Would I lie to you, baby?

Many fallacies based on irrelevant appeals have earned their own name, which is helpful to remembering the type of mistaken assumption being made.

Appeals to Ignorance

It is false to assume that the mere absence of a reason for (or against) an idea should itself count as a reason against (or for) the idea. Consider these examples:

- We know we have a corporate spy someplace in the organization, probably on the management team itself. There is no evidence that it is Francesca. In fact, she's too clean, if you know what I mean. We should fire Francesca; she's the spy.
- Someone here took my computer and I need it back. Who was it, John? Was it you? No, you say. Well prove it! Aha, you have no proof to offer. Well then, John, it was you. And I want it back now!
- Impressionism, and especially French Impressionism, is the best form of art. You can't name any other form that has been proven to be more beautiful. Can you?

Thinking Critically *The Practice*: Wrongful Termination

In an episode of a once-popular 1990s TV series, *The Practice,* called "The Battlefield" that aired October 15, 1998, the owner of a small dry-cleaning business is being sued by his former employee. The former employee, a smart and competent Iranian woman, alleges that her former employer fired her in violation of anti-discrimination laws. Her lawyer claims that she was fired because of her national origin. This is called a wrongful termination civil suit, and, if she wins, she would be entitled to financial compensation for lost income and additional payments for punitive damages. Her former employer would have to pay if he loses. But he may win because his defense attorney's strategy is to argue to the jury that they would have made the same decision, were they in her former employer's shoes. Watch the episode and transcribe the arguments presented by the defense attorney. Identify fallacies of relevance as may be included in that attorney's arguments. The jury's decision in this case is unexpected, as is the judge's final response. Access this episode at www.mythinkinglab.com. The reference the defense attorney in the video clip makes to a bomb in the *World Trade Center* is not about September 11th. The reference is to a prior attack. On February 26, 1993, a Ryder rental truck loaded with 1,500 pounds of explosives was detonated in the underground garage below the World Trade Center's North Tower. The bombing killed six people, injured more than a thousand, and shocked the nation. This episode of *The Practice* asks us to think about whether our fears should be permitted to override our rights. By the way, the memorial to that 1993 attack was destroyed on September 11th.

Watch the Video on mythinkinglab.com

Use Creative Questioning to Challenge the Relevance of Reason to Claim

	Here are six examples of arguments we might hear in everyday situations. In each case the reason offered may in fact be true, and the claim might be true in a few cases as well. But the reason given is not relevant to the claim being asserted.	By applying the fundamental concern, "What does the reason actually have to do with the claim?" to the six examples, we can focus the issue of relevance in each case.
1	John, a world-famous violin virtuoso, endorses Brand XYZ motor oil. So, Brand XYZ motor oil is an excellent product.	What about being a great violinist qualifies one as an expert on motor oil?
2	On the Internet I saw that lots of students said they liked Professor Smith's classes. She's really popular. So, Professor Smith must do an excellent job getting her students to learn the material.	What about being popular implies that a professor is effective in getting students to learn? What if the professor was just an easy grader or funny or likable, but actually a lousy teacher?
3	I can't think of any practical alternatives to gasoline as a vehicle fuel. So, there is no practical alternative automotive fuel.	Are the limits of the possibilities for alternative fuels to be equated with the limits of my imagination?
4	Yesterday in class when we were working on our project, you didn't say a word. So, you must not know anything about the topic.	Could there not have been many reasons, other than ignorance of the topic, why a person does not speak up during group project time in class?
5	If we look around us, we see that people everywhere value human life. So, it is right that we should defend this value over all others.	Why does the fact that many people value something make it imperative that it be regarded as the highest of all possible values? Would we say the same for other things people everywhere value, such as a true friend, a respectful and appreciative supervisor, or satisfying dinner followed by delightful entertainment and a good night's sleep?
6	We chose to go to the moon not because it is easy, but because it is hard.	Just because something is difficult, should we now choose to do that thing? Yes it was difficult, but that was not the basis for our decision to choose to go to the moon.

Appeals to the Mob

It is false to assume that because a large group of people believes something or does something that their opinion or their behavior is necessarily correct or appropriate. Here are two examples of the Fallacy of Appeal to the Mob, also known as the *Bandwagon Fallacy*.

- Everyone knows that a black quarterback will not be able to lead an all-white team. So we will not put Doug Williams at the quarterback position.[xiv]
- All the kids at school are getting tattoos. Every one of my friends has one, and some have two. I see adult men and women with tattoos. So, I'm thinking that it's about time that I get a tattoo.

Appeals to Emotion

It is false to assume that our initial emotional response to an idea, event, story, person, image, or proposal is necessarily the best guide for forming reflective fair-minded judgments. Chapter 10 discusses this in greater detail, because the relationship between our emotional responses and our decisions about what to believe and what to do are complex. Because gut reaction and reasoned reflection are both real factors in human decision making, strong critical thinkers learn to draw on both of those resources. But, at times, people offer fallacious arguments that provide nothing more by way of a reason than an appeal to one's unreflective emotional response. Here

If you cannot name a superior art form, does that imply that French Impressionism is the best art form?

Thinking Critically — Should DUI Homicide be Prosecuted as Murder?

A prosecuting attorney in New York is bringing charges of murder against individuals who have killed other people while driving under the influence. The attorney argues that everyone understands that driving while under the influence poses risks for the driver and for other people, including the risk of a fatal accident. The statutes provide for charges of "depraved indifference" when one's behavior results in the unintended but foreseeable death of another human being. Defense attorneys argue, among other things, that the laws pertaining to murder were never intended to be applied in this way. The debate was captured by CBS's *60 Minutes* in a segment that aired on August 2, 2009. Review that segment and map out the reasoning for both sides of this debate. Evaluate the reasoning using the four tests for evaluating arguments. After completing your evaluation, present your own reasoned views on the matter. Access this segment at www.mythinkinglab.com.

Watch the **Video** on **mythinkinglab.com**

are some examples of the Appeal to Emotion fallacy, which tends to rely on emotionally loaded words and expressions.

- I love you like the son I never had, and because of that I believe you. No, I must believe you. Love leaves no other option.
- He's a lousy, rotten terrorist. One of those people. So, there's no question but that he deserves to die.
- Watch out—the political right is populated by a dangerous pack of hate-mongering jackals. They will destroy this nation because they have no respect for the truth or common decency. You can't believe anything they say.
- Watch out—the political left is a goose-stepping gaggle of dangerous tax-and-spend liberals. They will destroy America with bloated, ineffective social programs hardworking taxpayers can't afford. You can't believe anything they say.
- I know you have your heart set on going to Stanford; it's something you talked about since you were in the ninth grade. You kept up your grades, aced the SATs and did everything you could to be admitted. And, I'm so proud of you, you did it. Everyone is. And you know what, I don't care what it takes or what the family has to do, we'll mortgage the house, get another job, anything. But somehow, some way, whatever it takes and whatever the consequences for me or for your younger brothers and sisters, we are going to find the money so you can go to Stanford. I've made up my mind. That's what we'll do!

Ad Hominem Attacks

It is false to assume that because the person making the argument is deficient in some real or imagined way, the person's argument, work product, or views should not be accepted on their own merits. *Ad hominem* is Latin for "against the person" and it expresses the error this fallacy makes, which is to claim that a person's ideas must be tainted because the person has some vice or flaw. The opposite would be equally fallacious, which is to assume that because the person making the argument is virtuous the argument must be good, too. Strong critical thinking no more obliges us to reject every argument a convicted felon makes than to accept every argument the Dali Lama might make. Arguments are to be judged on their own merits, not on the merits of their producers. Here are some examples.

- I don't trust you because of what you did last week at the party. Don't bother trying to explain yourself. As far as I'm concerned, anything you say is a lie.
- He worked for Clinton and Carter. How can we believe that the legislation he's proposing will do anything but ruin this country?
- The Governor was spotted drunk in a Brazilian bordello. There are pictures on the Web already. So we can't believe anything he says about environmental problems or clean energy solutions.
- You have nothing of value to contribute to this conversation about minority race relations. You're not black, Latino, Asian, Native American, or anything. You're white.
- I'm sorry, but I don't find his income and expense projections credible. I don't see how he could have done those numbers correctly. After all, we know he's looking for another job. He has no company loyalty.

Straw Man Fallacy

This fallacy relies on the false assumption that, by refuting a weaker argument among several reasons given in support of claim, one has successfully refuted all the reasons for that claim. For example:

- Look, we can't approve your request for additional advertising funds. You said that one of the four marketing options you were reviewing was Web page design. But we have a policy not to support any further Web-based development.
- You said in Chapter 1 that legalizing drugs was a good idea, because then they could be regulated for quality and taxed. And you said it would permit us to shift law enforcement resources toward preventing other more harmful criminal behaviors. But I'm opposed to new taxes of any kind. So, I cannot agree with you about legalizing drugs.

A variation on the theme, also called the Straw Man Fallacy, is the pernicious practice of attributing to the opposition an argument that is not theirs, and then demolishing that argument. The misattribution may be mistaken, or worse, intentional. From this the person committing the fallacy misleadingly then argues that he or she has destroyed the opposition's position entirely. Besides being intellectually dishonest and inconsistent with the critical thinking virtue of truth-seeking, this practice violates the values of objectivity and fair-mindedness. And, adopting the strategy of trying to make an idiot out of the opposition can be risky, too. To use straw men and misrepresentations when presenting the opposition's arguments can lead one's listeners, and at times one's self, to the mistaken belief that there is little or no merit to the opposition's view. In the health care reform debates during the summer of 2009, those opposed to "death panels" demonized the proposed legislation for a provision that, as it turned out, was already part of existing Medicare law. The actual provision to which they objected provided for reimbursement to health care providers if patients voluntarily sought end-of-life counseling about such matters as living wills, power of attorney, DNR orders, or hospice care. When the dust settled, even some who had raised the specter of government death panels backed away from that overly dramatic straw man criticism. Others, however, continued to believe that the proposed legislation would mandate euthanasia.

Underestimating one's opponent in a debate or dispute can backfire. One reason is that listeners can be alienated when they realize that we have not been fair or objective. A second reason is that we may become overconfident. Strong critical thinkers try not to mislead themselves. They school themselves to follow the political adage, "Never believe your own press releases." In so doing, strong critical thinkers try not to confuse defeating a straw man argument with giving due consideration to the opposition's arsenal of worthy arguments.

Playing with Words Fallacy

In Chapter 4 we saw how vagueness and ambiguity can be problematic in certain contexts. The Playing with Words Fallacy exploits stereotyping, problematic vagueness, problematic ambiguity, donkey cart expressions, or slanted language in attempting to support a claim. Because Playing with Words Fallacies are so varied and so vexing, we devoted that chapter to learning how to apply our critical thinking skills to resolve those problems. Here are three more quick examples of arguments that are fallacious because they exploit problematic uses of key terminology.

- Everyone who is in prison can still be free, for true freedom is the knowledge of one's situation. The more one knows about one's self, the more one is truly free.
- I'm selfish, you're selfish. When you really look at it, everybody tries to meet their own needs. So, we are wrong to be so harsh on a guy just because he spends all his money on nice clothes and fine food for himself while letting his children run around hungry and in rags.
- We cannot know that others experience the world as we do. To truly know is to be inside the minds of others. And that is simply not possible.

Thinking Critically Bluster, Badger, Interrupt, Whine, and Scoff

Strong critical thinkers lament the incivility, degradation, and degeneration of today's political discussions in the media. Too often the best-known political commentators engage in fallacious argumentation. They can be recognized by their reckless and irresponsible rhetorical tactics: Instead of carefully presenting the best arguments for both sides of an important issue, these commentators stridently, if irrationally, defend one side and verbally assault the other. Their opinions are laced with ridicule and *ad hominem* attacks. They dismiss out of hand any evidentiary facts which the opposition might present, and often they insist their own untrue "facts" instead. They opine loudly. They interrupt often, and talk over any representative of the other side who might be present. They whine about being victimized by the other side and yet they complain that the other side whines about being victimized. They scoff at divergent opinions. And they disrespect anyone and everyone who disagrees. To see examples of these abusive and misleading tactics in action watch the 10 video clips at **http://www.askmen.com/top_10/celebrity/top-10-crazy-political-commentators_10.html**

In episode 203 (February 18, 2011) of *Real Time*, the political commentator Bill Maher takes on Liberals for their wishy-washy relativism in regard to the rights of women in the Middle East. Watch his commentary after the "New Rules" segment that comes toward the end. As a challenge exercise, map and evaluate Maher's arguments. While you have episode 203 cued up, look for elements of bluster, badger, interrupt, whine, and scoff in that episode. One of the biggest risks to effectively analyzing and evaluating the strength of the other side's perspectives is to regard those who disagree as either "evil" or "stupid." Does Bill Maher or any of his guests in that episode make this mistake? State your argument by providing reasons and evidence. **www.mythinkinglab.com**

Watch the **Video** on **mythinkinglab.com**

Thinking Critically Is Competitive Cheerleading a Sport?

Many activities that are recognized as sports include artistic and musical components—for example, synchronized swimming and figure skating. With hundreds of thousands of junior high school, high school, and college students participating in cheerleading, why is cheerleading, at least in its competitive format, not a recognized varsity sport? Cheerleading is as physically demanding as many varsity sports (more than some, such as golf) and certainly every bit as dangerous as football and hockey in terms of the number of serious injuries each year. Is it tradition, gender politics, pressure by the companies that make money off of cheerleading competitions, what?

Research the arguments for and against recognizing cheerleading as a high school and college sport. Map and evaluate the arguments on both sides of this issue. Be on the lookout for the fallacies discussed in this section, you should spot a few. You might begin with the debate on Varsity.com, **http://varsity.com/event/1252/cheer-as-a-sport.aspx** and view "Cheerleading: Controversy and Competition" from the ESPN series, *Outside the Lines* on **mythinkinglab.com**.

Watch the **Video** on **mythinkinglab.com**

Misuse of Authority Fallacy

One version of Misuse of Authority Fallacy relies on the false assumption that if a powerful or popular person makes a claim, then the claim must be true. In addition to this error, there are other ways that expertise can be misrepresented and misused, as we saw in Chapter 6. In that chapter we talked about the many characteristics of an authority whose word should, in all probability, be accepted. Because reliance on the word of another is such an important part of how people decide what to do or what to believe, critical thinkers are alert to the fallacies of Misuse of Authority. In addition to the many given in Chapter 6, here are a couple more examples:

- When asked why the curriculum had been changed, the Superintendent of Schools replied that the city's Chamber of Commerce had advised that the students in the Junior High School would be educationally better served if all teachers spent more time during class preparing the students to take standardized math tests and less time on American History, Creative Writing, Social Studies, Art, Leisure Reading, or Health Education.
- In the annual NCAA March Madness office pool, the boss picked North Carolina State to win it all. I'm going to pick the same team she picked. After all, she's the boss.

The written historical record shows that the question of how to evaluate arguments goes back at least 2,500 years to the birth of the field study today known as logic. Logic, with its historical roots in rhetoric and argumentation, explores the question of how to decide whether or not the claims based on various kinds of arguments should be accepted. More specifically, it focuses on one of the presumptions of the practice of argument making: If the premises of an argument are taken to be true, that implies that the argument's conclusion is probably or necessarily true as well.[xv] The wisdom and intellectual treasures of many of the world's great cultures and civilizations are evident in the rich history of logic. Fortunately, there are many important and enduring lessons that critical thinking can draw from the study of logic with regard to testing the logical strength of different kinds of arguments, recognizing common fallacies, and understanding the conditions for using inductive and deductive reasoning methods correctly. Drawing on those enduring lessons, we have begun to assemble our tool kit for evaluating arguments in this chapter. We will add some precision tools for the evaluation of arguments in the next two chapters.

Better than Memorizing—Analyze, Internalize, and Explain

Here and in the next two chapters we introduce a great many names traditionally used to categorize reliable argument patterns and unreliable fallacious varieties of arguments. The terminology of logicians and other scholars who study arguments is valuable to the extent that it helps us remember the underlying ideas. But the key to learning is to practice and internalize the process of interpreting people's words correctly so that we can understand exactly what their arguments are, and then evaluating those arguments fair-mindedly. People with strong critical thinking skills are good at evaluating arguments because they can recognize logically correct forms of arguments as well as common mistakes that make an argument invalid, unjustified, or fallacious. And, they can explain in their own words why one form is reliable and another is fallacious. All around the planet, there are people who are skilled at evaluating arguments, but who may never have learned the academic terminology to classify arguments. Unfortunately, there are others who can recite the textbook definitions of the rules and terms from memory but yet, in practice, lack skill at evaluating arguments.

Being able to explain why an argument is unworthy of acceptance is a stronger demonstration of one's critical thinking skills than being able to remember the names of the different types of fallacies. Exercising one's skills in analysis and explanation leads to stronger critical thinking and better communication of one's thinking in daily life. Rote memorization, which is valuable for other things, is not a critical thinking skill.

REVIEW

Study and Review on mythinkinglab.com

The natural human practice of reasoning with a friend or colleague to seek the truth reveals how, in argument making and reason giving, four important presumptions support the expectations and responsibilities that make that practice work in real life. The reasons we give should be true. The arguments we use should be logical. The reason given should be the relevant basis for accepting the truth of the claim. And the claim should not be used to lend support or credence to the reason. These four conditions ground the application of four straightforward tests to determine whether an argument is worthy of being accepted. The four are the Test of Truthfulness, the Test of Logical Strength, the Test of Relevance, and the Test of Non-Circularity. The tests, which are to be applied in a particular order, must all be passed if an argument is to be worthy of acceptance as a demonstration that its conclusion is true or is very probably true.

To help with the application of the Test of Relevance, we examined seven common fallacies of relevance. Arguments that manifest these fallacious approaches to presenting reasons and claims often beguile and mislead us. In the next two chapters we will explore in greater detail the application of the Test of Logical Strength with special attention to deductive reasoning and inductive reasoning. There we will expand the discussion of fallacies as well, for there are some that masquerade as valid deductive arguments and others that masquerade as strong inductive arguments.

KEY TERMS

good argument/worthy argument is an argument that merits being accepted as a proof that its conclusion is true or very probably true. (p. 136)

sound argument is an argument with true premises that also passes the Test of Logical Strength. (p. 136)

fallacies are deceptive arguments that appear logical, but upon closer analysis, fail to demonstrate their conclusions. (p. 140)

FIND IT ON MYTHINKINGLAB.COM

In this chapter we invited you to work three exercises using video clips you could access at www.mythinkinglab.com.

Watch the Video on mythinkinglab.com

- On page 135 we used the argument that the monk was not killed by the devil in *The Name of the Rose*. Later in the story, the real killer is identified. Watch the film in its entirety and then map out the reasoning Sean Connery's character uses to solve this captivating murder mystery.
- On page 142 we used an episode of *The Practice*, and our focus was on the arguments the defense attorney made. The jury ended up agreeing with the defense in that story. View that episode again and this time focus on the arguments the plaintiff's lawyer made. Evaluate those arguments using the four criteria presented in this chapter. The case in favor of the plaintiff's claim of wrongful termination appears strong. Why were those arguments less effective with the jury?
- On page 144 we discussed the *60 Minutes* report on prosecuting homicide by drunk driving as murder. What about the person who sold the driver alcoholic drinks in a bar or restaurant just prior to the fatal accident? If that bartender suspected that the driver was drinking too much to safely operate the car, should he or she have refused service? Did the person have an affirmative obligation to call a taxi or to take away the driver's car keys? If so, then should the person who sold the drinks be prosecuted too as an accessory or an accomplice to the murder? When making your arguments, be sure to present them in ways that will satisfy all four tests for the worthiness of arguments that we learned in this chapter.

Exercises

REFLECTIVE LOG: THE ETHICS OF FALLACIOUS ARGUMENTATION

What if we discovered that we could manipulate the voting public more effectively by the use of fallacious arguments than by the use of worthy arguments? Consider the political impact of the "death panels" issue described under the Straw Man Fallacy on pages 144–145. The entire episode generated more heat than light. And, yet, it may have achieved its political purpose. Many who heard and believed that the proposed legislation envisioned a eugenics program akin to that advanced by Nazi Germany showed up at town meetings to vent their anger and voice their objections. If the goal was to delay or derail the Democratic legislative agenda, then the strategy succeeded. This is only one example of using one's skills at argument making to achieve one's goals. Defense attorneys who get juries to acquit criminals is another, as are prosecuting attorneys who get juries to convict innocent people accused of crimes. The ethical question for all critical thinkers is: To what purposes ought I to put my powerful critical thinking skills? This question is analogous to the question: To what purposes ought I to put my college education? These are, in part, ethical questions and, in part, questions about one's sense of how to make the meaning of one's life. And what are your answers? Why?

GAYS IN THE MILITARY

Over many years public opinion has slowly shifted to the extent that the "Don't Ask Don't Tell" legislation, which enabled the U.S. military to discharge openly gay or lesbian soldiers, has been repealed. I have discussed this issue with groups of U.S. Special Forces master sergeants and can attest to the fact that not all enlisted personnel agree that the regulations should be changed. Research the arguments for and against the "Don't Ask Don't Tell" military policy. Map and evaluate the arguments on both sides using the four tests of the worthiness of arguments presented in this chapter. You might include in your examination of this issue the article "Gays in the Military," published in the *Rand Review 35*(1) (Spring 2011): 14–20.

Read the **Document** on **mythinkinglab.com**

GROUP VIDEO EXERCISE: ASSISTED SUICIDE

Assisted suicide is legal in Oregon and in Sweden, but not in many other places. There are arguments pro and con. Begin this exercise by familiarizing yourself with those arguments. Map and evaluate the most common arguments on both sides. Then interview four people over the age of 60, four people between the ages of 18 and 30. With their permission, videotape the interviews so that you can check the accuracy of your analysis and interpretation of their perspectives. Ask each person to consider whether or not they would agree with a law that permitted a competent adult to seek and to receive suicide assistance from a licensed health care professional, if that adult knew with a very high level of confidence that she or he had a medical condition that would result in painful death in less than three months. Map and evaluate, using the four tests of the worthiness of arguments presented in this chapter, the set of arguments you collect from the eight people. Is there a pattern? You might find it interesting in conjunction with this exercise to watch the July 13, 2009 "Tiny Bubbles" episode of the Showtime series, *Nurse Jackie* (episode 6, season 1).

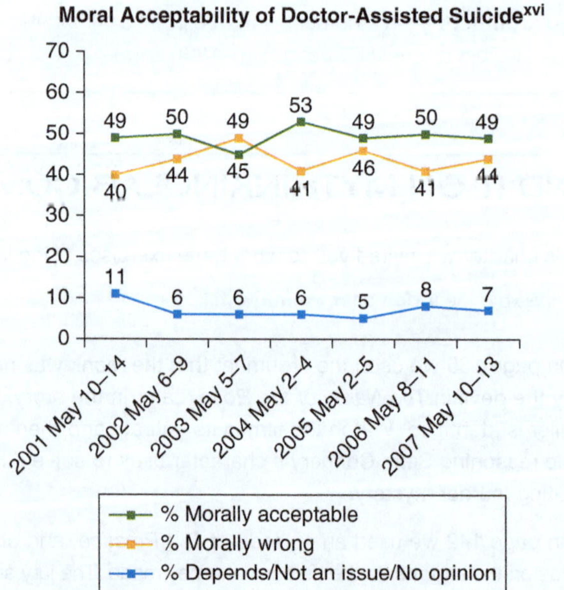

FIVE-PERSON GROUP PROJECT: WHAT DO OTHERS THINK?

Each member of the group, having seen the *60 Minutes* video and worked on the exercise on page 144, will have thoroughly considered the issue of homicidal DUI as murder. But for this project, you must first set aside your own individual opinions on this matter. This project involves interviewing people for whom this issue is much more than a textbook's abstraction. So you and the other members of your group need to focus on what you hear in the interviews without letting your personal opinions get in the way.

Your group will conduct four sets of interviews. You must always have at least two members of your group participate in each interview. This is so that you can help each other remember what the person being interviewed said.

First set of interviews: Locate at least one person—two or three if possible—who has been arrested for driving while under the influence of alcohol or drugs even if not for homicide. Find out what that person or those people think. Listen to their arguments, and then write them down and evaluate those arguments. Be objective and fair-minded in your evaluation, regardless of whether you agree or disagree with the person's position.

Second set of interviews: Locate at least one person—two or three if possible—who is a former drinker. Interview that person the same way. Get his or her views on the matter, write down the person's arguments, and evaluate those arguments objectively and fair-mindedly.

Next, contact MADD or some other volunteer organization that is known for its stance on issues relating to drunk driving. Follow the same drill. Get that organization's arguments down and evaluate them.

Finally, contact the office of your local prosecuting attorney, or the state police and, again, conduct your interview and evaluate the arguments you hear.

Having talked directly with people who are close to this issue, your group must now assemble all the arguments that came forward in the various interviews. In light of these perspectives, take a stance individually and as a group on whether or not homicide by DUI should be prosecuted as murder. Write out the group's opinion and give the reasons. Write out your individual opinion, if you disagree, and give your reasons. Whatever you finally decide, use strong critical thinking and sound reasons.

Read the Chapter on mythinkinglab.com

Listen to the Chapter Audio on mythinkinglab.com

Why should

she have to die? All she wanted was to surprise her brother.

There is precious little margin for error on the boundless emptiness of outer space as Thomas Barton, pilot of the tiny emergency dispatch ship, discovers. Thinking he was on a rescue mission to deliver vitally needed vaccine to an outpost colony, he soon finds he must decide who will live and who will die.[i]

Unless the vaccine reaches the colony in time, everyone at the outpost will surely die. Barton's little craft must get through. No other emergency dispatch vessel can reach the colony in time. A young woman, upon learning that Barton's ship was headed for the distant colony, stowed away aboard his ship. She thought maybe she would have to pay a small fine. But it would be worth it to be able to visit her brother who is stationed at the outpost. When the ship's computer detects the additional weight of her body, Barton is able to locate the young stowaway. Her hopes turn to dust when she learns that standing military orders require stowaways aboard emergency dispatch ships to be summarily executed.

Barton does not want to execute the young woman. But the computer says that the craft does not have sufficient fuel to land safely with her aboard. The immutable physics of mass and velocity require that 120 pounds must be jettisoned into space.

<<< The distressing dilemma that opens this chapter follows Thomas Barton, a fictional pilot of the emergency dispatch ship in the 1954 sci-fi classic "The Cold Equations," by Tom Godwin. The story was later made into an episode of the CBS television series *The New Twilight Zone.* Check for it on YouTube.com.

CHAPTER 08

Evaluate Deductive Reasoning and Spot Deductive Fallacies

HOW do we evaluate deductive arguments?

HOW can we recognize common fallacies masquerading as deductive arguments?

Desperately, Barton and the young woman pile everything that is not welded down into the airlock. Binders, tools, eating utensils and everything else they find is jettisoned into space to lighten the load. But it is not enough. With nothing else left to jettison, except one of the two of them, the cold equations become all too real.

The mission will fail, the colonists will all die, and so will Barton and the young woman unless the excess weight is shed before the craft enters the atmosphere. Barton considers sacrificing himself. But that will not work. The young woman cannot possibly land the craft safely. If Barton sacrifices himself, he will guarantee that she and all the colonists will die.

The logic of the situation makes Barton's dilemma inescapable. No matter what choice he makes, someone must die. Deciding not to decide is the equivalent of deciding that everyone should die. All the options are bad. The story draws to a close with the young woman stepping into the airlock. The hatch is sealed. Barton reaches for the red handle that will jettison her into space. Cold as this logic may be, only with her death can others live.

Although at times we all have wished otherwise, none of us can suspend the laws of nature or the laws of logic. In business, a company that is losing money may have no choice but to lay off good employees. In a medical emergency, health care professionals have to triage those needing care. Military leaders have to send brave soldiers into combat knowing that some will not return. Regardless of our feelings in the matter, there are times in our lives when the facts and the logic of a given situation force us to entertain options we had hoped never to face. In those situations we cannot afford to be wrong about the facts or about the logical strength of our reasoning.

In this chapter and the next we drill into the Test of Logical Strength more deeply than in the previous chapter. We will focus on evaluating the logical strength of deductive arguments in this chapter and inductive arguments in the next. Recall that in Chapter 2 we characterized the distinction between deductive arguments and inductive arguments this way: Deductive arguments present their conclusions as necessarily true, if all the premises are true. By contrast, inductive arguments present their conclusion as probabilistic, given the truth of the premises. Within each of the two broad classifications of arguments, we will find many varieties. So, to extend our skill of argument evaluation, we will explore these different kinds of deductive arguments and inductive arguments more deeply.

Because this chapter and the next focuses on the second of the four tests for evaluating arguments, the Test of Logical Strength, we are going to assume that the examples used here have already passed the first test, the Test of the Truthfulness of the Premises. We are going to assume that the premises of the example arguments are true. This will be a lot to swallow, because some of the premises are patently false. But, for the purposes of focusing on the logic of the arguments, let us entertain the fiction within the context of these two chapters.

The current chapter begins with positive examples of logically correct forms of deductive arguments and then continues with fallacies that masquerade as deductive arguments, but are not logically correct. We then do the same with inductive arguments in the next chapter. We first examine the positive examples and then the misleading fallacies that mimic those more reliable inductive reasoning strategies.

Deductive Validity and Language

For an argument to be evaluated as a **deductively valid argument**, it must be impossible for the premises all to be true and the conclusion false. In other words, an argument is deductively valid if there is no possibility, real or imaginable—short of changing the very meanings of the terms and the rules of grammar—that will make the premises all true and the conclusion false. Deductively valid arguments satisfy the Test of Logical Strength.

As you'll see in a moment, certain configurations of language form deductively valid argument templates. By their very form and structure these argument templates reliably generate valid, deductive arguments as long as we do not change the meanings of the words or the rules of grammar. This is why the premises of a valid deductive argument are said to make the truth of the conclusion necessary. Without violating the meanings of the words or the grammatical rules of the language, there is no possible way for the premises all to be true and the conclusion false.

REASONING DEDUCTIVELY ABOUT DECLARATIVE STATEMENTS

The first group of valid deductive argument templates we will consider include those that derive their valid structures from the way simple statements interact grammatically when we use prepositions or adverbs that have logical force. These include the words *and*, *or*, *not*, and *if . . . then. . .*

Denying the Consequent[ii]

One valid deductive argument template we rely on regularly produces arguments structured like this:

Premise #1: If A, then B.
Premise #2: Not B,
Conclusion: Therefore, not A.[iii]

The argument template uses the capital letters *A* and *B* to stand for simple positive declarative statements, like **A = "The Nissan Titan gets good gas mileage."** And **B = "The Dodge Ram 3500 gets outstanding mileage."** Substituting those two statements in the template for A and for B produces this argument:

- Premise #1: If **the Nissan Titan gets good gas mileage**, then **the Dodge Ram 3500 gets outstanding mileage**.
- Premise #2: It is not the case that **the Dodge Ram 3500 gets outstanding mileage**.

Conclusion: Therefore, **the Nissan Titan gets good gas mileage**.

In each of the examples below, **the blue statement** is A and **the orange statement** is B" Here are three more examples of valid deductive arguments built by substituting declarative statements into the "denying the consequent" argument template.

- If **Richard graduated with honors**, then **Richard maintained a GPA of 3.2 or higher.**
  It is not the case that **Richard maintained a GPA of 3.2 or higher.**
  Therefore, **Richard did** not **graduate with honors.**
- If **you have been promoted to the rank of captain,** then **you have served for at least a year.**
  You have not **served for at least a year.**
  It follows then that **you have** not **been promoted to the rank of captain.**
- If **the sun shines on the far side of the moon**, then **red roses grow inside the barns in Iowa.**
  It is not true that **red roses grow inside the barns in Iowa.**
  So, it is not true that **the sun shines on the far side of the moon.**

This last example is curious because it is structurally valid, but in fact we would not rely on it as a proof that the sun does not shine on the far side of the moon. The argument is not acceptable because even if the second premise were true, which is highly doubtful, the first premise is not. This example is a quick reminder that logical strength, while essential, is not the only consideration that strong critical thinkers have in mind when evaluating arguments in real life. Again, in all the examples here and to follow we are maintaining our focus on the logic while assuming that all the premises are true.

Yes, it can be challenging to assume that the premises are true, especially considering the notoriously dreadful gas mileage that gas guzzlers like the Nissan Titan and the Dodge Ram actually get. But that is why we separated the Test of the Truthfulness of the Premises from the Test of Logical Strength. Facts and logic are two different things.

It is the mark of an educated mind to be able to entertain a thought without accepting it.[iv]

—Aristotle *Greek critic, philosopher, physicist, & zoologist (384–322 BC)*

Fill in the argument template to create two deductively valid examples of your own.

If ____________________, then ____________________.
It is not the case that ____________________.
Therefore, it is not the case that ____________________.

If ____________________, then ____________________.
It is not the case that ____________________.
Therefore, it is not the case that ____________________.

Affirming the Antecedent

A second very commonly used deductive argument template also relies on the meaning and grammatical power of "if ______, then ______" expressions. In this case, however, the second premise affirms that the "if ______" part is true.

Premise #1: If A, then B.
Premise #2: A.
Conclusion: Therefore, B.[v]

Here are three examples of arguments that are valid on the basis of affirming the antecedent deductive argument template.

- If **the price quote from College Insignias is lower than the price quote from University Logos**, then **we will get the T-shirts for our AIDS walk team printed at College Insignias.**

The price quote from College Insignias is lower than the price quote from University Logos.
Therefore, we will get the T-shirts for our AIDS walk team printed at College Insignias.

- If you are eligible to graduate with honors, then you will receive notification from the Registrar.
  You are eligible to graduate with honors.
  So, it follows that you will receive notification from the Registrar.
- If the sun shines on the far side of the moon, then carrier pigeons are raised in Denver.
  The sun shines on the far side of the moon.
  So, carrier pigeons are raised in Denver.

As with pre-algebra, we are substituting values for the variables in the formula. In pre-algebra the result was an equation; here the result is a valid argument. Fill in the "affirming the antecedent" argument template to create two deductively valid examples of your own.

If ____________________, then ____________________.
____________________.
Therefore, ____________________.

If ____________________, then ____________________.
____________________.
Therefore, ____________________.

Disjunctive Syllogism

When we are presented with various alternatives and then learn that one or more of those alternatives will not work, it is logical to reduce our options. The argument template for this deductively valid structure produces arguments with this pattern:

Premise #1: Either **A** or **B**.
Premise #2: Not **A**.
Conclusion: Therefore, **B**.

Here are two examples of arguments that are valid by virtue of the "disjunctive syllogism" argument template.

- Either we'll go to Miami for spring break, or we will go to Myrtle Beach.
  We are not going to Miami for spring break.
  So, we will go to Myrtle Beach.
- Either I'll take organic chemistry over the summer, or I'll register for that course next fall.
  No way will I be able to take organic chemistry over the summer.
  So, I'll register for that course next fall.

The next example is a variation on the second. Instead of the first alternative being eliminated so that the second emerges as the only remaining option, in this case the second alternative

Grammatically Equivalent Structures			
These pairs of logically equivalent grammatical structures . . .		. . . give us two ways to say the same thing.	
A unless B	A or B	The dishwasher is still full unless you emptied it.	Either the dishwasher is still full or you emptied it.
Not A unless B	If A then B	The table is not set unless Grandma set it.	If the table is set, then Grandma set it.
A only if B	If A then B	It is time to eat only if Dad is done grilling the steaks.	If it is time to eat then Dad is done grilling the steaks.
If A then B	Either A or not B	If it is time to clear the table then we are done eating our meal.	Either it is time to clear the table or we are not done eating our meal.
Neither A nor B	Not A and not B	Neither Bill nor Sue likes singing.	Bill does not like singing and Sue does not like singing.
Not both A and B	Either not A or not B	We cannot buy both a car and a boat.	Either we cannot buy a car or we cannot buy a boat.
A if and only if B	If A then B, and if B then A	We will rent a cottage if and only if our vacations coincide.	If we will rent a cottage, then our vacations coincide, and if our vacations coincide we will rent a cottage.
If A then not B	If B then not A	If the rent is due then we cannot afford to go out to dinner.	If we can afford to go out to dinner, then the rent is not due.

Thinking Critically *Neither*, *Unless*, and *Only*

There are other terms that, when used correctly, can be used in valid deductive argument templates. Create 10 arguments by first filling in the templates using the 3 declarative statements provided.

Statement A: College tuition increases will average more than 8 percent.

Statement B: I will earn my degree sometime within the next three years.

Statement C: I have legal access to unlimited amounts of cash.

1 Either A, B, or C. Not C. So, A or B.

2 It is not the case that both A and B are true. So, either A is not true or B is not true.

3 Neither B nor C is true. So, B is false.

4 B unless C. Not B. So, C.

5 A only if B. A. Therefore, B.

6 Not A unless C. Not C. Therefore, not A.

7 If A then C. If B then C. Either A or B. So, C.

8 It is not the case that if B then C. Therefore, B, but not C.

9 It is not possible that not B. Therefore, B.

10 A if and only if B. Not B. So, not A.

On some topic of your own choosing, write 3 declarative statements. Fill in the 10 templates using your statements. Now evaluate each of the arguments created by the first 10 fill-ins and the second 10 fill-ins. Is it possible in any of those cases that the argument's conclusion could be false if you assume that all argument's premises are true? The answer should be "no" in all 20 cases.

was eliminated so that the first emerged logically as the only remaining option. The template for this is:

Premise #1: Either **A** or **B**.
Premise #2: Not **B**.
Conclusion: Therefore, **A**.

- Either **I'll take organic chemistry over the summer**, or **I'll register for that course next fall**.
  No way can **I take organic chemistry next fall**.
  So, **I'll take that course over the summer**.

In context "that course" refers to organic chemistry. In actual practice, when we make arguments, we seldom repeat statements verbatim. Instead, we use internal references that are contextually unproblematic.

A special chapter entitled "The Logic of Declarative Statements" extends the discussion above into the discipline of Logic. That chapter presents a method for expressing the key logical relationships between simple declarative sentences using symbols. And it provides a surefire way of evaluating the validity of arguments expressed in that symbolic notation. Pearson Education includes the "The Logic of Declarative Statements" custom designed versions of *THINK Critically*.[vi]

REASONING DEDUCTIVELY ABOUT CLASSES OF OBJECTS

Other deductive arguments derive their valid structures from the meanings of words in the language used to show the interaction of groups of objects. Words like *some* and *all* are used to express our ideas about how individual objects and groups of objects relate.

Applying a Generalization

Consider this example of reasoning about individual objects and groups of objects:

- All the books by Michael Connelly feature his fictional hard-boiled LAPD detective, Hieronymous Bosch. *Echo Park* is a book by Michael Connelly. So, *Echo Park* features Detective Bosch.

In this example the first premise states every member of a class of objects (books by Connelly) has a specific attribute (features Detective Bosch). The second premise identifies a specific member of that class (*Echo Park*). And the conclusion that follows necessarily from those two premises is that *Echo Park* features Detective Bosch. Whenever we have a generalization that asserts that a given characteristic applies to each of the members of a class of objects, we can logically assert that a given individual or subgroup of individuals that are members of that class has that characteristic. For example:

- Everyone who installs attic insulation runs the risk of inhaling potentially harmful dust and fiberglass particles. Angela and Jennifer install attic insulation. This means that both of them run that risk.
- Anyone who plays in a rock band knows that after you play a set lasting 40 minutes, you need a short break. Angela plays drums and Jennifer plays bass guitar in the Blazing Sunsets, a rock band at our college. So Angela and Jennifer know that after playing a set lasting 40 minutes, they need a short break.

If *F* and *G* stand for classes of objects, and if *X* stands for an individual object, then the argument template for "applying a generalization" would be this:

Premise #1: Every member of **F** is a member of **G**.
Premise #2: Individual object **X** is a member of **F**.
Conclusion: So, **X** is a member of **G**.

The figure top left on page 156 illustrates this argument structure. The oval represents all the things that are F. The circle represents all the things that are G. The red area of F that is outside of circle G is empty, because premise #1 states if anything is an F then it is also a G. As premise #2 says, X is the member of F. So, the only place we can put X is in the region where F and G overlap. This establishes pictorially that the conclusion cannot be false. Any other placement of X would violate what the premises state.

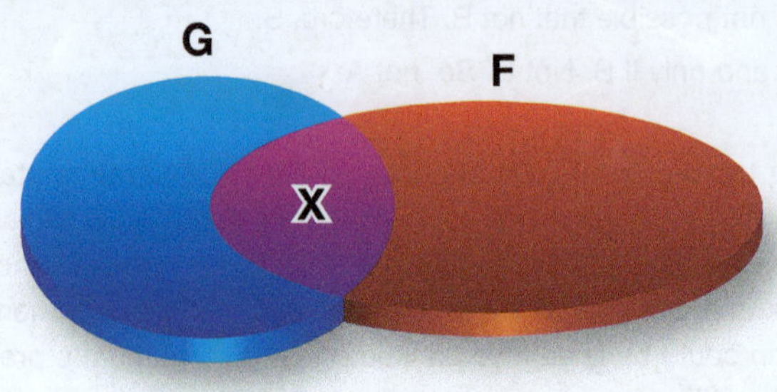

Applying an Exception

If we know that every member of a given class of objects has a certain characteristic, and we also know that one or more specific objects do not have that characteristic, we can logically infer that they are not members of that class. For example:

- Everyone who waits tables has experienced the challenge of trying to be respectful to a rude customer. Alexander has never experienced that challenge. That implies that Alexander has never worked as a waiter.
- Everyone who installs attic insulation runs the risk of inhaling potentially harmful dust and fiberglass particles. Angela and Jennifer have jobs that do not put them at risk for inhaling anything that is potentially harmful. So, Jennifer and Angela do not install attic insulation.
- The numbers 5, 7, 13, and 37 are not divisible by 2 without a remainder. Every even number is divisible by 2 with no remainder. So, 5, 7, 13, and 37 are not even numbers.

The argument template for "applying an exception" looks like this:

Premise #1: Every **F** is a **G.**
Premise #2: The object **X** is not a **G.**
Conclusion: So, **X** is not an **F.**

In the figure at the top of the right hand column premise #1 assures us that the red area of **F** that is outside of the circle **G** is empty. If there are any members of **F**, then they will all be inside circle **G**. But, because of premise #2, the only place to put **X** is outside of **G**. This establishes pictorially that the conclusion must be true. We cannot locate **X** in any place inside oval **F** without violating one or the other of the premises.

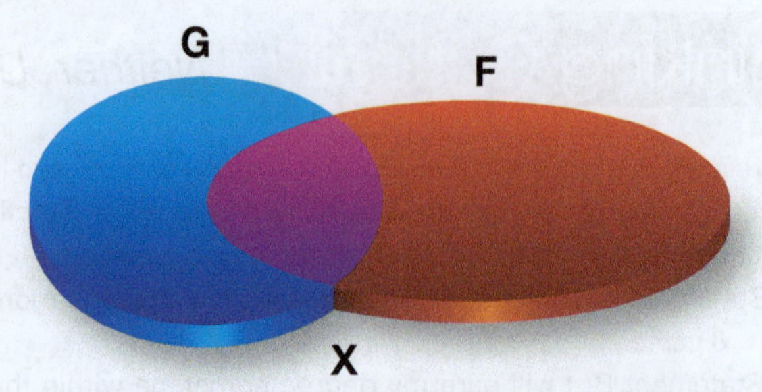

The Power of *Only*

Only is one of the most interesting words in the language. That word has the power to change the meaning of a sentence depending on where it is placed. Consider this four-part example. Here, first, is a simple sentence:

- Some people objected to being forced to attend.

Now watch how the meanings change depending on where *only* is positioned.

Location of *Only* to Change Meaning	Interpretation of New Statement
Only some people objected to being forced to attend.	Others people did not object.
Some people only objected to being forced to attend.	They did not quit, go on strike, or boycott.
Some people objected only to being forced to attend.	They would have preferred to have been asked or invited to attend voluntarily.
Some people objected to being forced only to attend.	They wanted to do more than attend; they wanted to participate actively.

Here is another example, but this time you fill in the left-hand side of the table showing where the word *only* would be located to enable the interpretation on the right.

- Some who are students pursue excellence.

Location of *Only* to Change Meaning	Interpretation of New Statement
some who are students pursue excellence.	They do nothing but pursue.
some who are students pursue excellence.	The one thing they pursue is excellence.
some who are students pursue excellence.	Some students do not pursue excellence.
some who are students pursue excellence.	They have no other identity besides being students.

Thinking Critically Classes and Objects

Let ***F*** be fun-loving people.
Let ***G*** be college graduates.
Let ***H*** be high-paid professionals.
Let ***X*** stand for Xavier.
Let ***Y*** stand for Yolanda.

Create arguments using each of these templates. Some of the arguments will turn out to be valid, and others will not. Evaluate each using the Test for Logical Strength to determine which are not valid deductive arguments. If you can think of a counterexample, then the argument is not deductively valid.

1 If anyone is an **F**, then that person is a **G**. Both **X** and **Y** are **G**. So, **X** is an **F**, and **Y** is also.

2 Some who are **F** are also **G**. Some who are **G** are also **H**. So, some who are **F** are **H**.

3 If **X** is an **F** and a **G**, then **X** is an **H**. As it turns out, **X** is an **F** but not a **G**. So, **X** is not an **H**.

4 Few **H** are **F**. But **Y** is an **H** and a **G**. If anyone is a **G**, then he or she is an **F**. So, **Y** is an **F**.

5 All **F** are **H**. All **G** are **H**. So, all **F** are **G**.

6 No **F** are **H**. No **G** are **F**. So, no **F** are **G**.

7 Some **H** are not **G**. All **G** are **F**. So, some **H** are not **F**.

8 Only some **F** are **H**. So, some **F** are not **H**.

9 Not all **F** are **H**. So, at least one **F** is not an **H**.

10 Only some **F** are not **H**. So, some **F** are **H**.

REASONING DEDUCTIVELY ABOUT RELATIONSHIPS

Natural languages are rich with terms that describe relationships. We use our understanding of the meanings of these terms to make deductive inferences about the objects to which the terms apply. For example, the arguments below are deductively valid because of the meanings of the relational terms like *sibling*, *brother*, *sister*, *shorter than*, *older than*, *taller than*, *younger than*, *greater than*, or *equals*. Notice that in ordinary discourse it is not necessary to specify generalizations like "Anyone who is a person's brother is that person's sibling," because those relationships are part of the meanings of the terms. Our understanding of the logical implications of relational terms is part of our comprehension of language. We seldom, if ever, attend to the deductive logical complexity embedded in natural language. Here are some examples of valid deductive arguments built on the meanings of the relational terms these arguments use.

- John is Susan's younger brother. So, they must have the same mother or the same father.
- Fresno is north of Bakersfield. Bakersfield is west of Phoenix. So, Phoenix is southeast of Fresno.
- Six is greater than five. Five is greater than four. Therefore, six is greater than four.
- $(4 + 6) = 10$. $(2 \times 5) = 10$. Therefore, $(4 + 6) = (2 \times 5)$.

Transitivity, Reflexivity, and Identity

Three relational characteristics we rely upon regularly when using deductive reasoning are named Transitivity, Reflexivity, and Identity. Here are two examples of valid deductive arguments based on each, beginning with two examples of transitivity:

- Tomas is taller than Jose. Jose is taller than Miguel. So, Tomas is taller than Miguel.
- Susan is Joan's ancestor. Joan is Philip's ancestor. So, Susan is Philip's ancestor.

Transitivity Relationship = *If x has a transitive relationship to y, and y has the same transitive relationship to z, then x has the same transitive relationship to z.*

- David is Stanley's neighbor. So, Stanley is David's neighbor.
- Sara is Helena's roommate. So, Helena is Sara's roommate.

Reflexivity Relationship = *If x has a reflexive relationship to y, then y has the same reflexive relationship to x.*

- Meryl Steep played Julia Child in the 2009 film *Julie and Julia.* The actress who played Julia Child in that film was nominated for an Oscar. So, Meryl Streep received an Oscar nomination for her performance in that film.
- The President of the United States was assassinated in 1963. People still remember where they were and what they were doing when they heard that shocking news. John F. Kennedy was the President who was killed that tragic November day in Dallas. So, people still remember where they were and what they were doing the day they heard that Kennedy had been assassinated.

Identity Relationship = *If x is y, then y is x.*

Fallacies Masquerading as Valid Deductive Arguments

Just as there are valid argument templates, there are fallacious argument templates. In every case, an analysis of the meanings of the terms used and the grammatical rules of the language reveal the source of the error. Precision of thought and expression is the key to avoiding these mistakes in our own argument making and also in our evaluation of the arguments offered to us. Often, a counterexample that mirrors the fallacious argument template will have the power to reveal the illogical structure, expose the fallacy, and squelch the argument's apparent persuasiveness. As before, in this section please assume that the premises of the example arguments are all true, so that we can focus on their logical flaws rather than their factual inaccuracies.

FALLACIES WHEN REASONING WITH DECLARATIVE STATEMENTS

We saw that affirming the antecedent and denying the consequent were two logically correct ways of reasoning with declarative statements. There is a pair of familiar fallacies that mimick those logically correct templates.

Affirming the Consequent

Suppose it is true that "If the river continues to rise, then the carpet will get wet." And suppose that we observe that the carpet is wet. It does not follow that the water that wet the carpet came from the river. The wetness may have come from an entirely different source, for example, the dishwasher overflowing, a pitcher of water being spilled, rain coming in an open window, or even old and sadly confused Uncle Joe bringing in the garden hose yet again to water the sofa with flower-patterned upholstery.

The fallacy of Affirming the Consequent follows this invalid pattern:

Premise #1: If **A**, then **B**.
Premise #2: **B**.
Conclusion: Therefore, **A**.

But **A** may not be the only condition that brings about **B**. So, it does not make logical sense to believe that **A** must be true simply because **B** is true. Here are more examples of the fallacy of Affirming the Consequent.

- If **we put an American on Mars before the end of the twentieth century, then we have a successful space program. We do have a successful space program**. So, **we put an American on Mars before the end of the twentieth century.**
- If **I am a good person, then God favors me with good friends, wealth, and fame. God has favored me with good friends, wealth, and fame**. Therefore, **I must be a good person.**

Thinking Critically The *House M.D.* Fallacy

Between abusing his subordinates, manipulating his friends, and being rude to his boss, Dr. House, played by Hugh Laurie, is called on to diagnose and treat some of the most rare and exotic diseases in the TV series *House M.D.* The question that drives the drama in each episode is whether or not House will make the right diagnosis before his trial-and-error treatments kill the patient. In the initial scenes of every show Dr. House gives his approval for his team to start medications or do surgeries based on their mistaken ideas about what is really wrong with the patient. Why all the mistakes—apart from there would be no story if he got the diagnosis right the first time? Answer: the fallacy of affirming the consequent. The reasoning pattern the junior physicians on House's team apply goes more or less like this: "If the patient has condition X, then we would see symptoms A, B, C, and D. We do see symptoms, A, B, C, and D. So the patient must have condition X." Watch an episode of *House M.D.* and see if you can pick out the fallacy.

Police dramas often rely on the same fallacy to drive the plot. Early in the stories the detectives reason more or less like this: "If suspect X did the deed, then we would find evidence A, B, C, and D. And, yes, look, here is evidence A, B, C, and D. So suspect X is the felon."

What saves the patient or exonerates the suspect? Strong diagnostic reasoning, which is a thinking strategy aimed at trying to rule out possibilities deductively. For example, something in a medical test—e.g., a given protein showing up in a blood test—implies that the patient could not possibly have condition X. Or the fact that a person was at some other location when the crime was committed definitely rules that person out as a suspect. Strong diagnostic reasoning is based on the deductive argument pattern we described as denying the consequent.

Apart from making for enjoyable drama, what problems in real life can result from the fallacy of affirming the consequent? Well, if missed medical diagnoses leading to expensive but ineffective medical treatments and the arrests of innocent people were not bad enough already, how about adding comparable mistakes made by other professionals? Have you ever paid an auto mechanic for a repair job only to find out that the mechanic's diagnosis of your car's problem was an honest mistake?

Getting the problem right just might be the most important step in problem solving. We know how to solve all kinds of problems. But applying a solution that does not fit the problem can result in making things worse, not better.

Thinking Critically *Therefore . . .*

Complete each argument below by using your deductive reasoning skills to draw a logically correct conclusion from the premises given.

1 If I put sugar in my coffee, then I enjoy it more. I put sugar in my coffee. Therefore ______________________.

2 David and Sharon both love cats. Anyone who loves cats is a friend of mine. Therefore ______________________.

3 Barbara and Bill are planning to marry. No couples planning to marry want to live in poverty and squalor. Therefore ______________________.

4 Alex is William's father. William is Kirk's father. And Kirk is Patricia's father. Therefore, Alex is Kirk's ______________ and Patricia's ______________________.

5 Apartment vacancy rates in town exceed 15 percent. Every time the rate exceeds 12 percent, you can be certain that there are some great deals on rentals near campus. Therefore ______________________.

6 Triangle ABC is congruent to triangle XYZ. Triangle XYZ is congruent to triangle PQR. Therefore ______________ is congruent to ______________________.

7 Mary's sister's mother is Genevieve's aunt. Therefore, Genevieve and Mary are ______________________.

8 Harry bought a used car at Sam's Used Cars. All the cars sold at Sam's Used Cars are junk on wheels. Therefore ______________________.

9 Among Women's National Basketball Association (WNBA) Western Division teams, the Phoenix Mercury are better than the Minnesota Lynx. And the Minnesota Lynx are better than the San Antonio Silverstars. Therefore ______________________.

10 In the Eastern Division of the WNBA the Connecticut Sun, the Washington Mystics, and the Chicago Sky are very competitive with one another. The Atlanta Dream is very competitive with the Connecticut Sun. Therefore the Atlanta Dream is ______________________.

Denying the Antecedent

Suppose the same hypothetical as before: "If the river continues to rise, then the carpet will get wet." And suppose that we receive the good news that the river has crested and is now receding. It does not follow that the carpet will not get wet. We still must contend with the leaky dishwasher, the open window, and dear old Uncle Joe, the sofa watering man.

The fallacy of Denying the Antecedent follows this invalid pattern:

Premise #1: If **A**, then **B**.
Premise #2: Not **A**.
Conclusion: Therefore not **B**.

As before, **A** may not be the only condition that brings about **B**. So, it does not make logical sense to think that just because **A** does not happen, **B** cannot happen. Here are two more examples of the fallacy of Denying the Antecedent.

- If **everyone who lived in Mississippi drank red wine daily,** then **the wine industry would be booming**. But **some Mississippians never drink red wine**. So, **the wine industry in not booming**.
- If **we see a light in the window**, **we know that there is someone at home**. But **we do** not **see a light in the window**. So, **no one is home**.

FALLACIES WHEN REASONING ABOUT CLASSES OF OBJECTS

Just as there are logically correct ways of reasoning about classes of objects and their members, there are familiar mistakes we often hear being made. Here are examples of fallacious reasoning about classes of objects. These common errors have earned their own names.

False Classification

Suppose "Criminals enjoy mafia movies" and "Cassandra enjoys mafia movies" are both true. It does not follow that Cassandra is a criminal. The same feature or attribute can be true of two groups or two individuals without requiring that one group can be classified as part of the other group or that the two individuals can be classified as the same person. The facts that Emile attended the campus concert and so did 50 students from the local high school does not make Emile a high school student.

Yet examples of False Classification seem remarkably abundant. Here are three examples of this fallacy.

- A good number of residents of Utah enjoy reading popular fiction. Some who enjoy popular fiction also enjoy windsurfing. So, a good number of residents of Utah enjoy windsurfing.
- The police profiler said that the rapist was a white male, age 25–35, and aggressive. The suspect is a white male, 28 years old, and aggressive. This establishes that the suspect is the rapist.
- There are ways of telling whether or not she is a witch. Wood burns and so do witches burn. So how do we tell if she is made of wood? Well, wood floats. And ducks float. So, if she floats, then she weighs the same as a duck and therefore she is made of wood. And therefore . . . , she is a witch! (Condensed from *Monty Python and the Holy Grail* Scene 5: "She's a Witch," 1975.)

Millions have enjoyed the humor that Monty Python created out of this fallacy in the famous "She's a Witch" scene from *Monty Python and the Holy Grail.* Go to **www.mythinkinglab.com** to access the clip.

Watch the **Video** on **mythinkinglab.com**

The knight's deductive reasoning implies certain death for the poor woman accused of witchcraft, but only if all three premises are true.

Premise #1:	If she floats she is a witch and we shall burn her.
Premise #2:	If she does not float, she'll drown.
Premise #3:	Either she will float or she will not float. [Unspoken.]
Conclusion:	Ergo, she dies.

Fallacies of Composition and Division

Reasoning about the relationships of parts and wholes can appear to be deductively valid, but fail because the attribute that applies to the parts may not apply to the whole, or vice versa. Here are some examples:

- It is in each person's financial interest to cheat a little on his or her income tax return. So, it is financially good for the nation if people cheat on their taxes.
- No muscle or joint or organ or cell in your body has the right to give its individual informed consent to a medical procedure. So, why should you, who are composed entirely of those many parts, have such a right?

In the first example, an attribute of individual people who pay taxes is being illogically attributed to the class of objects ("the nation"). The good of each is not necessarily the good of all. The second attempts to withhold from individuals the right to give informed consent because none of our body parts have that right. These examples of the Fallacy of Composition, so called because these fallacious arguments err by reasoning that a group has exactly the same attributes that each of its members have. "I don't know, Bill. Everyone on the Budget Committee is really smart. But, wow, that Committee makes stupid decisions. How can that be?" Simple. What is true of individuals is necessarily true of groups, including how well the group performs. Now consider these three examples:

- The president of the large corporation sent a memo to every vice president, director, manager, and supervisor saying, "In corporations of our size with hundreds of employees we can be certain that 10 percent of our total workforce is performing at a substandard level. Therefore, I am directing everyone in charge of a unit of 10 or more people to immediately terminate one person of every 10 in the unit. Forward the names of your substandard employee to Human Resources by 5:00 PM tomorrow."
- The United States of America has the right to enter into treaties and to declare war. Therefore each of the 50 states has the right individually to declare war or to enter into treaties.
- The average class size at the university is 35 people. Therefore, every class you are taking this term must have 34 other people enrolled in it.

These three examples illustrate the Fallacy of Division, which is the same error, but committed in the opposite direction. Fallacies of Division attribute to each individual member of a group a characteristic that is true of the group as a whole. In the first, an attribute of the class of objects known as the corporation's total workforce is being illogically attributed to each individual small department or unit. In the second, an attribute of human beings—the right to informed consent—is being attributed to each individual part of a human being, each cell. In the third, the average class size, which is an attribute of the university, is illogically attributed to each and every class being offered, as if small seminars and large lectures did not exist.

FALLACIES OF FALSE REFERENCE

Fallacies of false reference that occur when reasoning about relationships like identity, reflexivity, or transitivity most often occur when people think they are talking about the same thing, but in fact are not. The ambiguity of the expressions like "When did we see it?" or "I did it yesterday." can be the source of a mistaken inference if different people interpret "it" to be referring to different things. In Chapter 4 we used an example from *My Cousin Vinny* to illustrate the miscommunication that can arise out of just such an error. In that film the sheriff thought that a young man was confessing to murder when, in fact, he was only saying that he had inadvertently shoplifted a can of tuna fish. A comparable reasoning mistake occurs when people are not aware that the same object, person, or event may be identified using muliple descriptions.

An Act of Mercy?

Any sparks of humor we might find in the Monty Python silliness are quickly extinguished by the realization that witch burning really happened. Innocent women suspected of witchcraft were interrogated to the point of exhaustion. Misfortunes that may have befallen others in their community were interpreted as evidence that the accused had put a witch's evil spell on that unfortunate person. Any blemish on the accused woman's body—a bruise, a birthmark, or a scar from an old wound or burn—could be interpreted as the "mark of Satan," for further confirmation of her guilt.

As the video clip from *The Day the Universe Changed* illustrates, given our twenty-first-century worldview, the burning of a woman alive is a horrific killing of an innocent person. But, given their seventeenth-century worldview, the people living in Scotland only four centuries ago interpreted the very same event as an act of mercy. The laws of logic are the same here and now as they were then and there. What has changed? The differences in how the event is seen result from the vastly divergent set of implicit unspoken assumptions that constitute the two worldviews. It is within the context of our "truths" about the world that the laws of logic function. Today in parts of the world where a non-scientific worldview prevails, beliefs in voodoo and magic have a very real influence over the lives and decisions people make. In those communities, it would be "common sense" to fear that some might have the power to cause harm or misfortune simply by thinking evil thoughts and incanting spells.

Learning to make logical inferences is vital. But logic alone is not enough. Strong critical thinking requires more than skillful inference, analysis, explanation, and interpretation. It requires courageous truth-seeking and the intellectual honesty to reflect from time to time on our own most cherished beliefs and unspoken assumptions. Which of our twenty-first-century practices that we see as righteous and sensible will the people in the twenty-fourth century look back on in horror? Access the video clip at **www.mythinkinglab.com**. Be advised that the images in this clip may be disturbing.

Watch the **Video** on **mythinkinglab.com**

Suppose that "The dean knows that this year the School of Engineering award for Best Senior Project should go to Team Steelheads." And suppose that "The four members of the team are Karen, Anna, Dwight, and Angela" is true. It does not follow that the dean knows that Karen, Anna, Dwight, and Angela are winners of this year's award. Why? Because the dean may not know that they are the members of Team Steelhead. Knowing, believing, wanting, or intending something when it is described or named in one way does not imply that the person necessarily knows, believes, wants, or intends that very same thing as described or named in another way. That is, unless we add that the person is aware that the two descriptions actually refer to the same thing. Here are two more examples of the fallacy of False Reference.

- Tyler at age 10 has often told Mom that in college he wanted to learn how big buildings and bridges are built. These are subjects addressed in civil engineering. Therefore, Tyler has announced that he plans to major in civil engineering in college.
- Anthony heard that a winner of the Tour de France used banned performance-enhancing substances. Australian rider, Cadel Evans, won the 2011 Tour de France. Therefore, Anthony heard that Cadel Evans used banned performance-enhancing substances.

Thinking Critically — Create Your Own Deductive Reasoning Examples

Write two valid arguments based on each of these deductive templates:

- Denying the Consequent
- Affirming the Antecedent
- Disjunctive Syllogism
- Applying a Generalization
- Applying an Exception
- Transitivity Relationship
- Reflexivity Relationship
- Identity Relationship

Write two fallacious arguments exemplifying each of these errors:

- The Fallacy of Affirming the Consequent
- The Fallacy of Denying the Antecedent
- The Fallacy of False Classification
- The Fallacy of Composition
- The Fallacy of Division
- The Fallacy of False Reference

CHAPTER 08 REVIEW

Study and Review on mythinkinglab.com

The evaluation of reasoning is a ubiquitous part of everyday life. We evaluate inferences when talking with friends, working on projects, enduring television commercials, or reasoning through a decision. In this chapter we worked to strengthen our critical thinking skill of evaluation of deductive arguments in two ways: First, we examined a number of deductive reasoning patterns that derive their validity from the meanings of terms and the grammar of our shared language. Second, we reviewed a roster of fallacies that masquerade as valid deductive arguments in order to arm ourselves against their tempting deceits. In the next chapter we will do the same with inductive reasoning.

KEY TERM

deductively valid argument is an argument such that it is impossible for all of its premises to be true and its conclusion to be false. (p. 152)

FIND IT ON MYTHINKINGLAB.COM

- Evaluating deductive arguments made in real life introduces the added elements of context, purpose, social customs, and all the unspoken implicit assumptions that constitute our view of the world. The witch-burning scene from *The Day the Universe Changed* (p. 161) brings this home for us every time we see it. That's why we included it for you at www.mythinkinglab.com.

Watch the Video on mythinkinglab.com

- We love Monty Python's humor too. But that "She's a Witch!" clip (p. 160), also found at www.mythinkinglab.com, needed to be put into perspective. With unerring logic we humans too often do such violence to each other, fully confident in our beliefs.

Exercises

EVALUATE ARGUMENTS

Determine which of these arguments is a valid deductive argument and which is fallacious. In each case assume that all the premises are true, even if it strikes you that one or another of them is actually rather implausible. In each case indicate which valid deductive argument template or which fallacy is exemplied.

1. Everyone who owns a car needs car insurance. Joe just purchased a car. Therefore Joe needs car insurance.
2. Gatorade® is thirst quenchting. Tap water is thirst quenching. So Gatorade is tap water.
3. If we drive on the Pacific Coast Highway near San Francisco we can see islands off the Pacific Coast. We can see islands off the Pacific Coast. So we are driving on the Pacific Coast Highway near San Francisco.
4. "I believe the one who brings the hotdogs is supposed to bring the buns too. Sombody messed up," said John. "So, what you're saying is that my mother messed up," said Mary.
5. There are a lot of repossessed condos on the market. The one on Maple Street is less expensive than the place we saw on Palm Ave. And that cute one on Oak Blvd. is priced even lower than that. So the most expensive of the three is the place on Maple.
6. Twitter tweets are short, at most 140 characters. I counted the characters in your last e-mail and there were 1,400, which means that your last e-mail is nothing but 10 tweets.
7. "Either we'll finish the yard work in time to go to the movie, or we'll enjoy a quiet evening at home," said John. "I don't see us finishing in time for the movie," said Malaya. "It's a quiet evening at home then," said John.
8. If Pepsi tasted better than Coke, then more people would select Pepsi in a blind taste test. And that's just what happened. So, it must taste better.
9. If Pepsi tasted better than Coke, then it would outsell Coke. But Pepsi does not taste better than Coke. So it will not outsell Coke.
10. If the tuition goes up next year, then next fall the freshmen class enrollment will drop. But the freshmen class enrollment will be as high as ever next fall. Therefore next year the tuition will not increase.

REFLECTIVE LOG: GETTING THE PROBLEM WRONG

The risks associated with what the Fallacy of Affirming the Consequent (which we renamed in honor of the TV character "The *House M.D.* Fallacy") were the extra expense, unnecessary trauma, and risk of death associated with mistaken diagnosis. Review that Thinking Critically box (p. 158) and think about whether you might have ever committed that fallacy or whether you might have been victimized by that fallacy. In either or both cases, describe the situation. What was the fallacious reasoning? What happened as a result? What might you have done differently to have avoided making that mistake? What might the other person have done differently so that you would not have been victimized by their fallacious reasoning?

BONUS EXERCISE: DEVIL AND ANGEL

Having died, you find yourself in a room with no windows. You see two identical doors in front of you. There is someone guarding each door. The two guards are wearing identical uniforms. They look exactly alike. A voice which you recognize as the voice of God suddenly fills the room. God says, "Welcome. An angel guards the door to Heaven. A devil guards the door to Hell. The angel never lies. The devil never speaks the truth. You may ask one of the guards one question only. If you ask correctly, the door to Heaven will be opened for you. Good luck, I hope to see you soon." What one question do you ask in order to identify the door to Heaven with absolute certainty? To see this puzzle worked out watch the episode of the *Ricky Gervaise Show* that was broadcast on HBO on January 28, 2011.

Read the Chapter on mythinkinglab.com
Listen to the Chapter Audio on mythinkinglab.com

"Why would you think that Indiana State is less expensive than Butler University?" said Justin.

"Easy," replied his brother Silas. "The in-state tuition at ISU is around $8,000, and at Butler, which is private, the tuition is something like $30,500.[i]

Advantage ISU by $23,000 per year! You have to figure that the cost of room and board is a wash. So it comes down to tuition."

"That's not true. You have to figure financial aid into the mix. My grades are good enough, maybe I can get some financial aid. I've talked with the financial aid offices and they are saying I'd probably get about $10,500 in scholarship money from Butler, which would bring the tuition down to $20,000. The ISU people are talking about maybe $2,000 in scholarships. So my ISU tuition would come down to $6,000. Now the difference is only $14,000 per year."

"So? That's still a lot."

"Yes, but they said that since I'm not being claimed as a dependent on anyone's income tax return, I would probably qualify for a lot of support from student loans too. Both places just about guaranteed that I could make up the rest of what I'd need that way," said Justin.

Silas said, "Which means you can defer starting to pay back the loans until six months after you graduate, right?"

"Right. And let's look at how long it will take me to graduate. I'll transfer in from Ivy Tech with enough credits to be a junior. I could graduate from Butler in two years for sure."

<<< Indiana State University's signature campus fountain, a favorite place for students, faculty and staff to visit and enjoy the day. Is there a signature location, building, piece of public art on your campus?

Evaluate Inductive Reasoning and Spot Inductive Fallacies

HOW do we evaluate inductive arguments?

HOW can we recognize common fallacies masquerading as inductive arguments?

"Well," said Silas, "then it would be two years at ISU too."

"Not necessarily," replied Justin. "I've heard that there can be problems getting courses at ISU because the state has cut back on its funding of higher education. There's nothing ISU can do about that. But private colleges like Butler work hard to get everyone graduated on time."

"Alright, let's assume that it would take you three years to graduate from ISU, but only two to graduate from Butler. So looking only at the tuition minus the scholarships, you're still looking at $14,000 for two years at Butler as compared to $6,000 for three years at ISU. It seems clear to me that $28,000 in loans is a bigger problem than $18,000. All in all ISU looks like the better deal financially by about $10,000."

"No, you forgot one other thing," said Justin.

"What?" said Silas.

"If I graduate from Butler a year earlier, then I can get a full-time job that much sooner. And suppose I find a job that pays $30,000. In one year of working I will have covered that $10,000 spread. I realize that there are risks and uncertainties. I could be wrong. But financially speaking Butler is probably the better choice given my particular situation."

In contrast to the structural necessity of valid deductive reasoning, inductive reasoning is probabilistic. An **inductively justified argument** (or **"warranted argument"**) is an argument such that if all of its premises were true then its conclusion would most likely or very probably be true. Here is an example, based on a story from the CBS series *CSI*.[ii]

- A man is found dead of a gunshot wound to the stomach, his body in a seated position at the base of a tree in a forest. It is deer hunting season. Except for not wearing an orange safety vest, he is dressed like a hunter. His hunting rifle, never having been fired, lies on the ground at his side. The evidence strongly suggests that his death resulted from a hunting accident. The investigator infers by inductive reasoning that had the man been wearing his orange safety vest, he probably would be alive today.

The investigator's inductive inference is plausible. Although we can imagine alternative scenarios, in the absence of any further information, we have no basis for evaluating the investigator's induction as other than warranted.

In contrast to *deductions*, which depend on the meanings of words and rules of grammar, *inductive reasoning depends on the evidence at hand*. New information can lead us to revise conclusions reached using inductive inferences. Take the *CSI* story, for example. Suppose we come to learn the following additional facts:

- The time of death was mid-afternoon, a time when deer are not hunted. Deer are hunted at dawn and at dusk. The dead man had not purchased a hunting license. There was gunshot residue on the man's clothing, which indicates that he was shot at very close range. The gun that shot him could not have been more than a foot or two from his body. A $1,000,000 insurance policy had been purchased on his life only two weeks prior to his death. The policy had been paid for with his wife's credit card. The wife is the beneficiary who would receive the money if he should die by illness or by accident.

The initial inductive conclusion, death by accident, looks mistaken in the light of this new information. Now a more plausible conclusion would be that the man had been murdered by his wife or perhaps by someone she hired. Her motive, of course, would be the insurance money.

Conclusions accepted on the basis of justified inductive arguments remain subject to revision or possible rejection based on new information. The *CSI* example is fiction, of course. But there are real-life examples, too. A person may be found guilty beyond a reasonable doubt based on the circumstantial evidence presented to the jury at the time of the trial. A great many people who are found guilty really are guilty. Even so, new information may come to light years later to demonstrate that, in some cases, the guilty verdict was mistaken. The Innocence Project, which has exonerated hundreds of innocent people wrongly convicted, is a sobering reminder to us all about how difficult and yet how important it is to evaluate the logical strength

How does the Innocence Project use critical thinking to free dead men walking who are innocent?

of inductive arguments carefully. A strong but fair criminal justice system is essential to the rule of law. But a weak or unfair system undermines respect for law enforcement and trust in the court system. To learn more about the causes of wrongful convictions, such as eye witness misidentifications, improper forensics, and false confessions, visit **http://www.innocenceproject.org/understand/** Read the Document on mythinkinglab.com

Inductions and the Evidence at Hand

As we did in Chapter 8 when discussing deductive arguments, in this chapter we begin with positive examples of strong critical thinking using inductive reasoning, and then later in the chapter we will look at deceptively fallacious inductive arguments.

EVALUATING GENERALIZATIONS

A generalization may be based on data gathered systematically or unsystematically. We would be wise to place greater confidence in the claim if it were supported by data gathered more systematically, rather than on simply one or two happenstance personal observations. Consider the following three inductive generalizations. The claims, which are **bolded,** are supported by premises that report personal experiences, conversations focused on these topics, or information derived from historical records or opinion surveys.

1. **People over the age of 60 tend to prefer to listen to oldies.** This claim is based on the data gathered in telephone surveys of persons between the ages of 60 and 90, which were conducted in Florida, Arizona, Ohio, and Connecticut. In all, 435 interviews were conducted. Participants were asked to identify which type of music they preferred to listen to most. They were given eight choices: Classical, Pop, R&B, Country, Oldies, Broadway, Religious, and Top 40.

2. In May, inspectors from the city sanitation department made unannounced visits to all 20 hotels in the downtown area and to 10 of the other 30 hotels within the city limits. The 10 were representative of the type and quality ratings of those other 30 hotels. The inspectors by law could demand access to any room in the hotel to look for pests and to evaluate cleanliness. Careful records were kept of each room inspected. In all, 2,000 beds were examined for bedbugs. 1,460 beds tested positive. Based on the data from these inspections, we estimate that **73 percent of the hotel room beds in this city are infested with bedbugs.**

3. I have visited San Francisco maybe seven times over the past 25 years. It is one of my favorite vacation cities. I've gone in the summer and in the winter. And I can tell you one thing, bring a coat because **it's probably going to be cloudy and cold in San Francisco if you go in August.**

It is easy to imagine scenarios in which the information in the premises is true but the conclusion may not apply. We can conjure the possibility that someone over 60 does not like oldies. We can imagine that there may be one hotel in the city where most of the beds are not infested. It is no problem to think of the possibility that there should be at least one warm sunny August day in San Francisco. But, developing a possible counterexample does not necessarily diminish the logical strength of an inductive argument. A single counterexample is sufficient to invalidate a deductive argument, but not an inductive generalization. Notice that in the first example we have a somewhat modest assertion about what people over the age of 60 "tend to" prefer. The second says that it applies to 73 percent of the hotel beds, but not that the infected beds are evenly distributed among the city's 50 hotels. And the third says that it is "probably" going to be cold in San Francisco in August.

To evaluate the logical strength of inductive generalizations, we need to do more than find a single counterexample. We must, instead, examine whether the sampling of cases reported in the premises is adequate to support the probabilistic inferences that are drawn. This means asking four questions and finding satisfactory answers to each of them.

- **Was the correct group sampled?**
- **Were the data obtained in an effective way?**
- **Were enough cases considered?**
- **Was the sample representatively structured?**

If one counterexample invalidates a deductive argument, can one hotel bed bug or one sunny August day in San Francisco invalidate example 2 or 3?

Was the Correct Group Sampled?

The first example makes a claim about people over the age of 60. The premises tell us that adults between the ages of 60 and 90 were sampled. That is the correct group to sample if one wishes to make generalizations about persons in that age range. It would not do, obviously, to sample people under the age of 60 and then present those data as a basis for a claim about people over that age. One would think that sampling the wrong population would not be a mistake commonly made. But for years, pharmaceutical companies made inferences about children's drug dosages and the effects of various medications on women based largely on studies conducted on adult males. More recently, we have learned that there are genetic factors that affect the rate at which common pain relievers, like the ibuprofen in Motrin, are metabolized. This new finding should influence dosage recommendations for those who are poor metabolizers (e.g., 6 to 10 percent of Caucasians).[iii]

Were the Data Obtained in an Effective Way?

In our example about the music listening preferences of adults over 60, we see that the data were obtained via telephone surveys. We might think that a telephone survey may not be as efficient as using a Web-based survey, which would reach many more people and be much more cost-effective. But, upon reflection, it does not seem unreasonable to use the telephone to reach older adults, many of whom may not be comfortable with the use of computers and Web-based survey tools. Finding an effective method to gather data from the sample is often a major challenge for researchers.[iv] For example, consider how difficult it is to gather high-quality data about the state of mind of combat veterans in the year after their return from a war zone.

Were Enough Cases Considered?

In general, the more cases the better. But there comes a point of diminishing returns. If we are trying to make a reasonable generalization about millions of people who live in major metropolitan areas like Boston, New York, Chicago, or Los Angeles, it is neither necessary nor cost-effective to survey even one percent of a group so large. At some point the distribution of responses simply adds numbers, but the proportions of responses selecting each possible answer do not change significantly. Social scientists have worked out sophisticated statistical methods to provide a precise answer to the question of sample size. The answer establishes a minimum necessary depending on the kinds of statistical analysis to be conducted and the degree of accuracy needed for the question at hand. For example, to keep us up to date on the likely voting patterns in a forthcoming election, it is sufficient to track what likely voters are going to do within a margin of error of plus or minus 2 percent. Called a "power analysis," the calculations social scientists make begin with a projection of the number of cases expected to fall randomly into each possible category. Scientists can then determine whether the observed distribution varies significantly from the expected random distribution.[v] As a rough rule of thumb, they would want at least 25 cases per possible response category. In our "Oldies" example there are eight categories of music. So, we would need a sample of at least 200 individuals. We have 435, so the sample size is adequate. But we do not have a claim that reports a percentage. In our example the claim reports a *tendency*. Social scientists would not regard a tendency as being a strong enough deviation from random to be called "statistically significant."

Was the Sample Representatively Structured?

We said that 435 was an adequate sample size for our example, but were the 435 representative of the population being talked about in the claim? The claim talks about everyone over the age of 60. Because more than half of the people between 60 and 90 are women, and because women might have different preferences with regard to the music they like to listen to, we would need to be satisfied that the 435 reflected the actual ratio of women and men in that age group. We do not know that from the information given. If we hypothesize that music-listening preferences might be related to educational background, race, ethnicity, or socioeconomic status, then we would want to assure ourselves that the sample of 435 was representative of the distribution of those factors among the target population. Because we do not know if 435 is a representative sample, we cannot answer this fourth question in the affirmative. And, as a result, example #1 is not logically strong.

COINCIDENCES, CORRELATIONS, AND CAUSES

Decades ago scientists first observed that there were a number of cases of heart disease where, coincidentally, the person was a smoker. Further systematic research demonstrated a strong positive correlation between smoking and heart disease. Scientists hypothesized that perhaps smoking was a contributing factor. However, before making a defensible argument that quitting smoking would reduce a person's chances of heart disease, researchers had to explain scientifically how smoking caused heart disease. Researchers demonstrated scientifically that nicotine constricts blood vessels in the heart, which reduces blood flow to the heart muscle, thus causing heart attacks.

The progression from coincidence to correlation to causal explanations marks our progress in being able to explain and to predict events. At first we may observe two events and think that their occurrence is a chance coincidence. Then, as more data are systematically gathered and analyzed, we may discover that the two events are statistically correlated. And, with further experimental investigation, we may learn that in fact what had at first seemed like only a coincidence

Thinking Critically — Which Report Should We Believe and Why? The Devil is in the Details!

Mid-career median salaries of full-time employees with undergraduate degrees in engineering, applied mathematics, physics, computer science, statistics, economics, and the like are at or above $90,000, according to PayScale.com. Not surprising. But what did catch our attention were the mid-career median salaries for some of the other academic degree areas. Here is a partial listing of what we saw:

Chemistry	$80,900	Political Science	$80,100
American Studies	$78,600	Information Technology	$78,400
Accounting	$75,700	Philosophy	$75,600
Advertising	$74,700	Biology	$71,900
Business	$70,500	Nursing	$69,300
History	$69,000	Communications	$66,900
English	$65,800	Psychology	$61,300
Criminal Justice	$58,500	Education	$54,700
Art	$52,400	Athletic Training	$52,000
Social Work	$44,000	Child and Family	$40,500

Whoa! We said, how can Philosophy be above popular majors like Business, Nursing, Communications, and Psychology? Where did these data come from? Was the sample representative, did they look at enough cases, how did they get the data in the first place? The full listing is published at **http://www.payscale.com/best-colleges/degrees.asp** Follow the link on the PayScale.com Web site to the methodology used. The URL is **http://www.payscale.com/best-colleges/salary-report.asp**

What's It Worth? The Economic Value of College Majors, a study by the Center on Education in the Workforce at Georgetown University, looked at full-time full-year workers who had completed bachelor's degrees in different fields. That report paints a very different picture. In the Georgetown report, for example, the median salary for business majors as a group is $60,000, which is also where nursing comes in. Both are about 10K lower. Communication comes in at $50,000, education at $42,000—in other words nearly $15,000 lower. And the humanities including History, English, Philosophy, and the like come in at $47,000. For Philosophy that's $28,000 lower. The URL for the methodology is **http://www9.georgetown.edu/grad/gppi/hpi/cew/pdfs/majorsmethodology.pdf**

Why such huge differences? Which one is closer to the truth? Assuming both sources have provided accurate information based on the data available to them, how can we make sense out of the huge differences between what each says about the median salary by major? Hint: "The devil is in the details." Check out the sample sizes and the sources of the information each report uses. This will help you evaluate which is the more credible source.

The Georgetown report showed earnings by major and gender and by race. How do we explain the differences by gender as reflected in this chart from the Georgetown report? You can obtain this report from **http://cew.georgetown.edu/whatsitworth/**

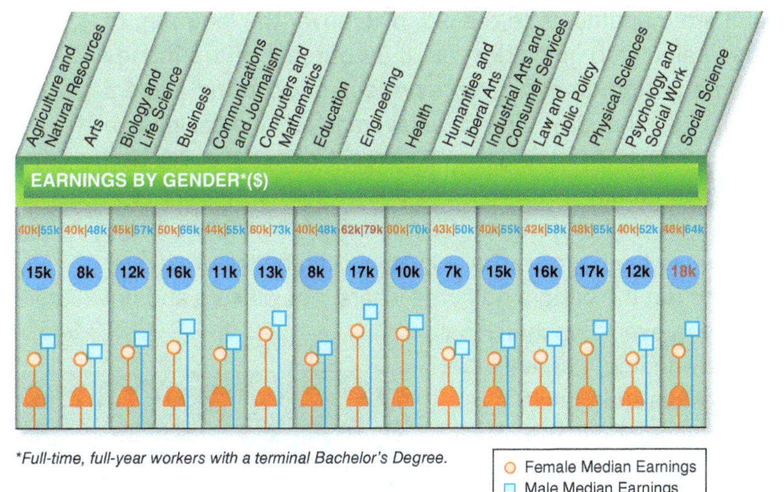

*Full-time, full-year workers with a terminal Bachelor's Degree.

Read the **Document** on **mythinkinglab.com**

actually occurs because of important causal factors. When and if we reach that stage we will have generated a causal explanation.

Coincidences

If two events happen to occur together by chance, we call that a coincidence. For example, annually in the United States on average 90 people are killed by lightning. That comes to one death for every 345,000 flashes in the United States.[vi] What are the chances that a given individual will be killed by lightning in a given year in the United States, given that the population is roughly 306,000,000? That coincidence has roughly one chance in 3,400,000 of occurring, all else being equal. The qualifier "all else being equal" means that weather patterns do not change substantially and that the people do not behave in ways which increase or decrease their chances of being killed by lightning in the United States, such as becoming permanent residents of some other country or standing in an open field holding aluminum rods in the air during lightning storms. But, all things being equal, we can use inductive reasoning and statistical facts to calculate the probabilities that a given coincidence might occur.

Thinking Critically Hotel Bedbugs and August Cold

Evaluate the bedbug example and the San Francisco in August weather example. In each case ask:

- Was the correct group sampled?
- Were the data obtained in an effective way?
- Were enough cases considered?
- Was the sample representatively structured?

When the premises do not provide enough information for a satisfactory answer, explain what information one would have to find, as we did when we noted what would be needed for the sample of 435 to be considered representative of the population of people over the age of 60.

Although we cannot predict with certainty that the next time you flip a coin it will come up heads, we can predict with a high level of confidence what will happen 50 percent of the time in the long run. We know how to calculate mathematical probabilities for events such as these because we know that each individual outcome occurs randomly with equal frequency. If we roll two regular dice, the result will be two 6s 1 time out of 36 rolls over the long haul. We calculate that by multiplying the chance of rolling a 6 on die #1, which is 1 out of 6, times the chance of rolling a 6 on die #2, which is also 1 out of 6. Then we multiply those odds to get the mathematical probability of both outcomes happening together—the product is 1 out of 36.

The luxurious casinos in Atlantic City and other gambling hubs are monuments to the reliability, over the long run, of these calculated coincidences. If 98 percent of the money bet in a casino on any given day goes back to the players as winnings that day, then on an average day the casino can be very confident of retaining 2 percent of every dollar bet. The more money bet, the more dollars that 2 percent represents. Unless more than 100 percent of the money bet is returned to the bettors as winnings, we can be sure that over the long run the bettors go home losers, not winners and not "breaking even." An individual person winning a specific bet is, considered in itself, a random coincidence. The totality of all those coincidences can be aggregated into a large and highly predictable profit margin for the casino. The best generalization to infer is that, in the end, the casino will very likely separate the chronic gambler from more and more of his or her money.

Correlations

As in the smoking and heart attack example, when the same coincidence is observed over and over again, people begin to suspect that the events may be related by something more than pure random chance. Even before knowing that one event may be the cause of another, we can determine whether the two are correlated. Correlations, calculated using statistical analyses, describe the degree to which two different sets of events are aligned. For example, scores on critical thinking skills tests are positively correlated with student success on state licensure exams in a number of health sciences professions.[vii] We might wish to speculate about the possible causal relationships of critical thinking skill to academic or professional success. But simply having the correlation in hand can be valuable to those professional programs that have more applicants than can be accepted. The admissions committees can use an applicant's critical thinking skills test score in the way that it uses GPAs or letters of reference, namely as another valuable data point to consider when making its decision to admit or not to admit an applicant.[viii]

When a research project reports that a statistically significant correlation has been found between events of kind #1 (scores on a critical thinking skills test) and events of kind #2 (scores on a state's professional licensure examination), that means that the relationship between the two kinds of events is viewed as not likely to be happenstance or chance. Of course, there could be an error in this estimate, but the threshold for this error is 5 percent. So, we can be 95 percent confident that the two events are really correlated. Even greater confidence that the events reported did not happen by mere chance can be found in many fields of research in which statistical significance is reported with 99 percent confidence, at 1 percent, or even less (0.001) chance of error. Even so, we remain in the realm of inductive reasoning because the inference, which is logically very strong, holds open the possibility that the findings reported may have happened by mere

Is it only luck that generated the hundreds of millions of dollars needed to build these lavish hotel casinos?

chance. The odds are very definitely against that possibility, however. If the 0.001 confidence level is reached, then the odds that the conclusion is mistaken are 1 in 1,000.

Using statistical correlations as their basis for confidence in their products, manufacturers of over the counter medical test kits do a thriving business. Walgreens sells home tests kits for pregnancy, paternity, colon disease, illegal drugs, blood alcohol levels, and ovulation. These products are used millions of people. And although these products can be highly reliable, most advertising themselves as 99 percent accurate, that still leaves a 1 percent chance for mistakes. At 1 percent, that comes to 10,000 errors out of 1,000,000 tests. Although the possibilities are remote, a test might be a false positive, meaning that that the test indicates that someone is a biological parent, is pregnant, is using, is drunk, or has ovulated when those results are not true. Or a test might come back false negative, meaning that the test failed to indicate that the person was in fact a biological parent, pregnant, using, etc. Rare as false positives and false negatives are, they illustrate the difference between "highly confident but possibly mistaken" inductive inferences and the certainty which characterizes valid deductive inferences. Depending on one's appetite for risk, with 1 chance in 100 of the test results being wrong, a person might be wise to double check before basing a major life decision on a single test's outcome.

Well-researched correlations can be powerful tools. Consider this possibility. Suppose that writing assignments, which employ grammatically complex constructions, use expected words and expressions, include sentences with greater average word counts, and include fewer spelling mistakes are statistically significantly correlated with higher grades. And suppose that assignments that are missing one or more of those features are statistically correlated with lower grades. Based on this, we can design computer programs that assign grades by parsing grammar and counting words.[ix] The computer does not need to understand the meaning of the essay nor does it have to evaluate the quality of arguments used. The grades assigned by computers can then be checked against the grades that human evaluators assign to those same essays. Refinements can then be made in the computer program's grading algorithms to achieve ever closer approximation to the results human beings would have produced. When the computer program is refined to the extent that it assigns the same grades as well-qualified human beings to 99.9 percent of the essays, then essay grading can be automated. To assign you the grade your professor would have assigned, the computer never needs to understand what you wrote. This is not science fiction. Automated grading is used by the Educational Testing Service.[x]

Causes

Documenting that a causal relationship exists between events requires more than demonstrating a strong correlation. The intellectual challenges of designing research capable of revealing the causal mechanisms at work in nature is important and interesting work. Perhaps this is why many strong critical thinkers find careers in scientific and technical fields

Grading Written Submissions

If the purpose of grading is to identify which essays fall into which broad groups—e.g., "Fail, Pass, High Pass" or "F, D, C, B, A"—and if a computer can manage this faster, with greater consistency, and with an accuracy that matches a well-trained human reader, it seems reasonable to use the computer.

If, on the other hand, the purpose of grading is to advance learning through commenting on the content and presentation of the student's written work, then automated grading does not seem to be a feasible nor desirable alternative. To provide useful feedback, the grader must understand the content being presented, follow the reasoning and the evidence presented, and be able to interpret, evaluate, and comment accurately and usefully.

Well-programmed computers and well-trained graders may assign different grades under certain conditions. These represent threats to the validity of the assigned grade. For example, essays that use information that is not factual may receive higher grades from the computer than human readers who recognized those factual errors. Essays that rely on irony, hyperbole, sarcasm, and humor may receive very different grades from humans and from machines, which presumably would neither recognize nor attend to those stylistic differences. Essays that use plagiarized material might receive a lower grade from the computer because it can check for the replication of text published elsewhere, as compared to a human grader who may not recognize the plagiarized material.

There are threats to the reliability of human graders because humans can become fatigued and less attentive as they grade written submissions for long periods of time. Different human graders may give the same essay different grades because they disagree on the relative importance of various elements in the essay. Humans may be influenced by their own personal beliefs, tending to give somewhat higher grades to essays that reflect their point of view. Computers do not suffer from these problems.

If the purpose of grading written submissions is to determine which candidates shall be admitted to highly competitive programs and which shall be excluded, then the threats to validity identified here may lead to unfortunate mistakes. If the purpose of grading written submissions is to determine who shall receive honors, awards, financial support, grant funding, publication, or special privileges, then categorizing essays into broad groups must be refined so that the most meritorious can be validly and reliably identified.

No one would want to be denied admission, funding, or the honor she or he was due because the grader (computer or human) failed to give a written submission its true score.

attractive. Causal explanations are desirable because they enable us to explain, predict, and control parts of the natural world. In Chapter 14 on Empirical Reasoning we will explore the powerful inductive investigatory methods used by scientists to achieve causal explanations.

It is not always possible to move all the way from coincidence to correlation to causal explanation in every field of inquiry. For example, predicting the behavior of the stock market remains a hazardous and uncertain adventure. Because we do not really know how all the factors that influence the market interact, we are not able to predict with high levels of confidence what the market will do on any given day. Some financial analysts turn out to be right, while others are wrong. Often, it seems as though the analysts announce why the market reacted as it did on a given day only after the day's trading is completed. Then, we hear that the market responded to changes in the jobless rate, the prime interest rate, consumer confidence level, or something else. But those same analysts are not able to use those same factors to predict accurately what the market will do in the future. If their explanations of the past behavior of the market were correct, one would expect that they would be able to make reliable predictions about the market's future behavior. That we are not able, yet, to make good predictions about the future leads us to suspect that we do not yet know, beyond the level of coincidences and correlations, what causal factors, individually or in combination with other causal factors, are relevant to explaining the behavior of the stock market. One can only wonder how relevant the factors those prognosticators identify as causes really are.

Fallacies Masquerading as Strong Inductive Arguments

Just as some fallacies are presented as valid deductive arguments, others are presented as justified inductive arguments. They draw their power to deceive and persuade from how closely they resemble the genuine article. A closer analysis often helps us avoid being misled by the following fallacies.

Erroneous Generalization

Generalizations, even those based on solid evidence, can be deceptively fallacious, too. At times, we generalize from too little information, exaggerating the claim beyond what the data support. At other times, the exaggeration results from sampling errors. Consider these examples:

- The paper showed a picture of the CEO in chains doing the perp walk as he was being led off to jail. Another middle-aged white guy with a $400 haircut! Same as Bernard Madoff, the guy who swindled 170 million dollars out of rich people with his phony investment Ponzi scheme. All those corporate thieves are overpaid white guys.
- Many medical professionals recommend a healthy diet and regular exercise. More is always better, right? So the way to be super healthy is to go on a crash diet and exercise as much as possible! Right?
- Seventy-one percent of the students enrolled in my educational methods course are women. So, women really like my courses.

In each of these cases, even if the premises were true, the conclusion goes unjustifiably beyond what those premises could support. Review each of these three examples and amend them by refining the conclusion so that it is logically justified by the premises given.

Playing with Numbers

Arguments, which use raw numbers when percentages would present a more fair-minded description, or use percentages when the raw numbers would present the more fair-minded description, can be evaluated as fallacies of Playing with Numbers. Arguments that cite statistics or numbers but do not provide sufficient information to make a good judgment about the significance of those numerical data are species of the Playing with Numbers Fallacy as well. For example:

- Six hundred people are affected by the decision you made prohibiting pythons as pets in this apartment complex. I

Thinking Critically — Group Project Challenge: The U.S. Census

There are two ways to conduct a census. Contact everyone and gather the data being sought, or generalize from well-structured representative samples. This group project invites you to evaluate the methodology used by the U.S. government for conducting the 2010 Census. You are invited to make recommendations for improving that methodology. If you come up with some good suggestions, offer them to your Congressional representatives and the U.S. Census Bureau. Begin your investigation here: **http://www.census.gov/popest/topics/methodology/**. **Read the Document on mythinkinglab.com**

To fully evaluate the methodology and make reasonable recommendations, your group will want to consider first and foremost the logical strength of the two alternatives (count absolutely everyone possible vs. make estimates based on samples.) When considering the sampling alternative, keep in mind the importance of sample size and representative structure. For both alternatives, keep in mind the question of the method of gathering data. For example, going door to door will ensure that homeless Americans are systematically excluded.

Other considerations that may weigh on your ultimate recommendations may include the cost (money and time) of the two alternatives, the political consequences of each, and the social value associated with enlisting volunteers in an effort of national scope.

Statistically, who is more at risk, car drivers or motorcyclists?

want you to know that 80 percent of the people surveyed said that they wanted you to reconsider your decision. How many people was that, you ask? Well, I personally talked to my four roommates and three agreed with me, which makes 80 percent.

- The average salary for postal workers is 5.6 percent higher than the average salary for the employees of the Transportation Safety Administration. This establishes that postal workers are overpaid.
- The National Highway Traffic Safety Administration reports that there were 24,474 automobile fatalities in 2009. That same year there were 4,462 motorcyclist fatalities. This means that driving or riding in a car is five and a half times more dangerous than riding a motorcycle.

Review these examples and add premises or restate the conclusion, or do both in order to transform each into an inductive argument that gives reasonable justification for believing that the claim—as you may have restated it—is now very probably true. For the third example about traffic fatalities visit http://www-fars.nhtsa.dot.gov/Main/index.aspx to get the relevant details. For example on the ratio of automobiles to motorcycles, or the ratio of total miles per year driven by the two different types of vehicles. **Read** the **Document** on **mythinkinglab.com**

False Dilemma

A real dilemma is a situation in which all our choices are bad. In the story, "The Cold Equations," the story that opened the previous chapter on deductive reasoning, Thomas Barton faced a real dilemma. Every option was undesirable; no matter what he decided, someone would have to die. But, at times we may think we are facing a dilemma when we are not. The world often offers more options than we may perceive at first. At times, the consequences of one or another of our options may not be nearly as dreadful as we initially imagine them to be. As the following examples indicate, at times what appears to be a real dilemma turns out upon closer analysis to be a false dilemma.

- The kidnappers have taken eight people hostage and are holding them at a farmhouse just outside town. If the SWAT team assaults the farmhouse, the hostages could be killed. But if we give into the kidnappers' demands for ransom and safe passage out of the country, we'll only be encouraging more kidnappings of innocent people. What can we do? There are no good alternatives.
- If I go to the job interview laid-back and unprepared, I'll blow it. But if I prepare for the interview I could overdo it and be so nervous that I'll blow it anyway. I'm a mess. There's no way to get ready for this interview.

As these examples show, another good name for this fallacy is "The Either/Or Fallacy" because the situations often appear to be limited to one option or another, but on further examination, additional options emerge. This is true of the first example. Assaulting the farmhouse and giving in are not the only possible options. Negotiating for the release of some or all of the hostages is an option. Waiting until those inside the farmhouse run out of food or water is another option. Blasting the farmhouse with mega decibels of sound and shooting tear gas in through the windows might force the occupants out. In other words, a little creativity can often reveal a way out of a false dilemma.

The Gambler's Fallacy

Random events, by definition, are not causally connected. But, at times, we make arguments that wrongly assume that what happens by chance is somehow connected or correlated with things we can control. We can use "Gambler's Fallacy" as an umbrella term to remind ourselves that random events are, in fact, random and that drawing inferences based on the assumption that they are correlated or causally connected is a mistake. Here are some examples of fallacious inferences that attribute more to mere coincidences than strong inductive reasoning would warrant.

- If we're going to Vegas, I'm going to bring my blue socks and I'm going to wear them in the casino. They're my lucky socks. Although I've lost money plenty of times wearing them, I've never won at slots without those blue socks on. So, I won't win a dime from the slots if I don't wear those socks!
- Whenever I leave the apartment, I rub the tummy of the little statue of Buddha we have on the table near the door. It makes me happy to do that because I know that it brings me good karma.
- I just flipped a coin twice and it came up heads both times. So, the next two times I flip it, the coin will come up tails because the chances are 50/50.

Thinking Critically Using Dilemmas to Heighten the Drama

The 2010 film *Extraordinary Measures* is based on the true life story of a father's desperate struggle to find a cure for Pompe Disease, a form of Muscular Dystrophy that limits a child's life span to about nine years. Harrison Ford plays the part of Dr. Robert Stonehill, who believes his research may lead to a cure. But Stonehill's research takes a lot of money, more than the father, played by Brandon Frasier, and the researcher are able to get from donations alone. So they formed a research company and then persuaded a venture capitalist to back them with ten million dollars. But the work was difficult and the expenses were high. There is a dramatic scene about 57 minutes into the story where the father and the researcher face a bitter dilemma. The venture capitalist gives them a choice: Meet an impossibly short deadline to complete their work or sell their company to pay back the venture capitalist. Both options are terrible from the perspective of Harrison Ford's character. He sees this as a dilemma from which there is no escape. But Brandon Frasier's character, the father of the sick children, sees it as a false dilemma. Locate that scene in the movie and see how Frasier's character and Ford's character grapple with the decision they must make.

- Cabrera is batting for the Detroit Tigers. Cabrera's batting average this year is .333. This is his third trip to the plate this game. He grounded into a double play his first trip and struck out his second time. So, he's going to get a hit this time.

False Cause

When two events occur one right after the other, we may mistakenly infer that the first is the cause of the second.

- Look, I put the CD into the player and the windshield wipers wouldn't turn on. It has to be that the problem with the wipers is somehow connected to the CD player.
- It's hard to know exactly what made her so angry. She seemed fine when we were talking earlier about what a jerk her former boyfriend was. Then you came in and boom! She exploded. I think it's your fault.

Called "*Post hoc, propter hoc*" ["After this, because of this"], confusing temporal proximity with causality is one of several mistakes grouped together under the heading of False Cause Fallacies. Another mistake is to confuse a correlation with a cause.

- Our information shows that in times of economic growth, the hemlines on women's skirts go from below the knee to above the knee. And in times of a bear market when the economy slows down, the hemlines that are considered stylish go down below the knee, at times to mid-calf or even ankle height. I know how we can cure the current recession! All we need to do to pull out of the current recession is to make the fashion designers raise hemlines.

Other mistakes often grouped under the broad heading of False Cause Fallacies result from confusing symptoms, outcomes, or intentions with causes. Here are examples:

- The pressure was intense that day. I had to get from the university to my job, a drive that normally took 25 minutes. But the professor kept us late and then my car wouldn't start. You know there had to be a traffic jam on the freeway that day. And I needed to get to work because I had to make this major presentation. My head was aching and my heart was beating so fast. I felt all sweaty and it was getting harder and harder to breathe. I think that it was all because I couldn't get any air. That's where the pressure was coming from. No air.
- Three years ago we instituted a policy of Zero Tolerance for binge drinking in campus-controlled housing units. Simultaneously, we instituted a non-punitive program of substance abuse counseling. Today we have been honored by the state legislature because the reported incidents of binge drinking have dropped 32 percent compared to numbers from three years ago. The counseling program is why. That program has greatly reduced the

Thinking Critically Create Your Own Inductive Reasoning Examples

Write three fallacious arguments exemplifying each of these errors:

The Erroneous Generalization Fallacy
The Playing with Numbers Fallacy
The False Dilemma Fallacy
The Gambler's Fallacy
The False Cause Fallacy
The Slippery Slope Fallacy

number of incidents of binge drinking in campus-controlled housing.

- We wanted it more than they did! And that's why we won.

Slippery Slope

Everyone knows that simply beginning something is no assurance that it will be completed. For a variety of reasons, too many good students never finish their degree programs. Not everyone who takes a drink becomes an alcoholic. Not everyone who buys a gun becomes a killer. The Slippery Slope Fallacy makes the false assumption that discrete events are linked together so that the first step in the process necessarily results in some significant, usually bad, result way down the road somewhere. The image conjured by this fallacy is of walking along the edge of a muddy wet ridge. One step over that edge and we slide on our butts all the way to the bottom. Another image associated with this fallacy is the "camel's nose under the tent" image. Once the camel gets its nose under the tent, there is no way to prevent the whole, huge clumsy animal from entering one's well-ordered abode.

- If you ever smoke a joint, then you are on the path to perdition. One puff and there is no stopping the inevitable fall. Next it will be snorting coke, then shooting up heroin, leading to addiction with track marks in your arms and hepatitis or worse from contaminated needles.
- I warn you, you had better come to every training session. We start lessons Monday. If you miss the first day, then you'll be behind and you will never catch up.

A person can make a mistake and recover from it. And some of the initial stages that are alleged to be dreadful turn out not to be problems at all. And the middle ground is often the best place to make one's stand. To quote Terence of ancient Rome, "Moderation in all things."

Fallacies—Common Yet Misleading Errors of Reasoning (Chapters 7, 8, & 9 Combined)			
Arguments that Fail the Test of Relevance	**Fallacies of Relevance**	Appeals to Ignorance Appeals to the Mob Appeals to Emotion Ad Hominem Attacks	The Straw Man Fallacy Playing with Words Misuse of Authority
Arguments that Fail the Test of Logical Strength	**Fallacies Masquerading as Valid Deductive Arguments**	Affirming the Consequent Denying the Antecedent False Classification	Fallacy of Composition Fallacy of Division False Reference
	Fallacies Masquerading as Warranted Inductive Arguments	Erroneous Generalization Playing with Numbers False Dilemma	Gambler's Fallacy False Cause Slippery Slope
Fail the Test of Non-Circularity		Circular Reasoning	

Study and Review on mythinkinglab.com

The evaluation of probabilistic inductive reasoning occurs each day of our lives. We evaluate inferences when talking with friends, working on projects, enduring television commercials, or reasoning through a decision. In this chapter we worked to strengthen our critical thinking skill of evaluation as applied to inductive arguments that offer to generalize from a limited number of experiences and samplings of data to reach justified claims about the characteristics of larger populations. To protect ourselves from being easily deceived, we reviewed the collection of common fallacies that masquerade as justified inductive arguments.

We are human. Our own experience and the scientific research come together on one important point: We humans often make important decisions about what to believe or what to do without reflection and despite the arguments. In the next two chapters we will explore why we do this, and, more importantly, how we can use critical thinking to help ourselves individually and in groups to be more reflective and more attuned to the power of worthy arguments as we make important decisions.

KEY TERM

inductively justified (or **"warranted"**) **argument** is an argument such that were all of its premises true then its conclusion would most likely or very probably also be true. (p. 166)

FIND IT ON MYTHINKINGLAB.COM

- Strong inductive reasoning depends on full and accurate information. Throughout the chapter you found opportunities to visit **www.mythinkinglab.com** and to connect to sources of useful information about important topics such as the causes of wrongful conviction, the relationships between academic majors and salaries, achieving an accurate census upon which to base policy decisions and political representation, and national statistics about motor vehicle accidents.
  Watch the Video on mythinkinglab.com
- The grittiness of real-life critical thinking about issues affecting millions of people comes out again in two of the exercises. When we apply our critical thinking to evaluating the arguments, we should come out with very similar assessments if we are working from the same set of assumptions and premises. In the exercises we invite you to engage these urgent and difficult issues through the *To Kill a Mockingbird* and the *Real Time with Bill Maher* "New Rules." Visit **www.mythinkinglab.com**.

Exercises

REFLECTIVE LOG: *TO KILL A MOCKINGBIRD*

Gregory Peck plays the defense attorney, Atticus Finch, in the film *To Kill a Mockingbird*. The story is about a young man accused of rape. In this clip, Atticus Finch is giving his summation to the jury. He must be careful not to alienate the members of the jury, whom he regards as potentially biased against the defendant because of his race. Atticus first argues that the prosecution has not proved that a crime was actually committed. He then claims that the accused, Tom Robinson, could not physically have done the things that the prosecution claims. Atticus, believing that he must do more than make claims and logical arguments establishing reasonable doubt, then addresses a key question. Why would the accuser have lied about being raped by the accused? Atticus says he has pity for the victim and then he argues that by accusing Tom Robinson, she was attempting to rid herself of her own guilt. The defense then attempts to challenge the prejudicial assumption: In the language of those days, "Negros cannot be trusted." Listen carefully to the claims and arguments made by Atticus Finch. Transcribe them, use the techniques in Chapter 5 to analyze and map them and, using what you learned in Chapters 7, 8 and 9, evaluate them. Explain your analysis and your evaluation. Would you have made the summation differently? If so, how? Access the video at www.mythinkinglab.com.

Watch the Video on mythinkinglab.com

EVALUATE ARGUMENT WORTHINESS AND EXPLAIN

Assume that all the premises that are asserted in the arguments below are true. Apply the remaining three tests to evaluate each argument to determine which are worthy of acceptance. Begin with the Test of Logical Strength. Remember, if the argument fails a test you do not have to apply any further tests because, at that point, the argument has been found to be unworthy of acceptance. In each case, give a detailed explanation to support your evaluation. State in your own words why each argument is worthy or unworthy of acceptance. Hint: Be prepared to add implicit but unspoken premises and assumptions. This exercise draws on your skills at evaluating deductive as well as inductive reasoning.

1. Anthony was at risk of dying from the severe fall that he took when he was climbing. Many who had the same near-fatal experience become averse to climbing afterward. So, Anthony will become averse to climbing after his fall.
2. Susan is John's younger sister. Linda is John's elder sister. So, Linda is Susan's elder sister.
3. I want to buy a boat and you want to buy a car. If we buy a car we can't use it for fishing or to go tubing. But if we buy a boat we can't use it in the city or anywhere else but at the lake. Either way we're stuck.
4. Blood samples taken from the crime scene were type AB. The accused person's blood is type AB. Therefore, the accused was at the scene of the crime.
5. Either we'll study together tonight for tomorrow's exam, or we will both blow it off. I'm too tired to study tonight. So, we're going to blow it off.
6. Whenever I play the lottery, the number I put in is my birthday. If that's not my lucky number, then I don't have one.
7. Randolph knows that John Glenn was a senator. John Glenn was an astronaut. Therefore Randolph knows that John Glenn was an astronaut.
8. Every member of the House of Representatives is under the age of 90. Therefore, the House of Representatives is an organ of government that was created less than 90 years ago.
9. Seventy-three percent of the people surveyed said that they wanted universal health care coverage. Fifty-four percent said that they were worried about the cost of the program or the quality of the care that would be provided. Therefore, the American people are opposed to the President's health care reform legislation.
10. The Mayor has been in office for three months, and our city's economic recession has not gone away. The Mayor needs to take full responsibility for the sorry state of the city's economy.
11. My dear old Uncle Joe has a statue of the Red Faced Warrior on his kitchen table. It faces the side door, and he says that it keeps bad people from coming into his house. He also has a picture of St. Christopher taped to the dashboard of his old Buick and a rosary draped over the rearview mirror. More protection he claims. On the other hand, he never locks his house, and he needs to get his eyes checked!
12. But if we don't study together, then I'm not going to get through the course. And if I don't get through the course,

then I'm going to ruin my GPA and lose my financial aid. So if we don't study together tonight, then I'm going to lose my financial aid.

13. We've lost six games in a row; our luck has to change today.
14. We didn't know what to do to improve sales. So, we all started wearing bow ties and navy blue sweaters to work. And look, three weeks later sales are way up. I'm sure it's our new office dress code.
15. It's January tenth and already six people have ordered new glasses with plastic frames. Last year only four people had ordered plastic frames by this date. That's an increase of 50 percent. We had better stock up. It's going to be a busy year.
16. Everyone loves ice cream. Children love ice cream. So, everyone's a child.
17. Water is our most precious resource. So, a towel on the rack means "I'll use it again" and a towel on the floor means, "Please replace."

WHAT'S THE TRUTH ABOUT COLON CLEANSING?

"The devil is in the details." Just as with the median annual salary by academic major discussion, we can find seemingly credible sources presenting substantially different information. A weak critical thinker substantially at that point, uncertain which source to believe and either unwilling or unable to evalute the arguments and reasons being presented. The weak critical thinker is apt to be suckered into buying something that does not work, or believing something that will only lead to bad decisions. But a strong critical thinker sees it as a challenge when two apparently credible sources present highly divergent information: Which is closer to the truth? If selecting an academic major based on faulty information about potential future earnings is not bad enough, making personal health care decisions based on faulty information and weak arguments only adds to one's problems. A service increasingly offered by spas and clinics that seems to be growing in popularity is colon cleansing or colonic hydrotherapy. Lots of colon cleansing products are marketed with celebrity endorsments. The arguments and reasons in support of colon cleansing include enhancing personal well-being, weight loss, and flushing bodily toxins. But there are reasons why colon cleansing is not recommended—e.g., that the process itself can cause internal injuries and that its alleged benefits cannot be demonstrated. In the end the burden of proof ought to be on those promoting the practice or selling the products and services.

You be the judge. Research the arguments and reasons given for and against the practice and evaluate them. Figure out which side in this issue is closer to the truth. See, for example, "The Dangers of Colon Cleansing," published in the *Journal of Family Practice*,[xi] **http://www.jfponline.com/Pages.asp?AID=9783&issue=August_2011&UID=**

Read the **Document** on **mythinkinglab.com**

CHALLENGE EXERCISE: WHAT'S THE TRUTH ABOUT CLIMATE CHANGE?

In November 2011 the United Nations Intergovernmental Panel on Climate Change (IPCC) released "The Special Report on Managing the Risks of Extreme Events and Disasters to Advance Climate Change Adaptation." More than 800 authors, selected from thousands of nominations, participated in preparing additional reports for release in 2013, 2014, and 2015. Scientific reports suggest that climate shifts are affecting global food production, for example "Climate Trends and Global Crop Production Since 1980" by Stanford professor David Lobell, published in *Science*.[xii] The IPCC is taking the view that climate change is a reality and that the question now is how our species will adapt. Review the IPCC 2011 report. Evaluate the IPCC arguments in support of the claim that climate change is occurring, that one major contributing factor is human activity, and that steps need to be taken to manage the risks of extreme events and disasters resulting from climate change.

GROUP EXERCISE: 2009 AND THE DEBATE OVER THE "PUBLIC OPTION"

At the end of the July 24, 2009, episode of HBO's *Real Time with Bill Maher*, Maher argues in support of the "public option" to be included in the health care reform legislation which at that time was being fiercely debated. The "public option" provision would provide the tens of millions of uninsured and underinsured Americans the option of purchasing health care insurance at an affordable price. Either the government would provide the program through a not-for-profit agency, or the legislation would permit the establishing of co-ops. Maher's barbed statements included these: "If conservatives get to call universal health care 'socialized medicine,' I get to call private, for-profit healthcare 'soulless, vampire bastards making money off human pain." "I would love to have some journalist ask a Republican who talks about socialized medicine: If it's so awful, how come it's what we have for our veterans?"

Using these quotes and other Bill Maher quotes you can locate in episode 161 at www.mythinkinglab.com, present, in as fair-minded and non-incendiary a way as possible, his main reasons, as revealed by the quotes, for supporting the "public option" provision. Map his reasons using the techniques presented in Chapter 5. Then evaluate each of his arguments for using the four-tests process presented in Chapter 7. Remain objective. Resist permitting your personal views on the subject to interfere with the objectivity of your analysis of his views or your evaluation of his arguments.

During the summer of 2009 many conservative political commentators spoke out against the "public option." Research the web for videos and written editorials by political conservatives like Bill O'Reilly, Dennis Miller, and Sean Hannity. With the same concern not to be caught up in the rhetoric, but instead to dig for their reasons and evidence, analyze and map their main arguments in opposition to the "public option." Once you have those arguments analyzed, apply all four of the tests for evaluating arguments. As with the arguments offered by Maher, here too arguments may fail because one or more of their premises are untrue, because the argument is illogical, because the reason is irrelevant, or because the argument is circular. To assist with these tests you might search for commentaries on the arguments, since many media outlets published editorials during those days to refute the arguments of the other side. One example is posted at http://mediamatters.org/research/200910080006

Watch the **Video** on **mythinkinglab.com**

Read the Chapter on mythinkinglab.com
Listen to the Chapter Audio on mythinkinglab.com

CHAPTER 10

Think Heuristically: Risks and Benefits of Snap Judgments

HOW does human decision making work, and where does critical thinking fit?

WHAT are cognitive heuristics and how do they help or harm decision making?

Many good judgments we make every day are automatic or reactive, rather than reflective. Well-trained pilots can fly complicated machines and take millions of us to our destinations every day. Through training and repetition, veteran pilots have internalized and made automatic a series of complex analyses, inferences, and quick effective judgments that novice pilots often find mentally all-consuming. Automatic reactions are also seen in more "grounded" drivers and in other situations. For example, bike riders often pedal along, paying more attention to the beauty of the surrounding fields, trees, and streams than on trying to maintain their balance. The process of e-mailing friends is another example. Our fingers tap the keys, but our minds are focused on composing our messages, not on locating the letters on the keyboards. Human beings do not make all their decisions using only their capacity for deliberative reflective thought. Human decision making is more complex.[i] Some judgments, including many good ones, are quick and reactive, not deliberative or reflective. Although some judgments are best made more automatically or reactively, some are best made reflectively.[ii] Our real-life critical thinking question is "Which of our reactive judgments ought we to make reflectively?"

For any of us to maximize our personal potential for developing and applying critical thinking to real-life decision making, we first must understand how human problem solving and decision making function

<<< To become a trusted, well-trained professional, like this pilot, one must combine knowledge, practice and reflection. There is no other way to transition the slow, halting and uncertain efforts of a novice into the swift, smooth, and effective work of a competent professional.

in real life. We know that critical thinking, or reflective purposeful judgment, can and ought to be applied to a very large array of vital issues and important decisions. And we know from our experience that we do not always use critical thinking. The fact that we *do* not use critical thinking does not imply that we *ought* not to be using critical thinking.

This chapter and the next one focus on the skill of self-regulation, because monitoring our own decision making and correcting our own decision making turn out to be essential. Taking a moment to "stop and think" is excellent advice for every one of us, authors included. We begin this chapter with a brief synopsis of the cognitive science research on decision making so that we can position critical thinking, and in particular the skill of self-regulation, within that context. We will learn that many reactive judgments are good judgments. But, in some circumstances, reactive judgments can lead to unnecessary risks and mistaken biases. Our work in this chapter is to use self-regulation to become more aware of those circumstances so we can correct ourselves reflectively, using critical thinking, before we make a mistake.

Human Decision-Making Systems

Human decision making emerges from the interplay of two cognitive drivers. One is our human propensity toward self-explanation known as argument making. The other driver is the influence on our decision making of mental "shortcuts" known as cognitive heuristics. *Argument making*, as we saw in the previous chapters, is the effort to be logical—that is, to rely on the relevant reasons and facts as we see them when making our decisions. In general, humans value making important decisions as rationally as the circumstances, significance, and content of their judgments permit. This is not to say that we are always successful in this effort. In fact, we often are not. And yet we explain our choices and judgments to ourselves, if not to others, in terms of the relevant reasons and facts—again, as we see them. For example, you ask me why I stayed overnight at a friend's house in another city instead of driving home. I reply that it was late and I was very tired, too tired to drive.

Heuristic thinking is the tendency, which is at times quite useful, of relying on highly efficient and generally reliable cognitive shortcuts when reaching a decision. In the research literature, these mental shortcuts are known as *cognitive heuristics*. These mental maneuvers are as much a part of the human reasoning process as argument making. Cognitive heuristics often enable us to make judgments and decisions more expeditiously and efficiently. Their influences, while often positive, can introduce errors and biases into human decision making.

THE "TWO-SYSTEMS" APPROACH TO HUMAN DECISION MAKING

Research on human decisions made in naturalistic, everyday contexts, describes the interaction of two overlapping decision-making systems.[iii] One is reactive, instinctive, quick, and holistic (System-1). The other is reflective, deliberative, analytical, and procedural (System-2). Both valuable systems function simultaneously, often checking and balancing each other.

Reactive (System-1) Thinking

System-1 thinking relies heavily on situational cues, salient memories, and heuristic thinking to arrive quickly and confidently at judgments, particularly when situations are familiar and immediate action is required. Many freeway accidents are avoided because drivers are able to see and react to dangerous situations quickly. Good decisions emerging from System-1 thinking often feel intuitive.[iv] Decisions good drivers make in those moments of crisis, just like the decisions practiced athletes make in the flow of a game or the decisions that a gifted teacher makes while interacting with students, are born of expertise, training, and practice. Often we decide first, quickly, and reactively, and then, if asked about our decisions, we explain how we analyzed the situation and we provide the reasons and arguments to explain those snap judgments, which are System-1 decisions. Overt explanations using argument making in the case of System-1 decisions are retrospective. We look back at the decision and explain the inferences we made at the spur of the moment.

Reflective (System-2) Thinking

System-2 thinking is useful for judgments in unfamiliar situations, for processing abstract concepts, and for deliberating when there is time for planning and more comprehensive consideration. Humans use heuristic maneuvers in System-2 thinking as well, often integrated as components of their logical arguments. Argument making is often part of the inference and deliberation process when making System-2 decisions. And, of course, explanations involve making arguments and giving the reasons we used during our deliberations. When we share our reflective interpretations, analyses, evaluations, and inferences, we are offering explanations. Because of this, critical thinking is self-regulated System-2 thinking. Critical thinking is System-2 thinking focused on resolving the problem at hand and at the same time monitoring and self-correcting one's own process of thinking about that problem.

MAP > it > OUT 1

Model of Two-System Human Decision Making

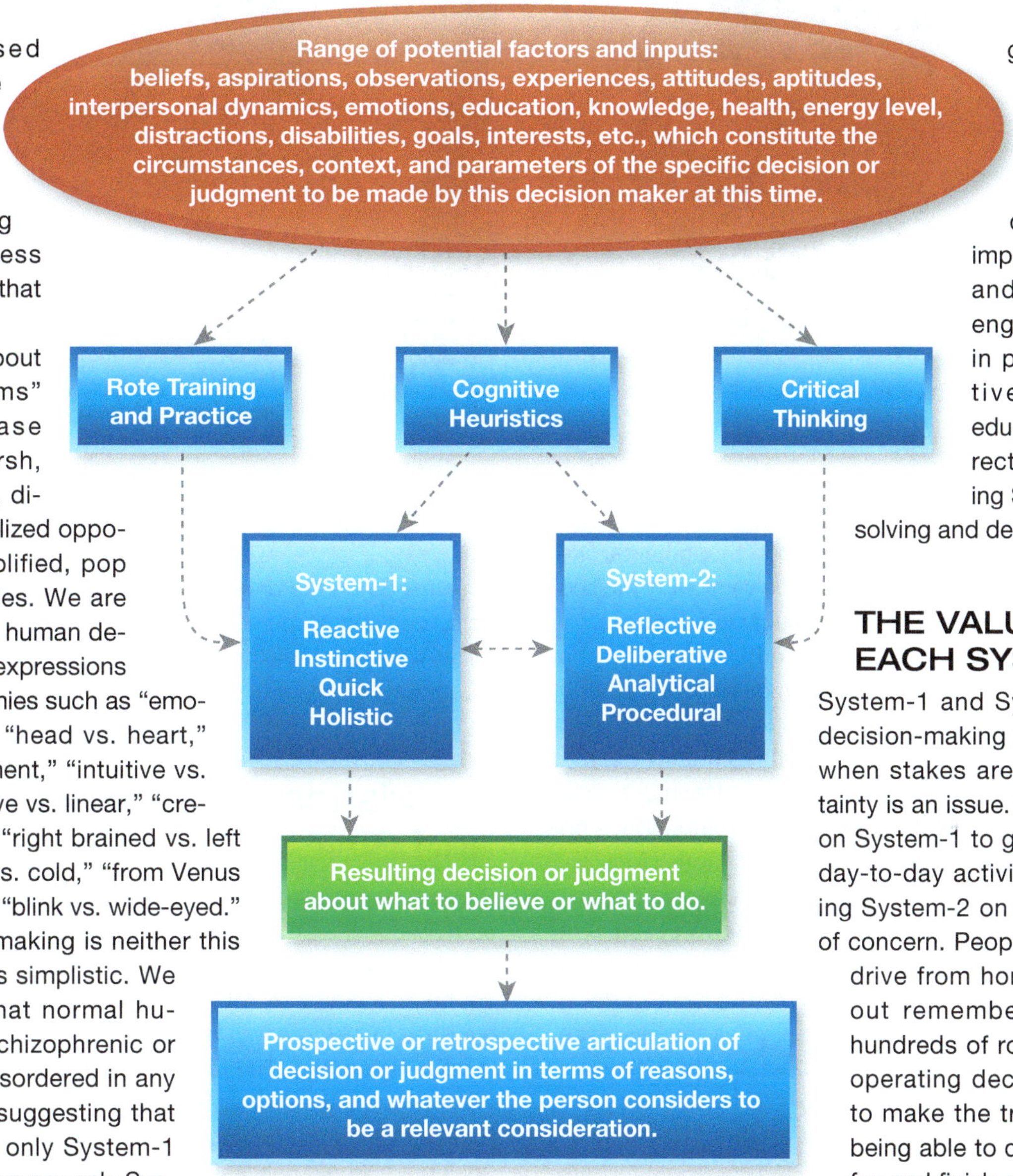

Range of potential factors and inputs: beliefs, aspirations, observations, experiences, attitudes, aptitudes, interpersonal dynamics, emotions, education, knowledge, health, energy level, distractions, disabilities, goals, interests, etc., which constitute the circumstances, context, and parameters of the specific decision or judgment to be made by this decision maker at this time.

Rote Training and Practice

Cognitive Heuristics

Critical Thinking

System-1: Reactive Instinctive Quick Holistic

System-2: Reflective Deliberative Analytical Procedural

Resulting decision or judgment about what to believe or what to do.

Prospective or retrospective articulation of decision or judgment in terms of reasons, options, and whatever the person considers to be a relevant consideration.

As you think about the "two-systems" approach, please avoid all the harsh, rigid, stereotypic, divisive, commercialized oppositional, oversimplified, pop culture dichotomies. We are not characterizing human decision making by expressions and false dichotomies such as "emotion vs. reason," "head vs. heart," "feeling vs. judgment," "intuitive vs. logical," "expansive vs. linear," "creative vs. critical," "right brained vs. left brained," "warm vs. cold," "from Venus vs. from Mars," or "blink vs. wide-eyed." Human decision making is neither this superficial nor this simplistic. We are not saying that normal human thinking is schizophrenic or psychologically disordered in any way. We are not suggesting that some people are only System-1 thinkers while others are only System-2 thinkers.

Normal human beings have and use both systems in problem solving and decision making every day. The two-systems approach to understanding human decision making accounts for the pushes and pulls that normal human beings often describe as part of their decision making. System-1 is the rapid-fire decision making we all experience on some occasions, while System-2 is the more reflective decision making we all experience on other occasions.

Because it is considered more useful for addressing novel and complex problems in a reflective and methodical way, System-2 is the mode of reasoned, informed and thoughtful problem solving and decision making that a broad undergraduate liberal arts and sciences education cultivates. System-2 is also the mode addressed by the evidence-based practice and research methods components of one's professional or graduate studies. All levels of education which aim at improving one's critical thinking—improving one's skills and dispositions to engage successfully in purposeful reflective judgment—is education focused directly on strengthening System-2 problem solving and decision making.

THE VALUE OF EACH SYSTEM

System-1 and System-2 are vital decision-making tools, particularly when stakes are high and uncertainty is an issue. We can often rely on System-1 to get us through our day-to-day activities while engaging System-2 on some other topic of concern. People report they can drive from home to work without remembering any of the hundreds of routine automobile operating decisions necessary to make the trip. Others report being able to drink a cup of coffee and finish a bowl of breakfast cereal almost without noticing because they are so engrossed in the morning newspaper. Have you ever had any of these kinds of experiences in your life—experiences where you did something "without really thinking about it" while your mind was preoccupied with a completely different problem or issue?

We do not store the memories of our System-1 guided actions if we are simultaneously engaged in deliberating about something using System-2. For example, when we are thinking about something else, like a work assignment, a relationship issue, or a financial problem, we are distracted from the simpler System-1 decision making we may be doing, like walking in a familiar place, driving home on a familiar route, or eating lunch. Our mental focus is on the System-2 work, and, during those times, System-1 operates in the background. This is

System-1: A soldier reacting under fire based on sound training.

System-2: Experienced policy makers considering possible responses to budget challenges.

why we may not remember routine System-1 judgments, like why we've walked into a room, whether we've already passed our freeway exit, or if we've already put sugar in our coffee.

System-1 functions in the background or "behind the scenes" more than System-2, but each system is capable of overriding the other. Conflicted decision-making contexts have, through the ages, been described in different ways—"temptation" being only one example. We are drawn one way, but at the same time, pulled the other way. Although we do not accept the implication that the colloquial expressions are scientifically accurate, we can spot oblique references to the behind-the-scenes pushes and pulls of the two systems in the way people ordinarily talk about their decision making. We have all heard people say things like "My gut says to do X, but my brain says to do Y"; "We looked at all the evidence and all the options and yet we don't feel comfortable with where the deliberations are heading"; or "Emotionally I want to do this, but rationally I think I should do that." Some theorists suggest these common ways of talking are evidence that, in certain kinds of ambiguous or complex situations, the two systems might conflict, drawing the decision maker in different directions. In general, this is thought to be an advantage that reduces the chance of making poor, suboptimal, or even dangerous errors in judgment—a natural system of checks and balances, as it were.

Even a good thinker makes both System-1 and System-2 errors from time to time. We misinterpret things, overestimate or underestimate our chances of succeeding, rely on mistaken analogies, reject options out of hand, trust feelings and hunches, judge things credible when they are not, etc. Often mistakes like these are directly related to the influences and misapplications of cognitive heuristics. We all share the propensity to use these heuristics as we make decisions, because at times the heuristics seem to be hardwired into our species. Since the critical thinking skill of self-regulation can help us avoid some of these errors if we become more familiar with how they look in practice, let's examine several in closer detail.

Heuristics: Their Benefits and Risks

Shakespeare called humans the paragon of animals. Aristotle said "rational animals." For Plato, "featherless bipeds" was good enough. Perhaps not the most honorific descriptions, yet humbling and useful reminders that there are times when we base our judgments on unfounded assumptions and fallacious reasoning. The long list of argument fallacies in the table at the end of Chapter 9 does not include all the ways that our decision making can go astray. In this chapter we consider a whole new set of biases and errors emerging from the *misapplication* of those ordinarily reliable reasoning maneuvers known as "heuristics." Given the natural limitations of human rationality, it turns out that errors in heuristic thinking can result in serious problems when the risks are great and the stakes are high.

The correct application of cognitive heuristics is absolutely essential for day-to-day living. We would exhaust ourselves mentally and accomplish very little if every single judgment was a full-blown reflective decision. We get through the routine parts of our day making quick, automatic reactive heuristic judgments. We rely on these snap judgments because (a) most of the time they are good enough for the purpose at hand; (b) we need to conserve our mental energy for bigger, more important, and less familiar problems that life throws our way; and (c) often, we have no time for reflective thought. This will be clearer as you review the examples and do the exercises in conjunction with each of the following heuristics.

INDIVIDUAL COGNITIVE HEURISTICS

Cognitive heuristics are natural human decision-making shortcuts we all rely upon in real life to expedite our judgments about what to believe or what to do. There are potentially beneficial consequences associated with relying on the cognitive shortcuts we'll discuss. In each case we examine the heuristic shortcut or maneuver itself and note potential advantages and disadvantages of relying on the heuristic. A brief, true-to-life vignette and other examples illustrate how that heuristic looks in real life. In most cases a short exercise invites you to apply your critical thinking—and in particular your skill at reflective self-regulation—to occasions in your own life when reliance on that particular heuristic may have resulted in outcomes that were less successful than you had hoped. There are 17 common heuristics described in this chapter. Each is likely quite familiar.

1. Satisficing and 2. Temporizing

"The first time he was at the beach, my 3-year-old grandson darted down to the wet sand and watched as a small wave washed up toward him. A wave came in and lapped at his toes and ankles, the chilly wet water sending him scurrying up the sand. He turned and cautiously approached the water a second time. Again he got close enough to just let the water touch the tips of his toes, and scooted up the sand. But not nearly as far as the first time. The third time he approached the surf he anticipated the wave as it approached and, instead of turning to run, he back-pedaled a few steps. Just far enough not to be hit by the salty bubbles. He went just far enough! The kid satisficed, I thought, and, more interestingly, nobody taught him how.

To the child, the water is captivating, inviting and yet dangerous? How far away from danger is "far enough" in our own lives?

The *Satisficing Heuristic*: Having found an option that is good enough, we take it. We human beings typically do only what must be done to achieve our purposes. In day-to-day living, when faced with choices, instead of expending the resources necessary to identify and then attain the maximally optimal alternative, we decide in favor of an alternative we deem satisfactory.[v] How many times have we read the whole menu in a restaurant compared to reading along only until we spot an entrée that strikes our fancy? We tend to divide the world into "good enough" and "not good enough" and search for a solution until a solution is found that is good enough to attain the desired outcome. Truisms like "If it isn't broken, don't fix it," and "Perfect is the enemy of good" reflect the satisficing cognitive maneuver.

- Example (System-1): Being thirsty, how much water would we drink? Only enough to slake our thirst.
- Example (System-2): Seeking a new job, how hard would we look? Hard enough to find one that meets whatever are our basic criteria for pay, proximity to home, nature of the work, etc.?
- Example (System-2): Having arrested a suspect who had the means, motive, and opportunity to commit the crime, how hard can we expect police detectives to strive to locate other suspects? Satisficing suggests hardly at all. The question of the actual guilt or innocence of the subject becomes the concern of the prosecuting attorney and the courts.

The *Temporizing Heuristic*: Deciding that a given option is "good enough for now," or temporizing is satisficing's running mate. We often move through life satisficing and temporizing. At times, we look back on our situations and wonder why it is that we have settled for far less than we might have. If we had only studied harder, worked out a little more, or taken better care of our relationships and ourselves, perhaps we would not be living as we are now. But at the time, each of the decisions along the way was "good enough for the time being."

We must not overlook the important potential advantages to satisficing. These include conserving time, money, and energy.[vi] If you have to put in 10 percent more effort and time to gain only 1 percent more value, your return on that investment of effort may not be worth the cost. The main disadvantage of satisficing is that we may be mistaken in our estimation of how much is "good enough." Why did the better team lose the game? Because, in underestimating its opponent, the team failed to play up to its own potential. Why did we have trouble on the exam? Because we did not do the homework exercises and study hard enough. Why did my boss not give me a better evaluation compared to my peers? Because I was not productive enough, even though I had thought all along that I was doing just fine. Using our critical thinking in real time, we should take a moment in key situations to be sure our heuristic estimate of "good enough" is really accurate. To achieve greater success we will have to self-correct and recalibrate our sense of how much is enough.

Thinking Critically How Good is Good Enough?

Think of two recent occasions when you were disappointed by how your efforts turned out because of misestimating how much on your part was necessary to achieve your goals. Use your critical thinking skills to make a reasoned judgment regarding how to adjust your sense of "good enough" to increase your likelihood of success in the same endeavors the next time.

3. Affect: "Go with Your Gut"

"I proposed on our first date. She said no. But somehow we both knew that her response was not going to be her final answer. A few months later we were engaged. More than 40 wedding anniversaries later, we are still in love. Perhaps we have been lucky; our marriage could have been a disaster. Whatever was reflective and rational about that decision—as I recall trying to explain it to her folks and mine—had to have been an effort to build a case for a decision we had already made."

The *Affect Heuristic*: Making a decision based on your initial affective ("gut") response.[vii] There is no question that many different kinds of experiences can cause us to respond with joy or sorrow, with desire or revulsion, with enthusiasm or dread. A "gut reaction," that is, an affective response, is a strong System-1 impetus, either positively or negatively, toward the object.[viii] It is natural to have the response.[ix] That response may be the "first word" on the matter, but System-2 self-regulation demands that we ask ourselves whether that should necessarily be the final word on the matter.

- Example: "Oh, I like those shoes. . . . You know, they would look great with the blue jacket I bought."
- Example: "Did you see his eyes? Pure evil! Made my blood run cold. Believe me, a guy like that, no way should you trust him."
- Example: "Forget it. I don't want to hear about how you think we can balance the budget. You said the 'T' word and I won't have anything to do with that. Read my lips, 'No new taxes!' We all pay too much in taxes as it is."

Our natural, initial affective response to ideas, questions, images, people, events, etc., can have obvious advantages and disadvantages. Research on the relationship between facial and body symmetry, perceived attractiveness, and physical health suggests that first affective impressions we have about another human being as a possible mate are evolutionarily selected for and contributes to the survival of the species. Our System-1 affective reaction can influence us toward embracing a choice that "just feels right" or away from an option that appears frightening or repugnant when our System-2 decision making gets bogged down with too many factors to consider, too many divergent criteria, and too much uncertainty. Were it not for this, some of us might never get unstuck and make a decision when one is needed.

But, what if that initially frightening option is actually the best and most reasonable? For example, what if our fear of the anticipated consequences of radiation or chemotherapy influenced us to reject those options when one or both of them were the best possible cancer treatment options? It may take significant amounts of reflective System-2 reasoning to overcome a powerful System-1 affective response to an idea, but it can be done. And at times it should happen, because there is no guarantee that our affective responses are necessarily always true. Strong critical thinking demands that we check our affective responses. Simply having them is not nearly enough for wise, reflective decision making.

The affect heuristic influences us to make judgments and decisions based on our initial impulsive and subliminal responses. Knowing this, marketing experts coined the

Based on your reaction when you first see these two dorm rooms, which residence hall would you prefer? Did you ever make a mistake by trusting your first reaction?

Thinking Critically Emotional Jolts

Think of two recent occasions when you had a strong initial affective response to an idea, proposal, opportunity, person, or event. Find one that was positive and one that was negative. Did you reflect on that response, evaluate it, and verify that it was the correct response? If not, this exercise provides the opportunity. Apply your System-2 reflective critical thinking skills to both of those responses. Gather needed information and analyze your response in the light of that new information. Call on your habits of truth-seeking and open-mindedness to support your effort to be as objective as possible in evaluating your initial responses.

expression, "The package is the product," to indicate how important the wrapping, the container, and the initial appearance of a product are to making the sale.[x] Certainly a broken residence hall window and an unkempt campus lawn are not necessarily indicative of an academically substandard college. But college recruiters know that these things had better be fixed before prospective students show up for the campus tour. And on reflection, no one would argue that a cabernet in an attractively designed bottle with a classy label is necessarily superior to a cabernet in a generic bottle with a plain looking label.[xi] There is no question that first impressions count when choosing a college, choosing a wine, or choosing a mate.

4. Simulation

"I was in center field, my favorite position, and the runner at third was itching to tag up and dash for home if the batter hit a fly ball. I imagined what I would do if it were hit to me, how I would run in, position my body, make the catch and fire the ball to the plate on one hop so the catcher could handle the throw easily and tag out the runner. The odds were overwhelming that the batter would hit the ball someplace else. But no! The ball was in the air arcing over the infield and sailing out toward center. I darted to my right, took the fly out of the air with my gloved left hand and made my throw toward the plate. The runner had tagged, leaving early I think. But he didn't have a chance. My throw, just up the third base line from home, was on target and on time. The catcher put the tag on the runner for the third out. It was like I had made a movie, watched the movie, and then lived the scene almost exactly."

The *Simulation Heuristic*: Estimating the likelihood of a given outcome based on how easy it is to imagine that outcome.[xii] Simulation is a mental process of imagining ourselves doing something successfully or unsuccessfully. Before giving a speech we might "see ourselves" at the podium talking to the audience with confidence, making our point, and delivering our message effectively. Or we may simulate the opposite, seeing ourselves messing up, getting flustered, and forgetting to say things we had wanted to say. If we experience ease in processing a simulation, this influences us to believe that achieving the anticipated outcome is more likely.[xiii] A person choosing among several options might simulate what it would be like to select an option and then, like making a movie in his or her mind, imagine what life would be like having selected that option. Unless we are being reflective about the actual probabilities that what we picture will actually happen, the simulation heuristic can influence us to select an option that plays out in our minds as the one offering the most desirable result. This might be called "wishful thinking," but whatever it is called, it is not a reflective and well-informed System-2 decision about the actual probability. The same would be true of pessimistically overestimating the likelihood of a bad outcome.

- Example: "You know, I didn't go there to buy a car. But when I was on the lot looking, this salesman came up to me and invited me to sit behind the wheel. Then we went on a test drive, and I could really see myself tooling along I-70 in this baby. So, here it is. My new set of wheels."
- Example: "I don't know what happened, sir!" said the sales representative to the manager after the failed presentation. "Yesterday I could see myself closing that deal."
- Example: "Day trading. I took it up for a while. Lost a lot of money, too. You know it just seemed like it was going to be so easy. All I had to do was invest in some stocks in the morning and watch them increase in value as the day went along. Then sell them just before the market did its typical end-of-day little dip. Well. Things didn't turn out that way at all. I think the only people who made money on my day trading were the guys who work at the brokerage house."

Psychologist Albert Bandura's research on social learning demonstrates the value and power of simulation to increase attitudes of self-efficacy.[xiv] Mentors and coaches use the simulation heuristic, (they may call it *visualization*) as a technique to improve performance and to help people anticipate being able to succeed at challenging things. Successful advertising often depends on stimulating simulation. Car ads, for example, often show someone with demographics just like the intended buyers taking great pleasure in driving the model of car the ad is promoting. The idea is that if you match those demographics, you would then be led to see yourself in that car and then want to buy it. The process of simulation is quick, easy, and need not be reflective. In fact, it might be better for the advertiser if you do not reflect too much on the actual costs and benefits of buying that new car. The obvious disadvantage of simulation is the potential to err in estimating the likelihood of the imagined outcomes. This can result in misplaced confidence and unwarranted optimism.

Everyone knows that simulating academic success is not a replacement for actually studying, doing the assignments, and doing well on exams. But along with those things, simulation can be very helpful. Take a moment and see yourself being a successful student by simulating how you will structure your time so that you can read the textbook and do all the exercises and assignments. Simulate how you will be organized, focused, and highly efficient in your use of that study time. See yourself going to class or taking tests justifiably confident in what you have learned, well prepared and ready to demonstrate your knowledge on exams and assignments. Oh, yes, and the critical thinking skill of self-regulation requires that we remind ourselves that we have to carry out the study plans that we have simulated, if we are to have a reasonable shot at achieving the learning and enjoying the success we anticipate.

5. Availability

"I was doing 75+ heading eastbound on I-96 from Michigan State back home to Detroit, alone, late at night. Darkness had engulfed the rural stretch of interstate. Occasionally, a car heading west passed by on the other side of the wide grassy median. Eastbound was two lanes, and I liked driving in the left lane because it was smoother since the heavy 18-wheelers had not furrowed and gnawed the pavement. But for reasons I'll never know, I decided that night to do the right thing, the thing I'd been taught in driver's education back in high school, and I moved back into the right-hand lane. Then, ahead, just over a slight rise in the interstate, I saw the glare of an approaching vehicle's high beam headlights. It didn't make sense—there shouldn't be any traffic heading west directly in front of me. I sped on, never reducing my speed. The lights grew brighter and brighter. I reached the crest of the rise in the freeway just as the other vehicle did. In a shocking blur it roared by, easily doing 75+. Heading west. On the eastbound side of I-96. And, thank God, he was in his right lane too. Moral of the story. Stay to the right, son, or you'll never know what hit you."

The *Availability Heuristic*: Estimating the likelihood of future events based on a vivid memory of a past experience that leaps easily to mind. Let's experiment with a memory. Imagine a conversation you may have had about foods you can't stand. Does a particularly awful experience with that food leap to mind? For example: "I hate mushrooms. Once when I was a kid I got sick on mushrooms at a restaurant." That quick, automatic connection is a manifestation of the availability heuristic. "No mushrooms on my pizza! Please." This heuristic leads us to estimate the likelihood of a future event based on the vividness or ease of recalling a similar past event.[xv] Because a past experience leaps vividly to mind or because it was so important, we overestimate the probability that future outcomes will be the same as they were back then. People tell stories of things that happened to them or their friends all the time as a way of explaining their own decisions and warning or advising their friends and family about the future. Often these are helpful because they vicariously increase our own range of experiences. The use of stories makes it much easier for us to remember their lessons or morals. Aesop's fables have more than entertainment value; they remind us not to "cry wolf," not

Thinking Critically Simulate

Simulate yourself hang gliding off the wind-swept cliffs along the Pacific Ocean. First, see yourself gliding up into the beautiful blue sky, enjoying the grand vistas and the glorious ocean, smelling the salty warmth of the sea air, swooping with silent grace toward the surf, and then lifting effortlessly and joyously on a vector of warm wind with the gulls and pelicans. Take your time. Enjoy the flight. Then when you are ready, ease yourself toward the soft sand and glide slowly to a perfect landing and the admiring approval of your friends. On a scale of 1 to 10, with 10 being "Yes, absolutely," how much did playing that movie in your mind incline you toward wanting to try hang gliding? On a scale of 1 to 10, with 10 being "easy," how easy would hang gliding be?

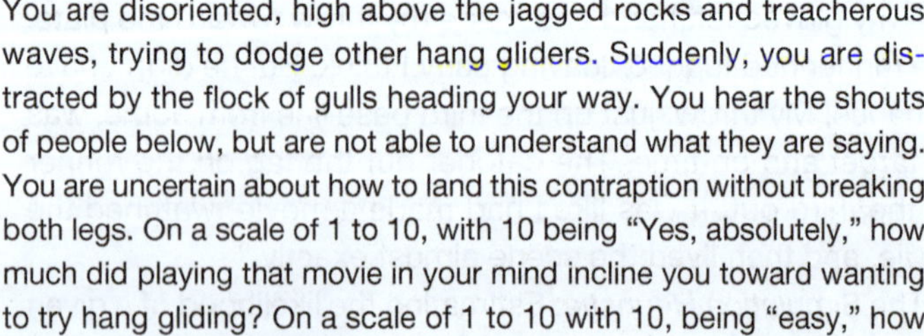

Now envision a second scenario. See yourself blown along, out of control, harnessed below a tissue-thick nylon wing attached to a flimsy aluminum frame, mentally on the edge of panic, your arms aching, and your back muscles knotted with tension. You are disoriented, high above the jagged rocks and treacherous waves, trying to dodge other hang gliders. Suddenly, you are distracted by the flock of gulls heading your way. You hear the shouts of people below, but are not able to understand what they are saying. You are uncertain about how to land this contraption without breaking both legs. On a scale of 1 to 10, with 10 being "Yes, absolutely," how much did playing that movie in your mind incline you toward wanting to try hang gliding? On a scale of 1 to 10 with 10, being "easy," how easy would hang gliding be?

Notice that neither simulation supplied any concrete information about hang gliding. Neither detailed the actual risks associated with the sport. Neither explained how one learns to hang glide, whether there are safer or more dangerous places to hang glide, or anything else that would have enabled one to make a reasoned and reflective System-2 analysis and evaluation in response to the question about how easy or difficult it would be.

But, on reflection, are we really more likely to become tornado victims simply because we see how a twister demolished this man's home?

to devalue what we have by coveting something we cannot get (as did the fox with the grapes), and many other solid bits of wisdom. On the other hand, there is always the risk that in the retelling, the actual events may be mistakenly remembered, misunderstood, or misinterpreted. Whether accurate or not, stories have an unwarranted amount of influence on decisions about what to expect, what to believe, and what to do.

Availability sells. The news media, knowing the power of a compelling narrative, regularly "put a human face" on news reports. They know it is boring to hear newscasters drone on about statistics and abstractions—for example, about how many homes were damaged by a tornado or how many families lost electric power due to the storm. So instead, the news crew will interview an emotionally distraught person. They will take pictures or video of the person, the damaged home and felled trees in the background, looking lost among the scatterings of furniture and the family's ruined and irreplaceable mementoes. This makes the abstraction "terrible tornado" vividly available to us. And because of the availability heuristic, we, unreflectively, jack up our estimate of the chances that we too might become a hapless storm victim—just like that sad person we're seeing in the news report.

So vivid were the images of the collapsing towers of NYC's World Trade Center, and so deep was the trauma to the nation's psyche in the days, weeks, and months immediately following September 11th, that estimates of imminent terrorist attacks skyrocketed. And not only in places that, upon reflection, one would consider high-threat targets, like transportation hubs in major metropolitan areas. So high were the estimates that all across the nation in tiny towns and villages where the actual chance of a terrorist attack was substantially lower than any of hundreds of other dangers—like storms, floods, epidemics, food contamination, drunk driving, loaded guns kept in unlocked drawers where children can get them—that were being ignored on a regular basis, Americans gave serious thought to the possibility of terrorist attacks and spent time and money to protect themselves against that extremely unlikely eventuality. I would submit that at the time we were making decisions about this possibility in a less than fully reflective and rational way. We do need to think carefully about terrorist attacks, not reactively, but with our System-2 critical thinking skills fully engaged.

The disadvantage of basing judgments on the availability heuristic is that we will wrongly estimate the actual probabilities that a given outcome will occur.[xvi] In the aftermath of the horrendous killings of over 30 people at Virginia Tech (VT) in April 2007, parents, students, faculty, and staff at the nation's more than 4,200 colleges and universities sharply revised their estimates of the probabilities of a similarly deranged killer's assault on their own campuses. Campus security increased, counseling centers received more funding, legislators held hearings at the state and national levels, and campus authorities updated emergency plans and conducted readiness drills. Although these might have been good things to do, resources are finite. Were these the most urgent things for a campus to do, given all the other risks and threats out there? Probably not. Fire preparedness, weather disaster preparedness, theft detection and prevention, rape and assault protection, food poisoning prevention, and flu epidemic preparedness are just a few projects that address tragically lethal and somewhat more probable eventualities. But all the attention was on the VT situation. It was vividly in mind for administrators, students, parents, and the media. Those other more likely dangers were not on their minds right then. Hence, the disproportionate allocation of time, money, and attention.

What are your chances of being struck by lightning this year? 1 in 1,000? 1 in 10,000? 1 in 100,000? 1 in 1,000,000? For stats on lightning strike deaths in the U.S. visit <http://www.lightningsafety.noaa.gov/medical.htm> Are your chances more or less than winning the Powerball Jackpot? Find out at <http://mathforum.org/library/drmath/view/56122.html>

6. Representation

"Uncle John did not smoke cigars at the track, he chewed them. Today he liked the filly—a sleek 3-year-old who looked fast. He would have to find her name in the racing form. But just watching her in the paddock, she reminded him of a horse he'd seen run so well at Bay Meadows a couple of years back. Same markings, same look of a winner in her dark, intense eyes. Hadn't he'd won a couple of Benjamins at 8 to 1 on that filly? To Uncle John it only made sense to put down a bet on this one to win." Uncle John made the snap judgment that because this horse looked like that other horse, this horse would perform like the other horse.

The *Representation Heuristic*: Making the snap judgment that X is like Y in every way upon noticing that X is like Y in some way. A perceived similarity becomes the basis for assuming that there is an analogical relationship between two things, an analogy that may or may not be warranted.[xvii] For example, someone might say, "My father and I were alike in so many ways—in our lifestyles and how we thought about things. Dad died a few years ago of lymphoma. He was only 69. You know, as much as I don't like the idea, I probably have about 30 years before lymphoma gets me, too." The speaker in this example is overestimating the probability of contracting a fatal lymphoma or even of dying at age 69. This thinking is disconnected from any System-2 analytical reflection on the scientific evidence regarding the genetic and environmental factors that estimate a person's cancer risks. But absent that self-corrective reflection, we risk allowing the analogical representation heuristic to influence our beliefs and choices unduly.

If the similarity between two things is fundamental and relevant, it's more likely that the analogy will be reliable. For example, suppose your co-worker was fired for missing sales targets. You might draw the reasonable conclusion that you are no different in relevant respects from your co-worker. Thus, if you miss your sales targets, you'll be fired too. Good thinking.

Or the similarity might be superficial or not connected with the outcome, which would make the analogical inference much weaker. For example, we see a TV commercial showing trim-figured young people enjoying fattening fast foods and infer that because we're young, too, we can indulge our cravings for fast foods without gaining excess, unsightly poundage. This is another example showing that heuristic thought needs to be monitored when it is used to make important decisions. As we develop our critical thinking skill of self-regulation, we become more adept at noticing when our decisions hinging on the analogical representation heuristic. And we can correct ourselves before making a decision that is not well thought out. Self-monitoring and self-correcting one's thinking can help ensure that conclusions are warranted. In Chapter 12, we will explore comparative reasoning and the criteria for the evaluation of analogical inferences in detail.

Looking like a winner doesn't make this horse a winner. Finding the key points of comparison that really make a difference requires sound critical thinking, as we'll see in Chapter 12.

Thinking Critically — Estimate Your Chances

Watch the local news on TV this evening and look for the story in which the victim of a crime, a disease, an economic misfortune, or an accident is interviewed. The more empathetic the victim, the better. The more the victim is like you in terms of age, gender, socioeconomic status, the better. On a scale of 1 to 1,000, with 1,000 being "extremely likely," estimate the chances of the same or a similar event happening to you. After making your estimate, check on the Internet to find the actual statistical likelihood that such an event will happen to you. Is it less than 1 chance in 1,000? For example, if the event is poisoning from contaminated food, the U.S. government estimates that there are about 5,000 deaths nationally each year. So, if you are living in the United States, your chances are 5,000 divided by 315,000,0000 (estimated 2012 population of the United States), which is less than 1 in 60,000. On a 1 to 1,000 scale, that is too small to register. But the sales of peanut butter, tomatoes, and spinach have not fully recovered from the nationwide food poisoning scares that were so well publicized by the media. If you estimated your chances of an event happening at a higher rate than 1 in 1,000 after watching the vivid personification of the danger on the evening news, and then learned that your actual chances were less than 1 in 1,000, this would help you appreciate how our System-1 thinking can be wrongly influenced by the availability heuristic. And it reinforces the need for the use of the System-2 critical thinking skill of self-regulation to balance our natural impulse to misestimate the actual risks.

From "pit bull" to "eagle"? System-1, loosened from sound critical thinking, takes full flight with the association heuristic.

7. Association

"We were having a good time, probably on our third beer, ESPN's *Sports Center* was on TV someplace nearby but we're not really paying attention because Bill was talking about how the girl he was seeing really liked dogs, and he did, too. So, he's saying that she has a pit bull. And I have no idea what Harry was thinking but he says, 'How do you think Michael Vick will do this season? He was amazing his first year back in the NFL, but can he do it again?' So we all look at Harry because he's on some other planet and say, 'Where did that come from?' And he's like, 'Pit bulls, dogs, dog fights, illegal, prison, Michael Vick.' And then I'm like, 'I wonder if Tiger Woods will pull off a comeback.' And now they're all looking at me. So I'm like, 'Hey, you know! Michael Vick, troubled athlete, big comeback after major issues. Can Tiger do the same? Which reminds me, are we all still on for golf this weekend?"

The *Association Heuristic*: Connecting ideas on the basis of word association and the memories, meanings, or impressions they trigger. We all have experienced conversations in which one comment seems connected to another by nothing more than word association. Someone might suggest, "Let's take our drinks outside to the picnic table." To which someone else might respond, "Remember the picnic three years ago when Grandpa had his heart attack? I'm never going to that park again." The representativeness, or associational heuristic maneuver, is triggered when a word or idea reminds us of something else. Typically, this is System-1 thinking: reactive, associational, and not critically reflective. For example, one person might associate sunshine with happiness, and another person might associate sunshine with sweaty work picking strawberries. Or, as in the example above, "picnic" with Grandpa's heart attack. The salient negative experience brought to mind by the mere use of the word *picnic* influenced the speaker to assert the decision never to return to the park where the sad event occurred. This unreflective decision emerged from the System-1 reaction triggered by the word association in this person's mind.

Associational thinking, an unmonitored nearly stream-of-consciousness twitter-blab of ideas, is of very little value, logically speaking. But if the associational thinker is also saying out loud everything that comes to mind, it can be creative, frustrating, and entertaining all at the same time. And way too personal! It is rather commonplace in today's culture, and yet we seem unconcerned that judgments made using associational thinking can be very flawed. Instead the media report the results of causal twitter fests and "instant polls" as though these represented our best and most informed thinking on a given topic.

8. Stereotyping

"Did I tell what happened when I went to D.C.? So I rented a car and Hertz gives me a Toyota Venza. Never drove one before, won't drive one again. I thought Toyotas were supposed to be good cars. Forget that. So, anyway, I get to the Hampton

Thinking Critically — Last Word to First Word

Listen attentively to a conversation. But do not focus on the topic being discussed, instead focus on the words as they are said. Pay special attention to the last word or expression in a sentence and count how many times the next speaker uses that word or expression as the first thing they say. An associational thinker—and we use the term *thinker* advisedly—often interacts conversationally by connecting what he or she says to the last word in the sentence that the previous speaker uttered. No, this doesn't make any logical sense. But listen for it nonetheless. Keep a log of which person in the conversation does it the most frequently. And keep track of whether or not the topic of the conversation is actually altered from whatever it was before to whatever topic the associational thinker introduces. Put a clock on the topic. See if any topics at all can last more than three minutes when the associational thinker is in full form.

Tweets, rolling update lists, and bottom of the screen news scrawls encourage discrete observations, like disjointed color pixels flashing independently. The full image, the big picture that includes the why as well as the what, is difficult to assemble in our minds. It is easy to zone out and watch the flashing colors but miss their meaning. Like snowflakes, each bit is captivating for a second, but is melted and gone the next.

Inn and that night while I'm sending e-mail I see some bug walking across the bedspread. A roach! What kind of dumps are those Hampton Inns? Won't stay in one of them anymore, I'll tell you. But, on the good side, I met this Marine, a young corporal, and he was an impressive young man. I could tell just talking to this young soldier that our servicemen and servicewomen are wonderful people."

The *Stereotyping Heuristic*: Making a snap judgment about an entire group based on a single instance. Although an anecdote is not data, we have all heard people draw conclusions about whole groups of people based on their experience with only one or two people who are members of that group. We call this stereotyping or profiling. There are advantages to stereotyping, because it is a highly efficient way of thinking. For example, I enjoyed the Grand Slam breakfast at Denny's the first time I ordered it, and I'll order it again and again. From that one experience, I make the snap judgment that it's the breakfast for me. On the other hand, there are risks associated with stereotyping. Profiling groups of people based on a single unfortunate experience with one member of that group can lead to bigotry, prejudice, misunderstanding, and mistrust, to name only a few.

Humans do not have the time to make systematic scientific surveys of everything we may need to know. So, we take the shortcut of basing decisions on relatively few instances. This is what we are doing when we ask a friend if she or he knows a good dentist, doctor, real estate broker, or lawyer. Or if we ask an alumna to tell us how good her college experience was when we are trying to decide where to go to school. The trade-off between effort expended and the reliability of the information derived makes this approach risky. Yes, it's a starting point to get some preliminary information, but it is not an ending point of a thorough investigation. Here again, monitoring one's habits of mind is a good idea.

The tendency to think that our personal experience of a single instance is predictive of what we would find were we to sample more systematically a whole class of individuals can undermine decision making in almost any context. We eat a burger at a fast food restaurant and make a snap judgment about everything on the menu there and at every other restaurant in the same chain. Does this work for paintings by a given artist, songs by a given songwriter, and novels by a given author? What about courses taught by a given professor, patient problems treated by a given health care provider, or building proposals by a real estate developer?

One example of negative stereotyping in contemporary America is the idea that all Muslims are terrorists. Like other negative stereotypes based on race, ethnicity, religion, or nationality, this one fuels fear and hatred. In our more reflective moments we realize that Muslim Americans were victims in the 9/11 attacks on the Twin Towers along with Jewish Americans, Christian Americans, and Americans who practiced no religion. We know that Muslim Americans serve with distinction in our armed forces, including side by side with soldiers of other faiths in combat in Afghanistan and Iraq.

Does the media play a role in promoting the heuristics of stereotyping and "us vs. them" thinking? Media professionals gathered for the 10th Arab Medial Forum to discuss how negative images of Arabs in Western media contribute to Islamophobia in the United States and Europe.

And we know that millions of American Muslims go to work every day, take care of their families, pay their taxes, and contribute in numerous ways to the quality of our communities. But even if we do not all agree about those observations, as Americans we treasure our First Amendment right of freedom of religion. Historically this Constitutional right has been the basis for the doctrine of the "Separation of Church and State," which stops government from enacting laws aimed specifically to limit the freedom of any American to worship as he or she chooses.

But our System-2 reflective considerations about freedom of religion and the rights of others can evaporate if System-1 kicks into overdrive. Negative stereotyping can trigger just that kind of kneejerk defensive hostility. And when that happens, occasionally System-2 is dragged into the skirmish, because all of us are naturally inclined to seek rationalizations in support of our unreflective reactions. Consider the tumult surrounding the "Ground Zero Mosque" a Muslim community center located just blocks from the World Trade Center site. The proposal fit within the permissible uses of the real estate according to the prevailing city zoning ordinances. But some people vigorously protested. One explanation of their reaction is that their System-1 decision making, triggered by a negative stereotype, led them immediately to be hostile toward the very idea of such a project. The furor went global. Arguments were presented pro and con. Bloggers opined. Eventually, after the zoning ordinances were closely examined and everyone's legal rights were duly considered, the project went forward.

Weak critical thinking makes us vulnerable to manipulation based on our unreflective snap judgments. Knowing this, political strategists often advise candidates to take advantage of negative racial, ethnic, religious, or national stereotypes to garner votes. Regrettably our prejudices have been played upon too frequently in the history of our democracy. Unfortunately we see examples of political pandering to our negative stereotypes even today. For example, one candidate for high office in 2011 advocated laws blocking a proposed Islamic mosque from being built in one town in Tennessee.[xviii] Perhaps unfamiliar with the document or its amendments, this candidate was running for President, the very office responsible for upholding and defending the Constitution, including the right of freedom of religion.

We know that it is difficult to root out the System-1 reactive stereotypic responses. On occasion it takes encountering a remarkable person or story to help us realize that our kneejerk stereotypes about people can get in the way of good judgment. Recently, for example, a 6-year-old little girl was rescued from a kidnapper by a brave man and his wife. Seeing the kidnapper snatch the child, they took immediate action. He chased the kidnapper while she called the police. The man who pulled the child out of the grasp of the kidnapper was honored by the mayor as a hero. The national news picked up the story. Oh, and, as it turns out, he is an illegal immigrant.[xix]

Speaking about jarring counterexamples that challenge strong critical thinkers to examine their unreflective stereotypes about people, do you know who Ayaan Hirsi Ali is? Yes, exactly, she is the former member of the Dutch Parliament, native of Somalia, ex-Muslim, feminist who advocates Islamic–Christian dialogue in America.[xx]

9. "Us vs. Them"

"I went to Congress to lobby for the reauthorization of the Higher Education Act and to support increased funding for Pell Grants and other forms of student aid. I explained that higher education is a benefit to the person who is fortunate enough to afford to go to college. Research shows consistently higher earnings for college graduates than for those who have not gone to college. But, I said, college education provides benefits to society as a whole. The teachers, nurses, businesspeople, engineers, journalists, social workers, and the like, who attained access to those professions through their college education, provide much needed services for everyone in the community. I was told by one member that he simply did not agree with that. His reason was simple: 'I've heard all that before because it's what the other side says.' I asked the member to help me understand his thinking better and he replied, 'You see, on the Hill, it's good guys vs. bad guys. They're the bad guys. Whatever they say, whatever they want, whatever argument they make, I don't buy it'."

The *"Us vs. Them" Heuristic*: Reducing decisions to the choice between two starkly opposing options and then rejecting the option your opposition favors. This could be named the "good guys vs. bad guys" heuristic as well because applying this heuristic results in an automatic competitive and oppositional relationship. And our tendency, evolving from the earliest survival instincts of our species, is to band together with "our own people" to fight "those other guys." Battle lines are drawn with phrases like "Those who are not with me are against me"; "There can be no middle ground"; "Never compromise"; and "There can be no negotiations."[xxi]

Have You Ever Been Stereotyped?

Were you ever the object of someone else's use of the stereotyping heuristic? To answer this, think of a time when you might have been treated a certain way, either positively or negatively, by someone else simply because of something about your age, gender, style of clothing, race, or accent.

2010 Election Results – US Senate

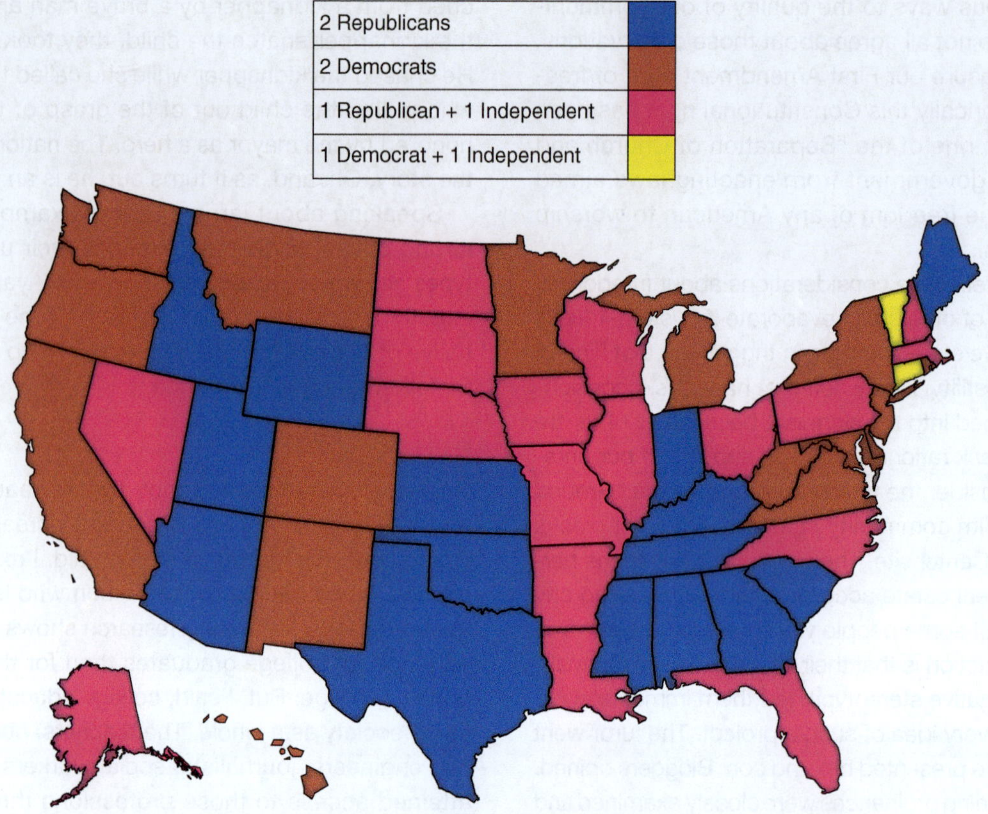

112th Congress-Post-Election Senate Control

Party	Seats Won	Seats Not Up	Total Seats
Democratic	13	38	51
Republican	24	23	47
Independent	0	2	2

As this post-election map reveals, political control turns on changing the minds of small percentages of people. A shift of 5% one way or the other can empower one party or the other. Visit http://uselectionatlas.org/RESULTS/seats.php?year=2010&off=3&elect=0&f=0 for details. Wedge issues, like gay marriage, immigration, and marijuana legalization, play on our System-1 Us vs. Them heuristic. Can our collective System-2 critical thinking overcome the divisiveness with reasoned judgment?

Once our minds apply the Us vs. Them heuristic to a situation, many other decisions about the people or issues involved become very simple. We have no obligations toward "them" or toward anything they want or anything they represent. But, if you are one of "us" we will stand by you through thick and thin.[xxii] In its most extreme manifestations, the Us vs. Them heuristic can set up the tendency to regard "them" as non-persons, objects off the ethical radar screen, "others" who can be manipulated or removed without ethical concern. As a nation, we saw this in the torture and prisoner abuses at Abu Ghraib. Called the false polarization effect,[xxiii] this tendency to divide the world into two opposing camps can be a very dangerous approach to problem solving and a potentially explosive and negative strategy for a society or a leader to take.

Let us not be naïve about this. If humans are strongly influenced by Us vs. Them thinking, then it would be foolish of us not to take that into consideration when approaching others for the first time. Generosity of spirit and openness are wonderful virtues, but venturing into potentially hostile territory with caution thrown to the wind is seldom likely to be the optimal choice. An advantage of this heuristic is that it orients our thoughts and actions in support of our family, our team, our platoon, our business, our community, "our kind." And, obviously, the disadvantage is that we lose objectivity and impartiality, and we can be prone toward bias and prejudice if we are not reflective. In instances like these, our critical thinking (System-2) must override the pull toward prejudice arising from the misapplication of the Us vs. Them heuristic.

Go to **www.mythinkinglab.com** and view the 3-minute "Pep Talk" scene from *Glory Road*. The coach begins by antagonizing his players with racial stereotyping, and their gut response (affect heuristic) is silent anger and resentment. The coach says that they cannot win the national championship, because they cannot think. He describes them losing the game, they can see it happening (simulation) in their minds, and they become even more agitated because he is the authority figure and he is saying they will lose. They do not want to lose. This is not "just a game." Then the coach changes his tone and evokes the Us vs. Them heuristic to rally the players and unify the team. The short scene ends with one of the players making the point to his teammate that he needs to play good defense (not satisfice), because the usual effort will not be good enough. **Watch** the **Video** on **mythinkinglab.com**

How does the coach use the Us vs. Them heuristic to motivate the team? Is this manipulation or leadership, or both? Can you give three personal experience examples of effective leaders achieving group goals by using their followers' System-1 reactions?

Journalists, politicians, zealots, coaches, and evangelists of all stripes use our natural tendency to mistrust "those other people"—the ones who are not part of "us," the ones who are different, the ones with whom we disagree. Unscrupulous people make an enemy of the opposition and ascribe to them evil and dangerous intentions. This rallies the troops against the external threat and makes it unnecessary to take seriously what "they" have to say. In the cut-throat competition for high office, campaigners strive to marginalize or even demonize their opposition, engender fear in "us," lest "they" should "get what they want," "come to power," or "take what is rightfully ours." The risks associated with dualistic thinking are serious, and these risks are compounded when fear and mistrust are set in opposition to loyalty and group identity.

The Us vs. Them Heuristic is a favorite tool of zealots, extremists, hate-mongers and bigots. Why does it work for them? Too often because, fearing their wrath, the rest of us fail to muster the courage to challenge their caustic and divisive rhetoric with accurate information and sound reasoning. The positive critical thinking habit of truth-seeking requires the courage to ask tough questions and to follow reasons and evidence wherever they lead. History shows us how devastating and explosive religion in the blind service of nationalism can be. That has not changed. So it is not an exaggeration to say that the lives of tens of millions of people may depend on the courage and capacity of educated and truth-seeking men and women to stand up to those whose ambitions or beliefs demand the economic, political, or military annihilation of all of "them".

10. Power Differential

"I once worked on a senior management team that was headed by a CEO who was the personification of the 'alpha male.' I recall one meeting where the other nine vice presidents and I were sitting along both sides of a conference table, with the CEO at the head of the table. He wanted us to discuss a proposal he had come up with the night before. He presented his idea by handing out five pages single-spaced and talking non-stop for half an hour. Then he said, 'OK, now I'd like to hear from you.' Nobody spoke. Nobody believed he actually wanted to hear our views. Nobody wanted to rock the boat or risk crossing him by pointing out even the smallest flaw or raising even the most tentative counterargument. The CEO waited less than two seconds. When nobody responded, he said, 'OK, then. That's it. We'll implement this. Now, next topic."

The *Power Differential Heuristic*: Accepting without question a belief as stated by, a problem as presented by, or a solution as proposed by, a superior authority. Social hierarchies abound at home, at work, in government, in religion, and even in recreation. Many are benevolent and respectful. But even in these cases, and certainly in those that are manipulative and abusive, there is a tendency to defer to the individual (or subgroup) in charge. It may be something as benign as agreeing on when to eat dinner or which TV show to watch. The decision to defer—that is, not to dispute or challenge—the decisions of others higher in the social pecking order is natural. It manifests itself in our accepting what "those above us" may decide to have us do. This heuristic leads us to see the world and how

Thinking Critically Closer to Home

Clubs, community groups, and professional organizations are not immune to the dangers of the misapplication of the Us vs. Them heuristic. On the other hand, the benefits of this heuristic include that it gives people energy and a sense of urgency to be working to defend their own, to compete for resources, and to feel justified in their beliefs and actions. Recall the last decision-making meeting of a club or organization to which you belong. In what ways did the Us vs. Them heuristic influence your group's thinking about people, about threats or opportunities, about problems or issues? Reflect on those influences. How might your group's decisions have been different had it not been for the sense of "Us" vs. "Them" that this heuristic engendered?

our leaders see it and to understand problems and issues the way our leaders describe them to us. Middle managers in a corporate culture are susceptible to similar pressures from senior executives, as are second children from their elder sibling, or junior officers relative to their superiors. But "pressure" is not exactly the correct word, for this heuristic makes compliance with authority the automatic reaction. Thus, when one is out of step with one's "higher-ups," one often feels more discomfort than when one is "going along to get along." In a gang, for example, the power differential between the gang leader and his or her followers, when combined with the Us vs. Them heuristic for viewing the world, can strongly influence gang members to internalize gang rivalries and to agree with violent responses to perceived threats.

There are some advantages to recognizing the realities of power differentials and not bucking the system. Not only can this save cognitive resources, it might save your job and your domestic happiness as well. After all, if the boss wants the client list updated, why not update it? And if your partner wants to go to a movie that might not have been your first choice, why not go anyway? Having people see things your way may not be the highest of all values, even if you are smarter than they are about some things. Societal harmony and domestic tranquility are values, too.

On the other hand, how many times have we seen clearly that the boss was heading the department in the wrong direction, that the team captain was employing an ineffective strategy, that our elder sibling was wrong, or that our leaders were motivated more by self-interest than by the common good? Any full evaluation of the reasoning presented by those in power over us—coaches, teachers, ministers, managers, governmental authorities, or otherwise—should include consideration of whether the benefits derived from the current power structure relationship warrant continuing that relationship or whether it is time to consider seriously other options. In reviewing one's options, do not forget the influence that the satisficing heuristic, discussed earlier, can have on our sense that, however flawed our current situation may be, it is "good enough."

A Student Body president champions a new resolution. How does the power differential within student organizations affect the work of the group and the sense of group unity?

11. Anchoring with Adjustment

"The first book report I wrote as a ninth grader was about a novel entitled *Space Cadets*. My report earned a C-. The teacher, a lover of eighteenth- and nineteenth-century British literature, found scant merit in the silly novel I had chosen and even less merit in my futile attempt to state its theme and explore how its author had developed plot and characters. A friend of mind received an A on his report on George Elliot's 1863 novel, *Silas Marner*. About halfway through the academic year I was consistently making C-, C, or C+ on my

Thinking Critically Fostering a Group Culture of Critical Thinking

The capacity to cultivate a group culture that fosters reflective, respectful, and fair-minded decision making and problem solving can be a great asset to a leader. The leader, if trusted not to revile, belittle, or ridicule subordinates for their ideas and suggestions, can benefit immensely. Decisions can be openly discussed and refined before being implemented. Problems can be analyzed and options considered, with each person feeling encouraged to bring his or her best thinking forward. Based on your own experience, what are some specific things leaders can do to foster a climate that is highly receptive to critical thinking and self-regulation? What are some things that undermine that good climate? Give examples.

work, and my friend was doing A- or A work. So, we switched. I started writing reports using his name and he wrote reports using my name. My grades (that is, the grades he earned for me) edged up into the C+ and B- range. His grades (that is, the grades my reports earned for him) held steady except for one B+ late in April. Our analysis: In the mind of our teacher from the first paper we submitted in September and throughout that whole year, I was a C student and my friend was an A student."

The *Anchoring with Adjustment Heuristic*: Having made an evaluation, adjust only as much as is absolutely necessary and then only if new evidence is presented.[xxiv] When we are making evaluative judgments, it is natural to locate or anchor our evaluation at some point along whatever scale we are using. If we are being more reflective, we may have established some criteria and we may be working to apply them as fair-mindedly as possible. As other information comes our way, we may adjust our evaluation. The interesting thing about this cognitive maneuver is that we do not normally start over with a fresh evaluation. We have dropped anchor and we may drag it upward or downward a bit, but we do not pull it off the bottom of the sea to relocate our evaluation. First impressions, as the saying goes, cannot easily be undone.

One advantage of this heuristic is that it permits us to move on. We have done the evaluation; there are other things in life that need attention. We could not long endure if we were to constantly reevaluate everything anew. Part of developing expertise is learning to calibrate and nuance one's judgments, refine one's criteria, and adjust the criteria to fit the complexities of the circumstances of judgment. Anchoring with adjustment can reflect a progression toward greater precision, a way to refine not only judgments about particular things, but the criteria applied when making those judgments.

The unfortunate thing about this heuristic, however, is that we sometimes drop anchor in the wrong place; we have a hard time giving people a second chance at making a good first impression. How often have we seen it happen that a co-worker's performance is initially evaluated as sub-par (outstanding) and almost nothing that happens subsequently can move that initial evaluation marker very far from where it started? Subsequent outstanding work (poor work) is regarded as a fluke or an anomaly, not as genuine counterevidence that should result in a thorough reevaluation.

12. Illusion of Control

"They hired me because I was known as a corporate gunslinger. I know how to take a failing organization and turn it around in short order. I kick ass and take names. I hire people who want to bust their butts to get the job done, and I fire the deadwood and anyone who gets in the way of what we're trying to do. Within 90 days I had reorganized the finance division and the technology division. Sales needed major work. That took another three weeks, but I put in the right people and revised our marketing approach. Then it was time to increase productivity and decrease costs in our manufacturing operation. In six months I had stopped the bleeding. In nine, we had bottomed out and were starting to see the signs of a turnaround. We posted our first net profits at the end of my fourth quarter with the corporation. I stayed another two years and then the job got so boring that I had to move on. So, now I'm on the market looking for another company that needs my skill set to save its cookies." The gunslinger's constant references "I did this" and "I did that" gives no credit to the team effort it really takes to turn an organization around. Perhaps the gunslinger deserves praise and credit for his or her leadership contributions. But from my own personal experience, I assure you that turning around a large organization that is in real trouble is a group project, not a one-person show. The gunslinger in this example is looking back on the project with an exaggerated and illusory sense of his or her own personal control over how events turned out.

Our opinions of celebrities often anchor on our first impressions and then adjust, but oh so slowly. Robert Downey, Jr., drug addict and criminal? Or Robert Downey, Jr., Oscar-nominated movie star? Sherlock Holmes! Which was your anchor? How can some reflective thought help us hoist anchor and reposition our thinking?

The *Illusion of Control Heuristic*: Estimating the control you have over events by the amount of energy and desire you put into trying to shape those events. When used correctly, this heuristic helps calibrate estimates of our effectiveness and thus helps us gauge how hard we should try. When misapplied, the illusion of control heuristic leads us into snap judgments that are nothing more than wishful thinking. We frequently overestimate our actual ability to control the outcomes of events because we consistently fail to account for contingencies.[xxv] We overestimate our control of a situation because we underestimate the influences of other people and events. As a result, we imagine wrongly that there is a very strong relationship between whatever we might do and how things are going to ultimately turn out. Wanting a given outcome strongly, we tend to think that decisions we make or actions we take are genuinely instrumental in bringing about or failing to bring about that outcome regardless of the actual contingencies, forces, and factors at work.

Thinking Critically First Impressions

One's reputation, positive or negative, can be one of the most difficult anchors to raise. If you have had the misfortune of making a poor first impression at some point in your life, you may know firsthand just how difficult it can be to overcome that unfortunate beginning. But this exercise is about the impressions you have of others. Reflect on the people whom you have met over the past year or two. Think of some whom you initially thought highly of and others whom you did not like at first. Has your general impression of any of these people changed? If yes, describe what the person did or said that was so memorable that you hauled up your anchor from positive waters and dropped it in negative waters, or vice versa. Now reflect on the others, and ask yourself what it would take for you to radically revise your initial opinion of any of them.

13. Optimistic Bias and 14. Hindsight Bias

Please answer these two questions: Are you any more or less likely than others just like you to contract cancer at your age? Are you more or less likely than others just like you to suffer a debilitating injury in a traffic accident?

The *Optimistic Bias Heuristic*: Tendency to underestimate our own risks and overestimate our own control in dangerous situations.[xxvi] On the two questions above, approximately 75 percent of us will estimate our risks to be lower and about 25 percent will say higher. But, the true answer is that our risks are neither higher nor lower than persons just like us. This natural tendency toward optimistic bias has the evolutionary advantage for our species of providing us with the courage to move ahead in life. The constant dread of serious hazards could be mentally detrimental and debilitating. However, since our risk of hazard is actually no better and no worse than others', all things being equal, this built-in bias results in poorer and perhaps riskier judgments in some situations. Our sense that we will succeed where others have failed, or that we are not as likely as others to suffer misfortune or the ill effects of bad decisions can lead us to take unnecessary risks.

Please answer these questions: Have you ever felt that you did not receive your fair share of the credit for your contribution to a highly successful project? Were you ever unfairly blamed when things went wrong, even thought the unfortunate outcomes were beyond your control?

The *Hindsight Bias Heuristic*: Tendency to remember successful events as being the result of the decisions we made and actions that we took and past failures as having resulted from bad luck or someone else's mistakes.[xxvii] Our human need for accuracy, predictability, and self-justification is believed to motivate this hindsight-biasing behavior.[xxviii] Hindsight bias adds fuel to the fire of our false confidence, for it inclines us to believe that our decisions and actions had a strong positive impact on the outcome of events, or, if things did not turn out as hoped, the fault was not ours. The tendency to take undeserved credit for good outcomes or to shift responsibility to others for undesirable outcomes is something we humans seem to have in common.

We do not mean to suggest that we are mistaken every time we feel unfairly blamed nor that we are mistaken every time we feel in control of a situation. By noting these potentials for wrong judgments, however, we are able to anticipate the possibility of a mistake and correct our thinking before we dig in too deeply to the feelings of pride or resentment that come with being mistakenly praised or blamed. We can use our self-regulation critical thinking skills to monitor ourselves for optimistic bias and hindsight bias so that our estimations about how much we really can control or how much blame or credit we deserve are made more reflectively, and hopefully, more accurately.

Thinking Critically ATVs

Yamaha makes one of today's most popular ATVs, the Yamaha Rhino. Before going further in this exercise, answer this: Suppose you were given, free of charge, the offer to use as you wish a Yamaha Rhino all day and you had complete access to a beautiful recreational area with hills, streams, ravines, woodlands, and open meadows. Assume that you would not be charged any money, even if you brought the vehicle back damaged. On a scale of 1 to 100, with 100 being "Absolutely, yes!" how likely would you be to accept this offer? After marking down your answer, watch the video clip of the CBS news story about the Yamaha Rhino at www.mythinkinglab.com. Listen to the riders who are interviewed. Do any of them exhibit indications that they may be suffering the influences of the illusion of control heuristic? Explain why. Now, having seen the video, on the same scale of 1 to 100, how likely would you be to accept the offer of the free use of the Rhino? If you changed your answer from the first time, that is OK. Question: If you changed your answer, why did you change? Reflect on your second decision. Did any of these heuristics play a role: availability, simulation, representation, anchoring with adjustment? Did your sense of risk and possible loss increase or decrease having seen the news story?

Watch the **Video** on **mythinkinglab.com**

How does our natural optimistic bias affect our decision making in contexts of risk and uncertainty? In *Business Week*, Dan Ariely says it is great for society but a disaster for individuals![xxix]

15. Elimination by Aspect: "One Strike and You're Out"

"I went on four job interviews, which was great because many of my friends were having trouble getting any interviews. The interviewers all wanted me to make a PowerPoint presentation. And, of course, there was a lot of meeting individuals and groups of people. And the mandatory lunch when you have to remember to order lemonade instead of anything alcoholic. All those parts went fine. But at one place there was this guy who kept interrupting my PowerPoint to ask questions. I don't want to work there, not with jerks like him in my work group. This other place was OK, great new computers in fact, but the cubicles were gray and so was the carpet. I just didn't like how blah it looked—too institutional, you know. So, really, it's down to the other two places, and I'm hoping to get an offer from one or both of them real soon."

The *Elimination by Aspect Heuristic*: Eliminating an option from consideration upon the discovery of one undesirable feature. There are simply too many choices! The Excalibur Hotel in Las Vegas boasts a 500-dish smorgasbord. DIRECTV offers hundreds of channels, as does SiriusXM radio. Want to buy a car, a downtown condo, a fancy watch, or enroll in an MBA program? There are thousands from which to pick. How do we move efficiently through this maze of opportunities? Certainly not by giving our full attention and due consideration to every aspect of every option. Rather, we hack through the choices individually or in whole bunches at a time, pushing the clutter out of our cognitive path as quickly and efficiently as possible. Elimination by aspect is our heuristic strategy. As soon as we identify a "reason why not," we dump that option and options like it. The reason does not have to be monumental. I don't like brown cars or used cars. That's it. For me, the car-buying choices have just been reduced by tens of thousands. Don't like cream sauces? Great, that cuts the smorgasbord problem down by a huge percentage. Don't like to wait behind other folks grazing through the food line? Fine, step around them to an open spot along the smorgasbord and never worry about looking back at the dozens of culinary delights you may have skipped.

In situations where we enjoy a plethora of acceptable choices, the cognitive utility of elimination by aspect cannot be overestimated. However, the price we pay for conserving all that energy and time is clear, too. Applying this heuristic may result in a final selection that does not reflect the best holistic choice we might have made. The used car I refused to consider may have been just as good in every way as a new car of the same make and model, but thousands of dollars less expensive. I will never give that car its due consideration, having eliminated it entirely from view when I rejected it along with all others that were labeled "used." In situations where our choices are limited and where no option is perfect, this heuristic can be a major liability. Because nobody is perfect, balancing the good with the bad is a sign of wisdom. The one strike and you're out approach denies this reality. Political litmus tests, for example, could paralyze a pluralistic democracy. We would all soon become hermits if we tried to select our employees, friends, and leaders on the principle that any one flaw is a fatal flaw.

Thinking Critically — Two Decimal Places

Reflect on how often you approach key decisions with your own personal litmus test, sorting choices by looking for a single flaw or reason to eliminate as many as possible as quickly as possible. For example, reducing the list of job applicants this way, "Let's eliminate every applicant whose GPA is less than 2.70." In this example, the first important System-2 question is why should we look at GPA at all, and the next reflective question is why does 2.70 make the cut, but 2.69 misses? What is the evidence that GPA is such a precise measure as that? Going back to your own personal litmus test decisions, apply your critical thinking skills, and ask yourself whether there is good evidence to support using that single criterion as a make-or-break decision point?

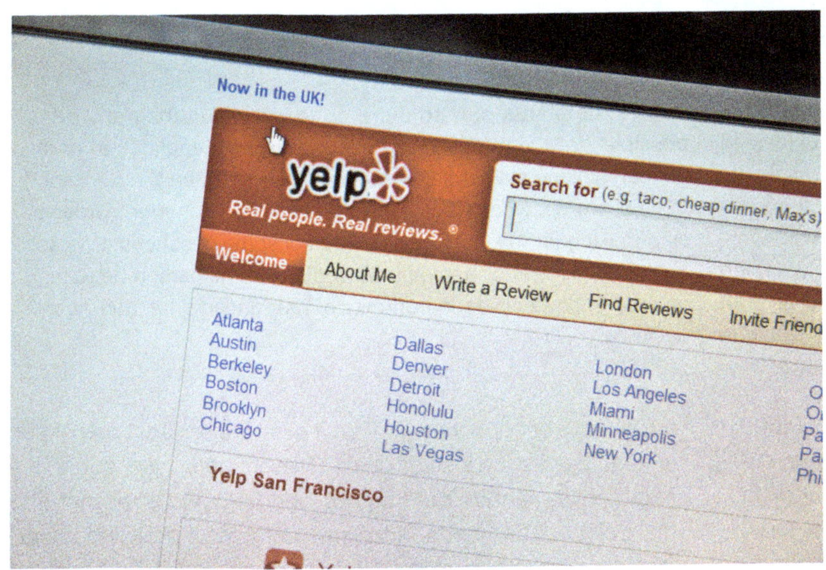

When you are choosing a restaurant for dinner, what characteristics do you consider vitally important? Does it take credit cards? Do I have to dress up? What is the noise level? What is the price level? Do they serve alcohol? Can I bring my dog? Web sites such as Yelp give diners all this info and more—they even have customer reviews! Ratings sites play to our tendencies to avoid risk and to use a "one strike and you're out" decision procedure. There are so many options that suffice, why not drop an option that has a negative rating? But, wait, what leads us to believe that the person who posted the rating is unbiased, informed and fairminded?

16. Loss and Risk Aversion

"Early in my career I was offered an entry-level management position with a new company in a new industry. The company was called Cingular Wireless. I didn't seek the job. And I was a bit surprised when the offer was extended one evening during a dinner party. It would have meant a lot more money than I was earning as a part-time instructor. A job like that would have been the ticket to a lucrative corporate career. But I had a job in the field of higher education, and, with a couple years of experience, I was becoming comfortable in the role of college teacher. I didn't want to lose the identity I had just begun to create for myself. I wasn't sure what it would be like to work in the corporate sector, having all my life been either a student or a teacher, and recently a new mother. My daughter was less than a year old at that time. What if the job with Cingular didn't work out? Somehow the idea of remaking myself into a corporate junior executive seemed too risky and there was too much to lose. So, I thanked the person but declined her offer."

The *Loss and Risk Aversion Heuristic*: Avoiding risk and avoiding loss by maintaining the status quo. Not losing anything, not going backward, at least staying where we are, for most humans, is the preferred default outcome, particularly under conditions of uncertainty. Research demonstrates that most humans are more likely to pass up an opportunity to make a gain rather than risk a loss.[xxx] Humans psychologically privilege the status quo. Whenever possible, humans take an incremental approach, seeking to avoid uncertainty and the difficult cognitive tasks of weighing and combining information or trading-off conflicting values, rather than opting for more dramatic change. Muddling through personal decisions, attempting to avoid any loss, is the norm rather than the exception. We've all heard the old adage "A bird in the hand is worth two in the bush."

Making decisions on the basis of what we do not want to risk losing can have advantages in many circumstances. People do not want to lose control, they do not want to lose their freedom, and they do not want to lose their lives, their families, their jobs, or their possessions. And so, in real life, we take precautions. Why take unnecessary risks? The odds may not be stacked against us, but the consequences of losing at times are so great that we would prefer to forgo the possibilities of gain not to lose what we have. Can you think of an example of this in your life?

We are more apt to endure the status quo, even as it slowly deteriorates, than we are to engage in change that we perceive as "radical" or "dangerous." Loss and risk aversion have the disadvantages of leading to paralysis or delay precisely when action should be taken. Having missed that opportunity to avert a crisis, we discover later that it requires a far greater upheaval to make the necessary transformations once the crisis is upon us. Worse, on occasion, the situation has deteriorated beyond the point of no return. In those situations we find ourselves wondering why we waited so long before doing something about the problem back when it might have been possible to salvage the situation. History has shown time and time again that businesses that avoid risks often are unable to compete successfully against those willing to move more boldly into new markets or into new product lines.

Uncertainty, risk, and fear of loss are the tools of those who oppose change, just as optimistic bias and simulation are the tools of the proponents of change. Consider the debate over health care reform in the United States. The August 2009 onslaught of organized opposition to health care reform legislation tried to prevent Congress and the Obama administration from "foisting expensive, risky, and ineffective programs" on the American people. More than "If it ain't broke, don't fix it," the campaign was "Leave well enough alone!"

17. "All or Nothing"

"I heard that there were going to be budget cuts and layoffs. We all knew that the economy was in the tank. But this is a big university with an annual operating budget over $230,000,000 and more than 1,800 faculty and staff members. So, I figured that the chances that they would cut the course that I was going to

Thinking Critically Why Do We Privilege the Status Quo?

Reflect on a recent experience in your life that involved making a decision that included some element of risk and potential loss. In a purely objective analysis the *status quo* is only one possibility among many and should not be given any more value than any other state of affairs. But, as you saw in the "Loss and Risk Aversion" section, for human beings, built as we are with an aversion to loss and risk seemingly in our DNA, that is easier said than done. How did you handle the decision you faced? Were you able to give the status quo no more or no less value than any other possible state of affairs? How might a stronger application of the critical thinking skill of self-regulation have affected the decision? In other words, what steps can you take to monitor your own decision making for loss aversion? Write out some questions a person might ask himself or herself that would help the person be able to make a good decision in contexts of risk, uncertainty, and potential loss.

take next semester out of the budget had to be about 100,000 to 1. I mean, they probably offer thousands of courses here every year. And there are so many other places to save money at a university without cutting academics. So, I planned my work hours and day care around taking that course. And then I go to register and it's not in the schedule. I learned they dropped it for budget reasons. Can you imagine! How am I supposed to complete my program if they cut required courses like that one?"

The *"All or Nothing" Heuristic*: Simplifying decisions by treating remote probabilities as if they were not even possibilities. By and large, when making decisions, we do not calculate Bayesian probabilities. Computers might, but humans do not. But over the millennia as a species, we humans have done reasonably well for ourselves (so far) by operating as if the exact probabilities did not really matter. Instead of thinking that there is precisely a 92 percent chance of this occurring or a 12 percent chance of that occurring, we tend to simplify our estimations and move them toward the extremes. In fact, we behave as if the odds were either 0 (no possibility at all), or 1 (it definitely will happen). Whether the chances are 1 in 100, or 1 in 10,000, do we really think about the mathematical differences in those situations? No. Instead we tend to treat both of them as if the odds were the same, and, in fact, as if they were both zero. The all or nothing heuristic treats these remote possibilities as if they were, for all practical purposes, "impossible." That is, as if the actual odds were 0 in 100 or 0 in 10,000.

When we stop and really think about things, there are all kinds of risky situations. A person walking across the street could be hit by a car. But, really, what are the chances? They are in fact *not* equal to zero. But if even the smallest risk of such a great loss as the loss of one's life were perceived, some of us might never venture out into the world. So, we push that decimal point out further and further in our minds, nullifying the risk, treating it as if it were not present at all. I've ice-skated hundreds of times, so what are the chances that tonight I'll fall and crack my skull? There are thousands of commercial flights each day, so what are the chances of a near miss involving my flight? Sadly, if one of those remote and unfortunate possibilities were to occur, we often think, "I never thought that would happen to me." A main advantage to the all or nothing heuristic is that it balances the paralyzing influences of loss and risk aversion.

HEURISTICS IN ACTION

In real-world conversations in which we focus on our own issues, cognitive heuristics expedite our thinking by generating ideas, but not necessarily reflectively. Here is an example of a person explaining why he decided to invest in high-tech stocks in late 2007. What could go wrong?

- "I know some businesses fail, particularly those based on technological innovation. But only 3 percent of new ventures failed last year, so I decided that the risk of failure was actually pretty small [All or Nothing], and I decided to go for broke and invest, and . . . you know. . . I'm pretty good at what I do, and I am really watching things closely now so that nothing happens that will threaten my investment. [Illusion of Control] I just don't think I can miss on this one." [Optimistic Bias]

True, it was smart to consider the percentage of businesses that failed, and to do all that one can to run a business well. And the business may not fail, but even the speaker himself would not be likely to invest with confidence were it not for the misuse of heuristic thinking, providing hope, a bit of confidence, and a sense of being in control of the investment. The economic recession of 2008 and 2009 demonstrated that the previous reasoning was a house built on sand.

Often, cognitive heuristics work in tandem with one another. For example, parents often worry about their children getting sick from germs that may be lurking in the environment, like on playground equipment, neighbors' houses, or in public bathrooms. The gut feeling "Germs = Bad!" is an example of the affect heuristic. Fueled on by the illusion of control heuristic, many parents set high standards for cleanliness, especially for their daughters. But research suggests that keeping little girls squeaky clean may in fact be the opposite of what they need.[xxxi]

Or take as another example the question of whether or not raising the minimum wage will kill jobs. This political "hot button" issue often triggers System-1 snap judgments from both sides of the political aisle. One side says, "Yes! More money for workers = good thing!" In this response we see a strong positive initial affective heuristic response. The other side counters with "No! Costs more, kills jobs, raises prices = bad." In this side's response we see loss and risk aversion, the loss of jobs and the risk of higher prices. What often happens is a compromise, the initial proposed increase is paired down, an example of anchoring with

adjustment. And occasionally the agreed-upon increase, if there is one, is delayed—an example of temporizing.[xxxii]

In the following example of a casual family conversation over morning coffee, several heuristics are in play, including association, affect, and stereotyping:

- Husband to wife: "I'm looking forward to retiring. I've worked for 35 years in offices without windows, and, when I'm retired I want to be outside. I can see myself on the fifth tee right now!"
- Wife replies: "Same as my Dad; he used to say how much he hated the winter especially—going to work when it was dark outside, working in a windowless office all day, and then coming home when it was dark."
- Mother-in-law: "That senior's apartment you showed me was terrible. Only one window! I need more light. I'm never moving to an apartment! You're going to have to drag me out of my house."

In the first paragraph, availability and simulation influence the husband immediately to link the idea of being outside to his vivid and happily remembered hobby [availability]. He sees himself golfing [simulation], projecting how much easier it will be to play golf when retired. As is common with the availability heuristic, he may be overestimating his opportunities to be on the fifth tee. Meanwhile, his wife is still thinking about the original topic, namely retirement. However, she connects her husband's expressed distaste for his windowless office with her father's similar expressions of distaste for the same work environment [representation]. At that point the mother-in-law introduces a new topic, her mind having jumped from "windowless" to an association with darkness [association] and from there to her vividly recalled [availability], negative [affect] experience of recently seeing one dark apartment. Clearly, she is overestimating the likelihood that all apartments will be dark. And, given that she has introduced this new topic, rather than join the conversation, this comment has the ring of a bolstering argument for a long-term debate about whether she will agree to move to an apartment. The option of moving to an apartment is off the table as far as she is concerned. And more, not wanting to lose control [loss aversion] over her own life, she expresses her decision to her children—regardless of their obvious age in this context—as a decision she will not permit them to override.

Heuristics and Possible Errors from Their Misapplication		
Heuristic	**Cognitive Shortcut**	**Possible Error from Misapplication**
Satisficing	Having found an option that is good enough, take it. We humans typically do only what must be done to achieve our purposes.	Underestimation of how much is required to satisfy objective
Temporizing	Decide that a given option is good enough for now.	Underestimation of the growing problems associated with failing to make a long-term adjustment in a timely way
Affect	Decide based on your initial affective ("gut") response.	First impressions and gut feelings may mislead.
Simulation	Estimate the likelihood of a given outcome based on how easy it is to imagine that outcome.	Overestimation of one's chance of success or likelihood of failure
Availability	Estimate the likelihood of a future event on the vividness or ease of recalling a similar past event.	Mistaken estimations of the chances of events turning out in the future as they are remembered to have turned out in the past
Representation	Make the snap judgment that X is like Y in every way upon noticing that X is like Y in some way.	The analogy may not hold.
Association	Connect ideas on the basis of word association and the memories, meanings, or impressions they trigger.	Jumping from one idea to the next absent any genuine logical progression and drawing confused and inaccurate inferences
Stereotyping	From a single salient instance, make a snap judgment about an entire group.	Profiling and misjudging individuals based on one's beliefs about the group
"Us vs. Them"	Reduce decisions to the choice between two starkly opposing options and then reject the option your opposition favors.	Unnecessary conflict, disrespect for others, polarization, undermining of the possibility of reasonable compromise
Power Differential	Accept without question a belief as stated by, a problem as presented by, or a solution as proposed by a superior authority.	Working on the wrong question or problem, applying a mistaken or inadequate solution
Anchoring with Adjustment	Having made an evaluation, adjust only as much as is absolutely necessary and then only if new evidence is presented	Failure to reconsider thoroughly, failure to evaluate fair-mindedly
Illusion of Control	Estimate the control you have over events by amount of energy and desire you put into trying to shape those events.	Overestimation of one's actual power to control or manage events—confusion of desire and effort with effectiveness
Optimistic Bias	The tendency to underestimate our own risks and overestimate our own control in dangerous situations	Taking unnecessary risks, putting one's self in unnecessary danger
Hindsight Bias	The tendency to remember successful events as being the result of the decisions one made and actions one took, and to remember past failures as having resulted from bad luck or someone else's mistakes	Misjudging the actual extent to which one's actions contributed either positively or negatively to past events and outcomes
Elimination by Aspect	Eliminate an option from consideration upon the discovery of one undesirable feature.	Failure to give due and full consideration to all the viable options
Loss and Risk Aversion	Avoid risk and avoid loss by maintaining the status quo.	Paralysis of decision making, stuck in the deteriorating status quo
"All or Nothing"	Simplify decisions by treating remote probabilities as if they were not even possibilities.	Failure to appreciate the possibilities that events could actually turn out differently than expected—the remote possibility may actually occur

Study and Review on mythinkinglab.com

Human decision making uses two cognitive systems: System-1 is reactive and automatic; System-2 is deliberative and reflective. System-1 enables us to get through the routine parts of our lives so automatically that we can focus mental energy on difficult problems using the deliberative and reflective powers of System-2. Argument making is an effort to be logical and to rely on relevant reasons and facts as we make deliberative decisions and as we explain our decisions to others. Heuristic thinking is the often quite useful tendency to rely on highly effective cognitive shortcuts when making judgments. This chapter examined seventeen common cognitive heuristics, noting the advantages and disadvantages of each. At times, we misapply one or more of those heuristic shortcuts and, so, run the risk that our snap judgments will be mistaken. We can avoid the misapplication of heuristics by applying our self-regulation critical thinking skill to monitor and to correct our judgment-making process.

KEY TERMS

System-1 thinking is reactive thinking that relies heavily on situational cues, salient memories, and heuristic thinking to arrive quickly and confidently at judgments. (p. 182)

System-2 thinking is reflective critical thinking that is useful for judgments in unfamiliar situations, for processing abstract concepts, and for deliberating when there is time for planning and more comprehensive consideration. (p. 182)

cognitive heuristics are human decision-making shortcuts people rely on to expedite their judgments about what to believe or what to do. (p. 185)

FIND IT ON MYTHINKINGLAB.COM

Watch the Video on mythinkinglab.com

- The "Pep Talk" scene in the film *Glory Road* (p. 195) is a classic "us vs. them" psychological ploy. I invited you to watch this scene at www.mythinkinglab.com.

  The coach's challenge the evening before the championship game was not only to motivate the team to give its best effort. He also wanted his players to know that they deserved to win and that their victory would mean something to a nation wrestling with a legacy of racial discrimination. The coach used critical thinking to identify a strategy whereby he might accomplish his motivational goal.

- There are other scenes in *Glory Road* where the coach needs to solve problems and make important decisions—for example, in his conversations with his wife, with the players individually, and with their parents. The coach's wife also displays strong critical thinking in how she deals with the pressures on her husband and family that come with the coach's recruiting and playing black athletes at a time and place in our history when racial prejudices and discrimination were strong. Watch the film in its entirety and pay special attention to how the coach and his wife think their way through socially awkward and personally stressful situations. Notice too the way that the screen writers rely on our heuristic expectations so that we viewers can sense the nature of the problems and feel the urges of our own heuristic responses.

Several things contributed to the basketball success chronicled in *Glory Road*. But one thing is for sure, had the coach or his wife, as depicted in the film, simply responded to events based on their unreflective heuristic guided responses, the championship would not have been won and their story never told.

Exercises

TWO- OR THREE-PERSON SMALL GROUP EXERCISE

Reflect on the choices you made today—for example, your choices of what you ate at one of your meals. Replay in your minds how you made that decision. Assuming that you are like the rest of us, you probably did not really give equal and due consideration to all of your potential options. That's OK. Heuristic snap judgments can be good things; for one, they are highly efficient and they conserve time and energy. Think now about the foods that you could have eaten, but decided not to choose. Share with the others in your conversation group the basis upon which you eliminated the ones you did not select. Was it by weighing all the pros and cons of each choice? Or was it via a snap judgment to reject a given option? For example, did association (memory of prior bad experience), affect ("looked gross"), or elimination by aspect ("too large a portion") play a role in your System-1 decision making? Talk about the choices you did make. Which cognitive heuristics played a role in those? For example, representativeness ("reminded me of something my Mom makes that tastes really good, so I thought this would taste good, too."), or satisficing ("I was in a hurry and I just grabbed the first thing that looked halfway edible").

REFLECTIVE LOG: TWO HOURS

Today or tomorrow keep a written record of all your actions, judgments, and decisions occurring within a 2-hour window that begins one hour before your main meal of the day. Make eight very brief log entries, one every 15 minutes. For each entry, list all the actions, judgments, and decisions you made in the prior 15 minutes. Keep track of what you are doing using your System-1 and System-2 thinking. Continue right up through preparing your meal, eating it, and whatever you do afterward until the 2-hour period is completed. For example, did you send a text, use the lavatory, think about a relationship, plan what to do on the weekend, open a can of soda, talk with a friend, imagine what it might be like to have more money, listen to music, fret over a problem, or go for a run? Whatever you did and whatever decisions or judgments you made, write them down.

Later, after a couple more hours have passed, go back and review your list of all your actions, judgments, and decisions you made. Count the number that you would classify as System-1 and the number you would classify as System-2. Are there any that you classified as System-1 that, in retrospect, you wish that you had reflected about more before acting or deciding as you did? In view of this little personal experiment, are their ways to build more critical thinking self-monitoring and self-correcting into your daily life?

CHALLENGE EXERCISE: EXPLAIN IT TO GRANDMA

Critical thinking is nothing new. Human beings have been relying on our reflective System-2 thinking from—well—from our beginning. Today we call this purposeful reflective judgment about what to believe and what to do "critical thinking." And we talk about its core skills and the positive habits of mind that incline us to use those skills. We caution ourselves against relying too heavily on snap judgments and we discipline ourselves to be reflective and thoughtful. The question is, do our grandparents use critical thinking or not?

If you are fortunate enough to be able to talk with one of your grandparents, please ask him or her if he or she uses critical thinking to solve problems and make decisions. Since the chances are overwhelming that he or she will not understand your question if you use the expression *critical thinking*, you will have to find some other way to ask the question. If you are not able to talk with any of your grandparents about critical thinking, then your challenge is to find someone else with whom you can have the conversation. The catch is that the person has to be at least 40 years older than you.

The challenges of this exercise, in addition to simply having the conversation, are to explain what you are learning about critical thinking and to see how much of what you describe is something that the older person may have also learned. Is there something the older person knows about strong critical thinking that you may not yet have learned?

WOULD YOU OR WOULD YOU NOT?

Make a snap judgment: Yes or No. Suppose you are thinking about having a child and you can be tested for hundreds of genetic diseases that you might pass on to that child. Assume the genetics test is free. Would you be tested? Now, reflect on the judgment you just made. Which heuristics in your case may have influenced you? Was there an element of fear and risk, afraid of knowing perhaps, even a quick association popping to mind about a genetic disease? Did a stereotype come to mind toward which you perhaps felt some aversion? OK, now put that initial snap judgment aside, and consider reflectively what a responsible person who is thinking about becoming a parent would do if given the opportunity. Before you decide this time, first learn more about the potential for genetic tests, and about the options for informed decision making once one has a fuller knowledge of one's own genetic heritage. Check out Christiane Benson's story, reported by NPR on January 13, 2011.[xxxiiii]

ALL-AMERICAN FAMILIES

TLC TV airs family reality shows which portray some of the diversity of family life in America. One show "19 Kids and Counting" features a conservative Christian family with a great many children. Another, "Sister Wives," shows domestic life in polygamist families, and a third, "All American Muslim" features the stories Muslim family life in Dearborn Michigan. One of the unspoken messages of these shows is the simple truth that whether Christian, Mormon or Muslim, most of the concerns that occupy your attention are those which all families understand, namely juggling career, child care, family chores and all the other common and familiar joys and sorrows of being a family in America in the twenty-first century.

So, why again did the Florida Family Association protest the "All American Muslim" series so vigorously, organizing a campaign that leading a national retailer, Lowe's, to withdraw its ads from that show? Why did Lowe's decide to withdraw its ads, given that it had received letters of support for the show from many other groups and individuals? And, given that a corporation is free to spend its marketing budget in any legal way it sees fit, why was there a boycott Lowe's backlash to the corporation's decision?

Research this complex issue beginning with the resources listed below. Then identify the all the heuristics which appear to have been at work in the decisions made by the Florida Family Association to voice its protest, by Lowe's to withdraw its advertising, and by those who decided to punish Lowe's by boycotting its stores. In retrospect, was there a more reasoned and reflective option that one or another of these decision makers might have pursued that would have been more effective for that organization, given its perception of the problem at hand? Link to these URL's at www.mythinkinglab.com.

TLC TV describes its eight-part "All American Muslim" series this way: "*All-American Muslim* takes a look at life in Dearborn, Michigan—home to the largest mosque in the United States—through the lens of five Muslim American families. Each episode offers an intimate look at the customs and celebrations, misconceptions and conflicts these families face outside and within their own community." Learn more about the five American families featured on "All American Muslim" on this TLC's web page: **http://tlc.howstuffworks.com/tv/all-american-muslim/all-american-muslim-families.htm**

Read about the objections voiced by the conservative Florida Family Association on this Time News Feed web page: **<http://newsfeed.time.com/2011/12/13/florida-group-fighting-all-american-muslim-has-history-of-protests/>**

Read Lowe's explanation for withdrawing its advertising at this New York Daily News web page: **<http://www.nydailynews.com/entertainment/lowe-explanation-bailing-all-american-muslim-high-comedy-premise-weren-t-sad-article-1.990400?localLinksEnabled=false>**

Read about the backlash against Lowe's for withdrawing its advertising on this Los Angeles Times web page: **<http://www.latimes.com/business/la-fi-lowes-muslim-20111213,0,5909694.story>**

Read the **Document** on **mythinkinglab.com**

Read the Chapter on mythinkinglab.com
Listen to the Chapter Audio on mythinkinglab.com

CHAPTER 11

Think Reflectively: Strategies for Decision Making

WHY do we feel so confident in our choices that we seldom change our minds?

WHAT specific critical thinking strategies can we use to improve our decision making?

Micky Wade,

"Irish" to his friends, is worried about what's going to happen to his older brother. Micky pleads with his professional trainer to keep his brother nearby, saying that his brother taught him everything he knows about fighting. Micky's trainer thinks that is a bad idea. All his life, Micky Wade, played by Mark Wahlberg in the 2010 biopic film *The Fighter,* has looked up to his half-brother Dicky Ekland, played by Christian Bale. Dicky, no longer fighting, has turned his focus to training and promoting his younger brother, and he's a crack addict. Everyone who knows Dicky, including Micky's girlfriend played by Amy Adams, views Dicky as unreliable and untrustworthy. But not Micky. No matter what, Micky refuses to give up on his brother. His loyalty to, belief in, and love for his older brother are unwaivering. As the story unfolds Micky slowly realizes that his brother Dicky and his controlling mother, who together serve as his promoters, have made a self-serving move that puts his boxing career in jeopardy. This is the final straw. Long after everyone else knew the truth, Micky finally accepts that he needs to break away from his brother and mother and seek professional trainers and promoters if he is to have any future in boxing. And yet, even in the face of this clear evidence that mom and brother are toxic, Micky cannot conceive of making his comeback without his brother by his side. Rent the film and look for those moments that portray how Micky tries to fortify his belief that he needs his brother by his side no matter how much evidence there is to the contrary.

Strong critical thinkers are able to entertain ideas without necessarily agreeing with them or rejecting them. They give ideas due consideration, even if those ideas are contrary to past decisions and commitments that the person may have made. In this chapter, our focus is on the commitment people have to their ideas, and our question is whether or not that commitment is warranted. But too often, by the time that we've made a commitment to an idea it is too late to undo the decision. The best opportunity to exercise our critical thinking is while we are still considering options. For reasons that will be explained in this chapter, it is very hard for human beings to reverse a decision once made.

This chapter is about how critical thinking can improve decision making by helping us hold off from making decisions prematurely and by monitoring and correcting our own decision making when necessary. In this opening example, as with the others in this chapter, the point is not whether the decision in the end turned out to be right or wrong. The key thing for the moment is the quality of the decision-making process. When there is time and when the issue is important, the best decisions are made reflectively by drawing on the full power of our critical thinking skills and habits of mind.

For the purposes of this chapter the key element in the "Irish" Micky Wade example is how absolutely self-assured Micky remains in the correctness of his decision. The Micky Wade character vividly displays an important psychological capacity of our species: We are able to make a decision, particularly one involving risk and uncertainty, and then to move forward on the basis of that decision without looking back. We become convinced we are right and that those who do not see things our way are wrong. We all are able to sustain our decision, reaffirm it, bolster it, and defend it. And many of us will keep right on believing that our decision is right even if our original reasons no longer apply. Yes, it is possible that we might reconsider or change our minds, but once we have locked in on our choice, the chances that we will change our mind are remote.

This chapter explores this phenomenon of locking into our decisions. This natural human tendency, called **dominance structuring,** is an extremely valuable characteristic. With confidence in the choice we have made, we are able to take action. Believing our decisions are right, we can persevere during difficulties. We would hardly be able to accomplish anything were we to constantly reconsider every decision and change our minds. Our natural tendency toward dominance structuring helps us to be resolute and to sustain our commitments. But with the benefits come risks. Because dominance structuring tends to lock us into a decision, this tendency can occasionally lock us into an unwise decision. The critical thinking skill of self-regulation and the habit of truth-seeking are our best hopes for identifying those occasions and guarding against hanging onto poor decisions. In this chapter we'll first unpack dominance structuring so we can see how it works. Then we'll consider critical thinking strategies for managing the occasionally negative influences and consequences of dominance structuring.

Dominance Structuring: a Fortress of Conviction

Once human beings have made a decision, they almost never change their minds. Looking back on our choice as compared to other options, we often feel that ours was so obvious and others were so poor that it is a wonder that we considered them possibilities at all. Maybe we do not need to work on the skill of self-regulation after all because we're seldom, if ever, wrong. We are likely to say to ourselves, "Others may disagree, but that's their issue." Things may not turn out as we had expected, but that's just bad luck or someone else's screw-up. Right? Be honest; there are plenty of times when

Thinking Critically What Can We Learn from Popular Fiction?

The Micky Ward character in *The Fighter* is not the only example of a fictional character willing to risk his career over the belief that someone they love is worthy of receiving committed loyalty, trust, and emotional investment. Enduring trust in the face of almost overwhelming contradictory evidence is true in life and a popular theme in literature. It is the dramatic engine in the *Girl with a Dragon Tattoo/ Millennium* trilogy by Stieg Larsson. In the second book of the trilogy, the protagonist Mikael Blomkvist is convinced that his estranged friend, Lisbeth Salander, has been wrongly accused of a triple murder. Despite compelling circumstantial evidence and shocking revelations about Lisbeth's psychological background, Blomkvist believes she is innocent of those crimes. Using his powerfully honed skills as an investigative reporter, he launches his own investigation into the murders. Fortunately for Blomkvist, the lead police investigator, Officer Bublanski, possesses strong critical thinking skills himself. So, while all the other police investigators appear to have locked in on the idea that Salander is guilty and while they have set about building the case for her arrest and prosecution, Bublanski at least tries to maintain an open mind, urging his colleagues to investigate other possible perpetrators—a fool's errand perhaps, given so much evidence of Salander's guilt. All three books in this trilogy are great reads, suspenseful, beautifully plotted, and artfully written. All three remind us about a danger we all risk, namely jumping to mistaken conclusions about other people and what motivates them. Did you ever discover that your judgments about a person were mistaken? How might one avoid making that kind of mistake?

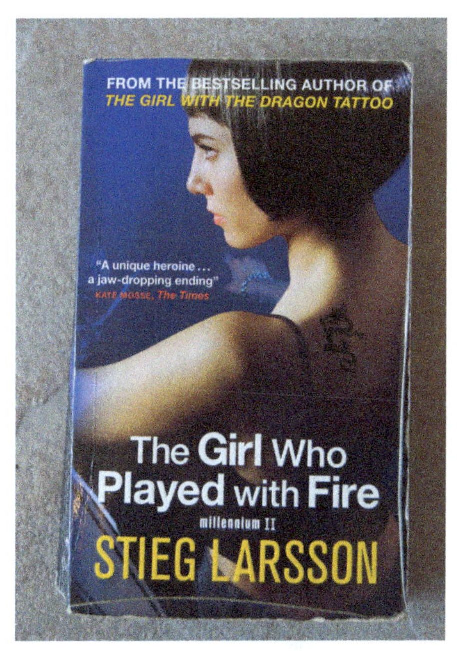

we all have thought exactly that. Why? Part of the answer may be that we really do a good job of making sound decisions. And part of the answer, whether our decisions are objectively wise or foolish, is our tendency toward dominance structuring. To appreciate the thought-shaping influences of dominance structuring, consider the arguments presented in this next example.

"I WOULD DEFINITELY GO TO THE DOCTOR"

This example is about a woman who, like Micky Wade, has made a decision. She has been asked to describe her decision making in detail to a trained interviewer. The narrative below is a brief excerpt from the transcription of that much longer interview.[i] The interviewer and the woman are talking about the possibility that she might discover a worrisome lump during a breast self-examination. The excerpt begins with the interviewer asking the woman whether she would go to see her health care provider if she were to discover a change in her body that caused her to worry about the possibility of breast cancer.

> **Interviewer:** "You're very religious. Could you see yourself waiting a while before going to the doctor and praying instead?"
>
> **Respondent:** "Oh, no. For one thing, God is a wonderful God; he made doctors. You know, my mother-in-law—I'm divorced, I was married then—she had had a heart attack. And, she definitely would pray instead of go to the doctor. She loved the Lord, and she remained in God's will [and was fortunate not to die]. But at times people have to understand that God doesn't make things as complicated as people kind of want to make it. And it's not about religion; it's about God, your personal relationship with Him. And God, He made some become doctors to want to help. You know that's how I feel. You know, I'll say this until the day I die and go back to the Lord. I'm a practicing Christian; I love the Lord. I just know God works within common sense. That's why He gave us a brain, you know. And I would definitely go to the doctor."

Review the decision map on page 212 showing the respondent's arguments. For this individual the option not selected ("I would pray for a while instead of going to the doctor") has virtually no support. She considers whether going to the doctor means that she is not being sufficiently trusting in God, but abandons that line of reasoning. She is pulled by the availability heuristic as she recalls what her mother-in-law would do, but she resists that pull, saying that God does not make things that complicated. Although in the end she offers only two arguments directly supporting her decision, it is clear from the interview and the map that all her thinking has moved inexorably and confidently in that direction. Not going to the doctor is, for her, not really an option. The problem in her mind was how to explain that to her deeply religious friends.

Were we to evaluate the arguments the woman makes using the standards and strategies presented in Chapter 7, we would find them wanting. For example, comparing herself to her mother-in-law could well have led the respondent

MAP > it > OUT 1

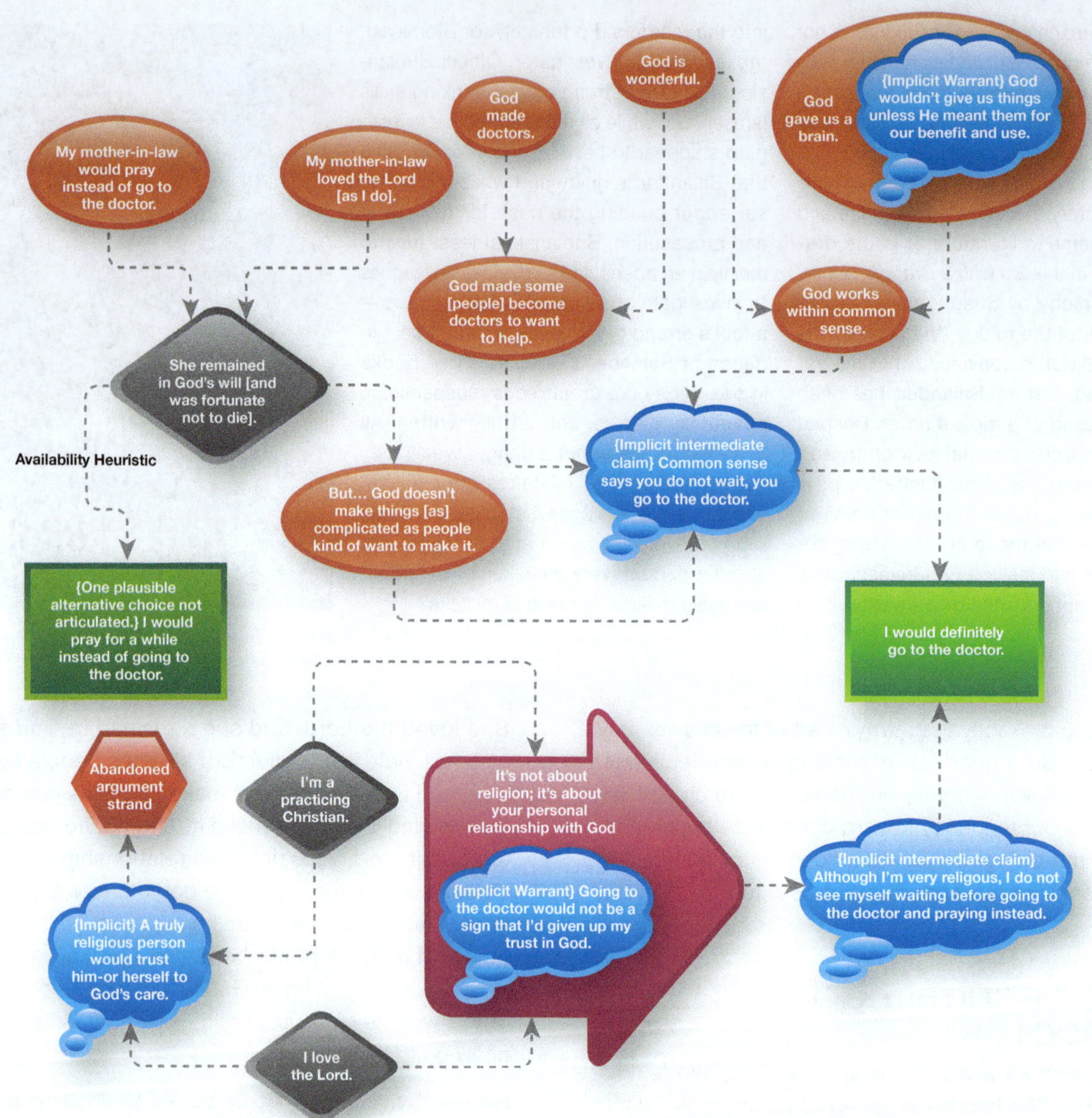

Decision Map—I would definitely go to the doctor

to infer that she did *not* need to see the doctor right away. The mother-in-law, a close family member, and, like herself, a woman of faith with a potentially severe illness, would delay seeking medical help. Ergo, following out the analogy, the woman being interviewed should also delay. The respondent's other arguments rely on belief statements about what God intends or how complicated God wishes things. But humans cannot know the mind of God. Therefore, we cannot establish the truth of premises about what God may want, intend, or think. This makes the soundness of those two arguments highly questionable. And yet, whatever their individual logical weaknesses might be, taken together her arguments are, for her, persuasive explanations that she would indeed go to the doctor. She is firm in that decision. From the longer narrative, which is not reproduced here, we can infer that she is not an uneducated or illogical person; therefore to understand what is happening we have to dig deeper into her purposes for telling the story as she does.

As it turns out, this woman is using her reasoning skills to explain a decision, not to make a decision. Going to the doctor was always to her the more sensible of the two choices. For her this was a System-1 decision—Sick? Go to the doctor! What she needed to do was explain that choice in the light of her deeply religious views and in the context of having relatives (and perhaps friends) who use religion to delay seeing a doctor for a possibly dangerous symptom. Her cognitive

Thinking Critically Pro or Con

Let's try a little thought experiment. Indicate whether you are pro or con on each of the following issues:

		PRO	CON
1	Legislation permitting assisted suicide	______	______
2	Banning abortion	______	______
3	The right to bear arms	______	______
4	Scholarships for immigrant college students[ii]	______	______
5	Decriminalizing prostitution	______	______
6	Capital punishment	______	______
7	Enforcing nondiscrimination policies for campus student groups[iii]	______	______

Pick one of the seven issues. Write down all the good reasons for your position, pro or con. All of them, please. After you have finished, write down all the good reasons for the other position, the one that is not your view of the matter. Thank you, and we'll come back to this in a moment.

challenge was actually rather formidable. She had to deal with the issue that some of her friends and the people at her church would interpret her going to the doctor as showing that her faith was weak. Notice that she does not bother to explain why going to the doctor would be valuable to her health, only why it's OK not to leave it to God. And also notice that she is not doubting her faith. But she does achieve her goal of creating a rationale to support her preferred option.

EXPLAINING AND DEFENDING OURSELVES

Our thinking capacities helped us survive as a species through the many millennia when we were anything but the most formidable species on the planet. Today our capacity for problem solving and decision making helps us achieve our personal goals, whatever they may be. If learning the truth helps achieve our goals, then we apply our skills to the problem of learning the truth. If needing to feel justified that we have made the right decision, particularly if that decision cost people their lives, is vital, we will apply our thinking skills toward creating and sustaining that justification.

Objectivity in decision making is something we prize. Yet objectivity can be very difficult for us when we already have a strongly held opinion on a given issue. Truth-seeking and open-mindedness incline us toward objectivity in the application of our skills of analysis, interpretation, evaluation, inference, and explanation. But unless we also invoke the sixth critical thinking skill, self-regulation, we may fail to achieve the objectivity we seek.

A Poorly Crafted Assignment

For many years I give my students critical thinking assignments expressed like this example: "Gun control is a controversial issue in our nation. Take a position for or against legislation banning all sales of handguns. Research the issue and defend your position with the best arguments possible. In doing so, please consider the arguments for the other side and explain why they are mistaken."

As it turned out, that was a terrible way to give a critical thinking assignment. Why? Because my students would do exactly what I had asked, in *exactly that order*. If they did not already have a point of view on the matter, they would first take one side or the other. Often their System-1 heuristic thinking played a big role in determining which side they took. Some were "pro gun" and some had poignant personal stories of gun violence that made them "anti gun." Some would knock one side or the other out of contention in their minds using the one-rule decision-making tactics of elimination by aspect: "If she'd had a gun to protect herself, she'd be alive today" or "You don't need an automatic pistol to hunt deer." Then, after they had taken a side in their minds, they would search for reasons and information that supported their point of view, but not reasons or information that opposed the view they had adopted. This was energetic investigation, but it was neither truth-seeking nor fair-minded. Their minds were pretty much already made up on the subject. Next they would write a paper laying out all the good reasons for their points of view. But, no matter which side they took, they struggled to say anything good about the opposing point of view. Their papers, by the way, were often well organized and logically presented. Like the woman talking about her decision to see the doctor, my students could explain their decisions and defend them. But they had not reflected on whether or not they were the best decisions. Critical thinking is not the holding of a belief; it is the process of reflective judgment by which we come to the belief.

"It is the mark of an educated mind to be able to entertain a thought without accepting it."

— Aristotle[iv]

The problem was my own, not my students'. I wanted my students to give due consideration to both sides of a controversial issue and to think about it in a fair-minded, objective, informed, and well-reasoned way. But that was not the instruction I gave. What I had done instead was invite them to build a dominance structure around one option and to bolster their perspective by fending off all counterarguments. I should have said, "The right to bear arms has become a major issue in our country. Come to class on Monday next week prepared to discuss this issue. I may ask you to take either the pro side or the con side with regard to a possible piece of legislation relating to gun control. Open your mind to either possibility. Be ready to present either side effectively. And be ready for the third possibility, which is that I will assign you to listen and then to adjudicate the class discussion by evaluating objectively the reasoning presented by your peers. Study the issue, inform yourself about the arguments in favor of and opposed to gun control. Be ready to speak intelligently and fair-mindedly on the topic of the right to bear arms and gun control legislation, no matter which of the three jobs I give you on Monday in class." If critical thinking is a process, then I should have found a way for my students to demonstrate that they are able to interpret, analyze, infer, explain, evaluate, and self-regulate. Only after the full, informed, and fair-minded discussion would it have made sense to invite students to then take a reasoned position on the matter.

The challenge for critical thinking is not unlike the problem of building a new house on a lot where an older house already stands. Without doing damage to the land or the neighborhood, we need to remove the old house, salvaging anything that may be of value, before we can build the new house. It takes similar skill and sensitivity to perform the same operation on opinions. Truth-seeking and open-mindedness need to be cultivated as much as possible so that we can be prepared to revisit our opinions with objectivity and judiciousness. In my life there have been more than a few times when my dearly held but ultimately mistaken opinions on controversial matters had to be abandoned so that sounder, more informed, and better-reasoned opinions could take their rightful place. But it is never easy to change one's mind about an opinion that has been firmly held—and this makes the job of self-regulation that much more difficult. To understand why most of us have a very hard time changing our minds, let's explore the psychological process of deciding on "the best available option."

MOVING FROM DECISION TO ACTION

Whenever we are presented with a problem, our cognitive heuristics and our capacity for logical reasoning play critical roles in the natural human quest to find some resolution that we can assert with plausible confidence to be our best available option. We shall call this option the *dominant or superior option* in any given context. In decision making we move, more or less quickly, through a process that includes sorting through options. We discard the implausible ones, identify one or more promising options, evaluate it or them on the basis of our decision-critical criteria,[v] and select the option we come to judge to be superior.[vi] Psychological research by Henry Montgomery and others, as we shall see, is consistent with the idea that both argument making and cognitive heuristics are central factors in our search for a dominant option—to move us from cognition to action. In times of uncertainty, when action

Thinking Critically — Pro or Con Revisited

Let's go back to the exercise in which we requested that you write down all the good reasons for your side of one of those seven issues. Please count up the number of good reasons you put down for your opinion and then do the same for the other side. If you are like most of the rest of us, it was easier to list more reasons in favor of your point of view than against it. Was that true? Did you list more in favor of your view than the opposing view? Most of us would have. Do you think you listed the strongest reasons against your point of view? Most of us do not take the time necessary to discover exactly what those are. Most of us act as if those who disagree with us have flimsy arguments when compared to our own. Never assume that those who disagree with you are idiots. That could be a costly error.

Poor Reflective Decisions

Reflective decisions are not always good decisions. Although reflective decision making often results in better choices, there are occasions when we make mistakes reflectively. Obviously, if we lack relevant knowledge, we are apt to make mistakes. Or if we do not anticipate the severe consequences that some options might produce, we are apt to make mistakes.

The tragic drowning deaths of three strong and healthy young men off the coast of Florida illustrate these problems. *The Tampa Tribune* summarized the basic facts this way:[vii] Two professional football players and two others, who played football at the University of South Florida, are lost at sea when their 21-foot boat capsizes about 35 miles west of Clearwater. Marquis Cooper, Corey Smith, and Will Bleakley are lost at sea and rescuers find Nick Schuyler clinging to the hull two days later. Months later, the lone survivor, Nick Schuyler gave an interview to HBO's *Real Sports*.[viii] In that interview Schuyler, clearly suffering emotionally from the tragic loss of his friends, told how the men, seeing a storm coming, made a series of decisions that resulted in their boat capsizing. The anchor had become stuck. They decided not to cut the rope because it would have cost a couple of hundred dollars to replace the anchor. Instead they moved the anchor line from the bow to the stern so they could try to pull the anchor free using the power of the boat's outboard motor. When they gunned the motor the anchor did not move; instead, the stern submerged and then their craft capsized. The men were thrown into the ocean. The storm hit, and over a period of two days three men succumbed to hypothermia. Had any of the men known that moving the anchor rope to the stern and gunning the engine would result in capsizing the boat, they would not have done that. But without the relevant knowledge the men made a poor decision. Or had they anticipated that deciding not to cut the anchor rope would put them at risk of dying, they certainly would have cut that rope.[ix]

A decision made by a 19-year-old driver in Michigan is a second equally tragic example of a poor decision made reflectively.[x] The *Detroit Free Press* reported that five young people were killed when an Amtrak train hit their car. A video camera mounted on the train captured the horrible final moments. Apparently, the car driver could see up ahead that the train signals were flashing and a train barrier had lowered blocking the right lane. One car had already stopped behind the barrier. As he approached the intersection, the driver had several seconds to consider his options. Instead of stopping behind the other car, he decided to try to cross the tracks. He accelerated into the left lane to go around the stopped car, intending to cut back into the right lane as he passed over the tracks. But the train, moving at high speed, collided with the car before it cleared the tracks. The train dragged the vehicle over 100 yards, crushing its five young passengers. Was it overconfidence that led the young driver to risk his life and the lives of his four friends? Or was it that he did not anticipate the dire consequences of failing to clear the intersection? We shall never know. But we do know that he had plenty of time to consider his options. And we know that the decision to risk everyone's life could have been changed at any second as he raced toward the intersection and began maneuvering around the stopped car and the train barrier.

Why are stories like these so important? Because it would be a mistake for us to believe that deliberation, in and of itself, is sufficient to ensure that we do not make mistakes. It may be our best hope, but without relevant knowledge, without the capacity to anticipate consequences, and without a good sense of what is at risk if we are wrong, we are apt to deliberate ourselves into major difficulties.

One final point: These are two tragic examples. We should have only compassion and sympathy for the victims, the survivor, and their families and friends. The analyses offered here are not intended as criticism of the people involved. We all can learn from these misfortunes.

is needed, dominance structuring is a necessary strategy for deciding between alternatives and swinging into action. Montgomery describes the human search for a single dominant option among our many possible choices in any given context as having four phases:

- pre-editing
- identifying one promising option
- testing that promising option for dominance
- structuring the dominance of the option selected.[xi]

Phase 1: Pre-Editing

In the pre-editing phase, we start by selecting a group of possible options and a number of attributes that we think are going to be important as we decide which option to finally pick. Take, for example, the problem of hiring one new employee from a large applicant pool. We want to interview only a small group of highly qualified candidates. We want them to have relevant work experience, education, letters of reference, and the like. We may have a concrete set of characteristics in mind for the final choice: someone with strong communication skills, enthusiasm for the position, and a schedule that permits that person to work the hours we might require. Our selection of these criteria shows good reasoning, for they are in fact crucial to finding the best person for the job. And we expect further evidence of reasoning in the systematic approach taken to identify potential candidates by advertising the position and screening the applicants to cull the list down to a group of interviewees. But when the applications come in, we don't exhaustively rate every candidate on every decision-critical attribute. Rather, at this early pre-editing stage we look for reasonable ways to make the decision easier and more efficient. We eliminate as many alternatives as possible with as minimal an expenditure of effort as must be committed to the task.

Typically, we use the elimination by aspect heuristic and the satisficing heuristic to make our work go more quickly. We toss every applicant who is missing any single qualifying condition (no letters of reference, insufficient education, or no relevant work experience), and we retain only those we judge to be good enough for a second look. We may cluster the applications into broad categories such as "well-qualified," "qualified," and "marginal." If we do cluster them like that, we will quickly eliminate all but the "well-qualified." Pre-editing can be brutally expeditious, and yet there is good reason for this. In real life we do not have the time or the resources to deliberate in detail about the cases we already know are not going to make the cut. What's the point?

Phase 2: Identifying One Promising Option

The second phase of the search for dominance is the identification of a promising option. We do this by *finding one* alternative that is more attractive than the others on at least one critically important attribute. There are many reasons why one choice may emerge as very attractive and be judged optimal. Perhaps this choice is most in tune with our values or current desires. Or perhaps the choice is the least threatening or the most economical. Whatever the source of the attraction, once this choice is identified, it becomes our superior or dominant option. Using our hiring example, suppose there are four finalists who have passed through our initial screening process, and we plan that a committee will interview them all. And suppose that candidate number one has the most job experience, number two is most energetic, number three is most analytical, and number four is the most congenial. It is possible the committee will immediately discover its consensus candidate. But it is more likely that different members of the committee will find different candidates to be optimal for different reasons. Each member of the committee has a different favorite. Thus, the stage is set for a difference of opinion as to which candidate should be the one hired.

Phase 3: Testing the Promising Option

Having identified a promising option, we begin almost immediately to test it against the other options. We do this by comparing our promising alternative to the other options in terms of the set of **decision-critical attributes**. Typically, we focus on seeing whether our promising option has any salient disadvantages or major drawbacks. Returning to our hiring example, suppose that five years of relevant work experience is a decision-critical criterion. If our favored candidate has seven years of relevant work experience, we will interpret that to mean that our candidate is not at a disadvantage on that criterion. That our candidate may not have as many years of experience as some other candidate is not a problem. We are not going to argue the potential positive advantage of more years beyond the minimum five. Our focus will only be to assure ourselves that our favored option does not fall short of the mark on any decision-critical factor. But what if our candidate does fall short? In that case some of us may argue that the disadvantage is not fatal to our favorite's candidacy. In fact, if we are attracted to candidate number four because of his or her congeniality, we are likely to argue that even if candidate four has only two years of experience, this is really more than enough. At this point, we are not looking to prove that our candidate is the best; rather we want to be sure that our candidate has no fatal flaws.

If our promising alternative is "comparable to the others," "about as good as the others," "neither better nor worse than the others," or "good enough" on the other decision-critical attributes, the promising alternative becomes the "to be chosen" alternative. Our initial preference for that candidate, *who was the first one we found whom we liked*, wins out. We become more and more firm in our choice. We will not abandon our "to-be-chosen" option easily. Once we begin to appraise and anchor on a given promising option, we seek to establish a

Job Candidate Options

Most Experienced

Most Energetic

Most Analytical

Most Congenial

Thinking Critically Recalling One of Your Own Decisions

Consider a time when you needed to deliberate over a decision under conditions of uncertainty about an important issue. Perhaps, for example, you pondered the question of which college to attend, which apartment to rent, or whether to accept a job offer. How well does the four-stage process described on pages 215–217 fit with your decision-making experience in that case? Were a number of conceivable options quickly eliminated in pre-editing? Did one option begin to appear rather attractive to you for some particular reason? Did you weigh that option against a few other possibilities to be sure that yours did not have any major disadvantages? Did you do any mental trading off, bolstering, grouping of criteria, or de-emphasizing of criteria that might initially have seemed important? In the end, after you had made your decision, do you recall thinking that the choice you made was rather obviously the best option among those realistically available at the time? If you answered "yes" to all the questions, which would be fine, then it would appear that you were dominance structured around that option. If you answered "no" to one or more of these questions, then reflect on what happened to derail the natural tendency toward dominance structuring in your particular case. If you do not feel that you were dominance structured around your preferred option, what new information or new considerations would have led you at the time to have made a different decision?

rationale for selecting this promising or "to-be-chosen" option over the others, and this means we transition nearly seamlessly into phase 4.[xii]

"A man hears what he wants to hear and disregards the rest."

***The Boxer*, sung by Simon & Garfunkel.**

Phase 4: Fortifying the To-Be-Chosen Option

In the final phase, we restructure our appraisals of the options so as to achieve the *dominance of one option over the others*.[xiii] This restructuring can be more or less rational, more or less in touch with reality, and, hence, more or less likely to lead to the intended and desirable results.[xiv] One way we restructure the decision so that our "to-be-chosen" candidate comes out on top is by de-emphasizing those decision-critical attributes on which our promising candidate may be weaker. Another way is to bolster our candidate by increasing the significance of an attribute on which our candidate is stronger. A third way is to collapse attributes into larger groupings; for example, we could combine education and job experience into the single attribute, "background experience." Now we can hire someone with more education but very little job experience, overriding our concern for job experience per se. Or, because we do not favor candidate number one who has the most job experience, we may need to diminish this apparent strength. We might argue that work experience is an advantage of candidate number one, but some detail about that work experience (for instance, that the person had never served in a supervisory role) is a disadvantage, so the one can be said to cancel the other. And, because of this, we might argue, candidate number one is not the person to hire.

The process of *de-emphasizing, bolstering, trading off, and collapsing* attributes continues until we find that one alternative stands above the others as the dominant choice. Acute reasoning skills are vital to this complex and dynamic process of making comparisons across attributes. Obviously, one might be able to quantify within a given attribute—for example, by comparing two candidates on the basis of their years of relevant background experience. But it is not clear how one would compare—for the purposes of possible trade-offs—communication skills against, say, energy or loyalty. And yet, we will make arguments in support of the to-be-chosen alternative as the decision-maker's search continues for a dominance structure to support this choice above all others.[xv] When the decision is being made by committee, and the stakes are high, this process can become interpersonally difficult, stressful, political, and, in the worst situations, ruthless.

The detective "began to worry that he was 'locking in,' a problem he saw with other cops all the time, the sure sense that something was just so, when it wasn't."

John Sandford, *Mortal Prey*

When is dominance structuring complete? There are three indicators. First, unless they are intentionally dissembling, people who have made their choice will tend to describe themselves as having decided, rather than as still thinking or as undecided. Second, people who are locked into a given choice tend to dismiss as unimportant, refute, or abandon all arguments that appear to be leading to a decision other than the one they embrace. Third, when asked to explain their choice, people who have built a dominance structure to fortify their selection often present with some enthusiasm a plurality of arguments supporting their chosen decision and they tend to recite rather unconvincingly a minimum number of arguments supporting any of the other possible options.

Thinking Critically Map Your Own Arguments

One more time, let's revisit the stance you took on one of those seven issues, where you were asked to list all the good reasons for both sides. Looking at your side of the matter, describe what information or what new considerations would lead you to change your mind. Please attempt to be as forthright and honest as possible. If nothing would lead you to change your mind, then write that down.

BENEFITS AND RISKS OF DOMINANCE STRUCTURING

The result of dominance structuring is confidence, whether reasonable or unreasonable, in the option we have decided upon. Dominance structuring supplies us with enough confidence to motivate us to act on our decisions and to sustain our efforts. Obviously, the more unreasonable, biased, irrational, and unrealistic we have been in our dominance structuring, the greater the risks of a poor decision. On the other hand, if we have made the effort to be reasonable, truth-seeking, informed, open-minded, and neither too hasty nor too leisurely in coming to our decision, then there is a greater chance that the decision will be a wise one. And we would be foolish not to be confident in it and not to act on the basis of such a decision. It is hard to know what more we could want when we need to make an important decision that involves elements of risk and uncertainty.

It would be a mistake to think of this human process as intentionally self-deceiving or consciously unethical or unfair. Rather, what cognitive scientists like Montgomery offer is a description of how human beings bolster confidence in their judgments under conditions of uncertainty. Humans seek to establish a strong and enduring rationale for the belief that one alternative dominates over others. This strong rationale impels us to act and sustains our continuing to act on the basis of that belief. We surround our choice with a rationale for its enduring superiority to the other choices. This strategy allows us then to move forward, with confidence in the quality of our decision.

Understanding the power of dominance structuring explains why it is so difficult for us to reconsider a choice once

Thinking Critically Organic Foods

Proponents of organic foods maintain that they're natural, they taste better, they are healthier for us, they are more environmentally sustainable, and purchasing them supports local small farmers. We should put aside the first reason, "they're natural." The Black Plague was natural, as are tornadoes, polio, and selfishness; thus, the argument "It is natural, therefore it is good" is fallacious. But the other reasons . . . well, those seem plausible. Of course, there's the issue of cost. Organic foods are expensive. So, for the sake of this exercise, let's eliminate that factor from the other side of the equation. Assume that you have plenty of money to spend on food. So, for this exercise, money is no problem. This leaves four reasons to go organic. And we only need one good reason to accept the claim that going organic is what we ought to do. Would you buy organic, if you had enough money? Yes or no? If no, why not? If yes, what would it take for you to change your mind? What if all four reasons were knocked down, would you still buy organic? What if all four reasons were knocked down and the assumption that you had plenty of money was removed? After you write your answers for this exercise, watch the clip "Organic" from *Penn and Teller: Bullshit!* (Showtime, Season 7, Episode 6). Remember, our focus in this chapter is not on the pro or con arguments about buying organic. For our purposes, what this video shows is that ordinary people can hold onto a decision (in this case, to buy organic foods) even though they come to believe that their reasons for doing so are misguided. Unscripted, they display how our shared, human psychological tendency to dominance structure around a decision continues to have the power to influence our behavior even after we no longer accept our original reasons for that decision. Nevertheless, a 2011 NPR-Thomson Reuters Health Poll[xvi] survey of 3,000 people about their attitudes regarding organic foods found that their reasons included "(36%) an eagerness to support local farms," "(34%) desire to avoid toxins," belief that organic foods were "(17%) better for the environment," and that organic foods "(13%) taste better." Why do we believe these things? Is it science or marketing? What would it take for us to change our minds?

Access the Penn and Teller video and the link to the survey at **www.mythinkinglab.com**.

Watch the **Video** on **mythinkinglab.com**

it has been made or why the criticisms of our choices seem unpersuasive. Once we have dominance structured around a choice, the virtues of other options are less compelling to us and their vices appear larger than they may in fact be. When the dominance structure has been created, it is not uncommon to hear people describe the results of their deliberations with phrases like "When we looked at it, we really didn't have any other choice," or "Hey, at the end of the day it was a no-brainer!" These mantras are evidence that the decision maker has elevated one option to the top position and discredited or discounted all other options. Having done that, it often is unclear to the decision maker why any of the other options were ever considered viable in the first place.

Searching for dominance in conjunction with elimination by aspect, satisficing, and anchoring with adjustment involves cognitive risks. First, the risk is in making poor decisions due to a lack of due consideration of all reasonable alternatives. Second, we risk that we are blind to the chance that our choice might be seriously flawed or need revision. At some level, we recognize these potential problems in human decision making. Our judicial system, for example, generally provides for appeals to be made to some person or judicial panel other than the one that rendered the initial decision. We know that once people have fixed their minds on given results, it is very difficult for them to change their judgment. In everyday life, who is there to review our decisions for us if we do not do have the habit of truth-seeking and the skill of self-regulation so that we can review them ourselves?

THE CLASSIC "O. J. DEFENSE" EXAMPLE

There are countless examples that display our natural human tendency toward dominance structuring. People engaged in group decision making have been known to revisit, and, at times, modify or reinterpret virtually every element involved in judging what to believe and what to do. Even if we assume that the decision makers are paragons of intellectual honesty, we should not underestimate the risks of dominance structuring around a mistaken choice if we are not careful. Although it may not make logical nor ethical sense to do so, there is no psychological limit on renegotiating the decision-critical attributes. We all want to be successful and solve our problems, and thus we are inclined, at times, to change our evaluations of competing options simply to reach a solution.[xvii] And when it comes to our enthusiasm for our to-be-chosen option, objectivity requires cognitive discipline—that is, strong critical thinking habits of mind.

So, we have two drivers to consider. One is our desire to achieve closure by making a decision. And the second is our psychological capacity, whether it is logical and ethical or not, to revisit and renegotiate every aspect of a decision to advance the to-be-chosen option. How might these two, in combination, make group decision making challenging? Well, consider what it might have been like to be a member of the jury for the O. J. Simpson murder trial.

Mr. Simpson, at that time, was one of the most widely known and admired college and professional American football stars of his era. Retired from football, he was an international celebrity who made movies and commercials. Then he was accused of murdering his wife and her alleged lover. What followed was a celebrity trial and media circus like only Los Angeles can produce. It filled the airwaves throughout 1995. People watched on television for days on end. In a time before Twitter, news reports appeared hourly in the CNN scroll and the progress of the trial was a daily topic in the tabloids and the mainstream media. Mr. Simpson retained a stellar defense team to represent him and vigorously to defend him from the accusations.

In Chapter 2, we said that critical thinking gave reasoned consideration to *evidence, methods, conceptualizations, standards*, and *contexts of judgment*. One way to interpret the "not guilty" verdict the jury returned for Mr. Simpson is to see how each of these five elements was addressed by the defense team. During Mr. Simpson's murder trial, the DNA *evidence* was questioned. "Was this really Mr. Simpson's DNA?" Some on the jury may have found it lacking. During the trial, the defense lawyers attacked the *methods* of the police investigation. "Was the chain of evidence secure or could there have been tampering?" Some on the jury may have judged those methods to be inadequate. The defense lawyers shifted the *context* of concern away from the violence done to the murdered people and onto the motives of potentially racist police officers and the moral character of those who were killed. Some on the jury may or may not have been distracted by this shift of attention. The *concepts* that were used by the defense went beyond jurisprudence to include those ideas and theories some associate with the politics of race. Perhaps some on the jury accepted that analysis and were influenced to be more sympathetic toward the accused because of that. The *standard* for a conviction—"beyond a reasonable doubt"—appeared to be given a new meaning by the defense team in which virtually every doubt might be conceived of as reasonable. Perhaps one or more of the jurors found the phrase problematically vague, resulting in a misapplication of the standard. Critical thinking in the context of group decision making is challenging even when the question is not as high-stakes as a potential murder conviction and even when the circumstances are less politically charged.

It would appear that to some of the jury members, the to-be-chosen alternative was that the accused was not guilty. Dominance structuring would suggest from that point forward some on the jury may have done whatever might psychologically be needed to restructure interpretations of evidence, analyses of motives, or the meaning of "reasonable doubt" to bring the option to dominance. To achieve this, it took more than just will power. It took considerable creativity and reasoning prowess to provide the jurors with the language and the conceptualizations that would permit them to go in the direction of the to-be-chosen alternative: "innocent." Arguments had to be made, data presented, reasons (contrived or otherwise) given, claims supported, and counterarguments refuted. Alternative explanations of the crime had to be simulated, effective responses favorable to the accused had to be engendered, options eliminated by aspect, and countless other opportunities for heuristic thinking made available. Eventually, the drive to come to a conclusion may have moved the jury to render the "not guilty" verdict, given that it became clear during their deliberations that one or more members of the jury were never going to be able to vote for "guilty." The drive for closure meant that the jury would not, could not deliberate indefinitely.

Mr. Simpson's defense team fulfilled its duty of putting on a vigorous defense. In so doing, the team demonstrated outstanding skills at being able to reframe the entire problem in the mind of at least some jurors. Mr. Simpson's lawyers persuaded some on the jury that in deciding Mr. Simpson's guilt or innocence they could send the message that juries would no longer passively condone the systematic oppression of African Americans by a criminal justice system rife with racism, incompetence, brutality, and evidence tampering.[xviii] We are *not* suggesting that any of the jurors in the Simpson trial thought he was guilty but voted "not guilty" simply to make a political statement. Dominance structuring does not work that way. We are saying that some jurors built a psychological dominance structure around their sincere belief that the state had failed to meet its burden of proof, "guilty beyond a reasonable doubt," because of the racism, incompetence, etc., in the system. And these jurors could not, in good conscience, vote a defendant guilty after having dominance structured around the belief that the burden of proof had not been met by the state.[xix]

Dominance structuring is a powerful influence on individual and group decision making, as the Simpson murder jury example illustrates. Our last discussion may seem a harsh critique of human decision making. However, no criticism is

O. J. Simpson's Murder Trial Defense Team

implied or intended. Nor is any praise. The description of dominance structuring is meant to be exactly that: a description of how human decision making works based on empirical investigations. At times we do well, at other times not.

OK, given that we humans engage in dominance structuring, and given that the process has many benefits but some risks, is that the end of the conversation? No. Developing strength in critical thinking is about improving our decision making. We are human beings, not machines, so we are not going to replace dominance structuring with some other process. The question for strong critical thinkers with a positive disposition toward truth-seeking becomes "What steps can we take to improve our decision making outcomes given that we tend toward dominance structuring?"

Self-Regulation Critical Thinking Skill Strategies

Because dominance structuring is an automatic System-1 tendency, we do not ask ourselves whether we wish to engage in dominance structuring or not. We just do it. And, again, for the most part that is a good thing, particularly in contexts of uncertainty when a decision is needed and action is required. But, sometimes, premature dominance structuring is a mistake. It can lock us into a less than optimal decision. Fortunately, System-2 decision making is capable of overriding and intervening. There are many strategies to mitigate the risks of dominance structuring around a less than optimal choice. These strategies rely on the critical thinking skill of self-regulation. Using self-regulation we can monitor our individual and group decision making, and we can make corrections in our decision-making processes to protect ourselves against premature dominance structuring around a lesser option. Some of these strategies will be familiar and obvious, but others may be new to you. What's important is that we use our self-regulation skills to monitor decision making and make mid-course corrections should we begin to waiver. And that can happen, because our preferred option, after all, appears to be rather strong as compared to the others. So, we will be tempted to take shortcuts and to achieve closure prematurely on our preferred option, fortifying it psychologically even against the onslaught of our original precautionary intentions.

CRITICAL THINKING PRECAUTIONS WHEN PRE-EDITING

Be Sure about "the Problem"

What we take to be the problem can limit our imaginations about possible solutions. For example, if the problem is "Our team is not going to meet the deadline," our solutions include working harder, putting in more time, or reducing the quality of the work to complete it on time. But if the problem is "Roy is not doing his share of the work," then our solutions include talking with Roy about the importance to the team of his fulfilling his responsibilities, giving some of Roy's work to other team members, replacing Roy on the team, or excluding Roy from the work effort and the resulting credit for the team's accomplishments. As we saw in the video that introduced Chapter 2, the crew of *Apollo 13* was able to identify the right problem; it was the oxygen. But if they had interpreted the problem to be instrumentation, it is difficult to see how they would have survived. Through training and experience, we learn all sorts of ways of solving all kinds of problems. But if we interpret the problem incorrectly, we are very apt to decide upon a solution that will be ineffective or inappropriate.

Specify the Decision-Critical Attributes

Before beginning to work on a solution, be clear about the standards to be applied when evaluating options and minimum thresholds that an acceptable option must meet. If two years of work experience is an expectation for hiring, then say so and stick to it. If a non-stop flight is, in your judgment, a requirement for your next vacation trip, then don't compromise on that standard. On the other hand, if a non-stop flight is desirable but not essential, then don't elevate a secondary criterion to the level of "mandatory." If the decision must be made after you hear from your friend next week on Monday, but before the opportunity lapses next week Thursday, then hold to that time frame. People with strong critical thinking skills and habits of mind protect themselves from making suboptimal decisions by establishing primary and secondary criteria and negotiating the secondary ones but holding firm to the primary ones.

Be Clear about Why an Option Is In or Out

Even at the pre-editing phase, make a reflective and deliberative judgment as to why each option should remain in contention or be eliminated. It will be impossible in most cases to give full consideration to every conceivable option. We need to eliminate large numbers of options early in the process so we can conserve time and energy to focus on those that remain. Real estate salespeople know this, and so they will ask prospective buyers and renters about their price range and how many bedrooms they need. These two parameters alone will enable agents to avoid wasting their own time and their clients' time on properties that are too expensive or not the right size.

Suppose you are looking to rent a two-bedroom apartment for less than $900 per month near school. A computer search or a friend who is a real estate agent can provide a list of a dozen apartments within minutes. Because you were clear about why an option was in (near the campus, two bedrooms) and why an option was out (cost more than $900), each and every one of the apartments will be a viable possibility. Your chances of making a poor decision or falling in love with a place you cannot afford or that does not meet your needs are reduced considerably. Suppose that a safe neighborhood and proximity to the metro system are also major considerations for you. Now, with clarity about five criteria, the choices become fewer and the next step, identifying the promising option, is more manageable.

"Apartment Must Haves"

- Under $900/mo
- Two bedrooms
- Near campus
- Near metro stop
- Safe neighborhood

CRITICAL THINKING PRECAUTIONS WHEN IDENTIFYING THE PROMISING OPTION

Scrutinize Options with Disciplined Impartiality

When you first start considering a problem, it is too soon to become the champion of one alternative over another, and you'll need to discipline yourself to assess strengths and weaknesses without becoming enamored of any specific option. If there are four apartments to look at, prepare your mind to look objectively at each. In practice, this can be more difficult than it seems, especially because many professional real estate agents often use the following tactics. First, an agent shows an acceptable property, a weaker one second, the best one third, and a lesser-quality property fourth. Psychologically, this puts the client at ease because, after two less-than-fully-desirable options, the third option looks really good, adjusting upward from where the client had first anchored. Seeing a less-acceptable fourth option helps lock the client in on the third option. Although the salesperson may never have heard of Professor Montgomery and dominance structuring, he or she knows how to wield these decision behaviors. The agent might ask the client to note the positives of one apartment over the other, guiding the dominance structuring process along. The agent will have a fifth to show, if the client insists, but the agent is hoping that the client will lock in on one that is "good enough." The way *not* to be shepherded into a decision we might later regret is to decide beforehand that we will not let ourselves make any decision about the options, not even a tentative decision, until we have examined each with equal scrutiny.

Listen to Both Sides First

A variation on the previous strategy is the mental discipline not to decide until we have heard the other side of the story. Judges instruct juries not to decide until after the prosecution and the defense have both completed presenting their cases and made their closing arguments. Parents discover that it is not good enough to hear one child's story about who started the fight and why. They know that they must hear the other child's side of the story. We all have a natural tendency to believe the first credible report we hear and then use that belief to critique subsequent reports. Has this ever happened to you? Can you think of a time when you were involved in a situation or a disagreement with another person that resulted in that other person telling a third party what happened, only to find that when you tried to explain your side of the story to that third party they seemed to have already made up their minds about you? We as authors can think of a few examples with co-workers, friends, and even some family members where this has happened to us in the past. It takes a set of practiced critical thinking self-regulation skills and a strong habit of open-mindedness to resist coming to a premature decision regarding which side to believe.

CRITICAL THINKING PRECAUTIONS WHEN TESTING THE PROMISING OPTION

Use All the Essential Criteria

As obvious as this seems, we often do not use all the decision-critical criteria after identifying our preferred option. We like the apartment in the complex that has the well-equipped workout room, and so we elevate that new factor to the status of a major consideration. But our initial set of essential factors did not include that consideration. It may have been on our desirable list, but it was not on the essentials list. Instead, we err by neglecting one or more of our initially essential criteria, for example, the proximity to the university or the cost. Strong critical thinking disciplines of mind incline us toward sticking to our initial criteria and applying all of them to this candidate and to all the other candidates. If a new and important criterion emerges during the decision-making process, then we would want to revise the list of decision-critical criteria and initiate a new search. There may be others that have great recreational spaces. As we first envisioned our set of criteria, great recreational space was not among them. Until we saw this apartment, that consideration was not an essential factor. No matter whether we stick with our initial set of criteria or initiate a new search with a new set of criteria, the important thing is that we apply all of them if they are all considered essential.

Treat Equals as Equals

The tendency toward dominance structuring privileges the promising option over all the other candidates by orienting our thinking around whether that one option has any obvious disadvantages. If the favored option has no obvious disadvantages, then it will become the to-be-chosen option. I like the apartment in the complex with the great fitness room. So, I ask myself whether it has any major disadvantages as compared to the other choices. It's pricey, but I can stretch. It isn't as close to the university, but it's not too far either. I wish the second bedroom were bigger, but I can live with that. Nope. No major disadvantages. Notice that in this process I did not give all four options a fair-minded evaluation, seriously comparing them on each criterion. Instead of truth-seeking, I threw objectivity to the wind and settled for an apartment that was more expensive, further from the university, and too small. And I did not even look at the other two criteria, safety and proximity to the Metro.

Diligently Engage in Truth-Seeking and Remain Impartial

Truth-seeking helps us follow reasons and evidence wherever they lead, even if they go against our preferred or favored option. This is an active process. We must discipline ourselves to go out and find the needed evidence and consider all the reasons, pro and con. Being diligent in truth-seeking means that we give fair-minded consideration to options and ideas even if they go against our preconceptions or cherished, but perhaps unreflectively held, beliefs. Impartiality helps us maintain our objectivity. But we all know that it is hard to be impartial in some situations. If the stakes are high for us or if people we care about are involved, it is very difficult. Strong critical thinking demands that we recognize contexts in which impartiality is difficult to maintain. In those cases, if others are involved, the judicious thing to decide is that someone else should decide.

Thinking Critically — Your Candidate in 2012

One's orientation toward a political party, either Democratic or Republican, runs deep. People often find themselves consistently voting for candidates from the same party. Dominance structuring explains part of this, and obviously the quality of the candidates and what they stand for explains part, too. Consider your preferred candidate in the 2012 presidential election. What would it have taken for you to support some other candidate? Make a decision map of your reasons for supporting your favored candidate and the reasons for voting for the other candidate. After you have finished your map, inspect it to see whether your decision map reveals a larger clustering of arguments around your favored candidate, with relatively fewer arguments supporting the other candidate. Evaluate the quality of those reasons using the standards presented earlier in the book in Chapters 7, 8, and 9.

In legal matters, when a potential juror is deemed to be at risk of not being impartial, that person is excused from being a juror. A judge who is at risk of not being impartial in a given case asks that the case be moved to a different judge. But in our daily lives, we cannot remove ourselves from judging or excuse ourselves from the responsibility of making decisions. We must, instead, make a conscious and deliberative effort to decide objectively. The habit of truth-seeking and the skill of self-regulation are irreplaceable assets in doing this.

CRITICAL THINKING PRECAUTIONS WHEN FORTIFYING THE TO-BE-CHOSEN OPTION

Be Honest with Yourself

The complex processes at work in the final stage of dominance structuring can be difficult to manage unless one is deeply committed to making honest evaluations. But, if there are good reasons, we can de-emphasize a given decision-critical criterion relative to another. In the apartment example, price may be more important than proximity to the campus. At other times, a criterion cannot be de-emphasized. Safety, for example, might have been a major consideration in the pre-editing phase. If that were the case, then it would be intellectually dishonest to argue at this point that it is no longer a factor to consider seriously. When bolstering we may be tempted to exaggerate the virtues of our to-be-chosen option and exaggerate the vices and shortcomings of the other options. But exaggeration would be less than fully honest. Yes, our favored candidate does have advantages, and yes, the other options have flaws, but we should use self-regulation to monitor our evaluation so that we do not blow these advantages or these flaws out of proportion. Trading off one criterion for another can be straightforward if the two have the same metric. For example, proximity to the university and proximity to the metro can both be measured in time and distance. So, we can more easily decide whether being a little closer to the metro and a little further from the university is acceptable or not. But when two criteria are measured on different metrics, the trade-offs can be more difficult. How much safety should one trade to get a lower rent? How much smaller can that second bedroom be in order to live closer to the university? Again, we need self-regulation skill to monitor and correct, if needed, our tendency to trade away too many important things to get that one feature that attracts us so much. Collapsing criteria is not going to work when the criteria are as different as those in the apartment example. It is hard to imagine price and safety as one criterion. But in the hiring example earlier in the chapter, it could be reasonable to collapse work experience, volunteer experience, and maybe service learning experience. If we can expect that the person learned job-relevant skills even though he or she may not have had a paying job, then collapsing makes sense.

CRITICAL THINKING STRATEGIES FOR BETTER DECISION MAKING

Task Independent Teams with the Same Problem

Military commanders, realizing the risks of poor decisions, occasionally set two independent teams to work on the same problem. The theory behind this strategy is that if the two teams make the same recommendations, then that recommendation is probably the best option. If the teams make divergent or conflicting recommendations, then that provides the commanding officer the opportunity to listen impartially and objectively as each team explains why its recommendation is superior.

Decide When It's Time to Decide

Particularly in group decision-making situations, there is a tendency to decide prematurely. Time for discussion is short, and some people always seem ready to decide faster than others do. People can become impatient, and the urgency of other matters can lead us into the trap of "Ready, Fire, Aim." We can mitigate the tendency toward premature decision making by first setting out a plan for making the decision that identifies all the steps that will be taken first. In group decision making, this can be very helpful, for it establishes a set of expectations and assures time for the diligent inquiry and deliberation that is due an important decision. Obviously, it would be equally unwise to fail to make the decision when opportunities are being missed and the costs of delaying are mounting up. Sticking to an initial plan for when and how a decision needs to be made, including the time frame, fact finding, option development, and consultation, can be very helpful.

Thinking Critically — Deciding Whether or Not a Man Should Die

In December 2005, Arnold Schwarzenegger, then governor of California, was faced with a difficult decision. Should he grant clemency to a high-profile inmate on death row, Mr. Stanley "Tookie" Williams? The death penalty, as a social policy, had come under considerable criticism. Many well-known Californians called for Governor Schwarzenegger to commute Mr. Williams's sentence to life without possibility of parole. Many Californians believed that Mr. Williams had demonstrated for several years that he was a "changed man." As a convicted murderer he deserved life in prison, but he was not the same person he had been decades earlier, and he did not, in their view, deserve at this time to be punished with death. Some saw him as a symbol of why the death penalty should be abolished. After deliberating on the matter, Governor Schwarzenegger decided against clemency, so Mr. Williams was executed. The governor posted a document on the Internet describing his decision-making process. Access that document at **www.mythinkinglab.com**.

Read the **Document** on **mythinkinglab.com**

The Governor's statement explains his decision. First, map that decision. Your map will show that the Governor provides two primary lines of reasoning supporting his decision. One ends in the claim that Mr. Williams is, in fact, guilty (as determined by the jury at his trial), and that there is no other basis for clemency given that he is guilty. The map should also show additional bolstering arguments supporting the conclusion that Mr. Williams should not be granted clemency: The gangs he formed continue to do violence; his attempted escape risked the lives of law enforcement officers; and the murders he committed were brutal in nature. The Governor entertained five considerations which indicated that a decision would be needed [mapped using diamond shapes]: (1) claimed innocence, (2) claimed redemption, (3) a lack of apology, (4) fairness of the trial, and (5) good works while in prison. Several of these were endorsed as important considerations in the public debate prior to the Governor's decision.

Second, examine the map that reflects your interpretation of this document to see if there is a discernible dominance structure surrounding and supporting the chosen option. Were the strongest arguments for the option not chosen identified and given due consideration? Does the map reflect that the Governor applied appropriate standards in an appropriate way? Discuss your response to these two questions with due consideration to maintaining your own objectivity, truth-seeking, and fair-mindedness. These are not easy questions because the chances are that you, like most of the rest of us, have an opinion about the death penalty. And, if so, then you, like the rest of us, have probably built a dominance structure to support your opinion on that policy question. Thus, objectivity and impartiality must be self-monitored during this discussion.

Third, evaluate the Governor's arguments individually and his decision holistically. Apply the criteria for evaluating arguments presented in Chapter 7, the Holistic Critical Thinking Scoring Rubric presented in Chapter 1, and what you have learned about heuristic thinking and dominance structuring in Chapter 10 and this one.

Analyze Indicators and Make Mid-Course Corrections

Health care and business professionals employ this strategy. They frequently measure progress and make necessary adjustments if the relevant outcome indicators do not show the expected improvements. This strategy is the critical thinking skill of self-regulation made operational. When a patient is in the hospital, the clinicians monitor all the patient's bodily systems to be sure that the treatment plan is having the desired effect. If any of the many tests that are performed show that the patient's condition is not improving, then the medical team makes changes in the patient's treatment. In business settings, people monitor sales revenues, expenses, cash flow, accounts payable, and accounts receivable on a regular basis. They review data to monitor progress toward revenue targets or to be sure they are staying within budget allocations. If any of the numbers look problematic, they make mid-course corrections. The same idea applies to decisions we make to improve or change our life situations. If we monitor the effects of those decisions and we do not see the results we planned, we need to make mid-course corrections.

Create a Culture of Respect for Critical Thinking

All of us, and leaders in particular, can increase the likelihood of better decision making by creating a culture of respect for critical thinking. We do this by modeling and encouraging positive critical thinking habits of mind. We do this by inviting, acknowledging, and rewarding the constructive use of critical thinking skills. We do this by showing respect for people even if they advance ideas and opinions that differ markedly from our own. We can model respecting people's effort to think well even if we do not accept their ideas. As leaders we would be wise to invite people to supply their reasons for their recommendations, rather than only their votes or their recommendations, as if the reasons were unimportant. As leaders we must give truth-seekers enough latitude to raise difficult questions without fear of reprisals. We must be willing to listen, to reconsider, and to be persuaded by good arguments. At the same time, we must use these same tools when presenting our final decisions—sharing not just the choice made, but providing the reasons for that choice.

CHAPTER 11 REVIEW

Study and Review on mythinkinglab.com

Dominance structuring is the natural tendency we have to fortify our decisions in our own minds so that we can move forward with confidence to act on those decisions, particularly in contexts of risk and uncertainty. The many advantages of dominance structuring include persistence when the going gets tough, confidence that we have made the right choice, and the courage to act even though some uncertainty may remain. With these advantages there are also risks. The choice may not have been a good decision in the first place. Or conditions may have changed, making the choice no longer optimal. But unless we are monitoring our decision making and self-correcting along the way, dominance structuring can lock us into a bad decision or prevent us from making needed changes. There are many critical thinking strategies that we can use to guard against the pitfall of poor decision making. These strategies share two common themes: cultivate and practice the critical thinking habits of mind, especially truth-seeking, and apply strong critical thinking skills, especially self-regulation. You can use these strategies to monitor decision making every step of the way and correct the process as often as needed.

KEY TERMS

dominance structuring is the psychological process through which humans achieve confidence in their decisions. The four phases of dominance structuring are pre-editing, identifying one promising option, testing that promising option for dominance, and structuring the dominance of the option selected. (p. 210)

decision-critical attributes are those criteria the decision maker deems to be important and relevant for the purpose of evaluating options. (p. 216)

FIND IT ON MYTHINKINGLAB.COM

- The decision to gun the boat engine to free a caught anchor in order to avoid the cost of replacing the expensive anchor equipment, or the decision to try and cross a train track even though the barriers are down and the lights are flashing to warn of the oncoming train in order to not be late for work can lead to horribly tragic outcomes—as we saw in the examples of the NFL players in Florida or the teens in Michigan. The strength or weakness of the original reasons was no match for the dominance structuring that sealed these individuals' commitment to their decided actions. View excerpts of the HBO interview with surviving boater Nick Schuyler at www.mythinkinglab.com. The Schuyler interview is hard to watch, although it is instructive, which is why we are providing the link. At www.mythinkinglab.com you will also find links to the video about the train crash that killed the five young people. That tragedy is instructive, if only to reinforce the life and death importance of making thoughtful decisions. But know before you decide to view these that you will be seeing a real event, one that is both tragic and disturbing. Watch the Video on mythinkinglab.com
- Life and death decisions are not limited to unfortunate tragedies. Governor Arnold Schwarzenegger wrestled with the question of whether or not to commute the death sentence of a man convicted of murder (p. 224). The Governor's reasoning is revealed in the document at www.mythinkinglab.com. Is this only a legal question? When does it become a question of conscience? After you've completed the exercise you may want to review our mapped analysis of the Governor's decision. See pp. 310–311 in the Appendix. Read the Document on mythinkinglab.com

- On a lighter note, popular culture abounds with deeply held, almost unshakable beliefs for which we have precious little hard evidence. The entertaining clip from one of Penn & Teller's broadcasts (p. 218) reveals that many of us have built almost impenetrable mental dominance structures around a belief in the superior quality, benefit, and value of organic foods. After seeing their analysis, we found ourselves seriously questioning some of our prior beliefs about organics. Perhaps you will too. Access the clip at www.mythinkinglab.com. Watch the Video on mythinkinglab.com

Exercises

REFLECTIVE LOG: POTENTIALLY LIFE-ALTERING DECISIONS

Picking an apartment is a relatively benign matter compared to decisions that have the potential to radically alter the course of your life. Imagine these four possibilities:

1. Considering whether you should get married
2. Deciding whether you need help with a drinking, gambling, or drug problem
3. Deciding whether to make an embarrassing apology to someone
4. Dealing with another request from a member of your family for a loan

Step 1: Select one of the four possibilities. Think about the problem as it might play out in your life and how you would go about deciding what you should do. Simulate the entire decision. Then, draw it out in a decision map or write a free-flowing essay.

Step 2: Examine your completed map or essay for dominance structure. Evaluate your decision process to see whether you applied the critical thinking strategies to ensure that you make as good a decision as possible.

SMALL GROUP DISCUSSION: WHAT WOULD IT TAKE?

You are on the governor's select committee of senior advisors, and the governor has asked you to make a recommendation and supply your reasons. Here's the situation: A serial killer who brutally rapes and tortures for days before murdering his victims was cornered by FBI agents and, while trying to escape, was shot and suffered a non-lethal head wound. Now lying in a private room in a state hospital, the killer, who is in a coma, is being kept alive by a feeding tube. Doctors say that he will never recover from the coma because of the severity of the head wound he suffered. Although there is no doubt about his guilt, he has never been arrested, indicted, or put on trial. The governor has been receiving political pressure from many sources saying that the killer should not be kept alive. They want the governor to order that the feeding tube be removed, which will cause the killer to starve to death. Others, hearing of this, have sent a flurry of messages to the governor that say that all human life must be respected, reminding the governor that this person has not been convicted of any crimes by a jury.[xx] The governor has asked you to advise on the question: "Withdraw the feeding tube or not?" After discussing this with your group, write down your recommendation and your reasons. Also write down your reasons for *not* recommending the opposite.

After you have written down your recommendation, write down what it would take for you to change your mind and recommend the opposite. If that is not a possibility, explain why not.

PREPARING FOR YOUR BIG DECISION

Consider a decision coming up in your life. Reflect on the issues and concerns that are leading you to make this decision. What exactly is "the problem" you must resolve with this decision? What are your decision-critical criteria? Which are essential and which are important but only desirable? Are there any minimum thresholds that must be met for an option to be considered viable? How do you plan to scrutinize your options? How will you be sure that you have heard all sides? Is there a way for you to assure yourself that none of the essential options will be dropped out of the equation before you make your decision? How do you plan to ensure that you have diligently engaged in truth-seeking, maintained your objectivity, and impartially evaluated all the options prior to selecting a favorite? How will you determine when the time has come to make the decision? What factors will you monitor after you have made your decision, so that you can know whether a mid-course correction is needed? This exercise does not invite you to make that important decision. It invites you to lay the groundwork for making that decision by applying the critical thinking strategies of self-regulation.

SMALL GROUP DISCUSSION: WISHY-WASHY FLIP-FLOPPERS

If judiciousness is a positive critical thinking habit of mind and if strong self-regulation skills and honest truth-seeking can guide us to revisit our decisions and change our minds, why is it that, in the United States, a leader who changes his or her mind is criticized for being wishy-washy? And why is it that a politician who learns new information and comes to a new position on an issue is criticized for flip-flopping?

OPTIONAL BONUS EXERCISE: *DEATH IN THE WEST*

In 1979, the BBC aired a documentary on smoking. It featured gut-wrenching interviews with American cowboys from Montana and other Western states that were dying of lung cancer, emphysema, and heart disease. Their doctors were interviewed and hypothesized that smoking was the cause of these men's illnesses. The documentary also shows interviews with executives from Phillip Morris, the manufacturer of Marlboro cigarettes, which used the "Marlboro Man," a handsome, rugged, healthy, independent-minded cowboy, on all their advertising. The executives offered reasons why we should not believe that cigarettes were causally connected to these diseases. Phillip Morris sued the BBC. The documentary was suppressed as part of the court settlement. It may be that only underground copies are available. If you happen to find a copy to watch, you will see dominance structuring in action. Even the independent clinical psychologist who is interviewed suggests that the Phillip Morris executives needed to think of themselves as people doing worthy labor, not as ruthless purveyors of disease and death. And this insight came several years before the initial research on dominance structuring was published. Watch the documentary, if you can locate a copy, and map the arguments made by the Phillip Morris executives in favor of smoking and opposed to those who would argue that smoking is dangerous.

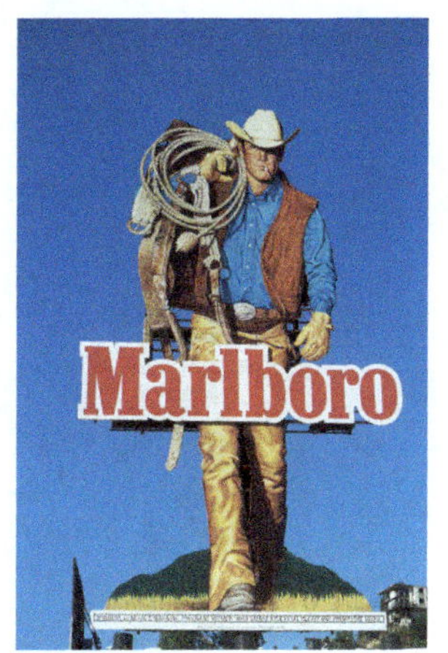

OPTIONAL CHALLENGE EXERCISE: QUESTIONING THE BELIEFS WE ARE BORN INTO

For many of us, the religion we say we belong to is the one into which we were born and raised. From childhood we were taught certain things and grew comfortable with the beliefs, rituals, and practices of a particular religion. Yes, there may have been questions and doubts, but somehow or other we fought though those. Abandoning the religion of our youth can feel like stepping into an abyss. We may have no sense of how we could replace it. What should we believe instead? What basis would we have for our sense of right and wrong, were it not connected to religion? What would we make of our place in the universe, if we were not somehow part of a Grand Plan, and watched over by a loving Creator? How would our family members respond? Who would we be, if we were not a _______?

There are answers to these questions. But make no mistake about it, the answers for any of us are not easily won. The first challenge of this exercise is to recognize how much we dominance structure around the religion of our youth. Meditate on that for some time. Ask yourself when, if ever, you actually sat down and compared point for point the religion of your youth in an objective, open-minded way with two or three of the other major world religions. For most of us, the answer is never. Oh, maybe we learned to defend our religion from the attacks and criticisms people may hurl at it. But, few of us have laid out the options side by side and reviewed their pluses and minuses point by point. Many of us fortify the dominance structure holding up our religious convictions by discounting objections and ignoring inconsistencies.

Part two is this challenge: Ask yourself what it would take for you to thoughtfully and intentionally examine the religion of your youth? Not reactively, not angrily ping-ponging off of some dreadful tragedy or upsetting news report. But with all due deliberation, considering the evidence as we know it, the reasons as we see them, the nature of the human condition as we understand it. One way for us to examine the religion we were born into would be to ask, what we would need to find, to learn, to know that would result in our reflective decision to say to ourselves in the privacy of our own heart and mind that, well, not to put too fine a point on it, sorry but as good as it might have been for our youth, the religion we were born into is simply untrue?

Read the Chapter on mythinkinglab.com
Listen to the Chapter Audio on mythinkinglab.com

CHAPTER 12

Comparative Reasoning: Think "This is Like That"

WHAT are the three most fundamental human reasoning patterns?

HOW can we recognize comparative reasoning?

HOW can we evaluate comparative reasoning?

WHAT are the uses, benefits, and risks of comparative reasoning?

"The reporter is supposed to shout, 'Americans, these guys are about to attack you,' and then you die. Is that the problem here?" demands veteran CBS News anchor Mike Wallace of Air Force general Brent Scowcroft. "Yes, you should warn our troops!" is the answer the general wants to hear. But that is not the answer Wallace gives. The hypothetical—you are an American TV news journalist who is embedded with enemy troops who are about to ambush a platoon of American soldiers. Your options—videotape the ambush for the evening news or warn the American platoon.

The program *Ethics in America* brought together military officers, journalists, and government officials to debate this hypothetical as a way of exploring the relationship between one's responsibilities as a professional journalist and one's responsibilities as a fellow American. Mike Wallace and Peter Jennings—at the time two of the best-known, most respected, and widely watched TV journalists in the nation—struggled mightily with the high-stakes hypothetical. As Mike Wallace is speaking, another panelist, USMC colonel George M. Connell, is seething with contempt for the journalist. The Marine colonel is wondering if he should order American Marines to rescue a reporter pinned down by enemy fire, if that same reporter didn't have the courage to risk his own life to save a platoon of Americans. To see how Wallace answers the general and whether the colonel would, in

<<< Marine Colonel George Connell, left, controls his contempt for the CBS journalist, Mike Wallace, center, who is arguing with Air Force General Brent Scowcroft, right.

fact, send Marines to rescue a journalist for whom he has "utter contempt," watch the video clip at **www.mythinkinglab.com**. Watch the **Video** on **mythinkinglab.com**

The clip begins with Harvard Law School professor Charles Ogletree presenting the hypothetical to Peter Jennings. After clarifying the question that Ogletree has put to him, Jennings refines the question; he struggles with the ethical dilemma. At one point, about three minutes into the clip, Jennings pauses nearly 12 seconds to ponder what he would do. No experienced television personality would knowingly create that much "dead air time." But, for Jennings, the problem is very high stakes. He infers that should he decide to warn the Americans about the ambush, the enemy will immediately kill him. Ogletree turns to Mike Wallace and presents the same problem. He too struggles. Unsure how to get a handle on the dilemma, Mike Wallace tries to use an analogy—he proposes that the ethics of the situation in the combat zone are comparable to ethical standards that would apply to a similar situation in a U.S. city. If a reporter knew that a murder was about to be committed on the streets of an American city, then the reporter would be ethically bound to call the police or to try to warn the victim. "Now," says Wallace, nervously moving his hands along the top of the table, "now . . . you take that and apply it to a war zone. And . . ." The video clip is a moving display of the challenges associated with reasoning through a novel high-stakes problem.

Comparative, Ideological, and Empirical Inferences

We human beings draw inferences and offer explanations in most situations using one of three fundamental reasoning strategies. We use *comparative reasoning* (this-is-like-that), *ideological reasoning* (top-down from core beliefs), or *empirical reasoning* (bottom-up from observations to generalizations). Each of the three offers advantages and disadvantages. In this chapter and the two that follow we will explore each of the three fundamental modes of human reasoning. In this way you will be able to make the most effective use of your critical thinking across the widest possible array of contexts.

Comparative reasoning (or **this-is-like-that thinking**) enables us to make interpretations, draw inferences, or offer explanations by relying on something that is more familiar in order to understand something that is less familiar. For example, one wintery bright February in Minneapolis–St. Paul two roommates were talking about climate change as they stepped

Thinking Critically — Preliminary Evaluation of Mike Wallace's Analogy

After you have watched Colonel Connell tell whether he would or would not "send Marines to save a couple of journalists," ask yourself if the comparison that Mike Wallace tried to make—between warning the soldiers and warning the potential murder victim—is a good analogy or not. Why or why not? In your arsenal of argument evaluation tools you already have the four tests for the acceptability of an argument. You also have the self-regulation skills we talked about in the last two chapters. Use those skills to keep your evaluation of Wallace's analogy tentative, at least for now. Moving forward, we will explore the specific criteria for evaluating comparisons, so let's put this analogy on the back burner for now.

Breaking Down Comparative Reasoning		
Elements	Mike Wallace's Example	Climate Change Example
Feature or features of interest	A journalist's ethical responsibilities	Proximity (lack of distance in space or time) to specific events
Less familiar object, event, concept, or experience	An American journalist warning an American platoon in a combat zone that it is about to be ambushed by the enemy	Achieving the perspective needed to perceive long-term global weather patterns
Assertion of useful likeness or similarity	is analogous to	is like
More familiar object, event, concept, or experience	an American journalist warning an innocent person in a U.S. city when the person is about to become the victim of a crime.	stepping back from a TV to see the whole picture rather than being so close to the screen that only a couple of pixels are in view.

through the residence hall doors and out into the brittle morning cold. "Climate change! Are you kidding me? Look around. We need snowshoes to get to class today!" The other, ever the serious student, replied, "Your problem is that you're too close to see the big picture. It's like you have your nose pressed up against the TV screen and can see only a couple of pixels. Step back and the pattern is as clear as Hi-Def."

We use comparative reasoning, as in the example, to explain abstract ideas. We use it when giving advice, too. For example, a grandparent might tell you a story that relates your current problem to something similar that happened to that grandparent and then use that to suggest how you might handle your current problem. The legal system's reliance on precedents is a form of comparative reasoning. In appealing to precedent a lawyer is arguing that the judge should treat the current case a certain way because it is so much like a previous case; it thus deserves to be handled the same way that case was handled. Imaginative engineers and scientific investigators use comparative reasoning when they develop and apply theoretical models in the creative search for novel solutions to problems. We will explore the creativity, complexities, and uncertainties of comparative reasoning in this chapter.

So that you know the plan, and so that you can get a preliminary sense of the contrasts between the three modes of reasoning, here's what we'll do in the next two chapters: In Chapter 13, we'll examine ideological reasoning, which is drawing inferences from axioms, principles, or core beliefs and values to determine their specific applications. In high school plane geometry, for example, we begin with a set of first principles—axiomatic assumptions—about lines and points, and from these we infer the theorems they imply. A person with strongly held political or religious principles will use this same mode of reasoning to draw inferences about specific legislative proposals. For example, if I begin with the principle that all human life is sacred, I am likely to oppose specific legislative proposals that would permit euthanasia because of the belief that euthanasia, the taking of a life, ought not to be permitted.

As we shall see in the next chapter, ideological reasoning is largely deductive, because we are looking for what the implications of our core beliefs must be. That it leaves very little room for doubt turns out to be both a strength and a weakness of ideological reasoning. The optional supplemental chapter on "Ethical Decision Making" examines how we use ideological reasoning and comparative reasoning when deliberating moral, ethical, or policy issues.

In Chapter 14, we explore empirical reasoning, which moves from particular observations toward hypotheses, generalizations, and theories intended to explain those observations. Because of the possibility that our theories, generalizations, and explanations might be false, this mode of reasoning is commonly associated with induction. In its most refined and sophisticated form, empirical reasoning is scientific investigatory reasoning that progresses, as we saw in Chapter 9, from coincidence to correlation toward causal explanations so accurate that we can predict and control events. Chapter 14 extends that discussion by exploring the rigor, power, and limitations of scientific investigatory reasoning. The optional supplemental chapters, "Think Like a Social Scientist" and "Think Like a Natural Scientist," take empirical reasoning into these two captivatingly interesting domains of human learning.

"This Is Like That"—Recognizing Comparative Reasoning

When using comparative reasoning, we make an interpretation, explanation, or inference about that which is less familiar by comparing it to that which is more familiar. As we saw in Chapter 10, on heuristic thinking, at times comparative reasoning can be automatic, reactive System-1 thinking. The representativeness heuristic, the simulation heuristic, and occasionally the affect heuristic are examples of making quick, reactive comparisons. The fruit of System-2 comparative reasoning, with its more deliberative effort to explicitly consider points of comparison and contrast, is often an analogical argument. Mike Wallace's effort in the opening video clip is an attempt to find a useful comparison when trying to solve a difficult and unfamiliar problem. Mike Wallace tried to understand his ethical responsibilities in a combat situation by considering his ethical responsibilities in a comparable, but not identical, situation that he had experienced before—namely warning an innocent person that he or she is about to become the victim of a crime.

Comparative reasoning, whether System-1 or System-2, is basically the reliance on a more familiar image, idea, or experience to shape or guide how we think about something that is less familiar. We are employing the word *reasoning* broadly in order to include comparisons used to illustrate, clarify, or explain our ideas as well as comparisons used to draw conclusions.

GARDENS OF COMPARATIVES

Just as there are myriad flowering plants in a well-tended garden, people cultivate an exceptional variety of ways to express comparative reasoning. To communicate our insights about why "this is like that" our species employs stories, metaphors, and similes. Most comparative reasoning does not appear as a fully developed argument with reasons and claims. But no matter how they are presented, comparisons can shape our judgments about what to believe or what to do. Judicious critical thinkers must be alert to the rich variety of ways we use comparisons to express our thinking. Here are several examples. Each is a bit different from the others, but they all do have one important feature in common: In each example, the speaker is attempting to interpret or to explain something, or to draw an inference about something, by comparing that thing to another thing the speaker believes to be more familiar to the listener.

- Think of the world as a clock. Just as a clock could not have come into existence unless there was a clockmaker, so there also must be a God who made this wonderfully complex world.
- You can make John the club's treasurer, if you want. But with the way he manages money doing that would be like skydiving without a parachute.
- Time is a great river. We float on that river, like leaves borne along by the rush of seasons, spun by the turbulence of events beyond our control, knowing only that we are being carried into the infinite sea of eternity.

- In the movie *Traffic,* Michael Douglas' character reminds us that in the war on drugs the so-called enemies may include our own children. How, he wonders, it is even possible to make war against your own children?[i]
- You pull the trowel over the wet cement with the same kind of motion you would use to apply frosting to a freshly baked cake.
- To explain how his murderous hatred for his wife ended up destroying the lives of everyone in his family, Willfred Leland James, a character in Stephen King's novella *1922,* says, "Poison spreads like ink in water."[ii]
- How do I know that my furry fireside friend, Blue, understands when I tell him it's time to go out for a walk? Well, I think that your average dog is about as smart as your average 2-year-old.
- Author Tom Franklin explains how an unexpected event can expose all the hidden secrets of a person's past life in his novel *Crooked Letter, Crooked Letter*: "Time packs new years over old ones but those old years are still in there, like the earliest, tightest rings centering a tree. . . . But then a saw screams in and the tree topples and the circles are stricken by the sun . . . and the stump is laid open for all the world to see."[iii]
- The people at the Family Bank care about each other. And we care about you. When you bank with Family Bank, you're not just customers, you're family.
- God forgives the sinner who repents in the same way that a loving father forgives a prodigal son who returns to the family.
- Animal rights activist: "We did not steal any animals from the lab. We rescued those monkeys because they were the helpless victims of torture."
- Last year, the CEO said we were all on the same team. Then the economy goes south and he wants our suggestions for downsizing. Sort of reminds you of asking for volunteers to play Russian roulette.
- One productive way of thinking about how our minds work is by using the computer model of list processing, as

suggested by Allen Newell. Just like computers, our minds store problems and tasks as lists, and our mind always works on the first thing in a list, the others coming to the fore only after the first is dealt with.[iv]

As the examples illustrate, comparative reasoning can rely on images, comparisons, parables, allegories, fables, models, metaphors, and similes. We can use comparative reasoning to illustrate ideas, to offer interpretations, to make arguments, to give reasons, to explain our thinking, and to simplify concepts. As Mike Wallace did in the video clip, we can use these skills to help ourselves understand new ideas, unfamiliar objects, and abstract concepts. Comparisons have the power to persuade people, to shape expectations, to alter attitudes, and to evoke emotions.

POWERFUL COMPARISONS CONNECT INTELLECT AND EMOTION

In his September 20, 2001 speech to the U.S. Congress former President George W. Bush said, "Al Qaeda is to terrorism what the Mafia is to crime."[v] By comparing al Qaeda to the Mafia, he communicated that al Qaeda was responsible for terrorism on a very large and organized scale, in the same way that the Mafia is responsible for crime on a large and organized scale. In addition, the former president's comparison evoked the same loathing toward al Qaeda that the public feels toward the ruthless, criminal Mafiosi. As a tool for communicating his ideas, Mr. Bush's comparison was powerfully effective, for it touched the American public at both an intellectual and an emotional level. Because they often communicate at the emotional level as well as the intellectual level, comparisons are among the most persuasively powerful devices in our culture.

Knowing that vivid comparisons can move hearts as well as minds, speechwriters strive to associate their ideas with memorable comparisons as these next two examples illustrate.

- A gift to the town's economy, the proposed metro line will ribbon our downtown business district and gracefully glide north to the airport.
- Like a knife thrust into the town's heart, the proposed metro line will sever existing transportation arteries and slice residential neighborhoods apart.

Although neither has supplied much by way of facts and figures, clearly the author of the first supports a proposal to build a metro line from the airport to the central city, while the author of the second opposes the proposal. Who would not want a gift wrapped in a beautiful ribbon? On the other hand, nobody would permit their streets and neighborhoods to be stabbed to death. Well-crafted comparatives, skillfully used, can dispose us for or against people, proposals, and points of view even before we have fully engaged our System-2 reflective judgment. As critical thinkers we must keep our guard up.

Evaluating Comparative Inferences

Comparisons are like a fine set of carpentry tools—you have to know a tool's purpose, or else it will be useless to you. Several factors contribute to the merit of a comparison (like the one in the previous sentence). Before specifying the evaluative criteria more formally, let's first look informally at how we might evaluate a couple of examples.

- "Competition in today's business climate is like war. Companies that have good strategic plans will out-compete their opposition; they will gain market share the way an army gains ground in a battle. Lean, mean, and nimble, they will be ready to attack new opportunities and defend against threats and assaults from all sides. Their loyal troops will do whatever it takes to make the business successful, including doing battle with marketing campaigns and orchestrating superior manufacturing productivity. And in the end, they will prevail. So if you want your company to win out over the competition, hire our consulting firm. We have the know-how to make you a winner."
- "A seagull is like a sailboat. The gull's tail is like the boat's rudder. The gull's body is shaped like the boat's hull. A lot of gulls are white, and so are a lot of sailboats. Gulls often fly in flocks, and sailboats are often seen in bunches, too, called regattas. The gull's feathery wings remind me of the billowing sails. Gulls probably float on the surface of the air the way a sailboat floats on the surface of the water."

The first comparison, "business is like warfare," is the stronger of the two. It is based on several points of comparison that seem both apt and central, specifically the struggle to gain market share, the importance of being able to adapt quickly to changing conditions, and the assets of good communications, efficient manufacturing, and loyalty. The analogy is productive in another way as well, for the maker of the analogy could have extended the comparison by adding comments about corporate espionage and sabotage but did not.

The second comparison is weaker. Yes, the gull's tail functions like a rudder. But the gull's body does not function like a hull; it only looks like a hull—and then, not very much like one, given the legs hanging down. Gulls do not float on the air by displacing their weight in that gaseous medium the way a boat displaces its weight in water. The similarities of color and visual appearance are superficial, not structural or functional. The hull of a sailboat holds up the mast, which lifts and holds the sail. When birds are in flight, the lifting is done by the wings, not the body. The physics of how a wing functions is the opposite of a sail. A sail catches wind and is pushed along. In contrast, the speed of the air passing over the top of a wing, as compared to the speed of the air passing under the wing, creates lift and pulls the wing upward. The physics of flight is not the same as the physics of floating. All in all, it is a rather poor analogy indeed.

DO THE FOUR TESTS OF ACCEPTABILITY APPLY?

The analyses and evaluations offered may appear to stray a bit from the four tests for the worthiness of arguments presented in Chapter 7. Let's apply those four tests to our two examples to see if they are as useful for evaluating comparative reasoning as they are for evaluating inductive and deductive reasoning.

First Test: Are the premises all true? The key premises in these two cases are the sentences that assert the similarities "business is like war" and "a seagull is like a sailboat." Based on the analyses, our first thought when applying this test would be to evaluate "business is like war" as true and "a seagull is like a sailboat" as false. Unfortunately, the words *true* and *false* are not optimal for evaluating a sentence that asserts a comparison. Those two terms offer us only two options when, in fact, our evaluations are more nuanced. Going back to our examples, we would want to say that "business is like war" is *more true* than "a seagull is like a sailboat." But expressions like *more true* or *more false* have no place in the world of logic. In addition, the two (waging war and sailing) are not connected in any way that would permit us to say that one is "more true" than the other. Words like *apt*, *insightful*, *vivid*, *silly*, and *superficial* are better words for evaluating sentences that assert comparisons. As we shall see, we use these insights to come up with more precise criteria for evaluating comparisons than "true" or "false."

Second Test: Are there counterexamples and how difficult is it to imagine them? Given that comparative inferences are inductive, this question helps gauge the logical strength of the analogy. We do not have refined statistical tests to apply to comparative inferences. But we can categorize comparisons as more or less plausible. And, yes, there are counterexamples to consider. Let's look at the stronger of the two analogies. Some businesses form partnerships with other businesses, and some acquire and merge with their competitors by purchasing their stock. Behaviors like these suggest that business is not always like war. Do these observations mean that the analogy is illogical? No, that would be too negative. What this *does* show is that comparative reasoning shows points of dissimilarity as well as points of similarity. We will need to make a more refined judgment about the utility of the points of comparison. We will build this insight into the more refined set of criteria provided in the next section of this chapter.

Third Test: Are the premises relevant to the truth of the conclusion? The conclusion is the assertion about the characteristics of the unfamiliar object (business in the first case and gulls in the second). At first, we may not see how warfare is relevant to understanding business or how boats are relevant to understanding gulls. The burden is on the maker of the analogy to show that the comparison is relevant. In both of our examples, the argument maker offers observations to establish the relevance of the comparison.

Fourth Test: Does the truth of any premise depend on the truth of the conclusion? This can be tricky, because for many of us, business is more familiar than warfare, and gulls or birds in general may be more familiar than boats. But comparative inferences should flow from what we know about war to what we can project to be true about business, and from what we know about boats to what we can project to be true about gulls. Both of our examples have problems with this test. Many businesspeople have never been in combat. Likewise, many people within the general public have no firsthand combat knowledge. Therefore, for many people, the comparison depends more on imagination of what war might be like than on actual warfare experience.

Based on the application of the four tests we developed in Chapter 7, neither comparison establishes that its conclusion is true or justified. But the purpose of comparative reasoning is to illustrate, illuminate, suggest, or hypothesize, rather than to prove that a conclusion is true. Our four tests of acceptability may be a little heavy-handed. Comparative inferences will almost always come up short on those four tests.

Yet some comparisons appear to be stronger and more useful than others. Why is that? Because in some cases, the points of comparison are based on shared functional, structural, central, and essential features. However, in other cases, the points of comparison are based on shared features, but they are unimportant, trivial, superficial, decorative, or happenstance. We'll analyze this generalization in the next section—to come up with five specific criteria to use when evaluating comparative inferences.

FIVE CRITERIA FOR EVALUATING COMPARATIVE REASONING

Why is comparative reasoning so potentially valuable? Its value comes from the possibility that comparative reasoning could lead to new insights, hypotheses, and dimensions as we try to understand something unfamiliar. If the comparison is reasonable, then some salient feature of the more familiar object is also a salient feature of the less familiar object. Evaluation depends on the congruence between the two objects. "Are they alike enough in important ways or not?" *The more pervasive the essential similarities are, the more relevant the comparison is, and therefore the more credibility a conclusion based on those similarities will have.* Comparative inferences, including analogical arguments, are inductive and probabilistic. They draw their power from the perceived relevance and pervasiveness of the fundamental parallelism between the situations or objects being compared. Superior comparative inferences are *familiar*, *simple*, *comprehensive*, *productive*, and *testable*.[vi] Let's break down each of these features in turn.

Familiarity

Suppose that a speaker offers this analogical argument: "Don't put John in charge of buying groceries! That would be like asking Queen Cleopatra to do the laundry." But suppose that the listener has no idea who Queen Cleopatra was. This lack of familiarity with the object of the comparison would quash the analogy like an elephant stepping on a snail. Familiarity is the first criteria for a successful comparative reasoning process. Successful comparisons direct the listener's attention to that which is more familiar. Consider this example:

- A coach trying to teach an 11-year-old how to swing a baseball bat: "The right way to swing a baseball bat is with the same motion you use when you swing a long-handled ax into the trunk of a pine tree."

These days, the number of children who learn to swing a baseball bat is higher than the number who learn to swing a long-handled ax. The coach's comparison fails because the child is probably entirely unfamiliar with ax swinging as the object of comparison. Maybe if the child was at summer camp and the camp counselor was trying to teach about chopping trees, the camp counselor could say, "Swing the ax like you would a baseball bat." This might work, because there is a better chance that the child is familiar with how to swing a baseball bat.

Earlier in this chapter, we looked at the following example about hiring John as the club treasurer.

- You can make John the club's treasurer, if you want. But with the way he manages money doing that would be like skydiving without a parachute.

This comparison works, but not because most of us have ever personally experienced skydiving. It works because most of us have seen people skydiving on television, so we can simulate the process. And we can easily realize that it would be suicidal to skydive without a parachute. The simulation heuristic makes skydiving familiar enough that we can understand the comparison. But for most listeners, it would be far less effective for the argument maker to have made this comment:

- You can make John the club's treasurer if you want to, but if you ask me it would be like ingesting massive quantities of sodium chloride.

The point is the same, but this comparison is less effective because most people are not as familiar with consuming toxic amounts of salt as a means of self-destruction. **Familiarity** is the quality of a comparison that expresses the degree of knowledge the listener has about the object to which the unknown is being compared.

Clichés

Like wearing good clothes to a wedding, comparisons dress up our conversation with memorable images and useful illustrations. At times, however, a given comparison can become so commonplace and overused that, like an old blouse or tie worn too often, it deserves to be retired. Here are a few that are simple, familiar, and, unfortunately, so overused that they have become clichés.

Can you add another five clichés to this list?

like riding a bike	costs an arm and a leg	out on a limb	old as the hills
tastes like chicken	luck of the draw	crazy like a fox	living the dream
fast as lightning	strong as an ox	sharp as a tack	pretty as a picture

Reserving a room online is like buying a book online.

Simplicity

Simplicity, a virtue for comparisons, is a measure of the relative complexity of the comparison. The less complicated—that is, the simpler—the comparison is, the better the comparison. Simpler comparisons are often more readily understood and remembered.

- Today our nation is declaring war on drugs.

The comparison of a policy to a war is simpler, more familiar, and easier to remember, and has more emotional impact than this description of the policy.

- Today I would like to announce a policy of concerted, long-term, resource-intensive, multi-agency interdiction of illegal substances and the associated criminal prosecution of persons found to be importing, manufacturing, distributing, selling, shipping, or possessing those substances.

Using a simple but effectively memorable image of "WAR!" the argument maker can more easily capture the imagination of the listener.

Consider the situation of a young American couple wanting to take a romantic vacation in Italy. Seeking advice about places to go and hotels to stay at, the couple is told, "You'll want to see Venice, Florence, Rome, and the Amalfi Coast. Not to worry, these days making hotel reservations in another country is as easy as buying books through Amazon.com." Suppose that the young couple is familiar with buying books on the Internet at Amazon.com, and because of that familiarity the couple knows that there are several initial steps. They had to establish an account and, in so doing, they had to enter a lot of personal data, such as their address and credit card information. Then they had to search for the book they wanted and wade through the ads and the suggestions, which appeared on their computer screen as they did so. Then they had to navigate through the checkout process. Familiar, yes. And, for this couple it is simple enough too. They have been through the Amazon.com registration and purchasing process successfully.

Comprehensiveness

The process of booking hotel reservations in another country may seem daunting for people who have never done it before. Comparing that process to the process of using Amazon.com

Thinking Critically — Keeping It Simple and Familiar

How are subscribing to podcasts and subscribing to newspapers similar and how are they different? How would you describe subscribing to podcasts to a less media-savvy friend or relative? How is reading a book on a iPad or tablet like reading a paperback you can hold in your hands? How are the two experiences different? How would you explain what it is like to read a book on an iPad or tablet to someone who has never read a book that way?

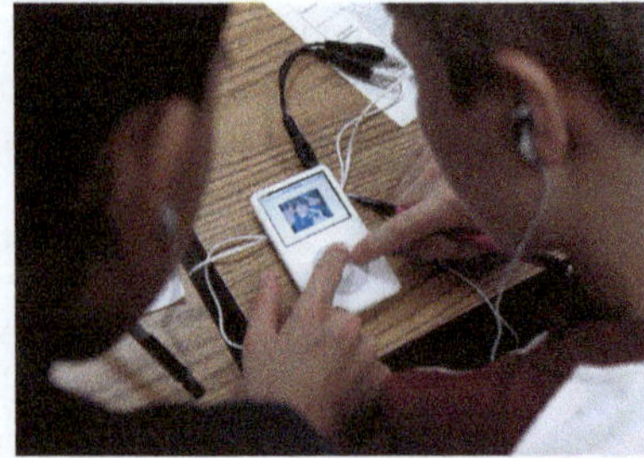

offers another benefit. It provides the young couple with a single comparison that includes all the major steps in the process. The virtue of simplicity must be balanced with the importance of **comprehensiveness**. One comparison is more comprehensive than another to the extent that it captures a greater number of central or essential features. The question is, "Does the comparison capture enough of the critical elements?" Let's revisit the example about the camp counselor teaching someone how to swing a long-handled ax into a tree.

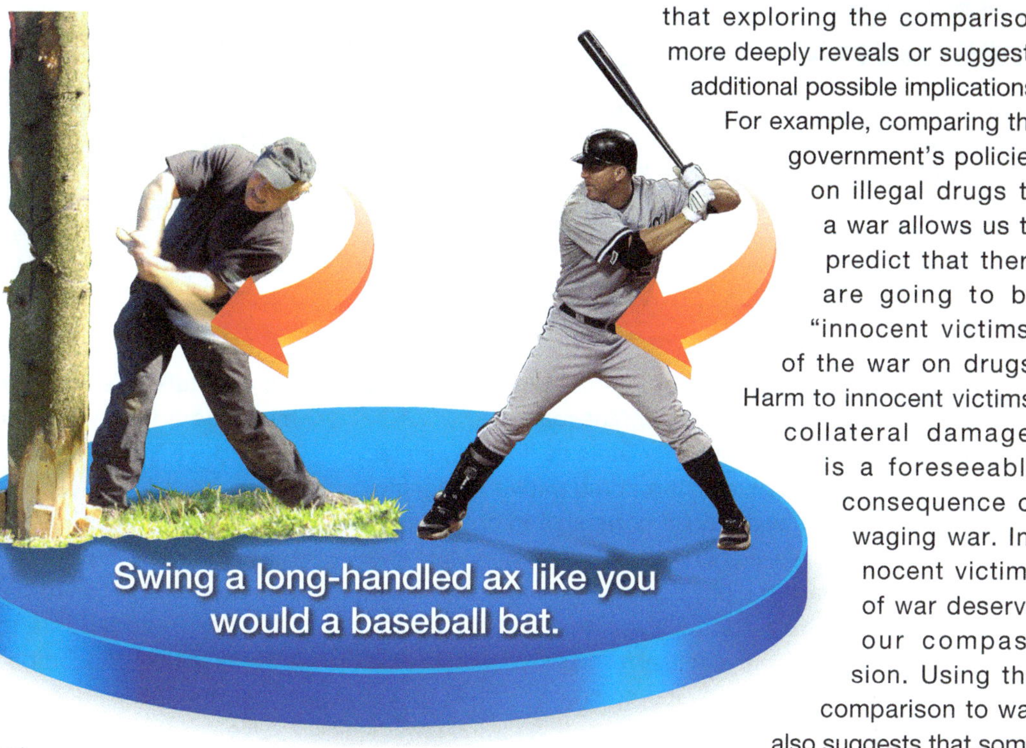

- Counselor to the camper: "Hold the handle like you would a tennis racket. Set your feet apart like you would if you were getting ready to push something heavy. And swing like you would if you were going to hit a nail with a heavy hammer."

Three comparisons were needed because none was comprehensive enough to apply to the whole effort. On the other hand, the counselor might have said:

- "Swing an ax like you swing a baseball bat."

That single comparison covers everything relevant, including how to hold the ax, how to stand, and how to swing.

Suppose that the counselor and the camper are in a gymnasium, not at the campground. And suppose that the camp counselor does not have an ax, but has a broom handle. And suppose instead of a tree, in the gym there is a volleyball net held up by two steel poles. The camp counselor could simulate the skill using the broom handle and pretending that one of the poles is a tree. The counselor might say, "Swing the ax like this." This demonstration would rely on the camper's capacity for comparative thinking, just as do the verbal explanations. This demonstration works as a comparative explanation because the camper can see the grip, the positioning of the feet, and all the relevant movements of the legs, hips, torso, arms, and wrists, even without an ax in hand or a tree in sight. And although swinging a broom handle into a steel pole only simulates swinging an ax into the soft wood of a living pine, the demonstration is a more comprehensive comparison than the words alone are.

Productivity

Productivity is the capacity of a comparison to bring to mind unexpected new ideas that go beyond the points of comparison initially mentioned. Productive comparisons are so rich that exploring the comparison more deeply reveals or suggests additional possible implications. For example, comparing the government's policies on illegal drugs to a war allows us to predict that there are going to be "innocent victims" of the war on drugs. Harm to innocent victims, collateral damage, is a foreseeable consequence of waging war. Innocent victims of war deserve our compassion. Using the comparison to war also suggests that some people are going to be regarded as "the hated enemies." In war, we use all of our military might to destroy the enemy. Wartime propaganda engenders hatred for a nation's enemy. So if we are waging war on drugs, we can expect to commit considerable effort to destroying the hated enemy—whomever that may turn out to be. This, in turn, raises an interesting problem: At times, a productive comparison can suggest something that is both unexpected and troubling. In non-metaphorical wars, the innocent victims are not the hated enemies. But what if one's brother or sister becomes a drug user and then, to support his or her habit, becomes a pusher? In situations like that, the "war on drugs" comparison does not help us understand what has happened or how we should behave toward our brother or sister. Should we have compassion for the person, hate the person, help the person, report the person to the authorities, or what?

Consider the productivity of comparing avatars to real people. In virtual worlds, like the galaxy we can explore through *Second Life*,[vii] I am my avatar. Avatars, however they may look and whatever they may do, tell us something about their creators. Researchers, noting the many points of comparison between avatars and their creators are studying avatar faces and avatar behavior to see whether it is possible to identify the people controlling them. In fact, because identity theft can happen to avatars too, there are proposals that virtual people should get ID checks.[viii] The solution applied in the familiar case to genuine people is being extended, by analogy, to the virtual world. And, why not go further? How about bank accounts and drivers' licenses too? With the integration of GPS technology, accident avoidance radar, infrared linkages, holographic projection systems, and on-board navigation systems, within a few short years we will be seeing avatars driving not

Thinking Critically Side-by-Side Comparison

Make a list of the major steps in the process of registering, locating, and buying a used copy of Agatha Christie's *Murder on the Orient Express* or Stephen King's *The Stand* on eBay. Locate a travel Web site, like Orbitz or Travelocity or one of the many European hotel reservation Web sites. Make a list of the major steps involved in registering, locating, and reserving a room at a three-star hotel in Paris, France. Place the two lists side by side. On the criterion of comprehensiveness, evaluate the comparison that says "reserving a room for a night at a three-star hotel in Paris is as easy as buying a used copy of an Agatha Christie or Stephen King novel on eBay." Were there any major steps in the process of reserving the room that were not part of the process of buying the book?

only along the virtual highways of Internet space, but along the potholed cement thoroughfares of the real world.

How productive is it to think of avatars as if they were real people? How can you extend the comparative reasoning? What else might your avatar need or be able to do? Perhaps climb a mountain or play a sport that you've always wanted to enjoy but did not have the physical strength to accomplish? Perhaps stand watch for you during an anxious time of fretful waiting? How about taking your final exam for you, or committing a crime for you? If your avatar commits a crime, do you go to jail or does your avatar? To explore this further rent the 2009 Bruce Willis sci-fi flick *Surrogates.*

Testability

The "war on drugs" comparison productively suggests consequences, including the unexpected and confusing one we just talked about—that a member of our own family might be both an "innocent victim" and a "hated enemy." Should we treat our addicted siblings or children who become small-time pushers as the hated enemy? We may not approve of what they are doing, and we may seek treatment for them, but most of us are not likely to think of them as "the enemy" or to treat them as such. That the comparison would lead us to do so diminishes its value. It is a weaker comparison because it implies this unacceptable consequence.

We call this criterion testability. **Testability** is the capacity of a comparison to project consequences that have the potential to be shown to be false, inapplicable, or unacceptable. If there is a war on drugs, then our siblings and children might be our hated enemy. For most of us, "hated enemy" does not apply to family members.

Thinking Critically Practice Using the Five Criteria on Two Analogies

Mike Wallace's Analogy

Reconsider the analogy Mike Wallace attempted to draw between warning American soldiers about the ambush and warning a person that he or she was a murderer's intended target. This time, apply the five criteria by asking:

1. How familiar, as compared to the combat zone situation, is the prospect of warning someone about a crime that is about to be perpetrated?
2. Is the comparison simple and straightforward enough for us to understand the basic idea and simulate what it would be like to warn the victim of the crime?
3. What are the critical elements in the two situations and how well are they captured by the comparison?
4. Is the comparison productive enough to provide useful guidance or indications of how we might behave in the unfamiliar combat zone situation?
5. Are there any crucial incongruities that undercut the comparison of the behavior of a civilian journalist in a combat zone to the behavior of journalists at home?

Father Tom's Story about the Man Who Lived by the River

Episode #14, "Take This Sabbath Day," from season 1 of *The West Wing*, first aired on February 9, 2000. In that episode, President Jed Bartlet, played by Martin Sheen, must decide whether or not to commute a murderer's death sentence. He has less than 48 hours to make his decision. The episode features an array of powerfully presented arguments—economic, ethical, political, religious, and legal. Pushed and pulled by those considerations, President Bartlet, a Catholic, eventually calls his wise old friend, a priest, played by Karl Malden, for guidance. The priest tells the president that he reminds him of a man who lived by a river. The man hears a radio report warning that the river was going to flood, possibly trapping the man in his own home. The story is, of course, meant as an analogy to Bartlet's situation. Evaluate that comparison using the standards of familiarity, simplicity, comprehensiveness, productivity, and testability. Access that episode at **www.mythinkinglab.com**.

Watch the **Video** on **mythinkinglab.com**

One tactic for testing a comparison is to ask if there are crucial incongruities between the objects being compared. Going back to an example from the beginning of the chapter, suppose that in response to the idea that stealing experimental animals is really a kind of rescuing of innocent victims, a person objected by saying, "No, under the law, animals are property, not persons. Therefore, they cannot be considered victims in any sense that would excuse you from the legal consequences of your having taken property without authorization." This objection points out that one of the consequences of that comparison does not apply—under the law, animals are property, not persons. This might change someday, but that day is not yet upon us. One of the other examples at the beginning of the chapter compared the CEO's request for downsizing options to Russian roulette. That comparison can be criticized as false in this way: "Not really, because in Russian roulette, you have to hold the pistol up to your own head, but what I plan to do is to recommend eliminating someone else's department, not my own."

The criterion of testability enables us to evaluate the acceptability of a proposed comparison. In general, we should prefer comparisons that have the potential to be testable as false, inapplicable, or unacceptable. Some comparisons simply cannot be falsified in principle. Consider this example: Like having a loving aunt or uncle, each of us has a guardian angel who watches over us, protects us from danger, and helps us know right from wrong. This comparison is familiar, simple, and productive. The many ways that a loving aunt or uncle might help us in our lives suggest a reasonable level of comprehensiveness as well. Unfortunately, there is no way, in principle, to test whether or not the comparison is true, applicable, or appropriate, at least none that these two textbook authors have been able to imagine so far.

SHAPING OUR VIEW OF THE UNIVERSE FOR TWO THOUSAND YEARS

Imagine a wooden wheeled cart, loaded with fresh vegetables, standing still on a flat and level country road. There are two ways to get the cart moving and keep it moving. One is to push it; the other is to pull it. Being very familiar with carts and the effort required for a man to push a cart along muddy country roads, Aristotle, and those influenced by his philosophical writings prior to Copernicus, drew comparative inferences about the movements of the Sun, the Moon, the planets, and the stars. The common sense, late fifteenth-century European view of the universe, which everyone in those days took to be God's design for things, placed Earth firmly in the center. Everyone could see these heavenly bodies moving in great circles above heads. Like the horse cart, they needed to either be pushed or pulled along their paths. A good job for angels, perhaps. How could we see them, if they were being pushed along a hard surface? The answer was that the surface was transparent, a "crystal sphere," totally encompassing Earth. Not familiar with crystal spheres? Think of a giant glass fishbowl. The heavenly object—for example, the Moon—was resting on a crystal sphere. An angel pushed it along, like a man pushing a cart. When we looked up, we saw the moon through the transparent crystal. And we could note the path it had traveled and predict where it was going because the path was a perfect circle. Heavenly motion was perfectly circular. On Earth, however, if you propel a cart along a flat and level path or drop a rock from a tower, you can see that the cart or the rock will move in a straight line. For two thousand years, Aristotle's views dominated our understanding of how the natural universe worked. Every object had its own particular nature,

Copernicus placed the sun at the center, with the earth and planets in elipical orbits—radical, crystal sphere shattering, stuff!

and it always behaved in certain predictable ways because its nature made it act that way.

Circular motion in heaven, straight-line motion on Earth, some Greek who's been dead for 2,500 years or so—who cares? Well, as it turned out, just about everyone of European heritage was affected in one way or another when the Aristotelian comparisons for understanding how the universe worked came undone. And who would have thought that it would be about the motion of Mars and the arc of cannonballs? Go to **www.mythinkinglab.com** and watch this clip from episode 5, "Infinitely Reasonable," of the BBC series *The Day the Universe Changed* to see how the Aristotelian model of the universe was unraveled. The clip begins with the astronomer-priest Copernicus and continues through Galileo and a letter he wrote to a female friend saying that Aristotle, and everything that depended on his view of the universe, was wrong. What do you imagine would be the immediate aftermath once Church authorities realized that the bulwark, upon which rested all European civil and religious power in those days, was wrong? **Watch** the **Video** on **mythinkinglab.com**

The comparative inference used by Aristotle—understanding the cause of motion in the way that you understand how a man pushes or pulls a cart—was a powerfully valuable comparison. It endured for two millennia as a scientific principle. The idea that an object is predictable because of how it is made remains a powerfully valuable idea, although today we do not appeal to an object's "nature." Instead, depending upon what the object is, we talk about its organic composition and function, its chemical structure, its genetic heritage or its physical properties.

THE MANY USES OF COMPARATIVE INFERENCES

Comparative reasoning is widely used in legal argumentation. Attorneys will appeal to precedents when arguing about the interpretation or the applicability of points of law. The basic character of the appeal to precedent is the assertion that the case now in question is so much like the prior case that the ruling that applied there should apply here. That argument depends on how much the new case is analogous to the prior case.

The short version of the appeal to precedent is used whenever we make an argument structured like this: "We had a situation sort of like this before and that time we did such-and-such." As in this example:

- Someone said we should turn off the air conditioner when we are stuck in a traffic jam on a blisteringly hot summer day. We didn't believe it until last summer when our car overheated on a day just like this. We were stuck in traffic and we kept the AC running. Not too smart of us. So I say this time we close that puppy down and just deal with the heat!

Comparative reasoning is used in discussions of ethics, such as to compare cases and infer obligations.

- Making a promise to help your sister rake the leaves is the same as when Daddy made the promise to take you to the zoo. Even though he was tired, Daddy had to keep his promise to you. He took you to the zoo. Remember? So you have to keep your promise to your sister. You go outside now and help her rake the leaves.

In the next example, the genetic similarity of human beings and human stem cells is used as a basis for the policy recommendation that the rights we accord to human beings should be accorded to stem cells.

- Because human stem cells can be cultivated and grown into human organs and potentially cloned into whole persons, we should think of stem cells as potential human beings. We are never justified in taking the life of an innocent human being. So geneticists should not be allowed to experiment with human stem cells.

In business and professional life, arguments like the following are commonplace.

- The CEO's misuse of corporate funds was bad enough, but the way upper management lied to keep the board from learning the truth was far worse. That deceit was a cancer that spread throughout upper management. And, like a cancer, it had to be mercilessly eradicated. Everyone had to go, even if it meant firing some people who never had any idea about what was going on. When you cut out a tumor, you have to remove good cells too, because you can't risk leaving a single bad cell or the cancer will return.

Thinking Critically — Simplicity and Hypothetical Entities

In the video clip from *The Day the Universe Changed*, the writer and presenter, James Burke, notes the application of the simplicity criteria by Copernicus. Can you spot how Copernicus used this criterion? First the Catholic Church was unconcerned about the "mere lines and circles" drawn by the astronomer-priest. Why? How are the hypothetical orbits of Earth and the sun, which Copernicus introduced, similar to other scientific ideas, like "atoms" and "germs"? Hint: Think of objects that exist "theoretically" and are used to explain observations but cannot themselves be observed—angels, for example. Can one test the existence of orbits, atoms, germs, and angels? In each case, why or why not?

MAP > it > OUT

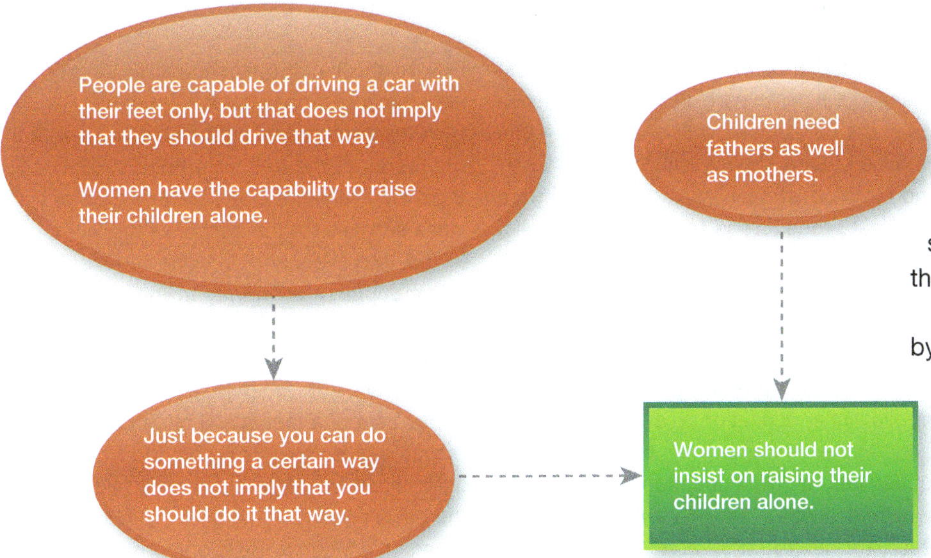

Throughout the chapter we have noted the persuasive power of comparative reasoning. This can be a major benefit of the use of comparative reasoning, and, at the same time it can be a serious liability. In the previous example, if we accept the characterization of the board's deceit as "a cancer," then it follows that we should treat that deceit with the same aggressive therapies. If we were to be persuaded that upper management did not lie to the board but that its failure to notify the board could be explained in some other reasonable way, then using the C word would only inflame passions and impel us toward responses that were disproportional, if not inappropriate.

A comparison's persuasive power depends heavily on the suggested parallelism. For example, consider this argument for the claim, "Women should not insist on raising their children alone."

- Comedian Chris Rock first acknowledged that women were fully capable of raising their children by themselves. Then he stated something almost everyone agrees with, namely that children need fathers. The he reminded the audience at the Apollo Theater that just because a person could do something does not mean that the person should do it. To make his point said that just because people *could* drive a car with their feet, it does not imply that people *should* drive a car with their feet.[ix]

The response Chris Rock received from the audience was loud and enthusiastic. The vivid comparison brought home his point. It was an easy and humorous image for the audience to visualize. And, if raising children alone is like driving your car with your feet, you can see how awkward, clumsy, risky, and foolish that would be.

To balance and complement the work done by the comparison on the negative side of the claim, the comedian bolstered the affirmative aspect of the claim with the observation about children needing fathers. From the other remarks he had made in the same context, it was clear to that audience that Chris Rock was really speaking to both of a child's parents, calling for them to stay in a parental relationship with their child.

The persuasive power of comparisons, analogies, and models derives in part from our natural propensity to use heuristics like simulation, representation, and association, which were explained in Chapter 10 on heuristic thinking. Comparisons are built into the language we use. We say that standard household electric current *flows* through the wiring in our homes and businesses. We know that if the wires are not connected to the sources, the electricity would not flow through them to our computers, lights, and appliances. The comparison is to water flowing through pipes. But if that were true, then electric current should be gushing out of every open socket in the wall. Obviously, there is more to it than what the simple and familiar image of flowing water conveys.

However persuasive they may be, logically speaking, comparative inferences are seldom, if ever, acceptable proofs of the truth of their conclusions. Comparing electricity to flowing water, as useful as that image might be for some purposes, does not prove that electricity can be expected to behave just like flowing water in all contexts. Comparisons are helpful for suggesting initially promising approaches to understanding unfamiliar things. Comparisons can be memorable and compelling. They have the power to shape individual and

Creative Suggestions vs. Solid Proofs

Comparative inferences are best used when making initial and tentative assumptions about new situations. They suggest explanations and hypotheses, which then should be analyzed and tested before being relied upon. Comparisons, termed "models," are relied upon in engineering to imagine possible solutions to structural puzzles. Models, not in a physical but in a conceptual sense, are used in science to suggest promising hypotheses for further testing. While creative comparisons can be richly suggestive of new ideas, comparative inferences are notoriously inadequate to the task of serving as final proofs of those ideas.

Thinking Critically

Group Discussion: The "Free Enterprise System" Model

One of the basic economic beliefs associated with doing business in the free enterprise system is the "law of supply and demand." When the supply of goods or services is greater than the demand, prices go down. When the demand is greater than the supply, prices go up. For example, in times of weather emergencies, merchants selling ordinarily plentiful commodities like food, electric generators, fuel, flashlights, tarps, and fresh water are beset by unquenchable demand because people are trying to stock up. So prices rise. Showing the reverse process, the prices of homes and automobiles dropped during the 2008–2009 recession because consumer demand fell sharply.

Two areas of our economy seem to defy the law of supply and demand. One is public higher education, where tuition and fees do not increase to the level that market demands would sustain. If this fit the free enterprise model, then the consumers—that is, the students—would be charged much more. The second area that does not appear to fit the model is health care. In the case of health care, the consumers, sick or injured people in need of care, do not "shop around" looking for the best deal. Also, the charge for a medical procedure is the same whether a lot of people or only a few people need that service.

First, evaluate the comparison of public higher education to the classic model of the free enterprise system. How can comparing public higher education to a business operating in the free enterprise system help us understand higher education better, and in what ways does the idea not fit? Second, evaluate health care services against the classic model of the free enterprise system. How does comparing the services provided by health care professionals, hospitals, emergency rooms, insurance providers, and pharmaceutical companies to businesses functioning in a free enterprise system help us better understand health care services? How might the comparison cause us problems because it does not fit?

A third enterprise that may or may not fit the model of the free enterprise system is organized religion. Organized religion provides services for the benefit of the faithful, including prayers and religious ceremonies. Many people give money to those organizations and receive those services. In some cases, the money is given voluntarily as contributions; in other cases, the money is in payment of a fee. In still other cases, the money is given voluntarily, but the amount is established by the religious organization on the basis of some metric, like 10 percent of a person's income. Religious organizations need the money they receive in order to pay their employees, rent or buy buildings used for worship, and acquire the equipment and supplies needed to provide services. Evaluate the comparison of organized religion to the free enterprise model and the applicability of the law of supply and demand.

group decisions. Comparisons can be humorous, emotionally evocative, and powerfully motivating. Their simplicity and familiarity often lead to a false sense of their relevance and applicability. The strong critical thinker with a healthy sense of skepticism and a good nose for weak logic will be cautious when comparisons and metaphors, rather than sound arguments, are used as substitutes for solid explanations or as calls to action.

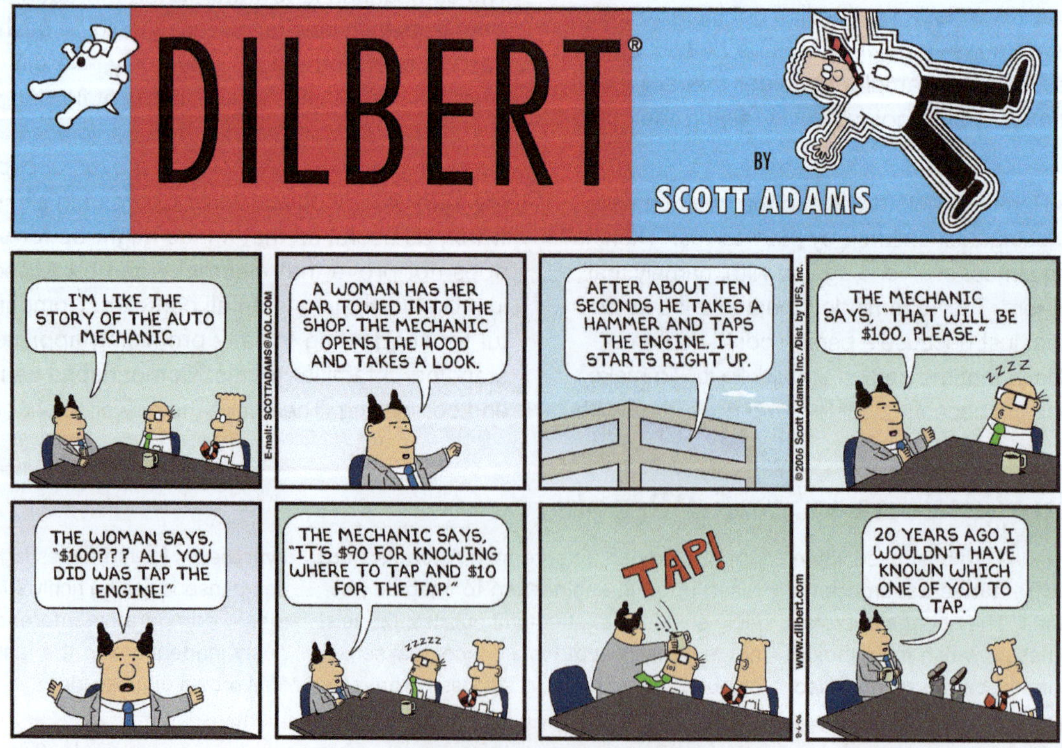

✓ Study and Review on mythinkinglab.com

Comparative reasoning projects aspects of things that are more familiar onto things that are less familiar. Using comparative inferences, we extend our understanding and our expectations about less familiar things by comparing them to things that are more familiar to us. Comparative reasoning is best used to make tentative projections, to propose hypotheses, and, at most, to offer imprecise probabilistic explanations. Although powerfully persuasive because of their appeal to familiar things and their connections to cognitive heuristics, comparisons are risky. Their soundness, logical strength, and relevance can easily be questioned. They are useful for suggesting new directions of inquiry or pointing the way to possible solutions to problems, if the comparison of the current problem to the past one is sufficiently parallel in its essential elements. Although they can captivate our imaginations and move us emotionally, comparative inferences are notoriously weak and unreliable, from a logical point of view. We can evaluate comparative inferences using five criteria: familiarity, simplicity, comprehensiveness, productivity, and testability. The most useful comparisons are those that are based upon structural, functional, central, and essential features in order to *suggest* how we might understand that which is less familiar based on what we know about that which is more familiar.

KEY TERMS

comparative reasoning (or **this-is-like-that thinking**) is the process of using what is more familiar to make interpretations, explanations, or inferences about what is less familiar. (p. 230)

familiarity, in the evaluation of comparisons, is the degree of knowledge the listener has about the object to which the unknown is being compared. (p. 235)

simplicity, in the evaluation of comparisons, is a measure of the relative absence of complexity. (p. 236)

comprehensiveness, in the evaluation of comparisons, is the extent to which a comparison captures a greater number of central or essential features. (p. 237)

productivity is the capacity of a comparison to suggest consequences that go beyond those mentioned in the initial comparison. (p. 237)

testability is the capacity of comparisons to project consequences that have the potential to be shown to be false, inapplicable, or unacceptable. (p. 238)

FIND IT ON MYTHINKINGLAB.COM

- As delicate shade-loving plants wither in direct sunlight, analogies and comparisons, while perhaps beautiful, at times cannot stand the bright analytical light of close logical examination and evaluation. And yet they seem so helpful, at least at first. We invite you to watch the *Ethics in America* video clip that opens this chapter (pp. 229–230). In it, the veteran TV journalist Mike Wallace struggles with the question of warning American troops that the enemy is about to ambush them. Access this remarkable *Ethics in America* segment of the episode "Under Orders Under Fire—Part II" at www.mythinkinglab.com. Start the clip at 30:13, which is where the interlocutor first asks Peter Jennings to consider what he would do if he realized that enemy troops were about to attack a platoon of American soldiers. The clip is 12 minutes long. Watch the Video on mythinkinglab.com

- We found *The West Wing* episode about capital punishment to be terrific, start to finish (p. 238). You can access the culminating highlight of that episode, a conversation between President Bartlet and his old friend, Fr. Tom, played by Karl Malden, at www.mythinkinglab.com. What do you think of the allegorical tale that the wise confessor spins?

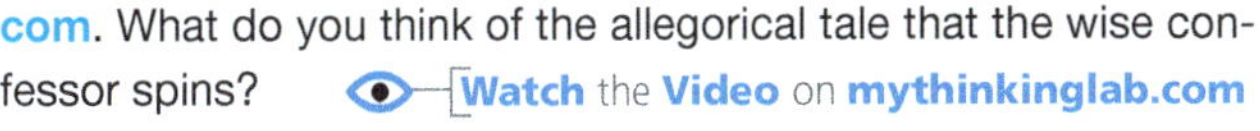
Watch the Video on mythinkinglab.com

- The entire *The Day the Universe Changed* series is worth watching through at least twice. It is perhaps the greatest and most readily understandable digest of the history and philosophy of science ever produced. We invite you to go to www.mythinkinglab.com and view a short clip from the episode where we learn about the power of Aristotle's "like a cart being pushed along its path" analogy (p. 240). This way of explaining why the Sun, Moon, and stars move about in the sky controlled how Europeans thought about the solar system for two millennia. **Watch** the **Video** on **mythinkinglab.com**

- Three video clips are connected to exercises. In one the liberal host of the *Daily Show*, Jon Stewart, admits he was wrong to disagree with conservatives, and particularly Charlton Heston, on gun control. The exercise after that one refers to a clip from the news show 20/20 which shows how journalists weave emotionally charged comparisons into their reports. The final video clip for this chapter found at www.mythinkinglab.com is from an HBO special about the slaughter of animals for human food production. Called *Death on a Factory Farm*, it is the basis for a Bonus Exercise. You'll find that exercise at www.mythinkinglab.com in the supplementary materials for this chapter. Some of the images in this HBO special report can be disturbing for some people.

Watch the **Video** on **mythinkinglab.com**

Exercises

REFLECTIVE LOG: TIME TRAVEL—EVALUATE THE EVALUATIONS

Time travel—the stuff of great science fiction! Is time travel really possible? If the time-space continuum loops back upon itself, like tangled yarn, then perhaps there are places so close together that passages from one point in the string to another point in the string would not be impossibly distant. Consider the following two comparisons. The first is by an advocate of the dynamic view of time, and the second is by an advocate of the static view of time.

Advocate of the dynamic view of time: Like wind rushing by our faces, time whisks from the past to the future, pausing but for the smallest instant in this moment we call the present. The past is unreal and the events it contains are no more. The future is unreal, and the events that will become are not yet. Only the fleeting present—that place where past and future join—is real. And even that reality is lost into the past as quickly as it is conceived. Think, you who flit on life's stage for your one tiny moment of existence—how should you use what precious little time you have?

Advocate of the static view of time: Time doesn't pass; we do. We move through time as if we were driving along an interstate highway. The highway stretches ahead of us and behind us to places we may never visit. We get on the highway at birth and exit at death. We move along, like those in the cars beside us, at a constant rate of speed. So, looking from car to car it seems we are not moving, but looking at the mileposts flashing by, like the weeks and months of our lives; we are steadily going along. Along this highway, there are places that came *before* or *after* or that occurred *simultaneously* with others. The past and the future are real places.

Before reading further, stop for a moment and write your own evaluation of the two comparisons, "time is like the wind" and "time is like an interstate highway."

After entering your own evaluations into your log, read the following two critiques. The first applies to the dynamic view and the second to the static view.

Critic of the dynamic view of time: Your analogies are charming, but your thinking is confused. If only the present is real, how can we measure the *passage of time*? Any measurement must be against some external standard. But do you want to argue that there is some kind of time outside of time? Also, consider the present. According to you, it is the point at which the unreal past touches the unreal future. In that case, it is so infinitesimally tiny as to have no duration in itself. Thus, the present is unreal too. But if time is the accumulation of present moments, you might as well say that time is entirely unreal. There is no past, future, or present.

Critic of the static view of time: You make it sound like all I have to do is make a U-turn and I can go back in time. That's absurd. Also, by your analogy, if I step on the accelerator, I can shoot ahead of the other cars and, in effect, speed myself into the future. That is also absurd. Your problem is that you are thinking of time as analogous to your concept of space. However, our movement in space from one place to another does not imply we can move in time from one present to another.

Evaluate the critics' evaluations. In what respects are the two critiques strong or weak? How might an advocate of each of the two views of time respond reasonably to the criticisms offered? If you disagree with both of the critics or if you agree with both of the critics, then explain what your view of time is. Just for fun: Is time travel possible?

JON STEWART: "I WAS WRONG—CHARLTON HESTON WAS RIGHT"

After the tragic massacre at Columbine High School in 1999, people advocating stricter gun control legislation protested against the National Rifle Association's planned convention in Colorado. They argued that it was disrespectful and insensitive of the NRA to meet so close to the site of such a tragedy. Jon Stewart, host of *The Daily Show*, admitted he was wrong to have supported those protesters since his views would have abridged the Second Amendment rights of law abiding citizens who were members of the NRA. In 2010 others protested the location of a Mosque near Ground Zero using very similar arguments. To see Stewart admit his mistake and to see the comparison of the 1999 arguments with the 2010 arguments watch the opening 9 minutes of the August 19, 2010 *Daily Show*. The sequence is entitled "Extremest Makover Homeland Edition."[x] There are two places in that sequence that Stewart uses comparative reasoning. The first, about 5 minutes in, has to do with hand-lettered highlighted index cards. The second, and more important, begins about 7 minutes and 20 seconds into the sequence, where Stewart invokes the arguments made by Charlton Heston in defense of the NRA's exercise of its First Amendment rights. Stewart says that the 2010 case of a Muslim Community Center is analogous and that Heston's arguments apply now as much as they did more than a decade ago. Evaluate both of the examples of comparative reasoning in the August 19, 2010 *Daily Show* opening sequence.

Visit www.mythinkinglab.com for the link to this episode.

Watch the **Video** on **mythinkinglab.com**

"TICKING TIME BOMBS"

A loving father buys what he believes are new tires and has the family car serviced so his 19-year-old son and some friends can take it on vacation. He gets the phone call all parents dread. There was an accident. His son was killed. The car's "new" tires had sat unsold in the retailer's stockroom for so many years that they were dangerously old. On the highway one exploded causing the driver to lose control. An emotionally gripping comparison leaps to the minds of parents and young people. "That could be my child." "That could be me!" Visit www.mythinkinglab.com for the link to this *20/20* news feature.[xi] Evaluate the commentator's use of comparisons like "ticking time bombs," "museum of death," and "cryptic code." What exactly are the statistics on auto crashes resulting from exploding tires? Why do the automobile manufacturers and the tire manufactures not agree on the recommendation that no tires should be sold as new if they are more than six years old? If selling a product that you know is dangerous is ethically wrong, which is what one of the attorney's in the video asserts, then what ethical responsibilities do retailers have regarding the sale of "aged tires"? Can you think of any comparisons that would support your position with regard to the ethics of that situation?

Watch the **Video** on **mythinkinglab.com**

GROUP EXERCISE: ARE VIRUSES LIVING THINGS?

We tend to compare "germs" to living things, like bugs, that infect our bodies and cause illnesses. Bacteria fit that comparison, except that not all bacteria are harmful. Digestion, for example, relies on bacteria in our mouths and gastrointestinal tracts. Without those bacteria, we would be less well nourished. But what about viruses? Are viruses living organisms? Do they reproduce, move around, and take in nourishment?

In a science textbook, locate a contemporary and scientifically precise definition of "living organism." Determine whether viruses are living organisms. What other comparisons might be useful to help the general public understand what viruses are?

If the question about viruses was not difficult enough once you got into the science, try this one: Are self-replicating nanabots living things? They move, they reproduce, and they performs specific functions once they have identified the correct location and objects upon which to act. What's missing?

THE POLITICS OF HEALTH CARE

Legal challenges to the 2010 Affordable Health Care Act emerged immediately upon passage of the legislation. Sensible arguments and powerful political interests were arrayed on both sides. In late September of 2011 the White House decided to invite the U.S. Supreme Court to rule on the constitutionality of that health care legislation. In a statement explaining the decision, a White House spokesperson compared the provision in the law requiring people to purchase health insurance to provisions in state laws requiring auto owners to purchase auto insurance.[xii] Review the story as presented in four or more separate news sources and identify how each represented the comparative reasoning used by the spokesperson. You might consider the reports provided by FOX, *USA Today*, the *Washington Post*, NPR, or the *New York Times*, for example. After you have analyzed that comparison, evaluate it using the standards presented in this chapter. Can you think of any other arguments based on comparative reasoning either for or against the provision in this legislation that requires the purchase of health care coverage?

Read the Chapter on mythinkinglab.com
Listen to the Chapter Audio on mythinkinglab.com

CHAPTER 13

Ideological Reasoning: Think "Top Down"

HOW can we recognize ideological reasoning?

HOW can we evaluate ideological reasoning?

WHAT are the uses, benefits, and risks of ideological reasoning?

"Only marriage between a man and a woman is valid or recognized in California," read Proposition 8, a ballot initiative that was approved by California voters 52 percent to 48 percent on November 4, 2008. And then the controversy really started to heat up.

Less than six months before that, in June 2008, the California Supreme Court had ruled that same-sex marriage was a fundamental right. More than 8,500 couples sought marriage licenses in the first week the ban was lifted, which was "more than two and a half times an average June week," reported the *Los Angeles Times*.[i] The California court's decision and the thousands of marriages it permitted deeply offended and angered religious conservatives who believed that marriage could only be a sacred bond between a man and a woman. The Alliance Defense Fund, a consortium of religiously conservative attorneys, drafted Proposition 8.[ii] At first, support for the proposition lagged far behind in the polls. But as the election approached, the movement gained momentum. In the media, in churches, in civic clubs, and on street corners throughout the state, backers and opponents presented their cases to the voting public. An unprecedented $83 million was raised by backers and opponents of Proposition 8, the largest amount ever for a battle over a single proposition in California history. And it isn't over yet! Not in California, not nationally.

"Top-Down" Thinking: Recognizing Ideological Reasoning

How divisive is the issue of gay marriage? After California's Proposition 8 passed in November 2008, supporters of the ban were delighted that their efforts had prevailed. But in the week after the election, angry opponents of Prop 8 marched in protest of the outcome in Los Angeles, San Francisco, Sacramento, San Diego, and other California cities. Immediately, legal challenges were filed with the California Supreme Court. One case requested that the court invalidate the same-sex marriages that had taken place between June 17 and Election Day. Another case asked the court to invalidate Proposition 8 itself. In August 2010 the proposition was ruled unconstitutional in California.[iii] Then the authority of the judge who made that ruling was contested on the grounds that he was gay.[iv] His ruling was upheld in June 2011.[v] This cleared the way for the case to move to the next level of appeal, but California's Governor Brown and Attorney General Harris decided not to appeal the decision. In effect they refused to defend Proposition 8. Angry and frustrated, the proponents of Proposition 8 appealed to the California Supreme Court for legal standing, which would enable them to act on behalf of the people of the State of California. Barring any delays, a ruling by the Court was made in December 2011.[vi]

While all the legal maneuvering and appeals in California run their course, the basic arguments for and against legislation banning or permitting gay marriage are essentially the same in 2012 as they were in the 1996, 2000, 2004, and 2008 election cycles. They are being repeated vigorously as gay marriage ballot initiatives reach voters in Maine, Minnesota, and Oregon in the 2012 cycle. Strategists for both major parties see gay marriage as a winning wedge issue for their candidate's presidential aspirations in November 2012.[vii] In as many as 10 states the gay marriage issue might bring out enough voters for one side or the other to determine the outcome of that state's presidential contest. With electoral votes and potentially the White House in the balance, the gay marriage issue is far from resolved.[viii]

For an analysis of the legal issues by CNN commentator and civil rights attorney Avery Friedman, go to **www.mythinkinglab.com**. Friedman frames the issue as a conflict of rights. On the one hand, there is the *right of the people of the state* to pass amendments to their state constitution. On the other hand, there is the *right of individuals* to marry the person whom they choose. If the court views the individual's right to marry the person of his or her choice as an "inalienable" right, then the court will reject Proposition 8. Inalienable rights cannot be stripped away, even by majority vote. But if the court determines that same-sex marriage is not an inalienable right, then Proposition 8 will stand, because of the right of the majority to amend the Constitution of the State of California. We can map out the court's decision, as envisioned by Friedman, this way:

Friedman's arguments begin with the idea that both sides in this issue have certain rights. This is an important first

Map the Concepts on mythinkinglab.com

MAP > it > OUT 1

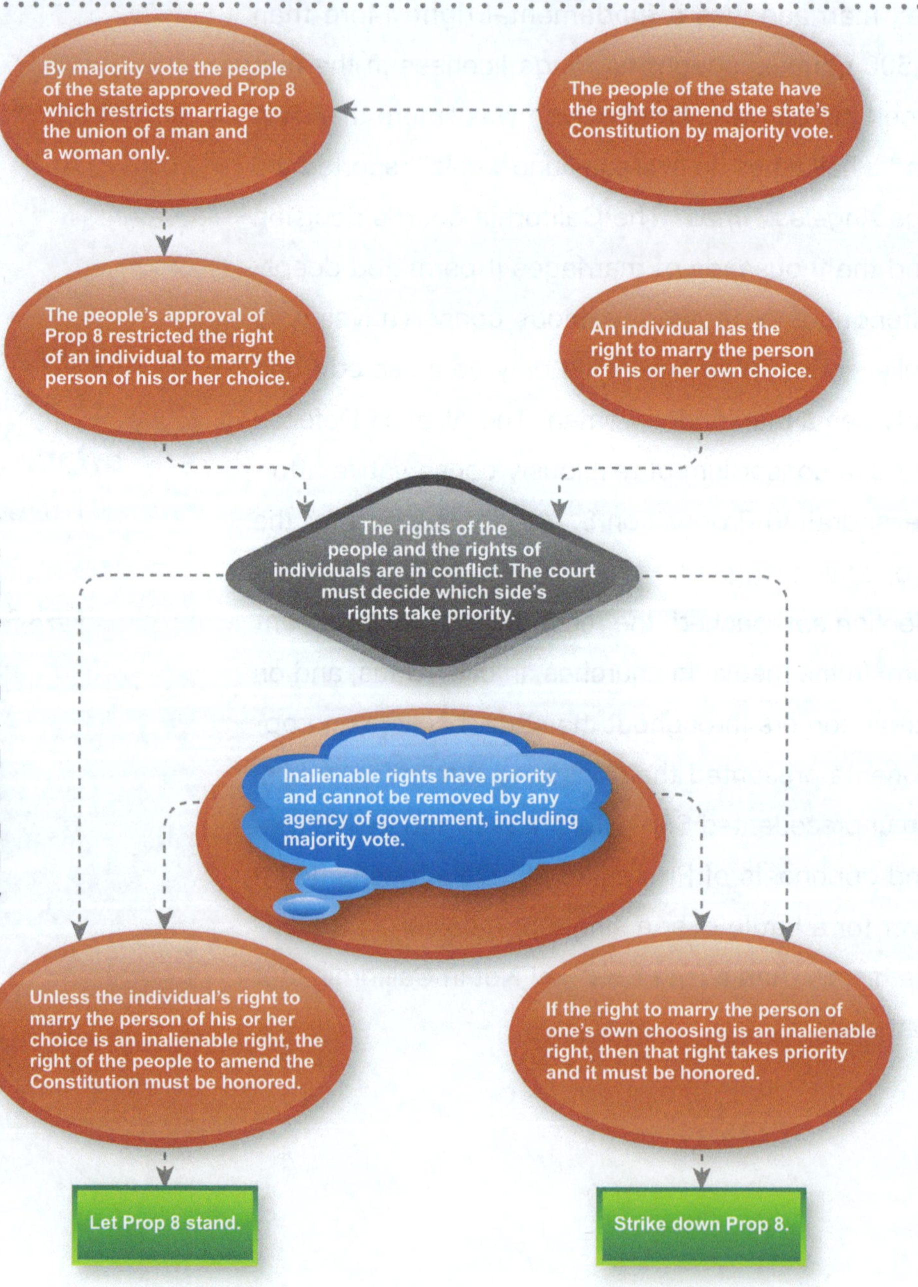

principle, for ascribing a right to a person implies that others cannot bar the person from exercising that right. The freedom to exercise one's rights is a core value in our society. Whenever the rights of different people come into conflict, it is necessary to consider which rights take priority. To help resolve the matter, Friedman suggests that the court will consider another high-level first principle, namely that inalienable rights cannot be removed from a person by any agency of government, including by majority vote. This is one of the basic principles of the American democratic system; it is affirmed in our Declaration of Independence. From these two broad and powerful absolutes ideals ("honor all rights" and "give priority to inalienable rights"), Friedman reasons down to the specific case at hand. If X is an inalienable right, then X cannot be removed by majority vote.

Is a single-parent family worse for children than a two-parent family?

Friedman's analysis is a model of **ideological reasoning** or **top-down thinking**. And that powerful mode of human reasoning is the focus of this chapter. Ideological reasoning begins, as illustrated by the previous arguments, with abstract generalizations and proceeds to apply these initial principles to specific situations.

Ideological reasoning is an important and widely used way of thinking. It offers many benefits, such as in the practice of law. This mode of reasoning comes into play whenever religion, ethics, politics, rules, regulations, or policy matters are the focus of concern. As we saw in the argument map on page 248 discussing Proposition 8, both sides in the same-sex marriage debate use ideological reasoning when making their respective cases in the courts. Lawyers for one side argue that the ideals associated with personal liberty and civil rights imply that same-sex marriage should be permitted. Lawyers for the other side argue that our democratic ideals imply that the majority's right to pass laws and constitutional amendments takes priority. Other people approach this question of same-sex marriage with their religious ideals in mind, or from a perspective based on fundamental beliefs about the purpose of marriage. Here is another example of an argument, as reported by CNN, which employs ideological reasoning:

- Miles McPherson, pastor of the Rock Church in San Diego, said the court "did the right thing." Voters in 28 other states have approved constitutional bans on same-sex marriages, and none has been rejected, he said. "God didn't create the family that way," McPherson said. "You can't have a family with a mother and a mother, because [children] need a mother and a father to nurture their personality and their character.[ix]

A short time ago the Evangelical Lutheran Church of America decided to allow congregations to support non-celibate same-sex relationships among their members and to allow individuals in same-sex relationships to assume positions as active members of the clergy. Here are two arguments, both of which begin from a religious ideology, the first in opposition to the decision, and the second in support:

- "Brothers and sisters, I ask you, before you dig yourselves deeper into this hole, if you are so absolutely certain that these behaviors are not sinful that you are willing to place yourselves and this church at the spiritual risk that comes from encouraging sin," said the Rev. Steven Frock of the Western Iowa Synod.
- Among those on the other side was Alan Wold of the Northern Illinois Synod. "If according to some I am going to be in error for supporting this . . . Let me err on the side of mercy, grace, justice, and love of neighbor. Let me err on the side of gospel, which makes all things new."[x]

If being parented by two adults is good for children, would having three parenting adults be even better?

Thinking Critically The Media and Politically Engendered Cynicism

One favorite tactic of politicians and ideologues is to try to assert that the media are biased. This way, if the person likes how he or she was treated in a certain news story, then ho-hum, that's how it should be. But if the person does not like a story, then the person can whine "See, I told you so. Look how I was misrepresented by the biased media."

Whatever the advantage or disadvantage to the individual, the net result is that the public's quotient of general cynicism increases. We've heard it all before. We tune out, disengage, decide it's all noise and that none of it makes any difference. The tragedy is that public cynicism undercuts reasoned public discourse and erodes a democracy.

The "outsider" political strategy also feeds public cynicism. Every self-styled "outsider" candidate claims that she or he will end the political finger-pointing and governmental gridlock that all Americans find so debilitating. The outsider paints the incumbents as incompetent or worse. But, if elected, the outsider becomes the incumbent whom the next outsider attacks the same way. The cumulative impact of all this negativity on the voting public is cynicism about the political process, apathy about voting, and reluctance to participate in government service. Why join an outfit everyone is criticizing? If the American public is told often enough that everything about government is messed up, some might just come to believe it. Of course, this is not what any of the candidates want. Yet it is the predictable result of the aggregation of each of their individual self-interested political strategies.

We authors are not cynics about the media, about politics or about government service. We want our democracy to flourish, our media to be trustworthy, and our public servants to be appreciated. There are many positive examples of exemplary public service by elected officials and heroic news reporting by brave and committed journalists. We see the power of the media to move hearts and minds when Americans respond to the victims of storms, tsunamis, earthquakes and wildfires. Would we have seen an "Arab Spring" without the social networking of individual news posts and grass roots Web sites? Would we have known about the protests in Libya, Egypt, and Syria without the main stream media reporting on the protests? Arguably the most significant social-political-religious shift in the Muslim world during the past 40 years would not have happened except for the media. It is difficult to be cynical when tyrannical governments topple because otherwise compliant citizens suddenly take to the streets by the tens of thousands, knowingly risking assaults and attacks by their own police and military in order to voice their protest.

We often hear that news coverage of ideologically controversial events is biased and slanted, rather than objective and fair-minded. People accuse news organizations of pandering, sensationalizing, and confusing hype and entertainment for solid reporting. And occasionally those accusations are true. Back in the day when there were only three national television networks, TV news departments could operate at a loss because ABC, NBC, and CBS made money from the other shows they produced. Entertainment revenues covered the expensive newsroom operations. Today, networks like CNN do not produce dramas, sitcoms, game shows, and variety shows. They cannot sell commercial time using entertainment programming. To survive, news networks need to find sponsors who will advertise on news shows. And, given that many advertisers do not want to be associated with political or ideological positions that they do not endorse, how can a news network, such as CNN, FOX News, MSNBC, or Current, survive economically without positioning itself either to the left or to the right of the political spectrum?

Question for discussion: Is today's glorious abundance of social and mainstream media—including television, print, Web, and social networking—a net benefit for reasoned public discourse and a flourishing democracy, or a net liability? If you could improve media coverage to make it more objective without suppressing free speech, what policies would you put in place?

Ideologically based reasoning, exemplified by both sides in this heated controversy over same-sex marriages, is pervasive and important in human affairs. We use it to make inferences and to explain our point of view on specific issues of the day. As strong critical thinkers, we must understand how it works, what its uses are, and what its potential benefits and risks are. Above all, we must learn to appreciate ideological reasoning for what it can achieve and, at the same time, be able to apply it and evaluate it objectively and fair-mindedly. Before we look at its evaluation and applications, both reasonable and unreasonable, we must learn to recognize ideological reasoning so we can distinguish it from comparative reasoning and from empirical reasoning. To help us be able to recognize ideological reasoning, we will first look briefly at three more sets of examples and then, based on the examples we've developed, we will be able to identify three distinguishing characteristics of ideological reasoning.

EXAMPLES OF IDEOLOGICAL REASONING

Consider the following pairs of ideological arguments. Beginning with broad axiom-like first principles and generalizations, each speaker reasons to specific applications. As is often the case with opposing ideological positions, there is precious little room for compromise.

Immigration Policy

1(a) By definition, if a person enters this country illegally, that person is breaking the law. All lawbreakers are criminals. Criminals should be prosecuted. I support legislation that is tough on crime. That is why I support a Constitutional amendment that requires the incarceration and deportation of all illegal immigrants.

1(b) Government policies and laws that destroy the family unit are bad. The family is sacred, and it is fundamental to our American way of life. That is why I oppose the Constitutional amendment, which would rip a family apart by deporting a parent, or even a child, if the person is not in this country legally.

God's Existence

2(a) The space-time continuum extends outward, forward, and backward infinitely from the present-here-and-now moment. It follows that there can be no reality whatsoever other than the universe, for there can be no time nor space outside the infinite vastness that is the space-time universe. Ergo, there is no God sitting outside our naturally infinite time-space continuum. Nor is there any such place as Heaven or Hell, nor any time when we shall receive eternal happiness or eternal pain. There is no place outside space nor any time after the end of time.

2(b) Every natural thing that exists today—the matter and energy that is this universe, this galaxy, this solar system, this planet, all the animals and plants, each one of us—every natural thing comes from prior natural causes. We would not exist were it not for our parents, for example. If we could go back in time, we would never find anything that came into existence on its own without a prior cause. Given that the natural world exists, it follows that something had to get this whole huge chain of causes going. Something had to set it all in motion. And that something had to be outside of the natural universe, for without a force outside nature, the whole long causal process would never have begun. Thus that first creative mover had to be supernatural. We call that First Cause by the name "God." Ergo, God exists.

What would the world have been like if God had created Eve first?

Is this a dad or a criminal? Blocking illegals vs. supporting families—exactly how should we frame the immigration policy question?

Human Nature

3(a) People are fundamentally good. Most people will keep their word and to try to do what is right for their fellow human beings most of the time. It is wrong to take away our freedom. This is why I support those who would maximize individual liberties and reduce the number of bureaucratic rules and regulations that legislators and administrators are constantly trying to impose on our personal and commercial interactions.

3(b) People are fundamentally bad. If they can get away with something they will; they can be counted on to exploit every advantage in an effort to advance their own interests. This is why we need tougher laws and detailed regulation of commerce. More individual liberty will lead only to greater societal disintegration and the inevitable exploitation of the poor by those who have the means to do so.

In the first pair of arguments about immigration policy, one speaker appeals to the value of enforcing our laws while the other appeals to the value of the family. Each comes up with a different conclusion. The first would deport people who entered the country illegally, without reference to the fact that a given person might be the parent or the child of someone else who is in the country legally. The second would attend to that family relationship and not deport the person. Starting the policy discussion from those two opposing positions will make a legislative compromise a challenge to negotiate. On the other hand, perhaps both speakers share both values. A first step might be agreeing that enforcing the laws and protecting families are both core commitments.

The second pair of arguments takes on a challenge that many regard as intellectually impossible: proving beyond a doubt either that God does exist or that God does not exist. Theological conceptualizations of God are not static; they have changed throughout human history and from culture to culture. So have our scientific conceptualizations and theories about the nature of the universe. Thus, in different historical eras and in different cultures, we may or may not find people making arguments for or against the existence of God or gods, as conceived of in those times and places. The Judeo-Christian monotheistic view of the universe dominated European culture for centuries. From that cultural perspective, many philosophers proposed arguments for God's existence. One question this pair of arguments raises for the critical thinker is "To what extent does or should our understanding of the universe influence our theological ideas?"

The arguments in the third pair both begin with a core belief about human nature. One says human nature is fundamentally good, another that it is fundamentally bad. The debate about our fundamental moral character goes back millennia. Are we the innocent creatures originally designed for life in a Garden of Eden, or are we self-indulgent brutes never more than the collapse of a government away from barbarism? The truth is probably some place between the two extremes. The issue is not likely to be resolved any time soon. And although there are anecdotes and historical examples, which might be cited to support both sides of that dispute, it is difficult to know when, how, or whether it can ever be fully resolved. But notice that, at the purely ideological level, one's stance on this question tends to propel one toward specific applications. If we're basically good, then trust us and give us more freedom. If we're basically bad, then protect us from each other with more governmental or religious controls on our behavior. Ideological reasoning, even about ideas that cannot be resolved, has important consequences for policies and practices that profoundly affect our lives.

How do our untested beliefs about human nature affect our behavior toward others?

THREE FEATURES OF IDEOLOGICAL REASONING

There are three distinguishing features of ideological reasoning: (1) It is deductive in character; (2) the ideological premises are axiomatic; and (3) the argument maker takes the ideology to be true more or less on faith. Before unpacking each of the three, we need to take note of the word "ideological." The root of *ideological* is "idea." The concept behind our use here of ideological as applied to reasoning is that the reasoning begins with ideas that express concepts, opinions, beliefs, or principles. The contrast would be reasoning that begins with descriptions of events, observations, or experiences. Our use of the term *ideological* is meant to be value-neutral. In other words, thinking is neither good nor bad simply because it is ideological as we are using the term here. Some people hear "ideological" or "ideology" and associate negative connotations with those words. And there is no question that some specific ideologies are quite dangerous. But *ideological thinking*, as we use the term, is not about a specific good or bad ideology. Rather, it refers to the way in which arguments are made beginning with general ideas, such as concepts, opinions, beliefs or principles, and moving down from these abstractions to their specific applications.

Ideological Reasoning Is Deductive in Character

For the most part, the conclusions of ideological arguments are presented as certainties. Qualifiers like *probably*, *maybe*, or *perhaps* are seldom, if ever, found in ideological arguments. There might be a citation of a book, author, or other "authoritative" source. There will seldom be references to correlations, data, experimentation, or systematic investigation unless those references support the author's preconceived ideas. Unlike courageous truth-seekers, ideologues look for facts that support their points of view, not facts that disagree. If research is cited, an example used, or a comparison made,

These images of Adam and Eve and the Vietnam War depict very different sides of human behavior. Are we all potentially devoted lovers or brutal warriors—or both? Explain why.

the purpose is anecdotal or illustrative, not evidentiary. For example, "Same-sex couples do not make good parents. Let me tell you about the sad case of little so-and-so who had two mommies, until they wanted to get a divorce."

Not all deductive reasoning is ideological. To categorize ideological reasoning as deductive is like categorizing trees as plants. Doing so does not imply that all plants are trees. Describing ideological reasoning as deductive focuses on the certainty with which ideological thinkers endow their conclusions. In Chapter 2 we defined *deductive* as "drawing an inference in which it appears that the conclusion cannot possibly be false if all of the premises are true." Ideological arguments fit that definition. Ideological thinkers have a strong sense that their conclusions must be true because their arguments move from general ideas to specific applications. If the general ideas are true, then their specific application must be true, too. We talked about this kind of deductive argument in Chapter 8's section "Applying a Generalization." There are other kinds of deductive arguments that have nothing to do with "general-to-specific," as the examples and discussions in Chapters 2 and 8 illustrate. In fact, our definition of deductive reasoning, cited above, never mentions "general" or "specific." The observations in this chapter about ideological reasoning, particularly about its benefits and risks, do not apply to all deductive arguments. There are many kinds of deductive arguments that are not ideological.

Ideological Premises Are Axiomatic

As in high school plane geometry, axioms are simply a set of *first principles, starting points, or assumptions*. For example, two straight lines on a plane can intersect at one and only one point. From the axioms we proved that other statements (theorems) were true. In ideological reasoning the key assumptions, whether spoken or unspoken, are those that embody a community's or individual's deeply held beliefs and core values. These, for that person and that community, are axiomatic. The ideas, concepts, principles, or beliefs that ideological thinkers use to initiate their arguments represent the axioms from which other ideas or specific applications follow, much like theorems in geometry. We saw absolute convictions, including those listed here, in the previous examples:

- Everyone should have the right to marry the person whom he or she chooses.
- God intended that marriage should be between a man and a woman.
- All lawbreakers are criminals.
- The family is sacred.
- The space-time continuum extends outward, forward, and backward infinitely.
- Every natural thing that exists today comes from prior natural causes.
- People are fundamentally good.
- People are fundamentally bad.

Ideological Reasoning or "Top-Down Thinking"

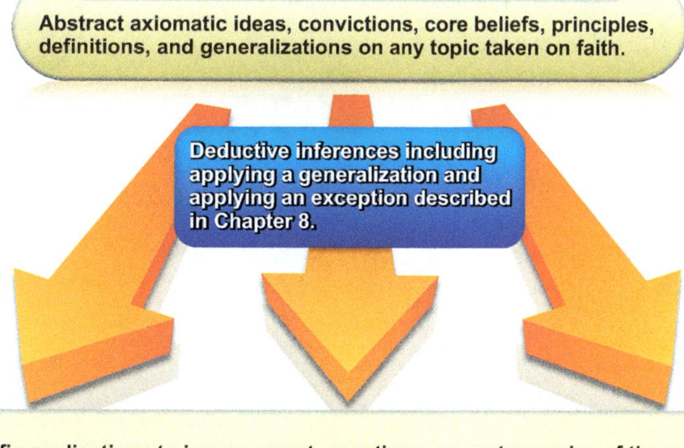

Metaphysical Claims

The term *metaphysical* refers to assertions that are regarded as being true or false, independent of physical facts or circumstances. A claim is metaphysical if there is no conceivable evidence that could establish whether the claim was true or false. The claims might be true, they might be false, or they may be nonsensical. But whatever they are, scientific inquiry cannot confirm or disconfirm them. The eight example claims in the "Ideological Premises Are Axiomatic" section below are all metaphysical in this sense of the word. One of them, "All lawbreakers are criminals," appears to be a tautology.[xi]

It may be impossible given the technology or the resources at hand in a given time or place to confirm or disconfirm a given claim, but those kinds of practical limitations alone do not make a claim metaphysical. For example, at one point it was technologically impossible to confirm or disconfirm the claim, "There was water on Mars." But today we have the technology and the resources to gather evidence to evaluate that claim. By contrast, there is no conceivable way, even if we had the technology and the funding, to confirm or to disconfirm a claim like "Pet cats have the same rights as pet angelfish." Some may wish to argue that the claim is true, but such an argument would depend on another metaphysical claim, perhaps, "All pet animals have the same rights." That argument would then qualify as ideological reasoning. And when we evaluate that argument, we would have problems with the very first test, the Test of the Truthfulness of the Premises, because we cannot know whether the axiomatic first principle about the equality of the rights of all species of pets is itself true.

The Argument Maker Takes the Ideological Absolutes on Faith

To the person or the community making an ideological argument, the first principles are so profoundly obvious that they require no demonstration. Ideological thinkers do not require or expect independent scientific confirmation of their first principles. Ideological reasoning begins with the conviction that the axiomatic first principles express good ideals and true beliefs. Similarly, ideological thinkers consistently regard their absolutes as immune from disconfirmation. Evidence scientifically gathered cannot, in principle, demonstrate to the argument maker that these absolutes are mistaken. Recall in our discussion about evaluating claims, back in Chapter 6, when we talked about the strategies of confirmation or disconfirmation as two independent ways to evaluate a claim. We might, for example, ask a person who believes that people are fundamentally good, "What would it take to convince you that you are wrong about that?" If the opinion is held by that person as a matter of faith, then the person would probably reply quite honestly, "Nothing. You could never convince me otherwise." We would expect the same reply from a person who holds as a matter of faith that people are fundamentally bad. The same holds for people who believe any of the other six statements in our list as matters of personal faith.

Because the argument maker sees the truth of his or her own ideology as self-evident, that person might at times become impatient, frustrated, or even angry with a listener who disagrees. A listener who cannot see the truth of those axiomatic first principles may appear to the argument maker to be uneducated, unintelligent, or perhaps even malevolent. This would be an unfair assumption on the part of the argument maker, of course.

Consider what we learned in Chapter 11 on reflective thinking about how dominance structuring gives us confidence to act on our choices and convictions. Once we realize that axiomatic convictions are held to be true independent of potential confirmation or disconfirmation, it is easier to understand how powerfully motivating they can be. In the grip of unquestioned axiomatic beliefs any community might readily become convinced that its particular view of the world is right and every other view is wrong. So powerful can a community's worldview be that some within that community are moved to become martyrs or warriors. They are willing to make the ultimate sacrifice to protect and defend their community's worldview.

"Do unto others as you would have others do unto you."

Thinking Critically — Assessing Our Convictions

All of us have beliefs that we hold with such conviction that they might be considered "immune" from being proven wrong, at least in our own minds. But a strong conviction might still be mistaken. Strong critical thinkers strive to protect themselves from the error of being strongly committed to mistaken beliefs. Critical thinkers ask themselves what evidence or arguments might be developed that should lead reasonable and fair-minded people to realize that one or another of their strongly held opinions is mistaken. Or they ask what possible life experience might come along to dislodge the dominance structuring that they have built in their minds to prop up a mistaken belief. This exercise invites you to ask yourself these same questions relative to your beliefs about each of the statements listed below. Some of the statements address serious topics; others address matters that may not be of great concern to you. But, whether the issue is profound or trivial, we can find ourselves holding beliefs with unwarranted conviction. And that is something that strong critical thinkers seek to avoid. This exercise unfolds in five steps.

Step 1: Mark "True," "False," or "Uncertain" by each statement below to reflect your current opinion about each.

1 Same-sex couples make excellent parents.

2 America is the greatest nation in the world.

3 Freedom is a fundamental right.

4 Every human being has a soul.

5 Every child deserves a high-quality free education.

6 The good of the many is more important than the good of the one.

7 Cheating on an exam is unethical.

8 Pets are people, too.

9 Children should honor and respect their parents.

10 Lazy people don't deserve handouts.

11 You should never wear a polka dot tie with a Hawaiian shirt.

12 Promises are meant to be kept.

13 Socialism is bad.

14 Geminis can't make decisions.

15 Cabernet goes better with beef than with fish.

16 Poker, as in Texas Hold'em, is not a sport.

Poker, as in Texas Hold'em, is not a sport.

17 Ronald Reagan was one of the five best presidents in U.S. history.

18 Our nation has an obligation to stop ethnic cleansing wherever it might happen.

19 Democracy is the best form of government.

20 God is love.

21 Humans, like other animals, are simply elements in the natural world.[xii]

22 Generosity of spirit engenders generosity in return.

23 The term *person* or *persons* includes every human being from the moment of fertilization, cloning or the functional equivalent thereof.[xiii]

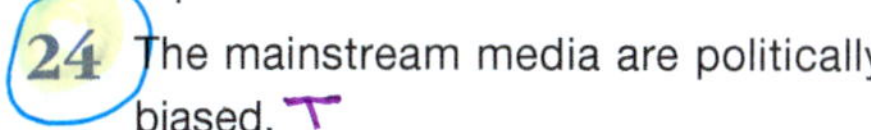

24 The mainstream media are politically biased.

25 Conscientious stupidity is more debilitating to a democracy than public cynicism.

Step 2: Having asserted your opinion about each statement, reflect on the risks associated with dominance structuring and create some mental space for yourself so that you can complete this exercise with your habits of truth-seeking, open-mindedness, and objectivity fully engaged.

Step 3: Looking only at the ones you marked "True," write down what evidence or arguments you would accept as proof that each statement is *false*. If no possible evidence or argument could persuade you that the statement is false, is there any experience you could imagine that would lead you to abandon your commitment to the truth of that statement?

Step 4: Looking only at those that you marked "False," write down what evidence or arguments you would accept as proof that each statement is *true*. If no possible evidence or argument could persuade you that the statement is true, is there any experience you could imagine that would lead you to abandon your commitment to the falsehood of that statement?

Step 5: Looking now only at the statements that you marked "Uncertain," write down the process you could use to gather information and make an informed, fair-minded, and reasoned judgment about what to believe with regard to the truth or falsity of that statement. That is, how would you use your critical thinking skills and habits of mind to make that purposeful reflective judgment?

Our level of faith and conviction is no measure of the truth of the beliefs we hold so dear. Our devotion to a cause is no measure of the worthiness of the values for which we may be prepared to die. We might be tragically mistaken, believing something that is not true, prizing something that is not worthy. Aristotle and the people of ancient Greece believed that slavery was an ethically acceptable practice. The economics of ancient Rome depended on slave labor as a given. Sending her mighty legions to conquer and enslave others was righteous and self-evidently reasonable. Slavery was accepted as part of the

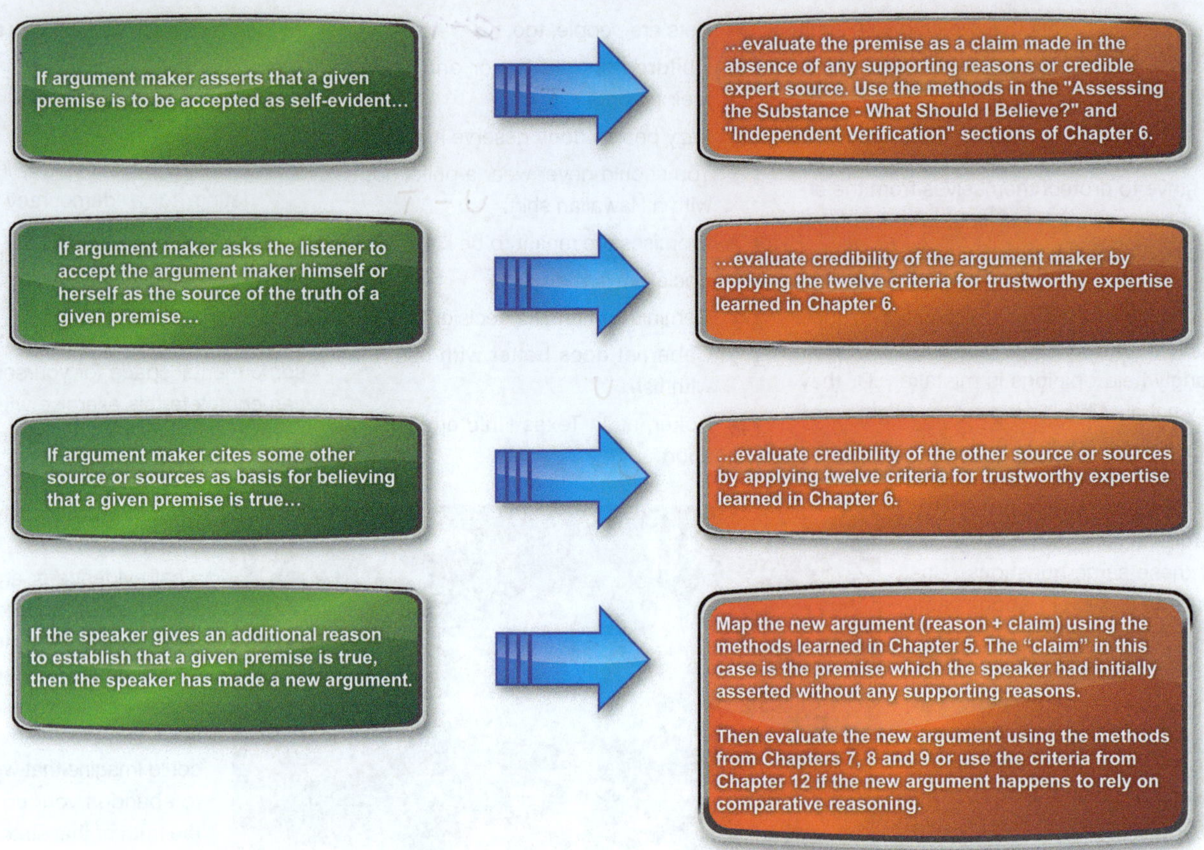

cultural fabric of several of the original 13 colonies that formed the United States. There were men and women of those times and places who were as convinced of the rightness of slavery as we, today, are convinced that it is wrong. By no means are we advocating relativism in this matter. Recall the "Levels of Thinking and Knowing" chart in the section on cognitive development in Chapter 6. There we said that "Truth-Seekers" and "Sages" were at higher and more sophisticated stages of intellectual development than "Relativists." To move beyond relativism, we need to expand the domain of critical thinking by courageously and objectively examining those beliefs that we hold as articles of faith. Perhaps some of the things that we hold to be true and righteous are as wrongheaded as slavery. That we believe them does not make them true.

As authors of a text book on critical thinking, we realize the importance of applying the critical thinking skill of self-regulation, guided by the habit of truth-seeking and a healthy sense of skepticism to ourselves as well. Yes, we are concerned to help you realize that there are pitfalls associated with unwittingly accepting any ideology as if it were immune from well-reasoned examination and thoughtful evaluation. But that same advice cuts both ways. As the authors we must ask ourselves, are we so blind to our own wrongheadedness on some issue—be it political, religious, social, cultural, or whatever—that we are being critical of the tiny speck in our brother's eye but missing the branch in our own eyes?

Evaluating Ideological Reasoning

To evaluate ideological reasoning, we will apply the four tests for the worthiness of an argument that we developed in Chapter 7. Recall that the four questions those tests ask are these: (1) Are all the premises true? (2) Is the argument logically strong? (3) Are the reasons relevant to the claim being made? and (4) Is the argument non-circular? Let us consider each question in sequence.

ARE THE IDEOLOGICAL PREMISES TRUE?

The test for the truthfulness of the premises is perhaps the most important test for ideological reasoning. If the premises are taken as true, then the listener could be well down the path to believing the conclusion. To apply this test, one must consider all the premises one after another. Some will be spoken and others will be implicit. Each needs individual attention. Given that strongly held beliefs and core values often function as the implicit but unspoken guiding ideology, it may be

Thinking Critically Faith in Adversity: The Book of Job

Critical thinking is not something invented by scientists or philosophers of the modern or postmodern eras. There is evidence of vigorous critical thinking, including lively debates and arguments, in many historically significant documents, the Bible among them, and in many religious traditions as well. The reasoning, as we would expect, particularly in prescientific times, tends to be ideological in character, but the skills of analysis, interpretation, inference, self-regulation, evaluation, and explanation are all evident. Consider, for example, the question "Why does God, who is all good and all powerful, permit innocent people to suffer evil?" The question has been around for thousands of years, and there are no easy answers. To say that evil is unreal is playing with words. To say that all evil is natural, like the tragic consequences of bad weather or unfortunate accidents, is to ignore the evil that men and women do to each other intentionally on occasion. To say that God gives us free choice so the evil we do is something God is permitting, but does not approve of, seems to contradict God's goodness. No loving parent would permit his or her children to rape and murder one another. This issue, known as "the problem of evil," is a classic concern of people raised in the Judeo-Christian tradition. It is addressed early in the Judeo-Christian Bible in a book called *Job*. That book contains the story of a wealthy and blessed man named Job. One day Satan and God decide to test his faith. They have a bit of a wager over the question of what it might take for Job to abandon his conviction and trust in God. Their approach is to test him by visiting upon him and his household all manner of evil and misfortune.

Read Job and consider how Job behaves in response to the adversity sent his way. Apply your critical thinking skills to the arguments used by the three main characters in the story: God, Job, and Satan. Map and evaluate their arguments. In the final analysis, is Job's faith an example of ideological reasoning or not—that is, does it have the three characteristics of being deductive, axiomatic, and immune from both confirmation and disconfirmation? Suppose God and Satan had tried a different ploy. Instead of taking away all the good things in Job's life, suppose that they only sent him more blessings. Would that have been a tougher challenge to his faith? Some might argue that it is more difficult for the coddled and comfortable to sustain their faith, than for the poor and desperate. Is there any experience or set of circumstances that can logically lead one to infer that if God does exist, then God is not currently taking an active interest in the lives and fortunes of all the individual human beings?

For a contemporary rendering of the story of Job, rent the 2009 Coen brothers film, A *Serious Man*. How to interpret that allegorical film's unexpected ending is a topic of considerable interest on the Internet. Question: In what respects does this film deviate from the classic Biblical version of the story of Job? Does that deviation alter or reinforce the core philosophical message about how difficult it is to understand why at times bad things happen even to those who try hard to be good people?

challenging to bring all the unspoken assumptions to the surface for examination. And yet, for ideological inferences, the key issues revolve around the truthfulness of those axiomatic ideological premises themselves. These are the very premises that the argument maker takes on faith and expects the listener to take on faith as well. For critical thinking, the question is, "How can we tell whether the premises expressing the speaker's ideology are true or false?"

The speaker may or may not wish to defend any given premise. The first possibility to consider in applying the Test of the Truthfulness of the Premises is that the speaker would provide no further backing. Instead, the speaker may regard the premise as self-evidently true. In this case we can use the methods described in Chapter 6 for evaluating claims to see whether or not we should agree that it is true. Asking the listener to have faith too is not likely to persuade a strong critical thinker with a healthy sense of skepticism.

The second possibility is that the argument maker would present himself or herself as the source that stands behind a given premise. The person might say, "Trust me when I tell you . . ." or "Based on all my experience I know that . . ." If the speaker wants us to believe the premise is true because of his or her own credibility, then we can apply the lessons from Chapter 6 about the twelve characteristics of a credible expert. We can use those lessons to assess whether the maker of an ideological argument is, in fact, a credible source whose word we should trust regarding the truth of a given premise.

The speaker's third option is to cite a source that the speaker trusts and that the speaker is asking the listener to also trust. Strong critical thinkers will then turn their evaluative attentions toward that source and inquire as to its worthiness. Suppose, for example, that the argument maker states, "It is in this reference book that XYZ," "I saw it on the Internet that XYZ," "My buddy at work says that . . . ," or "Someone on *Oprah* said XYZ." We would then demand reasons why any of these sources should be trusted as experts on the topic XYZ. In Chapter 6 we developed a full set of expectations for evaluating the credibility of sources, and we can apply those to see whether we should or should not trust the source that the speaker now offers.

The fourth possibility is that the argument maker could offer a reason why the ideological premise is true. In effect, this creates a new argument. The premise we had been questioning is now the conclusion of this new argument. Its reason is the reason newly given. This tactic of providing an additional reason simply pushes the problem one step back. For example, "I believe that chimpanzees and humans have the same rights because all animals that are self-conscious and can feel pain do have the same rights." Providing a reason for an ideological claim invites strong critical thinkers to evaluate that new argument. The first question might be "Why do you believe that all self-conscious animals that can feel pain have the same rights?" The next question might test the implications of that conviction by asking, "Do you really believe that worms, sparrows, kittens, small children, and carpenter ants have the same rights?" If the argument maker offers a reason or reasons why a given premise is true, we would simply apply our tools for evaluating arguments. We could map the argument,

Nineteenth-Century Ideologies and Twentieth-Century Wars

During the nineteenth century, remarkably different ideologies took heart from the expression "survival of the fittest" and the scientific weight that Darwin's evolutionary theory had already garnered. In the 1800s three writers whose ideas greatly influenced world leaders and world events a century later—Ernst Haeckel, William Sumner, and Karl Marx—pressed Darwinian ideas, misinterpreted and wrongly applied, into the service of their ideologies. To appreciate how each invoked evolution, watch the clip "Fit to Rule" from *The Day the Universe Changed*. You can access this clip at **www.mythinkinglab.com**.

The twentieth century saw tens of millions of human beings killed as these global ideologies clashed. Nazism, with its theory of Aryan supremacy and programs of "racial hygiene," manifested Haeckel's misuse of Darwin's ideas. Capitalism, which free of government regulation produces an ever widening gap between the very rich 1 percent and everyone else, manifested Sumner's misapplications of Darwin. And Communism, with its belief in the inevitability of the rise of the proletariat working class, revealed Marx's misconceptions about Darwin. As history has demonstrated, the power of ideologies like these not only to shape policies but to destroy tens of millions of human lives cannot be overestimated. Science made subservient to ideology will always pose a grave danger for us all.

Watch the **Video** on **mythinkinglab.com**

Haeckel's nineteenth-century misinterpretations of Darwin spawned the brutal genocides perpetrated by twentieth-century Nazism.

Sumner's nineteenth-century misinterpretations of Darwin spawned the greedy dog-eat-dog excesses and recurring market collapses of unrestricted twentieth-century capitalism.

Marx's nineteenth-century misinterpretations of Darwin spawned failed economics and the crushing misery of twentieth-century communism.

then use the four tests. If the speaker happens to use comparative reasoning to make a new argument that his or her original premise was true, we would apply the criteria from Chapter 12 for evaluating comparative thinking.

Depending on the context and the importance of the issue, we may decide not to push things this far. Good judgment is always a virtue. If the issue is trivial, we may not want to keep asking "Why should I believe you about that?" so aggressively that we end up risking an important friendship or relationship. But if the ideological argument is going to be costly and risky, then good judgment requires that we push the Test of the Truthfulness of the Premises with vigor. It is too easy to let ideological first principles slip by unchallenged. Strong critical thinkers do not want to do that. But because these first principles often express beliefs and values that we happen to share, we can drop our guard at times. And it is exactly in those times that we are vulnerable to making mistakes. We do not want to sing the critical thinker's lament, "Oh, but I should have asked more questions before I believed so-and-so or agreed to such-and-such. But it all sounded so sensible at the time."

LOGICAL STRENGTH AND IDEOLOGICAL BELIEF SYSTEMS

Ideological arguments, which are often the product of deductive reasoning, generally will pass the second test for evaluating arguments—the Test of Logical Strength. Although occasionally a fallacy slips in or a logical mistake occurs, many ideological arguments adhere to the valid reasoning patterns described in the section on deductive arguments in Chapter 8. They often use the templates for "applying a generalization" and "applying an exception." For example:

- Lazy people don't deserve handouts. Cecelia and street people like her who don't have regular jobs are lazy. So, you shouldn't give her any pocket change when you see her begging for a handout.
- Cheating is unethical only when the exam is important. But this course is not in my major and it's only a midterm, not the final. This exam is not important. So, it's OK to cheat on this exam.
- Jesus has made it clear that the most important commandment is to love our neighbors as we love ourselves. No nation that structures its health care policy so that 40 million of its citizens are systematically denied access to adequate health care is practicing love of neighbor.[xiv] Jesus would be very disappointed in all of us, voters and leaders alike, for our part in permitting so many millions of our neighbors to be treated so badly. This implies that Christians should be among the strongest advocates of universal health care.

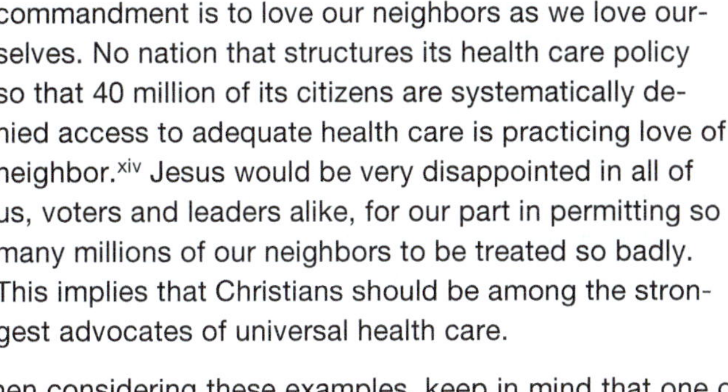

When should an ideology be set in stone?

When considering these examples, keep in mind that one or more of the premises may be false. But for the sake of illustrating the logical strength often found in ideological reasoning, let us, only for the moment, assume that they are all true.

Ideological belief structures often contain internal contradictions. Buddhism, Islam, Taoism, Newtonian physics, Aristotelian cosmology, Scientology, communism, fascism, democracy, Marxism, and feminism can all be reasonably described as ideological belief systems of one kind or another. Each contains inconsistencies, small or large, as is evident from the internal disagreements that theorists and proponents of those systems experience. Some, like Buddhism and Marxism, embrace inconsistency. Some, like Newtonian physics and Aristotelian cosmology, give way to superior conceptualizations, such as the theory of relativity. Some, like democracy and feminism, struggle with inconsistencies.

As a rule of thumb, all ideological belief systems that are "isms" are prone to internal inconsistencies. It is always possible that internal inconsistencies can be explained or resolved. As we shall see in the next chapter, the internal inconsistencies, called *anomalies*, in scientific belief systems often provide the impetus for further research and the generation of new knowledge. In ideologies that do not employ empirical investigation as a source of new knowledge, inconsistencies can be resolved by debate and the examination of founding documents. One belief will survive and be embraced as dogma, and the other will be branded a heresy.

What should we do if our beliefs lead to contradictions? In that case, strong critical thinking would require us to revise or abandon one or more of our beliefs. That is the only logical way to resolve the contradiction that inconsistent beliefs create. Unfortunately, in our opinion, proponents of ideological systems too often give themselves permission *not* to think critically about their own beliefs. Instead, they use escape clauses when challenged about the internal contradictions in their beliefs, using phrases such as "Well, we call that a mystery" or "If your faith were stronger, you would understand." The other unfortunate tactic ideological thinkers at times employ is resorting to donkey cart terms: "You see, true freedom means . . ." or "True racial supremacy means that we have . . ."

If the truth of their absolute convictions is challenged, weak critical thinkers are likely to try to fend off those challenges with fallacious or unverifiable rationales such as: "It's just common sense; everyone knows that . . ."; "Our tradition has always taught that . . ."; "It is a fundamental principle of our founders that . . ."; "Inspiration and revelation are the sources of . . ."; "I was brought up this way"; "It's what my parents always told me"; "It's what I learned in kindergarten"; or "We'll all find out the truth some day after we're dead."

But, having registered our concerns about how weak critical thinkers respond when problems are evident in their ideological reasoning, it is important to note that people with stronger critical thinking skills respond differently. When inconsistencies are found, there is a strong tendency on the part of those with stronger reasoning skills who are advocates of the ideology to address them and remove those inconsistencies. Understanding the power of dominance structuring to bolster their preferred opinion, we would expect those advocates not to abandon ship if they can plug the leak. Their efforts generally take the form of reframing the definitions of key terms, modifying or qualifying core beliefs, or refining the language used to express the ideology to remove the "apparent" contradiction. Notice that in this paragraph, we are talking about advocates who are devoted to the ideology and who have strong thinking skills. We did not say that they also had strong critical thinking habits of mind and a healthy skepticism.[xvi] If they did, then their responses would also have to include the possibility of abandoning the ideology in whole or in part. And some people do exactly that. For example, a recent study focused on the religious beliefs of ordained clergy in the Protestant Church of the Netherlands. Traditional Christian beliefs, for example belief in life after death, a personal God, or the Divinity of Jesus, were not universally affirmed. In fact, one in six of the clergy in that denomination were agonistics or atheists.[xvii]

"I do not feel obligated to believe that the same God who has endowed us with sense, reason, and intellect has intended us to forgo their use."

Galileo Galilei[xv]

RELEVANCY, NON-CIRCULARITY, AND IDEOLOGICAL REASONING

For the big "isms," our third test for evaluating arguments, the Test of Relevancy, tends to yield unambiguously positive results. Why? Proponents of large-scale ideological systems, like religions, metaphysical worldviews, and political and economic worldviews declare their ideologies to be relevant to everything. In the United States, commentators advocating liberalism and conservatism provide strongly held opinions on virtually all topics. The initial problems that some Christian theologians had with Darwin, for example, grew out of a belief system that presumed that, in the act of creation, God must have made every animal at the same time. Later theologians refined their theory of creation so that it would be consistent with the scientific evidence. The inconsistency was resolved, and the Church and its belief system could continue to be presented as relevant to all God had created, which of course, is everything. We saw in one of the previous examples that a plausible case can be made that Jesus would have expected his followers to support universal health care.

Our fourth test, non-circularity, produces consternation as well. The arguments used by ideological thinkers typically pass this test. They are not circular for the most part. Yes, it would be circular to argue that God exists because the Bible says so, and then to argue that the Bible is true because it is the word of God. But that is not generally how strong critical thinkers who are religious people would frame their arguments. And, yes, it would be circular for a Marxist to argue that the proletariat will prevail over other economic classes because that is the inevitable result of world historical economic forces, and then to argue that belief in those forces is based on the expectation that the proletariat will prevail. But, again, that is not how strong critical

How could a study of beetles and birds cause so much trouble?

thinkers who are Marxists would frame their arguments. In our experience, conversing with advocates of ideological systems often feels like a ride on a merry-go-round—a lot of movement but not much progress! To those watching from the side, the riders appear to be going no place fast, but they are generally enjoying the experience. To those riding, the spectators seem to be rushing by, while the merry-go-round represents the steady and predictable force of their well-ordered universe with every other horse and rider exactly in the place where they belong.

Uses, Benefits, and Risks of Ideological Reasoning

Ideological reasoning offers many benefits. First and foremost, our shared ideologies define and shape our communities and give individuals a strong sense of identity. We know who we are by reference to our ideological belief systems. For example, "I am a liberal, a member of the Democratic Party, and a Christian." Second, ideological convictions enable us to escape the suffocating malaise of relativism. The core values of an ideological belief system guide our thinking about right and wrong, good and bad, and obligatory and optional. Third, ideological reasoning offers an efficient way of addressing novel questions. Our "isms" often provide ready answers to new questions we may not have the time or the expertise to answer for ourselves. Suppose, for example, that we genetically modify food grains so that rice, corn, and wheat provide nourishment that is the equivalent of the protein from eating meat. People with deep convictions that anything God did not create naturally is probably bad might advocate bans on the genetic manipulation of foods. People deeply convinced that God intended human beings to use their powers of reason to solve problems, like world hunger, might advocate expanding the use of genetically altered foods.

The benefits are also the risks. Ideological reasoning is pervasive in our culture, and it can be powerfully persuasive. We noted that our ideologies shape the character of our communities and our personal identities as members of those communities. Ideological belief structures are socially normative—those who disagree are seen as outsiders, ignorant, mistaken, abnormal, or dangerous. Socrates (470–399 BCE.) was convicted of the capital offense of corrupting the youth of ancient Athens because he taught them to reason for themselves and to question the unsubstantiated beliefs of the leaders of that city-state.[xviii] Take heed, you who write books about critical thinking!

"Fix reason firmly in her seat, and call to her tribunal every fact, every opinion. Question with boldness . . ."

—Thomas Jefferson[xix]

Because ideological convictions often seem to be immunized against scientific confirmation or disconfirmation, it can be difficult for us to see them as mistaken. For example, we know of no scientific test to determine whether the individual is more important than the social collective. We have not found

Thinking Critically — Group Project: Conflicting Principles and Conflicting Positions

Select one of the following conflicts and prepare a well-researched report on the core beliefs, values, and assumptions that fuel each side in the dispute:

1. The conflict between Israel and Palestine in the Middle East
2. The conflict over legislation permitting assisted suicide
3. The conflict between property developers who want to build communities and create jobs and preservationists who want to protect the environment by limiting development

Thinking Critically — Value Judgments

We all make judgments that express priorities. We authors, like many of you, prefer clean water to impure water, moderate exercise to a couch potato's sedentary existence, and intelligent discourse to loudmouthed stubbornness. And, as you know, we give priority to all of the positive critical thinking habits of mind over their negative polar opposites. But we have not asked you to agree with us about the positive critical thinking habits of mind as a matter of faith. Instead, in Chapter 1, we considered several reasons why critical thinking was valuable for you individually and for us as a society. We connected the skills and the habits of mind to that core idea of critical thinking in Chapter 2. Therefore, the value of the habits of mind, like the value of the skills, comes from the value of critical thinking as purposeful reflective judgment. If there are superior ways to judge what to believe and what to do, we do not know what they are.

Taking it a step further, we have recommended that you should strengthen your skills and fortify your habits of mind. These recommendations are based on the value that we see for you and for all of us in using critical thinking. More than that, this book contains a number of other value judgments about critical thinking. We have urged that we try to be more reflective and use self-regulation to protect ourselves against premature dominance structuring and from risky reliance on System-1 judgments when more reflection should be used. To support our advice and explain our value judgments, we have used arguments, examples, and research. Some people might think that value judgments are automatically unreliable, false, or nonsense. We do not agree with that assumption. And we do not know how a rational person could argue for that assumption. Arguing that value judgments should neither be made nor accepted is arguing for a specific value judgment! So, let's agree that people make value judgments. The question critical thinking raises is the question of judiciousness. Are our value judgments reasonable, well founded, carefully considered, and thoughtfully applied with sensitivity to the complexities of real-world situations? Recall the "Sage" level of cognitive development we talked about in Chapter 6. That is the quality of value judgment we should be striving to attain.

To explore some interesting personal value judgments and moral dilemmas and to see whether you would make the bargains with the devil (or is he an angel?) that are offered, watch an episode or two of *The Booth at the End*. This remarkable show, somewhat reminiscent of the more thought provoking episodes of the classic *Twilight Zone*, can be seen on hulu.com **http://www.hulu.com/search?query=The+Booth+at+the+End&st=0&fs=null**

a scientific way to verify or falsify the belief that knowledge is superior to ignorance, but most of us believe it is. There is no scientific way to investigate the claim that it is the will of God that America be destroyed. Ideological convictions that are neither testable nor falsifiable can be called "metaphysical," as explained earlier in the chapter.

Ideological reasoning constrains and empowers. Our axiomatic core convictions have life-shaping consequences. Differing political orientations generate dramatically divergent visions of human society. Not surprisingly, people who are deeply convinced that their way is "the only right way" often seek to change or to destroy those institutions and people who

Thinking Critically — Group Exercise: Why Do We Believe What We Believe?

Discuss each statement or set of statements below in turn and, as a group, examine as objectively as possible the reasons why the statement or set of statements may be true or may be false.

1. Just like people, computers can think for themselves.
2. Chimpanzees have the same rights as humans.
3. Life is fundamentally unfair.
4. Management and labor are natural adversaries.
5. Over 2 million aliens, originally from some other planet, are being secretly held in a concentration camp 200 kilometers outside Johannesburg, South Africa.[xx]
6. The world will end on the winter solstice in 2012.[xxi]
7. When humans and machines elegantly merge, a singularity will pour to end the ravages of old age, illness, and perhaps even death.[xxii]
8. God created the world and watches over everyone. God wants us all to be nice to each other, which is what all religions teach. The goal of life is to feel good about oneself and to be happy. God needs to be involved with your life only when you really need something, otherwise not. Don't worry because when we die we all will go to heaven if we were good. Whatever.[xxiii]
9. And now these three remain: faith, hope, and love. But the greatest of these is love.[xxiv]

The Courage to Challenge the Ideologue

It takes courage to challenge powerful people who are using their ideological stance to cause harm. That decision is never an easy one, because there is always the risk that you will be targeted. The film *Good Night and Good Luck* reenacts a conversation that might have occurred at CBS when the journalists Edward R. Morrow and Fred Friendly decided to take on Senator Joseph McCarthy. This clip also includes actual footage of the Senator using innuendo and insinuation when questioning people whom he had called to testify before his Committee. Access this clip at **www.mythinkinglab.com**.

Because our ideological convictions generally operate in the background of our consciousness, we do not often question our fundamental axiomatic beliefs. And yet, they are powerful but subtle influences that shape our interpretations of events and experiences. For example, it is easy for a person with an ideological belief system to interpret questions that challenge that system as hostile and to regard the person who asks those questions as an enemy. Belief structures determine the scope of what we imagine to be possible. If we believe that all human beings have immortal souls, then we can imagine that it is possible that our souls might survive after our bodies die. Ideological systems shape the questions we ask. If we believe in souls surviving after bodily death, then it makes sense to ask where they go and what that disembodied survival might be like. Our belief systems, like filters on a camera, color our view of the world.

Watch the **Video** on **mythinkinglab.com**

What would today's parallel be to the ideology-busting, truth-seeking courage John Howard Griffin displayed?

threaten "the only right way." History offers many examples: the Christian Crusaders, the Taliban, the Nazis, the Stalinists, the Klan, racists, zealots, true-believers, and bigots of all stripes, shapes, and stenches who use ideological reasoning to motivate their followers and try to destroy those who disagree.

The benefits and risks of ideological thinking revolve around the power of ideologies to structure our individual and collective way of seeing the world. In the middle of the twentieth century many Americans saw the world as a place of conflict between two global powers, the United States and the Soviet Union, each dominated by opposing ideologies: constitutional democracy and communism. The film *Good Night and Good Luck* shows what can happen when unscrupulous ideological bullies, like Senator Joseph McCarthy, gain political power. True, McCarthy regarded himself as doing battle against the communists, who were regarded as ideologues and enemies of the United States. Although his goal may have been consistent with the defense of the rule of law and individual freedom, McCarthy's methods turned out to violate those very ideals.

Hundreds of years ago, the English statesman and philosopher John Locke described the habit of talking and listening only to those who agreed with the beliefs and opinions one already holds as a basic type of flawed thinking.[xxv] Today the critical thinking community refers to the habit first described by Locke as a failure of courageous truth-seeking. James Howard Griffin's extraordinary book, *Black Like Me*,[xxvi] describes the power of ideologies to shape our perceptions of reality. In that book, he tells about his life-shaping experiences as a white man living as a black man in America's deep South in the late 1950s. There are many other powerful examples in literature and film that help us simulate what the world is like from another's perspective. Trying to see the world through the eyes of another is a valuable way of expanding our sensitivities and monitoring our tendency to accept beliefs uncritically.

David Strathairn won an Oscar for his portrayal of Edward R. Morrow in *Good Night and Good Luck*

CHAPTER

13 REVIEW

Study and Review on mythinkinglab.com

Ideological reasoning begins with our deeply held convictions, core values, and assumptions about the world. From these we reason, top down, to specific implications about how we should live and what to think about issues of the day. Ideological reasoning is deductive in character, the ideological premises are axiomatic, and the argument maker takes the ideology to be true more or less on faith. Ideological reasoning is important and useful because it shapes our community and individual identities. It guides our thinking on policy questions and reflects our value judgments. It helps us know what we should think when we do not have the time or the expertise to address new questions on our own. The risks associated with ideological reasoning are as great as the benefits. Because strong convictions may be mistaken, we can easily find ourselves advocating and defending views that are ill-conceived and harmful. History shows the dangers of ideological reasoning though the wars, genocides, and human misery caused by ideologues and their followers.

KEY TERM

ideological reasoning (or **top-down thinking**) is the process of thinking that begins with abstractions or generalizations that express one's core beliefs, concepts, values, or principles and proceeds to reason top down to specific applications. Ideological reasoning is deductive and axiomatic. The argument maker takes the ideological premises on faith. (p. 249)

FIND IT ON MYTHINKINGLAB.COM

Watch the Video on mythinkinglab.com

- We open this important chapter with CNN reports about California's divisive Proposition 8. By visiting www.mythinkinglab.com, you can access the legal analysis CNN's Avery Freeman provides (p. 248). There, too, you can access the CNN news story describing the protests and demonstrations sparked by the court rulings. Wherever you live, we invite you to follow the issue of same-sex marriage closely. This could turn out to be one of those issues we will all look back on decades from now with wonderment. We can imagine a conversation about same-sex marriage in the year 2050 that includes the sentence, "What were they thinking back then in 2012?"

- The "Fit to Rule" episode (p. 258) from the series *The Day the Universe Changed* is an insightful analysis of how Darwinism was misused to advance ideological preconceptions. Visit www.mythinkinglab.com to access this remarkable video, and then ask yourself whether hundreds of millions of us are today being guided toward mutual destruction by "true believers" and unexamined ideological worldviews. Is our consumerist culture ideologically driven too? Why do we believe that we need to own so many nice, new things? Are we being led to believe that we can purchase happiness? If so, why and by whom?

Watch the Video on mythinkinglab.com

- Not all bullies lurk in playgrounds. Unfortunately, some are ensconced in government agencies, religious organizations, workplaces, universities, medical centers, health clubs, and corporate offices. That clip from *Good Night, and Good Luck* we invited you to watch (p. 263) offers a look at considerations that often come to mind when one contemplates confronting a bully. Access this clip at www.mythinkinglab.com. In fact, we urge you to watch the entire movie. It is an excellent film. Do we have any journalists with the truth-seeking courage, ethical strength, and powerful skills of an Edward R. Murrow or a Fred Friendly today?

Watch the Video on mythinkinglab.com

Exercises

REFLECTIVE LOG: THE MILITARY DRAFT

A nation can legislate mandatory service in the armed forces. Known as "the draft," the United States used forced conscription to build the armies it needed to fight World War II, the Korean War, and the Vietnam War. If drafted, a person must leave his or her school, job, and family to serve for a specified period of time, typically two years, in the armed forces. Draftees become soldiers. And some soldiers give their lives in combat. Those who try to escape their duties, known as "draft dodgers" are prosecuted and imprisoned. Assume that the nation's military leaders evaluate the readiness of the armed forces and determine that the national defense requires that a military draft should be established now. Assume that men and women between the ages of 18 and 35 will be subject to the draft as recommended to the President and the Congress. Assume that the proposal to institute a draft is going to be taken up by Congress next week and that you have the opportunity to offer your advice to your state's representatives and senators. Although the nation may or may not be at war at the moment when the legislation is being considered, it is reasonable to assume that the nation could be at war at some point in the future. Considering what you know about the nation, its ideological convictions, and its history, what would you recommend and why? Assume that you are the right age to be drafted into the military and that you are otherwise fully qualified and eligible to serve. That is, assume that whatever law is passed, if there is a draft, you may be one of the people conscripted to serve.

GROUP DISCUSSION: WHAT IDEALS WOULD YOU GO TO WAR TO DEFEND?

Throughout history people have gone to war. On many occasions, religious ideologies, political ideologies, or economic ideologies have been at the root of those conflicts. The Crusades, World War II, and the American Civil War might be seen as examples of such conflicts, at least in the minds of some leaders and some combatants; ideological reasoning played a major role in explaining why each war was unavoidably necessary. Discuss with your peers the ideological beliefs and core values that, in your considered judgment, would make war unavoidably necessary. Beyond self-defense and the defense of the lives of your family and other members of your community, are their principles, fundamental beliefs, and core values worthwhile to defend with your life and to protect the lives of those you love by waging war? Is freedom worthwhile? Is democracy? Would you go to war to end slavery, to prevent genocide, to free children from forced labor, to rescue fellow citizens from illegal detention in a foreign country, to protect commercial shipping on the high seas, or to save whales from being slaughtered for human food? Would you fight to regain your homeland, or to gain access to clean water? Would you go to war to free your ethnic group from an oppressor nation? If none of these is a worthwhile endeavor to you, is there anything that you personally would go to war to defend or to protect? Remember that whatever your group's answer might be, you should expect that your answer works in reverse as well. That means that you should expect others to do no more and no less, should they perceive your behavior as demanding from them an identical bellicose response. Be prepared to give the very best reasons possible for either the view that war would be the appropriate response of last resort in a given situation or that war is never an appropriate response no matter what the situation. When considering the "no matter what" alternative, be sure to include in your reflections "self-defense and the defense of the lives of your family and other members of your community."

WHEN IDEOLOGIES CLASH: MONEY, GOD, AND SEX

1 MONEY. In the 2009 film *Capitalism: A Love Story*, writer Michael Moore strongly suggests that contemporary American Capitalism is at odds with Christianity, Socialism, and Democracy. Whatever your personal beliefs, these four ideologies are, in fact, influencing your life, your leaders, and the laws by which we live. We recommend you view the film as part of your effort to learn about these major ideologies. But, keeping an open mind, do not limit your learning to one filmmaker's interpretation of these four ideologies. Develop a reasoned and factually informed analysis of each. In light of your learning and in light of the actual facts as can be demonstrated by trustworthy scientific studies, evaluate the claim that contemporary American Capitalism is at odds with Democracy, Christianity, and Socialism. If it is your view that it is at odds with any one of them (and it cannot be compatible with all of them because of the differences between the three), then how should we reconcile these ideological conflicts in real life—that is, what government policies and personal practices would be the wisest to pursue?

2 GOD. Bill Maher's 2008 film, *Religulous*, features interviews with several believers representing several different major world religions. The film, a comedic documentary about a serious subject, challenges viewers to examine the assumptions behind their own beliefs. The film culminates in the claim that today's conflicting religious ideologies clash so violently that they could trigger global nuclear war. Map the reasons developed throughout the film which support that dire warning. Remember that the reasons may be demonstrated more than spoken, e.g., that in spite of their claims to be peace loving, some religious leaders treat non-believers as if they deserved to be purged from the planet. Evaluate the film's major argument using the criteria developed in Chapter 7. Given that human nature has not changed much in 100 years, today are we as much at risk of global ideological war as were the people of the twentieth century?

3 SEX. In June 2011 New York legalized same-sex marriage. But before that legislation was passed, people were lining up on both sides of the issue. Always a lightning rod, Keith Olbermann's political commentaries feature high rhetoric, vigorous affect, and challenging analyses. On his June 23, 2011 installment of *Countdown*, he took on the topic of gay marriage. As challenging as it may be, keep an open mind as you watch his editorial on this controversial topic. Analyze his arguments using the mapping techniques we developed in Chapter 5. Then apply the four tests of the quality of arguments to the case that Olbermann makes in that commentary. One place you can find the video is YouTube.[xxvii]

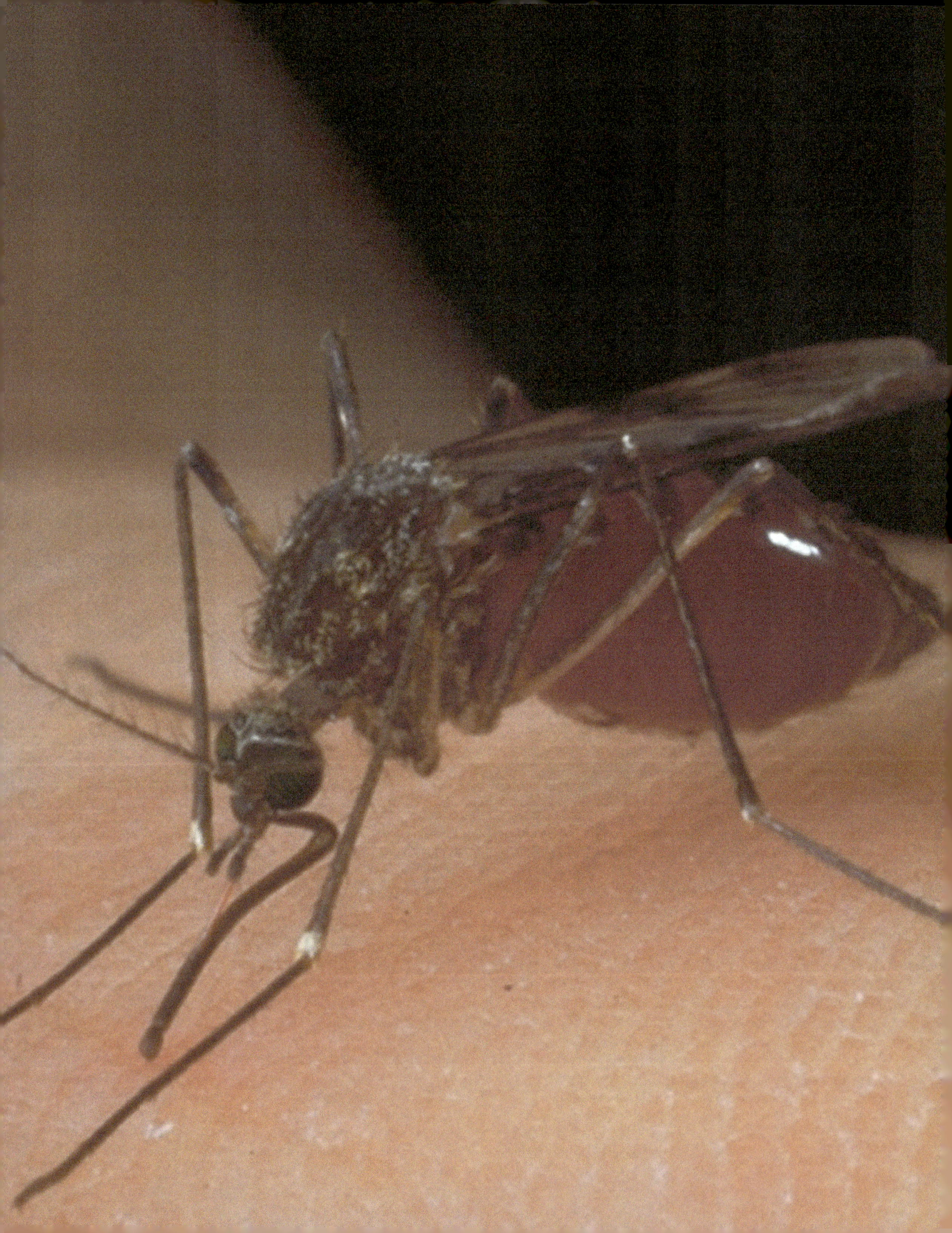

Read the Chapter on mythinkinglab.com
Listen to the Chapter Audio on mythinkinglab.com

CHAPTER 14

Empirical Reasoning: Think "Bottom Up"

HOW can we recognize empirical reasoning?

WHAT are the steps in conducting an investigation scientifically?

WHAT are the benefits and risks of empirical reasoning?

"Yellow fever!"

The cry struck dread and panic into the hearts of the residents of port cities from New Orleans to Philadelphia during the eighteenth and nineteenth centuries. Epidemics of yellow fever ravaged the population. Its symptoms include nausea and vomiting, chills, headaches, restlessness, prostration, and pain throughout the body. Victims suffer irregular fever, jaundice, bleeding from every bodily orifice, delirium, convulsions, coma, and death.[i] Once the disease took hold of a city, it spread throughout, mysteriously killing some but not others. The epidemics raged, and tens of thousands died until the first frosts of late autumn.

Called "Yellow Jack," no one knew where the disease came from, how to treat it, or how to stop its spread. Quarantines did not work. Closing doors and windows did not work. Burning tar to "disturb the miasma" did not work. The disease seemed to jump from house to house through the city, afflicting men and women, old and young, black and white, prosperous and poor.[ii] People fled cities by the thousands in fear. Commerce collapsed; cities declared bankruptcy. Ministers advocated moral reform and closing dance halls. Physicians treated the sick with purging and bleeding. Nurses and family members tried to ease the pain, to comfort, and to console. Many, but not all, of those physicians, ministers, nurses, and family members contracted the illness themselves. Why? Was it by touching the sick person, by breathing the same air, by handling the filthy bed linens? Was the contamination in the blood, the feces, the food, the furniture, or the air? Nobody knew. But unless someone could figure out exactly how the disease was transmitted, there would be no hope of containing or controlling it.

In the late 1870s a Cuban physician, Carlos Juan Finley, presented a theory about the cause of the disease. He hypothesized that the dreaded fever, which annually plagued his homeland, was carried from person to person by, of all things, a mosquito. He had gathered empirical data and mapped the locations where the mosquito was prevalent and where the fever occurred. Looking at the two maps, he realized that the locations correlated. But a correlation is not a cause, and the physicians of his day did not believe a disease could be transmitted by a mosquito. He presented his work in 1881 at a scientific meeting in Havana and was completely ignored.

That is, until 1900. That year the U.S. Army marched into Panama and faced the same enemy that had destroyed other armies sent by Spain and by Napoleon. The generals knew that the U.S. troops being sent to Panama risked annihilation by Yellow Jack. To lead the effort to combat yellow fever, the Army appointed a young major named Walter Reed. Reed and his colleagues thought that the mosquito transmission theory might have some value. They worked to refine the theory, but in October 1900 there had been only two cases to examine. Without more data, Reed's group could not rule out other possible causes. One particular explanation was regarded as much more plausible: the idea that germs transmitted by the filthy clothing and bedding of yellow fever victims caused the epidemic. *The Washington Post* labeled Reed's ideas about mosquitoes "silly and nonsensical."

To test his hypothesis that mosquitoes were the cause, Reed needed to create an experiment that would show two things: First, that the disease was transmitted by contaminated mosquitoes and, second, that it was not transmitted by contact with filthy, germ-infested clothing and bedding. To obtain the volunteer human subjects his experiment would require, he offered each willing person $100 in gold. At a remote location known as Camp Lazear, Reed set up two identical huts and divided the volunteers randomly, sending some to live for several days in Hut #1 and others to live for several days in Hut #2. Both huts were screened to prevent the entry of any mosquitoes. Hut #1 was loaded with filthy clothing and bedding in which yellow fever victims had slept, bled, vomited, and died. No one in Hut #1 became sick with yellow fever. Hut #2 was divided into two chambers by a screen that permitted the air to circulate between the two chambers. Infected mosquitoes were released into one side but not the other. As predicted, only the volunteers in the chamber where the infected mosquitoes had been released became ill. None of the other volunteers in Hut #2's other chamber contracted yellow fever, even though they were breathing the

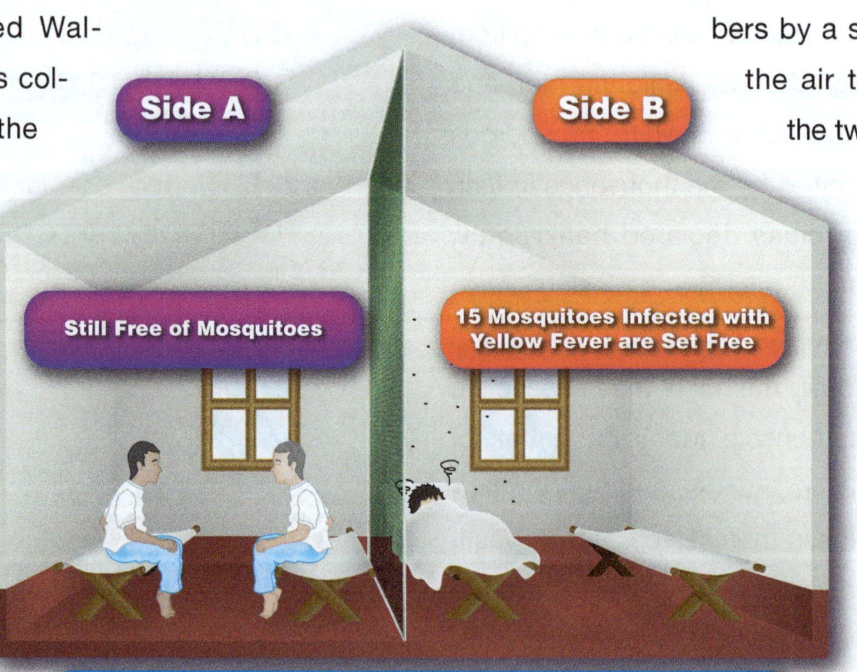

Interior of Walter Reed's experimental Hut #2. Why the screen creating Chamber A and Chamber B?

same air as the sick volunteers. Walter Reed was able to design a test that demonstrated that a widely held idea was probably false and that another idea (mosquitoes can bring sickness and death to humans) must be regarded as a vital new insight. It was an insight of great importance to public health. Go to www.mythinkinglab.com for details about the objective, preparation, protocol, data, and conclusions from Walter Reed's classic use of empirical reasoning in his Camp Lazear experiment.[iii] Read the Document on mythinkinglab.com

Recognizing Empirical Reasoning

Our capacity to anticipate what comes next and then to devise ways to affect the outcomes of events and processes is absolutely fundamental to our survival as a species and to our current planetary dominance. We look for cause-and-effect relationships to explain, and hence to predict and control. The opening sequence of *2001: A Space Odyssey*[iv] dramatizes the basic idea: You hit your rival over the head hard enough and he dies! But your arm is not long enough and your fist is not hard enough, so you make a tool, a club, to get the job done. The film suggests that progress from the bone used as a club to interplanetary space travel is simply a matter of filling in the blanks.[v]

Tens of thousands of years later we are still working on filling in those blanks. Today our species is using the map of the human genome and research on gene expression to mount a genetic counterattack on diseases like cancer. Advances gained through empirical reasoning permit us to ask ourselves questions that eclipse the understanding of scientists working in Reed's or Finley's day. What makes a cancerous cell's DNA express itself in different ways at different points in the tumor's growth? What are the mechanisms that turn the protein receptors off and on and, hence, make one kind of therapy effective and another ineffective at different points along the way?

"The kernel of scientific outlook is a thing so simple, so obvious, so seemingly trivial, that the mention of it may almost excite derision. The kernel of scientific outlook is the refusal to regard our own desires, tastes, and interests as affording a key to the understanding of the world."

Bertrand Russell[vi]

The correct answers to these questions and to others like them come only as the fruit of empirical arguments. Investigators, using the same kind of reasoning that Reed and Finley used, begin with a theory about how or why something happens in the natural world. They form a testable hypothesis, gather data by observation and experimentation, and use those data to confirm or disconfirm their hypothesis. In the process, they strive to disconfirm competing hypotheses. In this chapter we will explore this kind of "bottom up" thinking, known as empirical reasoning. The thinking we are examining in this chapter is explored in greater depth in two different supplemental chapters that your instructor may have included in your textbook. In the supplemental chapters, "Think like a Social Scientist" and "Think like a Natural Scientist," we take this discussion of the features of empirical reasoning further by exploring what questions are asked by social scientists and natural scientists, how they use empirical research methods to answer those questions, and the standards by which these scientists evaluate the answers. In other words, we really get into what it means to think like a social scientist or to think like a natural scientist.

CHARACTERISTICS OF EMPIRICAL REASONING

Empirical reasoning is *inductive in character, open to self-corrective revision*, and *the argument makers take their empirical premises to be true on the basis of interpersonally verifiable experience*. Thus empirical reasoning contrasts with ideological reasoning on all three key characteristics. Recall that in the previous chapter we described ideological reasoning as deductive, axiomatic, and taken on faith.

Empirical Reasoning Is Inductive

Describing scientific investigations as inductive in character means that the conclusions reached are probabilistic. Scientists would be the first to insist on this. They strive to remain open to the possibility that the conclusions they reach based on empirical reasoning might need to change! Recall our discussion of coincidences, correlations, and causes in the section on inductive reasoning in Chapter 9. We noted there that the analytical and inferential tools used in empirical reasoning, like statistical tests, produce confidence levels that approach 1 in 100 or 1 in 1,000. But even with such high levels of confidence, the conclusions drawn remain inductive. Scientists use observations and statistical analyses to draw inferences with varying levels of confidence. The inferences drawn remain probabilistic even when our statistical analyses permit us to have very high levels of confidence.[vii] Although it turned out that Finley was right about the mosquito being the vector that transmitted the yellow fever virus from one person to another, he *might* have been wrong. His correlations that mapped the mosquito's habitat and the areas where the disease was found may have been correct, but there just might have been some third factor he had overlooked.

Just as not all deductive reasoning is ideological, not all inductive reasoning is empirical. In Chapters 2, 9, and 12[viii] there are many examples of inductive arguments that are not instances of empirical reasoning. Just as deductive reasoning is not defined in terms of "general" and "specific," neither is inductive reasoning. Examples of comparative reasoning illustrate that induction can also go from general to general ("Fashion models are like thoroughbreds, beautiful to see but expensive to maintain and difficult to control") or from specific to specific ("Bill's tastes in desserts is like his sister's, so if Sue doesn't like rhubarb pie, Bill probably doesn't like it either"). The characterizations in this chapter about empirical reasoning do not necessarily apply to all of inductive reasoning because empirical reasoning is only one kind of inductive reasoning.

Empirical Reasoning Is Self-Corrective

The second important feature of empirical reasoning, namely that it is self-corrective, is vital to the progress made using investigative methods. Crime dramas like *CSI* and *Law & Order* unfold like mystery novels. They reveal clues and bits of information along the way so that the viewer can form hypotheses about "who done it." Clever writers arrange the story so that the criminal's identity is concealed as long as possible. But the writers organize the flow of information to the viewer so that various characters can be ruled out as the possible criminal. The viewer then revises his or her theory of the crime so that it explains all the data, old and new. The process of scientific inquiry is similar, except that there is nobody orchestrating the moment at which the data will be made known to the investigating researcher. The researcher is responsible for devising the means to acquire the kind of data that will be relevant and revise his or her hypothesis, if necessary, as new information is gained. To answer empirical research questions, investigators examine data gathered using instruments specifically designed to find the kinds of data that they expect might exist. We would not have invented the microscope had we not thought that perhaps there were important things to learn by looking at objects in more detail than the unaided human eye can reveal.

Empirical Reasoning Is Open to Independent Verification

A third feature of empirical reasoning is that premises that report data or the results of statistical tests are open to scrutiny and independent verification by the entire scientific community. Investigatory inquiry is a community activity. Other scientists are welcome to gather additional data, to re-create experiments, and to recalculate statistical findings. The observations, databases, and findings scientists use and report are subjected to the scrutiny of other investigators. Other scientists are welcome to scrutinize a colleague scientist's arguments, data-gathering methods, statistical analyses, and every other aspect of the empirical reasoning. Replication is a way of verifying that the observations and findings reported by the original scientist are true. If we were to replicate today the experiment Reed conducted in 1900, we should expect to find, as he did, that the only people who become infected are those who are exposed to yellow fever by the infected mosquitoes. Our belief in the truth of the premises, observations, and findings, does not depend on whether we have faith and trust in Reed. Science is not a matter of faith in the word of others. Science is based on the fact that if others conducted the same experiments, they would get the same results. The commitment of the scientific community to make the arguments, databases, analyses, and other aspects of the empirical reasoning process open to others for independent verification can lead to collaborations that advance our scientific understanding of phenomena. For example, unprecedented advances in Alzheimer's research have been achieved because of a 2003 agreement between The National Institutes of Health, the Food and Drug Administration, as well as industry, university, and non-profit researchers to combine their independent efforts into a shared database that the Alzheimer's research community could access.[ix]

Empirical Reasoning or Bottom-Up Thinking

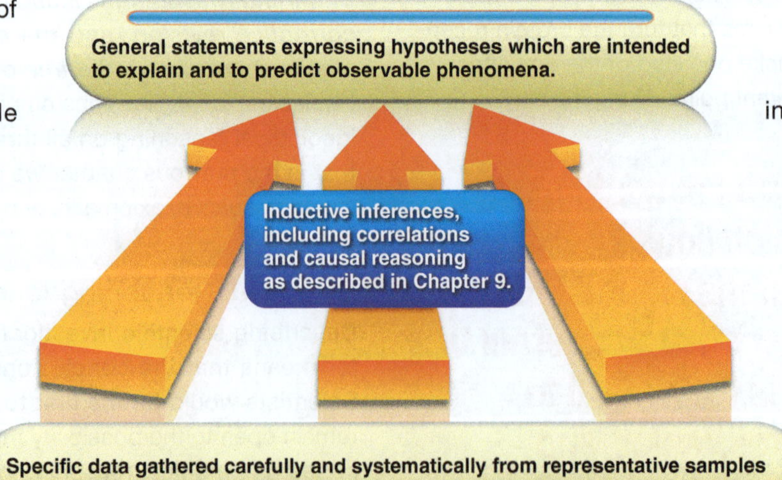

"One is always a long way from solving a problem until one actually has the answer."

Stephen Hawking[x]

HYPOTHESES, CONDITIONS, AND MEASURABLE MANIFESTATIONS

An empirical investigation begins with a hypothesis. The hypothesis often can be expressed as a hypothetical, such as "If things of a certain kind are placed under certain conditions, then we will be able to observe certain phenomena." Or a hypothesis can be expressed as a general statement: "Certain kinds of objects behave in certain ways under certain conditions." Here are some example hypotheses.

- If the *Salmonella* bacterium is exposed to temperatures greater than 140 degrees Centigrade for more than 30 seconds, it will die.
- Married couples who experience unanticipated severe financial problems will argue and fight more than they did prior to their financial problems.
- The reflexes of a person who drives a motor vehicle for five or more hours without a rest period will have deteriorated by 30 percent or more as compared to his or her reflexes after only one to four hours of driving.[xi]
- In our new program, we train sixth graders to tutor third graders in reading and math. Our hypothesis is that the test scores of the sixth graders and the third graders will be significantly higher than the scores of their peers who were not involved in this tutoring program.
- Green is big right now. So, if we promote the belief in the general public that our company has a sincere concern for the environment, we will see an increase in our market share.
- If the Federal Reserve reduces the prime interest rate, there will be a proportional reduction in short-term interest rates on consumer credit card purchases. And, if this happens, it will stimulate the economy, since consumers will tend to spend more, thus leading to an increase in manufacturing and the creation of more jobs.

Arguments expressing empirical reasoning include statements describing the particular states of affairs that the researchers strive to create experimentally or to measure in their natural settings. The advantage of creating specific conditions in the lab is that potential influences of extraneous factors can be reduced. Yet that tends to weaken the *generalizability* of the findings because the highly controlled conditions achieved in a science lab might not be found in the real world. The scientist's ultimate purpose is to explain and to predict real-world phenomena. There is always a trade-off between the strict controls possible in a laboratory experiment and the generalizability of that experiment to the real world. Automobile companies crash test their vehicles in lab experiments controlling for speed, mass, and direction of impact, and using computerized mannequins instead of human beings. That's good enough for me. They do not have to kill a lot of innocent people in "real-world" experiments to prove that one way of designing an airbag or door frame is better than another. Here are two examples in which the investigators note the difference

Thinking Critically — Measurable Manifestations

The six example hypotheses above illustrate measurable manifestations of hypotheses in six different subject areas: biology, psychology, human performance, education, marketing, and economics. Here are five more examples that are only partially completed. Please complete each one by expressing one or more measurable manifestations of the hypothesis proposed. Add additional statements that clarify or expand upon the descriptions of the exact conditions under which the behavioral manifestations you predict will occur. Explain, in your own words, why the clarifications or expanded descriptions are helpful.

- If we apply a solution made up of water and laundry bleach to mold growing on the surface of a glass dish, then the mold, which is a fungus, will ________________.
- In our experimental teacher training program, we have each college student spend a semester as a math and science tutor for seventh or eighth grade students. Our regular teacher training program does not include the semester tutoring. Our hypothesis is that the college students in our experimental program will ________________ as compared to the students in our regular program.
- One of the sources of energy consumption is household electricity usage. Electricity is used to heat water, cook or refrigerate food, and to operate lights and consumer appliances. Compact fluorescent light bulbs last six times longer than comparable incandescent bulbs and use less energy. So, we can predict that if the average consumer were to replace household light bulbs with compact fluorescent bulbs, he or she would save ________________.
- Fashion magazine models, many of whom are teenagers, risk malnourishment and severe eating disorders. If the fashion industry were to adopt mandatory body mass requirements to protect the health of these people, ________________.
- Domestic dogs, like their pack animal ancestors, behave in accord with a social hierarchy. The lesser animals in a pack will follow the lead of the dominant animal. Obedience and subservience are expected, and violation of the rule of the pack is punished. We can expect that if dog owners displayed more ________________, then their pet dogs would ________________.

Thinking Critically — A Relationship Between Symmetry, Attractiveness, and Smell?

Hypothesis: Women find men whose faces are more physically symmetrical to be more sexually attractive and to smell better than men whose faces are less physically symmetrical.

What is your first reaction to this hypothesis? How might we test it?

Suppose you had access to a sufficient number of willing volunteers including men whose facial and physical symmetry you could measure and women who were willing to provide you with their opinions about which of these men looked more sexually attractive and smelled better. Design an experiment to test the hypothesis expressed above. The challenge is to describe the steps your experiment would follow, if it were conducted. You do not have to actually conduct this experiment, just design it.

Remember to find some way not to let extraneous factors confound your data. For example, control for the possible influences of cologne or certain foods, like garlic. Be sure too that the women are not influenced by a man's facial expressions, weight, height, or personal charm. Find a strategy for gathering data, which will prevent the women from being influenced by something that a lab assistant might say or do.

After you have recorded the design for your experiment, visit **www.mythinkinglab.com** to access recent articles on symmetry and sexual attractiveness, including one peer-reviewed published study conducted by a Stanford undergraduate.

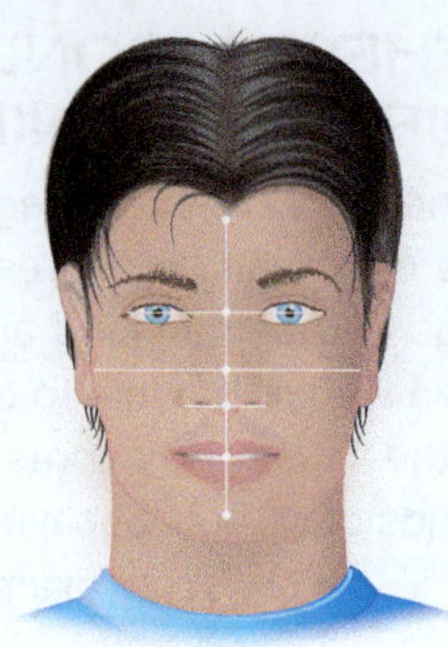

Simulate the **Experiment** on **mythinkinglab.com**

between the controlled experimental environment and the real world. Under the circumstances, trade-offs must be made.

- Rather than risk accidents on the open road where our subjects and other people as well might be injured or killed, we can check the reflexes of men and women of different ages by having them drive on a closed track in dry weather. Of course, driving on a closed track in dry weather is boring compared to driving on the open road under differing weather and traffic conditions.
- If we divide the sixth graders and third graders into two groups each, we can train one group of sixth graders to tutor one group of third graders. If we ensure that all other known relevant factors are held constant (for example, that otherwise they receive instruction in the same subjects by equally competent teachers in identical learning environments), then we should see statistically significantly higher test scores for the experimental group students [third graders who were tutored and their sixth grade tutors] as compared to the control group students [third graders who were not tutored and sixth graders not in the tutoring program]. But how can we ensure that the other known relevant factors are held constant?

Conducting an Investigation Scientifically

There are many steps involved in investigating an empirical question logically, systematically, and in a way that allows others in the scientific and professional community to verify the results through replication. Any place along the way an investigator can introduce error through technical, conceptual, methodological, or reasoning mistakes. And yet, because the process can be monitored and corrected by the investigator or others on the research team, science is exceptionally robust from the perspective of the reasoning to be used. All our critical thinking skills and habits of mind are engaged when we set out to determine, using empirical reasoning, what we should believe. And as in Reed's situation, it turns out that a measure of cleverness and bit of creativity are needed just to figure out how to test one's hypothesis.

PERHAPS THE FIRST RECORDED EMPIRICAL INVESTIGATION

A driving sense of scientific curiosity impelled the Head Librarian of Alexandria in North Africa to wonder how to explain this extraordinary observation: on one day each year, June 21st, that at noon on June 21st in a city 800 kilometers to the south, the sun cast no shadows. "Would I see this same lack of shadow everywhere?" To approach an answer to this question, the librarian first had to ask the question with more specific detail. "Do sticks, towers, columns, and obelisks cast shadows in Alexandria at noon on the summer solstice?" wondered that librarian. He experimented and observed that they do. "But how is that possible?' he wondered, given that the Earth is flat?"

At high noon on June 21st, the sun casts no shadows down the walls of this well. But it casts shadows at other places at that same date and time. Aristophanes asked, "Why?" 2,200 years ago.

"There are in fact two things, science and opinion; the former begets knowledge, the latter ignorance."

Hippocrates, Greek Physician[xii] (460–377 BCE)

That librarian, whose name was Aristophanes, was a person of extraordinary accomplishment and learning. Although 2,200 years ago science as we know it did not yet exist, inference, analysis, and truth-seeking were alive and well in Egypt and its greatest center of learning, Alexandria. Aristophanes drew the inference that the only way that there could be a shadow in the one city and not in the other is if the Earth were curved, instead of flat. He needed more data to either disconfirm his idea that the Earth was curved or to find evidence that supported his insight. It was easy to measure the length of the shadows in Alexandria at the appointed date and time. But, without any other way to measure the distance, Aristophanes had to hire a man to pace out the exact distance between Alexandria and the city to the south where the sun cast no shadows on June 21st at noon. Aristophanes needed that datum to calculate the curvature of the Earth. Then by using geometry (thank you, Euclid), he could estimate the Earth's circumference. Watch the explanation provided by Carl Sagan in the series *Cosmos* to appreciate Aristophanes' empirical reasoning as he tried to explain the phenomenon he was so curious about. Access this clip at www.mythinkinglab.com. As it turned out, Aristophanes was able to infer that the Earth was approximately 40,000 kilometers in circumference, an amazingly accurate calculation. (Oh, and for some reason, we forgot and then needed to rediscover more than a millennium and a half later that the world was round. Oops! Our bad!)

Watch the **Video** on **mythinkinglab.com**

STEPS IN THE PROCESS OF AN EXTENDED EXAMPLE

At some point during their college years, or soon after, many students find themselves working in an office as an administrative assistant. They may work in an office on campus, or during a summer job, or perhaps after graduation to pay the bills before they land a job closer to their intended career field. Many people work in group office environments for many years. The job can have its good points and its bad points. Lately, the collective productivity of office workers, which in the past may have been taken for granted, has become a serious concern for cost-conscious employers. With millions of men and women working in group offices, even a small increase or decrease in productivity can have an unexpectedly large impact on the nation's economy as well as the company's bottom line. How much does the workplace

environment affect the motivation and the productivity of group office workers?

Some might leap to the conclusion that improvements in the workplace environment would mean predictable increases in motivation and productivity. Others might be skeptical about that. Whatever one's initial thoughts, the question cannot be satisfactorily resolved without investigating the facts. Spending money to improve the workplace environment for group office workers may or may not make cost-effective positive changes in their motivation and productivity. Merely speculating about the issue is not an adequate response, not if you are the owner of the company and greater productivity would mean more profits for you.

The "Steps in a Scientific Investigation" table on pages 274–275 describes in detail how a team of researchers would scientifically investigate this question.[xiii] One column describes the steps in an empirical investigation. The next column applies that step to our example question. In the first step, the investigators articulate the question they are expecting to investigate. Unless the investigator expects to fund the research work himself or herself, simply raising a question is not adequate to secure the funding for conducting that research. Today researchers must explain why a question is significant enough to warrant attention and a commitment of resources. This real-world financial reality is reflected in the table. **Critical thinking** is the tool one uses to take into consideration all the problems that need to be overcome in order to engage in a productive empirical inquiry.

In the earlier paragraphs we already addressed Step 1, the importance of the question of the productivity of workers in group office settings. Investigating a factor that might improve motivation and productivity for millions of people is a worthy inquiry. Undertaking an investigation that involves the application of our knowledge of psychology to answer this question could be useful to millions of people and businesses.

If all the work described in the table looks difficult, that is because it is difficult to design a strong plan to test a complicated idea. But the table shows that reasoning through the

Steps in a Scientific Investigation			
The Steps in the Investigation		Group Office Example	The Investigator's Argument-Making Responsibilities
Identify a problem of significance.	(1)	How does the office environment affect the productivity and job motivation of employees working in a group office setting?	Explain why this problem is important. We did this in the text leading up to this table.
Form a hypothesis that describes what we can expect to happen under certain conditions.	(2)	The more noise and distractions, the more confined and the less personal the workspace, the lower the productivity and motivation of workers will be.	Explain that the hypothesis asserts that as the environment deteriorates, productivity and motivation decrease, but as the environment improves, productivity and motivation improve. This is a correlational hypothesis at this point, not a causal hypothesis.
Review the scientific literature to see what can be learned from the work of others about this hypothesis or similar hypotheses.	(3)	The lit review is for the purpose of informing our investigation. It can help with many practical problems in future steps (e.g., we may learn how those investigators measured "noise," "distractions," "productivity," and "motivation"). The lit review is not for the purpose of proving we are right.	Before accepting its conclusions, evaluate the scientific merit of each study. Are the premises true? Are the arguments logically strong? Were all the relevant factors considered? Was the research non-circular?
Identify all the factors related to the hypothesis and the phenomenon of interest that it will be important to measure, control, or monitor.	(4)	We will measure noise, distractions, personalization of the workstation, window view, productivity, and motivation. And we will measure things about the workers that might also affect motivation and productivity (e.g., years of experience, knowledge of the job, the importance the worker attaches to his or her assignments).	Explain why each of the factors to be measured is potentially relevant to the hypothesis (e.g., people with more experience may be more productive. People who are new to the job may be more motivated. People who think their assignments are "unimportant" may be less motivated.).
Make each factor measurable.	(5)	We will measure noise as decibels, personalization of the workstation as number of family pictures and personal knickknacks displayed, window views as simply the presence or absence of an unobstructed view out through an exterior building window located within 7 feet of the person's chair. Productivity as phone and e-mail messages sent and received in a randomly selected 1-hour period, and motivation as statements affirming desire to work as recorded during a personal interview.	Justify the chosen method of making each factor measurable. For example, why use an interview, instead of a survey questionnaire, to gather data about motivation?
Ensure that the experimental conditions can be met.	(6)	We will determine that there will be a sufficient number of office workers about whom data can be collected, that their supervisors have authorized the research, that the research has been reviewed and approved by relevant human subjects review boards, that the provision has been made to secure the informed consent of the persons who will be the experimental subjects. We will decide how we will gather the measurable data, including the information on work experience, who will conduct the interviews, who will count the personal items in each workstation, who will count the phone calls and e-mails, etc.	Answer why and how questions for every decision made about setting up these experimental conditions.

(continued)

Steps in a Scientific Investigation (*continued*)			
The Steps in the Investigation		Group Office Example	The Investigator's Argument-Making Responsibilities
Design a procedure to ensure that the data gathered will reveal the full range of possible observations.	**(7)**	We will study an equal number of workers in three settings: Group A will remain at their current workstations and data regarding noise, personal items, distance from exterior windows, and productivity will be gathered without any change in their work environments. Group B will be assigned new workstations that are optimally configured for the purposes of this study and encouraged to personalize those workstations to suit their own tastes. Group C will be assigned new workstations that are negatively configured according to the hypothesis of this study (noisy, no-window, not private) and be advised that they are not allowed to personalize those workstations.	Explain why and how the three groups will be created. Show that the investigator has considered all the ways that the data being gathered might be discounted as irrelevant or as misleading, and then has taken steps to guard against those problems.
Construct reliable measuring devices and test them.	**(8)**	E-mails processed will be measured by an automated count of messages opened and messages sent from each person's desktop PC through the network servers. Messages greater than 100 words will be counted as 1.5 messages. Privacy will be measured by counting the number of persons who pass within 3 feet of the person's chair. Interviews will follow a protocol of questions to be asked. Etc.	Demonstrate that whatever amounts of error the measurement tools themselves might introduce is an acceptably small amount.
Conduct the experiment/ gather the data.	**(9)**	Divide the workers into three groups. Make all the measurements and conduct the interviews. Record the data for future analysis.	Anticipate practical problems and justify the decisions about those problems (e.g., explain why in one case a person who sent an unexpected long, 300-word e-mail was given credit for 2 messages).
Conduct appropriate analyses of the data.	**(10)**	Statistical analysis shows that productivity for Group B is statistically significantly higher than for Group C. Distractions and noise together account for 31 percent of the variance in productivity. Differences in motivation were not statistically significant. Etc.	Demonstrate that the experimental conditions were satisfied, that the data were recorded correctly, that the correct analyses were used, and that the math is right.
Interpret the findings and discuss their significance.	**(11)**	If workplace distractions are limited, noise is reduced, and privacy is ensured, then one can expect modest increases in productivity. These findings may be of interest to interior design architects and supervisors who configure group workplace settings.	Demonstrate that the interpretations being made are reasonable and justifiable, given the data. The claims must not exaggerate the findings.
Extend the research by articulating new hypotheses.	**(12)**	We might inquire whether higher productivity will reduce costs of employee recruitment through increased retention of productive workers. Or might it reduce costs potentially by increasing the ratio of workers to supervisors on the assumption that fewer supervisory personnel are needed to manage an office staffed with more productive and satisfied workers?	Explain why the additional research would be valuable in its own right or because of its potential to refine applications of the current findings.
Publish the research. Contribute to our better understanding of the world by making the investigation known to others in the scientific and professional community.	**(13)**	We will submit a paper reporting this investigation for possible publication in the *XYZ Journal of Office Productivity*. Our paper will describe each step of our question, or methods, our measurement tools, our results, and our interpretation of those results.	The investigator must reason through questions such as "Who may need to see the results of this investigation?" in order to decide on an appropriate scientific or professional journal in which to seek publication.

process is not impossible. Within each step along the way, we benefit from the refinements made because previous investigators may have learned the hard way that this or that step was essential to making a tightly reasoned empirical inquiry. We can ask important questions and we can test important ideas using empirical methods. It takes training in research methods—often a requirement of undergraduate and graduate programs—to learn how to apply the broad sketch of empirical science provided here to the specific context of one's professional field and academic discipline. But, in general, the specific investigatory steps are more or less the same for empirical disciplines.[xiv] The critical thinking skills and habits of mind apply across the board.

"Measure what is measurable, and make measurable what is not so."

Galileo Galilei[xv]

EVALUATING EMPIRICAL REASONING

A rigorous and thorough investigatory process, like the one described in the "Steps in a Scientific Investigation" table, takes into consideration all four tests for the worthiness of an argument.[xvi] The truthfulness of the premises is in part ensured by the accuracy of the measurements made and the descriptions of the conditions under which the investigation was conducted. There are additional theoretical assumptions being made, of course. In the example, which showed how to apply the psychological theories about human motivation and productivity to a workplace setting, the theoretical assumptions were presented as true. One might wonder if they are, of course. In the example we could choose to measure noise, distractions, and views of exterior windows, but not the color of the flooring or the height of the ceiling. When we do this we are making certain assumptions about whether those factors we choose not to measure could plausibly be relevant. Perhaps we should also measure the air temperature, on the theory that it is difficult to work when you are too cold or too hot. In an empirical investigation, even one that is tightly controlled and designed, there will always be assumptions that may be questioned. That said, any issues about the truthfulness of any of the premises should have been addressed by the investigator when the study was being designed and by the reviewers who evaluated the merit of the project's possible contribution to knowledge development. If all of those checks fail, empirical investigations are still open to independent verification through replication.

The test for logical strength is also addressed in the research design of a study. That is why the investigators consider which statistical tests are the appropriate ones to use, given the kinds of data they are gathering. That is also why they consider any and all possible factors that might have a relationship to the outcome of the investigation. The investigation, if it is thoughtfully designed and carefully conducted, should supply ample grounds for an inductive inference with regard to the probable truth or falsity of the hypothesis. But, again, if there are errors in logical strength, they should emerge when independent investigators endeavor to replicate the study. Suppose, for example, that an independent inquiry determines empirically that the air temperature (something not measured in our study) had an impact on productivity and more of an impact than any of the other environmental factors we measured. In that study, workers in a group office were less productive when the office was too hot or too cold. In this case we would refine our collective understanding about the relationship of workplace environment and worker productivity. Instead of saying that environment does not count, we would say that it continues to make a difference, but that the element in the environment that is most important to control appears to be the air temperature. We would suggest that management makes sure it is warm enough, but not too warm, in the winter, and cool enough, but not too cold, in the summer.[xvii] The same observations can be made about the test of relevancy and the test of non-circularity. All the factors relevant to testing the hypothesis or to observing the phenomenon in question should have been identified by the investigators as they designed their empirical research. If the investigators missed any or were not able to account for one or more factors, they should note this in their discussion of their research findings. Similarly, a well-designed and well-executed project can be expected not to be circular. But expectations can be mistaken. Ideally, if the empirical reasoning behind the research plan fails the test of relevancy or the test of non-circularity, that should be picked up by the investigative team or project reviewers very early in the process. The research study should not move forward until those issues are addressed.

An evaluation of a researcher's empirical reasoning also occurs as a part of Step 13, when the researcher submits her or his written findings for publication in a scholarly journal. A research manuscript undergoes a process known as *peer review*. Through the peer review process the researcher's ideas, methods, and inferences about the findings are scrutinized by others who are experts in the same field of study. These expert reviewers analyze the research in terms of the evaluation steps we have described in this chapter. The peer review process is designed to screen out research that violates one or more of the four tests of the worthiness of an argument. If the work is good, but not quite good enough to be published, the peer review process works to indicate to the researcher how the work might be revised so that it meets the scholarly journal's standards for rigorous research. The peer review process is generally accepted by the scholarly community as the best available means for ensuring the quality of a scientific investigation, but it has its critics too who point out that the peer review process can be slow, ineffective, or inconsistently applied.[xviii]

Even with the peer review process, errors happen. From time to time poor research ends up being published. So, it is always a good idea not to take for granted that any of these four tests are somehow automatically passed simply because the reasoning is empirical, or simply because a study appears in print. That would be a mistake. Just because something is published in a professional or scientific journal does not mean it passes the four tests. Of course, with all the checks and balances, especially the process of independent peer review, the chances are high that the material published in professional and scientific journals can be trusted. Even so, note that the table, in Step 3, calls for the investigators to make their own independent evaluation of the merits of the arguments in other published papers that may be found in the literature.

"Nothing in all the world is more dangerous than sincere ignorance and conscientious stupidity."

Martin Luther King, Jr.[xix]

Benefits and Risks Associated with Empirical Reasoning

Empirical reasoning is used when we want to explain, predict, or control what happens. These are three powerful and interconnected purposes. Explanation helps us understand why.

- Why do some people catch yellow fever and not others?
- Why does the sun cast a shadow at one place and not at another?
- Why does environment affect workplace productivity?

Predictions, accurately made, enable us to anticipate what is likely to happen under certain conditions. But consistently making precise and accurate predictions depends on knowing how to explain the causes that bring about the phenomenon of interest.

- If we eliminate the mosquitoes that carry yellow fever, we can prevent the disease from spreading.
- If we travel to a place 1,600 kilometers south of Alexandria, we will see shadows cast by the sun in the opposite direction of those we see in Alexandria on June 21st.
- If we eliminate distractions and keep the air temperature moderate, we will increase employee productivity among workers in group office settings.

We human beings want to ensure our health, safety, survival, and, to the extent possible, our happiness by controlling our lives and the world around us. If we can explain and predict a given phenomenon, then we may be able to prevent it from happening or make it happen when we want it to happen.

- If we can prevent the spread of the disease, we will save a lot of lives.
- Because the Earth is a sphere, we can save fuel by taking a polar route when flying from Chicago to Moscow.
- If we can increase employee productivity, we will make more money.

Empirical reasoning offers the promise of explanation, prediction, and control, but empirical reasoning can be complicated. And errors can occur. It would be a mistake to think that a hypothesis was not true simply because an empirical inquiry failed to provide us evidence that supports that hypothesis. Empirical reasoning is inductive and probabilistic. So, it would be a mistake to think that findings that have been established with a high level of confidence can never be rejected, revised, or refined. Confirmatory findings *support* a hypothesis. The scope of questions that guide empirical investigations is very broad, but not universal. For instance, some questions, like those involving policy matters, require good judgment in addition to good information.

Scientific inquiry, when executed by fair-minded, truth-seeking people, is exhaustively systematic and unwaveringly honest. It anticipates the consequences of choices and intermediary judgments and decisions. It demands well-reasoned justifications at every step from the beginning, through all the intermediary stages in the investigation, all the way to the presentation of the results. The cognitive skills required are the critical thinking skills of analysis, interpretation, drawing reasoned inferences, explanation, evaluation, and reflective self-correction. The habits of mind, such as following reasons and evidence wherever they lead, courageously pursuing the inquiry, being systematic, being confident in the power and process of reasoned inquiry, and so on, are the ideal attributes of a critical thinker.

Empirical investigation and the application of our critical thinking skills and habits of mind to scientific inquiry are fundamentally group endeavors. It is the community that determines what is most important to study. Science progresses when the entire scientific community can evaluate the merits of a scientific investigation through replications and refinements of the original investigation. Replication and refinement yield either disconfirmation of the original investigation's findings or generation of support and possible improvements of the original findings. Thus, the scientific community uses a process of reasoning that has a built-in capacity for objective self-monitoring and self-correcting through independent inquiry. It is this capacity that gives empirical reasoning an advantage over comparative reasoning and ideological reasoning. Empirical reasoning calls for the application of the four tests of the logical quality of arguments at every stage of scientific investigation. The results are evident in our increasing knowledge of how the natural world works, and in the technological, biomedical, and engineering benefits humans have achieved over centuries by using scientific inquiry.

CHAPTER

14 REVIEW

Study and Review on mythinkinglab.com

Empirical reasoning moves bottom up, from specific observations and measurable data to generalizations that explain why things happen. Empirical reasoning is inductive in character and open to revision. The argument makers take their empirical premises to be true on the basis of observations that other persons can verify and replicate. The steps in an empirical inquiry require the formation of a hypothesis, and the specification of the conditions under which the truth or the falsehood of the hypothesis would be manifested in measurable phenomena. Using strong critical thinking, the investigator must identify the factors that, according to prevailing understandings and scientific theories, might affect the phenomenon of interest. In experimental contexts, the investigator will endeavor to control and vary these factors to most accurately observe the phenomenon being studied. In empirical investigations that do not involve experiments, the investigator will observe and measure the natural variations in the factors and note their effects. Empirical investigators analyze and interpret their measurements, using those analyses and interpretations to draw inferences leading to an evaluation of their hypothesis. Good science requires connections to past research, which is the purpose of a solid literature review, and it requires the production of reports for the advancement of knowledge and to aid one's scientific and professional community.

The purpose of empirical investigation is to generate new knowledge through which we can explain, predict, and possibly control what happens. **Critical thinking** in real life is also about explanation, prediction, and control. The "purpose" in purposeful, reflective judgment is deciding what to believe and what to do. There would be little benefit in that were it not that what we believe and what we do have meaning in our lives and in the lives of others we care about or who care about us. From the time our hominid ancestors first clubbed their way to the top of the local food chain to today, we have been using our oversized brains to try to figure out what to believe and what to do.

In the next chapter we will work on how to pull together all that we have learned about strong critical thinking in order to write sound and effective arguments. As important as writing is, it is not the only venue where strong critical thinking matters. As authors, our hope for you is that you would expand the scope and range of critical thinking in all the problem solving and decision making in your life. And, as the preface says, that you would be "forever young."

KEY TERMS

empirical reasoning (or **bottom up thinking**) is that process of thinking that proceeds from premises describing interpersonally verifiable experiences in order to support or to disconfirm hypotheses, which, in turn, are intended to explain and predict phenomena. Empirical reasoning is fundamentally inductive, self-corrective, and open to scrutiny and independent verification by the entire scientific community. (p. 269)

critical thinking is purposeful, reflective judgment in the real world concerning what to believe or what to do. (p. 278)

FIND IT ON MYTHINKINGLAB.COM

Explore the Concept on mythinkinglab.com

- We invite you to visit www.mythinkinglab.com three times in this chapter: first to learn more about Walter Reed's experimental inquiry into the cause of yellow fever (p. 269); second to examine some of the research exploring the connections among facial symmetry, beauty, sex, and mental health (p. 272); and third to watch the clip from the *Cosmos* series in which Carl Sagan recounts the empirical investigation Aristophanes designed and carried out to satisfy his driving desire to know why there were no shadows down a well (p. 273). Critical thinking skills and positive habits of mind—vital tools for everyone who would seek to know . . . anything.

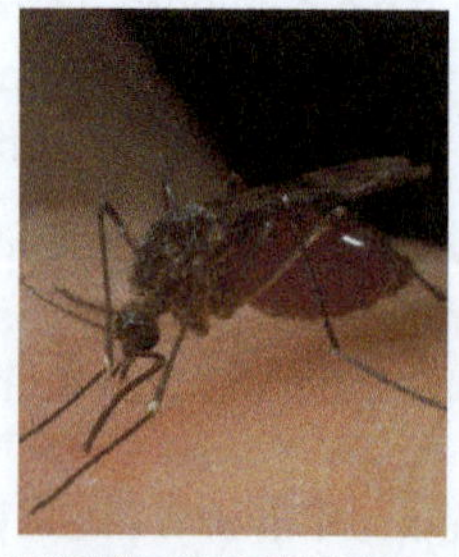

Exercises

GROUP EXERCISE: DESIGN THE INITIAL STEPS IN A SCIENTIFIC INVESTIGATION

Some claim that because of global warming, the sea level will rise by as much as 10 feet, or perhaps more, during the next two decades.

1. Is this a significant problem? Why do you make that judgment?
2. What testable hypotheses are implied by the claim, if it were true?
3. Let's assume that you have performed a thorough review of the scientific literature and that it has been helpful in suggesting factors to measure and ways of measuring them. And let's assume that, through this literature review, you have learned what other investigators have discovered about the potential implications of the sea level rising.
4. What factors related to these hypotheses should we measure either to disconfirm a given hypothesis or to acquire evidence that tends to support the hypothesis? Remember to think about all the ways that various factors might confound the evidence you might wish to gather.
5. How could those factors be measured?

EVALUATE REPORTS OF EMPIRICAL RESEARCH

Scientific studies are constantly being reported in newspapers, magazines, television, and the Internet. Because television synopses tend to provide the findings but not describe the methods or the data, we will focus this exercise on the fuller descriptions provided in newspaper, magazine, and Internet reports. Locate an article published within the last 30 days that reports on the findings of a scientific study. Read and analyze that article carefully. Using the table "Steps in a Scientific Investigation," determine how many of the steps are covered in the magazine or newspaper article. Based on what you learn about the scientific study from the article, evaluate the quality of that scientific research. To inform your evaluation you will want to judge how well the study, as reported by that magazine or newspaper, fulfills the demands of each step in the table. Remember that you are reading another person's synopsis of someone else's research.

Want more of a challenge? Find the scientific publication in which the research was originally reported. Evaluate the scientist's presentation of his or her research findings in light of the "Steps in a Scientific Investigation" table. Each step should be addressed someplace or other in that scientific publication, unless the scientific journal placed word limits on reports it would accept for publication.

REFLECTIVE LOG: COMPARATIVE, IDEOLOGICAL, AND EMPIRICAL REASONING

Chapters 12, 13, and 14 describe comparative, ideological, and empirical reasoning. Each of these major strategies of thinking is best suited for some applications, but not for others. Each has its strengths and weaknesses. As you probably detected from reading these three chapters, from the perspective of strong critical thinking, as the lead author I have major reservations about two of the three forms of reasoning. But even in my own life, I cannot do without using all three, at least on occasion.

I love comparative reasoning because of the fresh insights and novel and creative ways of looking at things it generates. I worry, however, that comparative reasoning can confuse people unless we remember that just because an idea is new does not mean its good! Comparisons aren't proofs, they are more like suggestions about how to look at things in a new light.

I admire empirical reasoning because it is self-corrective and is open to independent verification. When done well, it is systematic, modest, cumulative, useful and exhaustive. But even the highest levels of confidence do not provide some people the certitude that they crave. And I understand that some arguments, including those that capture my political and ethical stance on many issues I regard as vitally important, are best expressed using ideological reasoning.

Yet ideological reasoning, which does address those value-laden concerns, has many drawbacks when it comes to achieving accord among people. Perhaps this is because the starting points for ideological arguments must ultimately be taken on faith, and because, unlike empirical reasoning, ideological reasoning provides no agreed upon mechanisms for collaborative self-correction. Too much "my way or the highway" for me.

My comments are hardly exhaustive of the strengths and weaknesses of these three most common and powerful forms of human thinking. I ask you to reflect on what you have learned in Chapters 12, 13, and 14, and on everything you learned about critical thinking while studying this book. All things considered, what are the relative strengths and weaknesses of comparative, ideological, and empirical reasoning? As a truth-seeker who must make reasoned and purposeful judgments about what to believe or what to do in real life, which of these forms of reasoning is the most valuable? Explain why, give examples, and present your perspective as clearly as possible in your own words.

Read the Chapter on mythinkinglab.com
Listen to the Chapter Audio on mythinkinglab.com

CHAPTER 15

Write Sound and Effective Arguments

WHAT critical thinking questions do effective writers ask?

HOW do effective writers synthesize organize and develop their presentations?

HOW do writers evaluate the soundness and effectiveness of their written work?

A national economic crisis, health care reform, U.S. military presence overseas . . . What to do? President Obama presented his case to the nation in his 2010 State of the Union address[i] and then Virginia's governor, Bob McDonnell, delivered his party's response.[ii] Both likely used professional speech writers to lay out the arguments to make their cases to the American public. They were going for maximal logical and political effect. Each sought to persuade the American voting public that their approach was best and that their interpretation was most accurate. Each tried to position their party for the 2012 election. Although they disagreed strongly, each argued vehemently that their strategies were superior to the proposals coming from the other party. With the 2012 and 2014 general elections on the horizon, speech writers are helping incumbents and challengers frame the arguments for their campaign appearances. The main point of this opening example is not the content of the political speeches themselves but the thought processes used by writers who are striving to prepare sound and effective arguments to put before an audience. For example, what questions do speechwriters ask about the rhetorical situation? How do they build the case that their respective leaders will deliver? By what criteria can we evaluate the quality of their work as writers?

You can visit **www.mythinkinglab.com** for the transcripts of the 2010 State of the Union address and GOP response. Using the analytical techniques

described in Chapter 5, identify the major claims and map the arguments each makes.

Who comes to mind when you think about a highly effective and persuasive maker of strong arguments and persuasive speeches? Perhaps you think of Michelle Obama or a TV news anchor like Brian Williams, or one of your high school teachers, a professor, a coach, a lawyer, or perhaps a family member. What makes that person so successful? How do they organize their thoughts and build their case? How do they decide what to say and in what order, and what not to talk about at all? And how do they approach a reluctant listener with an unpopular idea? Surely they think about a lot more than grammar, spelling, and punctuation. But what?

Transforming learners into effective writers is education's holy grail.

That's what this chapter is about: thinking like an effective writer faced with the goal of making a sound and effective case for the truth of a given statement or for the virtues of a given recommendation. In college, professors expect competent literary analysis, well-researched term papers, effective oral presentations, persuasive speeches, and organized written reports that follow the rules of a particular style, such as APA, Chicago, or MLA. But obviously, just obeying the proper mechanics of writing—grammar, spelling, upside-down paragraph construction, and deciphering the minutiae of preparing accurate citations, to name a few—does not guarantee effective writing. And in professional life after college there are hardly any occupations that do not require a person to make effective arguments in writing in support of opinions or suggestions. Just about every boss out there can be heard telling an up-and-coming new hire, "Hey that's a good idea. Why don't you write it up for us?" To do well in college, and to find success in one's professional work, sooner or later we all realize that to be an effective writer we have to apply our critical thinking.

Think back for a moment about your experience as a developing writer. From the earliest grades, we are taught how to spell and formulate grammatically correct sentences. In middle school we are given repetitive practice in writing concise multi-paragraph essays (We can hear our junior high teachers' voices now: "it must be no longer than 1000 words!" "one paragraph for each idea" "where's the topic sentence?") In high school we were expected to use sources to support our opinions, to present reasons pro and con, and to develop "thesis statements." In our college-level basic writing courses we learn about the "rhetorical situation" as we discover how important it is to be mindful of the purpose of the writing we are asked to produce. Whether you are considering a major or a career in the social sciences, the natural sciences, mathematics or computer sciences, the arts, humanities, business, education, law enforcement, or engineering—or whatever—in college you are asked to write. But this chapter is not meant to cover the content of a college writing course, or to substitute for a course on writing across the curriculum or within your major. Rather, this chapter demonstrates how to use your critical thinking skills in creating sound and effective written arguments in your college work and in your chosen profession. To do this the chapter focuses on what it means to *think like an effective writer.*

What Critical Thinking Questions Do Effective Writers Ask?

Analyzing effective writing (and speaking) reveals certain basic elements. In all or almost all situations *a specific author* intends to *communicate* with a *specific audience* for a *specific purpose.* For the purpose of persuasive writing, the author's strategy is to communicate *reasons* that will lead the audience to believe that a *claim* is true and to decide to act on the truth of that claim. The claim may be a given statement that the author wants the audience to accept, or a recommendation that the author wants the audience to follow. Ideally the author's arguments are *worthy*, in the sense that concept is defined in Chapter 7 on evaluating arguments. Recall that a worthy argument passes the four basic tests of (1) truthfulness, (2) logical strength, (3) relevance, and (4) non-circularity. That means that each argument relies only on true premises and assumptions, demonstrates that its conclusion is true or very probably true, does not rely on fallacious reasoning, and that the flow of the reasoning goes one way only—from the premises toward the conclusion.

We've spoken about the need to make a case. An **author's case** can be thought of as all of the pros and cons along with the supporting evidence that the author presents to the audience in order to establish the truth of a given statement or the wisdom of a given recommendation. Using the decision mapping analytical tools presented in this book (especially in Chapter 5), we can map out the author's case. The resulting decision map will show the author's arguments pro and con, and their supporting reasons and counterarguments. With this analysis in hand, we can then evaluate the *soundness* of the author's case. Using a rubric for evaluating written argumentation, which we will present at the end of this chapter, we can evaluate the *effectiveness* of the author's case.

Before they set fingers to keyboard, effective writers already are thinking about the key elements: as the specific author they have an intention to communicate with a specific audience for a specific purpose. Effective writers know who they are as authors and they strive to understand exactly who their intended audience is. Effective writers have a clear sense of the context within which they are communicating, and they are clear about the purpose of the communication. Effective writers are systematic and thorough: They do the research and then they present well-reasoned arguments grounded in solid evidence. Effective writers are good critical thinkers who know what questions to ask and what methods to use. And they can evaluate their written product and apply their writing skills to real-world situations. To think like an effective writer we must apply our own critical thinking skills to discover our own answers for these same issues.

To become an effective writer the first thing we must do is apply our critical thinking skill of analysis to the rhetorical situation. **Rhetorical situation** refers to the interactive combination of four elements: a *specific author* using a specific mode of communication or *presentation* to engage a *specific audience* for the *specific purpose*. The purpose of persuasive writing is to make the author's case. The successful author who understands his or her audience and who has researched the topic well will organize and present a sound and effective case. The case will persuade a reasonable audience by means of presenting sound reasons and credible evidence. To achieve this, an effective writer asks himself or herself four key questions. The questions emerge directly from the rhetorical situation. Before doing anything else, the effective writer will ask:

1. Who am I, as author?
2. Who is the intended audience? What do they believe and value?
3. What is the purpose and what are the circumstances of my communication?
4. How should my case be developed and be presented?

Let's think about each one of these four broad and highly interconnected questions the way that a writer would.

THINK AUTHOR

Sound and effective writing comes from someone. It is not anonymous. A person gives the writing a voice. Voice is power. Voice communicates meaning, passion, and intensity. We can ignore words on a page. We can ignore "believe X." But it is very hard to ignore a voice that we respect. Voice says that there is a real person saying "I believe X." So now we have to take X more seriously because someone whom we respect believes X and wants us to believe X too. The first thing an effective writer must do is to discover his or her voice. The 2010 Academy Award–winning Best Film, *The King's Speech*, makes that point most eloquently. When you watch it, pay particular attention to the scene in which the king, played by Colin Firth, is finally able to break through his lifelong anger and

Honesty Works

Occasionally a writer fudges the truth. Writers of non-fiction have been discovered intentionally using false premises, claiming that their conclusions are logical when they knew that they were not, relying on fallacies to deceive a gullible audience, or using circular reasoning. We do not condone this. We think it is a mistake at many levels. We believe that sound and effective argument making should never knowingly employ falsehoods, be illogical, rely on fallacies, or build circular arguments. Not only is it manipulative, insincere, and disrespectful of the audience; it is also a sure way to alienate the strong critical thinkers in that audience. If an audience discovers that a writer is being deceitful, the audience will reject the message as well as the messenger. These admonitions hold true in social media as well! Like Bart Simpson on a bad day, authors of e-mails, blogs, tweets, Facebook posts, or other online comments may be prone to exaggerate the truth or outright fabricate the claims they are making about themselves or other individuals. Take for example the completely fictitious social media "reports" of actor Jackie Chan's death in 2011. And Mr. Chan is not the only celebrity who has been carelessly victimized in this way.[iii] Contrary to what some may think, outrageous, inaccurate, or irresponsible statements made in online environments are permanent. They cannot be revoked by clicking the delete button and, in fact, can become fodder for legal action.

frustration with the stunning realization that he indeed has a voice.[iv] The story is much more than a tale about a man overcoming the stammering and stuttering he had experienced since childhood. It shows how a king grows to understand that he has something he must say to his nation. It tells us all that we too can have an effective voice, if we learn how to control it.

We thought about who we were as authors in order to prepare to write this book for you. We shared our biographies with you because we wanted you to know that we were real people with a genuine desire to assist you to become stronger critical thinkers. Yes, we wanted you to know too that we had the academic and real-world professional creds to write a book like this. And we often shared personal anecdotes and stories in order to illustrate various ideas. It would be hard to miss that one of our concerns is to combat intolerance and hate, which explains many of the examples we elected to use. Another concern is to promote healthy living, which explains another bunch of examples. But more than either of those things, we really wanted to share our passion for learning, our belief that learning needs to connect to real-world experiences, and our commitment to the value of critical thinking in all dimensions of life. We hope that our voice has been clear and strong from Chapter 1 all the way through the book.

Find Your Voice

Suppose you are asked to write an editorial or blog for the college newspaper about "life as a college student." Your very first question needs to be: "Who am I, as author?" Take a moment and think about how you would respond. Here are some responses students have shared with us over the years.

- I am a female college student who just graduated from high school last year. I am majoring in International Relations and I want to work at the United Nations. My parents are alumni of this university. I attend full-time, and I am living on campus in the residence halls. I like to have fun, like anyone else, but I worry that there are some people in my residence hall that overdo it. There is too much drinking, at least that's what I'm seeing. Maybe I'm wrong and I shouldn't judge. But it bothers me.
- I am a 22-year-old male in ROTC and getting my college education. I come from a military family and look forward to serving my country after I graduate just like my father and my older brother and sister did. I'm hoping to deploy to Afghanistan. I'll be a second lieutenant and my unit's communications officer. It really bothers me that so few Americans understand why we're there. Either you take the battle to the bad guys or they will bring it to you.
- I am an Indian woman who is studying part-time to be an early childhood educator while raising my two children with my husband of 22 years. We moved to the United States a few years ago for my husband's work. I was a pre-school teacher in Mumbai for many years, but I must now become recertified in this country. This does not make sense to me. I know more than many of my teachers. But I will humbly comply, because I must get certified or I cannot do what I love, which is to take care of the little ones.
- I am the oldest of three children and the first person in my family to go to college. I live at home with my mom and dad, my little sister and brother, and my grandparents. I drive to campus for my classes then I leave to go to my job. Between that and my homework, I don't have a lot of time for my friends. Some of the people in my courses are full-time and will graduate years before me. Frankly I envy them at times. But other times I think that they have no clue about what it is like to make it in today's world. I'm the assistant night manager at a Chipotle restaurant now, but my major is chemical engineering and someday I'm going to own that restaurant and five more like it.

Effective writers think about themselves as authors as they prepare to draft a written case. They ask questions such as "How can I draw on my past experiences when talking about this topic?" "What makes me a credible person to argue for this claim?" "Do my attitudes about this topic make me unfairly biased, or can I be open-minded about this topic?" "What are my attitudes toward my intended audience—do I like them, respect them, trust them—and how do I want those attitudes to show through in my writing?" "What do I need to learn about the topic and about the audience before I start writing?" "What is my motivation for writing this—what do I want to get out of this communication?" "Why do I care about this topic?"

Ultimately, effective writers will consider how their backgrounds influence the assumptions that they make about the audience and the purpose for the communication. Effective authors consider the perspectives they will take on particular issues and make conscious decisions about how to present themselves and their positions on the topic.

Think about Who You Read

Along with thinking about what you like to read, think about who you like to read. Often we discover enjoyment in reading a particular author and we are eager to devour everything that author may have produced. Why? In part because we enjoy hearing that author's voice come through in her or his writing. As with our favorite film producers, musicians, and actors, we grow eager for our favorite author's next novel.

Identifying the author's voice is a key piece of enjoying and understanding what we read. We can apply our critical thinking skills to the author of a written piece in order to analyze and interpret a piece of writing. Thinking about the author's background, attitudes, and purpose can help us explain the decisions that the author made in constructing the piece. Why did the author take that position? Why did the author interpret this situation in the ways that he or she did? How did the author's assumptions about the world influence the analysis and evaluation of situational events and social relationships? These questions are particularly fascinating to ask when we are reading written argumentation intended to elicit a particular attitudinal or emotional response from the reading audience. Take for example the autobiographical narrative of Elizabeth Najeeb Halaby, the American-born woman who is the last wife and widow of the late King Hussein of Jordan. In *Leap of Faith: Memoirs of an Unexpected Life*, Queen Noor encourages the reader to see the Middle East through her eyes, providing a more sympathetic perspective on the history of that region, a region that may not be familiar to most of her reading audience.

THINK AUDIENCE

Effective writers do not write for themselves; they write for their audience. An effective writer seeks to establish a relationship with his or her audience. The relationship between author and audience is *grounded in the trust the author is able to engender in the audience*. Before putting pen to paper, the author must think critically about the intended audience. Who will be reading or hearing this? How do I get the audience's attention and keep it? What do I need to know about the audience in order to make good decisions about how to express my arguments, what to include, and what not to include? Is the audience friendly or hostile to the position I am going to take? Will this be my only chance to communicate to this audience?

What Does the Audience Care About?

Effective writers connect with the receptivity of their audience by appealing to the audience's core values, perspectives, and shared interests. To do this effective writers research their audiences. They learn about the background, experiences, interests, and goals of audience members. To craft a sound and effective case, an author draws on what is known or safely assumed about the audience in order to make critical thinking decisions about how to organize ideas and orchestrate the presentation of those ideas.

In order to formulate an effective argument, an author needs to know what will be convincing to an intended audience, what will move them to respond in the way the writer is seeking. Take for example the reality television show *Hell's Kitchen*, now in its ninth season on the Fox network. Each season, a group of chefs compete against one another in order to avoid elimination and win the ultimate prize: a coveted position as executive chef in a named fine-dining establishment. The case being made in the series is that there is a contestant worthy of winning this competition, and each episode serves as the evidence to support the claim that the best chef will be the winner. For any TV show to remain successful season after season the creators must demonstrate over and over again to its audience that it is worth watching. The creators consider their audience very carefully as they craft show after show. Will the viewing audience be interested in knowing how to prepare the dishes that are served in the *Hell's Kitchen* restaurant? Are viewers considering careers in the culinary arts? Do the viewers enjoy watching Gordon Ramsey yell at the bumbling chefs who seem to have forgotten all of their training and are ready to turn on one another at the drop of a fluffy white hat in order to win the competition? The importance of retaining and expanding the viewing audience (numbers of people, not waist sizes) certainly influences production decisions of many kinds, such as who will have the opportunity to be contestants.

Does it take strong critical thinking skills to solve the problems faced by expert chefs, like *Hell's Kitchen* star Gordon Ramsey?

How about editing decisions? Might audience analysis be influential in determining what footage will be seen in the episode? How do contestant elimination decisions and the interpersonal drama story lines shape the evocative language that is used to foreshadow next week's episode? Our point is that critical thinking skills are applied by the entertainment industry professionals who write, direct, act in, and produce successful shows. In so doing they are ever mindful of *audience* as an essential element among the four interconnected elements in their *rhetorical situation.* How can we writers, directors, actors, and producers create (author) TV show after TV show (presentation) on the same topic in a way that is fresh and entertaining for the viewers (audience) and persuades them to tune in again next time (purpose)?

Strong presentations and excellent purposes are not sufficient. Effective writers never take the audience for granted. Writers often prepare by asking themselves "Who cares and why?" "Who am I writing for, and why should I think that they will be interested in what I have to say about this topic?"

Writing for You

Yes, we asked ourselves these very same questions as we prepared to write this book. We (author-element) wanted to communicate the value of critical thinking (purpose-element) by writing a terrific book that teaches how to build critical thinking and apply critical thinking to real-world problems and decisions (presentation-element). But those three elements alone did not complete our rhetorical situation. We needed also to think a lot about *you.*

You, the college student, are our most important audience. We knew that we wanted to write this book for you. We knew that today's college student represents multiple and complex backgrounds in terms of age, race/ethnicity, religious affiliation, gender, health, family obligations, work responsibilities, interests, economic status, experiences, subject matter knowledge, skills, and belief systems. Because of the many faces in today's college classroom, we knew it was crucial for us to present many different real-world examples in the text scenarios and in the exercises. We also knew it was necessary to represent multiple perspectives on controversial issues; to show respect for the incredible diversity of the thousands of readers; to show sensitivity in our narratives, opening vignettes, and images you see on each page. We wanted you to see yourselves in the book and to know that it really was *written for you*.

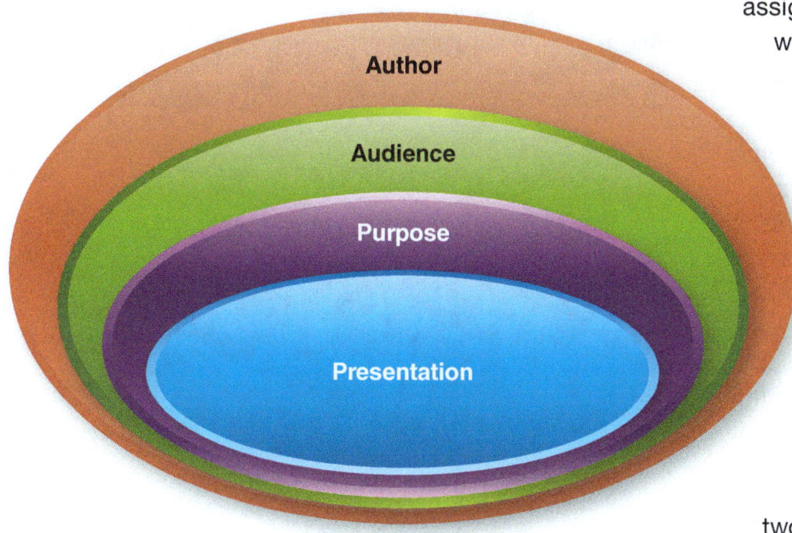

Rhetorical Situation –
The Interactive Combination of Four Elements

Written presentations often have multiple audiences, some not even intended by the authors. (We see that with tweets that go viral and "reply all—oops!" e-mails that circulate too widely and end up embarrassing their authors.) There was a *known* secondary audience for this book, namely your instructors. And so we authors thought a lot about how the book would be received and used by the faculty teaching critical thinking. For example, we wondered whether all the possible instructors would be familiar with the kinds of teaching tools and tactics that we planned to use in the book. Thinking that some instructors might be new to teaching for critical thinking, we wrote an instructors' manual to accompany this book. Because our main purpose was for you to build your critical thinking skills and develop strong critical thinking habits of mind, we decided to supply your instructors with all the support we possibly could provide so they, in turn, could help you get the most out of this book.

Who Is Your Audience?

"Write a paper on . . . !" One rhetorical situation you are highly likely to encounter as a college student is this: You (author) are asked by your instructor (audience) to write a paper (presentation) in which you research a topic and then take a position and defend your view (purpose). Many students, as they begin thinking about the topic they will write about, think about their opinion on that topic. We have two things to suggest. First, we suggest not taking one side or the other on an issue until after thoroughly researching it. This suggestion helps avoid the problem of locking-in prematurely, as described in Chapter 11 on reflective decision making. Our second suggestion: Think audience!

Who is the audience for the paper you are assigned to write? Many professors answer this question for you by identifying a target audience when they make the writing assignment. The professor might say, "Assume that you are writing a letter to the editor," or "Imagine that you are posting a blog for the whole world to see online," or "Write a paper that could be submitted for publication in a professional journal in your major." Or "Write a memo to your employer." Whenever the professor does specify the audience you can apply your analytical skills to determine how best to organize and express your ideas for that specific audience.

But what if the professor gives a writing assignment that does not include a specification of the intended audience? It is difficult to write for some imaginary, disembodied, unspecified audience about whom we know nothing. Professional writers would not attempt that. So, why should college students? We have two suggestions to offer. First, ask the professor to specify a target audience for the assignment. If that does not work, then as a last resort, imagine that the audience is the professor who made the assignment. Understand that college faculty are not entirely comfortable with being seen by their students as the rhetorical audience. So it is very likely that the first suggestion will work better.

However, if you are left with no option other than thinking of the professor as your audience, then proceed on the basis of that assumption. What do you know about that instructor and how can that knowledge help you to be more successful as a writer on this assignment? Begin with questions like this, "What can I assume that my instructor is looking for in this assignment?" Part of the answer to this will be in the grading criteria the instructor has described in the course syllabus and, more importantly, in any scoring rubrics and examples of the work of prior students that the instructor has shared. Another part of the answer to this comes from realizing what subject field standards the instructor is likely to apply. If the instructor is teaching writing or one of the humanities or arts disciplines, then the instructor is more likely to expect you to focus on analysis, interpretation, careful inference, and thoughtful evaluation. Your writing craft, important for all subject fields, may play a larger role in this instructor's assessment of your work. If the instructor is in the social or behavioral sciences or one of the professional fields then you can be sure that he or she will apply the standards appropriate to that discipline to your work. You'll find Chapters 12, 13, and 14, on comparative reasoning, ideological reasoning, and empirical reasoning, helpful—depending on which most applies to the instructor's discipline.

As you think about the instructor as your audience you will also want to ask yourself: what will get the instructor interested in your paper and make your paper stand out as compared to the other papers the instructor will also be reading. Writing is like golf: The best golfers compete against themselves, but golf is a sport, not just a pastime and competition with other players cannot be avoided. When a professor assigns a grade to a paper the professor typically uses an abstract grading standard like a scoring rubric, and the professor draws on his or her experience and expertise, measuring your work against the work of other students past and present. So it makes sense to ask yourself what will help your paper stand out as compared to the papers other students submit. What will keep the instructor focused and interested in what you have to say all the way through to the end of your paper? Instructors, being human, appreciate an engaging example, a clever turn of phrase, an apt metaphor, a concise and well-documented presentation, relevant quotations, well-crafted prose, accurate and informative graphics, insightful analyses, reasonable interpretations, and fair-minded presentations that offer a balanced, respectful, and objective approach to the topic at hand. Wit and irony are appreciated too, but only if all the other elements are present. You will also want to ask yourself what to avoid so the instructor will not respond negatively. For example, you will want to avoid grammatical errors, punctuation mistakes, and misspellings. Your instructor may react negatively to slang, profanity, and flippant comments. The instructor may have warned against overgeneralizations, claims that are not supported by evidence, or quotations that are inserted without appropriate citations. You can bet that the instructor will expect your work to be well organized and easy to follow, and be alienated by a paper that is nothing more than a swamp of mushy and marshy disjointed paragraphs.

Same Author and Audience, Different Purpose

Let's keep the same author (you) and the same audience (your professor) in this next example, but we'll change the purpose and the presentation. Suppose you want to communicate with one of your college professors that you are thinking of majoring in that professor's discipline and you wonder what careers people with that major are likely to pursue. Three elements in the rhetorical situation are clear. You (author) want to talk about (presentation) possibly majoring in the discipline so you can find out what career potentials it offers (purpose). The remaining element, the professor (audience), is more of an unknown now. Yes, you have been taking classes from this professor, but now you are going outside of that relatively well-defined context. Now you are seeking to communicate person-to-person about an academic discipline that might become your chosen major and shape your college studies and possibly your professional life after college. What do you know about this professor as a professional scholar and educator in that field? Maybe you sensed the professor's passion for the subject matter, or you were intrigued by the kinds of questions the professor's discipline explores. But talking with your professor is not like talking with a friend over coffee or with a family member around the kitchen table. So, strategize. How will you communicate with this professor? E-mail, text message, phone call, facebook, drop by during office hours, or catch the professor after class? And what will you say, (Probably not, "Yo, Dr. dude, your major is sick, man! Hook me up."). How will you communicate your interest in the subject area and your concern that the subject you decide to major in should also further your professional aspirations after graduation?

What if the machine grading your exam can't tell the difference between sense and nonsense?

Smart and strategic writers consider all of their audiences, including the non-human ones. This example may also apply to you. Suppose that your essay is going to be read and graded by a computer. Although abhorrent to faculty in a great many disciplines, this is happening more and more with group assessment instruments like the CLA.[v] And also with the college and graduate school entrance exams like the SAT and the GMAT that individuals take.[vi] What do computers look for when they evaluate an essay? Will the computer be able to tell that you are using irony, hyperbole, or sarcasm effectively? Will the computer be able to detect the differences in the quality of the critical thinking expressed in your analyses, interpretations, inferences, explanations, or evaluations? Or will the computer's scoring algorithm focus on syntax, spelling, average sentence length, average word length, sentence structure, and word choice?[vii] For more on the plusses and minuses of computer-graded written work visit "Thinking Critically—Grading Written Submissions" in Chapter 9 (p. 170).

THINK PURPOSE AND CIRCUMSTANCES

"What exactly am I trying to accomplish? And "How will I achieve it?" These are two of the most important questions an effective writer asks. Sound and effective writing is a matter of purpose and strategy, not just topic, word count, and sentence structure. A clear purpose is essential. Our advice: don't write it if you don't know why you're writing it.

But when you do know why, don't stop there. Make sure your audience knows too. When an author fails to communicate her or his thesis or goal, the audience is left to wonder "what's the point?" The audience is likely to tune out even if they care about the topic. They simply will not want to hear about it from that author.

Before producing words on the computer screen, effective writers clearly define the goal or purpose of their written communication and they think carefully about their strategy for achieving that goal. Imagine yourself creating a battle plan. "My goal is to persuade this audience of the truth of this claim. To achieve this goal I must do this, this, and this. And in accord with rules of engagement I will use sound and well-documented arguments." The overall strategy for leading the audience to believe that a claim is true and to act on the truth of that claim is communicating worthy arguments. As we noted, that concept is defined in Chapter 7, on evaluating arguments, where we describe the basic interpersonal expectations and responsibilities associated with the human practice of argument making and reason giving. Those are, in effect, what we have metaphorically here called the "rules of engagement."

Think Tactics

Strategy is the big picture approach. But successful campaigns are also tactical. Strong critical thinkers drill down into the details. As effective writers they ask tactical questions like these:

- "My case rests on three strong arguments, but which one will I put first and which one will I close with?"
- "I have a lot of abstract concepts and solid statistical information to build upon, but is there a vivid comparison or a gripping narrative that I can use to illustrate my point?"
- "This audience is apt to react negatively to me as an outsider unless I somehow let them know that I really do understand their issues and concerns, so how can I build that into my presentation?"
- "This audience is impatient, so how can I make my key point powerfully clear as early in my presentation as possible?"

Consider this example. Suppose you are taking a marketing course and the professor has made this assignment: *Prepare a 5–7-page paper with references addressing this topic: "How to improve brand X's recognition in television advertisements."* Right away you recognize that your professor is giving you some freedom in defining how you will approach your written response. What are some questions you could ask in order to think about your purpose when writing this paper? We can interpret this paper topic to mean that our paper has to include a marketing strategy for a brand of our choosing. To be effective you will need to write more than your personal opinions. At a minimum you will need some quotes from successful ad agencies' Web sites and from books describing the social science theories that apply to successful marketing. Ask yourself, what other source material might be useful? Perhaps a couple of extended examples showing what works when advertising the brand you decided to talk about.

Effective writing, like accomplishing one's mission, requires tactical problem solving and decision making.

Clues from Contextual Cues

Take advantage of situational and contextual cues. For example, you know you are writing a paper *for a college class*. Therefore a goal should be to present your written case using the format, language, and style appropriate for an academic paper.[viii] And since your professor declined to tell you anything about an intended audience, you infer that the audience is your professor. You also know that the professor is going to be reading lots of papers and so you will want yours to emerge as one of the best. Tactically it might make sense to select products from a brand that the professor might see himself or herself using and then to suggest a marketing approach that might appeal to the professor's demographic. This could help capture the professor's interest, as compared to talking about products and brands that the professor is not likely to care anything about. Again, this is a tactical suggestion. Every situation is different when we get to the level of tactics. You need to apply your critical thinking skills to plan your own approach, given what you know about *your* audience.

Another context cue: This paper is for this course, not some other course. So it makes sense to be sure to incorporate the ideas, theories, and concepts that this professor and the text for this course have been addressing in this part of the syllabus. Professors do not typically assign papers that are unrelated to the material they have been covering in that part of the course. Having shown your knowledge of this course, it is always useful to then think about how you will show that you can connect and integrate what you are learning in this course to other relevant knowledge gained in other courses.

Sound and effective written work typically revolves around one main controlling idea or purpose. Know your main claim. Write it out. Work it word for word until it expresses exactly what you intend to communicate. Of course, you cannot know what your main claim is with regard to a controversial topic until you research the topic open-mindedly, learn about it, and consider the various pros and cons objectively. But after you have engaged your powers of reasoned reflective judgment, set forth your considered opinion on the topic. Having done so, you can marshal your reasons and evidence, showing how you make the case for your claim and also how you consider and address the major counterarguments. Map everything out: claims, options rejected, reasons, assumptions,

"This book aims to strengthen critical thinking skills and nurture the courageous desire to seek truth by following reasons and evidence wherever they lead. . . .

"Our approach is simple, practical and focused. To strengthen critical thinking skills we have to use them. To build positive critical thinking habits of mind we have to engage our beliefs, intentions, and values around the importance of thinking critically as the optimal means of solving problems and making decisions, particularly in contexts of risk and uncertainty. [We use] questions, exercises, video clips, controversial examples, contemporary issues, practical life problems, classic questions, science, technology, religion, politics—all these and more . . . whatever it takes."

—From the Preface to *Think Critically*
Our message to you about our purpose and our strategy for achieving it.

counter-arguments and responses to them. Creating the outline for your paper is relatively straightforward from that point, *because you have done the thinking and organized your own ideas.* You have already worked carefully though your side and the other side in doing your background research.

Your paper becomes the document that presents the fruit of those mental labors in an orderly progression so that your audience can follow the path of your logic. A typical progression might be this:

- Here's the question or problem this paper is addressing.
- Here are the main possible options as discussed in the relevant literature.
- Here are the pros and cons of each of the main options.
- Because of the research I've done, this is where I come down on this topic, and here are my reasons.
- Yes, I am aware of potential problems and objections to my point.
- Here are the important ones and here is how I would propose to address them.
- Here is how we will know that the approach I am proposing is working.
- This is the bibliography of sources upon which this paper relies.

Think How to Organize and Develop Your Presentation

Whatever the medium, book, term paper, report, exam essay, e-mail, etc., a presentation cannot be effective unless it reaches out and grabs the audience's attention. To do this the author has to do more than lay out the facts like fish filets on crushed ice in the supermarket. The author has to share something of himself or herself—passion for the topic, concern for the audience, significance of the purpose, something real, something human, or something that communicates the value of the work. Even formal scientific publications include a paragraph addressing the reason why the research is important.

REACH OUT AND GRAB SOMEONE

"How will I get my audience's attention?" is a key question effective writers ask themselves. But it is slightly different from the question that hangs up many less experienced writers. They tend to ask, "How will I start my paper?" That question is almost on target because it focuses on the vitally important opening paragraph. But it is slightly off target too, because it focuses on the author instead of the audience. In general it is a good idea to eliminate "I" whenever possible. The audience should be the focus, not the author. You can see the contrasting results by comparing these two "draft opening paragraphs" to a paper about the economy.

Ho Hum Nap Time Draft	Okay, I'd Like to Read Some More Draft
In this paper I want to talk about the economy. There are a lot of things happening. I will first describe the current economic situation. The question for this paper is should a person invest in the stock market now or wait until the economy improves. I will say wait. Then I will explain why it is a bad time to buy stock and then talk about safer possibilities, like investing in government bonds.	Like hurricane Irene tearing up the East coast to pummel New York, massive economic storms are ravaging world markets, including our New York Stock Exchange. What do smart people do in a storm? They think safety first and hunker down. The economic equivalent is investing in government bonds. Now is no time to venture naively into the economic hurricane by buying stocks. This paper explains why.

Thinking Critically A Dozen Office E-Mail No No's

The tactics of successful written communication extend to the workplace and to its most prominent mode of sharing information and ideas, namely e-mail. Assume you are working in a typical office and suppose your boss has asked you a question by e-mail and expects an e-mail response. What are some of the do's and don'ts of that rhetorical situation? Having worked many years as administrators in large, complex organizations, we have learned, the hard way, some communication tactics:

1. Brevity is next to godliness—say it all on one screen.
2. Focus—no more than one topic per e-mail.
3. Never delegate problems or work upward to your boss—do the work, solve the problems, communicate solutions.
4. State the benefits of your proposal, not the shortcomings of someone else's.
5. Never propose something that is against company policies.
6. Don't display ignorance of management directives.
7. Be upbeat and positive, but not unreasonably optimistic.
8. Make your case using good reasons and accurate information.
9. Get it right the first time—follow-up corrections only make you look bad.
10. Irony does not play well in e-mails, nor do snarky comments.
11. Don't assume everyone has read the relevant background material.
12. Expect that if the higher-ups like your idea you will be asked to write it up in greater detail.

If there are tactics for successful e-mail communications at work, are there also tactics for effective workplace tweets between employees and bosses? If so, what are they?

There are many ways to grab your reader's attention. Vivid images, like hurricane Irene tearing up New York City, work. Apt comparisons are effective. In the example draft venturing into the stock market is compared to venturing out into a hurricane. Mixing in short punchy sentences, along with longer more detailed sentences, works too. By contrast, limp, tepid prose, navel-gazing introspection, and pedantic elitism are likely to alienate even a willing audience.

Successful writers and presenters show the audience that they care about them and that they are passionate about their topics. The audience can tell if the caring is real and the passion is genuine. If so, the audience will most often connect. We know an extraordinary math professor who teaches statistics. The course is required and students are often leery of taking a statistics course. But across the board they all praise the effectiveness of this particular professor as being the reason for their academic success in a class they were dreading. We asked some students why they thought this professor was so effective. Their response was that she was both knowledgeable and passionate about statistics, and she had an uncanny ability to express her excitement about statistics while teaching the concepts the students needed to learn. Students said they looked forward to her classes because she was so enthusiastic about stats and energized to work with them on real-world examples. She made a hard subject understandable and doable. For her the key to a successful presentation was her love for her subject and her passion to help her students learn it and be able to apply it.

CRAFTING A PRESENTATION

As far as the technical aspects of a written presentation go, there are many fine sources offering useful guidance about the craft of writing. We derived this list, for example, from the College Board.[ix]

- Once you have selected your topic, keep your focus narrow and manageable.
- Establish a clear thesis statement early—be specific and compelling.
- Use headings and subheadings to guide the reader.
- Assemble evidence to support claims—include interpretations of evidence.
- Be fair-minded and balanced in presentation—be sure to give cons and pros.
- Cite sources using appropriate style (MLA, APA, Chicago, etc.). There are publication manuals and resources on the Internet to assist with the stylistic requirements.
- Never plagiarize. Use quotes or paraphrasing, depending on the style of the discipline, and always provide citations.
- Use appropriate terminology and vocabulary and consider word choice appropriate to your audience. Most professors prefer if students' papers avoid overgeneralizations, colloquialisms, idioms, slang, profanity, pretentious rhetoric, problematic vagueness, and problematic ambiguity.
- Avoid parenthetical expressions.
- Follow format requirements: margins size, sentence spacing, page numbering, font size, meaningful title, endnote styles, footnote styles, list of works cited at the end.
- Write, rewrite, and polish your writing.
- Proofread your work, read it aloud, ask someone else to check it too.

Crafting an effective presentation matters for textbook writers, too. Given our purpose and our audience, we then thought about the presentation itself. Here are four examples. You be the judge. Did they work?

- We knew we needed to include many varied examples of real-world situations and current events focusing on issues

Thinking Critically Writing for Thinking

Why do you suppose that every chapter of this book includes a reflective log exercise?

Yes, because writing is a great way to improve critical thinking, just like applying our critical thinking skills and habits of mind is a great way to improve our writing. The critical thinking skill of meta-cognitive self-correction is the key to becoming a better thinker and writer.

Hence the reflective log exercises. They demand that we exercise that particular critical thinking skill. Meta-cognition enables us to reflect on our own thinking. We can analyze, interpret, explain, and evaluate our own thinking by the standards of good reasoning. We are using our own critical thinking skills to monitor and to improve our own thinking, just like we use those same skills to review and improve our own writing.

Meta-cognitive self-correction is a remarkable human mental ability. It is the engine that drives an individual's and a collaborative team's growth in thinking. It helps explain why strong critical thinking is manifested by a great many people including those who have not had the benefit of formal education.

The opposite is true as well. One reason why some do not develop their critical thinking to the fullest extent possible is that they are not reflective. Even some who have received many years of schooling end up full of disjointed things they memorized and lots of scripted training, but they cannot tell you why the training makes sense or what to do with all the facts they crammed into their crania. Like computers that can only execute their programs, but cannot monitor, evaluate, or improve those programs, without meta-cognitive self-reflection people fail to grow and to mature as thinkers.

We sincerely hope that the reflective log exercises, an important feature of the presentation plans for this book, have been working well for you.

and situations that college students of all kinds could find interesting. Otherwise you might be less motivated to engage the examples and less likely to benefit as much from the book. So all the examples in Chapter 3, which is about problem solving, focus on college students and how they can achieve success by being better problem solvers.

- Not wanting to cause any readers to feel excluded because a given term or example related only to people who were in some major, we selected examples and exercises with great care and we explained all the key terms and technical vocabulary needed. Someplace or other in this book there is an example that fits your major, no matter what your major is, including undeclared.
- To keep the pages fresh and interesting to read we avoided bland droning discourse *about* critical thinking as an academic concept, and instead focused on writing *for* critical thinking. Hence the focus on application and integration of critical thinking into life and learning.
- Realizing that most people learn best "from examples to theories" instead of "from theories to examples," we opened each chapter with an illustrative example, and we often organized sections and paragraphs so that the examples came above the explanatory text.

GOOD NEWS: WRITING IS WORK

The great inventor Thomas Alva Edison said, "Genius is 1 percent inspiration and 99 percent perspiration."[x] We cannot speak about genius, but we can say from experience that sound and effective writing is at most 10 percent inspiration and at least 90 percent perspiration. We think this is good news, because it means that people who put in the required effort can become more effective. If writing were largely about inspiration, then we all would be in trouble because inspiration is difficult, if not impossible, to teach.

So, if writing is basically digging in and working hard, then what are the things that need to be done? Effective writers seeking to build a reasonable and credible case are diligently methodical. They take the time and spend the energy to do things like

Develop a plausible, clear, and precise thesis statement
Inform themselves about the topic by doing solid research
Draft a solid, well-organized outline
Double check the credibility of their sources
Prewrite, write, and rewrite their presentation

An Arguable Thesis Statement and Solid Research

Organizers use social media to notify people about the time, place, and purpose of protests and demonstrations. In the summer of 2011 organizers planned to hold a demonstration on one of the subway platforms used by San Francisco's Bay Area Rapid Transit (BART). Concerned about possible injuries or deaths if protestors or passengers should fall off the platform into the path of a train or on to the electric rail, BART officials made the decision to shut down cell phone coverage. Effectively this prevented planners from organizing their demonstration, which was to be held in protest to an earlier shooting of an individual by armed BART security guards.[xi]

Suppose the professor teaching your English course gives this assignment: "Write an arguable thesis statement about BART's decision to close down cellular communications. Was it a violation of the First Amendment or a prudent business decision?" Analyze the following draft thesis statements and distinguish the arguable statements from those which are off-topic or for which no plausible case can be developed.

1 Free speech protections extend to cellular communications.
2 A business has an obligation to protect its customers from foreseeable harm.
3 Freedom of speech is the cornerstone of an open society.

Critical Thinking Skills Questions Asked by Effective Writers

THINK AUTHOR (MYSELF)

Interpretation—What about me makes me a credible author on this topic?

Analysis—What biases might I have in relation to the topic or issue?

Inference—Why am I motivated to undertake this communication?

Evaluation—Do I have the necessary knowledge and experience to write about this?

Explanation—How is my background influencing my perspective on this issue?

Self-Regulation—How can I remain open to considering alternative points of view or counter-evidence?

THINK AUDIENCE

Interpretation—Who is the audience for this communication?

Analysis—Is the audience receptive to the argument?

Inference—What will build credibility and trust between me and the audience?

Evaluation—Was the desired response achieved?

Explanation—Why does the audience need to hear this argument?

Self-Regulation—How do shifts in the audience's mode or knowledge change the argument?

THINK PURPOSE

Interpretation—What is the cognitive or behavioral purpose of this communication?

Analysis—What situational factors enhance or limit the effectiveness of this communication?

Inference—If the purpose is achieved, what will the audience do?

Evaluation—Are the reasons presented appropriate to the audience and to the purpose?

Explanation—How does the historical (economic, cultural, interpersonal, etc.) context influence the evaluation of evidence?

Self-Regulation—What could be done to refine the purpose and adjust better to the circumstances influencing this communication?

THINK PRESENTATION

Interpretation—Should the argument be an oral, written, or visual communication?

Analysis—How should the argument be structured so that it is optimally persuasive?

Inference—If I use this rhetorical device, how will the audience react?

Evaluation—Are style requirements being met?

Explanation—How did word choice influence the impact of the communication?

Self-Regulation—Will further revision and rewriting improve the strength of the communication?

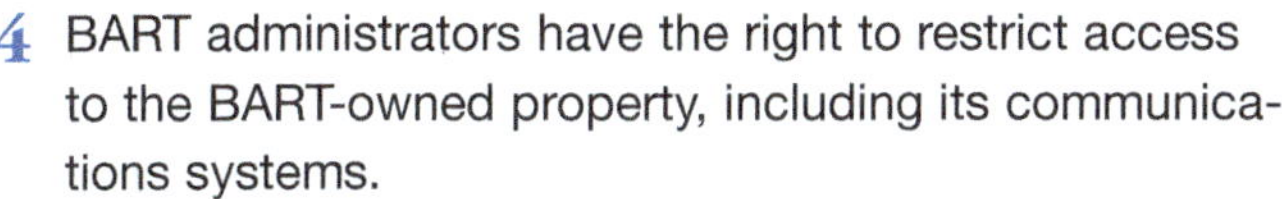

4 BART administrators have the right to restrict access to the BART-owned property, including its communications systems.

5 Concern for possible injury was not a sufficient cause for BART to have prevented peaceful protests.

6 The rain in Spain falls mainly on the train.

7 What is wrong with BART?

We can imagine developing arguments in support of the first six, but not #7. That one is a question, not a claim. It assumes that there is something wrong with BART. But the grammatical structure is wrong because it suggests that the paper is going to be an investigation, rather than the defense of your position on this issue. A careful interpretation of the professor's prompt is always in order. "What is the professor asking me to do?" An arguable thesis is going to be a *claim* as we have used the term throughout this book. A claim is a statement that the maker of an argument is endeavoring to show to be true or probably true. #7 does not fit that criterion. #6 can go too. Yes, we can conduct an empirical inquiry into the average annual distribution of precipitation on Spain's railroad equipment. But that is not relevant to the topic at hand.

The other candidates are contenders. But some are better than others. We suggest that #1, #2, and #3 do not meet the objective of the professor's assignment as well as #4 and #5 do. Here is why. Those first three, while relevant, are expressions of principles and values that could be useful as premises in top-down ideological arguments, but they are not focused on BART. The assignment calls for claims that assert that the decision made by the BART officials was either the right one or the wrong one. A clear and arguable thesis statement for a class assignment always draws upon a careful interpretation and analysis of the professor's question prompt. The professor said to talk about "BART's decision." Only #4 and #5 fit the demand. The next step, after researching the issue thoroughly and with an open mind to both sides of the issue, would be to analyze and then evaluate the reasons for and against the BART decision.

Map Out the Arguments Pro and Con—Then Outline Your Case

Our recommended tool for analysis is the argument and decision mapping process detailed in Chapter 5. Lay out the competing positions. What kinds of considerations would you expect to find in your review of the arguments in the BART example? In addition to doing the research, think about how you would make the strongest possible case for both sides. You might bring in principles like protecting innocent people from harm, affirming the rights of free speech, affirming the rights of business owners to control the use of their own property, and affirming the importance of laws which give priority to free speech over other lesser considerations.

As you do the research it is important to get all the reasons on the table. Work backward to dig out the reasons for the reasons and their implicit and explicit assumptions too. Diagram and color-code the counterarguments and statements that reveal invitations to further deliberation. Discover where lines of reasoning have been abandoned. Once you have mapped the terrain in detail you can add your own additional reasons, extend or defend arguments that have come under criticism, and amplify the map until you have fully expressed the relevant reasoning. And then, using the basic tests for the quality of arguments developed and for evaluating the credibility of claims, apply your critical thinking skills of evaluation to the elements in your decision map. Are the arguments worthy? Are the initial premises they rely upon credible?

To give you more of an idea of how a decision map related to the BART example might be developed, we've provided some preliminary ideas in the draft map. That map is underdeveloped. You'll see that four options are identified. Maybe there are more options. Arguments and counterarguments are anticipated only for two of the options in the map. A more refined map would explore arguments for and against the other options as well. There are unspoken assumptions that are not yet presented in the map. And the issue of the reason for the protests is not identified in the map either. Not to worry. Decision mapping, as we explained in Chapter 5, is a process of deeper and deeper analysis with maps being refined, revised, and improved as you go along.

After you have refined your analyses and filled out your decision map, then, with all the research, analysis, interpretation, inference, and evaluation as preparatory work in hand, you can make an informed, precise, and clear expression of your considered opinion regarding BART's decision. Now, having done the heavy lifting, you are ready to write your arguable thesis statement in light of your analysis. As you formulate your thesis statement, you may now want to offer an even more refined thesis statement. How about one of these?

- The BART decision, while it appeared to limit the corporation's financial liabilities, was a public relations disaster, a sure way to get sued, and an invitation to jurists and legislators to be clear that First Amendment protections do extend to cellular communications.
- Although legally and financially risky, in the end the BART decision to curtail cellular communications was the only mature and responsible choice, given the risks to innocent bystanders that the protestors appear to have disregarded.

And now, with your thesis statement clearly articulated and all the arguments mapped, you can readily outline your case. You know your reasons, the reasons for the other side, the counterarguments and the strengths and weaknesses of each.

EVALUATING THE CREDIBILITY OF SOURCES

If you are a registered voter then you probably have received voter materials about initiatives or measures that will appear on the ballot. Consider the following example of a parcel tax to be levied by the local school district to improve public education:

To provide stable funding for local high schools, maintain outstanding core academic programs in math, science, and English, retain highly qualified teachers, provide programs that prepare students for college and careers, and provide classroom materials like books and science lab equipment, shall the Mountain Ridge Joint Union High School District be authorized to levy $35 per parcel annually for six years, with citizen oversight, an exemption for seniors, no funds for administrators' salaries, and every dollar staying in local high schools? (Yes/No).

Five Suggestions for Identifying and Gathering Credible Source Material

1. Select appropriate databases. As powerful as it is, we suggest not limiting your searches to Google and Google Scholar. In addition, use the subject matter–oriented databases in your campus library.
2. Search for source material before formulating your thesis. One mark of a strong critical thinker is the realization that everyone has their point of view, including the investigator. To avoid biased searches that only produce evidence to support their preconceptions, strong critical thinkers intentionally discipline themselves to hold off taking sides or formulating their thesis until after the research is completed.
3. Be your own best critic. Once you have taken a tentative position on an issue, discipline yourself to search for relevant counter-evidence to that position. It will either strengthen your case to be able to account for the counter-evidence, or lead you to reconsider, which is what maturity of judgment and strong critical thinking would require.
4. It is better to list several good sources than to list every possible document that might remotely apply. Refine your search to produce a manageable number of sources. Narrow your keywords, define your audience, limit the time frame to only the past few years, seek sources that give even-handed overviews or that are fundamental or seminal works.
5. Evaluate the credibility of the sources. Find out who the author is, what the basis is for the claims being made, who manages the Web site where those claims are posted. Check the credentials of all proponents and opponents, evaluate the methods used in the source materials, establish that the material is authentic, reliable, and based on facts rather than a clever hoax. Remember Chapter 6; Don't end up on a blind date with Godzilla and don't send money to save the tree octopi of the Pacific Northwest.

MAP > it > OUT 1
BART'S Decision - DRAFT

"Thinking like an effective writer means carefully, thoughtfully, skeptically evaluating potential information resources for credibility, authority, and bias, being unwilling to settle for the borderline-relevant, easy-to-find, pops-to-the-top-of-a-Google-search source and taking the time to rigorously critique all the information that goes into your work."

—*Gail Gradowski, University Librarian*

Like most voters, you probably have had limited exposure to the actual language of this parcel tax proposal. Wanting to make an informed decision, you prepare to apply your critical thinking skills to the question by informing yourself about the issue. So, naturally, one place you look is to the voter materials that came in the mail. Government-prepared voter information materials provide useful examples of written arguments because they typically include three things: First an analysis of the ballot measure by an informed and impartial party, such as the county legal counsel; second statements pro and con supplied by interested individuals or groups; and third rebuttals to those statements that are provided by interested individuals and groups who have exercised their legal rights to review the arguments presented by the other side and to formulate responses.[xii] The point of all of this, of course, is to provide voters with information so that important decisions are not made by kneejerk System-1 snap judgments, but instead by reflective System-2 reasoned deliberation.

In our parcel tax example, the supporting statement is signed by five individuals: a local resident and city historian, the president of the Home and School Club, the co-president of the Parent Teacher Student Association, a local business owner, and an MD who is a former president of the State medical association. A rebuttal to the pro argument is presented by someone who describes himself simply as a concerned voter. This same individual submitted a position statement against the ballot measure. The rebuttal to the opposition is signed by the district school board president and its budget advisory committee members, two different chairmen of local charitable foundations that support education, as well as an alumnus of the district who is identified as a Rhodes Scholar. Without having access to the position statements of either side in this issue, but simply based on your life experience and what you learned in Chapter 6 about evaluating sources, which side of the issue appears to have more initial perceived credibility? Why?

Mindful of the risks as well as the benefits of System-1 heuristic thinking, we want to avoid jumping to the conclusion that the "concerned voter" is automatically less credible than the various individuals and groups that have come out in support of the ballot measure. By the same token, we don't want to jump to the conclusion that because it is a tax increase it is automatically a bad idea or that because the money is for schools that it is automatically a good idea. All of these "fast and furious" one-rule decisions can lead us to problems. In California, where we live, cleverly deceitful authors of ballot initiatives know that too many of us are likely to rely too heavily on our System-1 reactions instead of digging deeper into the ballot measures. So they disguise their intentions by using misleading titles for their initiatives. For all we know in California, some outfit with a title-nobody-could-be-against, like "Taxpayers Who Love Democracy," might sponsor an initiative perhaps named "The Freedom of Communication for All Act," which, if passed, would actually regulate or restrict various modes of communication. We never know. In our state it's important to apply System-2 and read the fine print.

How might we activate our System-2 thinking to evaluate the credibility of sources? Recalling the guidance in Chapter 6, we can start by asking whether the individual or group has the relevant expertise. Ideally our source, the person or people who are authoring the message, will enjoy all 12 of the positive characteristics of a trustworthy source as described in that earlier chapter. The list is straightforward. We've reproduced it here for you.

Twelve Characteristics of a Trustworthy Source

- Learned in topic X
- Experienced in topic X
- Speaking about X
- Up-to-date about X
- Capable of explaining the basis for their claim or their advice about X
- Unbiased
- Truthful
- Free of conflicts of interest
- Acting in accord with our interests
- Unconstrained
- Informed about the specifics of the case at hand
- Mentally stable

PREWRITING, WRITING, AND REWRITING

When the time comes to set fingers to keyboard, the actual process of writing an effective essay is commonly described as having three phases: *prewriting*, *writing*, and *rewriting.*"[xiii] Within each of these phases there are specific steps that can yield a higher-quality final written product. Here is what we and others suggest.[xiv]

PREWRITING: Organizing my thoughts – strategic decisions about presenting my case. Grab the audience's attention, explain your purpose, and describe the order in which your case will unfold the various arguments and counterarguments pro and con and the supporting documentation. Be sure to do the following:

1. Identify a topic, problem, or question as clearly as possible.
2. Develop a clear, focused, plausible, and arguable thesis statement.
3. Gather relevant evidence and credible source material.
4. Prepare a decision map that organizes all the arguments pro and con, from which you can then outline the entire presentation of your case, section by section.

WRITING: From the title to endnotes, put together one complete draft. Be sure to:

5. Draft a strong, clear, succinct introduction telling the reader what to expect.
6. Draft the body of your essay, focusing on main ideas and sub-ideas. Stick to your outline, or if a change is needed, change the outline too. Don't soar off into a free flight of opinions or irrelevant digressions after doing all the work of organizing your ideas and researching your topic.
7. Draft the conclusion which summarizes your views and reminds the audience of the issue, its importance, and the main thesis you have defended.

REWRITING: Check it. Fix it. Make it sing your song.

8. Rewrite the draft for clarity, flow, style, and interest. Delete repetitious material. Smooth out transitions. Be sure that the structural organization is clear to the reader so that the reader does not get lost in the details.
9. Check the craft before launching by reviewing the entire draft for mechanical or organizational errors, grammatical issues, misspellings, missing citations, sentence fragments, etc. Make edits as warranted and reread.
10. If available, incorporate feedback from peers, external reviewers, or the instructor.

TWO PRACTICAL TIPS

Extremely successful and influential writers, like George Orwell and Stephen King,[xv] offer interesting and candid guidance on how to practice the craft more effectively. We know we are not in their league. So, sticking with the theme that writing is 90-plus percent perspiration, we do have some practical tips to suggest.

We find it helpful to copy and paste the outline for our written work right into the document file that will become the first draft. This gives us the architectural structure, the red steel as it were, that we can then build upon. The outline provides us with the heading, subheading, and all the reminders of what we planned to say and where we planned to say it in the flow of the essay. The more detailed the outline, the better. Add notes that represent the evidence you plan on using in your case, a clever example or analogy that you want to use, quotes that fit well at various points. And don't forget to identify your sources. They can go into the outline too! There is nothing that wastes more time than placing an important quote or piece of evidence in your outline only to realize later that you have forgotten where you found it. Many of the

Thinking Critically Gullible, Uncritical Searchers Make the Internet a Liar's Paradise

Strong critical thinkers treat Internet sources with a healthy skepticism until they thoroughly check the credibility of those sources. Everyone who uses the Internet would be wise to keep their guard up. A poor job of evaluating the credibility of sources can be very embarrassing. Nobody wants to be tricked into including factual errors and outrageous inaccuracies in their written assignments.

A case in point: Suppose you have been given the assignment of writing a paper for your American History course on the effectiveness of Dr. Martin Luther King's non-violent, civil disobedience in undermining the culture of racial segregation in the United States. A search on the Internet produces the following possible sources:

—http://www.thekingcenter.org/
—http://www.martinlutherking.org/
—http://en.wikipedia.org/wiki/Martin_Luther_King,_Jr
—http://www.kinginstitute.info/

Visit each of these Web sites and evaluate their credibility using the tools presented in this chapter and in Chapter 6. Get past the home pages. Be sure to analyze each site completely (HINT: One of these is a hate site intended to mislead gullible searchers). What observations can you make about the author(s) and their credentials, organizational affiliations, accuracy of their "information," and hidden or not so hidden biases?

Does the Web address alone influence your perception of the credibility of the source? How accurate was that perception in light of what you observed by reviewing each Web site? How can we use our critical thinking skills of analysis and evaluation to determine whether these are sources that we should trust enough to cite in our written assignment?

"I think the following rules will cover most cases:
(i) Never use a metaphor, simile, or other figure of speech which you are used to seeing in print.
(ii) Never use a long word where a short one will do.
(iii) If it is possible to cut a word out, always cut it out.
(iv) Never use the passive where you can use the active.
(v) Never use a foreign phrase, a scientific word, or a jargon word if you can think of an everyday English equivalent.
(vi) Break any of these rules sooner than say anything outright barbarous."

—George Orwell, "Politics and the English Language," 1946

examples in this textbook started out as reminders typed in a different font color or as track-changes comment balloons so we would remember where to best use them. The endnotes and the Internet URLs were included so that the finished text could be enriched with real-world examples when we came back through to rewrite and to polish the rougher drafts.

Secondly, there is an arc to the quality of writing that can be produced in a single sitting. Much like it takes a runner time to warm up and settle into a comfortable pace, the effective writer is likely to notice that when she or he first sits down to write, the quality of the work may not be as strong as it will become once the writer has become more connected and engages with the writing activity. And again, like the runner who will experience fatigue over time that will inevitably compromise his or her pace, the writing will exhibit a peak in writing quality and ultimately begin to show signs of fatigue.

In our experience there are at least two lessons to be learned from becoming aware of this writing quality arc. First, it is highly improbable that a high-quality written communication can be produced in a single session. Second, to improve the weaker beginning and ending sections of a writing session it often works to start by reviewing, and editing the writing completed during the *previous* session. Like applying overlapping roof shingles to keep the rain out, each session overlaps the previous a bit and is, in turn, overlapped by the session that follows. Using reviewing and editing the previous session as a warm-up, it is easier to move forward into the new material, having settled in to a writing groove. Overlapping the arcs in writing quality is more likely to produce writing that is consistent in its quality from start to finish rather than work that is choppy, disconnected, and uneven.

A writing session arcs like a workout session: warm up, hit your stride, cool down.

Evaluating Effectiveness

We know how to evaluate the worthiness of arguments to be sure that they are sound, logical, non-fallacious, and non-circular. So if the arguments we produce in our written work meet those standards, then we have the "sound" part of "sound and effective" covered. But how do writers determine that their presentations are effective? To assess the potential for their written arguments to be effective, writers first assure themselves that they have correctly analyzed, interpreted, and addressed each element in the rhetorical situation. And secondly, as with all writing, the writers attend to the craft and mechanics of writing.

FEATURES OF SOUND AND EFFECTIVE WRITTEN ARGUMENTATION

Throughout this chapter we've suggested several strategies for crafting a sound written case that, if followed, increase the likelihood that the case will also be effective. So what are the features of effective written argumentation? We shared many of these features in the sections on analyzing the rhetorical situation and on the methods of developing the presentation. Here again are a few of the most important points to remember as you work to persuade reasonable people that your position on a given topic is the correct one or that your recommendations are worth accepting:

- An effective written presentation addresses a clear and manageable thesis in a way that is appropriate for the intended audience and the mode, purpose, and context of the communication.

- The reasons and claims are focused on supporting a focused and plausible thesis statement.
- The author has delivered a fair-minded and balanced discussion of the pros and cons, analyzed the relevant evidence, addressed key assumptions, and presented a credible case in a thorough and objective manner.
- The writing style is concise and coherent, and the author uses headings and an organized sequence of ideas and transitions to connect the paragraphs into a flowing essay.
- The author communicates a detectable voice, perspective, or personality and demonstrates respect for the audience and the audience's capacity to reach reasonable conclusions if presented with the relevant information.
- The written presentation is mechanically error free in terms of grammar, punctuation, spelling, and citations.

Practice is the key. This is very doable. As lead author of this book and many others, I speak from experience. I collected more than a few C's on high school and college written assignments before I learned that effective writing was largely a set of learnable skills. That's what the "90 percent perspiration" is about. Learning to write well, like building critical thinking skills, is a matter of doing the work: solid research; detailed outlines; carefully developed paragraphs; cohesive arguments; and attention to the details of correct, thoughtful, respectful, and accurate presentations. The approach we are recommending may not result in inspired prose and it may not garner many awards for creativity or eloquence, but following the suggestions we have presented will help you write a sound and effective case. And your case will be more persuasive because you will have clearly displayed the power of the critical thinking you will have applied to the topic.

A TOOL FOR EVALUATING CRITICAL THINKING AND WRITING

What standards do strong critical thinkers use when evaluating the soundness and effectiveness of their writing? Written presentations are generally evaluated in terms of the accuracy and efficacy of four domains: (1) *content,* which includes all assertions and supporting evidence; (2) *organization,* which includes the clarity of paragraph arrangement and effectiveness of transitions between paragraphs; (3) *mechanics,* which includes grammar, spelling, punctuation, and vocabulary; and (4) *style,* which includes formatting and, when appropriate, citation style. These domains can be further represented by two overarching categories: *the author's demonstration of critical thinking through the writing,* and *the author's command and competency at the craft of writing.* Strong critical thinking and masterful writing competency will be observed in a sound and effectively written argumentation. But, like any two independent but compatible sets of skills, strength in one does not ensure strength in the other. Both must be evaluated independently.

Let's assume you have organized, developed, and written a presentation that presents your well-researched best judgment about what to believe or what to do. And now you want to evaluate it yourself, before you hand it in to your professor or share it with whomever your intended audience may happen to be. We have an evaluation tool to share with you: The *Rubric for Evaluating Written Argumentation.*[xvi]

The *Rubric for Evaluating Written Argumentation* (REWA) is designed to provide detailed feedback on how written material that is intended to argue persuasively on behalf of a given claim, opinion, or recommendation might be improved. As you can see by reviewing the REWA, it addresses eight different aspects of sound and effective writing:

Purpose and Focus
Depth of Thought
Thesis
Reasoning
Organization
Voice
Grammar and Vocabulary
Mechanics of Presentation

How to Apply the *Rubric for Evaluating Written Argumentation*

Because each of the eight rows on the *Rubric for Evaluating Written Argumentation* addresses a different aspect of sound and effective writing, each aspect should be evaluated separately. When using the REWA give yourself a score on each

Top Ten Ways to Earn an F on a Writing Assignment

1. Plagiarize. Represent someone else's work as if it were your own.
2. Quote sources that are not credible or not even real.
3. String together direct quotes without adding context or interpretation.
4. Speed-write the essay and skip the proofreading.
5. Include gross factual errors or blatant misrepresentations of ideas.
6. Display close-minded hostility to opposing viewpoints.
7. Ramble aimlessly just to reach the required paper length.
8. Make errors in spelling, punctuation, grammar, and capitalization.
9. Use clichés, profanity, emoticons, jargon, and vacuous buzz words.
10. Misunderstand the assignment, disrespect the subject matter, insult your audience, and write on the wrong topic.

row separately. The REWA offers exactly four evaluative options. From highest to lowest the four are: *Highly Developed, Developed, Underdeveloped,* and *Substandard.*

For example, you might read an essay you have prepared for your Introductory English Composition course and realize that you should evaluate your Purpose and Focus, Depth of Thought, and Thesis (the first three rows) as "Developed," your Reasoning, Organization, and Voice (the middle three rows) as "Underdeveloped" but your Grammar and Vocabulary, and Mechanics of Presentation as simply "Substandard." You know right away that you need to spend more time on these last categories for sure. And you know that you could improve the middle ones as well. By engaging in this self-evaluation and addressing these categories you should be able to improve your essay and, in turn, improve your effectiveness as a writer—and your grade too!

As you can see, in the REWA each row can have a different evaluation decision. This is great! It tells you, the author, where your case needs more work to maximize its effectiveness. Contrast the REWA with the *Holistic Critical Thinking Scoring Rubric* (HCTSR) presented in Chapter 1. When applying the HCTSR to evaluate the quality of the critical thinking manifested in a presentation, we have to arrive at a holistic overall qualitative evaluation of *critical thinking* as either "strong," "acceptable," "unacceptable," or "weak." Unlike the HCTSR, the *Rubric for Evaluating Written Argumentation* does not provide an overall or composite score. Instead it yields eight separate scores, one on each aspect of the written argumentation.

Whenever you are evaluating a written presentation, whether your own work or the work of another person, we strongly recommend that the REWA and the HCTSR be used in tandem. This way a person can accurately focus their evaluative attention on each of the specific criteria as expressed in the two rubrics. Otherwise the tendency is to confuse, omit, or collapse the different individually important criteria. Employing both rubrics allows for both the holistic evaluation of the soundness of the critical thinking exhibited in a piece of writing (HCTSR) and a detailed analysis of the effectiveness of the writing (REWA). Remember that the HCTSR assigns a single rubric score or evaluation decision that represents the best overall characterization of the critical thinking being displayed. By contrast, the REWA analyzes eight separate aspects of the writing and so it provides for eight scores.

Rubric for Evaluating Written Argumentation

www.measuredreasons.com

	Highly Developed	Developed	Underdeveloped	Substandard
Purpose and Focus	The writer has made insightful and mature decisions about focus, organization, and content to communicate clearly and effectively. The purpose and focus of the writing are clear to the reader and the organization and content are well chosen, sophisticated, and/or persuasive.	The writer has made good decisions about focus, organization, and content to communicate clearly and effectively. The purpose and focus of the writing are clear to the reader and the organization and content achieve the purpose as well.	The writer's decisions about focus, organization, or content sometimes interfere with clear, effective communication. The purpose of the writing is not fully achieved.	The writer's decisions about focus, organization, or content interfere with communication. The purpose of the writing is not achieved.
Depth of Thought	The information presented reveals the writer's assimilation and understanding of the material. The writer is convincingly aware of implications beyond the immediate subject.	The information presented reveals the writer appreciates and understands the material. The writer seems aware of implications beyond the immediate subject.	The information presented reveals that the writer has only partially assimilated or understood the material. The writer shows some awareness of implications beyond the immediate subject.	The information presented reveals the writer's lack of assimilation and understanding of the material. The writer's assertions lack awareness of implications beyond the immediate subject.
Thesis	Has a highly developed, defendable assertion that provides focus and direction to the essay. Uses sources to support, extend, and inform, but not substitute for the writer's own development of ideas.	Has a clear recognizable assertion that provides focus and direction to the essay. Uses sources to support and inform writer's own development of ideas.	Uses relevant sources but lacks variety of sources and/or the skillful combination of sources necessary to support a central assertion.	Lacks a clear, recognizable assertion and/or lacks adequate sources.

	Highly Developed	Developed	Underdeveloped	Substandard
Reasoning	Substantial and well-reasoned development of ideas. All key assumptions are made explicit. Credible evidence is germane, and accurately analyzed and fair-mindedly interpreted. Displays strong critical thinking skills and habits of mind (See *Holistic Critical Thinking Scoring Rubric*.)	Offers solid reasoning. Most key assumptions are recognized or made explicit. Most inferences are accurate, most examples are on point.	Offers some supporting evidence. The case includes some examples that are too general, not interpreted, or not clearly relevant to thesis.	Offers simplistic, underdeveloped, fallacious, circular, or irrelevant arguments. Includes exaggerations, faulty reasoning, factual errors, biased statements, etc. (See *Holistic Critical Thinking Scoring Rubric*.)
Organization	Sequencing of ideas within paragraphs and transitions between paragraphs flow smoothly and coherently throughout the paper. The writer shows clear effort to assist the reader in following the logic of the ideas expressed.	Sequencing of ideas within paragraphs and transitions between paragraphs make the writer's points coherent and easy to follow.	Sentence structure and/or word choice sometimes interfere with clarity and coherence. Needs to improve sequencing of ideas within paragraphs and transitions between paragraphs to make the writing easy to follow.	Ineffective sentence structure, word choice, transitions, and/or sequencing of ideas make reading and understanding difficult.
Voice	The writer's tone or control of language consistently reflects a confident or authoritative central "voice" or "personality." The writer shows clear discernment of and effective engagement of intended audience.	The writer's tone or control of language generally reflects a confident or authoritative central "voice" or "personality." The writer shows appropriate and consistent awareness of intended audience.	A central "voice" or "personality" is evident, though inconsistent in minor ways. The writer shows little or inconsistent awareness of a particular audience.	The writer's tone or general control of language is so lacking in consistency that little central "voice" or "personality" is evident. The writer lacks awareness of a particular audience.
Grammar and Vocabulary	Sentence structure is complex and powerful. The writer has used vivid, purposefully crafted and varied sentence styles and lengths. The writer displays a broad range of vocabulary, with effective, accurate, and contextually appropriate word usage.	Sentences are effective and varied in style and length. Grammar or usage errors are minimal and do not distract the reader from understanding the intended meaning. The writer displays a satisfactory range of vocabulary and accurate and appropriate word usage.	Sentences show errors in structure. The writer uses limited variety in sentence style and length. The writer displays a limited range of vocabulary. Errors of diction and usage are evident but do not interfere significantly with readability.	Sentence structure is simple, with practically no variety in sentence style and length. Frequent errors in sentence structure interfere with readability. The writer displays an extremely limited vocabulary. Diction and syntax errors make communication confusing or unintelligible.
Mechanics and Presentation	Written response is virtually free of punctuation, spelling, or capitalization errors. The writer utilizes an appropriate and attractive format, presentation, and style (citations) for the assignment.	Written response contains only occasional punctuation, spelling, or capitalization errors. The writer utilizes an appropriate format, presentation, and style (citations) for the assignment.	Written response contains many punctuation, spelling, or capitalization errors. Errors interfere with meaning in some places. The writer makes some errors in format, presentation, or style (citations) for the assignment.	Written response contains many severe punctuation, spelling, or capitalization errors that hinder communication. The writer utilizes inappropriate format, presentation, or style (citations) for the assignment or the formatting is absent.

CHAPTER
15 REVIEW

Study and Review on mythinkinglab.com

Sound and effective written argumentation requires the consideration of four key elements of the rhetorical situation: Author, Audience, Purpose, and Presentation. Effective writers employ a number of strategies to synthesize evidence gathered from credible sources. They carefully and fair-mindedly articulate the reasons in support of the claim that is their central purpose in writing, whether it be to argue on behalf of an opinion or a recommendation. An effective written presentation addresses a clear and manageable thesis in a way that is appropriate for the intended audience and the mode and context of the communication. The reasons and claims are focused on supporting a focused and plausible thesis statement. The author has delivered a fair-minded and balanced discussion of the pros and cons, analyzed the relevant evidence, addressed key assumptions, and presented a credible case in a thorough and objective manner. The writing style is concise and coherent, and the author uses headings, an organized sequence of ideas, and transitions to connect the paragraphs into a flowing essay. The author communicates a detectable voice, perspective, or personality and demonstrates respect for the audience and the audience's capacity to reach reasonable conclusions if presented with the relevant information. The written presentation is mechanically error-free in terms of grammar, punctuation, spelling, and citations. Sound and effective writing is learnable because in the end it is only 10 percent inspiration, but 90 percent practiced effort. The *Rubric for Evaluating Written Argumentation* is a useful tool for assessing your own writing on eight essential dimensions and discovering which, if any, you can work on to make your presentation sound and effective. Use the REWA to evaluate effectiveness, use the HCTSR to evaluate soundness.

KEY TERMS

author's case includes all of the pros and cons along with the supporting evidence that the author presents to the audience in order to establish the truth of a given statement or the wisdom of a given recommendation. (p. 283)

rhetorical situation is the interactive combination of four elements: a specific author is using a specific mode of communication or presentation to engage a specific audience for the specific purpose. (p. 283)

FIND IT ON MYTHINKINGLAB.COM

Map the Concepts on mythinkinglab.com

- Analyze the major claims presented by President Obama in his July 2011 debt limit vote speech to the nation and the party rebuttal speech by Speaker of the House of Representatives Boehner. Use the analytical technique of argument mapping as described in Chapter 5 to create a visual display of these influential political figures' reasoning about the optimal response to the historic economic critical facing the United States.

- Explore Internet source material about Dr. Martin Luther King Jr.'s writings, speeches, and non-violent demonstrations of civil disobedience during the American Civil Rights Movement. Using the tools presented in this chapter and in Chapter 6, analyze the credibility of the Internet sources, focusing on the major claims and evidence provided by the authoring individuals or organizations.

Exercises

LETTERS TO THE EDITOR ABOUT COLLEGE APPLICATION ESSAYS

A front-page story on August 6, 2011 in the *New York Times* described how some high school students are seeking exceptional summer experiences to provide themselves with something that will make their college application essays stand out as special by contrast with the essays that other applicants might submit.[xvii] For this exercise, read the original news story and then read the letters to the editor about that story. Using the REWA, evaluate the soundness and effectiveness of the case presented by each letter to the editor.

LETTERS TO THE EDITOR OF THE CITY OR CAMPUS NEWSPAPER

Select an editorial published in your city or campus newspaper. Evaluate it with the REWA. Working individually or with a writing partner, research and write an opinion piece on the same topic. Submit it to campus or city newspaper as a letter to the editor.

PENN JILLETTE ON CONNECTING WITH THE AUDIENCE

On August 16, 2011, magician Penn Jillette, of the duo Penn & Teller, was interviewed on the NPR radio program *Talk of the Nation*.[xviii] Jillette was on the show to discuss his book, *God, No! Signs That You May Already Be an Atheist.* Listeners phone in during the interview and the host, Neal Conan, often puts them on the air. One caller identifies himself as a fellow magician and conveys the struggle he has forming an emotional or deep connection with his audience during his performances. The caller wonders if Jillette ever experienced a similar struggle. Review the discussion of audience and the importance of establishing a connection with the audience in order to make an effective case. Write up an analysis of this rhetorical context in terms of author (the magician), audience, purpose, and presentation. Explain how these four elements strain the soundness and effectiveness of the magician's case. Go to www.mythinkinglab.com to hear Penn Jillette's explanation and compare it to your own.

Listen to the **Podcast** on **mythinkinglab.com**

RESEARCH FOR THE CAMPUS PRESIDENT

Consider the following situation: You are the leader of a group of students known as the *President's Student Advisory Council*. An issue has come up on campus regarding food sold in the student cafeteria. The President of your institution is seeking your advice about the sale of genetically engineered foods on campus. The President wants you to prepare a written recommendation which responds to the following question: Should the campus sell or serve foods that have been genetically modified? The President has asked that you consider the arguments on both sides of this issue, and recommend whether to continue to offer genetically modified foods on campus. For this letter you must gather at least four credible sources of evidence. Your evidence must represent strong arguments for both the pro and con sides. Describe each source as well as how and where you obtained it. Provide an analysis of the source's credibility. After reviewing the source evidence, what recommendation would you make to the President and why?

REFLECTIVE LOG: ANALYZE YOUR OWN PRIOR WRITING

Select one research paper or persuasive essay that you have written for a course this term or in a previous term. Write a reflection about the process you went through when preparing and writing that paper/essay. As you write this reflective piece provide as many details as you can recall. How long did you spend working on the paper? What process of gathering evidence did you engage in? What sources did you use? Did you select the sources or were they provided to you? What planning steps did you use when preparing to write? How much editing and rewriting did you engage in? Using the HCTSR and REWA, evaluate the critical thinking and the writing that you displayed. Now, re-read your reflection and add a final paragraph: What is the relationship between my writing process and my critical thinking evaluation? How might I change my approach to preparing written cases in the future to reflect stronger critical thinking?

GROUP PROJECT: ARTIFICIAL SWEETENERS

In June 2011 a number of newspaper and Internet news sources reported the findings from a study linking the consumption of diet soda to increased waistlines over time and increased sugar levels in the blood stream. Researchers hypothesize that it may be the artificial sweeteners in the diet soda that are boosting people's appetites as well as blood-sugar levels.[xix] Assume that you are an intern in the legal department of Standard Sodas Inc. Your supervisor asks you to join her team in crafting a response letter to the public. The letter will be posted on the company's Web site. The team must develop a sound (logical and truthful) and effective (persuasive) written case for why consumers should continue to consume Standard Diet Soda.

EMPLOYER EXPLOITATION FASHION MODELS

This project is intended for a group of three to five students working collaboratively. It can serve as a cumulative final paper in a course on writing and critical thinking.

Hypothetical Question: *Should student leaders at your college initiate or join a national effort by college students to secure legislation regarding working age, body mass, nutrition, etc. to prevent the fashion industry employers from endangering the physical or mental health of runway models?*

Context: Ethical business practices suggest that employers should not put workers at unnecessary risk. The impact of culturally relative notions of physical beauty in our media-intensive society can have significant negative effects on the behavior and health of impressionable people of all ages, but particularly the youth. To what extent should an employer's freedom be limited, if at all, in the interests of the workers or of society? Employers who knowingly exploit workers, and industries that unnecessarily endanger impressionable young people, have traditionally come under scrutiny by college students seeking to build a more just and humane society. Often through boycotts and by seeking legislative changes or by insisting that the institution alter its investment practices, students at many of the nation's colleges have awakened their school's social consciousness to unacceptable business practices, whether in the United States or abroad. Some of the world's largest corporations and most entrenched business have been moved to alter their policies by the efforts initiated by college students. The fashion industry, in these respects, is no more formidable nor exceptional than other industries. And, more than the harm done to their workers, the images of men and women which the fashion industry presents as "desirable" and "beautiful" have potentially profound effects on people, particularly high school and college aged people. Hence efforts to secure legislative changes in the United States and in Europe initiated by that segment of the population would carry special economic and political significance for that industry.

Assignment: Fully research this topic in all of its historical, social, political, ethical, and scientific dimensions. Make a well-reasoned, fair-minded, scientifically complete and accurate, articulate, informed, well-organized, scholarly, ethically wise, humanly sensitive, and technically feasible recommendation that answers the *hypothetical question* stated above.

Audience: Write so that your recommendation may be transmitted to and read and understood by your colleague students, by intelligent college-educated members of the general public, the officials at your college, newspaper editors, and legislators. Your written presentation may include charts, images, video clips, or tables as your project team deems appropriate. There is no word limit or page limit on this assignment other than the limits you impose on yourselves when being mindful of your audience.

Due date: To be established by your instructor.

Extend Argument-Decision Mapping Strategies

The mapping strategies first introduced in Chapter 5 make the reasoning used in decision making clearer and much easier to follow. Argument and decision maps can be applied in many practical ways. In this section you'll see examples of maps used not only to analyze the relationships of claims and reasons, but to express the kinds of arguments being made, to express the evaluation of arguments, and to expose the reasoning strengths and weaknesses of important and complex multi-option decisions. This section builds the critical thinking skills and habits of mind that we've been strengthening all through this book. The key is that the mapping strategies work at a practical level because they reveal the thinking being used, and thus enable all of us to apply our interpretive and evaluative skills to that thinking—once we've secured a correct analysis, of course.

Mapping the Sequence of Arguments

Map A.1. This map displays an interviewee's explanation of why she cannot quit smoking *at this time*. As you can see, the map displays two possible conclusions and three watershed realizations that a decision was called for. One argument strand leading from one of the watershed ideas is abandoned. The interviewee who is providing this account of her ongoing decision offered five more arguments supporting quitting smoking now and four arguments for quitting later. This shows that she is seriously entertaining the idea of quitting and in fact is using the Temporizing Heuristic (described in Chapter 10) to sustain the ongoing, but shaky, decision to continue with smoking for the time being. We might infer from this that the dominance structuring (discussed in Chapter 11) around the "continuing to smoke" option may not be impervious.

The sequencing of a person's thoughts can often be a clue that a person is on the verge of a new decision or realization. *To capture the data about the order in which this interviewee presented her arguments we can add numbers inside the shapes.* The numbers represent the order of the interviewee's claims

MAP > it > OUT A.1
Quitting Smoking Someday

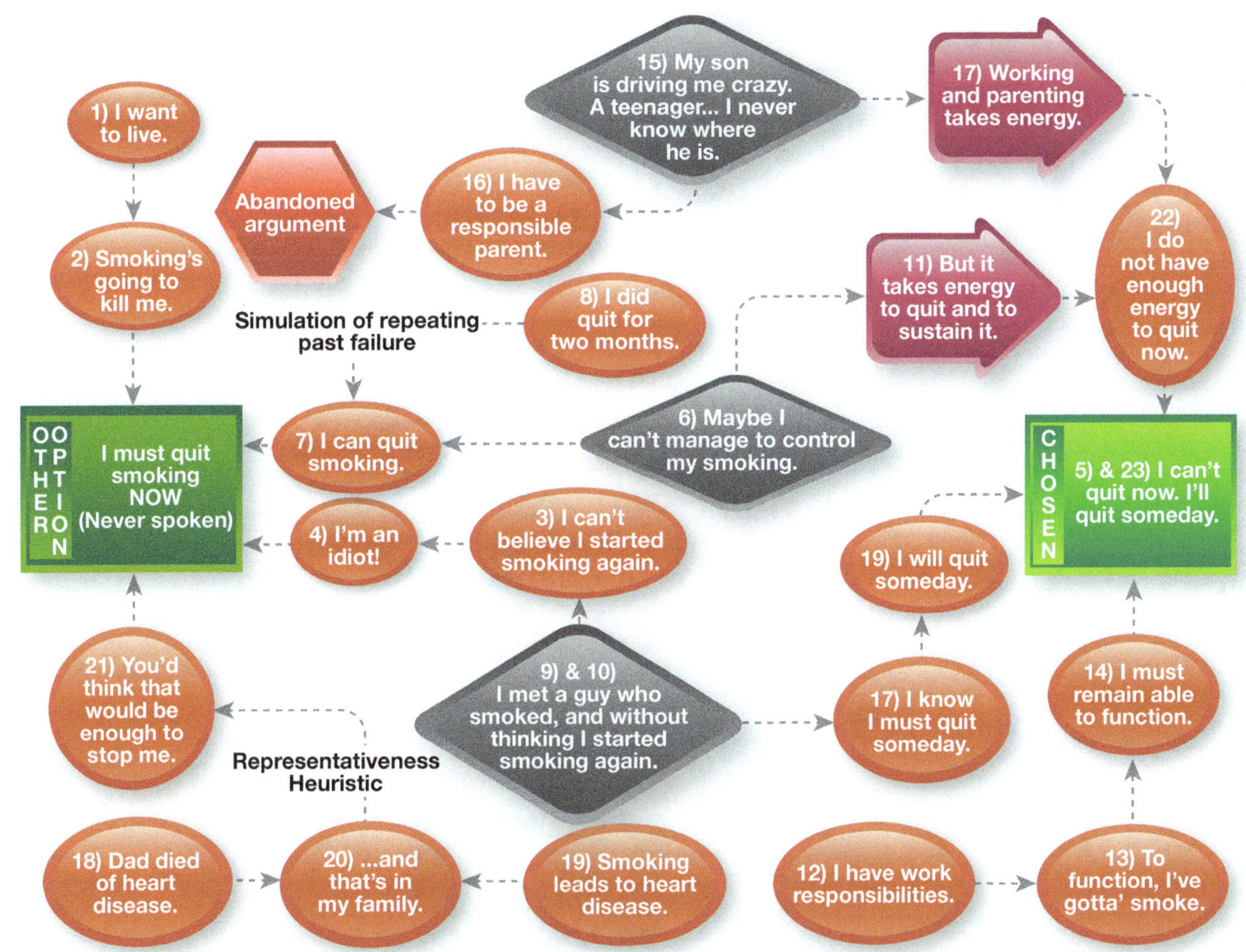

and reasons. This technique preserves the chronology of the interview, revealing how the interviewee first argues for quitting smoking (phrase 2: "Smoking is going to kill me"). Although the person never declares that she must stop smoking, it is an implicit statement in the first things she says (1: "I want to live, 3: "I can't believe I started smoking again," and 4: "I'm an idiot" [for doing so.]). But then the person's defenses begin to build. The temporizing starts rather early in the interview, as the person explains why this was not the time to try quitting (phrase 5). The interviewee's arguments also reveal unwarranted beliefs that there are beneficial effects of the nicotine addiction (phrase 13 "To function, I've gotta smoke"). If our purpose were to evaluate the reasoning, and not simply to analyze it, we could further augment the argument map by inserting "(True)" and "(False)" by each statement that we were sure was true or was false.

Mapping Forms of Inference

Look closely at Map A.1 and you'll spot another enhancement. On two of the arrow lines we've indicated the name of the reasoning used to move from one oval to the next. "Simulation of repeating past failure" indicates that the Simulation Heuristic described in Chapter 10 operated as the person's thinking moved from phrase 8 to phrase 7. She spoke phrase 7 first, then explained how she came to that idea with phrase 8, but without much self-confidence, having already revealed her relapse in phrase 3. *Introducing information on the arrow lines is a way of displaying how the analyst is interpreting what the interviewee is saying*. You'll see another interpretive insertion on the arrow line between phrase 20 and phrase 21. There the analyst suggests that the interviewee is using the Representativeness Heuristic, as the memory is fresh in her mind and close to her life.

Heuristics are not the only forms of inference that we can add by name to the arrow lines of an argument or decision map. We can insert the names of any fallacies, deductively valid argument templates, or inductive statistical tests that the argument maker uses to draw his or her inferences.

Map A.2. This map indicates the critical thinking skills used. In Map A.2 one of the deductively valid rules for drawing inferences

MAP > it > OUT A.2
We Need Groceries

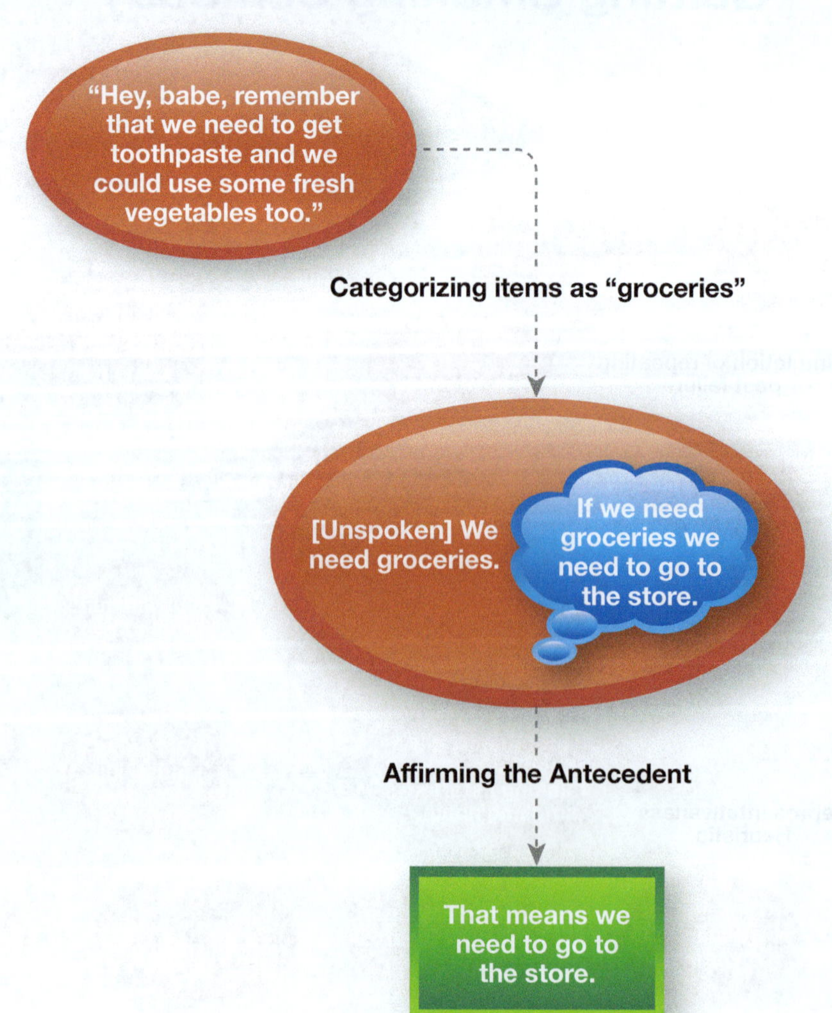

we discussed in Chapter 8, Affirming the Antecedent (also called "Modus Ponens"), is noted on the arrow line leading directly to the conclusion. The argument maker logically infers the conclusion without needing to speak aloud the two implicit statements in the intermediate claim. The argument maker reaches the first of those, "We need groceries," by applying a basic critical thinking sub-skill listed in Chapter 2, categorization. *Reference the logic used by the argument maker to infer the conclusion by inserting its name on arrow line.* Whether the argument maker used a logical argument pattern or a fallacious reasoning, if it has a name we can display it on the arrow line.

Mapping Supporting Explanatory Information

Map A.3. This map uses overlapping ovals, creating something that looks like an upside-down "Mickey Mouse" hat. The overlapping oval on the left shows that the data in the large central oval are supported by good methodology—specifically that the sample was representative. The right side's overlapping oval indicates that the claim in the center is based upon the application of a measurement instrument which the argument maker beliefs to have been valid and reliable. Argument makers often rely on well-established research methodologies or decision-critical factors in making a key claim. We can best interpret these elements as parts of a complex claim itself, rather than as separate reasons for the claim. *To display a complex claim that includes explicit justifications and explanations of that claim itself use overlapping ovals.*

Map A.3 also notes on the arrow line leading to the conclusion that the argument maker applied a commonly used analysis for statistical significance called a Chi-Square Test. As indicated with Map A.2, we can show this on the arrow line. The label on the arrow line in Map A.3 is shorthand for saying "The argument maker applied a Chi-Square statistical test to determine the likelihood that the observed results happened

MAP > it > OUT A.3
Which Students Value Truth-Seeking?

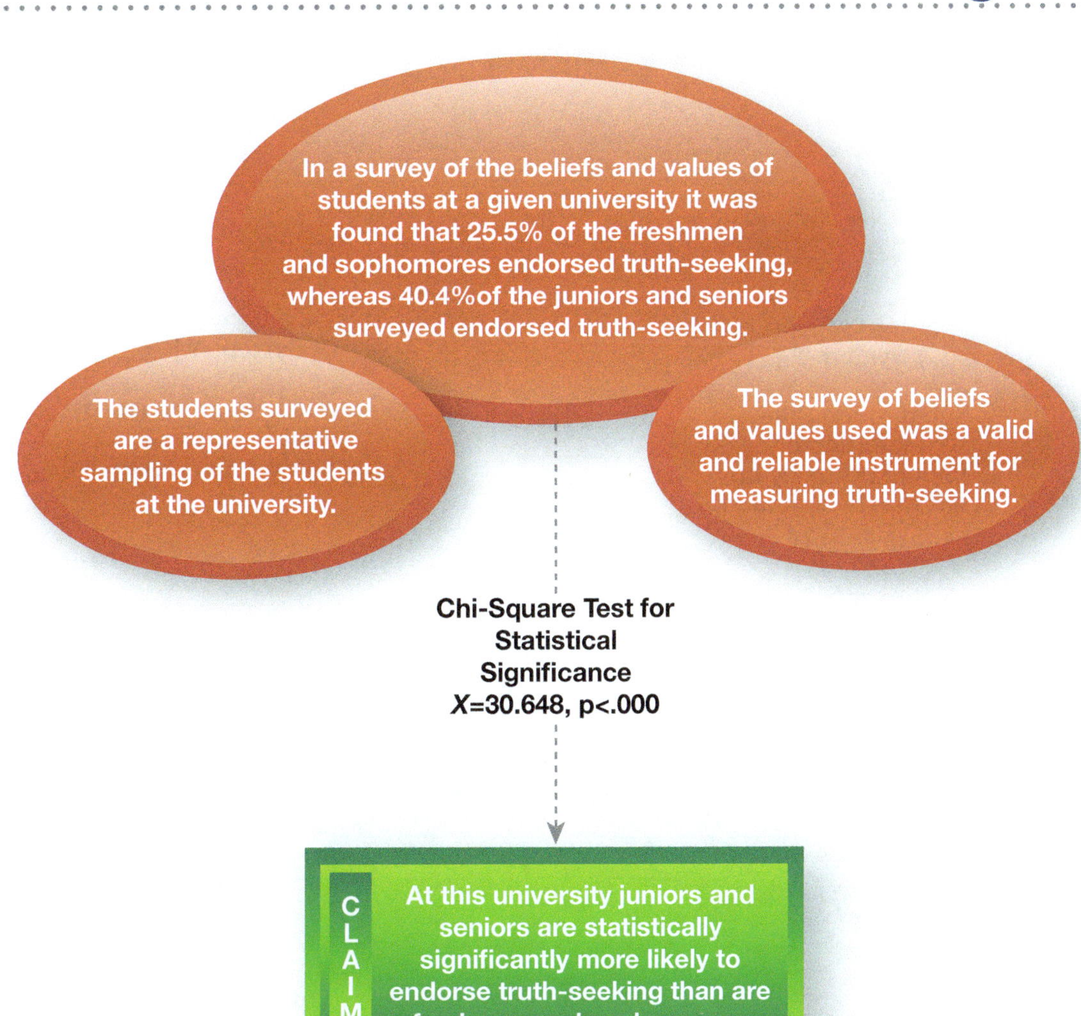

to come about merely by random chance is less than one chance in 1,000." Another option would have been to put this same information into a third oval that overlapped the larger oval above. Either way works to communicate the basis for the statistical analysis that, itself, then justifies our confidence in the conclusion. Breaking out each element and displaying it offers a map that better displays the complexity of the thinking yet keeps that reasoning easy to understand and interpret correctly. This is particularly helpful when the reasoning involves several complex steps, like scientific reasoning as described in the chapter on empirical reasoning, Chapter 14.

Mapping the Decision System

Map A.4. This augmented decision map draws from what we learned in Chapter 10 about systems of reasoning. Here, the notations of System-2 and System-1 reasoning are both present. The application of the rule called *substitution* is the more reflective System-2 inference that *would* have led the person to buy the car, but the System-1 negative affective response to its color gave the buyer pause. Ergo, this car was not purchased by this decision maker!

MAP > it > OUT A.4
Buying a Car

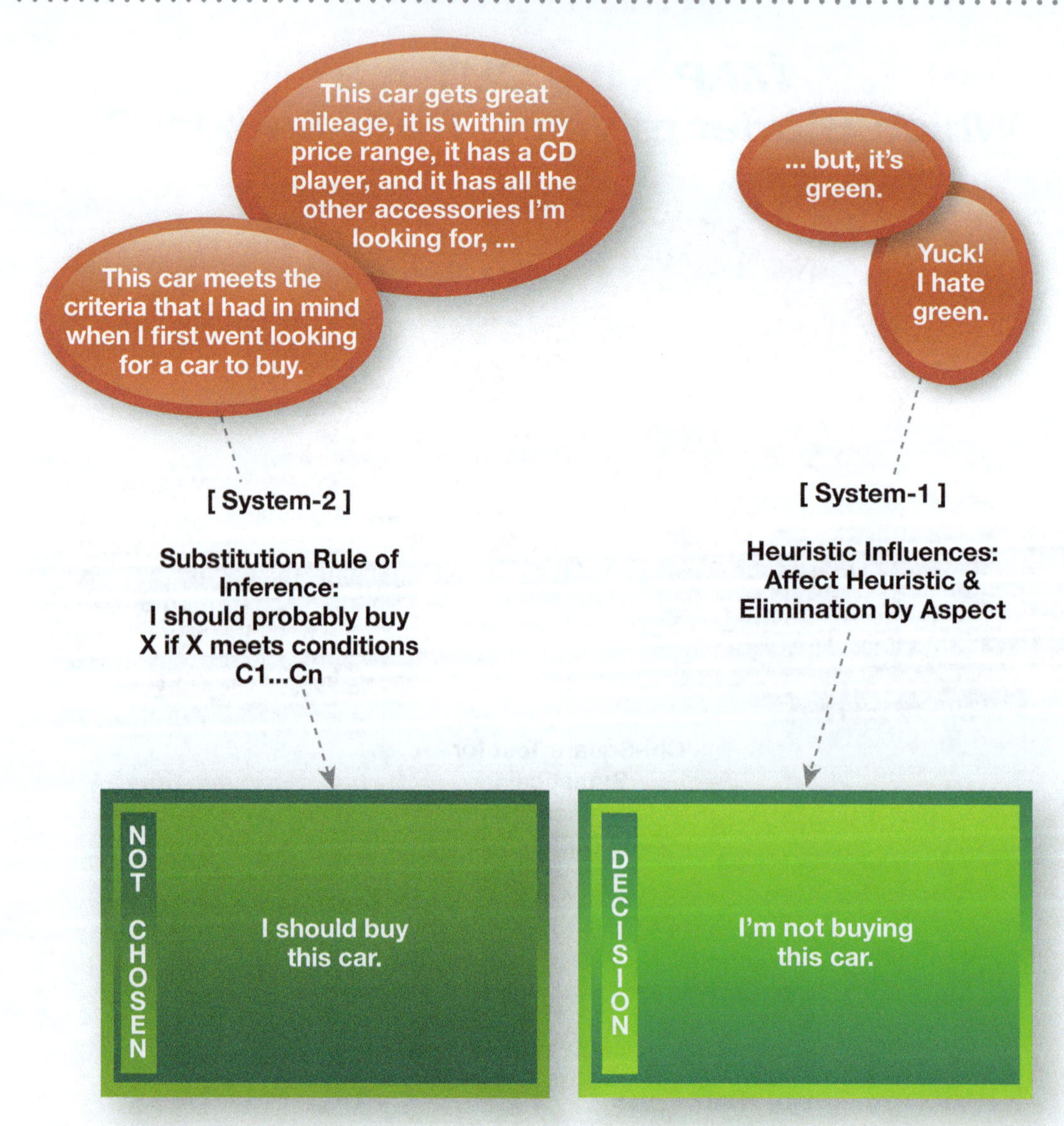

Less Is More

Map A.5. We can increase the information on a map or, if it helps in a given context, we can strip out information. In Map A.5 I have stripped out the arguments so that the map reveals the overall pattern of the decision making divorced from the specific content of the argument. The numbered "P" ovals are the reasons the speaker gave in favor of ("pro") attending a given college, and the "C" ovals are "con" arguments the speaker made concerning attending that college. And we've added evaluations of the arguments (discussed in Chapter 7) as "sound" or "unsound" based on the truthfulness of the premises and the logical strength of the speaker's original arguments. Now the map clearly shows which option was the one that was best supported, in our judgment, by the decision maker. The dominance structuring we talked about in Chapter 11 emerges strongly in this next map too. In the end, this person decided to attend Michigan State. What was particularly interesting was that a few of the arguments the person considered both for and against attending MSU were not sound. This is an instance of the fourth stage of dominance structuring, as we learned in Chapter 11, by a person who does not seem to be the world's best critical thinker.

MAP > it > OUT A.5
Which College Should I Attend?

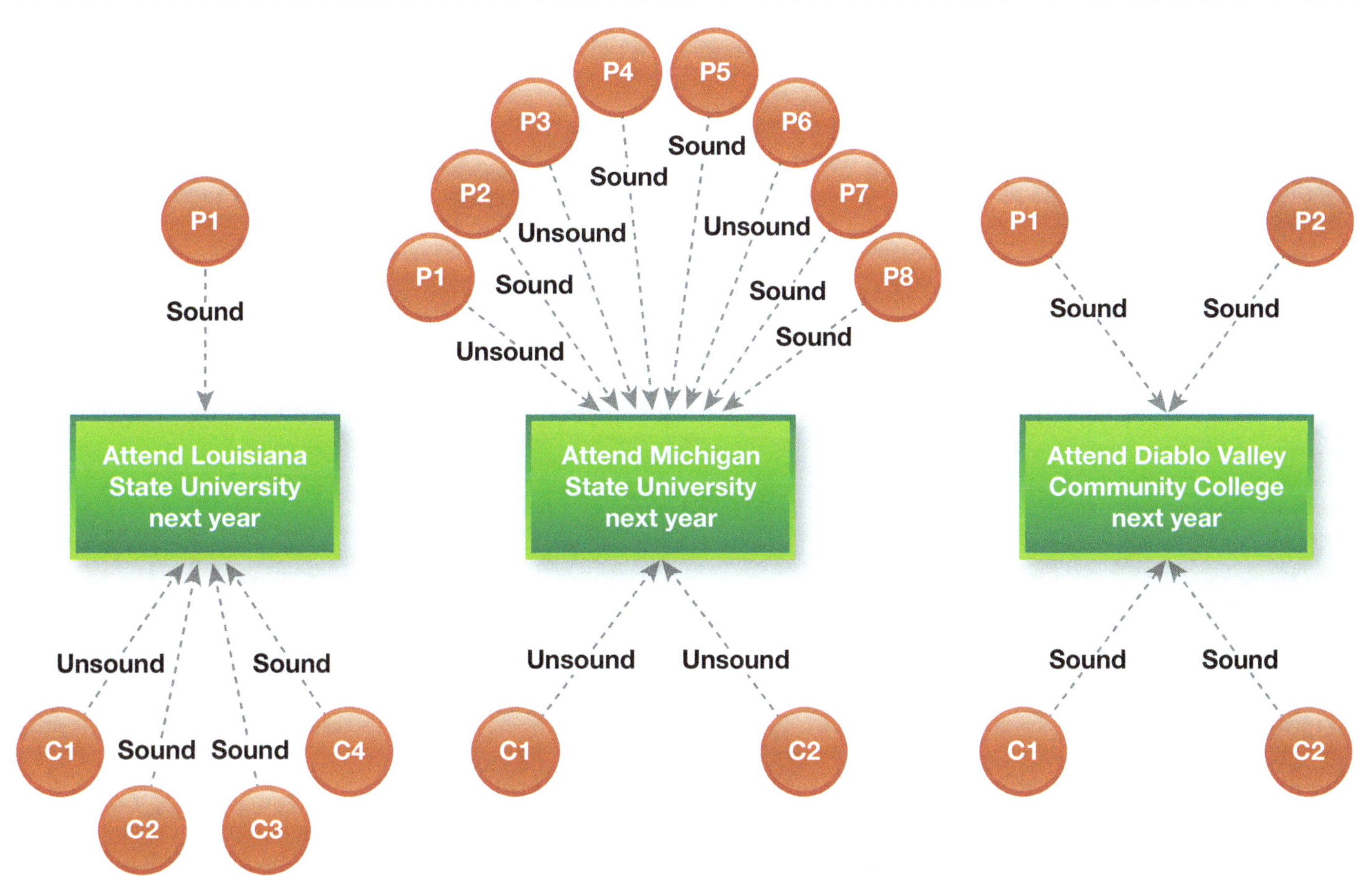

Schwarzenegger's Denial of Clemency

Map A.6. Here is a map of Governor Schwarzenegger's reasoning in his denial of clemency for Stanley "Tookie" Williams, explored in Chapter 11's exercise (page 224). We invited you there to map his reasoning as expressed in the statement he published. The map you produced would likely have been rather complex, since the reasoning you were mapping was itself rather complex. And you would probably have had to make

MAP > it > OUT A.6

Governor Arnold Schwarzenegger's Argument for Denying the Death Row Appeal for Clemency of Stanley "Tookie" Williams

more than a couple drafts before you were satisfied that your analysis was reasonable. Take a moment and study Map A.6.

Assuming this map is a reasonably accurate analysis, how would you evaluate that reasoning? In particular, what should we make of the two abandoned lines of reasoning? What would have been the result had they been more fully developed? Or, why should we assume that a person should apologize if the person believes he is not guilty? Similarly, why would an attempt to escape be interpreted as a reason to suppose that a person is guilty? A good argument map reveals both the strong points and the weak points of a decision maker's thinking.

Mapping Group Decision Making

Map A.7. Chapter 2 opens with the memorable scene from Apollo 13 where the crew and the people at the Houston Mission Control are trying to figure out what kind of problem the spacecraft was having. In that chapter we described the thinking by using words in sentence and paragraph form. Perhaps it was easy to follow. But it would have been even easier to trace the group's thinking as it made that vital decision had we used a decision map. Map A.7 begins with the realization that there is a problem on the spacecraft. This realization is communicated to Houston and then backed up by all the people on the spacecraft in Mission Control who report what their instruments are reading. Map A.7 illustrates that we need not confine our argument analysis and mapping strategies to displaying the thinking of a single individual. We can map group decisions too.

Mapping a group decision can be useful, but challenging too. As many college students and instructors know, figuring out how to best care for older parents and grandparents can be challenging for their children. About a year ago a family we know was working through the question of how best to help Grandpa Stanley relocate from Arizona to a new home closer to one of his adult children back in Chicago. He wanted to move because his wife had passed away as had many of his retirement friends. Over several weeks his four adult children discussed by phone and e-mail the various options. The decision was complex because Grandpa Stanley's needs and preferences were important, but so were the needs and abilities of the various adult children and their families. To sort out all the options and relevant considerations, a couple of huge decisions maps were drawn up and circulated. In the spirit of "let the chips fall where they may" the maps were accurate to a fault. All the options and reasons, weak and strong, were displayed, along with all the abandoned lines of reasoning. Which child was too busy with work, which had medical problems of his own to deal with, etc. all made it into the map. Given how families can be, all this truthfulness risked reopening old conflicts because the map exposed an unverifiable assumption and an occasional fallacy in the reasoning of one or another adult sibling. Eventually it was all happily resolved. Grandpa Stanley is resettled near two of his sons on the north side of Chicago. He occasionally rides the Red Line to Cubs games. With millions of other Cubs

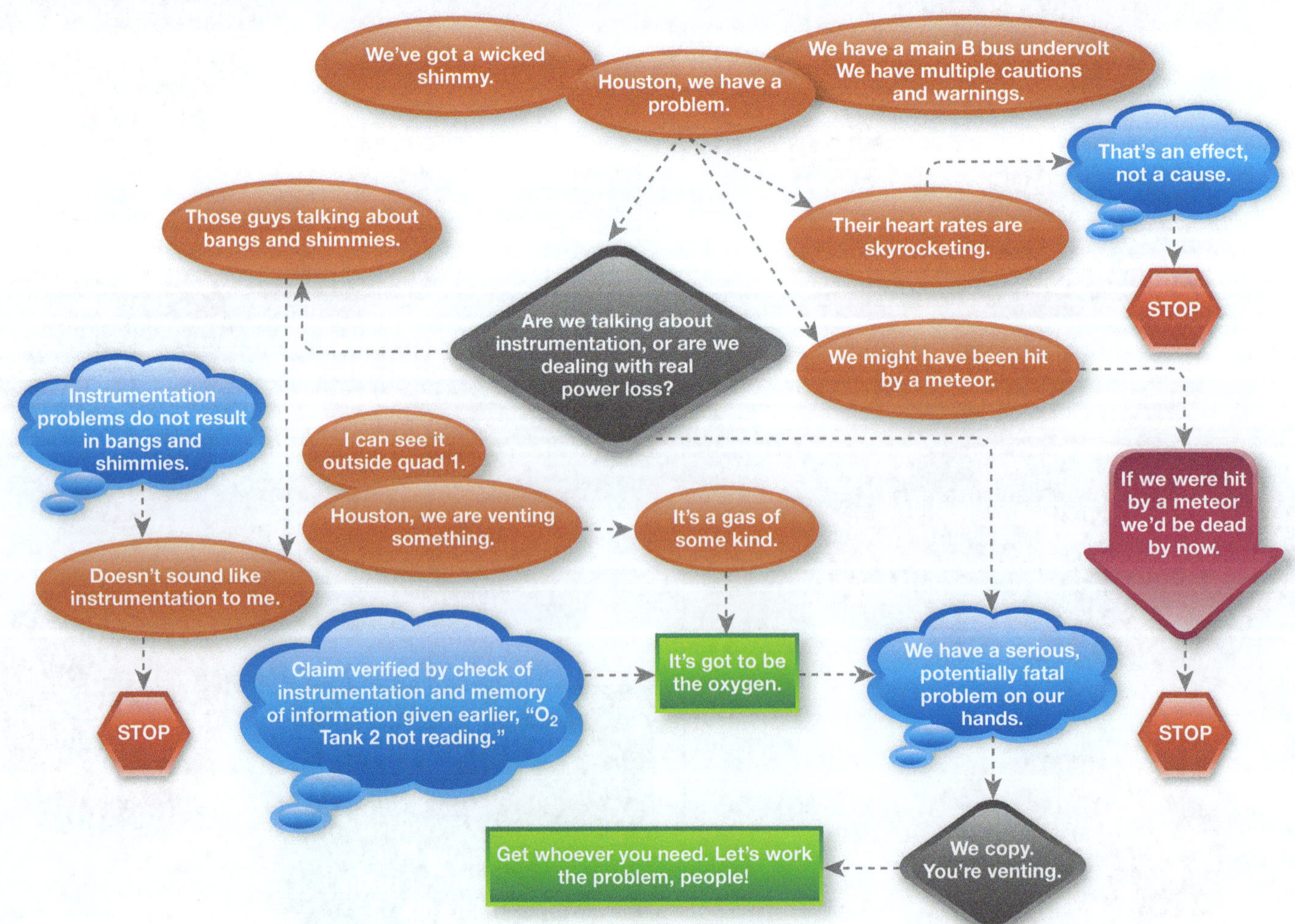

fans, Stanley yearns to cheer his team as World Series victors—someday. The adult siblings are all still close friends. The decision maps have been put away, perhaps someday to be shared with the great-grandchildren, but maybe not. There are things that are important, and then there are other things that are more important. Strong critical thinkers make judgments.

Research Applications

There are still other ways we can effectively use our mapping techniques for practical and for scholarly purposes. Advanced students interested in pursing the idea of using decision maps to compare how different people make comparable decisions, for example, would find the book *Thinking and Reasoning in Human Decision Making: The Method of Argument and Heuristic Analysis*, useful (Facione and Facione, The California Academic Press, 2007). The mapping techniques presented in this appendix and in Chapter 5 are drawn from that book; from our many years of collaborative research; and from our shared goal of making the analysis, interpretation, and evaluation of complex human decision making more scientifically objective and open to replication by other investigators. In this work, critical thinking and scientific inquiry, as discussed in Chapter 14, go hand in hand. When we use empirical reasoning, if our maps do not agree, we can compare our analyses to see what the best interpretation might be.

GLOSSARY

actions in social science research are processes or activities that bring about the conditions whereby something is done or accomplished.

ambiguity See **problematic ambiguity**

analysis the critical thinking skill that identifies the intended and actual inferential relationships among statements, questions, concepts, descriptions, or other forms of representation intended to express belief, judgment, experiences, reasons, information, or opinions.

analytical means that a person is habitually alert to potential problems and vigilant in anticipating consequences and trying to foresee short-term and long-term outcomes of events, decisions, and actions. "Foresightful" is another word for what "analytical" means here.

anomalies are solid scientific findings that are not consistent with prevailing theories.

argue (as in "to make an argument") is the process of giving a reason in support of a claim

argument is the combination of a person's claim and the reason a person presents in support of that claim.

author's case includes all of the pros and cons along with the supporting evidence that the author presents to the audience in order to establish the truth of a given statement or the wisdom of a given recommendation.

bottom up thinking See **empirical reasoning**.

claim refers to the statement that the maker of an argument is seeking to show to be true or probably true.

cognitive heuristics are human decision-making shortcuts people rely on to expedite their judgments about what to believe or what to do.

comparative reasoning (or **this-is-like-that thinking**) is the process of using what is more familiar to make interpretations, explanations, or inferences about what is less familiar.

comprehensiveness, in the evaluation of comparisons, is the extent to which a comparison captures a greater number of central or essential features.

conclusion is another way of referring to an argument's claim.

conditional is a grammatically correct construction used to assert that if an antecedent statement is true, then a consequent statement is true.

confident in reasoning means that a person is trustful of his or her own reasoning skills to yield good judgments. A person's or a group's confidence in their own critical thinking may or may not be warranted, which is another matter.

conjunction is a grammatically correct construction used to assert that two statements are both true.

contingent statement (in the Logic of Statements) means a grammatically correct expression that turns out to be true under at least one possible assignment of truth values to its component single statements and false under another other possible assignment of truth values to its component simple statements.

critical thinking is purposeful, reflective judgment that manifests itself in giving reasoned and fair-minded consideration to evidence, conceptualizations, methods, contexts, and standards in order to decide what to believe or what to do.

decision-critical attributes are those factors or criteria the decision-maker deems to be important and relevant for the purpose of evaluating options.

deductive reasoning is drawing inferences in which it appears that the conclusion cannot possibly be false if all of the premises are true.

deductively valid argument is an argument such that it is impossible for all of its premises to be true and its conclusion to be false.

disjunction is a grammatically correct construction used to assert that one or both of two statements are true.

dominance structuring is the psychological process through which humans achieve confidence in their decisions. The four phases of dominance structuring are pre-editing, identifying one promising option, testing that promising option for dominance, and structuring the dominance of the option selected.

empirical reasoning (or **bottom up thinking**) is that process of thinking that proceeds from premises describing interpersonally verifiable experiences in order to support or to disconfirm hypotheses, which, in turn, are intended to explain and to predict phenomena. Empirical reasoning is fundamentally inductive, self-corrective, and open to scrutiny and independent verification by the entire scientific community.

equivalence (in the Logic of Statements) means that two statements always have the same truth values. Two statements, A and B, are equivalent if, and only if, the biconditional (A = B) is a tautology.

ethical imperatives are intended to shape or guide behavior by expressing core values and beliefs about what is morally right or morally wrong. Ethical imperatives express behavioral ideals and moral principles by pointing out what we ought to do or ought to refrain from doing.

ethics refers to a set of behavioral ideals or moral principles that guide us in determining right and wrong. We can think of these ideals and principles as a set of core values and beliefs.

evaluation the critical thinking skill that assesses the credibility of statements or other representations that are accounts or descriptions of a person's perception, experience, situation, judgment, belief, or opinion; also assesses the logical strength of the actual or intended inferential relationships among statements, descriptions, questions, or other forms of representation.

expert refers to someone who is both experienced and learned in a given subject matter or professional practice area.

explanation the critical thinking skill that states and justifies reasoning in terms of the evidential, conceptual, methodological, criteriological, and contextual considerations upon which one's results were based; also presenting one's reasoning in the form of cogent arguments.

fallacies are deceptive arguments that appear logical, but upon closer analysis, fail to demonstrate their conclusions.

familiarity, in the evaluation of comparisons, is the degree of knowledge the listener has about the object to which the unknown is being compared.

good argument (or a **worthy argument**) is an argument that merits being accepted as a proof that its conclusion is true or very probably true.

ideological reasoning (or **top down thinking**) is the process of thinking that begins with abstractions or generalizations that express one's core beliefs, concepts, values, or principles and proceeds to reason top down to their specific applications. Ideological reasoning is deductive and axiomatic. The argument maker takes the ideological premises on faith.

implication (in the Logic of Statements) Statement A implies statement B if there is no interpretation of the statements letters of A and B such that A is true and B is false. Alternatively, statement A implies statement B if the grammatical expression generated by the structure (A → B) is a tautology.

inconsistent statement (in the Logic of Statements) means a grammatically correct expression that turns out to be false under every possible assignment of truth values to its component simple statements.

inductive reasoning is drawing probabilistic inferences regarding what is most likely to be true or most likely not true, given certain information.

inductively justified argument (or **warranted argument**) is an argument such that were all of its premises true then its conclusion would most likely or very probably also be true.

inference the critical thinking skill that identifies and secures the elements needed to draw reasonable conclusions; it forms conjectures and hypotheses, considers relevant information, and it educes or draws out the consequences flowing from data, statements, principles, evidence, judgments, beliefs, opinions, concepts, descriptions, questions, or other forms of representation.

inquisitive means that a person habitually strives to be well-informed, wants to know how things work, and seeks to learn new things about a wide range of topics, even if the immediate utility of knowing those things is not directly evident. An inquisitive person has a strong sense of intellectual curiosity.

interpretation the critical thinking skill that is an expression of the meaning or significance of a wide variety of experiences, situations, data, events, judgments, conventions, beliefs, rules, procedures, or criteria.

judicious means that a person approaches problems with a sense that some are ill-structured and some can have more than one plausible solution. A judicious person has the cognitive maturity to realize that many questions and issues are not black and white and that, at times, judgments must be made in contexts of uncertainty.

justified argument See **inductively justified argument**

language community is a community in which people share an understanding of the meanings of words and icons. Dictionaries were invented to record a language community's conventions for what its words *shall* mean.

make an argument is the process of giving a reason in support of a claim.

motivation in social science research is a term used to represent the internal or external forces that stimulate, maintain, and regulate human behavior and influence our decisions for action or reaction in social situations.

natural science refers to the systematic empirical inquiry into the causal explanations for the observed patterns, structures, and functions of natural phenomena from the sub-atomic to the galactic in scope.

negation is a grammatically correct construction used to assert that a statement is false.

null hypothesis is the hypothesis that two events, factors, or phenomena are not related.

open-minded means that a person is habitually tolerant of divergent issues and sensitive to the possibility of his or her own possible biases. An open-minded person respects the right of others who have different opinions.

participant in social science research means an individual who performs, shares, or engages in something. In social science, research, participants are sometimes referred to as subjects, informants, or actors.

premises are the statements, explicitly asserted or contextually assumed and implicit, that comprise an argument's reason. Each reason is a separate set of premises.

problem solving is moving from the point at which we initially realize that we have a difficulty that requires our attention to that point where we regard the difficulty as being sufficiently resolved for the current time and circumstances.

problematic ambiguity is the characteristic of a word or expression referring to more than one object or as having more than one meaning in a given context or for a given purpose.

problematic vagueness is the characteristic of a word or expression having an imprecise meaning or unclear boundaries in a given context or for a given purpose.

productivity is the capacity of a comparison to suggest consequences that go beyond those mentioned in the initial comparison.

reason is the basis provided by the argument maker to show that the claim is true or probably true.

rhetorical situation is the interactive combination of four elements: a specific author is using a specific mode of communication or presentation to engage a specific audience for a specific purpose.

self-contradictory statement is a sentence that is false entirely because of the grammatical construction and the meanings of the words used to form the sentence.

self-regulation the critical thinking skill by which one monitors one's cognitive activities, the elements used in those activities, and the results educed, particularly by applying skills in analysis, and evaluation to one's own inferential judgments with a view toward questioning, confirming, validating, or correcting either one's reasoning or one's results.

simple statement is a grammatically correct construction in a given language used to assert that an idea is true.

simplicity in the evaluation of comparisons, is a measure of the relative absence of complexity.

situation in social science research means the physical, social, and cultural circumstances or surroundings that define the phenomenon of interest.

social science is the systematic empirical study of the patterns, structures, and functions of human behavior, individually or in groups, within society,

sound argument is an argument with true premises that also passes the Test of Logical Strength.

statistically significant is a term used in statistical analysis to represent the probability that an obtained result has not occurred by chance.

System-1 thinking is reactive thinking that relies heavily on situational cues, salient memories, and cognitive heuristics to arrive quickly and confidently at judgments.

System-2 thinking is reflective critical thinking that is useful for judgments in unfamiliar situations, for processing abstract concepts, and for deliberating when there is time for planning and more comprehensive consideration.

systematic means that a person consistently endeavors to take an organized and thorough approach to identifying and solving problems. A systematic person is orderly, focused, persistent, and diligent in his or her approach to problem solving, learning, and inquiry.

tautology is a statement that is necessarily true because of the meanings of the words.

tautology (in the Logic of Statements) means a grammatically correct expression turns out to be true under every possible assignment of truth values to its component simple statement.

testability is the capacity of comparisons to project consequences that have the potential to be shown to be false, inapplicable, or unacceptable.

testable hypothesis is an hypothesis that can be shown to be false by reference to empirical evidence.

this-is-like-that thinking See **comparative reasoning.**

top down thinking See **ideological reasoning.**

trusted source (on topic X) is a person (or the words of a person) who is learned in X, experienced in X, speaking about X, up-to-date about X, capable of explaining the basis for their claim or their advice about X, unbiased, truthful, free of conflicts of interest, acting in accord with our interests, unconstrained, informed about the specifics of the case at hand, and mentally stable.

truth-seeking means that a person habitually has intellectual integrity and a courageous desire to actively strive for the best possible knowledge in any given situation. A truth-seeker asks probing questions and follows reasons and evidence wherever they lead, even if the results go against his or her cherished beliefs.

vague See **problematic vagueness**

valid argument See **deductively valid argument**

warranted argument See **inductively justified argument**

worthy argument (or **good argument**) is an argument that merits being accepted as a proof that its conclusion is true or very probably true.

CHAPTER 1

i. Retired Navy Admiral Mike Mullen to the graduating senior military officers at the U.S. National Defense University, June 11, 2009. Quoted according to a story by Fred W. Baker III of the American Forces Press Service.
ii. Ray Marshall and Marc Tucker, *Thinking for a Living: Education and the Wealth of Nations* (New York: Basic Books, 1992).
iii. Quoted according to a story by Fred W. Baker III of the American Forces Press Service.
iv. Karl Popper, *The Open Society and its Enemies*, Vols. 1 & 2 (New York: Routledge, 1945, 2002).
v. "Thurgood Marshall Quotes," Brainy Quote, 8 Jul. 2009. <http://www.brainyquote.com/quotes/quotes/t/thurgoodma115747.html>.
vi. Anne Rice, *The Vampire Lestat* (New York: Ballantine Books, 1985).
vii. Karl Popper, *The Poverty of Historicism* (New York: Routledge, 1957, 2002).
viii. The Delphi method begins by inviting all the experts to respond to an initial set of questions about the topic of interest. The project's coordinating research director, who cannot be one of the experts, has responsibility for compiling results, sharing those results with the roster of participating experts, and asking whether they agree, disagree, or want to propose clarifications or revisions. The research director also moves the project forward by asking questions that arise from the material being generated by the experts. This process is repeated over and over again as the group slowly comes to consensus on major points. The research director keeps track of those points of consensus. The research director invites more comment on areas that are still unclear or on which there is disagreement. The experts may end up not agreeing on everything. But after several rounds, there usually is enough accord on key points that the process can be drawn to a close. To do this, the research director writes up the points of apparent agreement and verifies that the experts are in accord. In this particular Delphi research project focusing on critical thinking, it took six rounds of questioning and 16 separate group communications back and forth before consensus was achieved. One very important thing about the Delphi process in general, which was true of this particular project as well: Because the group is made up of experts whose names and reputations are well known to the other experts, the Delphi process calls for omitting their names when the research director circulates their remarks and opinions to the other members of the group. That way the group sees each expert's arguments and explanations, but not knowing who the author is, the others in the group will not be overly influenced by any positive or negative opinions they may have about that other expert. The ideas speak for themselves. This account of the Delphi research process comes from the person who was the project director for the effort to achieve an expert consensus regarding the meaning of critical thinking, namely the author of this textbook. As such, he was not a contributing expert on that 46-person panel.
ix. American Philosophical Association, *Critical Thinking: A Statement of Expert Consensus for Purposes of Educational Assessment and Instruction*, also known as *"The Delphi Report"* (ERIC Doc. No. ED 315 423) 1990. Executive summary and full report available through Insight Assessment/The California Academic Press, Millbrae, CA, <www.insightassessment.com>.
x. Some use the word "meta-cognitive" when referring to the skills of self-monitoring and self-correcting. We will unpack these ideas in much greater detail in Chapter 2.
xi. <http://www.bbc.co.uk/news/world-europe-14342877>.
xii. <http://www.dailymail.com.uk/news/article-2016864/Yosemite-National-Park-Vernal-waterfall-accident-3-hikers-presumend-dead.html>.
xiii. Ann Sanner, "Obama to Sign National Service Bill Today," Huffington Post, 21 Apr. 2009, 8 Jul. 2009 <http://www.huffingtonpost.com/ 2009/04/21/obama-to-sign-national-se_n_189407.html>.
xiv. <http://www.nationalservice.gov/pdf/10_0421_saa_implementation.pdf>.
xv. "A Call to Service," From The White House Blog, The White House, 8 Jul. 2009 <http://www.whitehouse.gov/blog/09/04/21/A-Call-to-Service/>.
xvi. Reprinted with permission from The California Academic Press/ Insight Assessment—Assessing Critical Thinking Worldwide www.insightassessment.com USA Phone: (650) 697-5628. © 1994, 2009, Peter A. Facione, Noreen C. Facione, and Measured Reasons LLC, Hermosa Beach, CA. USA Permission is hereby granted to students, faculty, staff, or administrators at public or nonprofit educational institutions for unlimited duplication of the *Holistic Critical Thinking Scoring Rubric* when used for local teaching, assessment, research, or other educational and noncommercial purposes, provided that no part of the scoring rubric is altered and that "Facione and Facione" are cited as authors. (PAF49:R4.3:052009).
xvii. <http://topics.nytimes.com/top/news/international/countriesandterritories/haiti/index.html>.

CHAPTER 2

i. Allen Newell, *Toward Unified Theories of Cognition* (Cambridge, MA: Harvard University Press, 1990); Paul Slovic, Baruch Fischhoff, and Sarah Lichtenstein, "Behavioral Decision Theory," *Annual Review of Psychology* 28 (Jan. 1977): Henry Montgomery, "From Cognition to Action: The Search for Dominance in Decision Making,"

Process and Structure in Human Decision Making, Ed. Henry Montgomery and Ola Svenson (Chichester, UK: John Wiley & Sons, 1989) 23–49; Allen Newell and Herbert Alexander Simon, *Human Problem Solving* (Englewood Cliffs, NJ: Prentice Hall, 1972).

ii. The descriptions of events in this paragraph and the paragraphs that follow are based on the 1994 book *Apollo 13*, by Jeffery Kluger and Jim Lovell (Boston: Houghton Mifflin) and on subsequent dramatizations of the events described in that book including the 1995 film *Apollo 13,* directed by Ron Howard with technical consultation provided by the book's authors, Lovell and Kluger.

iii. John Dewey, *How We Think*. (Boston: D.C. Heath & Co., 1910).

iv. Peter A. Facione, Noreen C. Facione, and Carol A. Giancarlo, "The Disposition Toward Critical Thinking: Its Character, Measurement, and Relationship to Critical Thinking Skill," *Informal Logic* 20(1)(2000): 61–84; Peter A. Facione, Noreen C. Facione, and Carol A. Giancarlo, "The Motivation to Think in Working and Learning," *Preparing Competent College Graduates: Setting New and Higher Expectations for Student Learning*, Ed. Elizabeth A. Jones (San Francisco: Jossey-Bass Publishers, 1997) 67–79; Peter A. Facione, Carol A. Giancarlo, and Noreen C. Facione, *Are College Students Disposed to Think?* (ERIC Doc. No. ED 368 311) Apr. 1994; Peter A. Facione, Noreen C. Facione, "Profiling Critical Thinking Dispositions," *Assessment Update* (5)2 (1993): 1–4; Carol A. Giancarlo and Peter A. Facione, "A Look across Four Years at the Disposition toward Critical Thinking Among Undergraduate Students," *The Journal of General Education* 50(1) (2001): 29–55.

v. H. C. Triandis, "Values, Attitudes and Interpersonal Behavior," *Beliefs, Attitudes, and Values. Nebraska Symposium on Motivation*, Ed. Herbert E. Howe (Lincoln, NE: University of Nebraska Press, 1980); Icek Ajzen and Martin Fishbein, "A Theory of Reasoned Action: Some Applications and Implications," *Beliefs, Attitudes, and Values. Nebraska Symposium on Motivation*, Ed. Herbert E. Howe (Lincoln, NE: University of Nebraska Press, 1980).

vi. Peter A. Facione, Carol A. Giancarlo, Noreen C. Facione, and Joanne Gainen, "The Disposition Toward Critical Thinking," *Journal of General Education* 44(1) (1995): 1–25; Peter A. Facione, Noreen C. Facione, and Carol A. Giancarlo, *Test Manual: The California Critical Thinking Disposition Inventory* (Millbrae, CA: California Academic Press, 1992, 1994, 2001, 2007); Noreen C. Facione and Peter A. Facione, "Externalizing the Critical Thinking in Knowledge Development and Clinical Judgment," *Nursing Outlook* 44 (1996): 129–136; Peter A. Facione, "Empirical Methods of Theory and Tool Development for the Assessment of College Level Critical Thinking and Problem-Solving," Report, Conference on Collegiate Skills Assessment, Washington, DC: NCES, U.S. Department of Education, 1992; Elizabeth A. Jones, Steven Hoffman, L. Moore, G. Ratcliff, S. Tibbetts, and B. Click, *Essential Skills in Writing, Speech and Listening, and Critical Thinking for College Graduates: Perspectives of Faculty, Employers, and Policy Makers*, Project summary, U.S. Department of Education, OERI Contract No. R117G10037, University Park, PA: National Center for Postsecondary Teaching, Learning, and Assessment, Pennsylvania State University, 1994; Elizabeth Jones, Steven Hoffman, L. Moore, G. Ratcliff, S. Tibbetts, and B. Click, *National Assessment of College Student Learning: Identifying the College Graduates' Essential Skills in Writing, Speech and Listening, and Critical Thinking,* Washington, DC: National Center for Educational Statistics, U.S. Department of Education, Office of Educational Research and Improvement, OERI publication NCES 93-001, 2005.

vii. Stephen D. Brookfield, *Developing Critical Thinkers: Challenging Adults to Explore Alternative Ways of Thinking and Acting* (San Francisco: Jossey-Bass Publishers, 1987); Lauren Resnick, *Education and Learning to Think* (Washington, DC: National Academy Press, 1987); Chet Meyers, *Teaching Students to Think Critically* (San Francisco: Jossey-Bass Publishers, 1986).

viii. The findings of expert consensus are published in *Critical Thinking: A Statement of Expert Consensus for Purposes of Educational Assessment and Instruction* (ERIC Doc. No. ED 315 423) 1990. The research was undertaken originally as a project of a committee of the American Philosophical Association (APA), published by The California Academic Press, Millbrae, CA. In 1993 and 1994, the Center for the Study of Higher Education at Pennsylvania State University undertook a study of 200 policy makers, employers, and faculty members from two-year and four-year colleges to determine what this group took to be the core critical thinking skills and habits of mind. That Pennsylvania State University study, under the direction of Dr. Elizabeth Jones, was funded by the U.S. Department of Education Office of Educational Research and Instruction. The Pennsylvania State University study findings, published in 1994, confirmed the expert consensus expressed in the APA report.

ix. The descriptions of what characters do and think in this paragraph and those that follow are based on the book *12 Angry Men: A Play in Three Acts*, by Reginald Rose (London: Penguin Books, 1955), and Reginald Rose's later adaptation of that book for the 1957 United Artists film *12 Angry Men*.

x. The United Artists 1957 film version of *12 Angry Men* was nominated for three Academy Awards. Fifty years later the film *12 Angry Men* was selected for preservation in the United States National Film Registry by the Library of Congress as being "culturally, historically, or aesthetically significant." Do not miss DVD scene #10 where the two main protagonists argue about how a streetwise killer would hold a switchblade knife.

xi. American Philosophical Association, *Critical Thinking: A Statement of Expert Consensus for Purposes of Educational Assessment and Instruction*, also known as *"The Delphi Report"* (ERIC Doc. No. ED 315 423) 1990. (Millbrae, CA: The California Academic Press).

xii. Why "we" some times and "I" other times? There are two of us co-authoring the second edition. But because the book often illustrates key points with personal stories and because the two of us have had different life experiences that we want to share with you, we occasionally use the work "I" for the sake of accuracy. When we use the word "I" we intend that one of us, but not both of us, have had a particular experience that we both want shared. Thanks for understanding the difference between what "we" authors are saying together and what one or the other of us is describing as a personal experience.

xiii. © 2007, Image from P. Facione "Critical Thinking: What It Is and Why It Counts." Rendition of an original design used with permission of the publisher, Insight Assessment/The California Academic Press.

xiv. Mathematicians and computer scientists would describe this as a "recursive function," meaning that the function can be applied to itself. We can analyze our analyses. We can evaluate our evaluations.

xv. Table © 2009. *Test Manual for the California Critical Thinking Skills Test*, published by Insight Assessment, Millbrae, CA. Used with permission of the publisher.

xvi. M. Neil Browne and Stuart M. Keeley, *Asking the Right Questions*, 9th ed. (Pearson, 2009).

xvii. Table © 2009, *Test Manual for the Test of Everyday Reasoning*, Insight Assessment, Millbrae, CA. Used with permission of the publisher. Critical thinking skill definitions cited are from American Philosophical Association, *Critical Thinking: A Statement of Expert Consensus for Purposes of Educational Assessment and Instruction*. Also known as *"The Delphi Report"* (ERIC Doc. No. ED 315 423) 1990.

xviii. William Calvert Kneale and Martha Kneale, *The Development of Logic* (Oxford, UK: The Clarendon Press, 1962).

xix. Albert Blumberg, "Modern Logic," *The Encyclopedia of Philosophy*, Vol. 5, Ed. P. Edwards (New York: Macmillan, 1967) 24–34.

xx. Jum C. Nunnally, *Psychometric Theory* (New York: McGraw-Hill Book Company, 1978).

xxi. S. E. Hankinson and W. C. Willett, principal investigators. Funding provided by the National Institutes of Health, 7 Jul. 2009 <http://www.channing.harvard.edu/nhs/>.

xxii. *Nurses' Health Study Newsletter* 16 (2009): 6. See also, The Nurses' Health Study, <www.nurseshealthstudy.org>.

xxiii. "Mark Twain Quotes," Quote DB, 2 Jul. 2009 <http://www.quotedb.com/quotes/117>.

CHAPTER 3

i. We use "IDEAS" as a mnemonic device to assist in remembering the five steps. Note that each step, as described above, has two parts. The two parts of each step supplement each other. We could have merged the two parts grammatically, but at the risk of losing one or the other of them. However, if it is easier to remember the steps, one might describe them this way:

- Identify the problem and the priorities.
- Deepen understanding of relevant information.
- Enumerate options and consequences.
- Assess the options and make a preliminary decision on which one appears to best fit the situation.
- Scrutinize the process carefully and self-correct as necessary before making a final decision.

ii. Arthur W. Chickering and Linda Reisser, *Education and Identity*, 2nd ed. (San Francisco: Jossey-Bass, 1993). Arthur Chickering's model and other approaches are discussed in *Student Development in College: Theory, Research, and Practice* by Nancy J. Evans, Deanna S. Forney, and Florence M. Guido. (San Francisco: Jossey-Bass, John Wiley & Son, 2009).

iii. Erik H. Erikson, *Identity: Youth and Crisis* (Austen Riggs Monograph) (New York: Norton, 1968) <http://www.quotationspage.com/quote/603.html>.

CHAPTER 4

i. Jerome Lawrence and Robert Lee, *Inherit the Wind* (New York: Random House, Ballantine Books, 1955).

ii. Paul E. Koptak, "What's New in Interpreting Genesis," *The Covenant Quarterly* LIII(1) (Feb. 1995): 3–16. <http://www.religion-online.org/showarticle.asp?title=19>.

iii. Bible defenders and Bible detractors will both find the article "The Bible is Dead; Long Live the Bible," by Timothy Beal most interesting. He speaks directly to the question how the Bible is read and interpreted. For example, does it have a single right meaning? Does it answer questions, or does it raise questions? What was its historical context and purpose? Professor Beal's article appeared online in the *Chronicle of Higher Education*, April 17, 2011. It is drawn from his new book, *The Rise and Fall of the Bible: The Unexpected History of an Accidental Book*, published by Houghton Mifflin Harcourt.

iv. Jared Diamond, *Guns, Germs, and Steel* (New York: Norton, 1997).

v. *My Cousin Vinny*, Palo Vista Productions, dir. Jonathan Lynn, writ. Dale Launer, perf. Joe Pesci, Ralph Macchio, and Marisa Tomei. 1992.

vi. Andreas Teuber "Original Intent or how Does the Constitution Mean? *The London Review of Books*, 10(7), (Mar. 1988) <http://people.brandeis.edu/~teuber/origintent.html>.

vii. For example, often the jury in a criminal case is asked to deliberate about the perpetrator's intent as one of the elements when determining guilt or innocence, as in the case of murder in the first degree.

viii. Roger Fisher, William L. Ury, and Bruce Patton, *Getting to Yes: Negotiating Agreement Without Giving In* (New York: Penguin Books, 1983).

ix. "Driving Under Influence of Drugs or Alcohol," California Department of Motor Vehicles, 25 Aug. 2009 <http://www.dmv.ca.gov/pubs/vctop/d11/vc23152.htm>.

x. Link to NBC *Nightly News with Brian Williams* specific story broadcast on September 20, 2011: <http://www.msnbc.msn.com/id/3032619/>.

xi. The findings of expert consensus are published in *Critical Thinking: A Statement of Expert Consensus for Purposes of Educational Assessment and Instruction* (ERIC Doc. No. ED 315 423) 1990. The research was undertaken originally as a project of a committee of the American Philosophical Association (APA). This report is often referred to as "The Delphi Report."

CHAPTER 5

i. "Measles Vaccination," Vaccines and Immunizations, Department of Health and Human Services: Centers for Disease Control, 20 Oct. 2009, 27 Oct. 2009 <http://www.cdc.gov/vaccines/vpd-vac/measles/default.htm>.

ii. "Argument," Merriam Webster's Online Dictionary, 22 June 2009 <http://www.merriam-webster.com/dictionary/argument>.

iii. "Parents' Guide to Childhood Immunization," Centers for Disease Control and Prevention, 22 June 2009 <http://www.cdc.gov/vaccines/pubs/parents-guide/default.htm>.

iv. There is a contextual element relating to scientific research that a fuller analysis of the reason might include; if the question "But if even 1 case occurs, then why not call it a side effect?" were raised, then the premise added might be, "When two events occur together so rarely that their coincidence cannot be distinguished from pure chance, then we do not have sufficient reason to regard either as the cause of the other."

v. Successful communication depends on the intentions of the speaker concerning what he or she is trying to convey and on the beliefs of the speaker with regard to the knowledge of the listener. If the speaker believes that the listener is not aware of information that is essential for correctly interpreting what is being said, then it would not be sensible for the speaker to expect that the listener should understand the message. For more on this the reader may wish to search and explore the rich literature regarding the intricate relationships between communicating, meaning, believing and intending, for example, P. Facione, "Meaning and Intending," *American Philosophical Quarterly* 10(4) (1973): 277–287.

vi. A 2010 Pew Research Center survey shows that nearly 75 percent of Americans favor legalizing medical marijuana and that just over 40 percent are of the opinion that all marijuana should be legal. According to a 2008 Gallup poll that percentage was 35 percent, which itself is about triple the 12 percent who held that view when Gallup surveyed Americans in 1969.

vii. BBC Monday, 9 May 2011, "Blurred lines in California's cannabis capital" as reported by Vishva Samani.

viii. Rose, Reginald, *Twelve Angry Men—A Play in Three Acts,* (London: Penguin Books, 1955). The 1957 film version was nominated for three Academy Awards and in 2007 the film was selected for preservation in the United States National Film Registry by the Library of Congress as being "culturally, historically, or aesthetically significant." The El Train scene begins roughly forty minutes into that United Artists film. The fair-minded juror who leads the reasoning is played by Henry Fonda.

ix. That people make arguments in their efforts to reason through their decisions is clear. The number of arguments can vary widely, particularly if the decision is one of those important ones that needs to be reaffirmed on a frequent basis, like deciding not to seek a diagnosis for a worrisome symptom, or deciding not to take disciplinary action against a problem employee. Noreen C. Facione and Peter A. Facione, "Analyzing Explanations for Seemingly Irrational Choices: Linking Argument Analysis and Cognitive Science," *International Journal of Applied Philosophy* 15(2) (2002): 267–286.

x. The mapping conventions presented here are drawn from Peter A. Facione and Noreen C. Facione, *Thinking and Reasoning in Human Decision Making: The Method of Argument and Heuristic Analysis* (Millbrae, CA: The California Academic Press, 2007). That book offers additional conventions that enable the analyst to display the reasoning relationships (logical or statistical inferences) or the heuristic relationships (satisficing, association, anchoring with adjustment, etc.) that connect the reasons and claims.

xi. Peter A. Facione and Noreen C. Facione, *Thinking and Reasoning in Human Decision Making* (Millbrae, CA: The California Academic Press, 2007) 58.

CHAPTER 6

i. Maureen Boyle, "Massachusetts Slayings Touch Cape Verde Community around the World," GateHouse News Service, 8 Feb. 2009, 27 Jul. 2009 <http://www.enterprisenews.com/news/special_report_luke/x1536017033/Grief-across-the-ocean>. Stories also in *The Examiner*, Brockton, MA, Jan. 21–22, 2009 <http://www.enterprisenews.com/news/special_report_luke/x148964404/THE-VICTIMS-Selma-Goncalves>.

ii. Larry Keller, "From Hate to Hurt," *Intelligence Report 134* (Summer 2009): 50–54, Published by the Southern Poverty Law Center, Montgomery, Alabama.

iii. Patricia M. King and Karen Strohm Kitchener, *Developing Reflective Judgment* (San Francisco: Jossey-Bass Publishers, 1994). My formulation presented here is a reformulation of work by King and Kitchener. Scholars who were instrumental in expanding our understanding of cognitive development include B. Bloom, W. Perry, L. Kohlberg, J. H. Flavel, M. Fischer, and J. Piaget, to name only a few of the many.

iv. "Expert," Wikipedia, the Free Encyclopedia, 27 Jul. 2009 <http://en.wikipedia.org/wiki/Expertise>.

v. In Chapter 10, we will revisit statements like this in the context of "heuristic thinking" and "System-1 decision making." Highly trained individuals have so internalized their problem-solving and pattern-recognition skills in the domain of their expertise that they make automatic, reactive decisions. Often, these are quite reliable and appropriate. The difficulty for critical thinking is that we cannot know that in a reflective and carefully explained way. But let's save this conversation for later.

vi. Plato, "*The Republic* Book III, 389 b-c," *The Collected Dialogues of Plato*, Ed. Edith Hamilton (New York: The Bollingen Foundation, 1961) 634.

vii. Benjamin Edelman, "Red Light States: Who Buys Online Adult Entertainment?" *Journal of Economic Perspectives* 23(1) (Winter 2009): 209–220.

viii. Enda Brady, "Image of Virgin Mary Found in Tree Stump," Sky News, 10 Jul. 2009, 21 Aug. 2009 <http://news.sky.com/skynews/Home/ World-News/Virgin-Mary-Tree-Stump-Depiction-Found-InRathkeale-Ireland/Article/200907215334913>.

ix. Steven Miller Design Studio, 27 Jul. 2009 <http://www.stevenmillerdesignstudio.com/>.

x. Mark Silva, "Obama, McCain: U.S. Citizens," The Swamp: Tribune's Washington Bureau, 25 Oct. 2008, 27 Jul. 2009 <http://www.swamppolitics.com/news/politics/blog/2008/10/obama_mccain_us_citizens.html>.

xi. Alex Koppelman, "Why the Stories about Obama's Birth Certificate Will Never Die," Salon.com, 5 Dec. 2008, 27 Jul. 2009 <http://www. salon.com/news/feature/2008/12/05/birth_certificate/>.

xii. Stephen Barrett, M.D., "Q-Ray Bracelet Marketed with Preposterous Claims," Quackwatch, 6 Jan. 2008, 27 Jul. 2009 <http://www.quackwatch.com/search/webglimpse.cgi?ID=1&query=Q-Ray>.

xiii. Michael Higgins, "Placebo Effect a Key Issue in Trial over Pain Bracelet," *Chicago Tribune* 23 Aug. 2006.

xiv. The power bracelet bankruptcy and Koby's lost $400K were reported by several news outlets. For example: <http://content.usatoday.com/communities/gameon/post/2011/11/kobe-bryant-400k-endorsement-company-bankrupt/1> <http://www.huffingtonpost.com/mobileweb/2011/11/21/power-bracelets-lawsuit_n_1105559.html> <http://www.ocregister.com/articles/company-328232-balance-power.html>.

xv. This exercise is based on Greg Brown, "Evaluating a Nutritional Supplement with SOAP Notes to Develop CT Skills," *Critical Thinking and Clinical Reasoning in the Health Sciences*, Ed. Noreen C. Facione and Peter A. Facione (Millbrae, CA: California Academic Press, 2008) 198–201.

CHAPTER 7

i. In Chapter 5 we said that the premises of an argument is the set of statements, explicitly asserted or contextually assumed and implicit, which comprise a reason offered on behalf of a claim. A person may offer more than one reason for a given claim. Each reason is a set of premises. The "Truthfulness" presumption about argument making says that we expect that each and every premise that constitutes a given reason to be, in fact, true.

ii. Mary Pettibone Poole quote <http://www.quotationspage.com/subjects/intelligence/>.

iii. Peter Facione and Donald Scherer, *Logic and Logical Thinking* (New York: McGraw-Hill Publishing, 1978).

iv. People studying logic learn that there are a couple of peculiarly paradoxical cases in which the premises cannot possibly all be true and the conclusion false. One is a case in which the premises are inconsistent with each other. In that case it is impossible for them all to be true, because if one of the inconsistent pair of premises is true, then the other in the pair will necessarily be false. In that odd situation, the argument will pass the test of logical strength. Not to worry—it will fail the test of the truthfulness of the premises. The other odd case is the situation in which the conclusion of the argument is a tautology, and again the argument will pass the test of logical strength, because it will not be possible ever for the conclusion to be false. Again, not to worry, because the test of relevance eliminates these kinds of arguments from being considered acceptable. The test of relevance requires that the basis for believing in the truth of the claim should be the reason given and not some independent consideration. A tautology is true no matter what reason is given; in fact, the reason is entirely irrelevant to the truth of the claim. Therefore, an argument with a tautological conclusion fails the test of relevance.

v. Irving M. Copi and Carl Cohen, *Introduction to Logic* (New York: Macmillan Publishing, 1990) 52–53.

vi. "National Safety Council Calls for Nationwide Ban on Cell Phone Use While Driving," National Safety Council, 27 Jul. 2009 <http://www.nsc.org/news/cellphone_ban.aspx>.

vii. There are many excellent summaries of Pythagoras and the Pythagoreans, among them the Stanford Encyclopedia of Philosophy <http://plato.stanford.edu/entries/pythagoras/>. Others can be found in the *Encyclopedia of Philosophy*, Ed. Paul Edwards (New York: Macmillan/Free Press, 1967).

viii. John Searle, *Speech Acts: An Essay in the Philosophy of Language* (Cambridge, UK: Cambridge University Press, 1969).

ix. A couple of these may seem familiar because they were used as examples for other purposes in other chapters. This is the only place in the book, however, where you are being invited to evaluate them.

x. Paraphrased from the novel, *Rough Country*, John Sandford (New York: Putnam's, 2009).

xi. William C. Rhoden, *Third and a Mile: The Trials and Triumphs of the Black Quarterback* (Bristol, CT: ESPN Books, 2007). This excerpt from Chapter 5 examines the fitful start to the 12-year NFL career of James Harris: William C. Rhoden, "The James Harris story: a long, painful road," 12 Feb. 2007, 27 Jul. 2009 <http://sports.espn.go.com/espn/blackhistory2007/news/story?id=2762569>.

xii. Many frequently repeated mistakes in reasoning have earned themselves names as fallacies. To list them all would not be possible. That is one reason for approaching the evaluation of arguments in terms of the four tests. There are many fallacies we will describe in Chapters 8 and 9 that fail the test of logical strength. Obviously, those seven fallacies described in this chapter are arguments that also fail the test of relevance. We could have named "circular reasoning" as a common fallacy as well, but we already have the test of non-circularity. Being able to recognize common fallacies is a way to become more proficient in applying the tests of logical strength, relevance, and non-circularity. And it is fun, too, to see how we all are, at times, misled by the clever fallacies that commonly infest everyday conversation.

xiii. Aristotle, *On Sophistical Refutations,* trans. W. A. Pickard-Cambridge, 350 B.C.E., 27 Jul. 2009 <http://classics.mit.edu/Aristotle/ sophist_refut.html>; J. Machie, "Fallacies," *The Encyclopedia of Philosophy*, Vol. 3, Ed. Paul Edwards (New York: Macmillan Publishing, 1967) 169–179
C. L. Hamblin, *Fallacies* (London: Methuen, 1970);
John Chaffee, *Thinking Critically* (New York: Houghton Mifflin, 2003).

xiv. The prejudicial belief expressed in the first sentence was widely accepted for decades. Doug Williams went on to lead the Pittsburgh Steelers to victory in Super Bowl XXII. He received the 1988 Super Bowl MVP award for his performance that day as quarterback.

xv. A. Prior, C. Lejewski, J. F. Staal, A. C. Gram, et al., "The History of Logic," *The Encyclopedia of Philosophy*, Vol. 4, Ed. Paul Edwards (New York: Macmillan, 1967) 513–571.

xvi. Chart reproduced from Gallup Poll information: <http://www.gallup.com/poll/27727/Public-Divided-Over-Moral-Acceptability-DoctorAssisted-Suicide.aspx>.

CHAPTER 8

i. "The Cold Equations," a sci-fi classic, is a short story by Tom Godwin. It appeared in 1954 in *Astounding Magazine*. Later it was made into an episode of the CBS television series *The New Twilight Zone*. That episode, the 16th in third seasons, first aired January 7, 1989. Unfortunately, the episode was not available for viewing on any of the major Internet TV show Web sites, or through CBS.com. The show (22 minutes) is posted on YouTube at <http://www.youtube.com/watch?v=oZWXGg4otlg>.

ii. The word *consequent* in "Denying the Consequent" refers to the second part of an "If _____, then _____" statement, that is the part after "then _____". The part that comes before is the "if _____" part, or the "antecedent." So, the hypothetical is constructed "If antecedent, then consequent."

iii. Logicians call this pattern *modus tollens*.

iv. Aristotle quote <http://www.quotationspage.com/quote/1152.html>.

v. Logicians call this pattern *modus ponens*.

vi. Instructors should contact Pearson Education about customized versions of *THINK Critically*.

CHAPTER 9

i. Indiana State University is located in Terre Haute, Butler is located in Indianapolis. The statistics cited in this opening story came from *US News and World Report*'s Education Web site: <http://colleges.usnews.rankingsandreviews.

com/best-colleges/indiana-state-university-9563>. Visit the web pages for their respective undergraduate admissions offices for more precise and up to date information on tuition and fees.

ii. The story is drawn from *CSI* episode 212, "You've Got Male" (episode #12, season 2), which first aired on December 20, 2001. The story as it is told in the *CSI* episode includes yet another twist that is not revealed as it is recounted here. Hint: "murder or accident" is a false dilemma if there are other possibilities.

iii. Margaret K. Ma, Michael H. Woo, and Howard L. McLeod, "Genetic Basis of Drug Metabolism: Genetic Polymorphisms in the CYP Isoenzymes," *American Journal of Health-System Pharmacy* 59(21) (2002). pp. 2061–2069. Also found at Medscape Today, 10 Aug. 2009 <http://www.medscape.com/viewarticle/444804_5>.

iv. Raymond M. Lee, *Doing Research on Sensitive Topics* (London: Sage Publications, 1993); Delbert Charles Miller, *Handbook of Research Design and Social Measurement* (London: Sage Publications, 1991).

v. Scott Maxwell and Harold Delany, *Designing Experiments and Analyzing Data* (Belmont, CA: Wadsworth Publishing, 1990).

vi. "Lighting Fatalities, Injuries, and Damage Reports in the United States from 1959–1994," National Oceanic and Atmospheric Association Technical Memorandum NWS SR-193, October 1997, 10 Aug. 2009 <http://www.nssl.noaa.gov/papers/techmemos/NWS-SR-193/techmemo-sr193-3.html#section3b>.

vii. Karen B. Williams, Colleen Schmidt, Terri S. I. Tilliss, Kris Wilkins, and Douglas R. Glasnapp, "Predictive Validity of Critical Thinking Skills and Disposition for the National Board Dental Hygiene Examination: A Preliminary Investigation," *Journal of Dental Education* 70(5) (2006): 536–544; Kenneth L. McCall, Eric J. MacLaughlin, David S. Fike, and Beatrice Ruiz, "Preadmission Predictors of PharmD Graduates' Performance on the NAPLEX," *American Journal of Pharmacy Education* 15; 71(1) (2007): 5; The CCTST total score is a prepharmacy predictor of successful licensure as a pharmacist (NAPLEX test). Age, advanced science education courses, and previous BS or MS degree were not significantly correlated with NAPLEX; J. Giddens and G. W. Gloeckner, "The relationship of critical thinking to performance on the NCLEX-RN," *Journal of Nursing Education* 44(2) (2005): 85–89. CCTST total scores were higher in participants who passed the NCLEX-RN.

viii. The power of a correlation to predict results depends on how strong the correlation is. Typically a correlation is reported as a decimal value between 0 and 1. For example, "the correlation of X and Y is 0.31." Researchers use this number to calculate how much the change in X can predict changes in Y, and vice versa. That calculation is simple. Called the "variance," it is correlation squared. If college success (measured as GPA) is correlated at 0.40 with critical thinking skill, then we could infer that 16 percent of the variation seen in college GPA is predictable based on differences in critical thinking skills.

ix. Randy M. Kaplan, "Using a Trainable Pattern-Directed Computer Program to Score Natural Language Item Responses," Educational Testing Service, Research Report #RR-91-31, 1992, 10 Aug. 2009 <http://www.ets.org/Media/Research/pdf/RR-91-31-Kaplan.pdf>.

x. Donald E. Powers, Jill C. Burstein, Martin Chodorow, Mary E. Fowles, and Karen Kukich, "Comparing the Validity of Automated and Human Essay Scoring," Educational Testing Service, Research Report #RR-0010, 2000, 10 Aug. 2009 <http://www.ets.org/research/policy_research_reports/rr-00-10>.

xi. R. Mishori, A. Otubu, and A. Jones, "The Dangers of Colon Cleansing," *Journal of Family Practice* 60(8) (2011): 454–457.

xii. Published Online 5 May 2011. Science Express Index <http://www.sciencemag.org/content/early/2011/05/04/science.1204531.abstract>.

CHAPTER 10

i. Herbert Alexander Simon, *Models of Man: Social and Rational* (New York: Wiley, 1957).

ii. Peter Facione and Noreen Facione, *Thinking and Reasoning in Human Decision Making* (Millbrae, CA: The California Academic Press, 2007).

iii. Thomas Glovitch, Dale Griffin, and Daniel Kahneman, eds, *Heuristics and Biases: The Psychology of Intuitive Judgment* (Cambridge, UK: Cambridge University Press, 2002); Daniel Paul Slovic Kahneman, and Amos Tversky, eds, *Judgment under Uncertainty: Heuristics and Biases* (Cambridge, UK: Cambridge University Press, 1982); Steven A. Sloman, "Two Systems of Reasoning," *Heuristics and Biases: The Psychology of Intuitive Judgment*, Eds. Thomas Glovitch, Dale Griffin, and Daniel Kahneman (Cambridge, UK: Cambridge University Press, 2002) 379–396; Daniel Kahneman and Dale T. Miller, "Norm Theory: Comparing Reality to Its Alternatives," *Heuristics and Biases: The Psychology of Intuitive Judgment*, Eds. Thomas Glovitch, Dale Griffin, and Daniel Kahneman (Cambridge, UK: Cambridge University Press, 2002) 348–366.

iv. My research colleagues and I recommend avoiding use of the word *intuition*. We are puzzled by claims of justified true beliefs—knowledge—that go beyond observations or direct personal experience and yet are not preceded or preconditioned by some degree of interpretation, analysis, or inference, whether reflective or unreflective. Perhaps there is such a thing as intuitive knowledge, ineffable, immediate, mystical, and true. Even so, by definition such knowledge, if it is indeed knowledge, is beyond the scope of inter-subjective verification and science. That which is said to be "known" by intuition is, by definition, placed outside possible connections with other evidence-based, replicable, or falsifiable knowledge. Hence, other humans cannot, in principle, confirm or disconfirm that what is asserted to be known by means of intuition. "Special knowledge," available only to one, is always and ever to be suspect. Healthy skepticism demands that it be rejected. We respectfully decline to drink that Kool-Aid. Another reason we have deep ethical concerns about appeals to "intuition" as a basis for justifying beliefs as true or decisions as reasonable is that we seek accountability for knowledge and for action. In matters of importance, including the decisions made in professional practice contexts—such as medicine, law, government, business, and the military—some appeal to "gut feelings" or "intuition" because they are either unable or unwilling to explain their judgments. In effect, they seek the cover of "intuition" because they do not wish to explain their judgments, they cannot explain their judgments, or they do not want to permit others to evaluate those judgments or those explanations. How do we know this? Our research team includes people with many decades of professional practice experience involving health care, management, legal, and leadership responsibilities. We realize the fundamental inadequacies of appeals to intuition and gut feeling. These experiences, in part, motivated us to look more deeply into decision making.

v. Shelly E. Taylor, "The Availability Bias in Social Perception and Interaction" *Judgment under Uncertainty: Heuristics and Biases*, Eds. Daniel Kahneman, Paul Slovic, and Amos Tversky (Cambridge, UK: Cambridge University Press, 1982) 190–200; Baruch Fischhoff, "Attribution Theory and Judgment under Uncertainty," *New Directions in Attribution Research*, Eds. John. H. Harvey, William John Ickes, and Robert F. Kidd (Hillsdale, NJ: Erlbaum, 1976); Herbert Alexander Simon, *Models of Man: Social and Rational* (New York: Wiley, 1957).

vi. Gerd Gigerenzer, Jean Czerlinski, and Laura Martignon, "How Good Are Fast and Frugal Heuristics?" *Heuristics and Biases: The Psychology of Intuitive Judgment*, Eds. Thomas Gilovich, Dale W. Griffin, and Daniel Kahneman (Cambridge, UK: Cambridge University Press, 2002) 559–581.

vii. Paul Slovic, Melissa Finucane, Ellen Peters, and Donald G. MacGregor, "The Affect Heuristic," *Heuristics and Biases: The Psychology of Intuitive Judgment*, Eds. Thomas Gilovich, Dale W. Griffin, and Daniel Kahneman (Cambridge, UK: Cambridge University Press, 2002) 397–420; Norbert Schwarz, "Feelings as Information: Moods Influence Judgments and Processing Strategies," *Heuristics and Biases: The Psychology of Intuitive Judgment*, Eds. Thomas Gilovich, Dale W. Griffin, and Daniel Kahneman (Cambridge, UK: Cambridge University Press, 2002) 534–547.

viii. Oswald Huber, "Information-processing Operators in Decision Making," *Process and Structure on Human Decision Making*, Eds. Henry Montgomery and Ola Svenson (Chichester, UK: John Wiley & Sons, 1989) 3–21; Allen Newell and Herbert Alexander Simon, *Human Problem Solving* (Englewood Cliffs, NJ: Prentice Hall, 1972).

ix. Paul Slovic, Melissa Finucane, Ellen Peters, and Donald G. MacGregor, "The Affect Heuristic," *Heuristics and Biases: The Psychology of Intuitive Judgment*, Eds. Thomas Gilovich, Dale W. Griffin, and Daniel Kahneman (Cambridge, UK: Cambridge University Press, 2002) 397–420.

x. Phillip Waite, "Campus Landscaping in Recruitment and Retention: The Package Is the Product," Presented at the 2007 annual Noel Levitz conference on enrolment management, Orlando, FL, 2007.

xi. Business students may be interested in how the Turning Leaf brand applied a "Blue Ocean" Business strategy to this and made tremendous gains in a very competitive market. W. Chan Kim and Renee Mauborgne, *Blue Ocean Strategy* (Boston, MA: Harvard Business School Corporation, 2005).

xii. D. J. Koehler, "Explanation, Imagination and Confidence in Judgment," *Psychological Bulletin* 110 (1991): 499–519; S. J. Koch, "Availability and Inference in Predictive Judgment," *Journal of Experimental Psychology, Learning, Memory and Cognition* 10 (1984): 649–662.

xiii. Daniel Kahneman, Paul Slovic, and Amos Tversky, Eds. *Judgment under Uncertainty: Heuristics and Biases* (Cambridge, UK: Cambridge University Press, 1982); Amos Tversky and Daniel Kahneman, "Availability: A Heuristic for Judging Frequency and Probability," *Cognitive Psychology* 5 (1973): 207–232.

xiv. Albert Bandura, "Self-Efficacy: Toward a Unifying Theory of Behavioral Change," *Psychological Review* 84(2) (1977): 191–215; Albert Bandura, "Self-Efficacy Mechanism in Physiological Activation and Health-Promoting Behavior," *Adaptation, learning and effect*, Eds. J. Madden, IV, S. Matthysse, and J. Barchas (New York: Raven Press, 1989).

xv. Norbert Schwarz and Leigh Ann Vaughn, "The Availability Heuristic Revisited: Ease of Recall and Content of Recall as Distinct Sources of Information," *Heuristics and Biases: The Psychology of Intuitive Judgment*, Eds. Thomas Gilovich, Dale W. Griffin, and Daniel Kahneman (Cambridge, UK: Cambridge University Press, 2002) 103–119; Daniel Kahneman, Paul Slovic, and Amos Tversky, Eds. *Judgment under Uncertainty: Heuristics and Biases* (Cambridge, UK: Cambridge University Press, 1982) 11.

xvi. Daniel Kahneman, Paul Slovic, and Amos Tversky, Eds. *Judgment under Uncertainty: Heuristics and Biases* (Cambridge, UK: Cambridge University Press, 1982); Irving Lester Janis and Leon Mann, *Decision-making: A Psychological Analysis of Conflict, Choice, and Commitment* (New York: The Free Press, 1977).

xvii. Paul Rozin and Carol Nemeroff, "Sympathetic Magical Thinking: The Contagion and Similarity 'Heuristics.'" *Heuristics and Biases: The Psychology of Intuitive Judgment*, Eds. Thomas Gilovich, Dale W. Griffin, and Daniel Kahneman (Cambridge, UK: Cambridge University Press, 2002) 201–216; Daniel Kahneman and Shane Frederick, "Representativeness Revisited: Attribute Substitution in Intuitive Judgment," *Heuristics and Biases: The Psychology of Intuitive Judgment*, Eds. Thomas Gilovich, Dale W. Griffin, and Daniel Kahneman (Cambridge, UK: Cambridge University Press, 2002) 49–81. In the early heuristics literature, "representativeness" covered a wide range of things. Here we use "representation" as the name for some and "association" as the name for others. At times, these heuristics are found in the literature under the title "similarity."

xviii. <http://www.telegraph.co.uk/news/worldnews/republicans/ 8644679/US-Presidential-candidate-Herman-Cain-says-Americans-have-right-to-ban-mosques.html>.

xix. <http://abcnews.go.com/US/illegal-alien-saved-child-center-debate-policy-illegal/story?id=14347821>.

xx. Deborah Solomon, "Questions for Ayaan Hirsi Ali, The Feminist," *New York Times Magazine,* May 21, 2010, p. 14 <http://www.nytimes.com/2010/05/23/magazine/23fob-q4-t.html>.

xxi. Dualistic thinking divides the world into black and white with no shades of gray. For dualistic thinkers, all problems have right answers or wrong answers only. But psychological dualism is a broader construct. It is better understood in the context of cognitive development. The "Us vs. Them" dynamic, as cognitive heuristic, can influence decisions made by people whose cognitive development has progressed beyond dualistic thinking in many domains.

xxii. David Berreby, *Us and Them: Understanding Your Tribal Mind* (New York: Little, Brown and Company, 2005).

xxiii. Robert J. Robinson, Dacher Keltner, Andrew Ward, and Lee Ross, "Actual vs. Assumed Differences in Construal: 'Naïve Realism' in Intergroup Perception and Conflict," *Journal of Personality and Social Psychology* 68 (1995): 404–417.

xxiv. Amos Tversky and Daniel Kahneman, "Judgment under Uncertainty: Heuristics and Biases," *Science* 185 (1974): 1124–1131; Gretchen B. Chapman and Eric J. Johnson, "Incorporating the Irrelevant: Anchors in Judgments of Belief and Value," *Heuristics and Biases: The Psychology of Intuitive Judgment*, Eds. Thomas Gilovich, Dale W. Griffin, and Daniel Kahneman (Cambridge, UK: Cambridge University Press, 2002) 122–138.

xxv. S. C. Thompson, W. Armstrong, and C. Thomas, "Illusions of Control, Underestimations, and Accuracy: A Control Heuristic Explanation," *Psychological Bulletin* 123(2) (1998): 143–161.

xxvi. T. R. Schultz and D. Wells, "Judging the Intentionality of Action-outcomes," *Developmental Psychology* 21 (1985): 83–89.

xxvii. Baruch Fischhoff and Ruth Beyth, "'I knew it would happen'—Remembered Probabilities of Once Future Things," *Organizational Behavior and Human Performance* 13 (1975): 1–16.

xxviii. Irving Lester Janis and Leon Mann, Decision-making: A Psychological Analysis of Conflict, Choice, and Commitment (New York: The Free Press, 1977).

xxix. Dan Ariely, "The Curious Paradox of Optimism Bias," *Business Week*, Aug. 2009, 24 and 31: 48.

xxx. James G. March and Chip Heath, *A Primer on Decision Making: How Decisions Happen* (New York: The Free Press, 1994); Daniel Kahneman, Paul Slovic, and Amos Tversky, Eds. *Judgment under Uncertainty: Heuristics and Biases* (Cambridge, UK: Cambridge University Press, 1982); Irving Lester Janis and Leon Mann, *Decision-making: A Psychological Analysis of Conflict, Choice, and Commitment* (New York: The Free Press, 1977); Daniel Kahneman and Amos Tversky, *Choices, Values, and Frames* (Cambridge, UK: Cambridge University Press, 2000); Paul Slovic, "Limitations of the Mind of Man: Implications for Decision Making in the Nuclear Age," *Oregon Research Institute Bulletin* 11 (1971): 41–49.

xxxi. <http://www.npr.org/blogs/health/2011/02/04/133371076/how-keeping-little-girls-squeaky-clean-could-make-them-sick?sc=17&f=1001>.

xxxii. <http://www.npr.org/2011/04/24/135638370/does-a-higher-minimum-wage-kill-jobs?sc=17&f=1001>.

xxxiii. <http://www.npr.org/2011/01/13/132908098/new-gene-test-screens-nearly-500-childhood-diseases?sc=17&f=1001>.

CHAPTER 11

i. The interview was conducted with the woman's informed consent and under a protocol approved by the Human Subjects Research Review Board of a major medical research university. The interview was audiotaped, again with the woman's full knowledge and consent. The interview excerpt and the associated decision map are published in Noreen C. Facione and Peter A. Facione, *Thinking and Reasoning in Human Decision Making* (Millbrae, CA: The California Academic Press, 2007) 108–111. Used with permission.

ii. California has passed legislation known as the "Dream Act" that legalizes private funding to attend state public colleges and universities for illegal immigrant children who came the United States before the age of 16 <http://www.reuters.com/article/2011/07/26/us-usa-california-dream-idUSTRE76O6FV20110726>.

iii. In 2010 the *Chronicle of Higher Education* reported on the details and potential ramification for colleges and universities of a case being heard by the U.S. Supreme Court that would allow a Christian law students' group in California to prevent membership to individuals who engage in homosexual behavior <http://chronicle.com/article/Supreme-Court-Appears-Split/65169/>.

iv. "Quotations by Author: Aristotle," The Quotations Pages, 15 Sept. 2009 <http://www.quotationspage.com/quotes/Aristotle/>.

v. "Decision-critical criteria" is a short phrase that refers to those criteria the decision-maker deems to be important and relevant for the purpose of evaluating options. Two people working together to make a decision often agree to use the same decision-critical criteria because they both think that the same things are important and relevant when evaluating options. That said, they may not agree on the relative priority or importance of their various criteria. "Tastes great!" NO, "Less filling!"

vi. Henry Montgomery, "From Cognition to Action: The Search for Dominance in Decision Making," *Process and Structure in Human Decision Making*, Eds. Henry Montgomery and Ola Svenson (Chichester, UK: John Wiley & Sons, 1989) 23–49.

vii. <http://www2.tbo.com/news/breaking-news/2009/mar/01/coast-guard-searching-4-missing-boaters-ar-115159/>.

viii. <http://www.hbo.com/real-sports-with-bryant-gumbel/episodes/0/149-august-18-2009/synopsis.html>.

ix. <http://www2.tbo.com/news/breaking-news/2009/mar/27/report-inexperience-led-boating-mishap-killed-3-fo-ar-103716/>.

x. <http://www.cbsnews.com/stories/2009/07/09/national/main5147200.shtml>.

xi. Henry Montgomery, "From Cognition to Action: The Search for Dominance in Decision Making," *Process and Structure in Human Decision Making*, Eds. Henry Montgomery and Ola Svenson (Chichester, UK: John Wiley & Sons, 1989) 24.

xii. Henry Montgomery, "From Cognition to Action: The Search for Dominance in Decision Making," *Process and Structure in Human Decision Making*, Eds. Henry Montgomery and Ola Svenson (Chichester, UK: John Wiley & Sons, 1989).

xiii. Henry Montgomery "Decision Rules and the Search for a Dominance Structure: Towards a Process Model of Decision Making," *Analyzing and Aiding Decision Processes*, Eds. Patrick Humphreys, Ola Svenson, and Anna Vari (Amsterdam/Budapest: North Holland and Hungarian Academic Press, 1983) 343–369.

xiv. Henry Montgomery, "From Cognition to Action: The Search for Dominance in Decision Making," *Process and Structure in Human Decision Making*, Eds. Henry Montgomery and Ola Svenson (Chichester, UK: John Wiley & Sons, 1989) 26.

xv. Henry Montgomery "Decision Rules and the Search for a Dominance Structure: Towards a Process Model of Decision Making," *Analyzing and Aiding Decision Processes*, Eds. Patrick Humphreys, Ola Svenson, and Anna Vari (Amsterdam/Budapest: North Holland and Hungarian Academic Press, 1983) 343–369.

xvi. <http://www.facts4healthcare.com/pressroom/NPR_report_organicFoods.pdf>.

xvii. Oswald Huber, "Information-processing Operators in Decision Making," *Process and Structure on Human Decision Making*, Eds. Henry Montgomery and Ola Svenson (Chichester, UK: John Wiley & Sons, 1989) 3–21.

xviii. We are not offering an opinion one way or the other on the political statement that the Simpson defense team urged that the jurors in that celebrated case might consider making. Nor are we offering an opinion on the legal defense strategy known as *jury nullification*. That strategy is to persuade a jury to set aside the facts of a case for any of a variety of reasons in order to vote not-guilty no matter what they believe about the actual guilt or innocence of the accused. Again, this chapter is about how we can use strong critical thinking to make better, more thoughtful decisions, by self-regulating the psychological process of dominance structuring.

xix. We are not suggesting that Mr. Simpson was guilty. In fact, the jury's verdict was "not guilty." This example is intended as an interpretive analysis of how questions about the evidence, methods, concepts, standards, and context of a judgment can enter a group's decision-making dominance structuring.

xx. This scenario about a serial killer was inspired by Michael Connelly's novel *The Scarecrow* (New York: Little, Brown and Company, 2008).

CHAPTER 12

i. *Traffic,* Hollywood, CA: Universal Studios, dir. Steven Soderbergh, perf. Michael Douglas, Don Cheadle, Benicio Del Toro, Dennis Quaid, and Catherine Zeta-Jones, 2000.

ii. S. King, *Full Dark, No Stars*, (New York: Gallery Books, 2011) 125.

iii. T. Franklin, *Crooked Letter, Crooked Letter*, (New York: Harper Perennial, 2010) 251.

iv. Allen Newell, *Toward Unified Theories of Cognition* (Cambridge, MA: Harvard University Press, 1990).

v. Carolyn Lochhead and Carla Marinucci, "Freedom and Fear Are at War," The *San Francisco Chronicle*, 21 Sept. 2001, 1 Sept. 2009 <http://www.sfgate.com/cgibin/article.cgi?f=/c/a/2001/09/21/MN48614.DTL>.

vi. Michael Scriven, *Reasoning* (New York: McGraw-Hill, 1976).

vii. <http://SecondLife.com>.

viii. <http://www.bbc.co.uk/news/technology-14277728>.

ix. Chris Rock, *Chris Rock: Bigger and Blacker*, HBO Productions, writ. Chris Rock, perf. Chris Rock, 1999.

x. <http://www.thedailyshow.com/watch/thu-august-19-2010/extremist-makeover---homeland-edition>.

xi. <http://abcnews.go.com/Video/playerIndex?id=4826897>.

xii. BBC News US & Canada, "White House ask Supreme Court to Rule on healthcare law," September 29, 2011. <http://www.bbc.co.uk/news/world-us-canada-15112200>.

CHAPTER 13

i. *The Los Angeles Times* cites research on marriage statistics conducted by the Williams Institute of the UCLA School of Law, "Spike in Marriage Licenses Statewide," *The Los Angeles Times*, 3 Feb. 2009, 2 Sept. 2009 <http://www.latimes.com/news/local/la-marriagesmap,0,6124834.htmlstory>.

ii. The group that drafted Prop 8 in California is the Alliance Defense Fund. Stuart Whatley in "The Group Behind Prop 8" described the ADF as a Christian conservative consortium of lawyers, founded in 1994 as an answer to the American Civil Liberties Union (ACLU). Whatley's article was published in *The American Prospect* on October 22, 2008. To view the full text, go to <http://www.prospect.org/cs/articles?article=the_group_behind_prop_8>.

iii. National Conference of State Legislatures <http:ncsl.org/default.aspx?tabid=16430>.

iv. Commenting on the ruling one contributor, user name Geeoo, wrote, "This was the correct decision. A female judge does not recuse herself, nor does an African American judge when the cases are gender or race-based. And I don't think heterosexual judges recuse themselves in sexual cases, nor do divorced judges in a divorce case." Geeoo is using comparative reasoning. Applying the criteria described in the previous chapter, what is your evaluation of this argument?

v. <http://content.usatoday.com/communities/ondeadline/post/2011/06/gay-judges-repeal-of-same-sex-marriage-ban-in-calif-is-upheld/1?loc=interstitialskip> The play *8*, by Dustin Lance Black, dramatizes the arguments in the federal trial which lead to the overturn of Proposition 8. Several media outlets track Proposition 8 legal developments on their web sites. One is the Huffington Post. That URL is: <http://www.huffingtonpost.com/news/prop-8>.

vi. Search the Web for the latest on the Proposition 8 legal controversies. December 14, 2011 was the last day to present legal arguments regarding the constitutionality of the proposition, the fitness of the judge to hear the case, and the legal standing of a citizens group to defend a voter approved proposition when the state government declines to do so. For a summary of those arguments see <http://www.windycitymediagroup.com/gay/lesbian/news/ARTICLE.php?AID=35217>.

vii. <http://www.usnews.com/news/articles/2011/07/27/both-sides-see-same-sex-marriage-as-winning-issue-in-2012>.

viii. <http://www.2012presidentialelectionnews.com/2011/07/gay-marriage-initiatives-in-2012-could-galvanize-like-2004/>.

ix. "California High Court Upholds Same-Sex Marriage Ban," CNN.com, 26 May 2009, 2 Sept. 2009 <http://articles.cnn.com/2009-05-26/us/california.same.sex.marriage_1_marriage-ban-same-sex-marriages-ruling?_s=PM:US>.

x. "Lutherans Accept Clergy in 'Lifelong' Same-Sex Relationships," CNN.com, 21 Aug. 2009, 2 Sept. 2009 <http://www.cnn.com/2009/US/08/21/lutheran.gays/index.html#cnnSTCText>.

xi. In Chapter 6 we defined a *tautology* as a statement that is necessarily true by virtue of the rules of grammar and the meanings of the terms used.

xii. S. Hirst, 2006, *I Am the Grand Canyon: The Story of the Havasupai People*, (Grand Canyon, AZ: The Grand Canyon Association) xiv.

xiii. This is the language of Mississippi ballot initiative "Proposition 26." It was designed by its supporters to put a stop to abortions. It implied that abortion is the taking of a human person's life, which would be a homicide. In November 2011 Mississippi voters rejected ballot initiative.

xiv. If a health care professional is making this argument, then to analyze it properly we should inform ourselves about the meaning of "access" in that language community. "Access to adequate health care" is more than "has some level of health insurance" or "can go to an emergency room." Adequate health care, as defined by health care professionals, includes three things: screening, diagnosis, and treatment. These three are necessary not only to manage a person's care but also to prevent illness and to mitigate the morbidity and mortality associated with disease discovered at an already acute or advanced stage.

xv. "Galileo Galilei," Wisdom Quotes, 2 Sept. 2009 <http://www.wisdomquotes.com/authors/galileo-galilei/>.

xvi. See Chapter 2 for the difference between critical thinking skills and critical thinking habits of mind.

xvii. R. Pigott, "Dutch Rethink Christianity for a Doubtful World," BBC News Europe. August 5, 2011 <http://www.bbc.co.uk/news/world-europe-14417362>.

xviii. Plato, *Euthyphro,* trans. Benjamin Jowett, 380 B.C.E., 2 Sept. 2009 <http://classics.mit.edu/Plato/euthyfro.html>; Ian Kidd, "Socrates," *The Encyclopedia of Philosophy*, Vol. 7, Ed. Paul Edwards (New York: Macmillan Publishing, 1967) 480–486.

xix. "Thomas Jefferson Quotes," Brainy Quote, 2 Sept. 2009 <http://www.brainyquote.com/quotes/quotes/t/thomasjeff141347.html>.

xx. The premise of the 2009 film *District 9.*

xxi. This claim reflects the premise of Roland Emmerich's 2009 adventure film, *2012*, which connected the end of days with an interpretation of the Mayan calendar. Predictions about the end of days are not uncommon. May 21, 2011 was predicted to be "Judgment Day," by Harold Camping, whose followers took out newspaper ads with the noble intention of warning everyone who would listen. That date came and went, and the world as we know it continued. But sooner or later our species, many others, perhaps all of them, and perhaps the earth as well will be destroyed. Perhaps it will be an assault by another species, e.g. a deadly virus. Perhaps aliens will destroy our species and our planet. Perhaps a meteor will collide with the earth. Or perhaps the earth will survive until our sun goes supernova. But sooner or later, it all will end for us, for other species, and for our little blue planet.

xxii. The "Singularity Movement" is a utopian vision of golden future when the human mind and technology interact at such a deep level that the two will have become one and a new and superior intelligence will have emerged from that union. See, Vance, A. "Merely Human? So Yesterday," *The New York Times*, Sunday Business section page. June 13, 2010.

xxiii. Known as "Moralistic Therapeutic Deism" this set of beliefs has been described as the "New American Religion." See the article by the same title by Mohler, R. A. published in the Christian Post, April 18, 2005. <http://www.christianpost.com/news/moralistic-therapeutic-deism-the-new-american-religion-6266/>.

xxiv. *Paul's First Letter to the Corinthians*, The Holy Bible, Chapter 13, verse 13.

xxv. John Locke, "Of Wrong Assent or Error" in *Essay Concerning Human Understanding*, 1690, Book IV, Chapter XX.

xxvi. John Howard Griffin, *Black Like Me* (New York: Signet, 1961).

xxvii. <http://www.youtube.com/watch?v=jBnbxYD6x08>.

CHAPTER 14

i. Richard L. DeGowin, *Diagnostic Examination*, 6th ed. (New York: McGraw-Hill, 1994) 945.

ii. Bob Arnebeck, "A Short History of Yellow Fever in the U.S.," 30 Jan. 2008, 3 Sept. 2009 <http://www.geocities.com/bobarnebeck/history.html>.

iii. Lest we think that plagues of unknown origin no longer ravage and kill, consider the thousands of young men dying of kidney disease in Central America. Nobody knows why. Pesticides, food poisoning, chronic dehydration, chronic fatigue, what? And why only the men, and not the women? For more on this medical mystery see the BBC Science report "Mystery Kidney Disease in Central America" published online Dec. 11, 2011. <http://www.bbc.co.uk/news/magazine-16007129>.

iv. *2001: A Space Odyssey*, Warner Brothers Studios, dir. Stanley Kubrick, perf. Gary Lockwood and Keir Dullea, 1968.

v. At three key places in this film an obelisk is visible on-screen. One interpretation is that the obelisk's presence indicates moments of extraterrestrial intervention into human affairs; another is that these are moments of supreme insight, or perhaps divine inspiration. The first appearance of the obelisk is just before the man-ape creature realizes that he can use a leg bone as a tool to club another creature to death. This fictional depiction of the first realization of leg-bone-as-killing-tool includes moments intended by the filmmaker to show deliberation and stimulation. Whether the idea came to the man-ape by insight, extraterrestrial intervention, or divine inspiration is immaterial. What is important is that the man-ape considered the notion and decided to act on the hypothesis that a leg bone could be used to kill. Whatever its source, subsequent events supported that hypothesis.

vi. Bertrand Russell, "The Place of Science in a Liberal Education." *Mysticism and Logic and Other Essays*, 1918. (Originally published in *The New Statesman*, May 24 and 31, 1913.) Republished 2007. (New York: Casimo Inc.) 42.

vii. Carl Gustav Hempel, *Philosophy of Natural Science* (Englewood Cliffs, NJ: Prentice-Hall, Inc., 1966); Stephen Edelston Toulmin, *The Philosophy of Science* (New York: Harper & Row, 1953).

viii. Comparative reasoning, discussed in Chapter 12, is inductive, but because the points of comparison may be conceptual rather than experiential, comparative reasoning is not empirical.

ix. <http://www.nytimes.com/2010/08/13/health/research/13alzheimer.html>.

x. "Quotes on Education," Solina Quotes, 3 Sept. 2009 <http://isgwww.cs.uni-magdeburg.de/~graham/quotes/sciencefaves.html>.

xi. It is not necessary that a hypothesis be expressed as an "if . . . then" statement, only that it can be converted into one. For example, "The reflexes of a person who drives a motor vehicle for five or more hours without a rest period will have deteriorated by 30 percent or more as compared to his or her reflexes after only one to four hours of driving" can be rewritten as "If a person drives a motor vehicle for five or more hours without a rest period, then the person's reflexes will have deteriorated by 30 percent or more as compared with only one to four hours of driving."

xii. "Quotations by author: Hippocrates," The Quotations Page, 3 Sept. 2009 <http://www.quotationspage.com/quotes/Hippocrates>.

xiii. Delbert Charles Miller, *Handbook of Research Design and Social Measurement*, 5th ed. (Newbury Park, CA: Sage Publications, Inc., 1991); John W. Creswell, *Research Design Qualitative and Quantitative Approaches* (Thousand Oaks, CA: Sage Publications Inc., 1994); Stephen B. Hulley, Steven R. Cummings, Warren S. Browner, Deborah G. Grady, and Thomas B. Newman, *Designing Clinical Research* (Philadelphia, PA: Lippincott Williams & Wilkins, 2001); Emanuel Mason and William J.

Bramble, *Understanding and Conducting Research* (New York: McGraw-Hill, 1989).

xiv. The "empirical disciplines" as used here refer to the full spectrum of social, behavioral, natural, and physical sciences and all the other areas of study or professional fields, by whatever name, that fundamentally rely on empirical reasoning in the generation of new knowledge.

xv. "Galileo Galilei Quotes," Brainy Quote, 3 Sept. 2009 <http://www.brainyquote.com/quotes/authors/g/galileo_galilei.html>.

xvi. Chapter 7 introduces and explains each test: truthfulness of the premises, logical strength, relevance, and non-circularity. Are all the premises true? If the premises were true, would the conclusion be true or very probably true? Does the truth of the conclusion depend on the truth of the premises? Does the truth of the reason (set of premises) not depend on the truth of the conclusion?

xvii. Critical thinking in real life: Since managers tend to wear jackets and administrative assistants do not, the wise office manager, on hearing this refined research finding, may wish to ask the administrative assistants, not the managers, whether or not the heating and cooling is set right.

xviii. <http://www.nature.com/nature/peerreview/debate/index.html>.

xix. "Classic Quotes," The Quotations Page, 3 Sept. 2009 <http://www.quotationspage.com/quote/24972.html>.

CHAPTER 15

i. Obama's 2010 State of the Union address: White House Transcript <http://www.whitehouse.gov/the-press-office/remarks-president-state-union-address>.

ii. Governor McDonnell's GOP response <http://www.cbsnews.com/stories/2010/01/27/politics/stateofunion/main6148483.shtml>.

iii. <http://www.christianpost.com/news/twitter-fans-angered-by-false-claims-of-jackie-chans-death-54101/>.

iv. <http://www.kingsspeech.com/cast.html>.

v. <http://www.collegiatelearningassessment.org/files/ComputerAssistedScoringofCLA.pdf>.

vi. <http://www.ets.org/research/topics/as_nlp>.

vii. <http://www.insidehighered.com/news/2011/02/21/debate_over_reliability_of_automated_essay_grading>.

viii. Since most college courses are organized into disciplines, professional fields, or departments, "academic paper" may still be too broad. You should think about what is required to write an academic paper that fits the writing conventions of the discipline/professional field/department that sponsors your course.

ix. <http://www.collegeboard.com/student/apply/essay-skills/9406.html>. But, if you end up on the home page for the College Board, simply put "write essay" into the search box there.

x. <http://en.wikiquote.org/wiki/Thomas_Edison>.

xi. <http://www.aclu.org/blog/free-speech-technology-and-liberty/free-speech-and-bart-cell-phone-censorship>.

xii. Some states and local governments do not supply voter information materials that are this complete. But many do. If you have never seen materials of this kind, you can locate examples on the Internet. For example, here is one from California's 2010 election <http://voterguide.sos.ca.gov/propositions/19/>.

xiii. <http://www.dartmouth.edu/~writing/materials/faculty/pedagogies/process.shtml>.

xiv. <http://knol.google.com/k/english-student/how-to-write-an-effective-essay/3iocn0q161tw0/1#>.

xv. Stephen King, *On Writing: A Memoir of the Craft,* (New York: Pocket Books, 2000).

xvi. C. A. Gittens and Measured Reasons LLC, *Rubric for Evaluating Written Argumentation*. (Millbrae, CA: Insight Assessment, 2012). Reprinted with permission of the authors and publisher.

xvii. <http://www.nytimes.com/2011/08/12/opinion/education-watch-how-to-make-that-college-essay-special.html?_r=1&scp=3&sq=education&st=Search>.

xviii. <http://www.npr.org/2011/08/16/139676171/magician-penn-jillette-says-god-no-to-god?sc=emaf>.

xix. <http://www.nypost.com/p/news/national/diet_soda_in_fat_shocker_ylZ9hr7cn6VA17iXiaLupM>.

PHOTO CREDITS

CHAPTER 01 PAGE 2: Win McNamee/Getty Images; **4:** HBO/Everett Collection; **5 (from top):** New Line Cinema/Everett Collection; Warner Brothers/Everett Collection; **9:** Measured Reasons LLC; **13:** arindambanerjee/Shutterstock.com; **16:** HBO/Everett Collection.

CHAPTER 02 PAGE 18: Universal/Everett Collection; **25:** Everett Collection; **29:** Everett Collection; **33:** Digital Vision/Getty Images; **35:** PBS/Everett Collection; **36 (left to right):** Brand X Pictures/Getty Images; Photos.com; **39 (left to right):** Universal/Everett Collection; Everett Collection; Everett Collection.

CHAPTER 03 PAGE 42: joefoxphoto/Alamy; **45 (from top):** Jaimie Duplass/Shutterstock.com; Fancy/Alamy; **47:** Monkey Business Images/Shutterstock.com; **48:** gualtiero boffi/Shutterstock.com; **51:** Gabe Palmer/Alamy: **52:** William Perugini/Shutterstock .com; **53:** Mika/Comet/Corbis; **54:** Tim Roberts Photography/Shutterstock.com; **56:** US Food and Drug Administration FDA; **58:** Gino's Premium Images/Alamy; **59:** Huntstock/Glow Images; **60:** imagebroker.net/SuperStock; **61 (left to right):** VladisChern/Shutterstock.com; karam Miri/Shutterstock.com; Ancient Art & Architecture Collection Ltd/Alamy; **62:** joefoxphoto/Alamy.

CHAPTER 04 PAGE 64: Everett Collection; **67 (left to right):** Vincent O'Byrne/Alamy; imagebroker/Alamy; Gary Vogelmann/Alamy; JoeFox/Alamy; **70 (from top):** Gregory Wrona/Alamy; 20th Century Fox Film Corp/Everett Collection; **71 (left to right):** Allstar Picture Library/Alamy; Thinkstock; **73:** The Granger Collection; **74:** Joe Corrigan/Getty Images; **75 (from top):** AP Photo/Bugatti, HO; Maksim Toome/Shutterstock.com; Kyodo/Landov; **78:** Graham Whitby/ZUMAPRESS/Newscom; **80:** Tom Grill/Corbis Premium/Alamy; **81** Pearson Education/PH College; **83 (top left to right):** Everett Collection; 20th Century Fox Film Corp/Everett Collection; **(bottom):** Graham Whitby/ZUMAPRESS/Newscom.

CHAPTER 05 PAGE 86: Golden Pixels LLC/Shutterstock.com; **92:** J.P. Wilson/Icon SMI/Corbis Sports/Corbis; **94 (from top):** Scott Gries/Getty Images Entertainment/Getty Images; AP Photo/Huckabee Campaign; **104 (from top):** Golden Pixels LLC/Shutterstock.com; Scott Gries/Getty Images Entertainment/Getty Images; **107:** Fred R. Conrad/The New York Times/Redux Pictures.

CHAPTER 06 PAGE 108: Mark Wilson/Getty Images News/Getty Images; **110 (left to right):** David Woolley/Stockbyte/Getty Images; Beverly Logan/Stockbyte/Getty Images; **113:** Everett Collection; **114 (left to right):** Digital Vision/Getty Images; Marcy Maloy/Digital Vision/Getty Images; Michael Hitoshi/Digital Vision/Getty Images; **115:** moodboard/Alamy; **116:** Columbia/Everett Collection; **119 (left to right):** Jorg Greuel/Photodisc/Getty Images; Dorling Kindersley Images; **120:** Photos.com; **122 (left to right):** Spencer Platt/Staff/Getty Images Entertainment/Getty Images; AP Photos/Julien Behal; **123:** Win McNamee/Staff/Getty Images News/Getty Images; **127 (from top):** Everett Collection; Columbia/Everett Collection.

CHAPTER 07 PAGE 130: Chris Salvo/Taxi/Getty Images; **134 (from top):** Andersen Ross/Stockbyte/Getty Images; Scott Adams, Inc/United Media/United Feature Syndicate, Inc; **135:** Everett Collection; **137 (left to right):** Scott Mansfield/UpperCut Images/Getty Images; Stewart Cohen/Blend Images/Getty Images; **139:** Frederic Lewis/Staff/Archive Photos/Getty Images; **143:** Waterlilies, 1908 (oil on canvas), Monet, Claude (1840-1926)/Private Collection/Photo © Christie's Images/The Bridgeman Art Library; **144:** CBS/Landov; **145 (clockwise):** n03/ZUMA Press/Newscom; Newscom; ROGER L. WOLLENBERG/UPI/Newscom; Randi Radcliff/AdMedia/Newscom; Shepard Sherbell/Corbis News/Corbis; Brooks Kraft/News/Corbis; Michael S. Wirtz/MCT/Newscom; **146:** michael rubin/Shutterstock.com; **147:** Everett Collection;

CHAPTER 08 PAGE 150: Jerry Lodriguss/Photo Researchers, Inc.; **153 (from top):** Business Wire/Handout/Getty Images Publicity/Getty Images; Taro Yamasaki/Time Life Pictures/Getty Images; **158:** AF archive/Alamy; **160:** Everett Collection; **162:** Everett Collection; **163:** Werner Dieterich/Alamy.

CHAPTER 09 PAGE 164: Andre Jenny Stock Connection Worldwide/Newscom; **166:** RYAN C. HENRIKSEN/MCT/Newscom; **167 (left to right):** Christoph Wilhelm/Digital Vision/Getty Images; Image Source/Getty Images; **170:** trekandshoot/Shutterstock.com; **173:** Imagebroker/Alamy; **174:** Photos 12/Alamy; **177:** Everett Collection; **179:** HBO/Everett Collection.

CHAPTER 10 PAGE 180: David R. Frazier Photolibrary, Inc.; **184 (left to right):** AP Photo/Jim MacMillan; Blend Images/Shutterstock.com; **185:** Image Source/Jupiter Images; **186 (left to right):** Mode Ian O'Leary/Mode Images Limited/Alamy; Imagic Urban World/Alamy; **188:** Dynamic Graphics Group/Jupiter Images; **189 (from top):** Larry W. Smith/Getty Images News/Getty Images; imagebroker.net/SuperStock; **190:** T. O'Keefe/PhotoLink/Photodisc/Jupiter Images; **191 (left to right):** Dave Porter/Alamy; DAVID FURST/AFP/Getty Images; HARAZ N. GHANBARI/UPI/Landov; Jim McIsaac/Staff/Getty Images Sport/Getty Images; **191 (bottom):** o44/ZUMA Press/Newscom; **192:** FRANCIS DEAN/FRANCIS J. DEAN/DEAN PICTURES/Newscom; **195:** Buena Vista/courtesy Everett Collection; **196:** Bob Daemmrich/PhotoEdit; **197:** Thinkstock; **198 (left to right):** AP Photos/NICK UT; Allstar Picture Library/Alamy; **199 (from top):** Photos.com; Steven Lam/Taxi/Getty Images; **200:** City Living/Alamy; **201:** Ingvar Bjork/Alamy; **202:** clive thompson people/Alamy; **203 (from top):** Getty Images; Dilbert.com by Scott Adams/Universal Uclick; **205:** Buena Vista/Everett Collection.

CHAPTER 11 PAGE 208: JOJO WHILDEN/PARAMOUNT/HO/EPA/Photoshot; **211:** Peter Forsberg/Alamy; **213:** AP Photo/Joe Marquette; **216 (left to right):** S.E.A. Photo/Alamy; Blue Jean Images/Alamy; Business Office Career/Alamy; Andres Rodriguez/Alamy; **218:** David Young-Wolff/PhotoEdit; **220:** AP Photo/

Reed Saxon, Pool; **221:** Photos.com; **222:** Photos.com; **223:** age fotostock/SuperStock; **224:** ROBYN BECK/AFP/Getty Images; **225:** ROBYN BECK/AFP/Getty Images; **227:** Carl Purcell/Terra/Corbis.

CHAPTER 12 PAGE 228: Columbia University Graduate School of Journalism; **231:** Nenad Tomic/Alamy; **232:** Smit/Shutterstock.com; **233 (from top):** USA Films/Everett Collection; Ulrich Baumgarten/vario images GmbH & Co.KG/Alamy; Nigel Hicks/Dorling Kindersley; **234:** Universal Unclick; **236 (clockwise):** John Heseltine/Dorling Kindersley; Alex Segre/Alamy; PSL Images/Alamy; Andy Manis/The New York Times; **237 (from left):** Alistair Scott/Alamy; Paul Spinelli/Major League Baseball/Getty Images; **238:** Kim Sayer/Dorling Kindersley; **239 (from top):** Nancy Greifenhagen/Alamy; INTERFOTO/Alamy; **242:** Scott Adams United Media/United Feature Syndicate, Inc.; **243:** Columbia University Graduate School of Journalism.

CHAPTER 13 PAGE 246: C.J. Gunther/Corbis; **249 (from top):** Morgan Lane Photography/Alamy; DreamPictures/Taxi/Getty Images; **251 (from top):** akg-images; AP Photo/Susan Sterner; **252:** Dynamic Graphics, Inc.; **253 (left to right):** North Wind Picture Archives/Alamy; AP Photo/Eddie Adams; **254:** Hulton Archive/Getty Images; **255:** Lee Foster/Alamy; **257:** Wm. Baker/GhostWorx Images/Alamy; **258 (clockwise):** SPL/Photo Researchers, Inc.; Sean Sprague/Age Fotostock; AP Photo/World Food Program, HO; Bettmann/CORBIS; Frances Roberts/Alamy; The Granger Collection, NYC; **259 (clockwise):** Nigel Hicks/Dorling Kindersley; Sean Gallup/Getty Images; Alex Segre/Alamy; Steve Allen/Brand X Pictures/Getty Images; Measured Reasons LLC; **260:** North Wind Picture Archives/Alamy; **261:** Penguin Putnam, Inc.; **262 (left to right):** Cosmo Condina/Mira.com; Mexico/Alamy; **263 (left to right):** Penguin Putnam, Inc.; Warner Independent Pictures/Everett Collection; **264 (left to right):** C.J. Gunther/Corbis; Warner Independent Pictures/Everett Collection.

CHAPTER 14 PAGE 266: Chuck Brown/Photo Researchers, Inc.; **269:** Everett Collection; **273:** TWPhoto/Corbis; **278:** Chuck Brown/Photo Researchers, Inc.

CHAPTER 15 PAGE 280: JIM WATSON/AFP/Getty Images/Newscom; **284 (clockwise):** Supri Suharjoto/Shutterstock.com; Paul Matthew Photography/Shutterstock.com; Shutterstock.com; Arvind Balaraman/Shutterstock.com; **285:** EVA/BO/Queen/ZUMA Press/Newscom; **286:** Oliver Knight/Alamy; **289:** Brooks Kraft/Sygma/CORBIS; **297:** Trinity Mirror/Mirrorpix/Alamy; **298:** Howard Kingsnorth/Cultura Creative/Alamy; **302 (left to right):** JIM WATSON/AFP/Getty Images/Newscom; Trinity Mirror/Mirrorpix/Alamy.

TEXT, TABLE, AND FIGURE CREDITS

CHAPTER 01 PAGE 6: From THE VAMPIRE LESTAT by Anne O'Brien Rice. Copyright © 1985 by Anne O'Brien Rice. Used by permission of Ballantine Books, a division of Random House, Inc. **7:** From Peter A. Facione, American Philosophical Association, Critical Thinking: A Statement of Expert Consensus for Purpose of Educational Assessment & Instruction, (also known as The Delphi Report). Copyright © 1990, The California Academic Press, 217 La Cruz Ave., Millbrae, CA 94030. All Rights Reserved. Permission to duplicate for noncommercial uses may be purchased for $0.80 per copy from The California Academic Press. Phone or Fax 650-697-5628; From Facione, P. A., "Critical Thinking: What it is and Why it Counts." p. 3. Copyright © 1992, 1998, 2004, 2006, 2011 Peter A. Facione, Measured Reasons and The California Academic Press, Millbrae, CA; **10:** Ann Sanner, "Obama to Sign National Service Bill Today," Huffington Post, 21 Apr. 2009, 8 Jul. 2009. http://www.huffingtonpost.com/2009/04/21/obama-to-sign-nationalse_n_189407.html. Reprinted by permission of the Huffington Post; **12:** From Facione, Peter A, and Noreen C. Facione, The Holistic Critical Thinking Score Rubric. Copyright © 1994, 2009, Peter A. Facione, Noreen C. Facione, and Measured Reasons LLC, Hermosa Beach, CA USA. Published by the California Academic Press/Insight Assessment, Millbrae, CA 94030. To download free copies of this rubric visit http://www.insightassessment.com/9HCTSR.html.

CHAPTER 02 PAGE 21: Copyright © 2009, Measured Reasons, LLC; **24:** Used with permission of Insight Assessment, "Measuring Critical Thinking Worldwide." www.insightassessment.com; **26:** Used with permission of Insight Assessment, "Measuring Critical Thinking Worldwide." www.insightassessment.com; **26** Used with permission of Insight Assessment, "Measuring Critical Thinking Worldwide." www.insightassessment.com; **27:** American Philosophical Association; Peter A. Facione, Critical Thinking: An Expert Consensus Statement for Purposes of Educational Assessment and Instruction, Table 5, page 25. Copyright © 1990, The California Academic Press, 217 La Cruz Ave., Millbrae, CA 94030. All rights Reserved. Permission to duplicate for noncommercial uses may be purchased for $0.80 per copy from The California Academic Press. Phone or Fax 650-697-5628; **29:** From Peter A. Facione, American Philosophical Association, Critical Thinking: A Statement of Expert Consensus for Purpose of Educational Assessment & Instruction, (also known as The Delphi Report). Copyright © 1990, The California Academic Press, 217 La Cruz Ave., Millbrae, CA 94030. All Rights Reserved. Permission to duplicate for noncommercial uses may be purchased for $0.80 per copy from The California Academic Press. Phone or Fax 650-697-5628; **30:** Used with permission of Insight Assessment, "Measuring Critical Thinking Worldwide." www.insightassessment.com; **32:** From The New York Times, March 20, 2011. © 2011 The New York Times. All rights reserved. Used by permission and protected by the Copyright Laws of the United States. The printing, copying, redistribution, or retransmission of this Content without express written permission is prohibited. http://www.nytimes.com/2011/03/20/world/americas/20bolivia.html?pagewanted=all#; **31:** From the Test Manual for the California Critical Thinking Skills Test, Copyright © 2009. Published by Insight Assessment. Used with permission; **33:** From Peter A. Facione, American Philosophical Association, Critical Thinking: A Statement of Expert Consensus for Purpose of Educational Assessment & Instruction, (also known as The Delphi Report). Copyright © 1990, The California Academic Press, 217 La Cruz Ave., Millbrae, CA 94030. All Rights Reserved. Permission to duplicate for noncommercial uses may be purchased for $0.80 per copy from The California Academic Press. Phone or Fax 650-697-5628.

CHAPTER 03 PAGE 45: From The Yogi Book: I really didn't say everything I said! Reprinted by permission of LTD Enterprises, a Berra Family Corporation; **46:** Reprinted courtesy of Woody Allen; **55:** Reprinted by permission of the Brookings Institution; **56:** From The New York Times, June 5, 2010 © 2010 The New York Times. All rights reserved. Used by permission and protected by the Copyright Laws of the United States. The printing, copying, redistribution, or retransmission of this Content without express written permission is prohibited. www.nytimes.com.

CHAPTER 06 PAGE 109: Reprinted by permission of GateHouse Media, Inc. d/b/a GateHouse Media News Service; **112:** This work is released under CC-BY-SA. http://creativecommons.org/licenses/by-sa/3.0/; **114:** From The Southern Poverty Law Center's Intelligence Report. Reprinted by permission; **116:** From Victoria

Jackson, "The Three Scariest Things About Obama." From World Net Daily, July 15, 2011. Copyright © 2011 World Net Daily. Reprinted by permission of World Net Daily. www.wnd.com; **118:** From "'Miracle drug' called junk science" By Trine Tsouderos, The Chicago Tribune, May 21, 2009. http://www.chicagotribune.com/health/chi-autism-lupron-may21,0,242705.story. Reprinted by permission of Tribune Media Services; **122:** Enda Brady, "Image of Virgin Mary Found in Tree Stump," SkyNews, 10 Jul. 2009, 21 Aug. 2009. http://news.sky.com/skynews/Home/World-News/Virgin-Mary-Tree-Stump-Depiction-Found-InRathkeale-Ireland/Article/200907215334913. Reprinted by permission of British Sky Broadcasting; Reprinted by permission of Steven Miller. Steven Miller Design Studio. www.stevenmillerdesignstudio.com; **123:** Reprinted by permission of Fortum Energy; **125:** The Endangered Northwest Tree Octopus, by Lyle Zapato. http://zapatopi/treeoctopus. Reprinted by permission of the author.

CHAPTER 07 PAGE 141: William C. Rhoden, Third and a Mile: The Trials and Triumphs of the Black Quarterback (Bristol, CT: ESPN Books, 2007). Copyright © 2007. Reprinted by permission of ESPN Books, a division of Random House, Inc.; **148:** Figure: "Moral Acceptability of Docto-Assisted Suicides," by The Gallup Poll. http://www.gallup.com/poll/27727/Public-Divided-Over-Moral-Acceptability-DoctorAssisted-Suicide.aspx. Reprinted by permission of The Gallup Organization.

CHAPTER 09 PAGE 169: From What's It Worth? The Economic Value of College Majors, by the Georgetown Center for Education & Workforce. http://cew.georgetown.edu/whatsitworth/. Reprinted by permission.

CHAPTER 10 PAGE 194: From Dave Leip's Atlas of U.S. Presidential Elections. Reprinted by permission.

CHAPTER 11 PAGE 217: Copyright © 1968 Paul Simon. Used by permission of the Publisher: Paul Simon Music.

CHAPTER 12 PAGE 229: Excerpts from Mike Wallace and US Air Force General Brent Scowcrost, ETHICS IN AMERICA: Under Orders, Under Fire, (Part 1). Copyright © 1989 by Columbia University Seminars on Media and Society. Reprinted by permission; **232:** From FULL DARK, NO STARS, by Stephen King. Copyright © 2010 by Stephen King. Reprinted by permission of Scribner, a division of Simon & Schuster, Inc.; From Tom Franklin, CROOKED LETTER, CROOKED LETTER, William Morrow (2010). Copyright © 2010 Tom Franklin. All rights reserved. Reprinted by permission of HarperCollins Publishers.

CHAPTER 13 PAGE 247: From the Los Angeles Times, "Spike in marriage licenses statewide," February 3, 2009. Reprinted by permission from The Los Angeles Times; **249:** From "California High Court Upholds Same-Sex Marriage Ban," CNN.com, May 27, 2009, Sept2,2009,http://www.cnn.com/2009/US/05/26/california.same.sex.marriage/index.html. Copyright © 2009 CNN. Reprinted by permission; From "Lutherans Accept Clergy in 'Lifelong' Same-Sex Relationships," CNN.com, Aug 21, 2009, Sept. 2, 2009. http://www.cnn.com/2009/US/08/21/lutheran.gays/index.htm Copyright © 2009 CNN. Reprinted by permission.

CHAPTER 14 PAGE 269: Published in Mysticism and Logic and Other Essays (Originally published in the New Statesman, May 24th and 31st, 1913). Copyright © Bertrand Russell. Reprinted by permission of The New Statesman; **277:** From Strength to Love, by Martin Luther King, Jr. Copyright © 1963 by Martin Luther King, Jr. Reprinted by permission of Writer's House, as agents for the Executor of the Estate of Martin Luther King, Jr.

CHAPTER 15 PAGE 299: Rubric for Evaluating Written Argumentation. © 2011 Gittens, C.A. & Measured Reasons LLC, Santa Clara, CA. Reprinted with Permission. www.measuredreasons.com

INDEX

Page numbers followed by *f* refer to figures. Page numbers followed by *t* refer to tables.

J

K

L

M

N

S

T

U

V

W

Y